Western Civilization

Ideas, Politics & Society   Second Edition

Volume I   To 1789

Marvin Perry
Baruch College, City University of New York

Myrna Chase
Baruch College, City University of New York

James R. Jacob
John Jay College of Criminal Justice, City University of New York

Margaret C. Jacob
Baruch College, City University of New York

Theodore H. Von Laue
Clark University

George W. Bock, Editorial Associate

Houghton Mifflin Company   Boston

Dallas   Geneva, Illinois   Hopewell, New Jersey   Palo Alto

The following authors are members of The Institute for Research in History: Marvin Perry, Myrna Chase, James R. Jacob, and Margaret C. Jacob.

Copyright © 1985 by Houghton Mifflin Company. All Rights Reserved.

No part of this work may be reproduced or transmitted in any form or by any means, electronic or mechanical, including photocopying and recording, or by any information storage or retrieval system, except as may be expressly permitted by the 1976 Copyright Act or in writing by the Publisher. Requests for permission should be addressed to Permissions, Houghton Mifflin Company, One Beacon Street, Boston, MA 02108.

Printed in the U.S.A.

Library of Congress Catalog Card Number: 84-81394

ISBN: 0-395-36538-4

Credits

Cover: Ambrogio Lorenzetti: *Good Government in the City*, a mural in Siena, Palazzo Pubblico. *Scala/Art Resource, New York*

Chapter Opening Photographs
Chapter 1: Detail, *Tomb of Nakht*; The Metropolitan Museum of Art, New York. *Chapter 2:* Arch of Titus, Rome; Ewing Galloway, New York. *Chapter 3:* Mycenaean mask; Robert Harding Picture Library. *Chapter 4:* Theater at Epidaurus; Bildarchiv Foto Marburg. *Chapter 5:* Coin of Alexander; Courtesy of The American Numismatic Society, New York. *Chapter 6:* Roman warship, relief; Vatican/Alinari/Art Resource. *Chapter 7:* Pont du Gard, Nîmes; Jean Roubier/Rapho. *Chapter 8:* Ivory panel of the crucifixion; The Granger Collection. *Chapter 9:* Coronation of Charlemagne; Scala/Art Resource. *Chapter 10:* Medieval street scene; Bibliothèque de l'Arsenal/Bibliothèque Nationale, Paris. *Chapter 11:* West doors, Chartres Cathedral; Jean Roubier. *Chapter 12:* The Jacquerie; Bibliothèque Nationale, Paris. *Chapter 13:* Palladio: Villa Rotonda; Alinari/Art Resource. *Chapter 14:* Rembrandt: *Family Portrait*, c.

1668; Herzog Anton Ulrich-Museum, Braunschweig; photo B. P. Keiser. *Chapter 15:* Velde: *Dutch Man-of-War Saluting*; The Wallace Collection. *Chapter 16:* Versailles; French Government Tourist Office. *Chapter 17:* Louis XIV at French Academy of Sciences; Courtesy Burndy Library. *Chapter 18:* Winter Palace, St. Petersburg; William Brumfield.

Text Credits
Page 16: Egyptian poem: From Adolf Ehrman, Editor, *The Ancient Egyptians,* by permission of Methuen & Co., publishers.
Page 19: From John A. Wilson, *The Culture of Ancient Egypt* (1951). Reprinted by permission of the publisher, The University of Chicago Press. Copyright © 1951 by The University of Chicago.
Chapter 2: The biblical excerpts in Chapter 2 are taken from The Holy Scriptures, published in 1917 by the Jewish Publication Society of America. Reprinted with permission of the Jewish Publication Society.
Page 81: From "A Girl" by Sappho, translated by C. M. Bowra, from *The Oxford Book of Greek Verse in Translation* edited by T. F. Higham and C. M. Bowra (1938), by permission of Oxford University Press.
Page 81: From Pindar from H. D. F. Kitto: THE GREEKS (Pelican Books, Revised Edition, 1957), pp. 174–175. Copyright © H. D. F. Kitto, 1951, 1957. Reprinted by permission of Penguin Books Ltd.
Page 82: From Sophocles, *Oedipus the King,* translated by Bernard M. W. Knox (New York: Washington Square Press, 1959), by permission of Simon & Schuster.
Page 83: From Anthony J. Podlecki, THE PERSIANS by Aeschylus, © 1970, pp. 49, 96–97. Reprinted by permission of Prentice-Hall, Inc., Englewood Cliffs, N.J.
Page 84: From Euripides, *The Medea,* translated by Rex Warner, in *The Complete Greek Tragedies,* Vol. 1, in David Grene & Richard Lattimore, eds. (Chicago: The Chicago University Press, 1955), by permission of The Bodley Head Ltd.
Page 84: From Euripides, *The Trojan Women,* translated by Gilbert Murray (New York: Oxford University Press, 1915), p. 16, by permission of Oxford University Press.
Page 117: Plautus, quoted from J. Wright Duff, *A Literary History of Rome* (Totowa, N.J.: Barnes &

Noble Books, 1960), by permission of Barnes & Noble Books.

Page 117: Catullus, quoted from Havelock, Eric Alfred, *The Lyric Genius of Catullus.* Originally published: 1939; reprinted, New York: Russell & Russell, 1967.

Page 136: From THE AENEID OF VIRGIL, a verse translation by Allen Mandelbaum. Copyright © 1973 by Allen Mandelbaum. Reprinted by permission of Bantam Books, Inc. All rights reserved.

Page 137: Adapted from THE SATIRES OF JUVENAL, translated by Hubert Creekmore. Copyright © 1963 by Hubert Creekmore. Reprinted by arrangement with New American Library, New York, New York.

Chapters 8, 11, and 14: Biblical excerpts in these chapters are used with permission from the Revised Standard Version of the Bible, copyrighted 1946, 1952, © 1971, 1973, by The National Council of Churches.

Page 242: Troubadours' song: Reprinted by permission of Schocken Books Inc. from SONGS OF THE TROUBADOURS by Anthony Bonner. Copyright © 1972 by Schocken Books Inc. Also with permission of George Allen & Unwin (Publishers) Ltd., Hemel Hempstead, England.

Page 244: From The Prologue from Chaucer: THE CANTERBURY TALES, trans. Nevill Coghill (Penguin Classics, Revised edition, 1977), pp. 27, 31. Copyright 1951 by Nevill Coghill; Copyright © Nevill Coghill, 1958, 1960, 1975, 1977. Reprinted by permission of Penguin Books Ltd.

Page 289: From *Hamlet, Prince of Denmark,* in *The Complete Plays and Poems of William Shakespeare,* ed. by William Allan Neilson and Charles Jarvis Hill (Boston: Houghton Mifflin, 1942), p. 1067. © 1942 by Houghton Mifflin Company, renewed 1969 by Caroline Steiner and Margaret N. Helburn. Used by permission of Houghton Mifflin Company.

Contents

List of Maps

Preface

Western civilization is a grand but tragic drama. The West has forged the instruments of reason that make possible a rational comprehension of physical nature and human culture, conceived the idea of political liberty, and recognized the intrinsic worth of the individual. But the modern West, though it has unravelled nature's mysteries, has been less successful at finding rational solutions to social ills and conflicts between nations. Science, the great achievement of the Western intellect, while improving conditions of life, has also produced weapons of mass destruction. Though the West has pioneered in the protection of human rights, it has also produced totalitarian regimes that have trampled on individual freedom and human dignity. And although the West has demonstrated a commitment to human equality, it has also practiced brutal racism.

Despite the value that Westerners have given to reason and freedom, they have shown a frightening capacity for irrational behavior and a fascination for violence and irrational ideologies, and they have willingly sacrificed liberty for security or national grandeur. The world wars and totalitarian movements of the twentieth century have demonstrated that Western civilization, despite its extraordinary achievements, is fragile and perishable.

Western Civilization: Ideas, Politics, and Society examines the Western tradition—those unique patterns of thought and systems of values that constitute the Western heritage. While focusing on key ideas and important issues, the text also provides a balanced treatment of economic, political, and social history for students in Western civilization courses.

Every chapter for the second edition has been reworked to some extent. Several major structural changes have been made. The section on Byzantium and Islam in Chapter 9, "The Rise of Europe," has been enlarged. Chapter 16, "The Rise of Sovereignty," has been reorganized to give it a more straightforward chronology. Additional political and diplomatic developments have been included in Chapter 18, "The Age of Enlightenment," along with a new section on the American Revolution. Chapter 21, "The Industrial Revolution," has been resituated from later in the text. Two new chapters on intellectual history have been added: Chapter 24, "Thought and Culture in the Mid-Nineteenth Century," and Chapter 33, "Thought and Culture in an Era of World Wars." Chapter 26, "Industrial Europe," has an added section on Austria-Hungary between 1866 and 1914. Chapter 28, "Modern Consciousness," contains a new section on modernism in the arts and a rewritten and enlarged section on modern physics. The final three chapters in the text—"Western Europe Since 1945," "Eastern Europe Since 1945," and "Globalism"—have been updated to take into account new political forces in Western Europe and give some attention to the post-Brezhnev years in the Soviet Union and to recent developments in Poland and the Middle East.

The text contains several pedagogical features. Chapter introductions provide comprehensive overviews of key themes and give a sense of direction and coherence to the flow of history. Many chapters contain concluding essays that treat the larger meaning of the material. Facts have been carefully selected to illustrate key relationships and concepts and to avoid overwhelming students with unrelated and disconnected data. Appropriate quotations, many not commonly found in texts, have been integrated into the discussion. The art program has been amplified, with many new photographs and several new maps. Four essays link crucial periods in the history of art and architecture to their wider cultural setting; these essays have been revised and added to, and now incorporate color photographs. Each chapter contains an annotated bibliography and review questions that refer students to principal points. More questions have been added in this edition, with an emphasis on eliciting thoughtful answers, rather than memorized facts.

The text is written with the conviction that history is not a meaningless tale. Without a knowledge of history, men and women cannot fully know themselves, for all human beings have been shaped by institutions and values inherited from the past. Without an awareness of the historical evolution of reason and freedom, the dominant ideals of Western civilization, commitment to these ideals will diminish. Without a knowledge of history, the West cannot fully comprehend or adequately cope with the problems that burden its civilization and the world.

In attempting to make sense out of the past, the authors have been careful to avoid superficial generalizations that oversimplify historical events and forces and arrange history into too neat a structure. But we have striven to interpret and to synthesize in order to provide students with a frame of reference with which to comprehend the principal events and eras in Western history.

Western Civilization: Ideas, Politics, and Society is available in both one- and two-volume editions. Volume I of the two-volume edition treats the period from the first civilizations in the Near East through the Age of Enlightenment in the eighteenth century (18 chapters). Volume II covers the period from the growth of nation-states in the seventeenth century to the contemporary age (22 chapters). Because some instructors start the second half of their course with the period prior to the French Revolution, Volume II incorporates the last three chapters of Volume I: "The Rise of Sovereignty," "The Scientific Revolution," and "The Age of Enlightenment." Volume II also contains a compre-

hensive introduction that surveys the ancient world, the Middle Ages, and the opening centuries of the modern era; the introduction is designed particularly for students who did not take the first half of the course.

The text represents the efforts of several authors. Marvin Perry, general editor of the project, wrote Chapters 1–12, 19, 20, 22–25, 28–30, and 32–34. James R. Jacob is the author of Chapters 13 and 15. Margaret C. Jacob provided Chapters 14 and 16–18. Myrna Chase wrote Chapters 21, 26–27, and the section on reform in Britain in Chapter 23. Theodore H. Von Laue is the author of Chapters 31, 35–37, and the section on Russia in Chapter 26. The four art essays were written by Katherine Crum, and some of the material on Gothic cathedrals and modern art that she wrote for the first edition has been incorporated into the text. Marvin Perry and George Bock edited the manuscript for clarity and continuity.

The authors would like to thank the following instructors for their critical reading of sections of the manuscript:

Melvin S. Amov, *Grossmont College*

Leon Apt, *Iowa State University*

John W. Bohnstedt, *California State University, Fresno*

Werner Braatz, *University of Wisconsin, Oshkosh*

James B. Briscoe, *University of Arkansas, Fayetteville*

Ronald D. Cassell, *University of North Carolina, Greensboro*

Ron Doviak, *Borough of Manhattan Community College*

Leonard Greenspoon, *Clemson University*

Charles D. Hamilton, *San Diego State University*

Alexandra S. Korros, *Miami University, Hamilton*

Lyle E. Linville, *Prince George's Community College*

David MacDonald, *Illinois State University*

Robert Michael, *Southeastern Massachusetts University*

Algis Mickunas, *Ohio University*

Howard Negrin, *Baruch College, City University of New York*

William E. Painter, *North Texas State University*

Richard Pierard, *Indiana State University*

Paul Pinckney, *University of Tennessee, Knoxville*

Kenneth W. Rock, *Colorado State University*

Bernice Glatzer Rosenthal, *Fordham University*

Julius R. Ruff, *Marquette University*

Seymour Scheinberg, *California State University, Fullerton*

Donald J. Wilcox, *University of New Hampshire*

Many of their suggestions were incorporated into the final version. We are also grateful to the staff of Houghton Mifflin Company who lent their considerable talents to the project. I would like to express my personal gratitude to George Bock who assisted in the planning of the text from its inception and who read the manuscript with an eye for major concepts and essential relationships.

M.P.

Western Civilization

I

The Ancient World: Foundation of the West

To A.D. 500

1

The Ancient Near East:
The First Civilizations

Civilization was not inevitable, it was an act of human creativity. The first civilizations emerged about 5,000 years ago, in the Near Eastern river valleys of Sumer and Egypt. Before that time stretched the vast ages of prehistory, when our ancestors did not dwell in cities and knew nothing of writing. Today, when civilization is threatened by a nuclear holocaust, we might reflect on humanity's long and painful climb to a civilized state.

The Rise to Civilization

The Paleolithic Age

In recent decades anthropologists and archaeologists have made important discoveries that have shed light on the prehistoric past. Richard E. Leakey speculates about one such find in East Africa:

Close to three million years ago on a campsite near the east shore of Kenya's spectacular Lake Turkana, formerly Lake Rudolf, a primitive human picked up a water-smoothed stone, and with a few skillful strikes transformed it into an implement. What was once an accident of nature was now a piece of deliberate technology, to be used to fashion a stick for digging up roots, or to slice the flesh off a dead animal. Soon discarded by its maker, the stone tool still exists, an unbreakable link with our ancestors.[1]

The period called the Paleolithic Age, or Old Stone Age, began with the earliest primitive tool-making human beings who inhabited East Africa nearly 3 million years ago. It ended 11,000 to 10,000 years ago in parts of the Near East when people discovered how to farm. Our Paleolithic ancestors lived as hunters and food gatherers. Because they had not learned how to farm, they never established permanent villages. When their food supplies ran short, they abandoned their caves or tentlike structures of branches and searched for new dwelling places.

Human social development was shaped by this 3-million-year experience of hunting and food gathering. For survival, groups of families formed bands consisting of around thirty people; members learned how to plan, organize, cooperate, trust, and share. The men hunted for meat, and the women cared for the young, tended the fires, and gathered fruits, nuts, berries, and grain. Hunters assisted each other in tracking and killing game, finding cooperative efforts more successful than individual forays. By sharing their kill and bringing some back to their camp for the rest of the group, they reinforced the social bond. Bands that did not cooperate in the hunt or distribute meat to everyone were unlikely to survive.

Hunting and food gathering also stimulated mental and physical development. Food gatherers had to know which plants were safe to eat and where to find them. Hunting required strength, speed, good eyesight and hearing, and mental ability. Hunters had to study and analyze the habits of their prey, judge weather conditions, recall the location of dens and watering places, and make better tools and weapons. The physically weak and mentally deficient, unable to track animals and to cope with new problems, did not survive long. Individuals with superior intelligence and physical qualities lived longer and had more opportunities to mate, passing on their characteristics and gradually improving the human species.

Although human progress was very slow during the long centuries of the Paleolithic Age, developments occurred that influenced the future enormously. Paleolithic people developed spoken language and learned how to make and use tools. Both accomplishments are evidence of behavior that sets human beings apart from other creatures. To be sure, primates such as apes and chimpanzees utter sounds that express emotions, but they cannot give a name to an object or describe things. And although chimpanzees use a twig as a tool to get at insects, they do not save it for future use nor progress in their toolmaking from generation to generation.

Paleolithic people, on the other hand, shaped bone, wood, and stone tools that corresponded to ideas in their minds. They preserved their creations and taught other people how to use them. Succeeding generations improved on what they had learned from their ancestors. With these simple but useful tools, Paleolithic human beings dug up roots, peeled the bark off trees, trapped, killed, and skinned animals, made clothing, and fashioned fishnets. They also discovered how to control fire, which allowed them to cook their meat, and provided warmth and protection.

Like toolmaking, language was a great human achievement. Language enabled individuals to share their knowledge, experiences, and feelings with each other. Thus, language was the decisive factor in the development of culture and its transmission from one generation to the next. Language helped parents teach their children rules of conduct and religious beliefs, as well as how to make tools and light fires.

Most likely, our Paleolithic ancestors developed mythic-religious beliefs to explain the mysteries of nature, birth, sickness, and death. To primitive peoples, the elements— sun, rain, wind, thunder, and lightning— were alive. The natural elements had spirit; they could feel and act with a purpose. To appease them, hunters and gatherers made offerings to these forces of nature. Gradually shamans, medicine men, and witch doctors emerged who, through rituals, trances, and chants, seemed able to communicate with these spirits. Also, Paleolithic people began the practice of burying their dead, sometimes with offerings, which suggests belief in life after death. Another belief is shown in the many small statues of women, made between 40,000 and 25,000 years ago, that have been found by archaeologists in Europe and Asia; fashioned from ivory, wood, and clay and often marked by huge breasts and distended stomachs, these fertility figurines represent a mother goddess who gave life, food, and protection.

Between 30,000 and 12,000 years ago, Paleolithic people sought out the dark and silent interior of caves and, with only torches for light, they painted remarkably skillful and perceptive pictures of animals on the cave walls. When these prehistoric artists drew an animal with a spear in its side, they probably believed that this act would make them successful in hunting; when they drew a herd of animals, they probably hoped that this would cause game to be plentiful.

The Neolithic Revolution

Some 10,000 to 11,000 years ago, the New Stone Age or Neolithic Age began in the Near East. During the Neolithic Age, human beings discovered farming, domesticated animals, established villages, polished stone tools, made pottery, and wove cloth. So important were these achievements that they are referred to as the Neolithic Revolution.

Agriculture—the deliberate planting and cultivation of crops—first developed in the hilly regions of the Near East, where wheat and barley grew abundantly in the wild. People there also began to domesticate the sheep and wild goats that roamed the hills. In other parts of the world, farming and the domestication of animals developed independently.

Agriculture and the domestication of animals revolutionized life. Whereas Paleolithic hunters and food gatherers had been forced to use whatever nature made available to them, Neolithic farmers altered their environment to satisfy human needs. Instead of spending their time searching for grains, roots, and berries, women and children grew crops near their homes; instead of tracking animals over great distances, men could slaughter domesticated goats or sheep nearby. Farming made possible a new kind of community. Because hunters needed to roam over large areas, hunting bands were by necessity small. If the band grew too large, some members formed a new band and moved on. In contrast, several hundred or even several thousand people might live in a farming community.

Since farmers had to live near their fields and could store food for the future, farming led to the rise of permanent settlements. Villages containing as many as 200 or 300 people had emerged in late Paleolithic times, before the discovery of agriculture. Hunter-gatherers built such villages in areas that had an abundant, stable food supply—near a river or lake well stocked with fish, or in a valley with plenty of wild wheat and barley and herds of gazelles or goats. The development of farming greatly speeded the shift to villages. It is likely that trade also impelled people to gather in village communities. Herdsmen, hunters, and food gatherers living in regions rich in salt (needed for preserving food), volcanic glass (used for mirrors, blades, and spearheads), or hematite (an iron ore that was a source of red coloring for pottery) formed trading settlements that exchanged raw materials for food.

Villages changed the patterns of life. A food surplus freed some people to devote part of their time to sharpening their skills as basket weavers or toolmakers. The demand for raw materials and the creations of skilled artisans fostered trade and the formation of trading settlements. An awareness of private property emerged. Hunters had accumulated few possessions, since belongings only presented a burden when moving from place to place. Villagers, however, acquired property that they were determined to protect from each other and from outsiders who might raid the village. Hunting bands were egalitarian; generally, no one member had more possessions or more power than another. In farming villages, a ruling elite emerged that possessed wealth and wielded power.

In recent years, archaeologists have uncovered several Neolithic villages, the oldest of which was established before 8000 B.C. Among the most famous of these sites are Çatal Hüyük in Anatolia (Turkey), Jericho in Palestine, and Jarmö in eastern Iraq. Scholars disagree on whether these communities were just highly developed villages or whether they were the first cities. The traditional view is that cities arose about 3000 B.C. in Sumer, the home of the earliest civilization. Some scholars argue that 5,000 years before the Sumerian cities, Jericho's 2,000 inhabitants had created urban life by engaging in trade and embarking on public works. Jericho's walls were 6 feet 6 inches thick at the base and in some places 20 feet high. Their construction required cooperation and a division of labor beyond the capacity of an agricultural village. Similar communities, or "primitive cities," spread throughout much of the Near East in late prehistoric times.

Neolithic people made great strides in technology. By shaping and baking clay, they made pottery containers for cooking and for storing food and water. The invention of the potter's wheel enabled them to form bowls and plates more quickly and precisely. Stone tools were sharpened by grinding them on rock. The discoveries of the wheel and the sail improved transportation and promoted trade while the development of the plow and the ox yoke made tilling the soil easier for farmers.

The Neolithic period also marks the beginning of the use of metals. First used was copper, which was easily fashioned into tools and weapons. Implements made from copper lasted longer than those made of stone and flint, and they could be recast and reshaped if broken. In time, artisans discovered how to make bronze by combining copper and tin in the proper ratio. Bronze was harder than copper, which made a sharper cutting edge possible.

During the Neolithic Age, the food supply became more reliable, village life expanded, and the population increased. Families that acquired wealth gained a higher social status and became village leaders. Religion grew more formal and structured; nature spirits evolved into deities, each with specific powers over nature or human life. Altars were erected in their honor, and ceremonies were conducted by priests, whose power and wealth increased as people gave offerings to the gods. Neolithic society was growing more organized and complex; it was on the threshold of civilization.

The First Civilizations

What we call *civilization* arose some 5,000 years ago in the Near East (in Mesopotamia and Egypt) and then later in the Far East (in India and China). The first civilizations began in cities that were larger, more populated, and more complex in their political, economic, and social structure than Neolithic villages. Because the cities depended on the inhabitants of adjacent villages for their food, farming techniques must have been developed sufficiently to produce food surpluses. Increased production provided food for urban inhabitants who engaged in nonagricultural occupations—merchants, craftsmen, bureaucrats, and priests.

The invention of writing enabled the first civilizations to preserve, organize, and expand knowledge; it allowed government officials and priests to conduct their affairs with greater efficiency. Civilized societies also possessed organized governments that issued laws and defined the boundary lines of their states. On a scale much larger than Neolithic communities, the inhabitants erected buildings and monuments, engaged in trade, and used specialized labor for different projects. Religious life grew more organized and complex, and a powerful and wealthy priesthood emerged. These developments—cities, specialization of labor, writing, organized government, monumental architecture, and a complex religious structure—differentiate the first civilizations from prehistoric cultures.

Religion was the central force in these primary civilizations. It provided satisfying explanations for the operations of nature, helped to ease the fear of death, and justified traditional rules of morality. Law was considered sacred, a commandment of the gods. Religion united people in the common enterprises needed for survival—for example, the construction and maintenance of irrigation works and the storage of food. Religion also promoted creative achievements in art, literature, and science. In addition, the power of rulers, who were regarded either as gods or as agents of the gods, derived from religion.

The emergence of civilization was a great creative act and not merely the inevitable development of agricultural societies. Many communities had learned how to farm, but only a handful made the leap into civilization. How was it possible for Sumerians and Egyptians, the creators of the earliest civilizations, to make this breakthrough? This question has intrigued and baffled historians, and no single explanation is entirely convincing. Most scholars stress the relationship between civilizations and river valleys. Rivers deposited fertile silt on adjoining fields, provided water for crops, and served as avenues for trade. But environmental factors alone do not adequately explain the emergence of civilization. What cannot be omitted is the human contribution—capacity for thought and cooperative activity.

Both the Tigris and Euphrates rivers in Mesopotamia and the Nile River in Egypt deposited fertile soil when they overflowed their banks. But before these rivers could be of any value in producing crops, swamps around them had to be drained, and dikes, reservoirs, and canals had to be built. To construct and maintain irrigation works required the cooperation of large numbers of people, a necessary condition for civilization. As anthropologist Robert J. Braidwood says:

It was not only a business of learning to control the rivers and making their waters do the farmer's work. It also meant controlling men. . . . This learning to work together for the common good was probably the real germ of the Egyptian and the Mesopotamian civilizations.[2]

In the process of constructing and maintaining irrigation networks, people learned to obey rules and developed administrative, engineering, and mathematical skills. The need to keep records stimulated the invention of writing. These creative responses to the challenges posed by nature spurred the early inhabitants of Sumer and Egypt to make the breakthrough to civilization, thereby altering the course of human destiny. By the time the Hebrews and the Greeks, the spiritual

Soundbox of Lyre from Ur. This soundbox, made of wood, gold, and lapis lazuli about 2600 B.C., suggests the artistic achievements of the Sumerians in the visual, musical, and literary realms. Animal motifs were a characteristic feature of ancient Near Eastern art. (*Reproduced by permission of The University Museum, University of Pennsylvania*)

ancestors of Western civilization, appeared on the stage of history, civilizations had been in existence for some two thousand years.

Civilization not only brought benefits, it also gave people the capacity to organize for destructive enterprises. The power generated by technology, the authority exercised by leaders, and the habits of discipline learned by the communities' inhabitants led to warfare, as well as to irrigation works. Lewis Mumford observes:

. . . War was not a mere residue of more common primitive forms of aggression. . . . In all its typical aspects, its discipline, its drill, its handling of large masses of men as units, in its destructive assaults en masse, in its heroic sacrifices, its final destructions, exterminations, seizures, enslavements, war was rather the special invention of civilization: its ultimate drama.[3]

The practice of warfare developed by the first civilizations has never been eradicated.

Mesopotamian Civilization

Mesopotamia is the Greek word for "land between the rivers." It was here, in the valleys of the Tigris and Euphrates rivers, where the first civilization began. The first to develop an urban civilization in Mesopotamia were the Sumerians, who colonized the marshlands of the lower Euphrates which, joined by the Tigris, flows into the Persian Gulf. The origin of the Sumerians is obscure; they spoke a language unrelated to the tongues of their Semitic neighbors who had migrated from Arabia into Mesopotamia and adjacent regions.

Through constant toil and imagination, the Sumerians transformed the swamps into fields of barley and groves of date palms. Their hut settlements gradually evolved into twelve independent city-states, each consisting of a city and its surrounding countryside. Among the impressive achievements of the Sumerians

were a system of symbol writing on clay tablets (cuneiform) to represent ideas; elaborate brick houses, palaces, and temples; bronze tools and weapons; irrigation works; trade with other peoples; an early form of money; religious and political institutions; schools; religious and secular literature; varied art forms; codes of law; medicinal drugs; and a lunar calendar.

Although they spoke a common language and shared the same customs and gods, the Sumerian city-states engaged in frequent warfare with each other, principally over boundaries and water rights. Weakened by warfare, the Sumerians lay open to foreign domination.

The history of Mesopotamia is marked by a succession of conquests. To the north of Sumer was a Semitic city called Akkad. About 2350 B.C., the people of Akkad, led by Sargon the Great, the warrior king, conquered the Sumerian cities. He built the world's first empire, which extended from the Persian Gulf to the Mediterranean Sea. The Akkadians adopted Sumerian cultural forms and spread them beyond the boundaries of Mesopotamia with their conquests. Mesopotamian religion became a blend of Sumerian and Akkadian elements.

Around 2180 B.C., invasions by the Guti, a semibarbaric people from Iran, along with internal dissension, caused the Akkadian empire to collapse. In the ensuing period, the Sumerian cities, though they paid tribute to the Guti, enjoyed a large measure of independence. Gutian power was short-lived, and a century later, the Sumerian city-state of Ur was able to assert its dominion over Sumer and Akkad.

From about 2135 to 2027 B.C., Sumer experienced economic expansion and cultural growth. Sumer extended its control northward into Assyria, Elam, and northwestern Mesopotamia. During this period, Sumer launched an extensive temple-building program, Sumerian literature reached its peak, and a code of laws was formed, a predecessor to the famous code of Hammurabi. But assaults by the Semitic Amorites from the

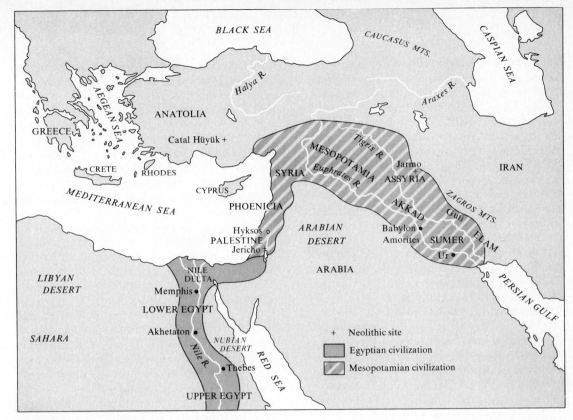

Map 1.1 Mesopotamian and Egyptian Civilizations

northeast and Elamites from Iran led to the disintegration of Sumerian power.

During the period of anarchy and war that followed, the Amorite city Babylon, northwest of Sumer on the Euphrates, became independent. Later, one of its rulers, Hammurabi (1792–1750 B.C.), launched conquests that brought Akkad and Sumer under his control.

During the centuries that followed, the Sumerian cities were incorporated into various kingdoms and empires. The Sumerian language, replaced by a Semitic tongue, became an obscure language known only to priests, and the Sumerians gradually disappeared as a distinct people. But their cultural achievements endured. Akkadians, Babylonians, Elamites, and others adopted Sumerian religious, art, legal, and literary forms. The Sumerian legacy served as the basis for a Mesopotamian civilization that maintained a distinct style for 3,000 years.

Religion: The Basis of Mesopotamian Civilization

Religion lay at the center of Mesopotamian life. Every human activity—political, military, social, legal, literary, artistic—was generally subordinated to an overriding religious purpose. Religion was the Mesopotamians' frame of reference for understanding nature, society, and themselves; it dominated and inspired all other cultural expressions. Wars between cities, for instance, were interpreted as conflicts between the gods of those cities, and victory ultimately depended on divine favor, not on human effort.

The Mesopotamians believed that people were given life so that they could execute on earth the will of the gods in heaven. No important decisions were made by kings or priests without first consulting the gods. To discover the wishes of the gods, priests sacrificed animals and then examined their livers; or the priests might find their answers in the stars or in dreams.

The cities of Mesopotamia were sacred communities dedicated to serving divine masters, and people hoped that appeasing the gods would bring security and prosperity to their cities. The Sumerians erected ziggurats—temples on huge multilevel mounds. The ziggurat in Ur measured 205 feet by 140 feet at the base and was about 70 feet high; staircases connected its levels and led to the top platform, on which stood a majestic temple.

The ziggurat was surrounded by low walls enclosing offices and houses for the priests, and shops where potters, weavers, carpenters, and tanners performed their crafts. The temple was the cultural and economic heart of the city. A particular city belonged to a god, who was the real owner of the land and the real ruler of the city; often a vast complex of temples was built for the god and the god's family. In the temple the god was offered shelter, food, clothing, and the homage of dutiful servants.

Supervised by priests, the temple was a vital part of the city's life. The temple owned land, probably most of the land in its city; temple priests collected rents, operated businesses, and received contributions for festivals. Most inhabitants of the city worked for the temple priests as tenant farmers, agricultural laborers, or servants. Priests coordinated the city's economic activity: supervising the distribution of land, overseeing the irrigation works, and storing food for emergencies. Temple scribes kept records of expenditures and receipts. By serving as stewards of the city's gods and managing their earthly estates, the priests sustained civilized life.

The gods—superhuman and immortal, invisible to human eyes but omnipresent—controlled the entire universe and everything in it. The moon, the sun, and the storm; the city, the irrigation works, and the fields—each was directed by a god. Mesopotamians saw gods and demons everywhere in nature.

There was a god in the fire and another in the river; evil demons stirred up sandstorms, caused disease, endangered women in childbirth. To protect themselves from hostile forces, Mesopotamians wore charms and begged their gods for help. Each Mesopotamian offered prayers and sacrifices to a personal god or goddess who provided protection against evil spirits.

Mesopotamians believed that they were manipulated by divine beings. When misfortune befell them, people attributed it to the gods. Even success was not due to their own efforts, but to the intervention of a god who had taken a special interest in them. Compared to the gods, an individual was an insignificant and lowly creature.

Life in Mesopotamia was filled with uncertainty and danger. Sometimes the unpredictable waters of the rivers broke through the dikes, flooding fields, ruining crops, and damaging cities. At other times an insufficient overflow deprived the land of water, causing crops to fail. Great windstorms left the countryside covered with a layer of sand, and heavy thunderstorms turned fields into a sea of mud that made travel impossible. Unlike Egypt, which was protected by vast deserts, Mesopotamia had no natural barriers to invasion. Feeling themselves surrounded by unfathomable and often hostile forces, Mesopotamians lived in an atmosphere of anxiety that permeated their civilization.

Contributing to this sense of insecurity was the belief that the gods behaved capriciously, malevolently, vindictively. What do the gods demand of me? Is it ever possible to please them? To these questions Mesopotamians had no reassuring answers, for the gods' behavior was a mystery to mere human beings:

What is good in a man's sight is evil for a god,
What is evil to a man's mind is good for his
    god.
Who can comprehend the counsel of the gods in
    heaven?
The plan of a god is deep waters, who can
    fathom it?

*Where has befuddled mankind ever learned
     what is a god's conduct?*[4]

A Mesopotamian man or woman hoped to experience the good life by being obedient to his or her older brother, father, foreman, priest, and king and to a personal god who could influence the decisions of the other gods. The rewards for obedience were long life, health, and worldly success. But the feeling persisted that happiness was either transitory or beyond reach—a pessimism that abounded in Mesopotamian literature.

A mood of uncertainty and anxiety, an awareness of the cosmos as unfathomable and mysterious, a feeling of dread about the nature of human existence and the impermanence of human achievement—these attitudes are as old as the first civilization. The *Epic of Gilgamesh*, the finest work of Mesopotamian literature, masterfully depicts this mood of pessimism and despair: "Where is the man who can clamber to heaven? Only the gods live forever . . . but as for us men, our days are numbered, our occupations are a breath of wind."[5]

Government and Law

The government of early Sumer may have been a "primitive democracy," that is, one in which a council of elders guided everyday affairs, and an assembly of citizens appointed a temporary king when war threatened. In time, kingship became hereditary and permanent, supplanting rule by the elders. The king's chief duties were to direct the construction and maintenance of temples and irrigation canals and to wage war.

Bestowed on a man by the gods, kingship was the central institution in Mesopotamian society. Unlike Egyptian pharaohs, Mesopotamian kings did not consider themselves to be gods, but great men selected by the gods to represent them on earth. Gods governed through the kings, who reported to the gods about conditions in their land (which

was the gods' property) and petitioned the gods for advice.

The Mesopotamians viewed earthly governments as exact replicas of the government of the gods. No one Mesopotamian god was all-powerful; instead, an assembly of gods made decisions as a group. Therefore, a mortal king could not be all-powerful either. For this reason, Mesopotamian kingship usually lacked the sureness, confidence, and absolutism of Egyptian kingship. This view of kingship also contributed to the anxiety in Mesopotamian life, for there was no assurance that a king, mortal and fallible, could correctly ascertain heaven's commands.

The king administered the laws, which came from the gods. Like everyone else in the land, the king had to obey divine laws. These laws provided Mesopotamians with a measure of security. The principal collection of laws in ancient Mesopotamia was the famous code of Hammurabi, the Babylonian ruler. Unearthed by French archaeologists in 1901–1902, the code has provided invaluable insights into Mesopotamian society. In typical Mesopotamian fashion, Hammurabi claimed that his code rested on the authority of the gods; to violate it was to contravene the divine order.

The code reveals social status and mores in that area and time. Women were subservient to men, although efforts were made to protect women and children from abuse. By making death the penalty for adultery, the code sought to preserve family life. Punishments were generally severe—"an eye for an eye and a tooth for a tooth." The code prescribed death for housebreaking, kidnapping, aiding the escape of slaves, receiving stolen goods, and bearing false witness, but it also allowed consideration of extenuating circumstances. Class distinctions were expressed in the code. For example, a person received more severe punishment if he had harmed a noble than he would if he had harmed a commoner. The code's many provisions relating to business transactions show the importance of trade to Mesopotamian life.

Couple from Nippur, 2500 B.C. Large eyes and geometrical beard and hair characterize Sumerian figures. The intimacy and stability of the pose contrast with the uncertainty and pessimism found throughout Mesopotamian literature. (*Courtesy of the Oriental Institute, University of Chicago*)

Business and Trade

The economy of Mesopotamian cities depended heavily on foreign and domestic trade. Whereas trade in Egypt was conducted by the state bureaucracy, in Mesopotamia there was greater opportunity for private enterprise. In addition to merchants, temple priests engaged in trade because they possessed surplus produce collected as rents from farmers using temple land. Early in Mesopotamian history, merchants were subservient to the king and the temple priests. Over the centuries, however, merchants began to behave as professionals—not just as agents of the palace or temple, but as private entrepreneurs.

Because of trade's importance to the life of the city, governments instituted regulations to prevent fraud. Business transactions had to be recorded in writing, and severe punishments were imposed for dishonesty. A system of weights and measures facilitated trade, and efforts were made to prevent excessive interest rates for loans.

Mycerinus and Queen, c. 2525 B.C. Swelling chests and hips idealize the royal couple's humanity, but the cubic feeling of the sculpture and the rigid con-fidence of the pose proclaim their unquestioned divinity. (*Courtesy Museum of Fine Arts, Boston*)

Mesopotamians imported resources not found at home—stone, silver, and timber; in exchange they exported textiles, fine handicrafts, and (less often because of difficulty in transporting them by donkey) agricultural products. They also imported copper from the Persian Gulf, precious metals from Afghanistan, ivory from Africa and the west coast of India, and cedar and cypress woods, oils, and essences from the Mediterranean coastal lands. Enterprising businessmen set up trading outposts in distant lands, making the Mesopotamians pioneers in international trade.

Writing, Mathematics, Astronomy, Medicine

The Sumerians established schools that trained the sons of the upper class in the art of cuneiform writing. Hundreds of tablets on which Sumerian students practiced their lessons have been discovered, testifying to the years of disciplined and demanding work required to master the scribal art. To assist their pupils, teachers prepared textbooks of word lists and mathematical problems with solutions. In translating Sumerian words into the Akkadian language, they compiled what was probably the world's first dictionary. Students who completed the course of study successfully were employed by the temple, the palace, the law courts, or merchants. The Sumerian system of cuneiform writing spread to other parts of the Near East.

The Mesopotamians made some impressive achievements in mathematics. They devised multiplication and division tables, including even cubes and cube roots. They determined the area of right-angle triangles and rectangles, divided a circle into 360 degrees, and had some understanding of principles that centuries later would be developed into the Pythagorean theorem and quadratic equations. But the Babylonians, who made the chief contribution in mathematics, barely advanced to the level of making theories; they did not draw general principles or furnish proofs for their mathematical operations.

By carefully observing and accurately recording the positions of planets and constellations of stars, Babylonian sky watchers took the first steps in developing the science of astronomy, and they devised a calendar based on the cycles of the moon. As in mathematics, however, they did not form theories to coordinate and illuminate their data. They believed that the position of the stars and planets revealed the will of the gods. Astronomers did not examine the heavens because of intellectual curiosity, but rather to discover what the gods wanted. With this knowledge, people could organize their political, social, and moral lives in accordance with divine commands, and they could escape the terrible consequences that they believed resulted from ignoring the gods' wishes. Consequently, Babylonian astronomy, despite its impressive achievements, remained essentially a mythical interpretation of the universe.

Consistent with their religious world-view, the Mesopotamians believed that disease was caused by gods or demons. To cure a patient, priest-physicians resorted to magic; through prayers and sacrifices they attempted to appease the gods and eject the demons from the sick body. Nevertheless, in identifying illnesses and prescribing appropriate remedies, Mesopotamian priest-physicians demonstrated some accurate knowledge of medicine and pharmacology.

Egyptian Civilization

During the early period of Mesopotamian civilization, the people of another river valley to the west put themselves on the path toward civilization. The Egyptians developed their civilization in the fertile valley of the Nile. For good reason, the Greek historian Herodotus called Egypt "the gift of the Nile," for without this mighty river, which flows more than 4,000 miles from central Africa northward to the Mediterranean Sea, virtually all Egypt would be a desert. When the Nile overflowed its banks, the floodwaters deposited a layer of fertile black earth that when cultivated, provided abundant food to support Egyptian civilization. The Egyptians learned how to control the river—a feat that required cooperative effort and ingenuity, as well as engineering and administrative skills.

Nature favored Egypt in a number of ways. In addition to water and fertile land, the Nile also provided an excellent transportation link between Upper (southern) and Lower (northern) Egypt. Natural barriers—mountains, deserts, cataracts in the Nile, and the Mediterranean Sea—protected Egypt from attack, allowing the inhabitants to enjoy long periods of peace and prosperity. Gold, copper, and stone were abundant, along with other natural resources. In addition, the climate of Egypt is dry and salutary. To the Egyptians, nature seemed changeless and beneficent. Thus, unlike Mesopotamians, Egyptians derived a sense of security from their environment.

Pyramids and Sphinx at Giza. In Egypt the afterlife dominated the thoughts of the living. Pharaoh's large pyramids and the lesser ones of his wives were built as monumental tombs. The colossal sphinx dates from the reign of Khafre (c. 2550 B.C.) and is a portrait of the pharaoh on the body of a lion. The sphinx continues as a royal portrait type through Egyptian history. (*Lee Boltin*)

From the Old Kingdom to the Middle Kingdom

About 2900 B.C., a ruler of Upper Egypt, known as Narmer or Menes, conquered the Nile Delta and Lower Egypt. By 2686 B.C., centralized rule had been firmly established, and great pyramids, which were tombs for the pharaohs, were being constructed. During this Pyramid Age, or Old Kingdom (2686–2181 B.C.), the essential forms of Egyptian civilization crystallized.

The Egyptians believed the pharaoh to be both a man and a god, the earthly embodiment of the deity Horus; he was an absolute ruler of the land and held his court at the city of Memphis. The Egyptians regarded the pharaoh as a benevolent protector who controlled the floodwaters of the Nile, kept the irrigation works in order, maintained justice in the land, and expressed the will of heaven. They expected that when the pharaoh died and joined his fellow gods, he would still help his living subjects.

In time, the nobles who served as district governors gained in status and wealth and gradually came to undermine the divine king's authority. The nobles' growing power and the enormous expenditure of Egypt's human and material resources on building pyramids led to the decline of the Old Kingdom. From 2181 to 2040 B.C., called the First Intermediate Period, rival families competed for the throne, thus destroying the unity of the kingdom. The civil wars and the collapse of central authority required to maintain the irrigation system cast a pall of gloom over the land, as is illustrated in this ancient Egyptian poem:

The wrongdoer is everywhere. . . .
Plunderers are everywhere. . . .
Nile is in flood, yet none plougheth for
*   him. . . .*
Laughter hath perished and is no longer made.
It is grief that walketh through the land,
*   mingled with lamentations. . . .*
The storehouse is bare.[6]

During what is called the Middle Kingdom (2040–1786 B.C.), strong kings reasserted pharaonic rule and reunited the state. With political stability restored, cultural life was reinvigorated and economic activity revived. Pharaohs extended Egyptian control south over the land of Nubia, which became a principal source of gold. A profitable trade was carried on with Palestine, Syria, and Crete.

About 1800 B.C., central authority again weakened. In the era known as the Second Intermediate Period (1786–1570 B.C.), the nobles regained some of their power, the Nubians broke away from Egyptian control, and the Hyksos (a mixture of Semites and Indo-Europeans) invaded Egypt. For centuries, desert and sea had effectively guarded Egypt from foreign invasion, but the Hyksos invaders, using horse and chariot and body armor, ended Egyptian complacency. The Hyksos succeeded in dominating Egypt for about a hundred years. Resentful of foreign rule, the Egyptians became more militant and aggressive; they learned to use the Hyksos' weapons and drove out the invaders in 1570 B.C. The period of empire building known as the New Kingdom (1570–1085 B.C.) then began.

The basic features of Egyptian civilization had been forged during the Old and Middle Kingdoms. Egyptians looked to the past, believing that the ways of their ancestors were best. For almost 3,000 years, Egyptian civilization sought to retain a harmony with that order of nature instituted at creation. Egyptians had no conception of progress. Believing that the universe was static and changeless,

the Egyptians valued the institutions, traditions, and authority that gave the appearance of permanence.

Religion: The Basis of Egyptian Civilization

Religion was omnipresent in Egyptian life and accounted for the outstanding achievements of Egyptian civilization. Religious beliefs were the basis of Egyptian art, medicine, astronomy, literature, and government. The great pyramids were tombs for the pharaohs, man-gods. Magical utterances pervaded medical practices, for disease was attributed to the gods. Astronomy evolved to determine the correct time to perform religious rites and sacrifices. The earliest examples of literature dealt wholly with religious themes. Pharaoh was a sacrosanct monarch who served as an intermediary between the gods and human beings. Justice was conceived in religious terms, something bestowed by a creator-god. The Egyptians developed an ethical code, which they believed had been approved by the gods.

Egyptian polytheism took many forms including the worship of animals, for Egyptians believed that gods manifested themselves in animal shapes. Consequently, crocodiles, cats, bulls, and other animals dwelt in temples and were mummified for burial when they died. Perhaps the Egyptians regarded animals with religious awe because an animal species continues from generation to generation without apparent change. To the Egyptian mind, says Henri Frankfort, a leading scholar in Near Eastern studies, the quality of changelessness made "animal life . . . appear superhuman . . . in that it shared directly, patently, in the static life of the universe."[7]

Certain gods were conceived by Egyptians as taking various forms. Thoth, for example, was represented as the moon, a baboon, an ibis, and an ibis-headed man. The god Amen was depicted both in human form and as a ram. To Egyptians, these different representations were not contradictory, for they did not seek logical consistency in religion. Egyptians also believed great powers in nature—sky, sun, earth, the Nile—to be gods. Thus, the universe was alive with divinities, and human lives were tied to the movements of the sun and the moon and to the rhythm of the seasons. In the heavens alive with gods, Egyptians found answers to the great problems of human existence.

A crucial feature of Egyptian religion was the afterlife. Through pyramid-tombs, mummification to preserve the dead, and funerary art, Egyptians showed their yearning for eternity and their desire to overcome death. Mortuary priests recited incantations to ensure the preservation of the dead body and the continuity of existence. Inscribed on the pyramids' interior walls were "pyramid texts" written in *hieroglyphics*—a form of picture writing in which figures, such as crocodiles, sails, eyes, and so forth, represented words, or sounds that would be combined to form words. The texts contained fragments from myths, historical annals, and magical lore and provided spells to assist the king in ascending to heaven.

At first, it was held that only the pharaoh and the royal family were immortal. In time, first the nobility and then commoners claimed that they too could share in the blessings of the "other world." Prayers hitherto reserved for the pharaoh were, for a fee, recited by priests at the burial of commoners. To Egyptians, the other world contained the same pleasures enjoyed on earth—friends, servants, fishing, hunting, paddling a canoe, picnicking with family members, entertainment by musicians and dancers, and good food. Because earthly existence was not fundamentally unhappy, however, Egyptians did not yearn for death.

Divine Kingship

"What is the king of Upper and Lower Egypt? He is a god by whose dealings one lives, the father and mother of men, alone by himself,

without an equal."[8] Divine kingship was the basic institution of Egyptian civilization. Perhaps the requirements of the Egyptian environment helped to fashion the idea of the pharaoh as a living god, because a ruler with supernatural authority could hold together the large kingdom and draft the mass labor required to maintain the irrigation system.

Through the pharaoh the gods made known their wishes for the Egyptian people. As kingship was a divine, not a manmade, institution, it was expected to last for eternity. The Egyptians rejoiced in the rule of an all-powerful, all-knowing god-king. To the Egyptians, the pharaoh was "the herdsman of everyone without evil in his heart."[9] They believed that divine kingship was the only acceptable political arrangement, that it was in harmony with the order of the universe, and that it brought stability and authority to the nation.

The power of the pharaoh extended to all sectors of society. Peasants were drafted to serve in labor corps as miners or construction workers. Foreign trade was a state monopoly conducted according to the kingdom's needs. Although private ownership of land was recognized in practice, all land in theory belonged to the pharaoh. As the supreme overlord, the pharaoh oversaw an army of government officials who collected taxes, supervised construction projects, checked the irrigation works, surveyed the land, kept records, and supervised government warehouses where grain was stored as insurance against a bad harvest. Because the pharaoh's word was regarded as a divine ordinance, Egypt, unlike Mesopotamia, had no need for written laws. All Egyptians were subservient to the pharaoh, and there was no conception of political liberty. Most pharaohs took their responsibilities seriously and tried to govern as benevolent protectors of the people.

Be not evil, it is good to be kindly. . . . Do right so long as thou abidest on the earth. Calm the weeper, oppress no widow, expel no man from the possessions of his father. . . . Take heed lest thou punish wrongfully. . . . Slay not a man

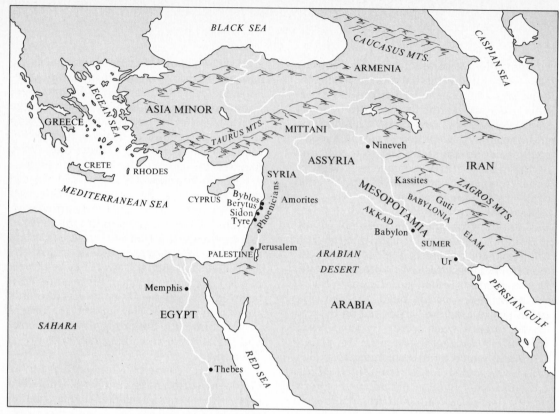

Map 1.2 Kingdoms and Peoples of the Ancient World

whose good qualities thou knowest. . . . Exalt not the son of one of high degree more than him that is of lowly birth, but take to thyself a man because of his actions.[10]

Egyptians derived a sense of security from the concept of divine kingship. It meant that earthly government and society were in harmony with the cosmic order. The Egyptians believed that the institution of kingship dated from the creation of the universe, that as part of the rhythm of the universe, kingship was necessary and beneficial to human beings, and that there was a divine order to the cosmos, which brought justice and security.

The pharaoh was seen as ruling in accordance with Ma'at which means justice, law, right, and truth. To oppose the pharaoh was to violate the order of Ma'at and to bring disorder to society. Because Egyptians regarded Ma'at as the right order of nature, they believed that its preservation must be

the object of human activity—the guiding norm of the state and the standard by which individuals conducted their lives. Those who did Ma'at and spoke Ma'at would be justly rewarded. Could anything be more reassuring than this belief that divine truth was represented in the person of the pharaoh?

Science and Mathematics

Like the Mesopotamians, the Egyptians made practical advances in the sciences. They demonstrated superb engineering skills in building pyramids and fashioned an effective system of mathematics that enabled them to solve relatively simple problems based more on experience than on reasoning. Noting that the Nile flooded after the star Sirius appeared in the sky, the Egyptians developed a calendar by which they could predict the time of the flood. The Egyptian 365-day solar calendar, based on the movements of the sun, was more accurate than the Babylonian lunar calendar.

In the area of medicine, Egyptian doctors were more capable than their Mesopotamian counterparts. They were able to identify illnesses; they recognized that uncleanliness encouraged contagion; they had some knowledge of anatomy and performed operations—circumcision and perhaps the draining of abscessed teeth. Although the progress of medicine was handicapped by the belief that gods caused illnesses, there is evidence that some Egyptian doctors examined the body in a scientific way. In a scroll, the Edwin Smith Surgical Papyrus (named after the nineteenth-century American Egyptologist who acquired it), the writer omitted all references to divine intervention in his advice for treating wounds and fractures. He described fractures in a matter-of-fact way and recommended healing them with splints and casts.

The New Kingdom and the Decline of Egyptian Civilization

The New Kingdom began in 1570 B.C. with the war of liberation against the Hyksos, which gave rise to an intense militancy and nationalism that found expression in empire building. Military-minded pharaohs conquered territory that extended as far east as the Euphrates River. From its subject states, Egypt acquired tribute and slaves. Conquests led to the expansion of the bureaucracy, the rise of a professional army, and the increased power of priests, whose temples shared in the spoils. The formation of the empire ended Egyptian isolation and accelerated commercial and cultural intercourse with other peoples. Egyptian art, for example, showed the influence of foreign forms during this period.

A growing cosmopolitanism was paralleled by a movement toward monotheism during the reign of Pharaoh Amenhotep IV (c. 1369–1353 B.C.). Amenhotep sought to replace traditional polytheism with the worship of Aton,

a single god of all men who was represented as the sun disk. Amenhotep took the name Akhenaton ("It is well with Aton"), and moved the capital from Thebes to a newly constructed holy city called Akhataten (near modern Tell el-Amarna). The city had palaces, administrative centers, and a temple complex honoring Aton. Akhenaton and his wife Nefertiti dedicated themselves to Aton—the creator of the world, the maintainer of life, and the god of love, justice, and peace. Akhenaton (or Ikhneton) also ordered his officials to chisel out the names of other gods from inscriptions on temples and monuments. With awe Akhenaton glorified Aton:

How manifold are thy works!
They are hidden from man's sight.
O sole god, like whom there is no other.
*Thou hast made the earth according to thy
    desire.*[11]

Akhenaton's "monotheism" had little impact on the masses of Egyptians, who retained their ancient beliefs, and was resisted by priests, who resented his changes. After Akhenaton's death the new pharaoh, Tutankhamen (1352–1344 B.C.) abandoned the capital at Amarna and returned to Thebes. Tutankhamen was succeeded by an elderly relative who reigned briefly. In 1340, Horemheb (1340–1315 B.C.), an army commander, seized power and had the monuments to Aton destroyed, along with records and inscriptions bearing Akhenaton's name.

Historians are not certain why Akhenaton made this radical break with tradition. Was he trying to strike at the priests whose wealth and prestige had increased considerably with Egypt's conquests? Did the break stem essentially from an intense religious fervor? But the most significant historical questions concerning Akhenaton are: Was his religion genuine monotheism, which pushed religious thought in a new direction? And if so, did it influence Moses, who led the Israelites out of Egypt about a century later?

These last questions have aroused controversy among historians. The principal limi-

Rosetta Stone. This ancient Egyptian stone (195 B.C.) bears the same decree in three forms—hieroglyphics in the top section, demotic (cursive Egyptian) characters next, and Greek at the bottom. The stone, which led to the deciphering of hieroglyphics, was found in August 1799 by a Frenchman serving under Napoleon; it passed into British hands with the French surrender of Egypt (1801). (*The British Museum*)

tation on the monotheistic character of Atonism is that there were really two gods in Akhenaton's religion—Aton and the pharaoh himself, who was still worshiped as a deity. Egyptologist John A. Wilson sheds light on this notion. Because Egyptians could not break with the central idea of their civilization, divine kingship, "one could say that it was the closest approach to monotheism possible within the thought of the day. That would still fall short of making it a belief in and worship of only one god."[12] Regarding the relationship of Atonism to a later Hebrew monotheism, Wilson says, "The mechanism of transmission from the faith of Akhena-

ton to the monotheism of Moses is not apparent."[13]

Late in the thirteenth century, Libyans, probably seeking to settle in the more fertile land of Egypt, attacked from the west, and the Peoples of the Sea, as unsettled raiders from the Aegean Sea area and Asia Minor were called, launched a series of strikes at Egypt. A weakened Egypt abandoned its empire. In the succeeding centuries Egypt came under the rule of Libyans, Nubians, Assyrians, Persians, and finally Greeks, to whom Egypt lost its independence in the fourth century B.C.

Egyptian civilization had flourished for almost 2,000 years before it experienced an almost 1,000-year descent into stagnation, decline, and collapse. During its long history the Egyptians tried to preserve the ancient forms of their civilization, revealed to them by their ancestors and representing for all time those unchanging values that are the way of happiness.

Empire Builders

The rise of an Egyptian empire during the New Kingdom was part of a wider development in Near Eastern history after 1500 B.C.—the emergence of international empires. Empire building led to the intermingling of peoples and cultural traditions and to the extension of civilization well beyond the river valleys.

Migration of Indo-Europeans

One reason for the growth of empires was the migration of peoples known as Indo-Europeans. Originally from a wide area ranging from southeastern Europe to the region beyond the Caspian Sea, Indo-Europeans embarked on a series of migrations around 2000 B.C. that eventually brought them into Italy, Greece, Asia Minor, Mesopotamia, Persia, and India. From a core Indo-European tongue there emerged the Greek, Latin, Germanic, Persian, and Sanskrit languages.

Several peoples established strong states in the Near East around 1500 B.C.—the Hurrians in northern Mesopotamia, the Hittites in Asia Minor, and the Kassites in southern Mesopotamia. Originally from the highlands of Armenia, the Hurrians had been infiltrating Mesopotamia for centuries. Aided by a wave of Indo-European invaders, they set up the Mitanni empire in northern Mesopotamia and adopted Mesopotamian civilization. In 1365 B.C., the Mitanni empire fell to the Hittites.

Penetrating Asia Minor, Indo-Europeans coalesced with native Hattic-speaking peoples to create the Hittite empire (1450–1200 B.C.). The Hittites ruled Asia Minor and northern Syria, raided Babylon, and challenged Egypt for control of Syria and Palestine.

The Hittites wanted to control the trade routes that ran along the Euphrates River into Syria. Mursilis I, a Hittite king, conquered part of Syria and sacked Babylon in 1595 B.C., ending the Amorite dynasty that had been established by Hammurabi four centuries earlier. Shortly after the attack, however, the Hittites withdrew from Babylon. In the 1300s, the Hittite empire reached its peak and included much of Asia Minor and northern Syria. The Hittites' success arose from their well-trained army. Mass attacks by light horse-drawn chariots demolished enemy lines, while foot soldiers made effective use of the battle axe and a short curved sword.

The Hittites borrowed several features of Mesopotamian civilization, including cuneiform, legal principles, and literary and art forms. Hittite religion blended the beliefs and practices of Indo-Europeans, native inhabitants of Asia Minor, and Mesopotamians. The Hittites were probably the first people to develop a substantial iron industry. At first, they apparently used iron only for ceremonial and ritual objects, and not for tools and weapons. However, because iron ore was more readily available than copper or tin (needed for bronze), after 1200 B.C. iron weapons and tools spread throughout the Near East, although bronze implements were still used. Around 1200 B.C., the Hittite empire fell, most likely to Indo-European invaders from the north.

By about 1460 B.C., the Kassites, assisted by Indo-Europeans, gained control over Babylonia, giving political unity to the area. The Kassites had originated in the Zagros Mountains to the east; like the Hurrians, they adopted Mesopotamian language and culture. They ruled Babylonia for some 400 years until subdued about 1150 B.C. by Elamites from Iran.

Small Nations

During the twelfth century there was a temporary lull in empire building, which permitted a number of small nations in Syria and Palestine to assert their sovereignty. Three of these peoples—Phoenicians, Aramaeans, and Hebrews*—were originally Semitic desert nomads. The Phoenicians were descendants of the Canaanites, a Semitic people who had settled Palestine about 3000 B.C. Those Canaanites who migrated northwest into what is now Lebanon were called Phoenicians.

Settling in the coastal Mediterranean cities of Tyre, Byblos, Berytus (Beirut), and Sidon, the Phoenicians were naturally drawn to the sea. These daring explorers established towns along the coast of North Africa, on the islands of the western Mediterranean, and in Spain, and they became the greatest sea traders of the ancient world. Phoenician merchants exported lumber, glass, copper and bronze utensils, and the purple dye produced from the murex, a mollusk that was plentiful in the coastal waters. The Phoenicians (or their Canaanite forebears) devised the first alphabet, which was a monumental contribution to writing. Since all words could be represented by combinations of letters, it saved memorizing thousands of diagrams and aided

---

*The Hebrews will be discussed in Chapter 2.

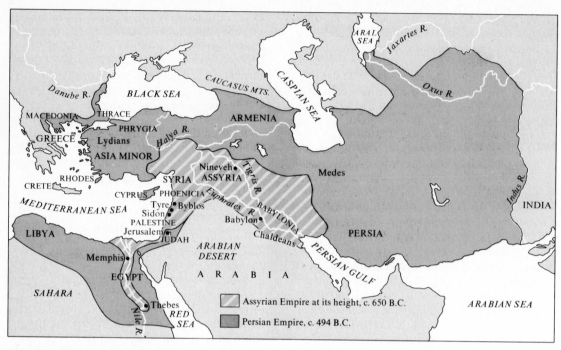

Map 1.3 The Assyrian and Persian Empires

the Phoenicians in transmitting the civilizations of the Near East to the western Mediterranean.

The Aramaeans, who settled in Syria, Palestine, and northern Mesopotamia, performed a role similar to the Phoenicians'. As great caravan traders they carried both goods and cultural patterns to various parts of the Near East. The Hebrews and the Persians, for example, acquired the Phoenician alphabet from the Aramaeans.

Assyria

In the ninth century, empire building resumed with the Assyrians, a Semitic people from the region around the upper Tigris River. Because their geographical position made them prey to other peoples in the area, the Assyrians emphasized military prowess to maintain their borders. The Assyrians care-

fully planned a military campaign and excelled in siege weapons, with which they subdued heavily fortified towns; their soldiers wore armor and wielded iron swords.

Although they had made forays of expansion in 1200 and 1100 B.C., the Assyrians began their march to "world" empire three centuries later. In the eighth and seventh centuries the Assyrians became a ruthless fighting machine that steamrolled through Mesopotamia—including Armenia and Babylonia—as well as Syria, Palestine, and Egypt. At its height, the Assyrian empire extended from the Iranian plateau in the east to the Egyptian city of Thebes.

How did the Assyrians administer such a vast empire? An Assyrian king, who was the representative and high priest of the god Ashur, governed absolutely. Nobles appointed by the king kept order in the provinces and collected tribute. The Assyrians improved roads, established messenger services, and engaged in large-scale irrigation projects to facilitate effective administration of their conquered lands and to promote prosperity. To keep their subjects obedient, the Assyrians resorted to terror and to deportation of troublesome subjects from their home territories. Assyrian kings boasted of their ruthlessness toward rebellious subjects:

13,000 of their warriors I cut down with the sword. Their blood like the water of a stream I caused to run through the squares of their city. The corpses of their soldiers I piled in heaps. . . . [The Babylonian king's] royal bed, his royal couch, the treasure of his palaces, his property, his gods and everything from his palace without number, I carried away. His captive warriors were given to the soldiers of my land like grasshoppers. The city I destroyed, I devastated, I burned with fire.[14]

Despite their harsh characteristics, the Assyrians maintained and spread the culture of the past. They copied and edited the literary works of Babylonia, adopted the old Sumerian gods, and used Mesopotamian art forms. The Assyrian king Ashurbanipal (669–626 B.C.) maintained a great library that contained thousands of clay tablets.

After a period of wars and revolts by oppressed subjects weakened Assyria, a coalition of Medes from Iran and Chaldeans, or Neo-Babylonians, sacked the Assyrian capital of Nineveh in 612 B.C. The conquerors looted and destroyed the city and the surviving Assyrians fled. Assyrian power was broken.

The Neo-Babylonian Empire

The destruction of the Assyrian empire made possible the rise of a Chaldean empire that included Babylonia, Assyria, Syria, and Palestine. Under Nebuchadnezzar, who ruled from 604 to 562 B.C., the Chaldean or Neo-Babylonian empire reached its height. A talented general and statesman, and a brilliant administrator, Nebuchadnezzar had Babylon rebuilt. The new Babylon that arose on the shore of the Euphrates had magnificent procession-ways that led to palaces and temples. On his palace grounds, Nebuchadnezzar created the famous Hanging Gardens for his Medean wife, according to legend. The 350-foot building was a series of vaulted terraces and was surrounded by a moat of flowing water. Trees, shrubs, and flowers decorated each terrace. In the interior, vaulted halls were stocked with vessels, fabrics, ornaments, and wines gathered from different regions of the empire. Here guests reclined on divans and were attended by slaves.

Persia: Unifier of the Near East

After Nebuchadnezzar's death, the Chaldean empire was torn by civil war and threatened by a new power—the Persians, an Indo-European people who had settled in southern Iran. Under Cyrus the Great and his son and successor, Cambyses, the Persians conquered all lands between the Nile in Egypt and the Indus River in India. This conquest took twenty-five years, from 550 to 525 B.C.

The Near Eastern conception of absolute monarchy justified by religion reached its culminating expression in the person of the Persian king who, with divine approval, ruled a vast empire, "the four quarters of the earth." Persian kings developed an effective system of administration—based in part on an Assyrian model—that gave stability and a degree of unity to their extensive territories. In so doing they performed a creative act of statesmanship. The Persian empire was divided into twenty provinces (satrapies), each one administered by a governor (satrap) responsible to the emperor. To guard against subversion, the king employed special agents— "the eyes and ears of the Emperor"—who supervised the activities of the governors. Persian kings allowed the provincials a large measure of self-rule. They also respected local traditions, particularly in matters of religion, as long as subjects paid their taxes, served in the royal army, and refrained from rebellion; and they deliberately tried to win the goodwill of priests in conquered lands.

Persepolis: Great Ceremonial Staircase and Audience Hall. Persepolis was the ceremonial center of the Persian empire. The repetitive geometric tribute bearers in bas relief along the staircase continue artistic traditions from distant Sumerian times. (*Courtesy of the Oriental Institute, University of Chicago*)

The empire was bound together by a uniform language, Aramaic (the language of the Aramaeans of Syria), used by government officials and merchants. Aramaic was written in letters based on the Phoenician alphabet. By making Aramaic a universal language, the Persians facilitated written and oral communication within the empire. The empire was further unified by an elaborate network of roads, an efficient postal system, a common system of weights and measures, and an empire-wide coinage based on an invention of the Lydians from western Asia Minor.

In addition to providing impressive political and administrative unity, the Persians fused and perpetuated the various cultural traditions of the Near East. Persian palaces, for example, boasted the terraces of Babylon, the colonnades of Egypt, the winged bulls that decorated Assyrian palace gates, and the craftsmanship of Median goldsmiths.

The political and cultural universalism of the Persian empire had its counterpart in the emergence of a higher religion, Zoroastrianism. Named for its founder, the Persian prophet Zoroaster, this religion taught belief in Ahura Mazda—the Wise Lord—god of light, of justice, wisdom, goodness, and immortality. But, in addition to the Wise Lord, there also existed Ahriman, the spirit of darkness, who was evil and destructive; Ahriman was in conflict with Ahura Mazda. People were free to choose whom they would follow. To serve Ahura Mazda, one had to speak the truth and be good to others; the reward for such behavior was life eternal in paradise, the realm of light and goodness. Followers of the evil spirit were cast into hell, a realm of darkness and torment. In contrast to the traditional religions of the Near East, Zoroastrianism rejected magic, polytheism, sacrifices, and temples, and instead stressed ethics.

Persia unified the nations of the Near East into a world-state, headed by a divinely appointed king, and synthesized the region's cultural traditions. Soon it would confront the city-states of Greece, whose political system and cultural orientation differed from that of the Near East.

The Religious Orientation of the Near East

All features of Near Eastern society—law, kingship, art, and science—were generally interpenetrated with, and dominated by religion. Religion was the source of the vitality and creativity of Mesopotamian and Egyptian civilizations. Near Eastern art was inspired by religion; literature and history dealt with the ways of the gods; science was permeated with religion. And priest-kings or god-kings, their power sanctioned by divine forces, furnished the necessary authority to organize large numbers of people in cooperative ventures.

A Myth-making World-View

A religious or mythopoeic (myth-making) view of the world gives Near Eastern civilization its distinctive form and allows us to see it as an organic whole. Myth-making was humanity's first way of thinking; it was the earliest attempt to make nature and life comprehensible. Appealing primarily to the imagination and emotions, not to reason, myth has been a fundamental formative element of human culture, which has expressed itself, often creatively, in language, art, poetry, and social organization.

Originating in sacred rites, ritual dances, feasts, and ceremonies, myths narrated the deeds of gods who, in some remote past, had brought forth the world and human beings. Holding that human destiny was determined by the gods, Near Eastern people interpreted their experiences through myths. Myths also enabled Mesopotamians and Egyptians to make sense out of nature, to explain the world of phenomena. Through myths the Near Eastern mind sought to give coherence to the universe, to make it intelligible. These myths gave Near Eastern peoples a framework with which to pattern their experiences into a meaningful order, justify their rules of conduct, and try to overcome the uncertainty of existence. Mythical explanations of nature and human experience made life seem less overwhelming, less filled with unbearable fears.

Religion determined the Near Eastern view of nature. Gods and demons resided within nature: the sun and stars, the rivers and mountains, the wind and lightning were either gods or the dwelling places of gods. To an Egyptian or a Mesopotamian, natural phenomena—a falling rock, a thunderclap, a rampaging river—were experienced as life facing life. They did not view nature as a physical entity, as an *it*, inanimate, impersonal, and governed by law; rather they saw every object in nature mythically, as a *thou*, suffused with life.

In other words, the ancients told myths instead of presenting an analysis or conclusions. We would explain, for instance, that certain atmospheric changes broke a drought and brought about rain. The Babylonians observed the same facts but experienced them as the intervention of the gigantic bird Imdugud which came to their rescue. It covered the sky with the black storm clouds of its wings and devoured the Bull of Heaven, whose hot breath had scorched the crops.[15]

Chronology 1.1 The Near East

3200 B.C.*	Rise of civilization in Sumeria
2900	Union of Upper and Lower Egypt
2686–2181	Old Kingdom; essential forms of Egyptian civilization take shape
2180	Downfall of Akkadian empire
1792–1750	Hammurabi of Babylon brings Akkad and Sumer under his control and fashions a code of laws
1570	Egyptians drive out Hyksos and embark upon empire building
1369–1353	Amenhotep IV; a movement toward monotheism
1200	Fall of Hittite empire
612	Fall of Assyrian empire
604–562	Reign of Nebuchadnezzar; height of Chaldean empire
550–525 B.C.	Persian conquests form a world empire

* Most dates are approximations.

The Egyptians believed that the sun rose in the morning, traveled across the sky, and set into the netherworld beyond the western horizon. After warding off the forces of chaos and disruption, the sun reappeared the next morning. For the Egyptians, the rising and setting of the sun were not natural occurrences—a celestial body obeying an impersonal law—but a religious drama.

The myth-making mind of the ancient Near East did not analyze nature systematically and rationally; it did not structure and explain reality by means of hypothesis, logical analysis, and general rules. Rather it saw the forces of nature as expressions of gods and demons; mythical relationships operated throughout the objective world.

Mesopotamians and Egyptians did not distinguish between the *subjective*—how nature appears to us through feelings, illusions, and dreams—and the *objective*, what nature really is, a system governed by laws that can be apprehended through intellectual analysis and

synthesis. Of course, Near Eastern people did engage in rational forms of thought and behavior. They certainly employed reason in building irrigation works, in preparing a calendar, and in performing mathematical operations. But, because rational or logical thought remained subordinate to a mythic-religious world-view, Near Eastern people did not arrive at a *consistently* and *self-consciously* rational method of inquiring into physical nature and human culture. They did not fashion a body of philosophic and scientific ideas that were logically structured, discussed, and debated.

Near Eastern civilization reached the first level in the development of science—observing nature, recording data, and improving technology in mining, metallurgy, and architecture. But it did not advance to the level of self-conscious philosophic and scientific thought—that is, logically deduced abstractions, hypotheses, and generalizations. These later developments were the singular achievement of Greek philosophy, which gave a "rational interpretation to natural occurrences which had previously been explained by ancient mythologies. . . . With the study of nature set free from the control of mythological fancy, the way was opened for the development of science as an intellectual system."[16]

Near Eastern Achievements

Sumerians and Egyptians demonstrated enormous creativity and intelligence. They built irrigation works and cities, organized governments, charted the course of heavenly bodies, performed mathematical operations, constructed large-scale monuments, engaged in international trade, established bureaucracies and schools, and advanced the level of technology considerably. And without the Sumerian invention of writing—one of the great creative acts in history—what we mean by *civilization* could not have emerged.

Many elements of ancient Near Eastern civilization were passed on to the West. The wheeled vehicle, the plow, and the phonetic alphabet—all important to the development of civilization—derive from the Near East. In the realm of medicine, the Egyptians knew the value of certain drugs, such as castor oil; they also knew how to use splints and bandages. The innovative divisions that gave 360 degrees to a circle and 60 minutes to an hour originated in Mesopotamia. Egyptian geometry and Babylonian astronomy were utilized by the Greeks and became a part of Western knowledge. In Christian art, too, one finds connections to the Mesopotamian art forms—for example, the Assyrians depicted winged angel-like beings.

In addition to concrete facts and artifacts, ideas and stories entered Western civilization from the Near East. One such idea was the belief that a king's power comes from a heavenly source. Mesopotamian literary themes were also borrowed, by both the Hebrews and the Greeks. For example, some biblical stories—the Flood, the quarrel between Cain and Abel, and the Tower of Babel—stem from Mesopotamian antecedents. A similar link exists between the Greek and the earlier Mesopotamian mythologies.

Thus, many achievements of Egyptians and Mesopotamians were inherited and assimilated by both Greeks and Hebrews. Even more important for an understanding of the essential meaning of Western civilization are the ways in which Greeks and Hebrews rejected or transformed elements of the older Near Eastern traditions to create new points of departure for the human mind.

Notes

1. Richard E. Leakey and Roger Lewin, *Origins* (New York: E. P. Dutton, 1977), p. 8.

2. Robert J. Braidwood, *Prehistoric Man* (Glenview, Ill.: Scott, Foresman, 1967), p. 141.

3. Lewis Mumford, *Transformation of Man* (New York: Harper Torchbooks, 1972), pp. 46–47.

4. Quoted in Sabatino Moscati, *The Face of the Ancient Orient* (Garden City, N.J.: Doubleday Anchor Books, 1962), p. 87.

5. *The Epic of Gilgamesh*, with an introduction by N. K. Senders (Baltimore: Penguin Books, 1965), pp. 69, 104.

6. Adolf Ehrman, ed., *The Ancient Egyptians* (New York: Harper Torchbooks, 1966), pp. 94, 97, 99.

7. Henri Frankfort, *Ancient Egyptian Religion* (New York: Harper Torchbooks, 1961), p. 14.

8. Quoted in ibid., p. 43.

9. John A. Wilson, "Egypt," in Henri Frankfort, et al., *Before Philosophy* (Baltimore: Penguin Books, 1949), p. 88.

10. Erhman, *The Ancient Egyptians*, pp. 76–78.

11. Quoted in John A. Wilson, *The Culture of Ancient Egypt* (Chicago: University of Chicago Press, Phoenix Books, 1951), p. 227.

12. Ibid., p. 225.

13. Ibid., p. 226.

14. Quoted in John Oates, *Babylon* (London: Thames and Hudson, 1979), pp. 110–111.

15. Frankfort, et al., *Before Philosophy*, p. 15.

16. S. Sambursky, *The Physical World of the Greeks* (New York: Collier Books, 1962), pp. 18–19.

Suggested Reading

Cook, J. M., *The Persian Empire* (1983). An up-to-date history of ancient Persia.

David, Rosalie A., *The Ancient Egyptians* (1982). Focuses on religious beliefs and practices.

Fagan, Brian M., *People of the Earth* (1980). A survey of world prehistory.

Frankfort, Henri, *Ancient Egyptian Religion* (1948). An interpretation of the origins and nature of Egyptian religion.

Frankfort, Henri, et al., *Before Philosophy* (1949). Brilliant discussions of the role of myth in the ancient Near East by distinguished scholars.

Gowlett, John, *Ascent to Civilization* (1984). An up-to-date study with excellent graphics.

Hallo, W. W., and Simpson, W. K., *The Ancient Near East* (1971). An authoritative survey of the political history of the Near East.

Leakey, Richard E. *Origins* (1977). What new discoveries reveal about the emergence of the human species.

Mertz, Barbara, *Red Land, Black Land* (1966). A social history of the people of Egypt.

Moscati, Sabatino, *The Face of the Ancient Orient* (1962). An illuminating survey of the various peoples of the ancient Near East.

Oates, John. *Babylon* (1979). A survey of the history of Babylon from its origin to Hellenistic times; includes a discussion of the legacy of Babylon.

Oppenheim, A. L., *Ancient Mesopotamia* (1964). Stresses social and economic history.

Roux, Georges, *Ancient Iraq* (1964). A balanced survey of Mesopotamian history and society.

Saggs, H. W. F., *The Greatness That Was Babylon* (1962). Strong on social and cultural history.

Wilson, John A., *The Culture of Ancient Egypt* (1951). An interpretation by a distinguished Egyptologist.

Review Questions

1. What progess did human beings make during the Paleolithic age?

2. Why is the development of the Neolithic Age referred to as the Neolithic Revolution?

3. What is meant by civilization? Under what conditions did it emerge?

4. The Sumerian achievement served as the basis for Mesopotamian civilization. Discuss.

5. How did religion influence Mesopotamian civilization?

6. What achievements did the Mesopotamians make in trade, mathematics, and science?

7. Define Old Kingdom, Middle Kingdom, and New Kingdom.

8. What role did the pharaoh play in Egyptian life? Do you think the pharaoh really believed that he was divine? Explain.

9. How did the Egyptians' religious beliefs affect their civilization?

10. What is the significance of Akhenaton?

11. The Egyptians would not have comprehended our concept of progress. Discuss.

12. What were the achievements of the Phoenicians and Aramaeans?

13. How did the Persians give unity to the Near East?

14. What advances in science were made by Near Eastern civilization? How was science limited by a myth-making view of nature?

15. Why has religion played such an important role in world history?

16. What were the accomplishments of the civilizations of the Near East? What elements of Near Eastern civilization were passed on to Western civilization?

2

The Hebrews: A New View
of God and the Individual

*A*ncient Mesopotamia and Egypt, the birthplace of the first civilizations, are not the spiritual ancestors of the West; for the origins of the Western tradition, we must turn to the Hebrews and the Greeks. As Egyptologist John A. Wilson says:

The Children of Israel built a nation and a religion on the rejection of things Egyptian. Not only did they see God as one, but they ascribed to him consistency of concern for man and consistency of justice to man. . . . Like the Greeks, the Hebrews took forms from their great neighbors; like the Greeks, they used those forms for very different purposes.[1]

In this chapter we examine one source of the Western tradition, the Hebrews, whose conception of God broke with the outlook of the Near East and whose ethical teachings helped to fashion the Western idea of the dignity of the individual.

Outline of Hebrew History

The Hebrews originated in Mesopotamia and migrated to Canaan, a portion of which was later called Palestine. The Hebrew patriarchs—Abraham, Isaac, and Jacob, so prominently depicted in the Old Testament—were chieftains of seminomadic clans that roamed Palestine and occasionally journeyed to Mesopotamia and Egypt. The early Hebrews absorbed some features of Mesopotamian civilization. For example, there are parallels between biblical law and the Mesopotamian legal tradition. Several biblical stories—the Creation, the Flood, the Garden of Eden—derive from Mesopotamian sources.

Some Hebrews journeyed from Canaan to Egypt to be herdsmen and farmers, but they eventually became forced laborers for the Egyptians. Fearful of becoming permanent slaves of pharaoh, the Hebrews yearned for an opportunity to escape. An extraordinary leader rose among them called Moses, who

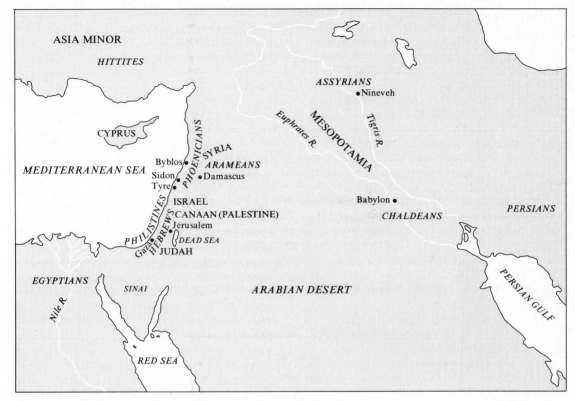

Map 2.1 Hebrews and Other Peoples of the Ancient Middle East

came to his people as a messenger of God. Leading the Hebrews in their exodus from Egypt in the thirteenth century B.C., Moses transformed them during their wanderings in the wilderness of Sinai into a nation, welded together and uplifted by a belief in Yahweh, the one God.

The Israelite Kingdom

The wandering Hebrews returned to Canaan to rejoin other Hebrew tribes that had not migrated to Egypt. The conquest of the Canaanites, who possessed a material culture superior to the Hebrews', took many generations. Settling in Canaan, the Israelites became an agricultural nation.

After the conquest, the Israelites did not form a state with a central government, but were loosely organized into a tribal confederation bound by a commitment to Yahweh. When enemies threatened, the elders of each of the twelve tribes would decide whether to engage in joint action. During emergencies, judges, who were leaders distinguished by their courage and empowered by "the spirit of Yahweh," rallied the clans against the common enemy. The tribal confederation lasted for about 200 years, until a threat by the Philistines in the late eleventh century B.C. led the Israelites to draw closer together under a king.

Originally from the islands of the Aegean Sea and the coast of Asia Minor, the Philistines (from whom the name Palestine derives) had invaded Canaan in the early part of the twelfth century B.C. From the coastal regions they expanded into the interior, extending their dominion over much Israelite territory. During this time of crisis, the twelve tribes united under the leadership of Saul, a charismatic hero whom they acclaimed as their first king. Under Saul's successor, David, a gifted warrior and a poet, the Hebrews (or Israelites) broke the back of Philistine power and subdued neighboring peoples.

The creation of an Israelite kingdom under David and his son Solomon in the tenth century B.C. was made possible by the declining power of other states in the Near East—Babylonia, Assyria, the Hittite Kingdom, and Egypt. Solomon's kingdom engaged in active trade with neighboring states, particularly Tyre (located along the Phoenician coast). Solomon's merchant fleet, built and manned by Phoenicians, traded with southerly lands bordering the Red Sea. Another sign of economic progress was extensive construction, especially in Jerusalem, the Hebrew spiritual center, where Solomon built a royal palace and beside it a magnificent temple honoring God.

New cities were built, and Jerusalem grew larger. The use of the iron-tipped plow improved agricultural productivity which, in turn, contributed to a significant population increase. Under Solomon, Israel also experienced a cultural flowering—some magnificent sections of the Old Testament were written and music flourished.

Old tribal patterns weakened as urban life expanded and some grew wealthy. Tribal society had been distinguished by a large measure of economic equality, but disparity between the rich and the poor grew, between those who considered themselves aristocrats and the common people.

Under Solomon, ancient Israel was at the height of its power and prosperity, but opposition to Solomon's tax policies and his favored treatment of the region of Judah in the south led to the division of the kingdom after his death in 922 B.C. The tribes loyal to

Solomon's son belonged to the Kingdom of Judah, while the other tribes organized the northern Kingdom of Israel. Both second-rate powers, neither Judah nor Israel could hold on to earlier conquests.

Conquest, Captivity, Restoration, and Rebellion

In 722 B.C., Israel fell to the Assyrians, who deported many Hebrews to other parts of the Assyrian empire. These transported Hebrews merged with neighboring peoples and lost their identity as the people of God. In 586 B.C., the Chaldeans conquered Judah, destroyed the temple, devastated the land, and deported several thousand Hebrews to Babylon. The prophets Isaiah, Ezekiel, and Jeremiah declared that the destruction of Judah was a punishment that the Hebrews had brought upon themselves by violating God's laws. This time was the darkest moment in the history of the Hebrews. Their state was gone, and neighboring peoples had overrun their land; their holy temple, built during the reign of King Solomon, was in ruins; thousands had died in battle or had been executed; others had fled to Egypt and other lands, and thousands more were in exile in Babylon. This exile is known as the Babylonian Captivity.

Still the Hebrews, in what is a marvel of history, survived as a people. Although many of the exiles in Babylon assimilated Babylonian ways, some remained faithful to their God Yahweh and the Law of Moses and longed to return to their homeland. Thus, their faith enabled them to endure conquest and exile. In Babylon another prophet, known as Second Isaiah, comforted the uprooted Hebrews. Isaiah declared that soon Yahweh, who controlled the course of history, would restore the erring but repentant Hebrews to their land in a second Exodus. When the Persians conquered Babylon, King Cyrus, in 538 B.C., permitted the exiles to return to Judah, now a Persian province, and to rebuild the temple.

The majority of Judeans preferred to remain in prosperous and cosmopolitan Babylon, but some of them did return to Judah, and in 515 B.C. the Hebrews, now commonly called Jews, dedicated the second temple at Jerusalem.

During the first half of the fifth century B.C. the restored Jewish community seemed on the verge of disintegration. Exploitation of the poor created internal tensions; intermarriage with non-Jews grew more frequent; and there was spiritual backsliding, including neglect of the Sabbath. Under the leadership of Nehemiah and Ezra in the second half of the fifth century B.C., administrative reforms were introduced and spiritual life was invigorated. Once again the Jews had overcome threats to their communal existence.

In the late fourth century B.C., Alexander the Great, commander of a Macedonian and Greek army, conquered the Near East, including Palestine. After Alexander's death his generals seized different parts of his empire. One general, Ptolemy, became ruler of Egypt; a second, Seleucus, became ruler of Syria. Palestine was seized by the Ptolemies, but in 198 B.C., Antiochus III the Great, a Seleucid king, defeated the Egyptians and annexed Palestine. His son Antiochus IV (175–163 B.C.) was insensitive to the religious feelings of the Jews; he suspended observance of the Sabbath, forbade the circumcision of children, destroyed copies of the Law, erected pagan temples, and forced the Jews, under penalty of death, to eat the flesh of pigs. In the most grievous insult to the Jews, he set an altar to the god Zeus in the holy temple. Under the leadership of Mattathias and his five sons, the Jews waged a patriotic religious struggle. When Mattathias died in 166 B.C., his third son Judas, called Maccabeus (which may mean "the hammer") assumed leadership of the revolt. Under Judas' brilliant generalship, the Jews retook control of Jerusalem and cleansed the temple of pagan symbols. The Feast of Hanukkah, in commemoration of the rededication of the temple, has been celebrated by Jews ever since.

Judaea Capta S(enatus) C(onsulto). With a commander's baton in hand and his foot upon a helmet, a victorious centurion proclaims Rome's victory over Judea, personified weeping at the foot of the palm tree. The destruction of the city of Jerusalem under Titus was complete, but the ethics of Old Testament writing would become part of the foundation of Western European culture. (*Courtesy of The American Numismatic Society, New York*)

The Old Testament

In the following centuries, the Jews would lose their independence to Rome and become a dispersed people. But they never relinquished their commitment to God and his Law as recorded in the Old Testament. Called Tanak by Jews, the Old Testament consists of thirty-nine books* by several authors who lived in different centuries. Jews call the first five books of the Old Testament—Genesis,

---

* In ancient times, the number of books was usually given as twenty-four. Certain books are now divided into two parts and the twelve works by the minor prophets are now counted as individual books.

Exodus, Leviticus, Numbers, and Deuteronomy—the Torah. Often the Torah is referred to as the Pentateuch, a Greek word meaning "five books."

The Old Testament represents Hebrew literary and oral tradition dating from about 1250 to 150 B.C. Compiled by religious devotees, not research historians, it understandably contains factual errors, imprecisions, and discrepancies. However, there are also passages that contain reliable history, and historians find the Old Testament an indispensable source for studying the ancient Near East. Students of literature study it for its poetry, legends, and themes, all of which are an integral part of the Western literary tradition. But it is as a work of religious inspiration that the Old Testament attains its profoundest importance.

The Old Testament is the record of more than 1,000 years of ancient Jewish history; containing Jewish laws, wisdom, hopes, legends, and literary expressions, it describes an ancient people's efforts to comprehend the ways of God. The Old Testament emphasizes and values the human experience; its heroes are not demigods, but human beings. Human strength as well as weakness is depicted. Some passages exhibit cruelty and unseemly revenge, while others express the highest ethical values. As set forth in the Old Testament, the Hebrew idea of God and his relationship to human beings is one of the foundations of the Western tradition.

God: One, Sovereign, Transcendent, Good

The Hebrew view of God evolved through the history and experiences of the Hebrew people. In the days of the patriarchs, before the sojourn in Egypt, the Hebrews most likely were not monotheists. They probably devoted themselves to the god of their particular clan and expressed no hatred for the idolatrous beliefs of neighboring peoples. The chief of each clan established a special attachment to the god of his fathers, hoping that the deity would protect and assist the clan. It is likely that the patriarchs' religion contained spiritual elements that later would aid in the transition to monotheism. But this probability cannot be documented with certainty, for much of patriarchal religion still remains a mystery.

Some historians say that Moses' religion was not pure monotheism because it did not rule out the existence of other gods. According to this view, not until the prophets, centuries later, did the Hebrews explicitly deny that other gods existed and that Yahweh stood alone. Other scholars believe that Moses proclaimed a monotheistic idea, that this idea became the central force in the life of the Hebrews at the time of the Exodus from Egypt, and that it continues to be central today. John Bright, an American biblical scholar, suggests a judicious balance. The religion of Moses did not deny the existence of other gods, says Bright, but it "effectively denied them status as gods."[2] The Hebrews could serve only Yahweh and "accorded all power and authority to Him." Consequently Israel was:

. . . forbidden to approach [other deities] as gods. . . . The gods were thus rendered irrelevant, driven from the field. . . . To Israel only the one God was God. . . . The other gods, allowed neither part in creation, nor function in the cosmos, nor power over events . . . were robbed of all that made them gods and rendered non-entities, in short, were "undeified." Though the full implications of monotheism were centuries in being drawn, in the functional sense Israel believed in but one God from the beginning.[3]

The Hebrew view of the one God marked a profound break with Near Eastern religious thought. Pagan gods were not truly free; their power was not without limits. Unlike Yahweh, Near Eastern gods were not eternal, but were born or created; they issued from some prior realm. They were also subject to biological conditions requiring food, drink, sleep, and sexual gratification. Sometimes they became ill, or grew old, or died. When they behaved wickedly, they had to answer to fate, which demanded punishment as retribution; even the gods were subject to fate's power.

The Hebrews regarded God as *fully sovereign*. He ruled all and was subject to nothing. Yahweh's existence and power did not derive from a preexisting realm as pagan gods' did. The Hebrews believed that no realm of being preceded God in time or surpassed him in power. They saw God as eternal, the source of all in the universe, and having a supreme will. He created and governed the natural world and shaped the moral laws that govern human beings. He was not subservient to fate but determined what happened.

Whereas Near Eastern divinities dwelt within nature, the Hebrew God was *transcendent*, above nature and not a part of it. Yahweh was not identified with any natural force and did not dwell in a particular place in heaven or on earth. Since God was the creator and ruler of nature, there was no place for a sun-god, a moon-god, a god in the river, or a demon in the storm. Nature was God's creation but was not itself divine. Therefore, when the Hebrews confronted natural phenomena, they experienced God's magnificent handiwork, not objects with wills of their own. The stars and the planets were creations of Yahweh, not divinities or the abodes of divinities. The Hebrews neither regarded them with awe nor worshiped them.

The Hebrews demythicized nature, but concerned with religion and morality, they did not create theoretical science. As testimony to God's greatness, nature inspired people to sing the praises of the Lord; it invoked worship of God, not scientific curiosity. When Hebrews gazed at the heavens, they did not seek to discover mathematical relationships, but admired God's handiwork. The Hebrews did not view nature as a system governed by natural law. Rather, they saw the rising sun, spring rain, summer heat, and winter cold as God intervening in an orderly manner in his creation. The Hebrews, unlike the Greeks, were not philosophers. They were concerned with God's will, not

Temple Floor Mosaic. Images in Hebrew art are extremely rare because of the biblical injunction against graven images. This floor mosaic from Beth Alpha synagogue in Israel is a zodiacal calendar, with the chariot of the sun in the middle. (*Consulate General of Israel*)

the human intellect; with the feelings of the heart, not the power of the mind; with righteous behavior, not abstract thought. Human mistakes stemmed not from ignorance but from disobedience and stubbornness.

Unlike the Greeks, the Hebrews did not speculate about the origins of all things and the operations of nature; they knew that God had created everything. For the Hebrews, God's existence was based on religious conviction, not on rational inquiry; on revelation, not reason. It was the Greeks, not the Hebrews, who originated rational thought. But Christianity, born of Judaism, retained the Hebrew view of a transcendent God and the orderliness of his creation—concepts that could accommodate Greek science.

The Hebrews also did not speculate about God's nature. They knew only that he was *good* and that he made ethical demands on his people. Unlike Near Eastern gods, Yahweh was not driven by lust or motivated by evil, but was "merciful and gracious, long-suffering, and abundant in goodness and truth . . . forgiving iniquity and transgression and sin" (Psalm 145:8).[4]* In contrast to pagan gods who were indifferent to human beings, Yahweh was attentive to human needs.

By asserting that God was *one, sovereign, transcendent*, and *good*, the Hebrews effected a religious revolution that separated them forever from the world-view held by the peoples of the Near East.

The Individual and Moral Autonomy

This new conception of God made possible a new awareness of the individual. In confronting God, the Hebrews developed an awareness of *self* or *I*. Each individual became conscious of his or her own person, moral autonomy, and personal worth. The Hebrews believed that God, who possessed total freedom himself, had bestowed on his people moral freedom—the capacity to choose between good and evil.

Fundamental to Hebrew belief was the insistence that God did not create people to be his slaves. The Hebrews regarded God with awe and humility, with respect and fear, but they did not believe that God wanted people to grovel before him; rather he wanted them to fulfill their moral potential by freely making the choice to follow or not to follow God's Law. Thus, in creating men and women in his own image, God granted them autonomy and sovereignty. In God's plan for the universe, human beings are the highest creation, subordinate only to God. Of all his creations, only they have been given the freedom to choose between righteousness and wickedness, between "life and good, and death and evil" (Deuteronomy 30:15).

God demanded that the Hebrews have no other gods and that they make no images

"nor any manner of likeness, or any thing that is in heaven above, or that is in the earth beneath, . . . thou shalt not bow down unto them nor serve them" (Exodus 20: 4–5). The Hebrews believed that the worship of idols deprived people of their freedom and dignity; people cannot be fully human if they surrender themselves to a lifeless idol. Hence the Hebrews had to destroy images and all other forms of idolatry. A crucial element of Near Eastern religion was the use of images—art forms that depicted divinities—but the Hebrews believed God, the Supreme Being, could not be represented by pictures or sculpture fashioned by human beings. The Hebrews rejected entirely the belief that an image possessed divine powers that could be manipulated for human advantage. Ethical considerations, not myth or magic, were central to Hebrew religious life.

By making God the center of life, Hebrews could become free moral agents; no person, no human institution, no human tradition could claim their souls. Because God alone was the supreme value in the universe, only he was worthy of worship. Thus, to give *ultimate* loyalty to a king or a general violated God's stern warning against the worship of false gods. The first concern of the Hebrews was supposed to be righteousness, not power, fame, or riches, which were only idols and would impoverish a person spiritually and morally.

There was, however, a condition to freedom. For the Hebrews, people were not free to create their own moral precepts or their own standards of right and wrong; freedom meant the voluntary acceptance of commands that originated with God. Evil and suffering were not caused by blind fate, malevolent demons, or arbitrary gods, but they resulted from people's disregard of God's commandments. The dilemma is that in possessing freedom of choice, human beings are also free to disobey God, to commit a sin, which leads to suffering and death. Thus, in the Genesis story Adam and Eve were punished for disobeying God in the Garden of Eden.

For Hebrews, to know God was not to

comprehend him intellectually, to define him, or to prove his existence; to know God was to be righteous and loving, merciful and just. When men and women loved God, the Hebrews believed, they were uplifted and improved. Gradually they learned to overcome the worst elements of human nature and to treat people with respect and compassion.

By giving devotion to God, the Hebrews asserted the value and the autonomy of human beings. Thus, the Hebrews conceived the idea of moral freedom, that each individual is responsible for his or her own actions. Also inherited by Christianity, this idea of moral autonomy is central to the Western tradition.

The Covenant and the Law

Central to Hebrew religious thought and decisive in Hebrew history was the covenant—God's special agreement with the Hebrew people:

And Moses went up unto God, and the Lord called unto him out of the mountain saying: "Thus shalt thou say to the house of Jacob and tell the children of Israel: Ye have seen what I did unto the Egyptians, and how I bore you on eagles' wings, and brought you unto Myself. Now therefore, if ye will hearken unto My voice indeed, and keep My covenant, then ye shall be Mine own treasure from all peoples; for all the earth is Mine; and ye shall be unto Me a kingdom of priests and a holy nation." [*Exodus 19:3–6*]

By this act the Israelites as a nation accepted God's lordship.

The Hebrews became conscious of themselves as a unique nation, as a "chosen people," for God had given them a special honor, a profound opportunity, and (as they could never forget) an awesome responsibility. The Hebrews did not claim that God had selected them because they were better than other peoples or because they had done anything special to deserve God's election. They believed that God, in a remarkable manner,

had rescued them from bondage in Egypt and had selected them to receive the Law so that their nation would set an example of righteous behavior and ultimately make God and the Law known to the other nations.

This responsibility to be the moral teachers of humanity weighed heavily on the Hebrews. They believed that God had revealed his Law—including the moral code known as the Ten Commandments—to the Hebrew people as a whole, and obedience to the Law became the overriding obligation of each Hebrew. Violating the Law meant breaking the sacred covenant—an act that could lead to national disaster. As the Law originated with the one God, the necessary prerequisite for understanding and obeying it was surrendering belief in other gods forever, for they were barriers to comprehending and carrying out God's universal Law.

Ethical concerns resulted in decrees dealing with economic, social, and political relationships, which were designed to give practical expression to God's universal norms of morality. And because the covenant was made with the entire Hebrew nation, society as a whole had a religious obligation to root out evil and to make justice prevail. Thus, there were laws to protect the poor, widows, orphans, resident aliens, hired laborers, and slaves. Israelite law incorporated many elements from Near Eastern legal codes and oral traditions. But by making people more important than property, by expressing mercy toward the oppressed, and by rejecting the idea that law should treat the poor and the rich differently, Israelite law demonstrated a greater ethical awareness and a more humane spirit than other legal codes of the Near East:

And a stranger shalt thou not wrong, neither shalt thou oppress him; for ye were strangers in the land of Egypt. Ye shall not afflict any widow or fatherless child. [*Exodus 22:20–21*]

If thy brother, a Hebrew man, or a Hebrew woman, be sold unto thee, he shall serve thee six years; and in the seventh year thou shalt let him go free from thee. And when thou lettest him go free from thee, thou shalt not let him go empty;

Masada. For four years the defenders of the hilltop fortress of Masada resisted the Roman forces that had earlier captured Jerusalem in A.D. 70. In the end, they preferred suicide to submission. The constancy of Jewish beliefs remained, in spite of internal political divisions, defeats, and dispersion. (*Consulate General of Israel*)

thou shalt furnish him liberally. . . . [Deuteronomy 15:12–14]

Thou shalt not curse the deaf, nor put a stumbling-block before the blind, but thou shalt fear thy God: I am the Lord. . . . thou shalt love thy neighbor as thyself. [Leviticus 19:14,18]

Hebrew law regulated all aspects of daily life including family relationships. The father had supreme authority in the family, extending to his married sons and their wives if they remained in his household. Although polygamy was permitted, monogamy was the general rule; adultery was punishable by death.

Like other Near Eastern societies, the Jews placed women in a subordinate position. The husband was considered his wife's master, and she often addressed him as a servant or subject would speak to a superior. A husband could divorce his wife, but she could not divorce him. Only when there was no male heir could a wife inherit property from her husband or a daughter inherit from her father. Outside the home, women were not regarded as competent witnesses in court and played a lesser role in organized worship.

On the other hand, the Jews also showed respect for women. Wise women and prophetesses like Judith and Esther were respected by the community and were consulted by its leaders. Prophets compared God's love for the Hebrews with a husband's love for his wife. The Book of Proverbs describes a woman of valor:

Strength and dignity are her clothing;
And she laugheth at the time to come.

She openeth her mouth with wisdom;
And the law of kindness is on her tongue.
She looketh well to the ways of her household,
And eateth not the bread of idleness.
Her children rise up and call her blessed;
Her husband also, and he praiseth her. . . .
[Proverbs 31:25–28]

Jewish law regarded the woman as a person, not as property. Even female captives taken in war were not to be abused or humiliated. The law required a husband to respect and support his wife and never to strike her. One of the Ten Commandments called for honoring both father and mother.

The Hebrew Idea of History

Their idea of God made the Hebrews aware of the crucial importance of historical time. Holidays commemorating such specific historical events as the Exodus from Egypt and the receiving of the Ten Commandments on Mount Sinai kept the past alive and vital. Egyptians and Mesopotamians did not have a similar awareness of the uniqueness of a given event: to them today's incident merely reproduced events experienced by their ancestors. To the Jews, the Exodus and the covenant were singular, nonrepetitive occurrences, decisive in shaping their national history. This historical uniqueness and importance of events derived from the idea of a universal God profoundly involved in human affairs—a God who cares, teaches, and punishes.

The Jews valued the future as well as the past. They envisioned a great day when God would establish on earth a glorious age of peace, prosperity, happiness, and human brotherhood. This utopian notion has become deeply embedded in Western thought. Two thousand years later when Karl Marx claimed that a golden age would be ushered in after the destruction of capitalism and the creation of a classless society, he was echoing an ancient Hebrew longing for utopia.

The Jews saw history as a divine drama

filled with sacred meaning and moral significance. Historical events revealed the clash of human will with God's commands. Through history's specific events, God's presence was disclosed and his purpose made known. When the Hebrews suffered conquest and exile, they interpreted these events as retribution for violating God's Law and as punishments for their stubbornness, sinfulness, and rebelliousness. The ancient Hebrews, says historian Millar Burrows, were convinced that history was "the work of a personal divine will, contending with the foolish, stubborn wills of men, promising and warning, judging and punishing and destroying, yet sifting, saving, and abundantly blessing those found amenable to disipline and instruction."[5] Because historical events revealed God's attitude toward human beings, these events possessed spiritual meaning, and therefore were worth recording, evaluating, and remembering.

The Prophets

Jewish history was marked by the emergence of spiritually inspired persons called *prophets*, who felt compelled to act as God's messengers. The prophets cared nothing for money or possessions, feared no one, and preached without invitation. Often emerging in times of social distress and moral confusion, the prophets pleaded for a return to the covenant and the Law. They exhorted the people and taught that when his people forgot God and made themselves the center of all things, they would bring disaster on themselves and their community.

The prophets saw national misfortune as an opportunity for penitence and reform. They were remarkably courageous men who did not quake before the powerful. In the late eighth century an angry Isaiah warned:

The Lord will enter into judgment
With the elders of His people, and the princes
thereof:
"It is ye that have eaten up the vineyard;

The spoil of the poor is in your houses;
What mean ye that ye crush my people,
And grind the face of the poor?" [Isaiah
    3:14–15]

Social Justice

The flowering of the prophetic movement—
the age of classical or literary prophecy—
began in the eighth century B.C. In attacking
oppression, cruelty, greed, and exploitation,
the classical prophets added a new dimension
to Israel's religious development. These
prophets were responding to problems em-
anating from Israel's changed social structure.
The general lack of class distinctions char-
acterizing a tribal society had been altered
by the rise of Hebrew kings, the expansion
of commerce, and the growth of cities. By
the eighth century, there was a significant
disparity between the wealthy and the poor.
Small farmers in debt to moneylenders faced
the loss of their land or even bondage; the
poor were often dispossessed by the greedy
wealthy. To the prophets, these social evils
were religious sins. Amos, a mid-eighth-cen-
tury prophet, felt a tremendous compulsion
to speak out against these injustices. In the
name of God, he denounced the heartless
rich, protested against the pursuit of luxury,
and warned that Israel would be punished
for its sins:

I hate, I despise your feasts,
And I will take no delight in your solemn
    assemblies.
Yea, though ye offer me burnt-offerings and
    your meal-offerings,
I will not accept them;
Neither will I regard the peace offerings of your
    fat beasts.
Take thou away from Me the noise of thy
    songs;
And let Me not hear the melody of the
    psalteries.
But let justice well up as waters,
And righteousness as a mighty stream. [Amos
    5:21–24]

God is compassionate, insisted the prophets. He cares for all, especially the poor, the

unfortunate, the sufferer, and the defenseless.
God's injunctions, declared Isaiah, were to:

Seek justice, relieve the oppressed,
Judge the fatherless, plead for the widow.
    [*Isaiah 1:17*]

Prophets de-emphasized sacrifices and rituals and stressed the direct spiritual-ethical
encounter between the individual and God.
It was the inner person more than the outer
forms of religious activity that concerned the
prophets. Holding that the essence of the
covenant was universal righteousness, the
prophets criticized priests whose commitment
to rites and rituals was not supported by a
deeper spiritual insight nor matched by a
zeal for morality in daily life. To the prophets,
an ethical sin was far worse than a ritual
omission. Above all, said the prophets, God
demands righteousness. To live unjustly, to
mistreat one's neighbors, to act without compassion—these actions violated God's law and
endangered the entire social order.

The prophets thus created a social conscience that has become part of the Western
tradition. This revolutionary social doctrine
states that everyone has a God-given right
to social justice and fair treatment; that each
person has a religious obligation to denounce
evil and oppose mistreatment of others; and
that the community has a moral responsibility
to assist the unfortunate. The prophets held
out the hope that life on earth could be improved, that poverty and injustice need not
be accepted as part of an unalterable natural
order, and that the individual was capable
of elevating himself or herself morally and
could respect the dignity of others.

Universalism

Two tendencies were present in Hebrew
thought: parochialism and universalism. Parochial-mindedness stressed the special nature, destiny, and needs of the chosen people,
a nation set apart from others. This outlook
was offset by universalism, a concern for all
humanity, which found expression in those
prophets who envisioned the unity of all

Dead Sea Scroll. The sacredness of the biblical text and the authority of the recorded word of God remain a theme and a unifying factor in ancient as well as modern Jewish history. Found in caves at Khirbet Qumran the Dead Sea Scrolls contained a version of an almost complete text of Isaiah that differed insignificantly from the modern version, yet the scroll dated from the second century A.D. and is the earliest version extant. (© *John C. Trever, 1970*)

people—a brotherhood of man under the fatherhood of God. All people were equally precious to God.

In that day shall there be a highway out of Egypt to Assyria, and the Assyrian shall come into Egypt, and the Egyptian into Assyria; and the Egyptians shall worship with the Assyrians. In that day shall Israel be the third with Egypt and with Assyria, . . . for that the Lord of hosts hath blessed him saying: "Blessed be Egypt My people and Assyria the work of My hands, and Israel Mine inheritance." [Isaiah 19:23–24]

Israel was charged with a sacred mission: to lead in the struggle against idolatry and to set an example of righteous behavior for all humanity.

The prophets were not pacifists, particularly if a war were being waged against the enemies of Yahweh. But some prophets denounced war as obscene and looked forward to its elimination. In a world where virtually everyone glorified the warrior, the prophets of universalism envisioned the day when peace would reign over the earth, when nations:

. . . shall beat their swords into plowshares,
And their spears into pruning-hooks;
Nation shall not lift up sword against nation,
Neither shall they learn war any more. [Isaiah 2:4]

These prophets maintained that when people glorify force, they dehumanize their oppo-

Chronology 2.1 The Hebrews

1250 B.C.*	Hebrew Exodus from Egypt
1024–1000	The reign of Saul, Israel's first king
1000–961	The creation of a united monarchy under David
961–922	The reign of Solomon; construction of the First Temple
750–430	The Age of Classical Prophecy
722	Kingdom of Israel falls to Assyrians
586	Kingdom of Judah falls to Chaldeans; the temple is destroyed
586–539	Babylonian Exile
538	Cyrus of Persia allows exiles to return to Judah
515 B.C.	Second Temple is dedicated

* Most dates are approximations.

responsibility of their religious inspiration and conviction.

Prophets emphasized the individual's responsibility for his or her own actions. In coming to regard God's law as a *command to conscience, an appeal to the inner person*, the prophets heightened the awareness of the human personality. They indicated that the individual could not know God only by following edicts and by performing rituals; the individual must experience God. Precisely this I-Thou relationship could make the individual fully conscious of self and could deepen and enrich his or her own personality. At Mount Sinai, God gave the Law to a tribal people who obeyed largely out of fear and compulsion; by the prophets' time, the Jews appeared to be autonomous individuals who heeded the Law because of a deliberate, conscious, and inner commitment.

Monotheism had initiated a process of self-realization and self-discovery unmatched by other peoples of the Near East. The prophets' ideals helped sustain the Jews throughout their long and often painful historical odyssey, and they remain a vital force for Jews today. Incorporated into the teachings of Jesus, these ideals, as part of Christianity, are embedded in the Western tradition.

nents, brutalize themselves, and dishonor God. When violence rules, there can be no love of god and no regard for the individual.

Individualism

The prophets' universalism was accompanied by an equally profound awareness of the individual and his worth to God. Before the prophets, virtually all religious tradition had been produced communally and anonymously. The prophets, however, spoke as fearless individuals who, by affixing their signatures to their thoughts, fully bore the

Notes

1. John A. Wilson, "Egypt—the Kingdom of the 'Two Lands'," in E. A. Speiser, *At the Dawn of Civilization* (New Brunswick, N.J.: Rutgers University Press, 1964), pp. 267–268. Volume I in *The World History of the Jewish People*.

2. John Bright, *A History of Israel* (Philadelphia: The Westminster Press, 1972), p. 154.

3. Ibid.

4. From *The Holy Scriptures* (Philadelphia: The Jewish Publication Society of America, 1917). The scriptural quotations are used in this chapter with the permission of the Jewish Publication Society of America.

5. Millar Burrows, "Ancient Israel," in Robert C. Dentan, ed., *The Idea of History in the Ancient Near East* (New Haven: Yale University Press, 1955), p. 128.

Suggested Reading

Albright, W. F., *The Biblical Period from Abraham to Ezra* (1963). Analyzes the culture and history of ancient Israel and explains the growing spiritual nature of the Hebrew conception of God.

Anderson, Bernhard, *Understanding the Old Testament*, 2nd ed. (1966) An excellent survey of the Old Testament in its historical setting.

Bright, John, *A History of Israel* (1972). A thoughtful, clearly written survey; the best of its kind.

de Vaux, Roland, *Ancient Israel*, vol. I, *Social Institutions* (1965). All phases of Israelite society—family, monarchy, law, war, and so on.

Ehrlich, E. L., *A Concise History of Israel* (1965). An interpretive essay covering the period from the Patriarchs to the destruction of the Jerusalem Temple in A.D. 70.

Heschel, Abraham, *The Prophets*, 2 vols. (1962). A penetrating analysis of the nature of prophetic inspiration.

Kaufmann, Yehezkel, *The Religion of Israel* (1960). An abridgment and translation of Kaufmann's classic multivolume work.

Kuntz, Kenneth J., *The People of Ancient Israel* (1974). An up-to-date introduction to Old Testament literature, history, and thought.

Muilenburg, James, *The Way of Israel* (1961). A discussion of biblical faith and ethics.

Scott, R. B. Y., *The Relevance of the Prophets* (1968). An introduction to the Old Testament prophetic tradition.

Snaith, N. H., *The Distinctive Ideas of the Old Testament* (1964). Discusses those central ideas that distinguish Hebrew religion from other religions of the Near East.

Review Questions

1. What role did each of the following play in Jewish history: Moses, Saul, David, Solomon, Babylonian Captivity, Judas Maccabeus?

2. How did the Hebrew view of God mark a revolutionary break with Near Eastern religious thought?

3. How did Hebrew religious thought promote the idea of moral autonomy?

4. How did the Hebrews interpret the covenant?

5. What was the Hebrew view of women? What was the significance of this view for Western history?

6. Provide examples showing that Hebrew law expressed a concern for human dignity.

7. Why did the Hebrews consider history to be important, and how did they demonstrate its importance?

8. Both parochialism and universalism were evident in ancient Hebrew thought and history. Discuss. Are both traditions also evident in modern Jewish history? Explain.

9. What role did the prophets play in Hebrew history? What is the enduring significance of their achievement?

10. Why are the Hebrews regarded as one source of Western civilization?

3

The Greek City-State:
Democratic Politics

*T*he Hebrew conception of ethical monotheism, with its stress on human dignity, is one source of the Western tradition. The other source derives from ancient Greece. Both Hebrews and Greeks absorbed the achievements of Near Eastern civilizations, but they also developed their own distinctive viewpoints and styles of thought that set them apart from the Mesopotamians and Egyptians. The great achievements of the Hebrews lay in the sphere of religious-ethical thought; those of the Greeks lay in the development of rational thought. As Greek society evolved, says British historian James Shiel, there

was a growing reliance on independent reason, a devotion to logical precision, progressing from myth to logos [reason]. Rationalism permeated the whole social and cultural development. . . . Architecture . . . developed from primitive cultic considerations to sophisticated mathematical norms; sculpture escaped from temple image to a new love of naturalism and proportion; political life proceeded from tyranny to rational experiments in democracy. From practical rules of thumb, geometry moved forward in the direction of the impressive Euclidian synthesis. So too philosophy made its way from "sayings of the wise" to the Aristotelian logic, and made men rely on their own observation and reflection in facing the unexplained vastness of the cosmos.[1]

The Greeks conceived of nature as following general rules, not acting according to the whims of gods or demons. They saw human beings as having a capacity for rational thought, a need for freedom, and a worth as individuals. Although the Greeks never dispensed with the gods, they increasingly stressed the importance of human reason and human decisions; they came to assert that reason is the avenue to knowledge and that people—not the gods—are responsible for their own behavior. In this shift of attention from the gods to the individual, the Greeks broke with the myth-making orientation of the Near East and created the rational outlook that is a distinctive feature of Western civilization.

Early Aegean Civilizations

Until the latter part of the nineteenth century, historians placed the beginning of Greek history in the eighth century B.C. Although the ancient Greek poet Homer had spoken of an earlier Greek civilization in his works, historians believed that Homer's epics dealt with myths and legends, not with a historical past. In 1871, however, a successful German businessman, Heinrich Schliemann, began a search for earliest Greece. Having been enthralled by Homer's epics as a youth, Schliemann was convinced that they referred to an actual civilization. In excavating several sites mentioned by Homer, Schliemann discovered tombs, pottery, ornaments, and the remains of palaces of what hitherto had been a lost Greek civilization. The ancient civilization was named after Mycenae, the most important city of the time. Mycenaean civilization pervaded the Greek mainland and the islands of the Aegean Sea for much of the second millennium B.C.

In 1900, Arthur Evans, a British archaeologist, made an equally extraordinary discovery; excavating on the island of Crete southeast of the Greek mainland, he unearthed a civilization even older than that of the Mycenaean Greeks. The Cretans, or Minoans, were not Greeks and did not speak a Greek language, but their influence on mainland Greece was considerable and enduring. Minoan civilization lasted about 1350 years (2600 B.C. to 1250 B.C.) and reached its height during the period from 1700 to 1450 B.C.

Religion and life were closely integrated in Minoan times, as they were in all the early civilizations. The king performed priestly functions, and sacred symbols were placed in palaces and homes. Cretan art expressed religious themes, and the worship of a mother goddess as well as other deities was common.

The centers of Minoan civilization were magnificent palace complexes, whose construction was evidence of the wealth and power of Minoan kings. That the palaces' architects and the artists who decorated the

Minoan Statuette of a Snake Goddess, Sixteenth Century B.C. Early Aegean religion still maintained elaborate ritual. In Crete, the female goddess was prominent. The exact meaning of the snakes is unknown, except for their link with ancient fertility cults. (*Courtesy Museum of Fine Arts, Boston*)

walls were sensitive to beauty is shown in the ruins that have been uncovered at various Cretan sites. The palaces housed royal families, priests, and government officials, and contained workshops that produced decorated silver vessels, daggers, and pottery for local use and for export. In Egypt, Syria, Asia Minor, and Greece, numerous Cretan artifacts have been found that attest to a substantial export trade.

Minoan creativity survived many disasters. Successive waves of destruction caused by earthquakes and accompanying fires shook the island. The palaces were probably all but destroyed three times during the late nineteenth and eighteenth centuries B.C. The last earthquake necessitated a complete reconstruction of the palaces. Cultural life, too, had to be renewed, along with economic life, for the palaces were central to Cretan civilization.

Despite these disasters, Minoan civilization recovered and progressed, aided by peaceful conditions. The palaces, swiftly rebuilt, were grander than ever—the palace at Knossos had more than 1,500 rooms. Cretan ships dominated the Aegean Sea. Economic and cultural contacts with the advanced civilizations of the Near East expanded, and art flourished. Cretan civilization had entered its golden age.

Judging by the archaeological evidence, the Minoans seemed peaceful. Minoan art did not generally depict military scenes, and Minoan palaces, unlike the Mycenaean, had no defensive walls or fortifications. Thus the Minoans were vulnerable to the warlike Mycenaean Greeks, who invaded and conquered Knossos. The Minoans never recovered from this blow, and within two centuries Minoan civilization faded away.

Who were these Mycenaeans? About 2000 B.C., Greek-speaking tribes moved southward into the Greek peninsula where, together with the pre-Greek population, they fashioned the Mycenaean civilization. In the Peloponnesus, the Mycenaeans built palaces that were based in part on Cretan models. In these palaces, Mycenaean kings conducted affairs of state and priests and priestesses carried out religious ceremonies; potters, smiths, tailors, and chariot builders practiced their crafts in the numerous workshops, much like their Minoan counterparts. Mycenaean arts and crafts owed a considerable debt to Crete. A script that permitted record keeping also probably came from Crete. The Mycenaeans were traders, too, exchanging goods with the peoples of Egypt, Phoenicia, Sicily, southern Italy, Macedon, and the western coast of Asia Minor.

At the apex of Mycenaean society was the king, who headed the armed forces, controlled production and trade, and was the highest judicial authority. Assisting the king were aristocrats who were officers in the army and held key positions in the administration. Also in the upper echelons of the society were the priestesses and priests, who supervised sanctuaries and other properties of the gods. Farmers, stockbreeders, and craftsmen constituted the bulk of the free population. Slaves, principally foreign prisoners of war, were at the bottom of the social pyramid.

Mycenaean civilization reached its height in the period from 1400 to 1230 B.C. Following that, constant warfare between the Mycenaean kingdoms (and perhaps foreign invasions) led to destruction of the palaces and abrupt disintegration of the Mycenaean civilization about 1100 B.C. But to the later Greek civilization the Mycenaeans left a legacy of religious forms, pottery making, metallurgy, agriculture, language, a code of honor immortalized in the Homeric epics, and myths and legends that offered themes for Greek drama.

The Rise of Hellenic Civilization

From 1100 to 800 B.C., the Greek world passed through the Dark Age, an era of transition between a dead Mycenaean civilization and a still unborn Hellenic civilization. The Dark Age saw the migration of Greek tribes from the barren mountainous regions of Greece to more fertile plains, and from the mainland to Aegean islands and the coast of Asia Minor. One group of invaders, the Dorians, penetrated the Peloponnesian peninsula in the south and later founded Sparta. Another group, called the Ionians, settled in Attica, where Athens is located, and later crossed to Asia Minor. During this period the Greeks experienced insecurity, warfare, poverty, and isolation. The bureaucratic system of Mycenaean government had disappeared, extensive trade had ceased, the art of writing had been forgotten, the palace workshops no longer existed, and art had reverted to primitive forms.

After 800 B.C., however, town life revived. Writing again became part of the Greek culture, this time with the more efficient Phoenician script. The population increased dramatically, there was a spectacular increase in the use of metals, and overseas trade expanded. Gradually Greek cities founded settlements on the islands of the Aegean, along the coast of Asia Minor and the Black Sea, and to the west in Sicily and southern Italy. These colonies, established to relieve overpopulation and land hunger, were independent, self-governing city-states, not possessions of the homeland city-states. During these two hundred years of colonization (750–550 B.C.), trade and industry expanded, the pace of urbanization quickened, and a new class emerged—the merchants, whose wealth derived from goods and money rather than from the land. In time, this middle class would challenge the landholding aristocracy.

Homer, Shaper of the Greek Spirit

The poet Homer lived during the eighth century B.C., just after the Dark Age. His great epics, the *Iliad* and the *Odyssey*,* helped to

---

* Many scholars hold that while Homer composed the *Iliad*, the *Odyssey* was probably the work of an unknown poet who lived sometime after Homer; some say that Homer composed both epics in their earliest forms and that others altered them.

shape the Greek spirit and Greek religion. Homer was the earliest molder of the Greek outlook and character.

For centuries Greek youngsters grew up reciting the Homeric epics and admiring the Homeric heroes. The *Iliad* deals in poetic form with a small segment of the last year of the Trojan War, which had taken place centuries before Homer's time during the Mycenaean period. At the very beginning, Homer states his theme:

The Wrath of Achilles is my theme, that fatal wrath which, in fulfillment of the will of Zeus, brought the Achaeans [Greeks] so much suffering and sent the gallant souls of many noblemen to Hades, leaving their bodies as carrion for the dogs and passing birds. Let us begin, goddess of song, with the angry parting that took place between Agamemnon King of Men and the great Achilles Son of Peleus.[2]

The story goes on to reveal the cause for this wrath. In depriving "the swift and excellent" Achilles of his rightful prize (the captive girl, Briseis), King Agamemnon has gravely insulted Achilles' honor and has violated the solemn rule that warrior heroes treat each other with respect. Achilles, his pride wounded by this offense to his honor, refuses to rejoin Agamemnon in battle against Troy. Achilles plans to retain his honor by demonstrating that the Achaeans need his valor and military prowess. Not until many brave men have been slain, including his dearest friend Patroclus, does Achilles set aside his quarrel with Agamemnon and enter the battle.

Homer employs a *particular* event, the quarrel between an arrogant Agamemnon and a revengeful Achilles, to demonstrate a *universal* principle—that "wicked arrogance" and "ruinous wrath" will cause much suffering and death. Homer grasps that there is an internal logic to existence, a significant order to human affairs. For Homer, says British classicist H. D. F. Kitto, "actions must have their consequences; ill-judged actions must have uncomfortable results."[3] People, even

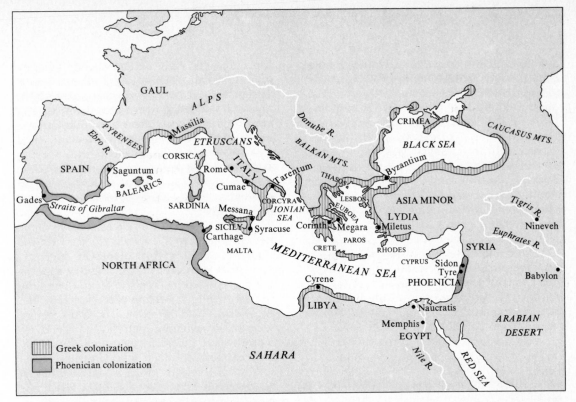

Map 3.1 Greek Colonization of the Mediterranean Basin

the gods, operate within a certain unalterable framework; their deeds are subject to the demands of fate, or necessity. With a poet's insight, Homer sensed what would become a fundamental attitude of the Greek mind: there is a universal order to things. Later Greeks would formulate it in philosophical terms.

Although human life is governed by laws of necessity, the Homeric warrior expresses a passionate desire to assert himself, to demonstrate his worth, to gain the glory that poets would immortalize in their songs—that is, to achieve *arete*, excellence. In the *Iliad*, Hector, prince of Troy, does battle with Achilles, even though defeat and death seem certain. He fights not because he is a fool rushing madly into a fray nor because he relishes combat, but because he is a prince bound by a code of honor and conscious of his reputation. In the code of the warrior aristocrats, honor meant more than life itself.

In the warrior-aristocrat world of Homer, *excellence* was principally interpreted as bravery and skill in battle. Homer's portrayal also bears the embryo of a larger conception of human excellence, one that combines thought with action. A man of true worth, says the wise Phoenix to a stubborn Achilles, is both "a speaker of words and a doer of deeds." In this passage, we find the earliest statement of the Greek educational ideal—the molding of a man who, says classicist Werner Jaeger, "united nobility of action with nobility of mind," who realized "the whole of human potentialities."[4] Thus, in Homer we find the beginnings of Greek humanism—a concern with man and his achievements.

To Mesopotamian and Egyptian minds, the gods were primarily responsible for the good or evil that befell human beings. To Homer, the gods are still very much involved in human affairs, but he also makes the individual a decisive actor in the drama of life. Human actions and human personality are very important. Homer's men demonstrate a considerable independence of will. Men pay respect to the gods but do not live in perpetual fear of them; they choose their own way, at times even defying the gods. As British classicist C. M. Bowra says, "the human actors . . . pursue their own aims and deal their own blows; the gods may help or obstruct them, but success or failure remains their own. The gods have the last word, but in the interval men do their utmost and win glory for it."[5]

Homer's works are essentially an expression of the poetic imagination and mythical thought. But his view of the eternal order of nature and his conception of the individual striving for excellence form the foundations of the Greek outlook.

Greek Religion

During the Dark Age, Greek religion was a mixture of beliefs and cults inherited from the Mycenaean past and from an even older Indo-European past imported from Asia Minor. The Greeks had no prophets or works of scripture in the manner of the Hebrews, but Homer's epics gave some clarity and structure to Greek religion. He did not intend his poetry to have any theological significance, but his treatment of the gods had important religious implications for the Greeks. In time, Homer's epics formed the basis of the Olympian religion accepted thoughout Greece. The principal gods were said to reside on Mount Olympus and on its highest peak was the palace of Zeus, the chief deity. The Olympian gods were recognized by all Greeks, but each city retained local gods and rituals that had been transmitted through generations by folk memory.

Many Greeks found an outlet for their religious feelings in the sacred ceremonies of mystic cults. Devotees of the cult of Dionysus, the god of wine and agricultural fertility, engaged in ecstatic dances and frenzied prayers for abundant harvests. Participants in the Eleusinian cult felt purified and reborn through their rituals and believed in a happy life after death. The Orphic cult, which was popular in the sixth century B.C., taught the unimportance of earthly life and the need to prepare for life after the grave. The Orphics believed that the soul, which once enjoyed a happy existence in another world, was imprisoned in the body for an unknown fault, and that if the individual controlled his or her bodily desires, the soul would be liberated after death.

In the early stages of Greek history, most people sought to live in accordance with the wishes of the gods. Through prayer, offerings, and ritual purification, they tried to appease the gods and consulted oracles to divine the future. Although religion pervaded daily life, the Greeks had no official body of priests who ruled religious matters and could intervene in politics. Instead, religious ceremonies were conducted by citizens chosen to serve as priests. But in time, traditional religion would be challenged and undermined by a growing secular and rational spirit.

Evolution of the City-State

The Break with Theocratic Politics

Greek society from 750 B.C. to the death of Alexander the Great in 323 B.C. comprised small independent city-states. The city-state based on tribal allegiances was generally the first political association during the early stages of civilization. Moreover, Greece's many mountains, bays, and islands—natural barriers to political unity—favored this type of political arrangement.

The scale of the city-state, or *polis*, was small; most city-states had less than 5,000 male citizens. Athens, which was a large city-state, had some 35,000 male citizens; the rest of its population of 350,000 consisted of women, children, resident aliens, and slaves, none of whom could participate in lawmaking. The citizens of the polis, many of whom were related by blood, knew each other well, and together they engaged in athletic contests and religious rituals. The polis gave individuals a sense of belonging, for its citizens were intimately involved in the political and cultural life of the community.

In the fifth century B.C., at its maturity, the Greeks viewed their polis as the only avenue to the good life—"the only framework within which man could realize his spiritual, moral, and intellectual capacities," in the words of Kitto.[6] The mature polis was a self-governing community that expressed the will of free citizens, not the desires of gods, hereditary kings, or priests. In the Near East, religion dominated political activity, and to abide by the mandates of the gods was the ruler's first responsibility. The Greek polis also had begun as a religious institution in which the citizens sought to maintain an alliance with their deities. But gradually the citizens de-emphasized the gods' role in political life and based government not on the magic powers of divine rulers, but on human intelligence as expressed through the community. The great innovation introduced by the Greeks into politics and social theory, says classicist Mason Hammond, was "the view that law did not emanate from gods, or divine rulers, but from the human community."[7]

The evolution of the Greek polis from a tribal-religious institution to a secular-rational institution was only a part of the general transition of the Greek mind from myth to reason. The emergence of rational attitudes did not, of course, spell the end of religion, particularly for the peasants, who remained devoted to their ancient cults, gods, and shrines. Greek commanders and statesmen, at times, were not beyond consulting omens and oracles before making decisions, and a considerable part of Athenian revenue went to the construction of temples and the observance of religious festivals. The Greeks were careful to show respect for the gods, for it was believed that these deities could aid or harm a city. Worshipping the god of the city was a required act of patriotism to which Greeks unfailingly adhered.

Thus, the religious-mythical tradition never died in Greece, but existed side by side with a growing rationalism. As Greek rationalism gained in influence, traditional religious beliefs and restrictions either were made to comply more with the demands of reason, or grew weaker through neglect and disuse. When Athenian democracy reached its height in the middle of the fifth century B.C., religion was no longer the dominant factor in politics. For many Athenians, religion had become largely ceremonial, a way of expressing loyalty to the city; they had actually come to rely on human reason, not divine guidance, in their political and intellectual life.

Greek political life was marred by violent party conflicts, demagoguery, intercity warfare, and the exploitation of weak states by stronger ones. Nevertheless, the Greek political achievement was extraordinary. What made Greek political life different from that of earlier Near Eastern civilizations, as well as of enduring significance, was the Greeks' gradual realization that community problems are caused by human beings and require human solutions. Thus the Greeks came to understand law as an achievement of the rational mind rather than as an edict imposed by the gods; law was valued because it expressed the will and needs of the community, not out of fear of the divine. The Greeks also valued free citizenship. An absolute king who ruled arbitrarily and by decree, who was above the law, was abhorrent to them.

The ideals of political freedom are best exemplified by Athens. But before turning to Athens, let us examine another Greek city, which followed a different political course.

Sparta: A Garrison State

Situated on the Peloponnesian peninsula, further inland than most Greek cities, Sparta had been settled by Dorian Greeks. While the other Greek city-states dealt with overpopulation and land hunger by establishing colonies, Sparta conquered its neighbors, including Messenia, in the eighth century B.C.

Instead of selling the Messenians abroad, the traditional Greek way of treating a defeated foe, the Spartans kept them as state serfs, or *helots*. Helots were owned by the state rather than by individual Spartans. Enraged by their enforced servitude, the Messenians, also a Greek people, desperately tried to regain their freedom. After a bloody struggle, the Spartans suppressed the uprising, but the fear of a helot revolt became indelibly stamped on Spartan consciousness.

To maintain their dominion over the Messenians who outnumbered them ten to one, the Spartans—with extraordinary single-mindedness, discipline, and loyalty—transformed their own society into an armed camp. Agricultural labor was performed by helots; trade and crafts were left to the *perioikoi*, conquered Greeks who were free but who had no political rights; and the Spartans learned only one craft, soldiering.

The Spartans were trained in the arts of war and indoctrinated to serve the state. Military training for Spartan boys began at age seven; they exercised, drilled, competed, and endured physical hardships. Other Greeks admired the Spartans for their courage, obedience to law, and achievement in molding themselves according to an ideal. Spartan soldiers were better trained and disciplined and were more physically fit than other Greeks. But the Spartans were also criticized for having a limited conception of arete.

Before converting itself into a military state, Sparta's cultural development had paralleled that of the other Greek cities. By isolating itself economically and culturally from the rest of Greece, however, Sparta became a closed provincial town and did not share in the cultural enlightenment that pervaded the Greek world. A culturally retarded Sparta paid a heavy price for military strength.

By 500 B.C., Sparta had emerged as the leader of the Peloponnesian League, an alliance of southern Greek city-states whose land forces were superior to those of any other combination of Greek cities. Sparta, though, was concerned with controlling its conquests, not with further imperialism.

Cautious by temperament and always fearful of a helot uprising, Spartans viewed the Peloponnesian League as an instrument for defense, not for aggression.

Athens: The Rise of Democracy

The contrast between the city-states of Athens and Sparta is striking. Whereas Sparta was a land power and exclusively agricultural, Athens was located on the peninsula of Attica near the coast, possessed a great navy, and was the commercial leader among the Greeks. Sparta's leaders were reluctant to send soldiers far from home, where they were needed to control the helots, so they pursued an isolationist foreign policy. The Athenians, daring and ambitious, endeavored to extend their hegemony over other Greek cities. Finally, Athenians and Spartans held different conceptions of freedom. To the Spartans, freedom meant preserving the independence of their fatherland; this overriding consideration demanded order, discipline, and regimentation. The Athenians also wanted to protect their city from enemies, but unlike the Spartans, they valued political freedom and sought the full development and enrichment of the human personality. Thus, while authoritarian Sparta became culturally sterile, the relatively free and open society of Athens became the cultural leader of Hellenic civilization.

Greek city-states generally moved through four stages: rule by a king (monarchy), rule by landowning aristocrats (oligarchy), rule by one man who seized power (tyranny), and rule by the people (democracy). In a monarchy, the first stage, the king, who derived his power from the gods, commanded the army and judged civil cases.

The second stage, an oligarchy, was instituted in Athens during the eighth century B.C. when aristocrats usurped power from hereditary kings. In the next century, aristocratic regimes experienced a social crisis. First, there was tension between the landholding nobility that dominated the govern-

Acropolis. On top of the rocky Acropolis stood Athens's most impressive structures, including the Temple of Athena Nike, and the majestic Parthenon. These monuments were a symbol of Athenian civic pride and creative genius. (*Greek National Tourist Organization*)

ment and the newly rich and ambitious merchants who wanted a share in governing Athens. Second, peasants who borrowed from the aristocracy, pledging their lands as security, lost their property and even became enslaved for nonpayment of their debts. In Athens the embittered and restless peasants demanded and were granted one concession. In 621 B.C., the aristocrats appointed Draco to draw up a code of law. Although Draco's code let the poor know what the law was and reduced the possibilities of aristocratic judges behaving arbitrarily, penalties were extremely severe, and the code provided no relief for the peasants' economic woes. Athens was moving toward civil war as the poor began to organize and press for the cancellation of their debts and the redistribution of land.

Solon, the Reformer In 594 B.C. Solon, a traveler and poet with a reputation for being wise, was elected chief executive. Two years later, the aristocrats, to avert open warfare, gave Solon the power to work out a solution to Athens's problems. Solon maintained that a principle of justice, *Dike*, underlies the human community, and that when people violate this standard of justice, they bring ruin upon the city. Thus, he held that the wealthy landowners, through their greed, had disrupted community life and brought Athens to the brink of civil war. A distinguishing feature of Greek intellectual life was the belief in the orderliness of the universe. For Solon (c. 640–559 B.C.), universal law also operated in the sphere of social life.

Originally, justice had been conceived in religious terms as the will of Zeus; in regarding justice as a principle operating within society, Solon withdrew justice from the province of religion and gave it a secular foundation. He initiated a rational approach to the problems of society by reducing the gods' role in human affairs: he attributed the city's ills to the specific behavior of individuals; he sought worldly remedies for these ills; and he held that written law should be in harmony with the natural order of things. In Solon's career can be detected the embryo of political thought and reform based on reason.

Underlying Solon's reforms was a concern for the interests of the community as a whole, a commitment to moderation, and an avoidance of radical extremes. Solon aimed at restoring a sick Athenian society to health by restraining the nobles and improving the lot of the poor. To achieve this goal, he canceled debts, freed Athenians enslaved for debt, and brought back to Athens those who had been sold abroad; but he refused to confiscate and redistribute the nobles' land as the extremists demanded.

Solon recognized that the aristocrats had abused their political power, but he did not believe that the common people were prepared for self-government. His political reforms rested on the assumption that aristocrats would continue to exercise a guiding role in government. He permitted all classes of free men, even the poorest, to sit in the Assembly, which elected magistrates and accepted or rejected legislation proposed by a new Council of Four Hundred, and opened the highest offices in the state to wealthy commoners, who had previously been excluded from these positions because they lacked noble birth. Thus, Solon undermined the traditional rights of the hereditary aristocracy and initiated the transformation of Athens from an aristocratic oligarchy into a democracy.

Solon also instituted ingenious economic reforms. Recognizing that the poor soil of Attica was not conducive to growing grain, he urged the cultivation of grapes for wine and the growing of olives, whose oil could be exported. To encourage industrial expansion, he ordered that all fathers teach their sons a trade and granted citizenship to foreign craftsmen willing to migrate to Athens. These measures and the fine quality of the native reddish-brown clay allowed Athens to become the leading producer and exporter of pottery. Solon's economic policies had transformed Athens into a great commercial center.

With imagination and intelligence, Solon had reformed Athenian society. His reforms completed, Solon retired from office. In refusing to use his prestige to become a tyrant, a one-man ruler, Solon demonstrated that his statesmanship rested on the highest moral principles—on a conception of justice. Believing that only the rule of law can hold the community together, Solon refused to act outside the law; wanting to imbue his fellow Athenians with a sense of responsibility, he refused to act irresponsibly. However, Solon's reforms did not eliminate factional disputes among the aristocratic clans nor relieve all the discontent of the poor.

Pisistratus, the Tyrant Pisistratus (c. 605–527 B.C.), another aristocrat, endeavored to take advantage of the general instability to become a one-man ruler. After two abortive efforts, he secured power in 546 B.C. and drove into exile those fellow aristocrats who had opposed him. Tyranny thus had replaced oligarchy.

Tyranny occurred frequently in the Greek city-states. Almost always aristocrats themselves, tyrants generally posed as champions of the poor in their struggle against the aristocracy, another indication that the government had to reckon with the needs of the entire community. To increase their own base of support, some tyrants extended citizenship to the landless and even to foreigners.

Pisistratus sought popular support by having conduits constructed to increase Athens's water supply; like tyrants in other city-states he gave to peasants land confiscated from exiled aristocrats, and granted state loans to small farmers. By concerning himself with the problems of the masses, Pisistratus continued the trend initiated by Solon. In a deliberate attempt to pacify the population, Pisistratus exercised personal power without abolishing the existing constitution.

Pisistratus' great achievement was the promotion of cultural life. He initiated grand architectural projects, encouraged sculptors and painters, arranged for public recitals of the Homeric epics, and founded festivals that included dramatic performances. In all these ways he made culture, formerly the province of the aristocracy, available to commoners. Pisistratus thus launched a policy that eventually led Athens to emerge as the cultural capital of the Greeks. In further weakening the power of the landed aristocracy, Pisistratus made the establishment of democracy under Cleisthenes possible.

Cleisthenes, the Democrat   After Pisistratus' death in 527 B.C., his power passed to his two sons. One was assassinated and the other driven from Athens by Spartans, whose intervention had been urged by exiled Athenian aristocrats who opposed one-man rule. In the power vacuum that ensued, a faction headed by Cleisthenes, an aristocrat sympathetic to democracy, assumed leadership.

By an ingenious method of redistricting the city, Cleisthenes ended the aristocratic clans' traditional jockeying for the chief state positions, which had caused so much divisiveness and bitterness in Athens. Cleisthenes replaced this practice, rooted in tradition and authority, with a new system devised by reason to ensure that historic allegiance to tribe or clan would be superseded by loyalty to the city.

Cleisthenes hoped to make democracy the permanent form of government for Athens. To safeguard the city against tyranny, he introduced the practice of *ostracism*. Once a year Athenians were given the opportunity to inscribe on a potsherd *(ostracon)* the name of anyone who they felt endangered the state.

An individual against whom sufficient votes were cast was ostracized, that is, forced to leave Athens for ten years.

Although some aristocratic features still existed in the government (notably the Council of the Areopagus, consisting of retired high officials), Cleisthenes had firmly secured democratic government in Athens. The Assembly, which Solon had opened to all male citizens, was in the process of becoming the supreme authority in the state. But the period of Athenian greatness lay in the future; the Athenians first had to fight a war of survival against the Persian Empire.

Athenian Greatness

The Persian Wars

In 499 B.C., the Ionian Greeks of Asia Minor rebelled against their Persian overlord. Sympathetic to the Ionian cause, Athens sent twenty ships to aid the revolt, an act that the Greek historian Herodotus said "was the beginning of trouble not only for Greece, but for the rest of the world as well." Bent on revenge, Darius I, king of Persia, sent a small detachment to Attica. In 490 B.C., on the plains of Marathon, the citizen army of Athens defeated the Persians—for the Athenians, one of the finest moments in their history. Ten years later, Xerxes, Darius' son, organized a huge invasion force of some 250,000 men and over 500 ships with the aim of reducing Greece to a Persian province. Setting aside their separatist instincts, most of the city-states united to defend their independence and their liberty. Herodotus viewed the conflict as a struggle for freedom.

The Persians crossed the waters of the Hellespont (Dardanelles) and made their way into northern Greece. Herodotus describes their encounter at the mountain pass of Thermopylae with 300 Spartans, who were true to their training and ideal of arete and "resisted to the last with their swords if they had them, and if not, with their hands and teeth, until the Persians, coming on from the front over the ruins of the wall and closing in from behind, finally overwhelmed them."[8] Northern Greece fell to the Persians, who continued south, burning a deserted Athens.

When it appeared that the Greeks' spirit had been broken, the Athenian statesman and general Themistocles (c. 527–460 B.C.) demonstrating in military affairs the same rationality that Cleisthenes had shown in political life, lured the Persian fleet into the narrows of the Bay of Salamis. Unable to deploy their more numerous ships in this cramped space, the Persian armada was destroyed by Greek ships manned by crews who understood what was at stake. In 479 B.C., a year after the Athenian naval victory at Salamis, the Spartans defeated the Persians in the land battle of Plataea. The inventive intelligence with which the Greeks had planned their military operations and a fierce desire to preserve their freedom had enabled them to defeat the greatest military power the Mediterranean world had yet seen.

The Persian Wars were decisive in the history of the West. Had the Greeks been defeated, it is very likely that their cultural and political vitality would have been crushed. The confidence and pride that came with victory, however, propelled Athens into a golden age, which became marred by the Athenian urge for dominance in Greece.

The Delian League

The Persian Wars ushered in an era of Athenian imperialism that had drastic consequences for the future. Immediately after the wars, more than 150 city-states organized a confederation, the Delian League, to protect themselves against a renewed confrontation with Persia. Because of its wealth, its powerful fleet, and the restless energy of its citizens, Athens assumed leadership of the Delian League. Largely because of the Athenian fleet, the league was able to drive both pirates and Persians from the Aegean Sea. Conceived as a voluntary association of independent Greek states seeking protection against Persia, the

league gradually came under the domination of Athens.

Athenians consciously and rapaciously manipulated the league for their own economic advantage, seeing no conflict between imperialism and democracy. They coveted the empire that gave them wealth, power, and glory, and they considered it natural for strong states to increase their might at the expense of weaker ones. Moreover, the Athenians claimed that the other city-states benefited from Athenian hegemony. Athens forbade member states to withdraw, crushed revolts, and stationed garrisons on the territory of confederate states. It used both tribute from members and the League's treasury to finance public works in Athens.

Although member states did receive protection, were not overtaxed, and enjoyed increased trade, they resented Athenian domination. As the Persian threat subsided, hatred for Athenian imperialism grew. In converting the Delian League into an instrument of Athenian imperialism, Athens may have lost an opportunity to perform a great creative act, as historian Arnold Toynbee suggests:

If the Athenians had resisted the temptation to abuse their trust, as the leading power in the confederacy, for their own narrow national advantage, the economic tide making for closer political union would probably have kept the confederacy of Delos in existence on a voluntary footing; and this might have led on, in time, to some kind of voluntary political unification of the Hellenic World as a whole. The course taken at this critical time, by Athenian policy under Pericles' leadership, led to a renewal of fratricidal warfare [and] the breakdown of Hellenic Civilization.[9]

The Mature Athenian Democracy

Athenian imperialism was one consequence of the Persian Wars; another was the flowering of Athenian democracy and culture. Democracy became more firmly entrenched when in 462 B.C. the aristocratic Council of the Areopagus was stripped of its political powers.

Map 3.2 The Aegean Basin

The Athenian state was a direct democracy, in which the citizens themselves, not elected representatives, made the laws. In the Assembly, which was open to all adult male citizens and which met some forty times a year, Athenians debated and voted on key issues of state—they declared war, signed treaties, and spent public funds. The lowliest cobbler, as well as the wealthiest aristocrat, had the opportunity to express his opinion in the Assembly, to vote, and to hold office. By the middle of the fifth century, the will of the people as expressed in the Assembly was supreme.

The Council of Five Hundred (which had been established by Cleisthenes to replace Solon's Council of Four Hundred) managed the ports, military installations, and other state properties and prepared the agenda for the Assembly. Because its members were chosen annually by lot and could not serve more than twice in a lifetime, the Council could never supersede the Assembly. Some

350 magistrates, also chosen by lot, performed administrative tasks. The ten generals, because of the special competence their posts required, were not chosen by lot, but were elected by the Assembly.

Athens has been aptly described as a government of amateurs; there were no professional civil servants, no professional soldiers and sailors, no state judges, no elected lawmakers. The duties of government were performed by ordinary citizens. Such a system rested on the assumption that the average citizen was capable of participating intelligently in the affairs of state; that he would, in a spirit of civic patriotism, carry out his responsibilities to his city. In fifth-century Athens, excellence was equated with good citizenship.

The introduction of pay for government officials marked a great democratic advance. It meant that a poor person could afford to leave his job for a year in order to serve on the Council of 500, on a commission overseeing the administration of the city, or in the law courts.

Although Athens was a democracy in form, in practice aristocrats continued to dominate political life for most of the fifth century. The generals elected by the people came from noble houses as did the leading politicians in the Assembly. This situation was not surprising, for aristocrats took for granted a responsibility to exercise leadership and acquired the education needed to perform this role. The economic expansion after the Persian Wars produced a wealthy class of tradesmen who eventually challenged aristocratic dominance in the Assembly during the last third of the fifth century B.C.

Athenian democracy undoubtedly had its limitations and weaknesses. Modern critics point out that resident aliens were almost totally barred from citizenship and therefore from political participation. Slaves, who constituted about one-fourth of the Athenian population, enjoyed none of the freedoms that Athenians considered so precious. The Greeks regarded slavery as a necessary precondition for civilized life; for some to be free and prosperous, they believed, others had to be enslaved. Whereas people today regard slavery and freedom as contradictory, to the Greeks they were complementary.

Slaves usually did the same work as Athenian citizens—farming, commerce, manufacturing, domestic chores. Some slaves—the 300 Scythian archers who made up the police force and those sufficiently educated to serve the state as clerks—enjoyed a privileged position. However, slaves who toiled in the mines suffered a grim fate. In Athens, some slaves were Greeks, but most were foreigners. Slaves were generally prisoners of war and captives of pirates.

Athenian women were another group denied legal or political rights. They were barred from attending the Assembly and holding public office, and generally they could not appear in court without a male representative. Like the Near Eastern societies, Greek society was male-dominated. Since it was believed that a woman could not act

independently, she was required to have a guardian—normally her father or husband—who controlled her property and supervised her behavior.

Ancient critics also attacked Athenian democracy. Having no confidence in the ability of the common people to govern, these aristocratic critics equated democracy with mob rule. The Assembly did at times make rash and foolish decisions and was swayed by the oratory of demagogues. For the most part, however, concludes British historian A. H. M. Jones,

the Assembly seems to have kept its head, and very rarely to have broken its rules of procedure. . . . Moreover, the people demanded high standards of its advisors. . . . It was informed advice, and not mere eloquence, that the people expected from rising politicians, and they saw to it that they got it.[10]

That the Athenians found democracy an indispensable form of government is proved by the paucity of revolts. In the almost two hundred years after Cleisthenes, there were only two attempts to undo the democracy. Both occurred under the stress of the Peloponnesian War, and both were short-lived.

The flaws in Athenian democracy should not cause us to undervalue its extraordinary achievement. The idea that the state represented a community of free citizens remains a crucial principle of Western civilization. Athenian democracy embodied the principle of the legal state—a government based on laws debated, devised, altered, and obeyed by free citizens.

This idea of the legal state could only have arisen in a society that had an awareness of and a respect for the rational mind. In the same way that the Greeks demythicized nature, they also removed myth from the sphere of politics. Holding that government was something that people create to satisfy human needs, the Athenians regarded their leaders neither as gods nor as priests, but as men who had demonstrated a capacity for statesmanship. Athens was unique, says Italian historian Mario Attilio Levi, for Athenians "had the audacity to maintain that human reason is itself the source of legitimacy and therefore of the right to govern and command, in a world in which the only recognized source of legitimacy was the gods."[11]

Both systematic political thought and democratic politics originated in Greece. There, people first asked questions about the nature and purpose of the state, rationally analyzed political institutions, speculated about human nature and justice, and discussed the merits of various forms of government. It is to Greece that we ultimately trace the idea of democracy and all that accompanies it—citizenship, constitutions, equality before the law, government by law, reasoned debate, respect for the individual, and confidence in human intelligence.

But there is a fundamental difference between the Greek concept of liberty and our own. We are concerned with protecting the individual from the state, which we often see as a threat to personal freedom and a hindrance to the pursuit of our personal lives. Identifying the good of the individual with the good of the community, the Greeks were not concerned with erecting safeguards against the state; they did not see the state as an alien force to be feared or to be protected against. To the Greeks, the state was a moral association, a second family that taught proper conduct and enabled them to fulfill their human potential.

Pericles: Symbol of Athenian Democracy

Pericles (c. 495–429 B.C.), a gifted statesman, orator, and military commander, was the central figure in Athenian life during the middle of the fifth century B.C. So impressive was his leadership that this period is called the Age of Pericles. The Athenians achieved greatness in politics, drama, sculpture, architecture, and thought during these decades.

In the opening stage of the monumental clash with Sparta, the Peloponnesian War

(431–404 B.C.), Pericles delivered an oration in honor of the Athenian war casualties. The oration contains a glowing description of the Athenian democratic ideal:

We are called a democracy, for the administration is in the hands of the many and not of the few. But while the law secures equal justice to all alike in their private disputes, the claim of excellence is also recognized; and when a citizen is in any way distinguished, he is preferred to the public service . . . as the reward of merit. Neither is poverty a bar. . . . a spirit of reverence pervades our public acts; we are prevented from doing wrong by respect for authority and for the laws. . . .[12]

Throughout the speech, Pericles contrasted the narrow Spartan concept of excellence with the Athenian ideal of the full development of the human personality. Unlike Sparta, Athens valued both political freedom and cultural creativity; indeed, as Pericles recognized, freedom released an enormous amount of creative energy, making possible Athens's extraordinary cultural accomplishments. "Our love of what is beautiful does not lead to extravagance, our love of the things of the mind does not make us soft," continued Pericles in praise of Athenian society.[13]

The Decline of the City-States

Although the Greeks shared a common language and culture, they remained divided politically. A determination to preserve city-state sovereignty prevented the Greeks from forming a larger political grouping, which might have contained the intercity warfare that ultimately cost the city-state its vitality and independence. But the creation of a Pan-Hellenic union would have required a radical transformation of the Greek character that for hundreds of years had regarded the city-state as the only suitable political system.

Youth Singing and Playing the Kithara (detail). This young man's figure presents an impressive picture of how ancient music was performed. The making of vases, ordinarily a craft, became high art in the archaic and classical periods of Greek civilization. Hundreds of examples of signed works allow us to talk of individual artists for the first time in history. This red-figured vase is by the "Berlin painter." (Attic, c. 490 B.C.) (*The Metropolitan Museum of Art, Fletcher Fund, 1956*)

The Peloponnesian War

Athens's control of the Delian League engendered fear in the Spartans and their allies in the Peloponnesian League. Sparta and the Peloponnesian states decided on war because they felt that their independence was threatened by a dynamic and imperialistic Athens. At stake for Athens was hegemony over the Delian League, which gave Athens political power and contributed to its economic prosperity. Neither Athens nor Sparta anticipated

the catastrophic consequences the war would have for Greek civilization.

The war began in 431 B.C. and ended in 404 B.C., with a temporary and uneasy interlude of peace from 421 to 414 B.C. Possessing superior land forces, the Peloponnesian League invaded Attica and set fire to the countryside. In 430 B.C., a plague, probably coming from Ethiopia by way of Egypt, ravaged Athens, killing about one-third of the population, including its leader, Pericles (in 429 B.C.). Because of Athenian sea power and Spartan inability to inflict a crushing defeat on Athenian ground troops, the first stage of the war ended in stalemate. In 421 B.C., the war-weary combatants concluded a peace treaty.

What led to the resumption of the war and the eventual defeat of Athens was the Athenian expedition against Sicily and its largest city, Syracuse. Athenians were intoxicated by an imperialist urge to extend the empire in the west and by prospects of riches. Swayed by speeches that stirred the emotions, the Athenian populace, believing disaster to be impossible and forsaking caution and reason, approved the Sicilian venture. In the words of Thucydides, the great fifth-century B.C. Athenian historian,

There was a passion for the enterprise which affected everyone alike. . . . The result of this excessive enthusiasm of the majority was that the few who actually were opposed to the expedition were afraid of being thought unpatriotic if they voted against it, and therefore kept quiet.[14]

In 415 B.C. the largest army ever assembled by a Greek city departed for distant Sicily. Unable to overcome the Syracusans, Nicias, the Athenian commander, appealed for reinforcements. Repeating their previous recklessness, the Athenians voted to send a second large expedition to Syracuse. Failure continued. Finally, as his army grew more dispirited and the Syracusans were reinforced by other Sicilian cities, Nicias consented to withdraw.

Then occurred an event that demonstrates

the persistence of the nonrational in Greek life. Just when the Athenians were ready to depart, there was an eclipse of the full moon, and Nicias took it as an omen. Heeding the advice of seers, Nicias postponed the evacuation for twenty-seven days, during which time the Syracusans blocked the mouth of the harbor. After failing in a desperate attempt to break out by sea, the Athenians tried to escape by land. It was a death march. Harassed on all sides by the Syracusans, the Athenians retreated in panic, leaving their wounded behind. They were trapped and were forced to surrender. Imprisoned in Sicilian rock quarries, they perished of hunger, thirst, and disease. Athens and its allies lost 50,000 men and 200 ships in the venture.

Launched with extravagant expectations, the Sicilian expedition ended in dismal failure and cost Athens all hope of victory in the struggle with Sparta. Fearful that victory in Sicily would increase Athenian manpower and wealth, Sparta had again taken up the sword. Strengthened by financial support from Persia and by the defection of some Athenian allies, Sparta moved to end the war. Finally, a besieged Athens, with a decimated navy and a dwindling food supply, surrendered. Sparta dissolved the Delian League, left Athens with only a handful of ships, and forced the city to pull down its long walls—ramparts designed to protect it against siege weapons; but the Spartans refused to massacre Athenian men and enslave the women and children as some allies had urged.

The Peloponnesian War shattered the spiritual foundations of Hellenic society. During the course of the long war, men became brutalized, selfish individualism triumphed over civic duty, moderation gave way to extremism, and politics degenerated into revolution. The moral basis of Hellenic society was wrecked. In the words of Thucydides:

Love of power, operating through greed and through personal ambition, was the cause of all these evils. To this must be added the violent fanaticism which came into play once the struggle had broken out. Leaders of parties . . . in professing to serve the

public interest . . . were seeking to win the prizes for themselves. In their struggle for ascendancy nothing was barred; terrible indeed were the actions to which they committed themselves, and in taking revenge they went further still. Here they were deterred neither by the claims of justice nor by the interests of the state. . . . Thus neither side had any use for conscientious motives; more interest was shown in those who could produce attractive arguments to justify some disgraceful action. As for the citizens who held moderate views, they were destroyed by both the extreme parties. . . . As the result of these revolutions, there was a general deterioration of character throughout the Greek World.[15]

Athens shared the political problems of the Greek world during the war. Pericles had provided Athenians with effective leadership in the three decades prior to the war; when the Assembly seemed to support unwise policies, he had won it over with sound arguments. After his death in 429 B.C., the quality of leadership deteriorated. Succeeding statesmen were motivated more by personal ambition than by civic devotion; rather than soberly examining issues, they supported policies that would gain them popularity. Without Pericles' wise statesmanship, the Assembly at times acted rashly, as it did in the case of the Sicilian expedition.

The deterioration of Greek political life was exemplified by conflicts between oligarchs and democrats. Oligarchs, generally from the wealthier segments of Athenian society, wanted to concentrate power in their own hands by depriving the lower classes of political rights. Democrats, generally from the poorer segment of society, sought to preserve the political rights of adult male citizens. Strife between oligarchs and democrats was quite common in the Greek city-states even before the Peloponnesian War. Both sides sought to dominate the Assembly and to manipulate the courts; both resorted to bribery and at times even assassinated opponents. During the Peloponnesian War these party conflicts erupted into civil war in a number of cities, including Athens.

Taking advantage of the decline in morale following the failure of the Sicilian expedition, oligarchs gained control of Athens in 411 B.C.; a body of Four Hundred citizens wielded power. Seeking to deprive the lower classes of political influence, the Four Hundred restricted citizenship to 4,000 men. But the crews of Athenian ships, loyal to democracy, challenged the authority of the Four Hundred, who were forced to flee.

After Athens's defeat in 404 B.C., oligarchs again gained control, this time with the support of Sparta. A ruling council of thirty men, the so-called Thirty Tyrants, held power. Led by Critias, an extreme antidemocrat, the Thirty trampled on Athenian rights, confiscating property and condemning many people to death. In the winter of 404–403, returned exiles led an uprising against the Thirty, who were unseated.

The Fourth Century

The Peloponnesian War was the great crisis of Hellenic history. The city-states never recovered from their self-inflicted spiritual wounds. The civic loyalty and confidence that had marked the fifth century waned and the fourth century was dominated by a new mentality that the leaders of the Age of Pericles would have abhorred. A concern for private affairs superseded devotion to the general good of the polis. Increasingly, the tasks of government were administered by professionals instead of by ordinary citizens, and mercenaries began to replace citizen soldiers.

The political history of the fourth century can be summed up briefly. Athens, the only state that might have conceivably imposed unity on the Greek world, had lost its chance. A culturally sterile, provincial-minded, and heavy-handed Spartan government lacked the talent to govern the Greeks. In many cities, Sparta replaced democratic governments with pro-Spartan oligarchies under the supervision of a Spartan governor. But Spartan hegemony was short-lived; before long the Greek city-

states had thrown off the Spartan yoke. The quarrelsome city-states formed new systems of alliances and persisted in their ruinous conflicts. Some Greek thinkers, recognizing the futility of constant war, argued that peace should be the goal of Greek politics. But their efforts were in vain.

In addition to wars between city-states, fourth-century Greece experienced a new outbreak of civil wars between rich and poor. Athens largely escaped these ruinous conflicts, but they engulfed many other cities. With good reason, Greek thinkers regarded social discord as the greatest of evils.

While the Greek cities battered each other in fratricidal warfare, a new power was rising in the north—Macedonia. To the Greeks, the Macedonians, a wild mountain people who had acquired a sprinkling of Hellenic culture, differed little from other non-Greeks whom they called barbarians. In 359 B.C., twenty-three-year-old Philip (382–336 B.C.) became Philip II, king of Macedonia. Having spent three years as a hostage in Thebes, Philip had learned the latest military tactics and had witnessed firsthand the weaknesses of the warring Greek states. He converted Macedonia into a first-rate military power and began a drive to become master of the Greeks.

Patient, deceitful, clever, and unscrupulous, Philip gradually extended his power over the Greek city-states. Not correctly assessing Philip's strength, the Greeks were slow to organize a coalition against Macedonia. In 338 B.C. at Chaeronea, Philip's forces inflicted a decisive defeat on the Greeks and all of Greece was his. The city-states still existed, but they had lost their independence. The world of the small, independent, and self-sufficient polis drew to a close and Greek civilization took a different shape.

The Dilemma of Greek Politics

There were deeper reasons why the Greek cities declined and fell victim to Macedonian

Chronology 3.1 The Greek City-State

1700–1450 B.C.*	Height of Minoan civilization
1400–1230	Height of Mycenaean civilization
1100–800	Dark Age
c. 700	Homer
750–550	Age of Colonization
621	Draco's code of law
594	Solon is given power to institute reforms
546–527	Under Pisistratus tyranny replaces oligarchy
507	Cleisthenes broadens democratic institutions
499	Ionians revolt against Persian rule
490	Athenians defeat Persians at Battle of Marathon
480	Xerxes of Persia invades Greece; Greek naval victory at Salamis
479	Spartans defeat Persians at Plataea, ending Persian Wars
478–477	Formation of Delian League
431	Start of Peloponnesian War
429	Death of Pericles
413	Athenian defeat at Syracuse
404	Athens surrenders to Sparta, ending Peloponnesian War
399	Execution of Socrates
387	Plato founds a school at Athens
359	Philip II becomes king of Macedonia
338 B.C.	Battle of Chaeronea; Greek city-states fall under dominion of Macedonia

* Some dates are approximations.

imperialism. Despite internal crisis and persistent warfare, the Greeks were unable to fashion any other political framework than the polis. The city-state was fast becoming an anachronism, but the Greeks were unable to see that in a world moving toward larger states and empires, the small city-state could not compete. An unallied city-state with its small citizen army could not withstand the powerful military machine that Philip had created. A challenge confronted the city-states—the need to shape some form of political union, a Pan-Hellenic federation, that would end the suicidal internecine warfare, promote economic well-being, and protect the Greek world from hostile states. Because they could not respond creatively to this challenge, the city-states ultimately lost their independence to foreign conquerors.

The waning of civic responsibility among the citizens was another reason for the decline of the city-states. The vitality of the city-state depended on the willingness of its citizens to put aside private concerns for the good of the community. Although Athens had recovered commercially from the Peloponnesian War, for example, its citizens had suffered a permanent change in character; the abiding devotion to the polis that had distinguished the Age of Pericles greatly diminished during the fourth century. The factional strife, the degeneration of politics into personal ambition, the demagoguery, and the fanaticism that Thucydides had described persisted into the fourth century and was aggravated by the economic discontent of the poor. The Periclean ideal of citizenship dissipated as Athenians neglected the community to concentrate on private affairs, or sought to derive personal profit from public office. The decline in civic responsibility could be seen in the hiring of mercenaries to replace citizen soldiers and in the indifference and hesitancy with which Athenians confronted Philip. The Greeks did not respond to the Macedonian threat as they had earlier rallied to fight off the Persian menace, because the quality of citizenship had deteriorated.

Greek political life evidenced both the best and the worst features of freedom, both the capabilities and limitations of reason. On the one hand, as Pericles boasted, freedom encouraged active citizenship, reasoned debate, and government by law. On the other hand, as Thucydides lamented, freedom could degenerate into factionalism, demagoguery, unbridled self-interest, and civil war.

Rationalism also presented problems. Originally the polis was conceived as a divine institution in which the citizen had a religious obligation to obey the law. As the rational and secular outlook became more pervasive, the gods lost their authority. When law was no longer conceived as an expression of sacred traditions ordained by the gods, but as a merely human contrivance, respect for the law diminished, weakening the foundations of the society. The results were party conflicts, politicians who scrambled for personal power, and moral uncertainty. Recognizing the danger, conservatives insisted that law must again be regarded as issuing from the gods; the city must again treat with reverence its ancient traditions. Although the Greeks originated the lofty ideal that human beings could regulate their political life according to reason, their history, marred by intercity warfare and internal violence, demonstrates the extreme difficulties involved in creating and maintaining a rational society.

Notes

1. James Shiel, *Greek Thought and the Rise of Christianity* (New York: Barnes & Noble, 1968), pp. 5–6.

2. Homer, *The Iliad*, trans. by E. V. Rieu (Baltimore: Penguin Books, 1950), p. 23.

3. H. D. F. Kitto, *The Greeks* (Baltimore: Penguin Books, 1957), p. 60.

4. Werner Jaeger, *Paideia: The Ideals of Greek Culture* (New York: Oxford University Press, 1945), 1:8.

5. C. M. Bowra, *Homer* (London: Gerald Buckworth, 1972), p. 72.

6. Kitto, *The Greeks*, p. 78.

7. Mason Hammond, *The City in the Ancient World* (Cambridge, Mass.: Harvard University Press, 1972), p. 189.

8. Herodotus, *The Histories*, trans. by Aubrey de Sélincourt (Baltimore: Penguin Books, 1954), p. 493.

9. Arnold Toynbee, *Hellenism* (New York: Oxford University Press, 1959), pp. 109–110.

10. A. H. M. Jones, *Athenian Democracy* (Oxford, England: Basil Blackwell, 1969), pp. 132–133.

11. Mario Attilio Levi, *Political Power in the Ancient World* (New York: Mentor Books, 1968), pp. 122–123.

12. Thucydides, *The Peloponnesian War*, trans. by B. Jowett (Oxford, England: Clarendon Press, 1881), bk. II, ch. 37.

13. Thucydides, *The Peloponnesian War*, trans. by Rex Warner (Baltimore: Penguin Books, 1954), p. 118.

14. Ibid., p. 382.

15. Ibid., p. 210.

Suggested Reading

Bowra, C. M., *The Greek Experience* (1957). An excellent introduction to Greek culture and society.

———, *Periclean Athens* (1971). A discussion of Athens at its height.

Claster, J. N., *Athenian Democracy* (1967). A useful collection of readings on the triumphs and failures of Athenian democracy.

Fine, John, V. A., *The Ancient Greeks* (1983). An up-to-date, reliable analysis of Greek history.

Finley, M. I., *The Ancient Greeks* (1964). An excellent popular account of Greek civilization.

———, *Early Greece* (1970). A survey of Minoan and Mycenaean civilizations and early Greek history.

Hammond, N. G. L., *The Classical Age of Greece* (1975). An interpretation of major developments in Greek history.

History of the Hellenic World (1974–   ). A multivolume history prepared by leading Greek scholars. It has been translated from the Greek and published by the Pennsylvania State University Press. The first volume, *Prehistory and Protohistory*, is excellent for Minoan and Mycenaean civilizations.

Hooper, Finley, *Greek Realities* (1978). A literate and sensitive presentation of Greek society and culture.

Kitto, H. D. F., *The Greeks* (1957). A stimulating survey of Greek life and thought.

Nilsson, M. P., *A History of Greek Religion* (1964). A highly regarded work on Greek religion.

Robinson, C. E., *Hellas* (1948). A useful short survey.

Taylour, William Lord, *The Mycenaeans* (1983). An account of all phases of Myceanean life.

Webster, T. B. L., *Athenian Culture and Society* (1973). Discusses Athenian religion, crafts, art, drama, education, and so on.

Willetts, R. F., *The Civilization of Ancient Crete* (1977). An account of all phases of Minoan civilization.

Review Questions

1. Describe the main features of Minoan and Mycenaean civilizations.

2. What was the legacy of the Mycenaeans to Hellenic civilization?

3. Why is Homer called "the shaper of Greek civilization"?

4. How did the Greek polis break with the theocratic politics of the Near East?

5. Contrast Spartan society with Athenian society.

6. What were the accomplishments of Solon? Pisistratus? Cleisthenes?

7. What was the significance of the Persian Wars?

8. What contradictions do you see between Athenian democratic ideals and Athenian imperialism? Why did no such contradiction exist for the Athenians?

9. Describe the basic features and the limitations of Athenian democracy.

10. Compare and contrast Athenian democracy with American democracy.

11. What were the causes and the results of the Peloponnesian War?

12. Give reasons for the decline of the polis.

13. What were the causes of the Peloponnesian War? What was the significance of the expedition to Sicily? What was the impact of the Peloponnesian War on the Greek world?

14. What problems did the city-states face in the fourth century B.C.?

15. Explain how Greek political life evidenced both the best and the worst features of freedom, both the capabilities and the limitations of reason.

4

*Greek Thought: From Myth
to Reason*

*T*he Greeks broke with the mythopoeic outlook of the Near East and conceived a new way of viewing nature and human society that is the basis of the Western scientific and philosophic tradition. After an initial period of mythical thinking, by the fifth century B.C. the Greek mind had gradually applied reason to the physical world and to all human activities. This emphasis on reason marks a turning point for human civilization.

The development of rational thought in Greece is a process, a trend, not a finished achievement. The process began when some advanced intellects became skeptical of Homer's gods and went beyond mythical explanations for natural phenomena. The nonphilosophic majority did not, however, totally eliminate the language, attitudes, and beliefs of myth from its life and thought. Even in the mature philosophy of Plato and Aristotle, mythical modes of thought persisted. What is of immense historical importance is not the degree to which the Greeks successfully integrated the norm of reason, but that they originated this norm, defined it, and applied it to their intellectual development and social life.

Philosophy

The first theoretical philosophers in human history emerged in the sixth century B.C. in the Greek cities of Ionia in Asia Minor. Curious about the essential composition of nature and dissatisfied with earlier creation legends, the Ionians sought physical, rather than mythic-religious, explanations for natural occurrences. In the process, they arrived at a new concept of nature and a new method of inquiry. They maintained that nature was not manipulated by arbitrary and willful gods and that it was not governed by blind chance. The Ionians said that underlying the seeming chaos of nature were principles of order— general laws ascertainable by the human mind. This discovery marks the beginning of scientific thought.

What conditions enabled the Greeks to make this breakthrough? Perhaps their familiarity with Near Eastern achievements in mathematics and science stimulated their ideas. But this influence should not be exaggerated, says Greek student of philosophy John N. Theodorakopoulos, for Egyptians and Mespotamians "had only mythological systems of belief and a knowledge of practical matters. They did not possess those pure and crystal-clear products of the intellect which we call science and philosophy. Nor did they have any terminology to describe them."[1] Perhaps the poets' conception of human behavior being subject to universal destiny was extended into the philosophers' belief that nature was governed by law. Perhaps the breakthrough was fostered by the Greeks' freedom from a priesthood and rigid religious doctrines that limit thought. Perhaps Greek speculative thought was an offspring of the city, because if law governed human affairs, providing balance and order, should not the universe also be regulated by principles of order?

Cosmologists: Rational Inquiry into Nature

Ionian philosophy began with Thales (c. 624–c. 548 B.C.) of Miletus, a city in Ionia. He was a contemporary of Solon of Athens, and concerned himself with how nature came to be the way it was. Thales said that water was the basic element, the underlying substratum of nature, and that through some natural process—similar to the formation of ice or steam—water gave rise to everything else in the world.

Thales revolutionized thought because he omitted the gods from his account of the origins of nature and searched for a natural explanation of how all things came to be. Thales also broke with the commonly held belief that earthquakes were caused by Poseidon, god of the sea, and offered instead a naturalistic explanation for these disturbances: he thought that the earth floated on water, and that when the water experienced turbulent waves, the earth was rocked by earthquakes.

Anaximander (c. 611–547 B.C.), another sixth-century Ionian, rejected Thales' theory that water was the original substance. He rejected any specific substance and suggested that an indefinite substance, which he called the Boundless, was the source of all things. From this primary mass, which contained the powers of heat and cold, he believed that there gradually emerged a nucleus, the seed of the world. He said that the cold and wet condensed to form the earth and its cloud cover, while the hot and dry formed the rings of fire that we see as the moon, the sun, and the stars. The heat from the fire in the sky dried the earth and shrank the seas. From the warm slime on earth arose life, and from the first sea creatures there evolved land animals, including human beings. Anaximander's account of the origins of the universe and nature understandably contained fantastic elements. Nevertheless, by offering a natural explanation for the origin of nature and life, it surpassed the creation myths.

Like his fellow Ionians, Anaximenes, who died about 525 B.C., made the transition from myth to reason. He also maintained that a primary substance—air—underlay reality and accounted for the orderliness of nature. Air that was rarefied became fire, while wind, clouds, and water were formed from condensed air. When condensed still further, water turned to earth, and when condensed even more, water turned to stone. Anaximenes also rejected the old belief that a rainbow was the goddess Iris; instead, he said that the rainbow was caused by the sun's rays falling on dense air.

The Ionians have been called "matter philosophers" because they held that everything issued from a particular material substance. Other sixth-century B.C. thinkers tried a different approach. Pythagoras (c. 580–c. 507 B.C.) and his followers, who lived in the Greek cities in southern Italy, did not find the nature of things in a particular substance but in mathematical relationships. The Pythagoreans discovered that the intervals in the musical scale can be expressed mathematically. Extending this principle of proportion found in sound to the universe at large, they concluded that the cosmos also contained an inherent mathematical order. Thus the Pythagoreans shifted the emphasis from matter to form, from the world of sense perception to the logic of mathematics. The Pythagoreans were also religious mystics who believed in the immortality and transmigration of souls. Consequently, they refused to eat animal flesh, fearing that it contained former human souls.

Parmenides (c. 515–450 B.C.), a native of the Greek city of Elea in southern Italy, challenged the fundamental view of the Ionians that all things emerged from one original substance. In developing his position, Parmenides applied to philosophic argument the logic used by the Pythagoreans for mathematical thinking. In putting forth the proposition that an argument must be consistent and contain no contradictions, Parmenides became the founder of formal logic. Reality is one, eternal, and unchanging, asserted Parmenides; it is made known not through the senses, which are misleading, but through the mind—not through experience, but through reason. Truth could be reached through abstract thought alone.

Democritus (c. 460–370 B.C.), from the Greek mainland, renewed the Ionians' concern with the world of matter and reaffirmed their confidence in knowledge derived from sense perception. But he also retained Parmenides' reverence for reason. His model of the universe consisted of two fundamental realities— empty space and an infinite number of atoms. Eternal, indivisible, and imperceptible, these atoms moved in the void. All things consisted of atoms, and combinations of atoms accounted for all change in nature. In a world of colliding atoms, everything behaved according to mechanical principles.

Concepts essential to scientific thought thus emerged in embryonic form with Greek philosophers: the mathematical order of nature (Pythagoras), logical proof (Parmenides), and

the mechanical structure of the universe (Democritus). By giving to nature a rational, rather than a mythical, foundation and by holding that theories should be grounded in evidence and be capable of being defended logically, the early Greek philosophers pushed thought in a new direction. Their achievement made possible theoretical thought and the systematization of knowledge—as distinct from the mere observation and collection of data.

This systematization of knowledge extended into several areas. Greek mathematicians, for example, organized the Egyptians' practical experience with land measurements into the logical and coherent science of geometry. Both Babylonians and Egyptians had performed fairly complex mathematical operations, but unlike the Greeks, they made no attempt to prove mathematical principles. In another area, Babylonian priests had observed the heavens for religious reasons, believing that the stars revealed the wishes of the gods. The Greeks used the data collected by the Babylonians, but not in religion; they sought to discover the geometrical laws that underlie the motions of heavenly bodies.

A parallel development occurred in medicine. No Near Eastern medical text explicitly attacked magical beliefs and practices. In contrast, Greek doctors, because of the philosophers' work, were able to distinguish between magic and medicine. The school of the Greek physician Hippocrates (c. 460–377 B.C.), located on the island of Cos off the Asia Minor coast, was influenced by the thought of the early Greek cosmologists. The following tract from the school of Hippocrates is on epilepsy, considered a sacred disease, and illustrates this growth of a scientific spirit in medicine:

I am about to discuss the disease called "sacred." It is not, in my opinion, any more divine or sacred than any other diseases, but has a natural cause, and its supposed divine origin is due to men's inexperience, and to their wonder at its peculiar character. Now . . . men continue to believe in its divine origin because they are at a loss to understand it. . . . My own view is that those who first attributed a sacred character to this malady were like the magicians, purifiers, charlatans, and quacks of our own day; men who claim great piety and superior knowledge. Being at a loss, and having no treatment which would help, they concealed and sheltered themselves behind superstition, and called this illness sacred, in order that their utter ignorance might not be manifest.[2]

The Sophists: A Rational Investigation of Human Culture

In their effort to understand the external world, the cosmologists had created the tools of reason. Greek thinkers then turned away from the world of nature and attempted a rational investigation of people and society. Exemplifying this shift in focus were the Sophists, professional teachers who wandered from city to city teaching rhetoric, grammar, poetry, gymnastics, mathematics, and music. The Sophists insisted that it was futile to speculate about the first principles of the universe, for such knowledge was beyond the grasp of the human mind; they urged instead that individuals improve themselves and their cities by applying reason to the tasks of citizenship and statesmanship.

The Sophists answered a practical need in Athens, which had been transformed into a wealthy and dynamic imperial state after the Persian Wars. Because the Sophists claimed that they could teach *political arete*—the ability to formulate the right laws and policies for cities and the art of eloquence and persuasion—they were sought as tutors by politically ambitious young men, especially in Athens. The Western humanist tradition owes much to the Sophists, who examined political and ethical problems, cultivated the minds of their students, and invented formal secular education.

Traditionally the Greeks had drawn a sharp distinction between Greeks and non-Greeks, and held that some people were slaves by nature. Some Sophists in the fourth century

Black-figured Athenian Vase. The black-figured vase style used a red background to outline form. Musculature could then be incised or painted in red on the light-colored bodies. Physical fitness and athletics were highly prized by the Greeks. Poets sang the praise of Olympic champions, and sculptors and vase painters captured the beauty of athletic physiques for an admiring public. (*The Metropolitan Museum of Art, Rogers Fund, 1914*)

B.C. arrived at a broader conception of humanity. They asserted that slavery was based on force or chance, that people were not slaves nor masters by nature, and they also held that all people, Greek and non-Greek, were fundamentally alike.

The Sophists were philosophical relativists; that is, they held that no truth is universally valid. Protagoras, a fifth-century Sophist, said that "man is the measure of all things." By this he meant that good and evil, truth and falsehood, are matters of individual judgment—there are no universal standards that apply to all people at all times.

In applying reason to human affairs, the Sophists attacked the traditional religious and moral values of Athenian society. Some Sophists taught that speculation about the divine was useless; others went further and asserted that religion was just a human invention to ensure obedience to traditions and laws.

The Sophists also applied reason to law with the same effect—the undermining of traditional authority. The laws of a given city, they asserted, did not derive from the gods; nor were they based on any objective and universal standards of justice and good, for such standards did not exist. Each community determined for itself what was good or bad, just or unjust. Beginning with this premise, some Sophists simply urged changing laws to meet new circumstances. More radical Sophists argued that law was merely something made by the most powerful citizens for their own benefit. This principle had dangerous implications: first, law did not need to be obeyed since it rested on no higher principle than might; second, the strong should do what they have the power to do, and the weak must accept what they cannot resist. Both interpretations were disruptive of community life, for they stressed the selfish interests of the individual over the general welfare of the city.

Some Sophists combined this assault on law with an attack on the ancient Athenian idea of *sophrosyne*—moderation and self-discipline—because it denied human instincts. Instead of moderation, they urged that people should maximize pleasure and trample underfoot those traditions that restricted them from fully expressing their desires. To these radical Sophists, traditions were only invented by the weak to enslave nobler natures.

In subjecting traditions to the critique of reason, the radical Sophists triggered an intellectual and spiritual crisis. Their doctrines encouraged disobedience to law, neglect of civic duty, and selfish individualism. These attitudes became widespread during and after the Peloponnesian War, dangerously weakening community bonds.

Socrates: The Rational Individual

In attempting to comprehend nature, the cosmologists had discovered theoretical reason. The Sophists then applied theoretical reason to society. In the process they created a profound problem for Athens and other city-states—the need to restore the authority of law and a respect for moral values. Conservatives argued that this restoration could only be accomplished by renewing allegiance to those sacred traditions undermined by the Sophists.

Socrates, one of the most extraordinary figures in the history of Western civilization, took a different position. Socrates was born in Athens, probably in 469 B.C., about ten years after the Persian Wars, and was executed in 399 B.C., five years after the end of the Peloponnesian War. His life spanned the glory years of Greece, when Athenian culture and democracy were at their height, as well as the tragic years of the lengthy and shattering war with Sparta.

Both the Sophists and Socrates continued the tradition of reason initiated by the cosmologists, but unlike the cosmologists, both felt that knowledge of the individual and society was more important than knowledge of nature. Socrates and the Sophists endeavored to improve the individual and thought that this could be accomplished through education. Despite these similarities, Socrates' teaching marks a profound break with the Sophist movement.

Socrates felt that the Sophists taught skills, but that they had no insights into questions that really mattered: What is the purpose of life? What are the values by which man should live? How does man perfect his character? Here the Sophists failed, said Socrates; they taught the ambitious to succeed in politics, but persuasive oratory and clever reasoning do not instruct a man in the art of living. He felt that the Sophists had attacked the old system of beliefs, but had not provided the individual with a constructive replacement.

Socrates' central concern was the perfection of individual human character, the achievement of moral excellence. Moral values, for Socrates, did not derive from a transcendent God as they did for the Hebrews. They were attained when the individual regulated his life according to objective standards arrived at through rational reflection, that is, when reason became the formative, guiding, and ruling agency of the soul. For Socrates, true education meant the shaping of character according to values discovered through the active and critical use of reason.

Socrates wanted to subject all human beliefs and behavior to the clear light of reason, and in this way to remove ethics from the realm of authority, tradition, dogma, superstition, and myth. Socrates believed that reason was the only proper guide to the most crucial problem of human existence—the question of good and evil. Socrates taught that rational inquiry was a priceless tool that allowed one to test opinions, weigh the merit of ideas, and alter beliefs on the basis of knowledge. To Socrates, when humans engaged in critical self-examination and strove tirelessly to perfect their nature, they liberated themselves from accumulated opinions and traditions and based their conduct on convictions that they could rationally defend. Socrates believed that people with critical minds could not be swayed by sophistic eloquence, nor delude themselves into thinking that they knew something when they really did not.

Dialectics In urging Athenians to think rationally about the problems of human existence, Socrates offered no systematic ethical theory, no list of ethical precepts. What he did supply was a method of inquiry called *dialectics*, or logical discussion. As Socrates used it, a dialectical exchange between individuals, a *dialogue*, was the essential source of knowledge. It forced people out of their apathy and smugness and compelled them to examine their thoughts critically, to confront illogical, inconsistent, dogmatic, and imprecise assertions, and to express their ideas in clearly defined terms.

Dialectics affirmed that the acquisition of knowledge was a creative act. The human mind could not be coerced into knowing; it was not a passive vessel into which a teacher poured knowledge. The dialogue compelled the individual to play an active role in acquiring the values by which he was to live. In a dialogue, individuals became thinking participants in a search for knowledge. Through relentless cross-examination, Socrates induced his partner to explain and justify his opinions through reason, for only thus did knowledge become a part of one's being.

Dialogue implied that reason was meant to be used in relations between human beings, and that they could learn from each other, help each other, teach each other, and improve each other. It implied further that the human mind could and should make rational choices. To deal rationally with oneself and others is the distinctive mark of being human. Through the dialectical method, people could make ethical choices, impose rules on themselves, and give form to their existence.

For Socrates, the ethical way of life required conscious choice as a prerequisite. The highest form of excellence was taking control of one's life and shaping it according to ethical values reached through reflection. Doing what was right either by accident or imitation was insufficient. Morality did not originate in the decrees of gods or in traditions, but within the individual. Through self-examination and self-discipline, a person could acquire moral values. The good life is attained by the exercise of reason, the development of intelligence— this precept is the essence of Socratic teaching. Socrates made the individual the center of the universe, reason the center of the individual, and moral worth the central aim of human life. In Socrates, Greek humanism found its highest expression.

The Execution of Socrates Socrates devoted much of his life to his mission—persuading

Porch of the Maidens, Attic Sculpture. The architect has incorporated the human form as a functional element in a rationally organized structure. The balance and harmony of the Porch of the Maidens weds humanity with art. (*Brown Brothers*)

For many years, Socrates challenged Athenians without suffering harm, for Athens was generally distinguished by its freedom of speech and thought. In the uncertain times during and immediately after the Peloponnesian War, though, Socrates made enemies. When he was seventy, he was accused of corrupting the youth of the city, and of not believing in the city's gods but in other new divinities. Underlying these accusations was the fear that Socrates was a troublemaker, a subversive, a Sophist who threatened the state by subjecting its ancient and sacred values to the critique of thought.

Socrates denied the charges and conducted himself with great dignity at his trial, refusing to grovel and beg forgiveness. Instead he defined his creed:

If you think that a man of any worth at all ought to . . . think of anything but whether he is acting justly or unjustly, and as a good or a bad man would act, you are mistaken. . . . If you were therefore to say to me, "Socrates, . . . We will let you go, but on the condition that you give up this investigation of yours, and philosophy. If you are found following these pursuits again you shall die." I say, if you offered to let me go on these terms, I should reply: . . . As long as I have breath and strength I will not give up philosophy and exhorting you and declaring the truth to every one of you whom I meet, saying, as I am accustomed, "My good friend, you are a citizen of Athens . . . are you not ashamed of caring so much for making of money and for fame and prestige, when you neither think nor care about wisdom and truth and the improvement of your soul?"[4]

Convicted by an Athenian court, Socrates was ordered to drink poison. Had he attempted to appease the jurors, he probably would have been given a light punishment, but he would not alter his principles even under threat of death.

Socrates did not write down his philosophy and beliefs. We are able to construct a coherent account of his life and ideals largely through the works of his most important disciple, Plato.

his fellow Athenians to think critically about how they lived their lives. "No greater good can happen to a man than to discuss human excellence every day,"[3] he said. Always self-controlled and never raising his voice in anger, Socrates engaged any willing Athenian in conversation about his values. Through probing questions, he tried to make people realize how directionless and purposeless their lives were.

Plato: The Rational Society

Plato (c. 429–347 B.C.) used his master's teachings to create a comprehensive system of philosophy that embraced both the world of nature and the social world. But Plato had a more ambitious goal than Socrates' moral reformation of the individual. Plato tried to arrange political life according to rational rules, and he held that Socrates' quest for personal morality could not succeed unless the community also was transformed on the basis of reason. Virtually all the problems discussed by Western philosophers for the past two millenniums were raised by Plato. We shall focus on two of his principal concerns, the theory of Ideas and that of the just state.

Theory of Ideas   Socrates had taught that universal standards of right and justice exist and that these are arrived at through thought. Building on the insights of his teacher Socrates and of Parmenides, who said that reality is known only through the mind, Plato insisted on the existence of a higher world of reality, independent of the world of things that we experience every day. This higher reality, he said, is the realm of Ideas or Forms—unchanging, eternal, absolute, and universal standards of beauty, goodness, justice, and truth. To live in accordance with these standards constitutes the good life; to know these forms is to grasp truth.

Truth resides in this world of Forms and not in the world made known through the senses. For example, a person can never draw a perfect square, but the properties of a perfect square exist in the world of Forms. Also, a sculptor observes many bodies, and they all possess some flaw; in his mind's eye he tries to penetrate the world of Ideas and to reproduce with art a perfect body. Again, the ordinary person only forms an opinion of what beauty is from observing beautiful things; the philosopher, aspiring to true knowledge, goes beyond what he sees and tries to grasp with his mind the Idea of beauty. Similarly, the ordinary individual lacks a true conception of justice or goodness; such

knowledge is available only to the philosopher whose mind can leap from worldly particulars to an ideal world beyond space and time.

Plato saw the world of phenomena as unstable, transitory, and imperfect, while his realm of Ideas was eternal and universally valid. An individual man partakes in an imperfect and limited way in the Idea of man; men may come and go, but the Idea of man persists eternally. Thus true wisdom is obtained through knowledge of the Ideas, not the imperfect reflections of the Ideas that are perceived with the senses.

Plato was a champion of reason who aspired to study and to arrange human life according to universally valid standards. In contrast to sophistic relativism, he maintained that objective and eternal standards do exist. Although Plato advocated the life of reason and wanted to organize society according to rational rules, his writing also includes a religious-mystical side. At times Plato seems like a mystic seeking to escape from this world into a higher reality, a realm that is without earth's evil and injustice.

Because Platonism is a two-world philosophy, it has had an important effect on religious thought. In future chapters we will examine the influence of Platonic otherworldliness on later philosopher-mystics and Christian thinkers.

The Just State   In adapting the rational legacy of Greek philosophy to politics, Plato constructed a comprehensive political theory. What the Greeks had achieved in practice—the movement away from mythic and theocratic politics—Plato accomplished on the level of thought: the fashioning of a rational model of the state.

Like Socrates, Plato attempted to resolve the problem caused by the radical Sophists—the undermining of traditional values. Socrates tried to dispel this spiritual crisis through a moral transformation of the individual, while Plato wanted the entire community to conform to rational principles. Plato said that if human beings are to live an ethical life, they must do it as citizens of a just and rational state.

In an unjust state, people cannot achieve Socratic wisdom, for their souls will mirror the state's wickedness.

Plato had experienced the ruinous Peloponnesian War and the accompanying political turmoil. He saw Athens undergo one political crisis after another; most shocking of all, he had witnessed Socrates' trial and execution. Disillusioned by the corruption of Athenian morality and politics, Plato refused to participate in political life. He came to believe that under the Athenian constitution neither the morality of the individual Athenian nor the good of the state could be enhanced, and that Athens required moral and political reform founded on Socrates' philosophy.

In his great dialogue, *The Republic*, Plato devised an ideal state based on standards that would rescue his native Athens from the evils that had befallen it. *The Republic* attempted to analyze society rationally and to reshape the state so that individuals could fulfill the best within them—to attain the Socratic goal of moral excellence. For Plato, the just state could not be founded on tradition (for inherited attitudes did not derive from rational standards), nor on the doctrine of might being right (a principle taught by radical Sophists and practiced by Athenian statesmen). A just state for Plato conformed to universally valid principles and aimed at the moral improvement of its citizens, not at increasing its power and material possessions. Such a state required leaders distinguished by their wisdom and virtue, rather than by sophistic cleverness and eloquence.

Fundamental to Plato's political theory as formulated in *The Republic* was his criticism of Athenian democracy. An aristocrat by birth and temperament, Plato believed that it was foolish to expect the common man to think intelligently about foreign policy, economics, or other vital matters of state. Yet the common man was permitted to speak in the Assembly, to vote, and, by lot, to be selected for executive office. A second weakness of democracy was that leaders were chosen and followed for nonessential reasons like persuasive speech, good looks, wealth, and family background.

A third danger of democracy was that it could degenerate into anarchy, said Plato. Intoxicated by liberty, the citizens of a democracy could lose all sense of balance, self-discipline, and respect for law:

The citizens become so sensitive that they resent the slightest application of control as intolerable tyranny, and in their resolve to have no master they end up by disregarding even the law, written or unwritten.[5]

As liberty leads to license, continued Plato, then the democratic society will deteriorate morally.

The parent falls into the habit of behaving like the child, and the child like the parent: the father is afraid of his sons, and they show no fear or respect for their parents, in order to assert their freedom. . . . To descend to smaller matters, the schoolmaster timidly flatters his pupils, and the pupils make light of their masters. . . . Generally speaking, the young . . . argue with . . . [their elders] and will not do as they are told; while the old, anxious not to be thought disagreeable tyrants, imitate the young and condescend to enter into their jokes and amusements.[6]

As the democratic city falls into disorder, a fourth weakness of democracy will become evident. A demagogue will be able to gain power by promising to plunder the rich to benefit the poor. To retain his hold over the state, the tyrant

begins by stirring up one war after another, in order that the people may feel their need of a leader, and also be so impoverished by taxation that they will be forced to think of nothing but winning their daily bread, instead of plotting against him.[7]

Because of these inherent weaknesses of democracy, Plato insisted that Athens could not be saved by more doses of liberty. He believed that Athens would be governed properly only when the wisest men, the philosophers, attained power.

Unless either philosophers become kings in their countries or those who are now called kings and rulers come to be sufficiently inspired with a genuine desire for wisdom; unless, that is to say, political power and philosophy meet together . . . there can be no rest from troubles . . . for states, nor yet, as I believe, for all mankind.[8]

Plato rejected the fundamental principle of Athenian democracy: that the average person is capable of participating sensibly in public affairs. People would not entrust the care of a sick person to just anyone, said Plato, nor would they allow a novice to guide a ship during a storm. Yet, in a democracy, amateurs were permitted to run the government and to supervise the education of the young— no wonder Athenian society was disintegrating. Plato felt that these duties should be performed only by the best people in the city, the philosophers who would approach human problems with reason and wisdom derived from knowledge of the world of unchanging and perfect Ideas. Only these possessors of truth would be competent to rule, said Plato. Whereas Socrates believed that all people could base their actions on reason and acquire virtue, Plato maintained that only a few were capable of philosophic wisdom, and these few were the state's natural rulers.

The organization of the state, as formulated in *The Republic*, corresponded to Plato's conception of the individual soul, of human nature. Plato held that the soul had three major capacities: reason (the pursuit of knowledge), spiritedness (self-assertion, courage, ambition), and desire (the "savage many-headed monster" that relishes food, sex, and possessions). In the well-governed soul, spiritedness and desire are guided by reason and knowledge—standards derived from the world of Ideas.

Plato divided people into three groups; those who demonstrated philosophic ability should be rulers; those whose natural bent revealed exceptional courage should be soldiers; those driven by desire, the great masses, should be producers (tradesmen, artisans, or farmers). In what was a radical departure from the general attitudes of the times, Plato held that men and women should receive the same education and have equal access to all occupations and public positions, including philosopher-ruler.

Plato felt that the entire community must recognize the primacy of the intellect, and sought to create a harmonious state in which each individual performed what he or she was best qualified to do and preferred to do. This would be a just state, said Plato, for it would recognize human inequalities and diversities and make the best possible use of them for the entire community. Clearly this conception of justice was Plato's response to the radical Sophists who taught that justice consisted of the right of the strong to rule in their own interest, or that justice was doing whatever one desired.

In *The Republic*, philosophers were selected by a rigorous system of education open to all children. Those not demonstrating sufficient intelligence or strength of character were to be weeded out to become workers or warriors, depending on their natural aptitudes. After many years of education and practical military and administrative experience, the philosophers were to be entrusted with political power. If they had been properly educated, the philosopher-rulers would not seek personal wealth or personal power; they would be concerned with pursuing justice and serving the community. The philosophers were to be absolute rulers. Although the people would have lost their right to participate in political decisions, they would have gained a well-governed state whose leaders, distinguished by their wisdom, integrity, and sense of responsibility, sought only the common good. Only thus could the individual and the community achieve well-being.

Plato repudiated the fundamental principles of a free community: the right to participate in government, equality before the law, and checks on leaders' power. Even freedom of thought was denied the great mass of people in Plato's state. Philosopher-rulers would search for truth, but the people were to be told clever stories—"noble lies," Plato called them—to keep them obedient. But the philosopher-rulers, said Plato, would not be seekers of power or wealth; as wise and virtuous people, the best products of polis education, it would not be in their character to behave like ruthless tyrants.

The purpose of *The Republic* was to warn Athenians that without respect for law, wise leadership, and proper education for the young, their city would continue to degenerate. Plato wanted to rescue the city-state from disintegration by re-creating the community spirit that had vitalized the polis—and he wanted to re-create it based not on mere tradition but on a higher level with knowledge and philosophy. The social and political institutions of Athens, Plato felt, must be reshaped according to permanent and unalterable ideals of justice.

Aristotle: Creative Synthesis

Aristotle (384–322 B.C.) stands at the apex of Greek thought because he achieved a creative synthesis of the knowledge and theories of earlier thinkers. Aristotle studied at Plato's Academy for twenty years. Later he became tutor to young Alexander, the son of Philip of Macedonia. Returning to Athens after Alexander had inherited his father's throne, Aristotle founded a school called the Lyceum.

The range of Aristotle's interests and intellect is extraordinary. He was the leading expert of his time in every field of knowledge, with the possible exception of mathematics. Even a partial listing of his works shows the universal character of his mind and his all-consuming passion to understand the worlds of nature and of humankind: *Logic, Physics, On the Heavens, On the Soul, On the Parts of Animals, Metaphysics, Nicomachean Ethics, Politics, Rhetoric,* and *Poetics.*

Aristotle undertook the monumental task of organizing and systematizing the thought of the Pre-Socratics, Socrates, and Plato. He shared with the natural philosophers a desire to understand the physical universe; he shared with Socrates and Plato the belief that

reason was a person's highest faculty and that the polis was the primary formative institution of Greek life. Out of the myriad of Aristotle's achievements, we shall discuss only three: his critique of Plato's theory of Ideas, his ethical thought, and his political thought.

Critique of Plato's Theory of Ideas   Like Democritus before him, Aristotle renewed confidence in sense perception; he wanted to swing the pendulum back from Plato's higher world to the material world. Possessing a scientist's curiosity to understand the facts of nature, Aristotle appreciated the world of phenomena, of concrete things. He respected knowledge obtained through the senses, as the following selection from his observations of the animal kingdom shows:

With the common hen after three days and three nights there is the first indication of the embryo. . . . Meanwhile the yolk comes into being . . . and, the heart appears, like a speck of blood, in the white of the egg. This point beats and moves as though endowed with life.[9]

Aristotle retained Plato's stress on universal principles. But he wanted these standards to derive from human experience with the material world; in this way they could be adapted to the requirements of the natural sciences. To the practical and empirically minded Aristotle, the Platonic notion of an independent and separate world of Forms beyond space and time seemed contrary to common sense. To comprehend reality, said Aristotle, one should not escape into another world. For him, Plato's two-world philosophy suffered from too much mystery, mysticism, and poetic fancy; moreover, Plato undervalued the world of facts and objects revealed through sight, hearing, and touch, a world that Aristotle valued. Like Plato, Aristotle desired to comprehend the essence of things and held that understanding universal principles is the ultimate aim of knowledge. But unlike Plato, he did not turn away from the world of things to obtain such knowledge.

For Aristotle, the Forms were not located

in a higher world outside and beyond phenomena, but existed in things themselves. He said that through human experience with such things as men, horses, and white objects, the essence of man, horse, and whiteness can be discovered through reason; the Form of Man, the Form of Horse, and the Form of Whiteness can be determined. These universals, which apply to all men, all horses, and all white things, were for both Aristotle and Plato the true objects of knowledge. For Plato, these Forms existed independently of particular objects, so the Forms for men or horses or whiteness or triangles or temples existed, whether or not representations of these Ideas in the form of material objects were made known to the senses. For Aristotle, however, without examination of particular things, universal Ideas could not be determined. Whereas Plato's use of reason tended to stress otherworldliness, Aristotle tried to bring philosophy back to earth.

By holding that certainty in knowledge comes from reason alone and not from the senses, Plato was predisposed toward mathematics and metaphysics—pure thought that transcends the world of change and material objects. By stressing the importance of knowledge acquired through the rational examination of sense experience, Aristotle favored the development of empirical sciences—physics, biology, zoology, botany, and other disciplines based on the observation and investigation of nature and the recording of data. Aristotle maintained that theory must not conflict with facts and must make them more intelligible, and that it was the task of science to arrange facts into a system of knowledge.

Ethical Thought   Like Socrates and Plato, Aristotle believed that a knowledge of ethics was possible and that it must be based on reason. Aristotle's ethical thought derived from a realistic appraisal of human nature and a common-sense attitude toward life. For him, the good life was the examined life; it meant making intelligent decisions when confronted with specific problems. Persons

Philosopher (Statuette), c. 280 B.C. Greek artists were the first to excel in realistic portraiture. The philosopher is neither a divinely inspired seer nor a divine king, but a person in quest of knowledge. (*The Metropolitan Museum of Art, Rogers Fund, 1910*)

could achieve happiness when they exercised the distinctively human trait of reasoning, when they applied their knowledge relevantly to life, and when their behavior was governed by intelligence and not by whim, tradition, or authority.

Aristotle recognized that people are not entirely rational, that there is a passionate element of the human personality that can never be eradicated or ignored. Aristotle held that surrendering completely to desire was to descend to the level of beasts, but that denying the passions and living as an ascetic was a foolish and unreasonable rejection of human nature. Aristotle maintained that by proper training, people could learn to regulate their desires. They could achieve moral well-being, or virtue, when they avoided extremes of behavior and rationally chose the way of moderation. "Nothing in excess" is the key to Aristotle's ethics.

Aristotle believed that the contemplative life of the philosopher would yield perfect happiness. The pursuit of philosophic wisdom and beauty, he stated, offered "pleasures marvellous for their purity and their endur-ingness."[10] But Aristotle did not demand more from an individual than human nature would allow; he did not set impossible standards for behavior, but recognized that all persons cannot pursue the life of contemplation, for some lack sufficient leisure or intelligence. But by applying reason to human affairs, all individuals could experience a good life.

Political Thought Aristotle's *Politics* complements his *Ethics*. To live the good life, he said, a person must do it as a member of a political community. Only the polis would provide people with an opportunity to lead a rational and moral existence. With this assertion, Aristotle demonstrated a typically Greek attitude. At the very moment when his pupil Alexander the Great was constructing a world-state that unified Greece and Persia, Aristotle defended the traditional system of independent city-states. Indeed, his *Politics* summed up the polis-centered orientation of Hellenic civilization.

Like Plato, Aristotle presumed that human affairs could be rationally understood and intelligently directed. In *Politics*, as in *Ethics*, he adopted a common-sense, practical attitude. He did not aim at utopia, but wanted to find the most effective form of government for most men in typical circumstances.

Aristotle emphasized the importance of the rule of law. He placed his trust in law rather than in individuals, for they are subject to passions. Aristotle recognized that at times laws should be altered but recommended great caution; otherwise, people would lose respect for law and legal procedure.

. . . For the law has no power to command obedience except that of habit, which can only be given by time, so that a readiness to change from old to new laws enfeebles the power of the law.[11]

Tyranny and revolution, Aristotle said, can threaten the rule of law and the well-being of the citizen. To prevent revolution, the state must maintain

the spirit of obedience to law, more especially in small matters; for transgression creeps in unperceived and at last ruins the state. [This cannot be done] unless the young are trained by habit and education in the spirit of the constitution. [To live as one pleases] is contradictory to the true interests of the state. . . .

Men should not think it slavery to live according to the rule of the constitution, for it is their salvation.[12]

Drama

In the sixth century B.C., lawgivers, tyrants, and artists demonstrated their individuality by announcing their names. Seventh- and sixth-century lyric poets and dramatists also gave expression to this rise of the individual through their awareness of human personality.

One of the earliest and best of the Greek poets was Sappho, who lived about 600 B.C.

on the island of Lesbos. Sappho established a school to teach music and singing to well-to-do girls and to prepare them for marriage. With great tenderness, Sappho wrote poems of friendship and love: "Some say the fairest thing on earth is a troop of horsemen, others a band of foot-soldiers, others a squadron of ships. But I say the fairest thing is the beloved."[13] And of her daughter Cleïs, she wrote:

I have a child; so fair
As golden flowers is she,
My Cleïs, all my care.
I'd not give her away
For Lydia's* wide sway
Nor lands men long to see.[14]

Pindar (c. 518–438 B.C.) was another Greek lyric poet. In his poem of praise for a victorious athlete, Pindar expressed the aristocratic view of excellence. Life is essentially tragic—triumphs are short-lived, misfortunes are many, and ultimately death overtakes all; still man must demonstrate his worth by striving for excellence.

He who wins of a sudden, some noble prize
In the rich years of youth
Is raised high with hope; his manhood takes
*   wings;*
He has in his heart what is better than wealth
But brief is the season of man's delight.
Soon it falls to the ground;
Some dire decision uproots it.
—Things of a day! such is man; a shadow in a
*   dream.*
Yet when god-given splendour visits him
A bright radiance plays over him, and how
*   sweet is life!*[15]

The high point of Greek poetry is the drama, an art form that originated in Greece. The Greek dramatist portrayed the sufferings, weaknesses, and triumphs of individuals. Just as a Greek sculptor shaped a clear visual image of the human form, a Greek dramatist

*Ancient country in Asia Minor.

brought the inner life of a human being into sharp focus and tried to find the deeper meaning of human experience. Thus, in both art and drama, the growing self-awareness of the individual was evident.

Drama originated in the religious festivals honoring Dionysus, the god of wine and agricultural fertility. A profound innovation in these sacred performances, which included choral songs and dances, occurred in the last part of the sixth century B.C. Thespis, the first actor known to history, stepped out of the chorus and engaged it in dialogue. By separating himself from the choral group, Thespis demonstrated a new awareness of the individual.

With only one actor and a chorus, however, the possibilities for dramatic action and human conflicts were limited. Then Aeschylus introduced a second actor in his dramas, and Sophocles a third. Dialogue between individuals thus became possible. The Greek actors wore masks, and by changing them, each actor could play several roles in the same performance. This flexibility allowed the dramatists to depict the clash and interplay of human wills and passions on a greater scale.

Because of the grandeur of the dramatists' themes, the eminence of their heroes, and the loftiness of their language, Greek spectators felt intensely involved in the tragedies of the lives portrayed. What they were witnessing went beyond anything in their ordinary lives, and they experienced the full range of human emotions.

A parallel development to Socratic dialectics—dialogue between thinking individuals—occurred in Greek drama. Greek tragedy evolved as a continuous striving toward humanization and individualization. Through the technique of dialogue, early dramatists first pitted human beings against the gods and destiny. Later, by setting characters in conflict against each other, dramatists arrived at the idea of individuals as active subjects responsible for their behavior and decisions, which were based on their own feelings and thoughts.

Aphrodite. One of the oldest of the gods, Aphrodite has come down through the centuries as the goddess of beauty. The Greeks humanized their gods, and in this graceful figure, the qualities of human beauty are evident. The pose dates this work to late Hellenistic times (mid-second century B.C.). On the other hand, the head and face recall prototypes of the fourth century B.C. (*Veroia Museum/TAP Service, Athens*)

Like the natural philosophers, Greek dramatists saw an inner logic to the universe, which they called Fate or Destiny; both physical and social worlds obeyed laws. When people were stubborn, narrow-minded, arrogant, or immoderate, they were punished. The order in the universe required it, said Sophocles:

The man who goes his way
Overbearing in the word and deed,
Who fears no justice,
Honors no temples of the gods—
May an evil destiny seize him.
And punish his ill-starred pride.[16]

In being free to make decisions, the dramatist says, individuals have the potential for greatness, but in choosing wrongly, unintelligently, they bring disaster to themselves and others.

Also like philosophy, Greek tragedy entailed rational reflection. The tragic hero was not a passive victim of fate. He was a thinking human being who felt a need to comprehend his position, to explain the reasons for his actions, and to analyze his feelings.

The essence of Greek tragedy lies in the tragic hero's struggle against cosmic forces and insurmountable obstacles that eventually crush him. But what impressed the Greek spectators (and today's readers of Greek drama) was not the vulnerability nor weaknesses of human beings but their courage and determination in the face of these forces.

Aeschylus

Aeschylus (525–456 B.C.), an Athenian nobleman, had fought in the battle of Marathon. He wrote over eighty plays, of which only seven survive. In these plays, there are common themes. As an Athenian patriot, he urged adherence to traditional religious beliefs and moral values. Like Solon, the statesman, Aeschylus believed that the world was governed by divine justice that could not be violated with impunity, and that when individuals evinced *hubris* (overweening pride or arrogance), which led them to overstep the bounds of moderation, they must be punished. Another principal theme was that through suffering, persons acquired knowledge: the terrible consequences of sins against the divine order should remind all to think and act with moderation and caution.

Aeschylus' play *The Persians* dealt with an actual event, the defeat of Xerxes, the Persian emperor, by the Greeks. Xerxes' intemperate ambition to become master of Asia and Greece was in conflict with the divine order of the universe. For this *hubris*, Xerxes must pay:

*A single stroke has brought about the ruin of
    great
Prosperity, the flower of Persia fallen and
    gone.*[17]

The suffering of Xerxes should make man aware of what he can and cannot do:

*And heaps of corpses even in generations hence
Will signify in silence to the eyes of men
That mortal man should not think more than
    mortal thoughts.
For* hubris *blossomed forth and grew a crop of
    ruin,
And from it gathered in a harvest full of tears.*
. . . .
*In face of this, when Xerxes, who lacks good
    sense, returns,
Counsel him with reasoning and good advice,
To cease from wounding God with overboastful
    rashness.*[18]

Whereas Aeschylean drama dealt principally with the cosmic theme of the individual in conflict with the moral universe, later dramatists, while continuing to use patterns fashioned by Aeschylus, gave greater attention to the psychology of the individual.

Sophocles

Another outstanding Athenian dramatist was Sophocles (c. 496–406 B.C.). His greatness as

a playwright lay in both the excellence of his dramatic technique and the skill with which he portrayed character. The people that he created possessed violent passions and tender emotions; they were human in their actions but noble in their nature. Sophocles consciously formulated a standard of human excellence: individuals should shape their character in the way a sculptor shapes a form—according to laws of proportion. Sophocles felt that when these principles of harmony were violated by immoderate behavior, a person's character would be thrown off balance and misfortune would strike. The physical world and the sphere of human activities obey laws, said Sophocles, and human beings cannot violate these laws with impunity.

Whereas Aeschylus concentrated on religious matters and Euripides dealt with social issues, Sophocles wrote about the perennial problem of well-intentioned human beings struggling valiantly but unwisely and vainly against the tide of fate. His characters, who were determined on some action fraught with danger, would resist all appeals to caution and unknowingly but inescapably meet with disaster.

In *Oedipus Rex*, Oedipus is warned not to pursue the mystery of his birth. But he refuses to give up the search: "Nothing will move me. I will find the whole truth." (He had unsuspectingly killed his father and married his mother.) For this determination, born more of innocence than arrogance, he will suffer. Events do not turn out, as Oedipus discovers, the way a person thinks and desires that they should; the individual is impotent before the relentless universal laws of human existence. It seems beyond imagining that Oedipus, whom all envied for his intelligence and good works, would meet with such a dreadful revelation.

But tragedy also gives Oedipus the strength to assert his moral independence. Although struck down by fate, Oedipus remains an impressive figure. In choosing his own punishment—self-inflicted blindness—Oedipus demonstrates that he still possesses the distinctly human qualities of choosing and acting, that he still remains a free man responsible for his actions. Despite his misery, Oedipus is able to confront a brutal fate with courage and to demonstrate nobility of character.

Euripides

The rationalist spirit of Greek philosophy permeated the tragedies of another Athenian, Euripides (c. 485–406 B.C.). Like the Sophists, Euripides subjected the problems of human life to critical analysis and challenged human conventions. It was this critical spirit that prompted the traditionalist Aristophanes to attack Euripides for introducing the art of reasoning into tragedy. Women's conflicts, the moral implications of adultery, the role of the gods, the rearing of children, and the meaning of war were carefully scrutinized in Euripides' plays. Euripides blends a poet's insight with the psychologist's probing to reveal the tangled world of human passions and souls in torment.

Euripides recognized the power of irrational, demonic forces that seethe within people—what he called "the bloody Fury raised by fiends of Hell."[19] A scorned Medea, seeking revenge against her husband by murdering their children, says:

I know indeed what evil I intend to do,
But stronger than all my afterthoughts is my
    fury,
Fury that brings upon mortals the greatest
    evils.[20]

In his plays, Euripides showed that the great tragedy of human existence is that reason can offer only feeble resistance against these compelling, relentless, and consuming passions. The forces that destroy erupt from the volcanic nature of human beings.

A second distinctive feature of Euripidean tragedy is its humanitarianism. No other Greek thinker expressed such concern for a fellow human being, such compassion for human suffering. In *The Trojan Women*, Euripides depicted war as agony and not glory, and the warrior as brutish and not noble. He described the torments of women for whom war meant the loss of homes, husbands, children, and freedom. In 416 B.C., Athens massacred the men of the small island of Melos, sold its women and children into slavery, and sacked the city. *The Trojan Women*, performed a year later, warned Athenians:

> *How are ye blind,*
> *Ye treaders down of cities, ye that cast*
> *Temples to desolation, and lay waste*
> *Tombs, the untrodden sanctuaries where lie*
> *The ancient dead; yourselves so soon to die!*[21]

By exposing war as barbaric, Euripides was expressing his hostility to the Athenian leaders who persisted in continuing the disastrous Peloponnesian War.

Aristophanes

Aristophanes (c. 448–c. 380 B.C.) was the greatest of the Greek comic playwrights. He lampooned Athenian statesmen and intellectuals, censured government policies, and protested against the decay of traditional Athenian values. Behind Aristophanes' sharp wit lay a deadly seriousness, for there was much in Athens during the Peloponnesian War that angered him. As an aristocrat, he was repelled by Cleon, the common tanner who succeeded Pericles. As an admirer of the ancient values of honor, duty, and moderation, he was infuriated by the corruption resulting from the Sophists' teachings. As a man of common sense, he recognized that the Peloponnesian War must end. In the process of serving as a social critic, Aristophanes wrote some of the most hilarious lines in world literature.

In *Lysistrata*, an antiwar comedy, the women of Greece agree to abstain from having sexual relations with their husbands and lovers to compel the men to make peace. Lysistrata reveals the plan:

For if we women will but sit at home,
Powdered and trimmed, clad in our daintiest
*   lawn,*
Employing all our charms, and all our arts
To win men's love, and when we've won it,
*   then*
Repel them firmly, till they end the war,
We'll soon get Peace again, be sure of that.[22]

After the plan has been implemented, many women become "husband-sick" and seek to desert the temple where they have gathered. But the men also suffer:

Oh me! these pangs and paroxysms of love,
Riving my heart, keen as a torturer's wheel![23]

Through these unorthodox methods, the women achieve their goal, peace. Performed during the darkest days of the war, this play reminded its audiences to concentrate their efforts in the real world on securing peace.

In *The Clouds*, Aristophanes ridiculed the Sophist method of education both for turning the youth away from their parents' values and for engaging the youth in useless, hair-splitting logic. To Aristophanes, the worst of the Sophists was Socrates, who is depicted in *The Clouds* as a fuzzy-minded thinker with both feet planted firmly in the clouds. Socrates is made to look ridiculous, a man who walks on air, contemplates the sun, and teaches such absurd things as "Heaven is one vast fire extinguisher" or "How many feet of its own a flea could jump." The Sophists in the play teach only how "to succeed just enough for my need and to slip through the clutches of the law." A student of these Sophists becomes a "concocter of lies . . . a supple, un-principled, troublesome cheat."[24]

To Aristophanes, Socrates was a subversive who caused Athenians to repudiate civil mo-rality and to speculate about nonsense ques-tions. Clearly, Aristophanes admired the Athens of the battle of Marathon and feared the rationalism that Euripides, the Sophists, and Socrates had injected into Athenian in-tellectual life.

History

The Mesopotamians and the Egyptians kept annals that purported to narrate the deeds of gods and their human agents, the priest-kings or god-kings. The Hebrews valued his-tory, but believing that God acted in human events, they did not remove history entirely from the realm of myth. The Greeks initiated a different approach to the study of history. As the gods were eliminated from the nature philosophers' explanations for the origins of things in the natural world, mythical elements also were removed from the writing of history.

Greek historians asked themselves ques-tions about the deeds of people, based their answers on available evidence, and wrote in prose, the language of rational thought. They not only narrated events but also examined causes. British philosopher and historian R. G. Collingwood states:

The Greeks quite clearly and consciously recognized both that history is, or can be, a science, and that it has to do with human actions. Greek history is not legend, it is research; it is an attempt to get answers to definite questions about matters of which one recognizes oneself as ignorant. It is not theocratic, it is humanistic; the matters inquired into are not of gods, they are of men. Moreover, it is not mythical. The events inquired into are not events in a dateless past, at the beginning of things; they are events in a dated past, a certain number of years ago. This is not to say that legend, either in the form of theocratic history or in the form of myth, was a thing foreign to the Greek mind. . . . But what is remarkable about the Greeks was not the fact that their historical thought con-tained a certain residue of elements which we should call non-historical, but the fact that side by side with these, it contained elements of what we call history.[25]

In several respects, however, the Greeks were unhistorical. To them history moved in cycles; events and periods constantly repeated themselves. Unlike the Hebrews, they had little awareness of historical uniqueness and progression. Nor was history as vital to the Greeks as it was to the Hebrews. Greek philosophers, fixing their minds on eternal truths, were largely indifferent to history.

Herodotus

Often called the "father of history," Herodotus (c. 484–c. 424 B.C.) wrote a history of the Persian Wars. Herodotus valued the present and recognized that it is not timeless but has been shaped by earlier happenings. To understand the conflict between Persia and Greece, the most important event in his world during his lifetime, he first inquired into the histories of these societies. Much of his information was derived from posing questions to natives of the lands he visited. Interested in everything, Herodotus frequently interlaced his historical narrative with a marvelous assortment of stories and anecdotes.

The central theme of Herodotus' *Histories* is the contrast between Near Eastern despotism and Greek freedom and the subsequent clash of these two world-views in the Persian Wars. Certain of their superiority, the Greeks considered the non-Hellenic world to be steeped in ignorance and darkness. But Herodotus was generally free of this arrogance. A fair-minded and sympathetic observer, tolerant of differences, he took joy in examining the wide range of human character and experience.

Though Herodotus found much to praise in the Persian Empire, he was struck by a lack of freedom and what he considered barbarity. Herodotus emphasized that the mentality of the free citizen was foreign to the East, where men were trained to obey the ruler's commands absolutely. Not the rule of law but the whim of despots prevailed in the East. When a Persian official urged some Greeks to submit to Xerxes, Herodotus wrote that the Greeks said: "You understand well enough what slavery is, but freedom you have never experienced, so you do not know if it tastes sweet or bitter. If you ever did come to experience it, you would advise us

to fight for it not with spears only, but with axes too."[26] Of all the Greek city-states, Herodotus admired Athens most. Freedom had enabled Athens to achieve greatness, said Herodotus, and it was this illustrious city that had rescued the Greek world from Persia.

Another theme evident in Herodotus' work was punishment for hubris. In seeking to become king of both Asia and Europe, Xerxes had acted arrogantly; although he behaved as if he was superhuman, "he too was human, and was sure to be disappointed of his great expectations."[27] Like the Greek tragedians, Herodotus drew universal moral principles from human behavior.

In several ways Herodotus was a historian rather than a teller of tales. First, he asked questions about the past, instead of merely repeating ancient legends; he tried to discover what had happened and the motivations behind the actions. Second, Herodotus at times demonstrated a cautious and critical attitude toward his sources of information:

The course of my story now leads me to Cyrus: who was this man who destroyed the empire of Croesus, and how did the Persians win their predominant position in Asia? I could, if I wished, give three versions of Cyrus' history, all different from what follows; but I propose to base my account on those Persian authorities who seem to tell the simple truth about him without trying to exaggerate his exploits.[28]

Third, while the gods appeared in Herodotus' narrative, they played a far less important role than they did in Greek popular mythology. Nevertheless, by retaining a belief in the significance of dreams, omens, and oracles, and by allowing for divine intervention, Herodotus fell short of being a thoroughgoing rationalist. Herodotus' writings contain the embryo of rational history; Thucydides brought it to maturity.

Thucydides

Thucydides (c. 460–c. 400 B.C.) also concentrated on a great political crisis confronting the Hellenic world—the Peloponnesian War.

Living in Periclean Athens, whose life blood was politics, Thucydides regarded the motives of statesmen and the acts of government as the essence of history. He did not just catalogue facts, but sought those general concepts and principles that the facts illustrated. His history was the work of an intelligent mind trying to make sense out of his times.

Thucydides applied a rationalist empiricism worthy of the Ionian natural philosophers to the sphere of political history. He searched for the truth underlying historical events and attempted to present it objectively.

Of the events of the war I have not ventured to speak from any chance information, nor according to any notion of my own; I have described nothing but what I either saw myself, or learned from others of whom I made the most careful and particular inquiry. The task was a laborious one, because eyewitnesses of the same occurrences gave different accounts of them, as they remembered or were [partial to] one side or the other. And very likely the strictly historical character of my narrative may be disappointing to the ear. But if he who desires to have before his eyes a true picture of the events which have happened, and of the like events which may be expected to happen hereafter in the order of human things, then I shall be satisfied.[29]

In Thucydides' history, there was no place for myths, for legends, for the fabulous—all hindrances to historical truth. He recognized that a work of history was a creation of the rational mind and not an expression of the poetic imagination. The historian seeks to learn and to enlighten, not to entertain.

Rejecting the notion that the gods interfere in history, Thucydides looked for the social forces and human decisions behind events. Undoubtedly, he was influenced by Hippocratic doctors who frowned on divine explanations for disease and distinguished between the symptoms of a disease and its causes. Where Herodotus occasionally lapsed into supernatural explanations, Thucydides wrote history in which the gods were absent, and he denied their intervention in human affairs.

In addition to being a historian, Thucydides was also a political philosopher with a specific view of governments and statesmen. He warned against the dangers of extremism unleashed by the strains of war, and he believed that when reason was forsaken, the state's plight would worsen. He had contempt for statesmen who waged war lightly, acting from impulse, reckless daring, and an insatiable appetite for territory. For this reason, he regarded the decision to attack Syracuse in Sicily as a gross political blunder. Although Thucydides admired Athens for its democratic institutions, rule of law, sense of civic duty, and cultural achievements, he recognized an inherent danger in democracy—the emergence of demagogues who rise to power by stirring up the populace.

Political scientists, historians, and statesmen still turn to Thucydides for insights into the realities of power politics, the dangers of political fanaticism, the nature of imperialism, the methods of demagogues, and the effects of war on democratic politics.

The Greek Achievement: Reason, Freedom, Humanism

Like other ancient peoples, the Greeks warred, massacred, and enslaved; they could be cruel, arrogant, contentious, and superstitious; and they often violated their ideals. But their achievement was unquestionably of profound historical significance. Western thought begins with the Greeks who first defined the individual by his capacity to reason. It was the great achievement of the Greek spirit to rise above magic, miracles, mystery, authority, and custom and to discover the means of giving rational order to nature and society. Every aspect of Greek civilization—science, philosophy, art, literature, politics, historical writing—showed a growing reliance on human reason and a diminishing dependence on the gods.

In Mesopotamia and Egypt, people had no clear conception of their individual worth and no understanding of political liberty. They were not citizens, but subjects who marched to the command of a ruler whose power originated with the gods; such royal power was not imposed on an unwilling population, but was religiously accepted and obeyed.

In contrast, the Greeks created political freedom. They saw the state as a community of free citizens who made laws in their own interest. The Greeks held that men are capable of governing themselves and valued active citizenship. For the Greeks, the state was a civilizing agent that permitted people to live the good life. Greek political thinkers arrived at a conception of the rational or legal state in which law was an expression of reason, not of whim or divine commands; of justice, not of might; of the general good of the community, not of self-interest.

The Greeks also gave to Western civilization a conception of inner, or ethical, freedom. People were free to choose between shame and honor, cowardice and duty, moderation and excess. The heroes of Greek tragedy suffered, not because they were puppets being manipulated by higher powers, but because they possessed the freedom of decision. The idea of ethical freedom reached its highest point with Socrates. To shape oneself according to ideals known to the mind, to become an autonomous and self-directed person, became for the Greeks the highest form of freedom.

Underlying everything accomplished by the Greeks was a humanist attitude toward life. The Greeks expressed a belief in the worth, significance, and dignity of the individual; they called for the maximum cultivation of human talent, the full development of human personality, and the deliberate pursuit of excellence. In valuing the human personality, the Greek humanists did not approve of living without restraints; they aimed at creating a higher type of man. Such a man would mold himself according to worthy standards; he would make his life as harmonious and flawless as a work of art. This aspiration required effort, discipline, and intelligence. Fundamental to the Greek humanist outlook was the belief that man could master himself. Although people could not alter the course of nature, for there was an order to the universe over which neither human beings nor gods had control, the humanist believed that people could control their own lives.

By discovering theoretical reason, by defining political freedom, and by affirming the worth and potential of human personality, the Greeks broke with the past and founded the rational and humanist tradition of the West. "Had Greek civilization never existed," says poet W. H. Auden, "we would never have become fully conscious, which is to say that we would never have become, for better or worse, fully human."[30]

Notes

1. John N. Theodorakopoulos, "The Origins of Science and Philosophy," in *History of the Hellenic World: The Archaic Period* (University Park: Pennsylvania University Press, 1975), p. 438.

2. Quoted in George Sarton, *A History of Science,* vol. 1 (Cambridge, Mass.: Harvard University Press, 1952), pp. 355–356.

3. Plato, *Apology,* trans. by F. J. Church and rev. by R. D. Cummings (Indianapolis: Bobbs-Merrill, 1956), Section 28.

4. Ibid., Sections 16–17.

5. Plato, *The Republic,* trans. by F. M. Cornford (New York: Oxford University Press, 1945), p. 289.

6. Ibid.

7. Ibid., p. 293.

8. Ibid., pp. 178–179.

9. *Historia Animalium* in *Works of Aristotle,* vol. 4, trans. by D'Arcy Wentworth Thompson (New York: Oxford University Press, 1962), p. 561.

10. *Nicomachean Ethics* in Richard McKeon, ed., *Basic Works of Aristotle* (New York: Random House, 1941), p. 1104.

11. *Politics,* in McKeon, *Basic Works of Aristotle,* p. 1164.

12. Ibid., pp. 1246, 1251.

13. Cited in Werner Jaeger, *Paideia: The Ideals of Greek Culture* (New York: Oxford University Press, 1945), 1:135.

14. "A Girl," in *The Oxford Book of Greek Verse in Translation*, T. F. Higham and C. M. Bowra, eds. (Oxford, England: Clarendon Press, 1938), p. 211.

15. Cited in H. D. F. Kitto, *The Greeks* (Baltimore: Penguin Books, 1957), pp. 174–175.

16. Sophocles, *Oedipus the King*, trans. by Bernard M. W. Knox (New York: Washington Square Press, 1959), p. 61.

17. Aeschylus, *The Persians*, trans. by Anthony J. Podlecki (Englewood Cliffs, N.J.: Prentice-Hall, 1970), p. 49, lines 250–251.

18. Ibid., pp. 96–97, lines 818–822, 829–831.

19. *The Medea*, trans. by Rex Warner in David Grene and Richard Lattimore, *The Complete Greek Tragedies, Euripides*, vol. 1 (Chicago: University of Chicago Press, 1955), p. 101.

20. Ibid., p. 96, lines 1078–1080.

21. Euripides, *The Trojan Women*, trans. by Gilbert Murray (New York: Oxford University Press, 1915), lines 95–97, p. 16.

22. *Lysistrata*, in *Five Comedies of Aristophanes*, trans. by Benjamin Bickley Rogers (Garden City, N.Y.: Doubleday Anchor Books, 1955), p. 292.

23. Ibid., p. 320.

24. *The Clouds*, in ibid., pp. 156–157, 169–170.

25. R. G. Collingwood, *The Idea of History* (New York: Oxford University Press, 1956), pp. 17–18.

26. Herodotus, *The Histories*, trans. by Aubrey de Sélincourt (Baltimore: Penguin Books, 1954), p. 458.

27. Ibid., p. 485.

28. Ibid., p. 53.

29. Thucydides, *The Peloponnesian War*, trans. by B. Jowett (Oxford, England: Clarendon Press, 1881), bk. I, ch. 22.

30. W. H. Auden, ed., *The Portable Greek Reader* (New York: Viking, 1952), p. 38.

Suggested Reading

Copleston, Frederick, *A History of Philosophy*, I (1962). An excellent analysis of Greek philosophy.

Cornford, F. M., *Before and After Socrates* (1968). The essential meaning of Greek philosophy clearly presented.

Dodds, E. R., *The Greeks and the Irrational* (1957). Analyzes the role of primitive and irrational forces in Greek culture.

Guthrie, W. K. C., *The Greek Philosophers from Thales to Aristotle* (1960). A short reliable survey of Greek philosophy.

Jaeger, Werner, *Paideia: The Ideals of Greek Culture* (1939–1944). A three-volume work on Greek culture by a distinguished classicist. The treatment of Homer, the early Greek philosophers, and the Sophists in volume I is masterful.

Jones, W. T., *A History of Western Philosophy*, I (1962). Clearly written; contains useful passages from original sources.

Kitto, H. D. F., *Greek Tragedy* (1954). A valuable introduction to Greek drama.

Lloyd, G. E. R., *Early Greek Science* (1970). A survey of Greek science from Thales to Aristotle.

Robinson, J. M., *An Introduction to Early Greek Philosophy* (1968). Combines original sources with lucid discussion.

Snell, Bruno, *The Discovery of the Mind* (1953). A collection of essays focusing on the Greek origins of European thought.

Taylor, A. E., *Socrates*. A discussion of the man and his thought.

Review Questions

1. What was the achievement of the Ionian natural philosophers?

2. How did Pythagoras, Parmenides, and Democritus contribute to the development of science?

3. How did the Sophists advance the tradition of reason initiated by the natural philosophers? How did they contribute to a spiritual crisis in Athens?

4. What was Socrates' answer to the problems posed by the Sophists?

5. What is the educational value of the Socratic dialogue?

6. How did Plato make use of Socrates'

thought? What does Plato mean by the realm of Ideas or Forms?

7. Describe the essential features of Plato's *Republic* and the reasons that led him to write it.

8. Discuss whether Plato's political thought has any value for us today.

9. How did Aristotle both criticize and accept Plato's theory of Ideas? What do Aristotle's political and ethical thought have in common?

10. Do you agree with Aristotle that "men should not think it slavery to live according to the rule of the constitution, for it is their salvation"?

11. What did the Greek dramatists have in common with Socrates?

12. Greek dramatists explored the inner life of the individual. Discuss this statement and give examples to support it.

13. The rationalist spirit of Greek philosophy permeated the tragedies of Euripides. Discuss.

14. Why do the Greek plays have perennial appeal?

15. Why is Herodotus called the "father of history"? How did Thucydides surpass Herodotus as a historian? Why is Thucydides still worth reading today?

16. The Greeks broke with the mythopoeic outlook of the ancient Near East and conceived a world-view that is the foundation of Western civilization. Discuss.

5

The Hellenistic Age:
Cultural Diffusion

*G*reek civilization, or Hellenism, passed through three distinct stages—the Hellenic Age, the Hellenistic Age, and the Greco-Roman Age. The Hellenic Age began in 800 B.C. with the early city-states, reached its height in the fifth century B.C., and endured until the death of Alexander the Great in 323 B.C. From that date the ancient world entered the Hellenistic Age, which ended in 30 B.C. when Egypt, the last major Hellenistic state, fell to Rome. The Greco-Roman Age lasted 500 years, encompassing the period of the Roman Empire up to the collapse of the Empire's western half in the last part of the fifth century A.D.

Although the Hellenistic Age had absorbed the heritage of classical (Hellenic) Greece, its style of civilization changed. During the first phase of Hellenism, the polis had been the center of political life. The polis had given the individual identity, and only within the polis could a Greek live a good and civilized life. With the coming of the Hellenistic Age, this situation changed. The city-state was eclipsed in power and importance by kingdoms. While cities retained a large measure of autonomy in domestic affairs, they had lost their freedom of action in foreign affairs. No longer were they the self-sufficient and independent communities of the Hellenic period.

Unable to stand up to kingdoms, the city-state had become an outmoded institution. The bonds between the individual and the city loosened. People had to deal with the feelings of isolation and insecurity produced by the decline of the polis.

As a result of Alexander the Great's conquests of the lands between Greece and India, tens of thousands of Greek soldiers, merchants, and administrators settled in eastern lands. Their encounters with the different peoples and cultures of the Near East widened the Greeks' horizon and weakened their ties to their native cities. Because of these changes, the individual had to define a relationship not to the narrow, parochial society of the polis, but to the larger world. The Greeks had to examine their place in a world more complex, more foreign, more threatening than the polis. They had to fashion a conception of a community that would be more comprehensive than the parochial city-state had been.

Hellenistic philosophers struggled with these problems of alienation and community. They sought to give people the inner strength to endure in a world where the polis no longer provided security. In this new situation, philosophers no longer assumed that the good life was tied to the affairs of the city; freedom from emotional stress—not active citizenship and social responsibility—was the avenue to the good life. This pronounced tendency of people to withdraw into themselves and seek emotional comfort helped shape a cultural environment that contributed to the spread and triumph of Christianity in the Greco-Roman Age.

In the Hellenic Age, Greek philosophers had a limited conception of humanity, dividing the world into Greek and barbarian. In the Hellenistic Age, the intermingling of peoples caused a shift in focus from the city to the *oikoumene* (the inhabited world); parochialism gave way to universalism and cosmopolitanism, as people began to think of themselves as members of a world community. Philosophers came to regard the civilized world as one city, the city of man. This was their response to the decline of the city-state and the quest for an alternate form of community.

By uniting the diverse nationalities of the Mediterranean world under one rule, Rome gave political expression to the Hellenistic philosophers' longing for a world community. But the vast and impersonal Roman Empire could not rekindle that sense of belonging, that certainty of identity, that came with being a citizen of a small polis. In time, a resurgence of the religious spirit, particularly in the form of Christianity, helped to overcome the feeling of alienation by offering an image of community that stirred the heart.

Alexander the Great

After the assassination of Philip of Macedon in 336 B.C., his twenty-year-old son, Alexander, succeeded to the throne. Alexander inherited a proud and fiery temperament from his mother. From his tutor Aristotle, Alexander acquired an appreciation for Greek culture, particularly the Homeric epics. Undoubtedly, the young Alexander was aroused by these stories of legendary heroes, particularly of Achilles, and their striving for personal glory. Alexander acquired military skills and qualities of leadership from his father.

Alexander also inherited from Philip an overriding policy of state—the invasion of Persia. Such an exploit attracted the adventurous spirit of the young Alexander; a war of revenge against the Persians, who were masters of the Greek city-states of Asia Minor, also appealed to Alexander's Pan-Hellenic sentiments. Alexander was heir to the teachings of the fourth-century orator, Isocrates, who urged a crusade against Persia to unite the Greeks in a common cause. Philip had intended to protect his hold on Greece by driving the Persians from Asia Minor. But Alexander, whose ambition knew no bounds, aspired to conquer the entire Persian Empire. Daring, brave, and intelligent, Alexander possessed the irrepressible energy of a romantic adventurer.

With an army of 35,000 men, Alexander crossed into Asia Minor in 334 B.C. After capturing the coast of Asia Minor, Alexander marched into Syria and defeated the Persian army at the battle of Issus. Rather than pursuing the fleeing Persian king, Darius III, Alexander stayed with his master plan, which included the capture of coastal ports to crush the Persian navy. He captured Tyre, thought to be an impregnable city, and advanced into Egypt. Grateful to Alexander for having liberated them from Persian rule, the Egyptians made him pharaoh. Alexander appointed officials to administer the country and founded a new city, Alexandria.

Having destroyed or captured the Persian

Mosaic of a Lion Hunt. This pebble mosaic floor may be an illustration of a rescue of Alexander by his friend Krateros; it was found at the Macedonian capital, Pella. The lion hunt as a theme in art appears in Egyptian, Assyrian, and Mycenaean cultures; the king is the guardian of his flock and must protect it from predators. Subduing lions may also be an allusion to one of the labors of Hercules. (*Pella Museum/TAPService, Athens*)

fleet, Alexander in 331 B.C. moved into Mesopotamia in pursuit of Darius and his army. The Macedonians defeated the numerically superior Persians at Gaugamela, just east of the Tigris River, but Darius escaped. After a stopover at Babylon and at Persepolis, which he burned (in revenge for Xerxes' destruction of Athens more than 150 years earlier), Alexander resumed the chase. When he finally caught up with Darius, the Persian king was dead, killed by Persian conspirators.

Alexander relentlessly pushed deeper into Asia, crossing from Afghanistan into north India where he defeated the king of Pontus in a costly battle. When Alexander announced plans to push deeper into India, his troops, exhausted and far from home in a strange land, resisted. Alexander yielded to their wishes, and returned to Babylon in 324 B.C. In these campaigns, Alexander proved himself to be a superb strategist and leader of men.

Winning every battle, Alexander's army had carved an empire that stretched from Greece to India. Future conquerors, including Caesar and Napoleon, would read of Alexander's career with fascination and longing.

The world after Alexander differed sharply from that existing before he took up the sword. Alexander's conquests brought West and East closer together, marking a new epoch. Alexander himself helped implement this transformation. He took a Persian bride, arranged for 80 of his officers and 10,000 of his soldiers to marry oriental women, and planned to incorporate 30,000 Persian youths in his army. Alexander founded Greek-style cities in Asia, where Greek settlers mixed with orientals.

As Greeks acquired greater knowledge of the Near East, the parochial-mindedness of the polis gave way in many ways to a world outlook. As trade and travel between West

Greek Art and Roman Reflections

Figure 1 The Parthenon, Athens, 447–432 B.C (*Art Resource*)

Figure 2 Procession of Horsemen, from the Parthenon Frieze. (*The British Museum*)

The concept of beauty formulated by Greek artists of the fifth century B.C. has challenged and inspired the Western world for over two thousand years. Around 450 B.C., the architects, painters, and sculptors of Athens created the new classic style. As the everyday use of the term suggests, *classic style* is idealized, calm, measured, and free of superfluous detail. All these adjectives fit the prototypical Greek classical temple, the Parthenon.

Built in Athens between 447 and 432 B.C., the Parthenon brought to perfection the architectural form that the Greeks had developed during the sixth century B.C. It replaced an unfinished temple, destroyed by the Persians when they sacked the city in 479 B.C. At the very first glimpse of the Parthenon, one can see that its proportions and placement fit the site perfectly. The temple seems sus-

pended before the distant hills, crowning the high plateau of the Acropolis (Figure 1).

Although the Parthenon's majestic site can still be seen, it takes imagination to picture the original appearance of the building. It once housed an immense statue of the goddess Athena made of ivory and gold. The temple front was painted, and the triangular spaces above the colonnades (called *pediments*) were filled with colored life-size sculptures.

Behind the temple colonnade, high above the temple floor, ran a continuous sculptured frieze depicting the great Panathenaic procession (Figure 2). Every four years, all the citizens of Athens re-affirmed their dedication to Athena, the patron goddess of the city, by participating in a procession that led from the city up through the single entrance gate to the Acropolis and around the temple.

Figure 3 *Top:* Black-figured Lekythos: Women Working Wool on Loom. 6 3/4 in. high. Athenian, sixth century B.C. (*The Metropolitan Museum of Art, Fletcher Fund, 1931*)

Figure 4 *Bottom:* Red-figured Column-Krater: Artist Painting a Statue of Herakles. 20 1/4 in. high. Early Apulian, early fourth century B.C. (*The Metropolitan Museum of Art, Rogers Fund, 1950*)

The ceremony culminated in the presentation to Athena of a sacred robe. The long frieze, a portion of which is shown here, forms an ideal image of the Athenian city-state. Citizens of all ages are shown moving along in the procession, some on foot, some on horseback, some moving quickly, others waiting. All of them show a calm, measured grace that befits Athena, the model of self-restraint and wisdom.

Greek craftsmanship and taste appear in the production of pottery vessels, as well as in the "high art" of the Parthenon. Although commonly called *vases* in modern times, Greek pottery vessels were intended for everyday use. A *lekythos* held olive oil; its narrow neck prevented the oil's flowing rapidly (Figure 3). A *krater* was used for mixing water with wine (Figure 4). The manufacture and export of pottery was an important source of income for Athens.

Decoration on the pottery provides much information about everyday life in ancient Greece. In the black-figured lekythos, women are depicted spinning wool and folding the finished cloth. On the krater is a sculptor's workshop, where a marble statue of Herakles is receiving a finishing coat of colored wax. The artist is applying a coat of pigment and wax to the hero's lion skin, while a shop assistant is heating a metal burnisher to melt the wax and cause the paint to penetrate the stone. Behind the artist, Herakles himself observes the work in progress, along with two other deities.

The Greeks left an enduring legacy in the classical figure style. Approximately one hundred fifty years separate the Metropolitan Museum's *Kouros* figure (Figure 5) of about

600 B.C. from Polykleitos' *Doryphoros* (Figure 6) of about 450 B.C. The obvious difference between the two nude male figures is that the later one looks more like a real human being. But increased naturalism is only one component of the change in style. It is more accurate to think of this development as a shift from a simple pattern to a more subtle and complex pattern.

Around 600 B.C., Greek sculptors began carving life-sized figures, borrowing a pose favored by the Egyptians. In this pose, the figure faces directly forward. Both legs are extended, one foot in front of the other; the arms are held close to the sides, fists clenched. Early Greek sculptures in this pose are called *kouros* figures from the ancient Greek word for *young man*.

Throughout the sixth and early fifth centuries, Greek sculptors adapted and refined the kouros figures. They retained the original pose, adding more and more observed detail. Then another pattern emerged, the classical figure style. Greek sculpture made between about 480 and 450 B.C. shows a new sense of individuality. In looking at such works as

Figure 5 Youth of the "Apollo type." Athenian marble statue, 615–600 B.C. (*The Metropolitan Museum of Art, Fletcher Fund, 1932*)

the famous *Doryphoros*, one is made aware of the vulnerability and sensitivity of an individual human being. The pathos and complexity of life, so profoundly revealed in Greek poetry and drama, is expressed in classical art as well. Such an attitude toward life and art stands in marked contrast to the chiseled, abstract formality of work produced in the Near East at the same time.

The *Doryphoros*, meaning *spear-carrier*, was probably made in Athens by Polykleitos around 450 B.C. The original was a bronze statue, which no longer exists. Its pose and structure are known only from Roman copies. In the *Doryphoros*, Polykleitos demonstrates the idealization that is such an important element of classical style. Although the statue looks lifelike, it resembles no one specific individual. Its features are naturalistic, but they are perfected and refined. The figure has no idiosyncratic details, no warts or wrinkles. Its beauty is distilled from many examples, a beauty transcending that of any single earthly individual.

Another important element of Greek classical style is the subtle balance of forces expressed through the pose. The pose of the

Figure 6 Polykleitos' Doryphoros. Roman marble copy. (*Alinari/Art Resource*)

Figure 7 Mosaic of Swan. Roman, fourth century A.D.; restored c. 1200. (*Robert Harding Associates*)

Doryphoros, and of many other fifth-century sculptures, describes a pattern that was copied and recopied for centuries afterward. The figure stands with one knee bent, one knee straight, so that an S-shaped axis curves through the body. One arm is flexed, while the other is extended; the shoulders and hips tilt; and the head is turned. The figure seems to stand in perfect balance—alert yet relaxed, still yet filled with potential movement. This impression of action and repose, of tension and relaxation, does not result from a "snapshot" pose. Standing in the pose of the *Doryphoros* is neither natural nor comfortable. The figure communicates the sense of ideal beauty not through strictly realistic representation, but through the use of a highly formalized pattern.

According to literary sources, Polykleitos consciously worked from a mathematical model. He wrote a book on ideal proportions, now lost, that was based on the Pythagorean theory of beauty. This theory held that ideal beauty could be revealed by re-creating in art the perfect mathematical ratios upon which the universe itself is structured.

When the Romans sought to develop culture, they looked to Greek models in the visual arts, just as they did in many other fields. Much of our knowledge about ancient Greek art stems from the enthusiasm of Roman connoisseurs. How did archaeologists know that the sculpture they unearthed at Pompeii was a copy of Polykleitos' *Doryphoros*? It bore no inscription, but it did accord with a description of Polykleitos' spear-carrier, mentioned by the Roman Pliny in his *Natural History* (first century A.D.).

Well-to-do Romans built villas in the countryside as retreats from the pressures of metropolitan life (Figure 9). One villa at Boscoreale, about a mile north of Pompeii, was

Figure 8 The Pantheon, Rome, c. A.D. 125. (*Anderson/Art Resource*)

preserved by ash from the eruption of Mount Vesuvius in 79 A.D. Its elaborate wall decoration interweaves reality and illusion. The walls are divided by fictive (painted) columns, so that one seems to be looking out from the interior through an open colonnade. The scenes beyond the columns include landscapes and complex architectural views, all rendered with illusionism that seems to recreate the effects of spatial perception. The mosaic floor combines geometric patterns with illusionistic scenes (*emblemata*). Many elegant mosaic floors have survived since Roman times. Among the most colorful is the swan in Figure 7.

The Pantheon, the most complete surviving building of Roman antiquity (Figure 8), was built by the Emperor Hadrian in the second century A.D. He was an educated man with a thorough appreciation of Greek culture. In the temple, Greek forms of ornamentation are combined with Roman building techniques. The vast hemispherical dome was constructed by pouring concrete into great wooden forms; then the interior was faced with marble. In contrast to a Greek temple, where the exterior is paramount, the Roman temple emphasizes interior space.

—KATHERINE CRUM

Figure 9 Cubiculum from Boscoreale. Roman, 40–30 B.C. (*The Metropolitan Museum of Art, Rogers Fund, 1903*)

and East expanded, as Greek merchants and soldiers settled in Asiatic lands, and as Greek culture spread to non-Greeks, the distinctions between barbarian and Greek lessened. Although Alexander never united all the peoples in a world-state, his career pushed the world in a new direction toward a fusion of disparate peoples and the intermingling of cultural traditions.

Hellenistic Society

The Competing Dynasties

In 323 B.C., Alexander, not yet thirty-three years of age, died of a fever. Alexander had built an empire that stretched from Greece to the Punjab of India, but he was denied the time needed to organize effective institutions to govern these vast territories. After Alexander's premature death, his generals engaged in a long and bitter struggle to see who would succeed the conqueror. Since none of the generals or their heirs had enough power to hold together Alexander's vast empire, the wars of succession ended in a stalemate. By 275 B.C., the empire was fractured into three dynasties: the Ptolemies in Egypt, the Seleucids in Asia, and the Antigonids in Macedonia. Macedonia—Alexander's native country—continued to dominate the Greek cities, which periodically tried to break its hold. Later, the kingdom of Pergamum in western Asia Minor emerged as the fourth Hellenistic monarchy. These Hellenistic kings were not native rulers enjoying local support (except in Macedonia), but were foreign conquerors. Consequently, they had to depend on mercenary armies and loyal administrators.

In the third century B.C., Ptolemaic Egypt—which ruled Cyprus, islands in the Aegean Sea, cities on the coast of Asia Minor, and southern Syria including Palestine—was the foremost power in the Hellenistic world. Its great fleet ensured access to its far-flung provinces and protected its trade. Internal revolts, court intrigues, and wars with the

kingdom of Seleucia weakened Ptolemaic power in the second century B.C.

The Seleucid Empire, like that of the Ptolemies, was an absolute monarchy in which the king was worshiped as a god. But the Seleucid Empire stretched from the Mediterranean to the frontiers of India and encompassed many different peoples, among them several warlike groups; thus this empire was more difficult to control. Attempts by the Seleucids to extend their power in the west were resisted by the Ptolemies. In the third century, these two Hellenistic kingdoms waged five long wars. Finally, the Seleucid ruler Antiochus III (201–198 B.C.) defeated the Ptolemaic forces and established Seleucid control over Phoenicia and Palestine. Taking advantage of Egypt's defeat, Macedonia seized several of Egypt's territories.

In 169–168 B.C., Seleucid Syria invaded Egypt with the intention of annexing it to the Seleucid Empire. This aim would likely have been realized except for the intervention of a new power to the west, Rome. Rome became increasingly drawn into the affairs of the quarrelsome Hellenistic kingdoms; by the middle of the second century B.C., Rome had imposed its will upon them. From this time on, the political fortunes of the western and eastern Mediterranean were inextricably linked.

Cosmopolitanism

Hellenistic society was characterized by a mingling of peoples and an interchange of cultures. Greek traditions spread to the Near East, while Mesopotamian, Egyptian, Hebrew, and Persian traditions—particularly religious beliefs—moved westward. The parochialism of the city-state was replaced by a growing cosmopolitanism. Although the rulers of the Hellenistic kingdoms were Macedonians and their high officials and generals were Greeks, the style of government was modeled after that of the ancient oriental kingdoms. In the Hellenic Age, the law had expressed the will of the community, but in

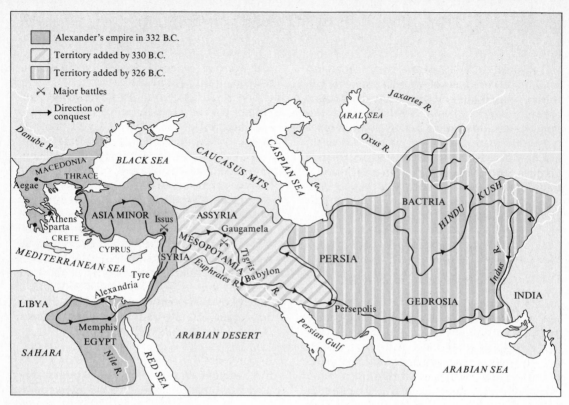

Map 5.1 Alexander's Conquests

this new age of monarchy, the kings were the law. The Macedonian rulers encouraged the oriental practice of worshiping the king as a god or as a representative of the gods. In Egypt, for example, the priests conferred on the Macedonian king the same divine powers and titles traditionally held by Egyptian pharaohs. Also, in accord with ancient tradition, statues of the divine king were installed in Egyptian temples.

The Seleucids, following Alexander's lead, founded cities in the east patterned after the city-states of Greece. Thousands of Greeks settled in these cities, which were Greek in architecture and contained Greek schools, temples, theaters, and gymnasia. Hellenistic kings brought books, paintings, and statues to their cities from Greece. Hellenistic cities, inhabited by tens of thousands of people from many lands and dominated by a Hellenized upper class, served as centers and agents of Hellenism, which non-Greeks adopted. The ruling class in each Hellenistic city was united

by a common Hellenism which overcame national, linguistic, and racial distinctions. *Koine*, a form of Greek, came to be spoken throughout much of the Mediterranean world.

Hellenistic cities engaged in economic activity on a much greater scale than the classical Greek city-states had. Increased trade integrated the Near East and Greece into a market economy, and business methods became more sophisticated. The middle and upper classes enjoyed homes, furniture, and jewelry more elegant than those of Periclean Athenians, and some people amassed great fortunes. In contrast to the ideal of citizenship that distinguished the fifth-century polis, many Greeks who settled in Egypt, Syria, and other eastern lands ran roughshod over civil law and moral values, and engaged in competitive struggles for wealth and power.

The greatest city of the time and the one most representative of the Hellenistic Age was Alexandria. Strategically located at one of the mouths of the Nile, Alexandria became a center of commerce and culture. The most populous city of the Mediterranean world, Alexandria at the beginning of the Christian era contained perhaps a million people— Egyptians, Persians, Macedonians, Greeks, Jews, Syrians, and Arabs. The city was an unrivaled commercial center; goods from the Mediterranean world, east Africa, Arabia, and India circulated in its marketplaces. This cosmopolitan center also attracted poets, philosophers, physicians, astronomers, and mathematicians.

In addition to the proliferation of Greek urban institutions and ideas, Hellenistic cosmopolitanism was expressed by an increased movement of peoples, the adoption of common currency standards, and an expansion of trade. International trade was facilitated by improvements in navigation techniques, better port facilities, the extension of the monetary economy at the expense of barter, and the rapid development of banking. The makeup of Hellenistic armies also reflected the cosmopolitanism of the age. Serving the Hellenistic kings were men from lands stretching from India to the little-known areas north of the Danube. The cities in Egypt and Syria saw the emergence of a native elite who spoke Greek, wore Greek-style clothing, and adopted Greek customs.

All phases of cultural life were permeated by cultural exchange. Sculpture showed the influence of many lands. Historians wrote world histories, not just local histories. Greek astronomers worked with data collected over the centuries by the Babylonians. The Hebrew Scriptures were translated into Greek for use by Greek-speaking Jews, and Jewish thinkers began to take note of Greek philosophy. Greeks increasingly demonstrated a fascination for oriental religious cults. Philosophers helped to break down the barriers between peoples by asserting that all inhabit a single fatherland. As the philosopher Crates said, "My fatherland has no single tower, no single roof. The whole earth is my citadel, a home ready for us all to live in."[1]

The spread of Greek civilization from the Aegean to the Indus River gave the Hellenistic world a cultural common denominator, but Hellenization did not transform the East and make it one with the West. Hellenization was limited almost entirely to the cities, and in many urban centers it was often only a thin veneer. In Alexandria, for example, conflicting customs often led to riots between different nationalities. Many Egyptians in Alexandria learned Greek, and some assumed Greek names, but for most, Hellenization did not go much deeper. In the countryside, there was not even the veneer of Greek culture. Retaining traditional attitudes, the countryside in the East resisted Greek ways. In the villages, local and traditional law, local languages, and family customs remained unchanged; and religion, the most important ingredient of the civilizations of the Near East, also kept its traditional character.

Hellenistic Culture

Literature and History

There was a great outpouring of literary works during the Hellenistic Age. Callimachus (c. 305–240 B.C.), an Alexandrian scholar-poet, felt that no one could duplicate the great epics of Homer or the plays of the fifth-century B.C. dramatists. He urged poets to write short, finely crafted poems, instead of composing on a grand scale.

Apollonius of Rhodes (third–second century B.C.) took issue with Callimachus and wrote the *Argonautica*. This Homeric-style epic tells the story of Jason's search for the Golden Fleece. Apollonius was a gifted poet, although the epic was not the best genre for expressing his talent. His poetic talent and psychological insight are shown in this description of how love for Jason takes possession of Medea:

Time and again she darted a bright glance at Jason. All else was forgotten. Her heart, brimful of this new agony, throbbed within her and overflowed with the sweetness of the pain. A working woman, rising before dawn to spin and needing

Nike and Two-Horse Chariot: Hellenistic Gold Earring. The Hellenistic Age broadened the outlook of Hellenic Greece. In cosmopolitan Hellenistic society, life became more complex. This elaborate earring is vastly different from the simple ornaments of the Periclean Age and mirrors the new complexities. (*Courtesy Museum of Fine Arts, Boston*)

light in her cottage room, piles brushwood on a smouldering log, and the whole heap kindled by the little brand goes up in a mighty blaze. Such was the fire of Love, stealthy but all-consuming, that swept through Medea's heart. In the turmoil of her soul, her soft cheeks turned from rose to white and white to rose.[2]

Theocritus (c. 315–250 B.C.), who lived on the island of Sicily, wrote pastorals that showed great sensitivity to natural beauty. With uncommon feeling, Theocritus responded to the sky and wind, to the hills, trees, and flowers, and to the wildlife of the countryside:

Amid the shadowing foliage the brown cicalas chirped

And chattered busily without pause; and far away was heard
From the dense bramble-thicket the tree-frog's fluted note.[3]

The Athenian playwright Menander (c. 342–291 B.C.) depicted Athenian life at the end of the fourth century. Menander's plays, unlike Aristophanes' lampoons of inept politicians, dealt little with politics. Apparently Menander reflected the attitude of his fellow Athenians who, bored with public affairs, had accepted their loss of freedom to Macedonia and were preoccupied with their own private lives. Menander dealt sympathetically with human weakness and wrote about stock characters: the clever slave, the young playboy, the elderly seducer, the heroine in trouble.

The leading historian of the Hellenistic Age was Polybius (c. 200–118 B.C.), whose history of the rise of Rome is one of the great works of historical literature. Reflecting the universal tendencies of the Hellenistic Age, Polybius endeavored to explain how Rome had progressed from a city-state to a world conqueror. As a disciple of Thucydides, Polybius sought rational explanations for human events. Also like Thucydides, he relied on eyewitness accounts (including his own personal experiences), checked sources, and strove for objectivity.

Science

During the Hellenistic Age, Greek scientific achievement reached its height. When Alexander invaded Asia Minor, the former student of Aristotle brought along surveyors, engineers, scientists, and historians, who continued with him into Asia. The vast amount of data in botany, zoology, geography, and astronomy collected by Alexander's staff stimulated an outburst of activity. To integrate so much information, scientists had to specialize in the various disciplines. Hellenistic scientists attempted a rational analysis of nature; they engaged in research, organized

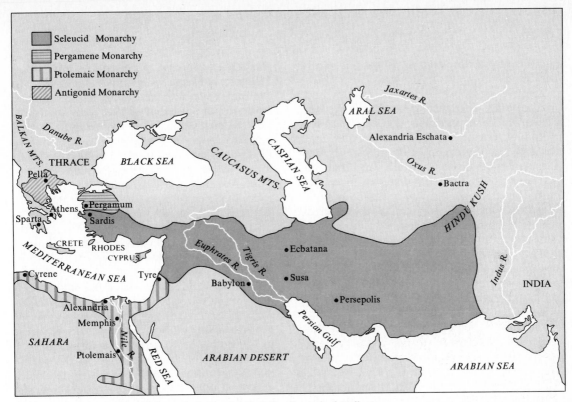

Map 5.2 The Division of Alexander's Empire and the Spread of Hellenism

knowledge in logical fashion, devised procedures for mathematical proof, separated medicine from magic, grasped the theory of experiment, and applied scientific principles to mechanical devices. Hellenistic science, says historian Benjamin Farrington, stood "on the threshold of the modern world. When modern science began in the sixteenth century, it took up where the Greeks left off."[4]

Alexandria was the principal center of scientific research, but Athens still retained some of its former luster in this area. After Aristotle's death in 322 B.C., he was succeeded as head of the Lyceum by Theophrastus and then Strato. Both wrote treatises on many themes—logic, ethics, politics, physics, and botany. Theophrastus systematized knowledge of botany in a manner similar to Aristotle's treatment of animals. Strato is most famous for his study of physics. It is likely that Strato, in his investigation of physical problems, did not rely on logic alone but

performed a series of experiments to test his investigations.

Because of its state-supported museum, Alexandria attracted leading scholars and superseded Athens in scientific investigation. The museum contained a library of more than half a million volumes, as well as botanical gardens and an observatory. It was really a research institute in which some of the best minds of the day studied and worked.

Alexandrian doctors advanced medical skills. They improved surgical instruments and techniques, and through dissecting bodies, they added to anatomical knowledge. Through their research, they uncovered organs of the body not known heretofore, made the distinction between arteries and veins, divided nerves into those comprising the motor and sensory systems, and identified the brain as the source of intelligence. Their investigations advanced knowledge of anatomy and physiology to a level that was not significantly improved until the sixteenth century A.D.

Knowledge in the fields of astronomy and mathematics also increased. Eighteen centuries before Copernicus, Alexandrian astronomer Aristarchus (310–230 B.C.) said that the sun was the center of the universe, that the planets revolved around it, and that the stars are situated at great distances from the earth. But these revolutionary ideas were not accepted, and the belief in an earth-centered universe persisted. In geometry, Euclid, an Alexandrian mathematician who lived around 300 B.C., creatively synthesized earlier developments. Euclid's hundreds of geometrical proofs, derived from reasoning alone, are a profound witness to the power of the rational mind.

Alexander's expeditions had opened the eyes of Mediterranean peoples to the breadth of the earth and had stimulated explorations and geographical research. Eratosthenes (c. 275–195 B.C.), an Alexandrian geographer, sought a scientific understanding of this enlarged world. He divided the planet into climatic zones, declared that the oceans are joined, and with extraordinary ingenuity and accuracy measured the earth's circumference.

Archimedes of Syracuse, who studied at Alexandria, was a mathematician, a physicist, and an ingenious inventor. His mechanical inventions, including war engines, dazzled his contemporaries. However, Archimedes dismissed his practical inventions, preferring to be remembered as a theoretician. In one treatise, he established the general principles of hydrostatics—a branch of physics that treats the pressure and equilibrium of liquids at rest.

Philosophy

Hellenistic thinkers preserved the rational tradition of Greek philosophy. Like their Hellenic predecessors, they regarded the cosmos as governed by universal principles intelligible to the rational mind. For the philosophers of both ages, a crucial problem was the achievement of the good life. And both Hellenic and Hellenistic thinkers sought rules for human conduct that accorded with rational standards; both believed that individuals attain happiness through their own efforts, unaided by the gods. In the tradition of Socrates, Hellenistic thinkers taught a morality of self-mastery. But although they retained the inheritance of the classical age, they also transformed it, for they had to adapt thought to the requirements of a cosmopolitan society.

In the Hellenic Age, the starting point of philosophy was the citizen's relationship to the city; in the Hellenistic Age, the point of departure was the solitary individual's relationship to humanity, his personal destiny in a complex world. Philosophy tried to deal with the feeling of alienation resulting from the weakening of the individual's attachment to the polis and to arrive at a conception of community that corresponded to the social realities of a world grown larger. Unlike Plato and Aristotle, Hellenistic philosophers were moralists, not great speculators and theorists. The Hellenistic schools of philosophy, in contrast to their predecessors, were far less concerned with the scientific understanding of nature. Philosophy was now primarily preoccupied with understanding the human condition, and it tried to alleviate spiritual uneasiness and loss of security; it aspired to make persons ethically independent so that they could achieve happiness in a hostile and competitive world.

In striving for tranquillity of mind and relief from conflict, Hellenistic thinkers reflected the general anxiety that pervaded their society. They retained respect for reason and aspired to the rational life, but by stressing peace of mind and the effort to overcome anxiety they were performing a quasi-religious function. Philosophy was trying to provide comfort for the individual suffering from feelings of loneliness and insignificance, and this attempt was an indication that Greek civilization was undergoing a spiritual transformation (the full meaning of which we will examine in Chapters 7 and 8). This gravitation toward religiosity in an effort to relieve despair gathered momentum in the centuries that followed. Thus Hellenistic philosophies helped prepare people to accept Christianity, which promised personal salvation. Ultimately the Christian answer to the problems of alienation and the need for community would predominate over the Greco-Roman attempt at resolution.

Epicureanism   Four principal schools of philosophy arose in the Hellenistic world: Epicureanism, Stoicism, Skepticism, and Cynicism. In the tradition of Plato and Aristotle, Epicurus (342–270 B.C.) founded a school at Athens at the end of the fourth century B.C. In significant ways Epicurus broke with the attitude of the Hellenic Age. Unlike classical Greek philosophers, Epicurus, reflecting the Greek's changing relationship to the city, taught the value of passivity and withdrawal from civic life. To him, citizenship was not a prerequisite for individual happiness. Wise persons, said Epicurus, would refrain from engaging in public affairs, for politics could deprive them of their self-sufficiency, their freedom to choose and to act. Nor would wise individuals pursue wealth, power, or fame, for the pursuit would only provoke anxiety. For the same reason, wise persons would not surrender to hate or love, desires that distress the soul. Nor could there be happiness when they worried about dying or pleasing the gods.

To Epicurus, fear that the gods interfered in human life and could inflict suffering after death was the principal cause of anxiety. To remove this source of human anguish, he favored a theory of nature that had no place for the activity of gods. Therefore he adopted the physics of Democritus, which taught that all things consist of atoms in motion. In a universe of colliding atoms, there could be no higher intelligence ordering things; there was no room for divine activity. Epicurus taught that the gods probably did exist, but that they were not involved in human affairs, so individuals could order their own lives. Epicurus embraced atomism, not as a disinterested scientist aspiring to truth, but as

Epicurus. The direct gaze of this marble head of Epicurus shows an inner calm, which was the goal of Epicurean philosophy. In the tradition of Greek philosophy, Epicurus maintained that happiness came from a rationally ordered life. But unlike fifth-century Greeks, Epicurus urged his followers not to engage in public affairs. (*The Metropolitan Museum of Art, Rogers Fund, 1911*)

a moral philosopher seeking to liberate emotional life from fear of the gods.

People could achieve happiness, said Epicurus, when their bodies were "free from pain" and minds "released from worry and fear." Although Epicurus wanted to increase pleasure for the individual, he rejected unbridled hedonism. Because happiness must be pursued rationally, he believed, those merely sensuous pleasures that have unpleasant aftereffects (such as overeating and overdrinking) are to be avoided. In general, Epicurus espoused the traditional Greek view of moderation and prudence.

By opening his philosophy to men and women, slave and free, Greek and barbarian, and by separating ethics from politics, Epicurus fashioned a philosophy adapted to the post-Alexandrian world of kingdoms and universal culture.

Stoicism   About the same time as the founding of Epicurus' school, Zeno (335–263 B.C.) also opened a school in Athens. Zeno's teachings, called Stoicism, became the most important philosophy in the Hellenistic world. By teaching that the world constituted a single society, Stoicism gave theoretical expression to the world-mindedness of the age. By arriving at the concept of a world-state, the city of humanity, Stoicism offered an answer to the problem of community and alienation posed by the decline of the city-state. By stressing inner strength in dealing with life's misfortunes, Stoicism offered an avenue to individual happiness in a world fraught with uncertainty.

At the core of Stoicism was the belief that the universe contained a principle of order, variously called the Divine Fire, God, and Divine Reason (*Logos*). This ruling principle underlay reality and permeated all things; it accounted for the orderliness of nature. The Stoics reasoned that because people are part of the universe, they too shared in the logos that operated throughout the cosmos. The logos was implanted in every human soul; it enabled people to act intelligently, and to comprehend the principles of order that governed nature. Since reason was common to all, human beings were essentially brothers and fundamentally equal. Reason gave individuals dignity and enabled them to recognize and respect the dignity of others. To the Stoics, all people, Greek and barbarian, free and slave, rich and poor, were fellow human beings, and one law, the law of nature, applied to all human beings. Thus the Stoics, like the Hebrews, arrived at the idea of the oneness of humanity.

Pericles had spoken of the Athenian's obligation to abide by the laws and traditions of his city; Stoics, viewing people as citizens of the world, emphasized the individual's duty to understand and obey the natural law that governed the cosmos and applied to all. Socrates had taught a morality of self-mastery based on knowledge; the Stoics spread Socrates' philosophy beyond Athens, beyond Greece, and enlarged it, offering it as a way of life for all. Like Socrates, the Stoics believed that a person's distinctive quality was the ability to reason and that happiness came from the disciplining of emotions by the rational part of the soul. Also like Socrates, the Stoics maintained that individuals should progress morally, should perfect themselves.

In the Stoic view, wise persons ordered their lives according to the natural law—the law of reason—that underlay the cosmos. This harmony with the logos would give them the inner strength to resist the torments inflicted by others, by fate, and by their own passionate natures. Self-mastery and inner peace, or happiness, would follow. Such individuals remain undisturbed by life's misfortunes, for their souls are their own. Even slaves were not denied this inner freedom; although their bodies were subjected to the power of their masters, their minds still remained independent and free.

Stoicism had an enduring impact upon the Western mind. To some Roman political theorists the Empire fulfilled the Stoic ideal of a world community in which people of different nationalities held citizenship and were governed by a worldwide law that accorded with the law of reason, or natural law that operated throughout the universe. Stoic beliefs—by nature we are all members of one family, each person is significant, distinctions of rank and race are of no account, and human law should not conflict with natural law—were incorporated into Roman jurisprudence, Christian thought, and modern liberalism. There is continuity between Stoic thought and the principle of inalienable rights stated in the Declaration of Independence.

Skepticism   The Epicureans tried to withdraw from the evils of this world and to attain personal happiness by reducing physical pain and mental anguish. The Stoics sought happiness by actively entering into harmony with universal reason. Both philosophies sought peace of mind, but the Stoics did not disengage themselves from political life and often exerted influence over Hellenistic rulers. Skepticism, another school of philosophy, attacked the Epicurean and Stoic belief that there is a definite avenue to happiness. Skeptics held that one could achieve spiritual comfort by recognizing that none of the beliefs by which people lived was true or could bring happiness.

Some Skeptics taught indifference to all theory and urged conformity to accepted views whether or not they were true. This attitude would avoid arguments and explanations. Gods might not exist, said the Skeptics, but to refuse to worship or to deny their existence would only cause trouble—therefore individuals should follow the crowd. The life of the mind did not bring truth or happiness; so why should one bother with it? Suspend judgment, recognize the inability to understand, do not commit oneself to a system of belief—by these means one could achieve peace of mind.

Metaphysical speculation, inquiring into the origin of things, and clever reasoning would bring neither assurance nor happiness. Instead of embracing doctrines, said the Greek writer Lucian, individuals should go their way "with ever a smile and never a passion."[5] This was the position of those Skeptics who were suspicious of ideas and hostile to intellectuals.

The more sophisticated Skeptics did not run away from ideas, but pointed out their limitations and weaknesses: they did not avoid theories, but disputed and refuted them. In doing so, they did not reject reason, but focused on a problem of reason—whether indeed it could arrive at truth. Thus, Carneades of Cyrene (213–129 B.C.) insisted that all ideas, even mathematical principles, must be regarded as hypotheses and assumptions, not as absolutes. Just because the universe showed signs of order, Carneades argued, one could not assume that it had been created

Veiled Dancer, Alexandrian, Third Century B.C. The twisting movement and the profusion of angles characterize Hellenistic art, which abandoned the simplicity, balance, and repose of classical Greek art. (*Metropolitan Museum of Art, bequest of Walter C. Baker, 1972*)

by God. The principles of religion rested on faith; they could not be rationally defended. Since there was never any certainty, only probability, morality should not derive from dogma, but from practical experience.

Cynicism   The Cynics were not theoretical philosophers but supreme individualists who rebelled against established values and conventions—against every barrier of society that restrained individuals from following their own natures. Cynics regarded laws and public opinion, private property and employment, and wives and children as hindrances to the free life. Extreme individualists, the Cynics had no loyalty to family, city, or kingdom and ridiculed religion, philosophy, and literature.

Cynics put their philosophy into practice. They cultivated idleness, indifference, and apathy. To harden themselves against life's misfortunes, they engaged in strenuous exercise, endured cold and hunger, and lived ascetically. Not tied down by property or employment, Cynics wandered shoeless from place to place, wearing dirty and ragged clothes and carrying staffs. To show their disdain for society's customs, Cynics grew long scraggly beards, used foul language, and cultivated bad manners. Diogenes, a fourth-century B.C. Greek Cynic, supposedly said: "Look at me, . . . I am without a home, without a city, without property, without a slave; I sleep on the ground; I have neither wife nor children, no miserable governor's mansion, but only earth, and sky, and one rough cloak. Yet what do I lack? Am I not free from pain and fear, am I not free?"[6]

In their attack on inherited conventions, Cynics strove for self-sufficiency and spiritual security. Theirs was the most radical philosophical quest for meaning and peace of soul during the Hellenistic Age.

The Hellenistic Age encompassed the period from the death of Alexander to the formation of the Roman Empire. During these three centuries, Greek civilization spread eastward as far as India, and westward to Rome. Peoples began to conceive of themselves as members of a world community, speaking a common Greek language and sharing a common Greek civilization. It was Rome, conqueror of the Mediterranean world and transmitter of Hellenism, that inherited the universalist tendencies of the Hellenistic Age and embodied them in law and institutions.

Notes

1. Quoted in John Ferguson, *The Heritage of Hellenism* (New York: Science History Publications, 1973), p. 30.

2. Apollonius of Rhodes, *The Voyage of Argo*, trans. by E. V. Rieu (Baltimore: Penguin Books, 1959), p. 117.

3. *The Idylls of Theocritus*, trans. by R. C. Trevelyan (London: The Casanova Society, 1925), p. 28.

4. Benjamin Farrington, *Greek Science* (Baltimore: Penguin Books, 1961), p. 301.

5. Quoted in J. H. Randall, Jr., *Hellenistic Ways of Deliverance and the Making of the Christian Synthesis* (New York: Columbia University Press, 1970), p. 74.

6. Epictetus, *The Discourses as Reported by Arrian, the Manual and Fragments*, trans. by W. A. Oldfather (Cambridge, Mass.: Harvard University Press, 1966), II:147.

Suggested Reading

Bonnard, Andre, *Greek Civilization*, III (1961). Self-contained chapters on various phases of late classical and Hellenistic periods.

Bury, J. B., et al., *The Hellenistic Age* (1970). First published in 1923; contains valuable essays by leading classicists.

Cary, M., *A History of the Greek World 323–146 B.C.* (1972). A standard survey of the Hellenistic world.

Ferguson, John, *The Heritage of Hellenism* (1973). A good introduction to Hellenistic culture.

Grant, Michael, *From Alexander to Cleopatra* (1982). A fine survey of all phases of Hellenistic society and culture.

Green, Peter, *Alexander the Great* (1970). A lavishly illustrated study.

Hadas, Moses, *Hellenistic Culture* (1972). Focuses on the cultural exchanges between East and West.

Peters, F. E., *The Harvest of Hellenism* (1970). A comprehensive treatment of Hellenistic history and culture.

Randall, J. H., Jr., *Hellenistic Ways of Deliverance*

and the Making of the Christian Synthesis (1970). An astute discussion of Hellenistic and early Christian thought.

Tarn, W. W., *Alexander the Great* (1956). A controversial interpretation.

Wallbank, F. W. *The Hellenistic World* (1982). A survey of the Hellenistic world that makes judicious use of quotations from original sources.

Review Questions

1. What were the basic differences between the Hellenic and Hellenistic Ages?

2. How did Alexander the Great contribute to the shaping of the Hellenistic Age?

3. Provide examples of Hellenistic cosmopolitanism.

4. In what ways is New York closer to Hellenistic Alexandria than to Hellenic Athens?

5. What was the significance of the Museum at Alexandria?

6. Hellenistic science stood on the threshold of the modern world. Explain.

7. What problems concerned Hellenistic philosophers?

8. What were the Epicurean, Stoic, Skeptic, and Cynic prescriptions for achieving happiness?

9. What was the enduring significance of Stoicism?

10. Which of the Hellenistic philosophies has the most appeal for you?

6

The Roman Republic:
City-State to World Empire

Rome's great achievement was to transcend the narrow political orientation of the city-state and to create a world-state that unified the different nations of the Mediterranean world. Regarding the polis as the only means to the good life, the Greeks had not desired a larger political unit and had almost totally excluded foreigners from citizenship. Although Hellenistic philosophers had conceived the possibility of a world community, Hellenistic politics could not shape one. But Rome overcame the limitations of the city-state mentality and developed an empirewide system of law and citizenship. The Hebrews were distinguished by their prophets, and the Greeks by their philosophers; Rome's genius found expression in law and government.

Roman history falls into two periods: the Republic began in 509 B.C. with the overthrow of the Etruscan monarchy; and the Empire started in 27 B.C. when Octavian (Augustus) became in effect the first Roman emperor, ending almost five hundred years of republican self-government. By conquering the Mediterranean world and extending its law and, in some instances, citizenship to different nationalities, the Roman Republic transcended the parochialism typical of the city-state. The Republic initiated the trend toward political and legal universalism, which reached fruition in the second phase of Roman history, the Empire.

Evolution of the Roman Constitution

By the eighth century B.C., peasant communities existed on some of Rome's seven hills near the Tiber River in central Italy. To the north and south stood Etruscan and Greek cities whose higher civilizations were gradually absorbed by the Romans. The origin of the Etruscans remains a mystery, although some scholars believe that they came from Asia Minor and settled in northern Italy. From them, Romans acquired architectural styles and skills in road construction, sanitation, hydraulic engineering including underground conduits, metallurgy, ceramics, and portrait sculpture. Symbols of authority and rule were also borrowed from the Etruscans—purple robes, ivory-veneer chariots, thrones for state officials, and a bundle of rods and an ax held by attendants. Etruscan words and names entered into the Latin language, and Etruscan gods were absorbed by Roman religion.

The Etruscans had expanded their territory in Italy during the seventh and sixth centuries B.C., and they controlled the monarchy in Rome. But the Etruscan city-states failed to establish a federal union with a centralized government. Defeated by Celts, Greeks, and finally Romans, by the third century B.C. the Etruscans had ceased to exercise any political power in Italy.

Rome became a republic at the end of the sixth century B.C. when the landowning aristocrats, or patricians, overthrew the Etruscan king. As in the Greek cities, the transition from theocratic monarchy to republic offered possibilities for political and legal growth. In the opening phase of republican history, religion governed the people, dictated the law, and legitimized the rule of the patricians, who regarded themselves as the preservers of sacred traditions. Gradually the Romans loosened the ties between religion and politics and hammered out a constitutional system that paralleled the Greek achievement of rationalizing and secularizing politics and law. In time the Romans, like the Greeks, came to view law as an expression of the public will and not as the creation of god-kings, priest-kings, or a priestly caste.

The impetus for the growth of the Roman constitution came from a conflict—known as the Struggle of the Orders—between the patricians and the commoners, or plebeians. At the beginning of the fifth century B.C., the patrician-dominated government was composed of two consuls together with the Centuriate Assembly and the Senate. Patricians owned most of the land and controlled the army. The executive heads of government were the two annually elected consuls who came from the nobility; they commanded the army, served as judges, and initiated legislation. To prevent either consul from becoming an autocrat, decisions had to be approved by both of them. In times of crisis the consuls were authorized by the Senate to nominate a dictator; he would possess absolute powers during the emergency, but these powers would expire after six months. The consuls were aided by other annually elected magistrates and administrators. The Centuriate Assembly was a popular assembly but, because of voting procedures, was controlled by the nobility. The assembly elected consuls and other magistrates and made the laws, which also needed Senate approval. The Senate advised the assembly but did not itself enact laws; it controlled public finances and foreign policy. Senators either were appointed for life terms by the consuls or were former magistrates. The Senate was the principal organ of patrician power.

The tension between patricians and commoners stemmed from plebeian grievances, which included enslavement for debt, discrimination in the courts, prevention of intermarriage with patricians, lack of political representation, and the absence of a written code of laws. Resentful of their inferior status, the plebeians organized and waged a struggle for political, legal, and social equality. They were resisted every step of the way by patricians, who wanted to preserve their own dominance. The plebeians had one decisive weapon: their threat to secede from Rome, that is, not to pay taxes, work, or serve in the army. Realizing that Rome, which was constantly involved in warfare on the Italian peninsula, could not endure without plebeian help, the pragmatic patricians begrudgingly made concessions. Thus the plebeians slowly gained legal equality.

Early in the fifth century the plebeians won the right to form their own assembly (the Plebeian Assembly when later enlarged was called the Tribal Assembly). This Assembly could elect officials called tribunes, who were empowered to protect plebeian rights. As a result of plebeian pressure, about 450 B.C. the first Roman code of laws was written; called the Twelve Tables, the code gave plebeians some degree of protection against unfair and oppressive patrician officials. Other concessions gained later by the plebeians included the right to intermarry with patricians, access to the highest political, judicial, and religious offices in the state, and the elimination of slavery as payment for debt. In 287 B.C., a date generally recognized as the termination of the plebeian-patrician struggle, the acts of the Tribal Assembly became binding on all and did not need Senate approval.

Although the plebeians had gained legal equality and the right to sit in the Senate and to hold high offices, Rome was still ruled by an upper class. True, the Tribal Assembly and the tribunes constituted democratic elements and, in theory, seemed to balance the power of the patrician-dominated Senate. In actual fact, however, power was concentrated in a ruling oligarchy consisting of patricians and influential plebeians who had joined forces with the old nobility. Marriages between patricians and politically powerful plebeians strengthened this alliance. As wealthy plebeians generally became tribunes, they tended to side with the old nobility rather than to defend the interests of poor plebeians. By using bribes, the ruling oligarchy maintained control over the Assembly, and the Senate remained a bastion of aristocratic power. In the Greek cities, tyrants had succeeded in breaking aristocratic dominance, thereby clearing a pathway for democratic government. But in the Roman Republic, the nobility maintained its tight grip on the reins of power until the civil wars of the first century B.C.

Regarding themselves as Rome's finest citizens, the ruling oligarchy led Rome during its period of expansion and demonstrated a sense of responsiblity and a talent for statesmanship. In noble families, parents and elders prepared the young for public service. They recounted the glorious deeds of ancestors and reminded youngsters of their responsibility to bring additional honors to the family.

During their two-hundred-year class struggle, the Romans forged a constitutional system based on civic needs rather than on religious mystery. The essential duty of government ceased to be the regular performance of religious rituals and became the maintenance of order at home and the preservation of Roman might and dignity in international relations. Although the Romans retained the ceremonies and practices of their ancestral religion, public interest, not religious tradition, determined the content of law and was the standard by which all the important acts of the city were judged. In the opening stage of republican history, law was priestly and sacred, spoken only by priests and known only to men of religious families. Gradually, as law was written, debated, and altered, it became disentangled from religion. Another step in this process of secularization and rationalization occurred when the study and interpretation of law passed from the hands of priests to a class of professional jurists, who analyzed, classified, systematized, and sought common-sense solutions to legal problems.

The Roman constitution was not a product of abstract thought, nor was it the gift of a great lawmaker like the Athenian Solon. Rather, like the British constitution, the Roman constitution evolved gradually and empirically in response to specific needs. The Romans, unlike the Greeks, were distinguished by practicality and common sense, not by a love of abstract thought. In their pragmatic and empirical fashion, they gradually developed the procedures of public politics and the legal state.

Undoubtedly, the commoners' struggle for rights and power did arouse bitter hatred on both sides. But unlike the domestic strife in Greek cities, Rome's conflict did not end in civil war. This peaceful solution testifies to the political good sense of the Romans. Fear of foreign powers and the tradition of civic patriotism prevented the patrician-plebeian conflict from turning into a fight to the death. At the time of the class struggle, Rome was also engaged in the extension of its power

Cinerary Urn, Etruscan, C. 160–140 B.C. The Etruscan influence on the Romans extended to portrait sculpture. The Etruscans had adopted the Greek style in portraiture to commemorate their ancestors. (*Worcester Art Museum, Massachusetts*)

over the Italian peninsula. Without civic harmony and stability, Rome could not have achieved expansion.

Roman Expansion to 146 B.C.

By 146 B.C., Rome had become the dominant power in the Mediterranean world. Roman expansion had occurred in three main stages: the uniting of the Italian peninsula, which gave Rome the manpower that transformed it from a city-state into a great power; the collision with Carthage, from which Rome emerged as ruler of the western Mediterranean; and the subjugation of the Hellenistic states, which brought Romans in close contact with Greek civilization. As Rome expanded territorially, its leaders enlarged their vision. Instead of restricting citizenship to people having racial kinship, Rome assimilated other peoples into its political community. As law had grown to cope with the earlier grievances of the plebeians, it adjusted to the new situations resulting from the creation of a multinational empire. The city of Rome was evolving into the city of humanity—the cosmopolis envisioned by the Stoics.

The Uniting of Italy

Frequent conflicts with hostile neighbors had forced Romans to develop militarily and to strengthen their commitment to Rome. These developments fostered expansion. During the first stage, Rome extended its hegemony over Italy, subduing in the process neighboring Latin kinsmen, semicivilized Italian tribes, the once dominant Etruscans, and Greek city-states in southern Italy. At the beginning, Roman warfare was principally motivated by the peasants' land hunger. As Rome grew stronger and its territory and responsibilities increased, it was often drawn into conflict to protect its expanded boundaries and its allies.

Rome's conquest of Italy stemmed in part from superior military organization and discipline. Copying the Greeks, the Romans organized their soldiers into battle formations; in contrast, their opponents often fought as disorganized hordes that were prone to panic and flight. Fighting as part of a unit strengthened the courage and confidence of the Roman soldier, for he knew that his comrades would stand with him. (Roman soldiers who deserted their post or fled from battle were punished and disgraced, an ordeal more terrible than facing up to the enemy.) Also, the promise of glory and rewards impelled the Roman soldier to distinguish himself in battle.

Ultimately, Rome's success was due to the character of its people and the quality of its statesmanship. The Roman farmer-soldier was dedicated, rugged, persevering, and self-reliant. He could march thirty miles a day laden with arms, armor, and equipment weighing sixty pounds. In the face of danger he remained resolute and tenacious, obedient to the poet Virgil's maxim: "Yield you not to ill fortune, but go against it with more daring." Romans willingly made sacrifices so that Rome might endure. In conquering Italy, they were united by a moral and religious devotion to their city strong enough to overcome social conflict, factional disputes, and personal ambition.

Despite its army's strength, Rome could not have mastered Italy without the cooperation of other Italian peoples. Instead of reducing adversaries to slavery and taking all their land—a not uncommon method of warfare in the ancient world—Rome endeavored, through generous treatment, to gain the loyalty of conquered people. Some defeated communities retained a measure of self-government but turned the conduct of foreign affairs over to Rome and contributed contingents to the army when Rome went to war. Other conquered people received partial or full citizenship. In extending its dominion over Italy, Rome displayed a remarkable talent for converting former enemies into allies and eventually into Roman citizens. No Greek city had ever envisaged integrating nonnatives into its political community.

The Italian Confederation formed by Rome was a unique and creative organization that conferred on Italians a measure of security and order previously unknown. Rome prevented internecine wars within the peninsula, suppressed internal revolutions within city-states, and protected the Italians from barbarians (Gallic invaders from the north). In the wars of conquest outside Italy, a share of the glory and plunder fell to all Italians, another benefit of the confederation.

By 264 B.C., Rome had achieved two striking successes. First, it had secured social cohesion by redressing the grievances of the plebeians. Second, Rome had increased its military might by conquering Italy, obtaining the human resources with which it would conquer the Mediterranean world.

The Conquest of the Western Mediterranean: The Punic Wars

When Rome finished unifying Italy, there were five great powers in the Mediterranean area: the Seleucid monarchy in the Near East, the Ptolemaic monarchy in Egypt, the kingdom of Macedonia, Carthage in the western Mediterranean, and the Roman-dominated Italian Confederation. One hundred and twenty years later—146 B.C.—Rome had subjected these states to its dominion, "an event for which the past affords no precedent," said the contemporary Greek historian Polybius.

Roman expansion beyond Italy did not proceed according to predetermined design. Indeed, some Roman leaders considered involvement in foreign adventures a threat to both Rome's security and its traditional way of life. But it is difficult for a great power not to get drawn into conflicts as its interests grow, and without planning it, Rome acquired an overseas empire.

Shortly after asserting supremacy in Italy, Rome engaged Carthage, the other great power in the western Mediterranean, in a prolonged conflict. Founded about 800 B.C. by Phoenicians, the North African city of Carthage had become a prosperous commercial center. Its wealth was derived from a virtual monopoly of trade in the western Mediterranean and along the west coasts of Africa and Europe. The Carthaginians had acquired an empire comprising North Africa and coastal regions of southern Spain, Sardinia, Corsica, and western Sicily. Carthaginians pursued a cautious foreign policy, preferring diplomacy to conflict and avoiding wars offering no promise of commercial gain.

War between the two great powers began because Rome feared Carthage's designs on the northern Sicilian city of Messana, whose ruling oligarchy had appealed to Rome for protection. Although it had no territorial or commercial interests in Sicily, Rome was apprehensive about the southern Italian city-states that were its allies, fearing that Carthage would use Messana either to attack them or to interfere with their trade. In 264 B.C., after much uncertainty and debate, Rome decided that the security of its allies required intervention in Sicily. Since Carthage would not surrender its claim to Messana, the two powers stumbled into a collision that neither had deliberately sought. As the war progressed, Rome's objectives amplified. No longer satisfied with driving Carthage from Messana, Rome wanted to expel Carthaginians from Sicily altogether, a decision that lengthened

the war by twenty years and turned it into a war of exhaustion.

Although Rome suffered severe losses—including the annihilation of an army that had invaded North Africa and the destruction of hundreds of ships in battle and storms—the Romans never considered anything but a victor's peace. Drawing manpower from loyal allies throughout Italy, Rome finally prevailed over Carthage, which had relied principally on a mercenary army and could not recoup its sea losses. Without the means of continuing the war, Carthage made peace in 241 B.C., surrendering Sicily to Rome. Three years later, Rome seized the islands of Corsica and Sardinia from a weakened Carthage. With the acquisition of these territories beyond Italy, which were made into provinces, Rome had the beginnings of an empire.

Carthaginian expansion in Spain precipitated the Second Punic War (218–201 B.C.). The Carthaginian army was commanded by Hannibal (247–183 B.C.), whose military genius astounded the ancients. Hannibal led a seasoned army, complete with war elephants for charging enemy lines, across mountain passes so steep and icy that men and animals sometimes lost their footing and fell to their deaths. Some 26,000 men survived the crossing into Italy; 15,000 more were recruited from Gallic tribesmen of the Po Valley. At the battle of Cannae (216 B.C.), Hannibal's army completely destroyed a Roman army of 60,000 soldiers, the largest single force Rome had ever put into the field.

Romans were in a state of shock. Mixed with grief for the dead was the fear that Hannibal would crown his victory with an attack on Rome itself. To prevent panic, the Senate ordered women and children indoors, limited mourning to thirty days, and prepared to raise a new army. Adding to Rome's distress was the defection of many southern Italian allies to Hannibal.

These were the Republic's worst days. Nevertheless, says the Roman historian Livy, the Romans did not breathe a word of peace.

Map 6.1 Roman Conquests During the Republic ▶

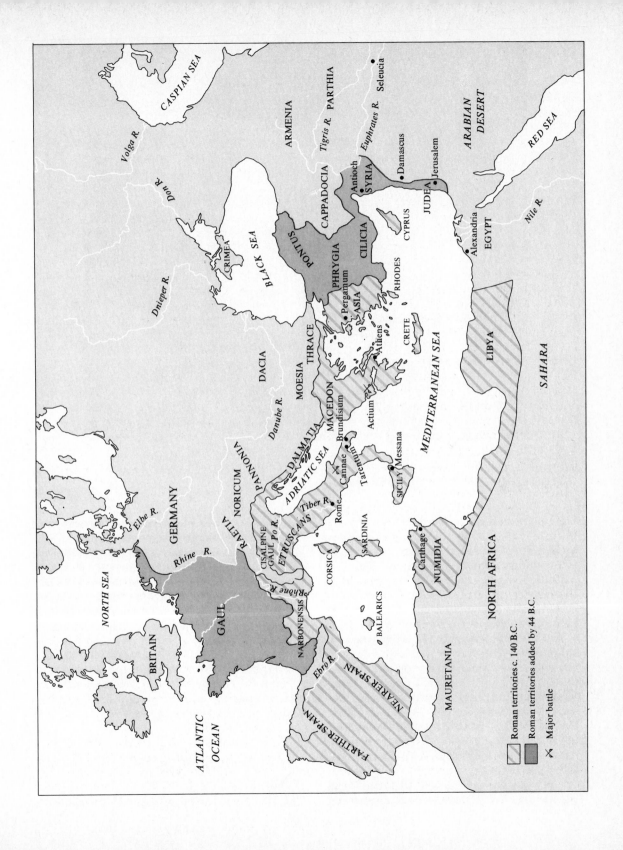

CASPIAN SEA

Volga R.

Don R.

Dnieper R.

CRIMEA

BLACK SEA

ARMENIA

PARTHIA

Tigris R.

Euphrates R.

Seleucia

ARABIAN DESERT

RED SEA

Nile R.

CAPPADOCIA

PONTUS

PHRYGIA

CILICIA

Antioch
SYRIA
Damascus

JUDEA
Jerusalem

Alexandria
EGYPT

CYPRUS

RHODES

ASIA
Pergamum

CRETE

Athens

MEDITERRANEAN SEA

LIBYA

SAHARA

THRACE

MOESIA

DACIA

Danube R.

DALMATIA

MACEDON

ADRIATIC SEA

Actium

Brundisium

Tarentum

Cannae

Messana
SICILY

Carthage

NUMIDIA

NORTH AFRICA

PANNONIA

NORICUM

RAETIA

GERMANY

Elbe R.

Rhine R.

Rhône R.

CISALPINE
GAUL
Po R.
ETRUSCANS

Tiber R.
Rome

GAUL

NARBONENSIS

Ebro R.

NEARER SPAIN

FARTHER SPAIN

SARDINIA

CORSICA

BALEARICS

NORTH SEA

BRITAIN

ATLANTIC OCEAN

MAURETANIA

Roman territories c. 140 B.C.

Roman territories added by 44 B.C.

× Major battle

Roman Forum, House of the Vestals, and the Capitol. The Forum was the center of Roman government and administration under both the Republic and the Empire. Here the *curia* (Senate house) and important basilicas were located. (*ENIT/Italian Government Travel Office*)

Hannibal could not follow up his victory at Cannae with a finishing blow, for Rome wisely would not allow its army to be lured into another major engagement. Nor did Hannibal possess the manpower to capture the city itself, particularly since the central cities remained loyal to Rome. But for nearly fifteen years, Hannibal's army ravaged Italy.

At the same time that Hannibal was devastating Italy, his brother Hasdrubal was engaging Roman forces in Spain, commanded by the brothers Publius and Cnaeus Scipio. Reinforced by troops from Carthage, Hasdrubal destroyed the divided armies of the Scipios, both of whom perished in battle. In 210 B.C., Publius Scipio's son, who bore the same name, was dispatched to Spain to redeem the defeat.

The younger Scipio possessed superior self-confidence, a trait that he conveyed to his troops. After completing the conquest of Spain by 206 B.C., Scipio invaded North Africa, threatening Carthage and forcing Hannibal to withdraw his troops from Italy in order to defend his homeland. Hannibal, who had won every battle in Italy, was defeated by Scipio at the battle of Zama in North Africa in 202 B.C.; this battle marked the end of the Second Punic War. Thus Rome's superior reserves of manpower, determination, and willingness to make sacrifices had overcome Hannibal's military feats. Carthage was compelled to surrender Spain and to give up its elephants and its navy.

The Conquest of the Hellenistic World

The Second Punic War left Rome the sole great power in the western Mediterranean;

it also hastened Rome's entry into the politics of the Hellenistic world. As in Rome's uniting of Italy and conquest of the western Mediterranean, its expansion in the East followed no predetermined plan. Rome did not deliberately seek territorial aggrandizement. As a great power, Rome was drawn into Greek affairs, fearing political disorder. Intervention in Greece then led to Roman involvement in the Hellenistic kingdoms of the Near East and Asia Minor—Seleucia, Egypt, and Pergamum. The inability of the Hellenistic states to settle their own disputes prompted Rome to attempt to impose its dominion over them; their failure to present unified resistance simplified Rome's military effort. Overcome by superior power, the Hellenistic states became client kingdoms of Rome and, they consequently lost their freedom of action in foreign affairs.

Roman imperialism is a classic example of a great power being snared into overseas adventures. To achieve security, Rome protected its allies, prevented endemic warfare, and thwarted any would-be conquerors of Italy. In the course of these actions came considerable spoils of war, but Rome's principal motives for expansion were strategic and political, not economic.

In 146 B.C., the same year that Rome's hegemony over the Hellenistic world was assured, Rome concluded the Third Punic War with Carthage. Although Carthage was a second-rate power and no longer a threat to Rome's security, Rome had launched this war of annihilation against Carthage in 149 B.C. The Romans were driven by old hatreds and the traumatic memory of Hannibal's near-conquest. Rome sold Carthaginian survivors into slavery, obliterated the city, and turned the land into the Roman province of Africa. Rome's savage and irrational behavior toward a helpless Carthage was an early sign of the failure of senatorial leadership; there would be others.

Rome had not yet reached the limits of its expansion, but there was no doubt that by 146 B.C. the Mediterranean world had been subjected to its will.

The Consequences of Expansion

Thousands of Greeks came to Rome; many were educated persons who had been enslaved as a result of Rome's eastern conquests. This influx accelerated the process of Hellenization begun earlier with Rome's contact with the Greek cities of southern Italy.

A crucial consequence of expansion was Roman contact with the legal experience of other peoples, including the Greeks. Roman jurists, demonstrating the Roman virtues of pragmatism and common sense, selectively incorporated into Roman law elements of the legal codes and traditions of these nations. Thus Roman jurists gradually and empirically fashioned the *jus gentium*, the law of nations or peoples.

Roman jurists then identified the *jus gentium* with the natural law (*jus naturale*) of the Stoics. The jurists said that law should accord with rational principles inherent in nature—universal norms that are capable of being discerned by rational people. As the Roman statesman Cicero said,

True law is right reason in agreement with nature; it is of universal application, unchanging and everlasting. . . . And there will not be different laws at Rome and at Athens, or different laws now and in the future, but one eternal and unchangeable law will be valid for all nations and all times.[1]

The law of nations combined Roman civil law—the law of the Roman state—with principles drawn from Greek and other sources, and it eventually replaced much of the local law in the empire. This evolution of a universal code of law that gave expression to the Stoic principles of common rationality and humanity was the great achievement of Roman rule.

Rome's conquests also contributed to the rise of a middle class of commoners. Their wealth was derived from contracts to supply the army, to construct public buildings, and to collect taxes in the provinces. Rome had no professional civil service, and the collection of public revenues was open to bidding—the highest bidder receiving a contract to collect customs' duties, rents on public lands, and tribute in the provinces. The collector's profit came from milking as much tax money as he could from the provincials. These financiers belonged to a group called the Equites, which also included prosperous landowners. Generally, the interests of the Equites paralleled those of the ruling oligarchy. At times, however, they did support generals—notably Julius Caesar—who challenged senatorial rule.

The immense wealth brought to Rome from the East gave the upper classes a taste for luxury. The rich built elaborate homes, which they decorated with fine furniture and works of art and staffed with servants, cooks, and tutors. They delighted in sumptuous banquets that contained all types of delicacies. Wealthy matrons wore fancy gowns and coiffures to match. These excesses prompted Roman moralists to castigate the people for violating traditional values.

Roman conquerors had transported to Italy hundreds of thousands of war captives, including Greeks, from all over their empire. The more fortunate slaves worked as craftsmen and servants; the luckless and more numerous toiled on the growing number of plantations or died early laboring in mines. Roman masters often treated their slaves brutally. Although slave uprisings were not common, their ferocity terrified the Romans. In 135 B.C., slaves in Sicily revolted and captured some key towns, defeating Roman forces before being subdued. In 73 B.C., gladiators led by Spartacus broke out of their barracks. Proclaiming a war for the liberation of all slaves, Spartacus was joined by tens of thousands of runaways. The slave army defeated Roman armies and devastated southern Italy before the superior might of Rome prevailed. Some 6,000 of the defeated slaves were crucified.

Republican Rome treated the people in overseas lands differently from its Italian allies. Italians were drafted into the Roman army, but provincials as a rule served only in emergencies, for Rome was not certain of their loyalty nor of their readiness to meet

Roman standards of discipline. Whereas Rome had been somewhat generous in extending citizenship to Italians, provincials were granted citizenship only in exceptional cases. All but some favored communities were required to pay taxes to Rome. Roman governors, lesser officials, and businessmen found the provinces a source of quick wealth; they were generally unrestrained by the Senate, which was responsible for administering the overseas territories. Exploitation, corruption, and extortion soon ran rampant. The Roman nobility proved unfit to manage a world empire.

Despite numerous examples of misrule in the provinces, there were many positive features of Roman administration. Rome generally allowed its subjects a large measure of self-government and did not interfere with religion and local customs. Usually the Roman taxes worked out to be no higher than, and in some instances were lower than those under previous regimes. And most important, Rome reduced the endemic warfare that had plagued these regions.

Rome used its power essentially for constructive ends—to establish order; to build roads, aqueducts, and public buildings; and to promote Hellenism. When Rome destroyed, it rebuilt creatively; when it conquered, it spread civilization and maintained peace. But no doubt its hundreds of thousands of prisoners of war, uprooted, enslaved, and degraded, would not have viewed Roman conquest as beneficial; nor would the butchered Spanish tribesmen or the massacred Carthaginians. To these hapless victims, Rome appeared as an evil oppressor, not as the creator of a cosmopolis that brought order and security.

Culture in the Republic

A chief consequence of expansion was increased contact with Greek culture. During the third century B.C., Greek civilization started to exercise an increasing and fruitful influence upon the Roman mind. Greek teachers, both slave and free, came to Rome and introduced Romans to Hellenic cultural achievements. As they conquered the eastern Mediterranean, Roman generals began to ship libraries and works of art from Greek cities to Rome. In time, Romans acquired from Greece knowledge of scientific thought, philosophy, medicine, and geography. Roman writers and orators used Greek history, poetry, and oratory as models. Adopting the humanist outlook of the Greeks, the Romans came to value human intelligence and eloquent and graceful prose and poetry. Wealthy Romans retained Greek tutors, poets, and philosophers in their households and sent their sons to Athens to study. Thus, Rome creatively assimilated the Greek achievement and transmitted it to others, thereby extending the orbit of Hellenism. To be sure, some conservative Romans were hostile to the Greek influence, which they felt threatened traditional Roman values, but the tide of Hellenism could not be stemmed.

Plautus (c. 254–184 B.C.), Rome's greatest playwright, adopted features of fourth- and third-century Greek comedy. His plays had Greek characters and took place in Greek settings; the actors wore the Greek style of dress. But the plays also contained familiar elements that appealed to Roman audiences—scenes of gluttony, drunkenness, womanizing, and the pains of love.

> *Not the throes of all mankind*
> *Equal my distracted mind.*
> *I strain and I toss*
> *On a passionate cross;*
> *Love's goad makes me reel,*
> *I whirl on Love's wheel,*
> *In a swoon of despair*
> *Hurried here, hurried there—*
> *Torn asunder, I am blind*
> *With a cloud upon my mind.*[2]

Another playwright, Terence (c. 190–159 B.C.), was originally from North Africa, and was brought to Rome as a slave. His owner, a Roman senator, provided the talented youth

with an education and freed him. Like Plautus, Terence was influenced by Menander, the fourth-century Athenian comic playwright. Terence's Latin style, graceful and polished, was technically superior to that of Plautus. But Terence's humor, restrained and refined, lacked the boisterousness of Plautus' writing that appealed to the Roman audience. For this reason, Terence's plays were less popular. Terence demonstrated more humaneness than Plautus did, a quality that is depicted in his attitude toward child rearing:

> *I give—I overlook; I do not judge it necessary to exert my authority in everything. . . . I think it better to restrain children through a sense of shame and liberal treatment than through fear. . . . This is the duty of a parent to accustom a son to do what is right rather of his own choice, than through fear of another.*[3]

Catullus (87–54 B.C.) is generally regarded as one of the greatest lyric poets in world literature. He was a native of northern Italy whose father had provided him with a gentleman's education. In his early twenties, Catullus came to Rome and fell in love with Clodia; she was the wife of the governor of Cisalpine Gaul, who was away at the time. For the older Clodia, Catullus was a refreshing diversion from her many other lovers. Tormented by Clodia's numerous affairs with other men, Catullus struggled to break away from passion's grip:

> *I look no more for her to be my lover*
> *As I love her. That thing could never be.*
> *Nor pray I for her purity—that's over.*
> *Only this much I pray, that I be free.*
>
> *Free from insane desire myself, and guarded*
> *In peace at last. O heaven, grant that yet*
> *The faith by which I've lived may be*
>   *rewarded.*
> *Let me forget.*[4]

The historian Sallust (c. 86–35 B.C.) sided with Caesar against the senatorial oligarchy. After Caesar's death, Sallust withdrew from public life, devoting himself to writing history.

His works contain brilliant character sketches. With a high moral tone, Sallust condemned the breakdown of republican values.

Growing love of money, and the lust for power which followed it, engendered every kind of evil. Avarice destroyed honor, integrity, and every other virtue, and instead taught men to be proud and cruel, to neglect religion, and to hold nothing too sacred to sell. Ambition tempted many to be false . . . At first these vices grew slowly and sometimes met with punishments; later on, when the disease had spread like a plague, Rome changed: her government, once so just and admirable, became harsh and unendurable.[5]

Lucretius (c. 94–c. 55 B.C.), the leading Roman Epicurean philosopher, was influenced by the conflict fostered by two generals, Marius and Sulla, which is discussed later in this chapter. Distraught by the seemingly endless strife, Lucretius yearned for philosophic tranquillity. Like Epicurus, he believed that religion prompted people to perform evil deeds and caused them to experience terrible anxiety about death and eternal punishment. In his work, *On the Nature of Things,* Lucretius expressed his appreciation of Epicurus. Like his mentor, Lucretius advanced a materialistic conception of nature and denounced superstition and religion for fostering psychological distress. He proposed that the simple life, devoid of political involvement and excessive passion, was the highest good and the path that would lead from emotional turmoil to peace of mind. Epicurus' hostility to traditional religion, disparagement of politics and public service, and rejection of the goals of power and glory ran counter to the accepted Roman ideal of virtue. On the other hand, his glorification of the quiet life amid a community of friends had great appeal to first-century Romans, who were disgusted with civil strife.

Cicero (106–43 B.C.), a leading Roman statesman, was also a distinguished orator, an unsurpassed Latin stylist, and a student of Greek philosophy. His letters, more than eight hundred of which have survived, provide modern historians with valuable insights into late republican politics. Dedicated to republicanism, Cicero sought to prevent one-man rule. He adopted the Stoic belief that natural law governs the universe and applies to all, and that all belong to a common humanity.

. . . there is no difference in kind between man and man; for . . . Reason, which alone raises us above the level of the beasts and enables us to draw inferences, to prove and disprove, to discuss and solve problems, and to come to conclusions, is certainly common to us all, and though varying in what it learns, at least in the capacity to learn it is invariable. . . . In fact, there is no human being of any race who, if he finds a guide, cannot attain virtue.[6]

Stoicism was the most influential philosophy in Rome. Its stress on virtuous conduct and performance of duty coincided with Roman ideals, and its doctrine of natural law that applies to all nations harmonized with the requirements of a world empire.

The Collapse of the Republic

In 146 B.C., Roman might spanned the Mediterranean world. After that year the principal concerns of the Republic no longer were foreign invasions, but adjusting city-state institutions to the demands of empire and overcoming critical social and political problems at home. In both instances the Republic was unequal to the challenge. Instead of developing a professional civil service to administer the conquered lands, Roman leaders attempted to govern an empire with city-state institutions that had evolved for a different purpose. In addition, the Republic showed little concern for the welfare of its subjects, and provincial rule worsened as governors, tax collectors, and soldiers shamelessly exploited the provincials.

During Rome's march to empire, all its classes had demonstrated a magnificent civic spirit in fighting foreign wars. With Carthage and Macedonia no longer threats to Rome, this cooperation deteriorated. Internal dissension tore Rome apart as the ferocity and drive for domination formerly directed against foreign enemies turned inward against fellow Romans. Civil war replaced foreign war.

The Romans had prevailed over their opponents partly because of their traditional virtues—resoluteness, simplicity of manners, and willingness to sacrifice personal interests for the good of Rome. But the riches flowing into Rome from the plundered provinces caused these virtues to decay, and rivalry for status and wealth overrode civic patriotism. The masses, landless and afflicted with poverty and idleness, withdrew their allegiance from the state.

In this time of agony, both great and self-seeking individuals emerged. Some struggled to restore the social harmony and political unity that had prevailed in the period of expansion. Others, political adventurers, attacked the authority of the Senate to gain personal power. And the Senate, which had previously exercised leadership creatively and responsibly, degenerated into a self-serving oligarchy that resisted reform and fought to preserve its power and privilege.

Neither the Senate nor its opponents could rejuvenate the Republic. Eventually it collapsed, a victim of class tensions, poor leadership, power-hungry demagogues, and civil war. Underlying all these conditions was the breakdown of social harmony and the deterioration of civic patriotism. The Republic had conquered an empire only to see the spiritual qualities of its citizens decay.

The Crisis in Agriculture

The downhill slide of the Republic was triggered by an agricultural crisis. In the long war with Hannibal in Italy, each side had tried to deprive the other of food supplies; in the process, they ruined farmlands, destroyed farmhouses and farm equipment, and slaughtered animals. With many Roman sol-

Detail of Wall Painting, Villa at Boscoreale, First Century B.C. The painter's illusionism draws the viewer into the crowded architecture of the city. The Romans built single-family dwellings (the *domus*), as well as apartment dwellings several stories in height. (*The Metropolitan Museum of Art; Rogers Fund, 1903*)

dier-farmers serving long periods in the army, fields lay neglected. Returning veterans with small holdings lacked the money to restore their land; they were forced to sell their farms to wealthy landowners at low prices.

Another factor that helped to squeeze out the small farmowners was the importation of hundreds of thousands of slaves to work on large plantations called *latifundia*. Farmers who had formerly increased meager incomes by working for wages on neighboring large estates no longer were needed. Sinking ever deeper into poverty and debt, farmers gave up their lands and went to Rome seeking work. The dispossessed peasantry found little to do in Rome, where there was not enough industry to provide them with employment and where much of the work was done by slaves. The once-sturdy and independent Roman farmer, who had done all that his country had asked of him, was becoming part of a vast urban underclass—poor, embittered, and alienated. The uprooting of a formerly self-reliant peasantry was Hannibal's "posthumous revenge" on Rome; it would prove more deadly than Cannae.

The Gracchi Revolution

In 133 B.C., Tiberius Gracchus (163–133 B.C.), who came from one of Rome's most honored families, was elected tribune. Distressed by the injustice done to the peasantry and recognizing that the Roman army depended on the loyalty of small landowners, Tiberius made himself the spokesman for land reform. He proposed a simple and moderate solution for the problem of the landless peasants: he would re-enact an old law barring any Roman from using more than 312 acres of the state-owned land obtained in the process of uniting Italy. For many years the upper class had ignored this law, occupying vast tracts of public land as squatters and treating this land as their own. By enforcing the law, Tiberius hoped to free land for distribution to landless citizens.

Rome's leading families viewed Tiberius as a revolutionary who threatened their property and political authority. They thought him a democrat who would undermine the Senate, the seat of aristocratic power, in favor of the Assembly, which represented the commoners. For one thing, Tiberius had proposed that the Assembly settle the affairs of Pergamum, Rome's newest province and dispose of its treasury. Surely that would violate the Senate's right to control the purse and to administer provinces, the senators said. When Tiberius sought re-election as a tribune, a

violation of constitutional tradition, the senators were convinced that he was a rabble-rouser who aimed to destroy the republican constitution and become a one-man ruler. To preserve the status quo, with wealth and power concentrated in the hands of a few hundred families, senatorial extremists killed Tiberius and some three hundred of his followers, dumping their bodies into the Tiber.

The cause of land reform was next taken up by Gaius Gracchus (153–121 B.C.), a younger brother of Tiberius. An emotional and gifted speaker, Gaius won the support of the city poor and was elected tribune in 123 B.C. A more astute politician than his brother, Gaius increased his following by favoring the Equites, the new class of plebeian businessmen, and by promising full citizenship to all Italians. He aided the poor by reintroducing his brother's plan for land distribution and by enabling them to buy grain from the state at less than half the market price. But like his brother, Gaius aroused the anger of the senatorial class. A brief civil war raged in Rome during which Gaius Gracchus (who may have committed suicide) and 3,000 of his followers perished.

By killing the Gracchi, the Senate had substituted violence for reason and made murder a means of coping with troublesome opposition. A governing class cannot behave like hoodlums with impunity. Soon the club and the dagger became common weapons in Roman politics, thereby hurling Rome into an era of political violence that ended with the destruction of the Republic. Though the Senate considered itself the guardian of republican liberty, in reality it was expressing the determination of a few hundred families to retain their control over the state. It is a classic example of a once-creative minority clinging tenaciously to power long after it had ceased to govern effectively, or to inspire allegiance. The Senate that had led Rome to empire had become a self-seeking, unimaginative, entrenched oligarchy that was leading the Republic and the Mediterranean world into disaster.

Rome in the first century B.C. was very different from the Rome that had defeated

Hannibal. Entranced by eastern luxuries and determined to retain oligarchic rule, the senatorial families neglected their responsibility to the state. Many upper-class Romans, burning to achieve the dignity that would mark them as great men, tried to climb onto the crowded stage of Roman politics, but the best roles were already reserved for members of the senatorial families. With so few opportunities, aspirants to political power stopped at nothing.

Roman politics in the century after the Gracchi was bedeviled by intrigues, rivalries, personal ambition, and political violence. Political adventurers exploited the issue of cheap grain and free land in order to benefit their careers. Whereas the Gracchi were sincere reformers, these later champions of social reform were unscrupulous demagogues, who cleverly charmed and manipulated the city poor with bread and circuses—low-cost food and free admission to games. These demagogues aspired to the tribunate of the plebes, an office possessing powers formidable enough to challenge the Senate and yet not too difficult to obtain, since ten tribunes were elected each year. By riding a wave of popular enthusiasm, these political adventurers hoped to sweep aside the Senate and concentrate power in their own hands. The poor, denied land and employment, demoralized, alienated and lulled into political ignorance by decades of idleness, food handouts, and free entertainment, were ready to back whoever made the most glittering promises. The Senate behaved like a decadent oligarchy, and the Tribal Assembly, which had become the voice of the urban mob, demonstrated a weakness for demagogues, an openness to bribery, and an abundance of deceit and incompetence. The Roman Republic had passed the peak of its greatness.

Rival Generals

Marius (157–86 B.C.), who became consul in 107 B.C., adopted a military policy that eventually contributed to the wrecking of the Republic. Short of troops for a campaign in Numidia in North Africa, Marius disposed of the traditional property requirement for entrance into the army and filled his legions with volunteers from the urban poor, a dangerous precedent. These new soldiers, disillusioned with Rome, served only because Marius held out the promise of pay, loot, and land grants after discharge. Their loyalty was given not to Rome but to Marius, and they remained loyal to their commander only as long as he fulfilled his promises.

Marius had set an example that other ambitious commanders followed. They saw that a general could use his army to advance his political career, that by retaining the confidence of his soldiers, he could cow the Senate and dictate Roman policy. The army, no longer an instrument of government, became a private possession of generals. Seeing its authority undermined by generals appointed by the Assembly, the Senate was forced to seek army commanders who would champion the cause of senatorial rule. In time, Rome would be engulfed in civil wars, as rival generals used their troops to further their own ambitions or political affiliations.

Meanwhile, the Senate continued to deal ineffectively with Rome's problems. When Rome's Italian allies pressed for citizenship, the Senate refused to make concessions. The Senate's shortsightedness plunged Italy into a terrible war, known as the Social War. As war ravaged the peninsula, the Romans reversed their policy and conferred citizenship on the Italians. The unnecessary and ruinous rebellion petered out.

While Rome was fighting its Italian allies, Mithridates, king of Pontus in northern Asia Minor, invaded the Roman province of Asia. In 88 B.C., he aroused the local population to massacre 80,000 Italian residents of the province. Mithridates and his forces crossed into Greece and occupied Athens and other cities. Faced with this crisis, the Senate entrusted command to Sulla (138–78 B.C.), who had distinguished himself in the Social War. But supporters of Marius, through intrigue and violence, had the order rescinded and the command given to Marius.

Sulla refused to accept his loss of command

and with his loyal troops proceeded to the capital. This was a fateful moment in Roman history: the first march on Rome, the first prolonged civil war, and the first time a commander and his troops defied the government. Sulla won the first round. But when Sulla left Rome to fight Mithridates in Greece, Marius and his troops retook the city and in a frenzy lashed out at Sulla's supporters. The killing lasted for five days and nights.

Marius died shortly afterwards. Then Sulla quickly subdued Marius' supporters on his return and became dictator of Rome. Sulla instituted a terror that far surpassed Marius' violence. Without legal sanction and with frightening and cold-blooded cruelty, Sulla marked his opponents for death; the state seized their property and declared their children and grandchildren ineligible for public office.

Sulla resolved to use his absolute power to revive and make permanent the overriding rule of the Senate. He believed that only rule by an aristocratic oligarchy could protect Rome from future military adventurers and assure domestic peace. He therefore restored the Senate's right to veto acts of the Assembly, limited the power of the tribunes and the Assembly, and reduced the military authority of provincial governors to prevent any march on Rome. To make the Senate less oligarchical, he increased its membership to six hundred. Having put through these reforms, Sulla retired.

Julius Caesar

But the Senate failed to wield its restored authority effectively. The Republic was still menaced by military commanders who used their troops for their own political advantage, and underlying problems remained unsolved. In 60 B.C., a triumvirate consisting of Julius Caesar (c. 100–44 B.C.), a politician, Pompey, a general, and Crassus, a wealthy banker, conspired to take over Rome. The ablest of the three was Caesar.

Recognizing the importance of a military command as a prerequisite for political prominence, Caesar gained command of the legions in Gaul in 59 B.C. The following year he began the conquest of that part of Gaul outside of Roman control. The successful Gallic campaigns and invasion of Britain revealed Caesar's exceptional talent for generalship. Indeed, his victories alarmed the Senate, which feared that Caesar would use his devoted troops and soaring reputation to seize control of the state.

Meanwhile the triumvirate had fallen apart. In 53 B.C., Crassus had perished with his army in a disastrous campaign against the Parthians in the East. The bonds between Pompey and Caesar were weak, consisting essentially of Pompey's marriage to Caesar's daughter Julia. After her death in 54 B.C., Pompey and Caesar grew apart. Pompey, who was jealous of Caesar's success and eager to expand his own power, drew closer to the Senate. Supported by Pompey, the Senate ordered Caesar to relinquish his command. Without his troops, Caesar realized that he would be defenseless; he decided instead to march on Rome. After Caesar crossed the Rubicon River into Italy in 49 B.C., civil war again ravaged the Republic. Pompey proved no match for so talented a general; the Senate acknowledged Caesar's victory and appointed him to be dictator for ten years.

Caesar realized that republican institutions no longer operated effectively and that only strong and enlightened leadership could permanently end the civil warfare destroying Rome. His reforms were designed to create order out of chaos. Caesar fought the corruption that had so angered provincial subjects by lowering taxes, making the governors responsible to him, preventing capitalists from exploiting the regions, and generously extending citizenship to more provincials. To aid the poor in Rome, he began a public works program that provided employment and beautified the city. He also relocated over 100,000 veterans and members of Rome's lower class to the provinces, where he gave them land. To improve administration, he reorganized town governments in Italy and reformed the courts.

In February of 44 B.C., Rome's ruling class—

jealous of Caesar's success and power and afraid of his ambition—became thoroughly alarmed when his temporary dictatorship was converted into a lifelong office. The aristocracy saw this event as the end of senatorial government and their rule, which they equated with liberty, and as the beginnings of a Hellenistic type of monarchy. A group of aristocrats, regarding themselves as defenders of republican traditions more than four and a half centuries old, assassinated Caesar on March 15 in the year 44 B.C. Cicero expressed the general feeling of the conspirators:

Our tyrant deserves his death, [for his] was the blackest crime of all. [Caesar was] a man who was ambitious to be king of the Roman people and master of the whole world. . . . The man who maintains that such an ambition is morally right is a madman, for he justifies the destruction of law and liberty.[7]

There was also a strong element of jealousy in the conspirators' motivation.

The Republic's Last Years

The assassination of Julius Caesar did not restore republican liberty, but plunged Rome into renewed civil war. Two of Caesar's trusted lieutenants, Mark Antony and Lepidus, joined with Octavian, Caesar's adopted son, and defeated the armies of Brutus and Cassius, two instigators of Caesar's death. After Lepidus was forced into political obscurity, Antony and Octavian fought each other with the empire as the prize. In 31 B.C., at the naval battle of Actium in western Greece, Octavian crushed the forces of Antony and his wife, Egypt's Queen Cleopatra. Octavian emerged as master of Rome and four years later became, in effect, the first Roman emperor. The Roman Republic, whose death throes had lasted for decades and kept the Mediterranean world in turmoil, had finally perished.

The Roman Republic, which had amassed power to a degree hitherto unknown in the ancient world, was not wrecked by foreign

Bust of Caesar. Julius Caesar tried to rescue a dying Roman world by imposing strong rule. He paved the way for the transition from Republic to imperial rule. (*Ewing Galloway*)

invasion, but by internal weaknesses: the personal ambitions of power seekers, the degeneration of senatorial leadership, and the willingness of politicians to use violence; the formation of private armies in which soldiers gave their loyalty to their commander rather than to Rome; the transformation of a self-reliant peasantry into an impoverished and demoralized city rabble; and the deterioration of those ancient virtues that had been the source of the state's vitality. Before 146 B.C., the threat posed by foreign enemies, particularly Carthage, forced Romans to work together for the benefit of the state, and the

Chronology 6.1 The Roman Republic

509 B.C.	Expulsion of the Etruscan monarch
449	Law of Twelve Tables
287	The end of the struggle of the orders
264–241	First Punic War; Rome acquires provinces
218–201	Second Punic War; Hannibal is defeated
149–146	Third Punic War; destruction of Carthage
133–122	Land reforms by the Gracchi brothers; they are murdered by the Senate
88–83	Conflict between Sulla and the forces of Marius; Sulla emerges as dictator
79	Sulla retires
73–71	Slave revolt is led by Spartacus
58–51	Caesar campaigns in Gaul
49–44	Caesar is dictator of Rome
31 B.C.	Antony and Cleopatra are defeated at Actium by Octavian

equilibrium achieved during the patrician-plebeian struggle was maintained. This social cohesion broke down when foreign danger had been reduced, and in the ensuing century of turmoil, the apparatus of city-state government failed to function effectively.

Thus, the high point of Roman rule was not achieved under the Republic. The city-state constitution of the Republic was too limited to govern an immense empire. Rome first had to surpass the narrow framework of city-state government before it could unite the Mediterranean world in peace and law. The genius of Augustus (Octavian), the first emperor, made this development possible.

Notes

1. Cicero, *De Re Publica*, trans. by C. W. Keyes (Cambridge, Mass.: Harvard University Press, Loeb Classical Library, 1928), 3. 22 (p. 211).

2. Quoted in J. Wright Duff, *A Literary History of Rome* (New York: Barnes & Noble, 1960), pp. 136–137.

3. Terence, *The Brothers*, trans. by H. T. Riley (London: Henry G. Bohn, 1853), pp. 202–203.

4. Catullus, quoted in E. A. Havelock, *The Lyric Genius of Catullus* (New York: Russell & Russell, 1929), p. 63.

5. Sallust, *The Conspiracy of Catiline*, trans. by S. A. Handford (Baltimore: Penguin Books, 1963), pp. 181–182.

6. Cicero, *De Legibus*, trans. by C. W. Keyes (Cambridge, Mass.: Harvard University Press, Loeb Classical Library, 1928), 1. 10 (pp. 329–330).

7. Cicero, *De Officiis*, trans. by Walter Miller (Cambridge, Mass.: Harvard University Press, Loeb Classical Library, 1913), 3. 21 (p. 357).

Suggested Reading

Badian, E., *Roman Imperialism in the Late Roman Republic* (1968). An interpretive essay on the interaction between Roman domestic politics and foreign policy.

Boren, H. C., *Roman Society* (1977). A social, economic, and cultural history of the Republic and the Empire; written with the student in mind.

Brunt, P. A., *Social Conflicts in the Roman Republic* (1971). Concerned with the discontents of the rural and urban poor and internal struggles within the propertied classes.

Crawford, M., *The Roman Republic* (1982). A recent and reliable survey, with many quotations from original sources.

Errington, R. M., *The Dawn of Empire: Rome's Rise to World Power* (1972). A study of Rome the reluctant imperialist.

Gelzer, Matthias, *Caesar: Politician and Statesman* (1968). A revised edition of a classic work first published in 1921.

Grant, Michael, *A History of Rome* (1978). A recent synthesis of Roman history by a leading classical scholar; valuable for both the Republic and the Empire.

Gruen, E., *The Last Generation of the Roman Republic* (1974). An account of the Roman Republic from Sulla to Caesar; stresses social history.

Homo, Leon, *Roman Political Institutions* (1962). Reprint of the 1929 classic study of the Roman constitution down to the fall of the Empire in the West.

Lewis, N., and M. Reinhold, eds., *Roman Civilization* (1966). A two-volume collection of source readings. Volume I covers the Republic.

Lintott, A. W., *Violence in Republican Rome* (1968). Deals with the corruption of politics through violence.

Mazzolani, L. S., *The Idea of the City in Roman Thought* (1970). How Roman philosophers, poets, and statesmen view the polis and the cosmopolis.

Scullard, H. H., *From the Gracchi to Nero* (1963). A reliable history of the death of the Roman Republic and the rise of the Roman Empire.

Starr, C. G., *The Emergence of Rome* (1953). A short, clearly written introduction to the emergence of Roman power in Italy and the Mediterranean.

Review Questions

1. What were the complaints of the Roman plebeians at the beginning of the fifth century B.C.? What was the outcome of the patrician-plebeian conflict?

2. The Romans forged a constitutional system based on civic needs, not on religious mystery. Discuss this statement.

3. What factors enabled Rome to conquer Italy?

4. Without planning it, Rome acquired an overseas empire. Explain.

5. What did the first two Punic Wars reveal about the character of the Roman people?

6. What were the consequences of Roman expansion?

7. How was Roman cultural life influenced by Greek civilization?

8. What were the causes of the agricultural crisis faced by Rome in the second century B.C.?

9. How did the Gracchi brothers try to deal with the agricultural crisis? Why were they opposed by Rome's leading families?

10. What was the significance of the struggle between Marius and Sulla?

11. How did Caesar try to cope with the problems afflicting Rome? Why was he assassinated?

12. Analyze the reasons for the collapse of the Roman Republic.

13. Discuss what the parallels are between the collapse of the Roman Republic and the downfall of Athens.

14. The institutions of the Roman Republic were not suited to governing a world empire. Discuss this statement.

7

The Roman Empire:
A World-State

Rome's republican institutions, designed for a city-state, proved incapable of coping with the problems created by the conquest of a world empire. Invincible against foreign enemies, the Republic collapsed from within. But after Octavian's brilliant statesmanship brought order out of chaos, Rome entered its golden age under the rule of emperors. For almost two hundred years, from 27 B.C. to A.D. 180, the Mediterranean world enjoyed unparalleled peace and stability. The Roman world-state—erected on a Hellenic cultural foundation and cemented with empirewide civil service, laws, and citizenship—gave practical expression to Stoic cosmopolitanism and universalism. But even this impressive monument had structural defects, and in the third century A.D., the Empire was wracked by crises from which it never fully recovered. In the fifth century, German tribesmen overran the western half of the Empire, which had by then become a shadow of its former self.

During its time of trouble, Rome also experienced an intellectual crisis; forsaking the rational and secular values of classical humanism, many Romans sought spiritual comfort in oriental religions. One of these religions, Christianity, won out over its competitors, and was made the official religion of the Empire. With the triumph of Christianity in the Late Roman Empire, Western civilization took a new direction. Christianity would become the principal shaper of the European civilization that emerged from the ruins of Rome.

Augustus and the Foundations of the Roman Empire

After Octavian's forces defeated those of Antony and Cleopatra at the battle of Actium in 31 B.C., no opponents could stand up to him. The century of civil war, political murder, corruption, and mismanagement had exhausted the Mediterranean world, which longed for order. Like Caesar before him, Octavian recognized that only a strong monarchy could rescue Rome from civil war and anarchy. But learning from Caesar's assassination, he also knew that republican ideals were far from dead. To exercise autocratic power openly like a Hellenistic monarch would have aroused the hostility of the Roman ruling class, whose assistance and good will Octavian desired.

Octavian demonstrated his political genius by reconciling his military monarchy with republican institutions—he held absolute power without abruptly breaking with a republican past. Magistrates were still elected and assemblies still met; the Senate administered certain provinces, retained its treasury, and was invited to advise Octavian. With some truth, Octavian could claim that he ruled in partnership with the Senate. By maintaining the façade of the Republic, Octavian camouflaged his absolute power and contained senatorial opposition, which had already been weakened by the deaths of leading nobles in battle or in the purges that Octavian had instituted against his enemies. Moreover, Octavian's control over the armed forces made resistance futile, and the terrible violence that had followed Caesar's assassination made senators amenable to change.

In 27 B.C., Octavian shrewdly offered to surrender his power, knowing that the Senate, purged of opposition, would demand that he continue to lead the state. By this act, Octavian could claim to be a legitimate constitutional ruler leading a government of law, not one of a lawless despotism so hateful to the Roman mentality. In keeping with his policy of maintaining the appearance of traditional republican government, Octavian refused to be called king or even, like Caesar, dictator; instead, he cleverly disguised his autocratic rule by taking the inoffensive title *Princeps* (First Citizen). The Senate also conferred upon him the semireligious and revered name of *Augustus*.

Augustus' reign signified the end of the Roman Republic and the beginning of the Roman Empire, the termination of aristocratic politics and the emergence of one-man rule. As the historian Tacitus recognized, Augustus had accomplished a profound revolution in Roman political life: "The country had been transformed, and there was nothing left of the fine old Roman character. Political equality was a thing of the past; all eyes watched for imperial commands."[1] Under Augustus the power of the ruler was disguised; in ensuing generations, however, emperors would wield absolute power openly. As Rome became more autocratic and centralized, it took on the appearance of an oriental monarchy.

Augustus introduced the practice of emperor worship. In the eastern provinces, where oriental and Hellenistic monarchs had been regarded as divine, the person of Augustus was worshiped as a god. In Italy, where the deification of leaders was alien to the republican spirit, divine honors were granted to Augustus's genius or spirit of leadership; once deceased, Augustus and his successors were deified. By the third century, Italians and other peoples in the western territories viewed the living emperor as a god-king.

Despite his introduction of autocratic rule, Augustus was by no means a self-seeking tyrant, but a creative statesman. Heir to the Roman tradition of civic duty, he regarded his power as a public trust delegated to him by the Roman people. He was faithful to the classical ideal that the state should promote the good life by protecting civilization from barbarism and ignorance, and he sought to rescue a dying Roman world.

To prevent a renewal of civil war and to safeguard the borders of the Empire, Augustus reformed the army. As commander-in-chief, he could guard against the reemergence of ambitious generals like those whose rivalries and private armies had wrecked the Republic. Augustus maintained the loyalty of his soldiers by assuring that veterans, on discharge, would receive substantial bonuses and land in Italy or in the provinces. By organizing a professional

Imperial Family in Procession. This relief is no procession of timeless gods as in the Greek Parthenon. Children tug at their parents' togas, and the imperial family fulfills its civic duties as visible embodiments of the state. The relief is from the altar of peace, which honors Augustus. (*Alinari/Art Resource*)

standing army made up principally of volunteers who generally served for twenty-five years, Augustus was assured of a well-trained and loyal force capable of maintaining internal order, extending Roman territory, and securing the frontier.

For the city of Rome, Augustus had aqueducts and water mains built that brought water to most Roman homes. He created a fire brigade that reduced the danger of great conflagrations in crowded tenement districts, and he organized a police force to contain violence. He improved the distribution of free grain to the impoverished proletariat, and financed out of his own funds the popular gladiatorial combats.

In Italy, Augustus had roads repaired, and fostered public works. He arranged for Italians to play a more important role in the administration of the Empire. For the Italians' security, his army suppressed the brigandage that had proliferated in the countryside during the preceding century of agony, and guarded the northern borders from barbarian incursions.

By ending the civil wars and their accompanying devastation and by ruling out forced requisition of supplies and extortion of money, Augustus earned the gratitude of the provincials. Also contributing to his empirewide popularity were his efforts to correct tax abuse and to end corruption through improving the quality of governors and enabling aggrieved provincials to bring charges against

Roman officials. Augustus also continued the sensible practice of not interfering with the traditional customs and religions of the provinces. During his forty-year reign, Rome overcame the chaos of the years of revolution. The praise bestowed on him by grateful provincials was not undeserved. One decree from the province of Asia called Augustus

the savior of all mankind in common whose provident care has not only fulfilled but even surpassed the hopes of all: for both land and sea are at peace, the cities are teeming with the blessings of concord, plenty, and respect for law, and the culmination and harvest of all good things bring fair hopes for the future and contentment with the present.[2]

The Pax Romana

The brilliant statesmanship of Augustus inaugurated Rome's greatest age. For the next two hundred years the Mediterranean world enjoyed the blessings of the *pax Romana,* the Roman Peace. The ancient world had never experienced such a long period of peace, order, efficient administration, and prosperity. Although both proficient and inept rulers succeeded Augustus, the essential features of the pax Romana persisted.

The Successors of Augustus

The first four emperors who succeeded Augustus were related either to him or to his third wife, Livia. They constituted the Julio-Claudian dynasty, which ruled from A.D. 14 to A.D. 68. Although their reigns were marked by conspiracies, summary executions, and assassinations, the great achievements of Augustus were preserved and strengthened. The Senate did not seek to restore republicanism, and continued to assist the Princeps; the imperial bureaucracy grew larger and more professional; the army, with some exceptions, remained a loyal and disciplined force.

The Julio-Claudian dynasty came to an end in A.D. 68 when Emperor Nero committed suicide. Nero had grown increasingly tyrannical and had lost the confidence of the people, the senatorial class, and the generals, who rose in revolt. In the year following his death, anarchy reigned as military leaders competed for the throne. After a bloody civil war, the execution of two emperors, and the suicide of another, Vespasian gained the Principate. Vespasian's reign (A.D. 69–79) marked the beginning of the Flavian dynasty. By rotating commanding officers and stationing native troops far from their homelands, Vespasian improved discipline and discouraged mutiny. By having the great Colosseum of Rome constructed for gladiatorial contests, he earned the gratitude of the city's inhabitants. Vespasian also had nationalist uprisings put down in Gaul and Judea.

In Judea, Roman rule clashed with Jewish religious-national sentiments. Recognizing the tenaciousness with which Jews clung to their faith, the Roman leaders deliberately refrained from interfering with Hebraic religious beliefs and practices. Numerous privileges, such as exemption from emperor worship because it conflicted with the requirements of strict monotheism, were extended to Jews not only in Judea but throughout the Empire. But sometimes the Romans engaged in activities that outraged the Jews. For example, Pontius Pilate, the Roman procurator in Judea from A.D. 26 to 36, at one point ordered a Roman army unit into Jerusalem with banners bearing the image of the emperor. The entire Jewish nation was aroused. To the Jews, this display of a pagan idol in their holy city was an abomination. Realizing that the Jews would die rather than permit this act of sacrilege, Pilate ordered the banners removed. Another explosive situation emerged when the Emperor Caligula (A.D. 37–41) ordered that a

Map 7.1 The Roman Empire under Augustus and Hadrian ▶

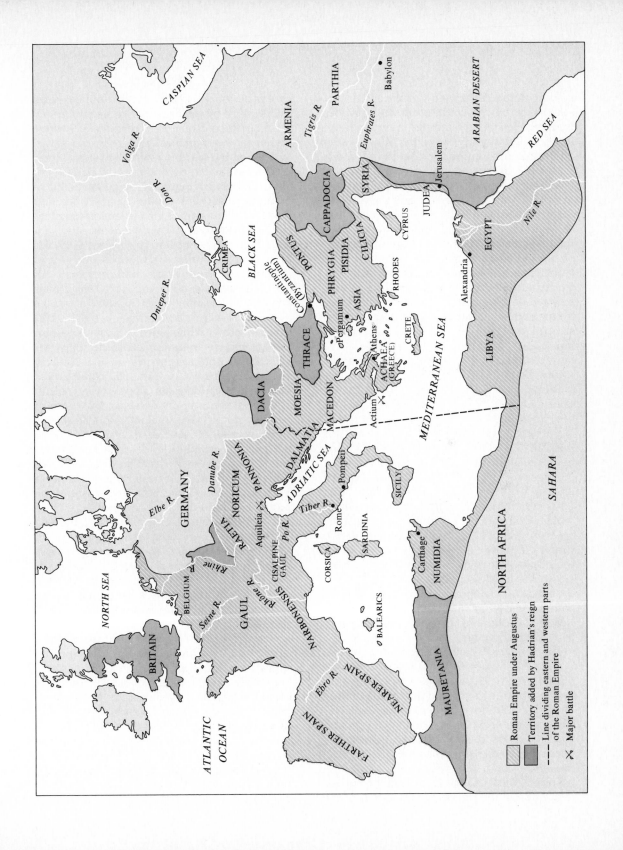

CASPIAN SEA

Volga R.

Don R.

Dnieper R.

ARMENIA

Tigris R.

PARTHIA

Euphrates R.

Babylon

ARABIAN DESERT

RED SEA

SYRIA

Jerusalem

JUDEA

Nile R.

CAPPADOCIA

PONTUS

CRIMEA

BLACK SEA

Constantinople (Byzantium)

PHRYGIA

PISIDIA

CILICIA

CYPRUS

EGYPT

Alexandria

ASIA

Pergamum

RHODES

THRACE

MACEDON

DACIA

MOESIA

Athens

ACHAEA (GREECE)

CRETE

MEDITERRANEAN SEA

LIBYA

Danube R.

DALMATIA

ADRIATIC SEA

Actium

Elbe R.

GERMANY

NORICUM

PANNONIA

RAETIA

Aquileia

Pompeii

SICILY

SAHARA

NORTH SEA

Rhine R.

BELGIUM

Seine R.

GAUL

CISALPINE GAUL

Po R.

Tiber R.

Rome

SARDINIA

CORSICA

Carthage

NUMIDIA

NORTH AFRICA

BRITAIN

Rhône R.

NARBONENSIS

BALEARICS

ATLANTIC OCEAN

Ebro R.

NEARER SPAIN

FARTHER SPAIN

MAURETANIA

Roman Empire under Augustus

Territory added by Hadrian's reign

Line dividing eastern and western parts of the Roman Empire

Major battle

golden statue of himself be placed in Jerusalem's temple. Again the order was rescinded when the Jews demonstrated their readiness to resist. Relations between the Jews of Judea and the Roman authorities deteriorated progressively in succeeding decades. Militant Jews who rejected Roman rule as a threat to the purity of Jewish life urged their people to take up arms. Feeling a religious obligation to re-establish an independent kingdom in their ancient homeland and unable to reconcile themselves to Roman rule, the Jews launched a full-scale war of liberation in A.D. 66. In A.D. 70, after a five-month siege had inflicted terrible punishment on the Jews, Roman armies captured Jerusalem and destroyed the temple. After the conquest of Jerusalem, some fortresses, including the Masada on the western side of the Dead Sea, continued to resist. The defenders of the Masada withstood a Roman siege until A.D. 73; refusing to become Roman captives, they took their own lives.

Vespasian was succeeded by his sons Titus (A.D. 79–81) and Domitian (A.D. 81–96). The reign of Titus was made memorable by the eruption of Vesuvius, which devastated the towns of Pompeii and Herculaneum. After Titus' brief time as Emperor, his younger brother Domitian became ruler. After crushing a revolt led by the Roman commander in Upper Germany, a frightened Domitian executed many leading Romans. These actions led to his assassination in A.D. 96, ending the Flavian dynasty. The Flavians, however, had succeeded in preserving internal peace and in consolidating and extending the borders of the Empire.

The Senate selected one of its own, Nerva, to succeed the murdered Domitian. Nerva's reign (A.D. 96–98) was brief and uneventful. But he introducd a practice that would endure until A.D. 180: he adopted as his son and designated as his heir a man with proven ability, Trajan, the governor of Upper Germany. This adoptive system assured a succession of competent rulers.

Trajan (ruled A.D. 98–117) eased the burden of taxation in the provinces, provided for the needs of poor children, and had public works built. With his enlarged army he conquered Dacia (parts of Rumania and Hungary), where he seized vast quantities of gold and silver, and made the territory into a Roman province, adding to the large frontier Rome had to protect. Trajan also made war against Parthia (a kingdom southeast of the Caspian Sea that had once been part of the Hellenistic kingdom of Seleucia), capturing Armenia and advancing to the Persian Gulf. Overextended lines of communication, revolts by Jews in several eastern provinces, and counterattacks by the Parthians, however, forced his armies to return to Rome.

Trajan's successor, Hadrian (A.D. 117–138) abandoned what remained of Trajan's eastern conquests. He strengthened border defenses in Britain, and fought the second Hebrew revolt in Judea (A.D. 132–135). After initial successes, including the capture of Jerusalem, the Jews were again defeated by superior Roman might. The majority of Palestinian Jews were killed, sold as slaves, or forced to seek refuge in other lands. The Romans renamed the province Syria Palestina; they forbade Jews to enter Jerusalem, except once a year, and encouraged non-Jews to settle the land. Although the Jews continued to maintain a presence in Palestine, they had become a dispossessed and dispersed people.

After Hadrian came another ruler who had a long reign, Antoninus Pius (A.D. 138–161). He introduced humane and just reforms, in particular, limits on the right of masters to torture their slaves to obtain evidence, and the establishment of the principle that an accused person be considered innocent until proven guilty. During Antoninus' reign the Empire remained peaceful and prosperous.

Marcus Aurelius (A.D. 161–180), the next emperor, was also a philosopher whose *Meditations* was an eloquent expression of Stoic thought. His reign was marked by strife. Roman forces had to fight Parthians, who had seized Armenia, a traditional bone of contention between Rome and Parthia. The Roman legions were victorious in this campaign but brought back from the East an epidemic that decimated the population of the Empire. Marcus Aurelius also had to deal with German incursions into Italy and the Balkan peninsula that were far more serious than any faced by previous emperors. Roman legions gradually repulsed the Germans, but the wars forced Marcus Aurelius to resort to a desperate financial measure—devaluation of the coinage.

From the accession of Nerva in A.D. 96 to the death of Marcus Aurelius in A.D. 180 the Roman Empire was ruled by the "Five Good Emperors." During this period the Empire was at the height of its power and prosperity, and nearly all its peoples benefited. The four emperors preceding Marcus Aurelius had no living sons, so they had resorted to the adoptive system in selecting successors, which served Rome effectively. But Marcus Aurelius chose his own son Commodus to succeed him. With the accession of Commodus, a misfit and a megalomaniac, in A.D. 180, the pax Romana came to an end.

The Time of Happiness

The Romans called the pax Romana the "Time of Happiness." This period was the fulfillment of Rome's mission—the creation of a world-state that provided peace, security, ordered civilization, and the rule of law. Roman legions defended the Rhine-Danube river frontiers from incursions by German tribesmen, held the Parthians at bay in the East, and subdued the few uprisings that occurred. Nerva's adoptive system of selecting emperors provided Rome with internal stability and a succession of emperors with exceptional ability. These Roman emperors did not use military force needlessly, but fought for sensible political goals; generals did not wage war recklessly, but tried to limit casualties, avoid risks, and deter conflicts by a show of force.

Constructive Rule Roman rule was constructive. The Romans built roads, improved harbors, cleared forests, drained swamps, irrigated deserts, and cultivated undeveloped lands. Goods were transported over roads made safe by Roman soldiers and across a Mediterranean Sea swept clear of pirates. A wide variety of goods circulated throughout the Empire: gold, silver, copper, tin, fruit, and salt from Spain; wool, cheese, ham, and glass products from Gaul; iron, hides, and tin from Britain; wine, honey, and marble from Greece and Macedonia; textiles, olive oil, carpets, and jewels from Asia Minor; leather goods, perfume, drugs, and timber from Syria, Judea, and Arabia, and grain from Egypt. From Parthia, China, and India—lands beyond the eastern borders of the Empire— came silk, spices, pearls, cotton, jewels, perfumes, and drugs; from African lands south of the Sahara came gold, ivory, and wild animals. A stable currency, generally not subject to depreciation, contributed to the economic well-being of the Mediterranean world.

Scores of new cities sprang up, and old ones grew larger and wealthier. Although these municipalities had lost their power to wage war and had to bow to the will of the emperors, they retained considerable freedom of action in local matters. Imperial troops guarded against civil wars within the cities and prevented warfare between cities—two traditional weaknesses of city life in the ancient world. The municipalities served as centers of Greco-Roman civilization, which spread to the farthest reaches of the Mediterranean, continuing a process initiated during the Hellenistic Age. Regions of North Africa, Gaul, Britain, and South Germany, hitherto untouched by Hellenism, were brought into the orbit of Greco-Roman civilization. Barriers between Italians and provincials broke down, as Spaniards, Gauls, Africans, and other provincials rose to high positions in the army and in the imperial administration, and even became emperors. Citizenship, generously granted, was finally extended to virtually all free men by an edict of A.D. 212.

Improved Conditions for Both Slaves and Women Conditions improved for those at

The Colosseum. The amphitheatrum Flavianum, which we call the Colosseum, was built during the reign of Vespasian (A.D. 69–79). It could seat some 50,000 spectators who came to watch the gladiator contests and the beast-hunts. (*Anderson/Art Resource*)

the bottom of society, the slaves. At the time of Augustus, slaves may have accounted for a quarter of the population of Italy. But their numbers declined as Rome engaged in fewer wars of conquest. The freeing of slaves also became more common during the Empire. Freed slaves became citizens, with most of the rights and privileges of other citizens; their children suffered no legal disabilities whatsoever.

During the Republic, slaves had been terribly abused; they were often mutilated, thrown to wild beasts, crucified, or burned alive. Several emperors issued decrees protecting slaves from cruel masters. Claudius forbade masters to kill sick slaves; Vespasian forbade masters to sell slaves into prostitution. Domitian prohibited the castration of slaves, and Hadrian barred the execution of slaves without a judicial sentence. The Stoic philosopher Seneca (c. 4 B.C.–A.D. 65) told Romans that slaves were not beasts of burden, but fellow humans: "Kindly remember that he whom you call your slave sprang from the same stock, is smiled upon by the same skies, and like yourself breathes, lives, and dies."[3]

The status of women had been gradually improving during the Republic. In the early days of the Republic, a woman had lived under the absolute authority of her husband. By the time of the Empire, a woman could own property and, if divorced, keep her dowry. A father no longer forced his daughter to marry against her will. Women could make business arrangements and draw up wills without the consent of their husbands. Roman women, unlike their Greek counterparts, were not secluded in their homes, but could come and go as they pleased. Upper-class women of Rome had far greater opportunities for education than did those of Greece.

The history of the Empire, indeed Roman history in general, was filled with talented and influential women. The historian Sallust said that Sempronia, the wife of a consul and the mother of Brutus, one of the assassins of Julius Caesar, was "well-educated in Greek and Latin literature. . . . She could write poetry, crack a joke, and converse at will . . . she was in fact a woman of ready wit and considerable charm."[4] Some wives and mothers became deeply involved in political life. Livia, the dynamic wife of Augustus, was often consulted on important government matters, and during the third century there were times when women controlled the throne.

Law and Order   From Britain to the Arabian Desert, from the Danube River to the sands of the Sahara, some seventy million people with differing native languages, customs, and histories were united by Roman rule into a world community. Unlike those of the Republic, when corruption and exploitation in the provinces were notorious, officials of the Empire felt a high sense of responsibility to preserve the Roman peace, institute Roman justice, and spread Roman civilization.

The achievement of the pax Romana found expression in law. Evolving gradually since the republican conquests, the law of nations (*jus gentium*) came to be applied throughout the Empire, although it never entirely supplanted local law. In the eyes of the law, a citizen was not a Syrian, or a Briton, or a Spaniard, but a Roman. Based on principles thought to be rational, just, and common to all humanity, jus gentium gave recognition to the Stoic conception of natural law.

In creating a stable and orderly political community with an expansive conception of citizenship, Rome resolved the problems posed by the limitations of the city-state— civil war, intercity warfare, and a parochial attitude that divided men into Greek and non-Greek. Rome also brought to fruition an ideal of the Greek city-state—the rational state that protected and promoted civilized life. By constructing a world community that broke down barriers between nations, by preserving and spreading Greco-Roman civilization, and by developing a rational system of law that applied to all humanity, Rome completed the trend toward universalism and cosmopolitanism that had emerged in the Hellenistic Age. The Roman world-state was the classical mind's response to the problem of community posed by the decline of the city-state in the era of Alexander the Great. Aelius Aristides, a second-century rhetorician, glowingly extolled the Roman achievement:

Neither sea nor any intervening distance on land excludes one from citizenship. No distinction is made between Asia and Europe in this respect. Everything lies open to everybody; and no one fit for office or a position of trust is an alien. . . . You have made the word "Roman" apply not to a city but to a universal people. . . . You no longer classify peoples as Greek or barbarian. . . . You have redivided mankind into Romans and non-Romans. . . . Under this classification there are many in each city who are no less fellow citizens of yours than those of their own stock, though some of them have never seen this city.[5]

Roman Culture During the Pax Romana

During the late Roman Republic, Rome had creatively assimilated the Greek achievement (see pages 87–88) and transmitted it to others, thereby extending the orbit of Hellenism. Rome had acquired Greek scientific thought, philosophy, medicine, and geography. Roman writers used Greek models; sharing in the humanist outlook of the Greeks, they valued human intelligence and achievement and expressed themselves in a graceful and eloquent style. Roman cultural life reached its high point during the reign of Augustus, when Rome experienced the golden age of Latin literature.

At the request of Augustus, who wanted a literary epic to glorify the Empire and his role in founding it, Virgil wrote the *Aeneid,* a masterpiece in world literature. The *Aeneid* is a long poem that recounts the tale of Aeneas and the founding of Rome. The first six books describing the wanderings of Aeneas show the influence of Homer's *Odyssey;* the last six books relating the wars in Italy show the *Iliad's* imprint. Intensely patriotic, Virgil ascribed to Rome a divine mission to bring peace and civilized life to the world, and he praised Augustus as a divinely appointed ruler who had fulfilled Rome's mission. The Greeks might be better sculptors, orators, and thinkers, said Virgil, but only the Romans knew how to govern an empire.

For other peoples will, I do not doubt,
still cast their bronze to breathe with softer
    features,
or draw out of the marble living lines,
plead causes better, trace the ways of heaven
with wands and tell the rising constellations;
but yours will be the rulership of nations,
remember, Roman, these will be your arts:
to teach the ways of peace to those you
    conquer,
to spare defeated peoples, to tame the proud.[6]

In his *History of Rome,* the historian Livy (59 B.C.–A.D. 17) also glorified the Roman character, customs, and deeds. He praised Augustus for attempting to revive traditional Roman morality, to which Livy felt a strong attachment. Modern historians criticize Livy for failing to utilize important sources of information in this work, for relying on biased authorities, and for allowing a fierce patriotism to warp his judgment. Although Livy was a lesser historian than Thucydides or Polybius, his work was still a major achievement, particularly in its depiction of the Roman character that helped make Rome great.

Horace (65–8 B.C.) was the son of a freed slave. An outstanding poet, he broadened his education by studying literature and philosophy in Athens, and Greek ideals are reflected in his writings. Horace enjoyed the luxury of country estates, banquets, fine clothes, and courtesans along with the simple pleasures of mountain streams and clear skies. His poetry touched on many themes—the joy of good wine, the value of moderation, and the beauty of friendship. Desiring to blend reason and emotion, Horace urged men to seek pleasurable experiences, but to avoid extremes and to keep desire under rational control.

Unlike Virgil, Livy, or Horace, Ovid (43 B.C.–A.D. 17) did not experience the civil wars during his adult years. Consequently he was less inspired to praise the Augustan peace. His poetry showed a preference for romance and humor, and he is best remembered for his advice to lovers. To the man who wants to win a woman, Ovid advised:

First of all, be quite sure that there isn't a woman who cannot be won, and make up your mind that you will win her. Only you must prepare the ground.

You must play the lover for all you're worth. Tell her how you are pining for her.

Never cease to sing the praises of her face, her hair, her taper fingers, and her dainty foot.

Tears too are a mighty useful resource in the matter of love. They would melt a diamond. Make a point, therefore, of letting your mistress see your face all wet with tears.

Women are things of many moods. You must adapt your treatment to the special case.[7]

The writers who lived after the Augustan age were of a lesser quality than the preceding men, although the historian Tacitus (A.D. 55–c. 118) was an exception. Sympathetic to republican institutions, Tacitus denounced Roman emperors and the imperial system in his *Histories* and *Annals.* In *Germania,* he turned his sights on the habits of the Germanic peoples. He describes the Germans as un-disciplined but heroic and brave, with a strong love of freedom.

The satirist Juvenal (A.D. c. 55–138) attacked evils of Roman society, such as the misconduct of emperors, the haughtiness of the wealthy, the barbaric tastes of commoners, the failures of parents, and the noise, congestion, and poverty of the capital.

. . .

a piece of pot
Falls down on my head, how often a
* broken vessel is shot*
From the upper windows, with what
* force it strikes and dints*
The cobblestones! . . .

. . .

But these aren't your only terrors.
* For you can never restrain*
The criminal element. Lock up your
* house, put bolt and chain*
On your shop, but when all's quiet,
* someone will rob you or he'll*
Be a cutthroat perhaps and do you
* in quickly with cold steel.*[8]

The two most prominent scientists during the Greco-Roman age were Ptolemy, the mathematician, geographer, and astronomer who worked at Alexandria in the second century A.D., and Galen (A.D. c. 130–c. 201), who investigated medicine and anatomy. Ptolemy's thirteen-volume work, *Mathematical Composition*—more commonly known as the *Almagest,* a Greek-Arabic term meaning the *greatest*—summed up antiquity's knowledge of astronomy and became the authoritative text during the Middle Ages. In the Ptolemaic system, a motionless, round earth stood in the center of the universe; the moon, sun, and planets moved about the earth in circles, or in combinations of circles. The Ptolemaic system was built on a faulty premise, as modern astronomy eventually showed; how-ever, it did work, that is, it did provide a model of the universe that adequately ac-counted for most observed phenomena.

As Ptolemy's system dominated astronomy,

so the theories of Galen dominated medicine down to modern times. By dissecting both dead and living animals, Galen attempted a rational investigation of the body's working parts. Although his work contains many er-rors, he made essential contributions to a knowledge of anatomy.

Romans borrowed art forms from other peoples, particularly the Greeks, but they borrowed creatively, transforming and en-hancing their inheritance. Roman portraiture continued trends initiated during the Hel-lenistic Age. Hellenistic art, like Hellenistic philosophy, expressed a heightened aware-ness of the individual. Whereas Hellenic sculpture aimed to depict ideal beauty—the perfect body and face—Hellenistic sculpture captured individual character and expression, often of ordinary people. This movement from idealism to realism was carried forward by Roman sculptors who realistically carved every detail of a subject's face—unruly hair, prominent nose, lines and wrinkles, a jaw that showed weakness or strength. Sculpture also gave expression to the imperial ideal. Statues of emperors conveyed nobility and authority; reliefs commemorating victories glorified Roman might and grandeur.

In architecture, the Romans most creatively transformed the Greek inheritance. The Greek temple was intended to be viewed from the outside; the focus was exclusively on the su-perbly balanced exterior. By using arches, vaults, and domes, the Romans built struc-tures with large, magnificent interiors. The vast interior, massive walls, and overarching dome of the famous Pantheon, a temple built in the early second century during the reign of Hadrian, symbolizes the power and majesty of the Roman world-state.

Despite its many achievements, Roman culture presents a paradox. On the one hand, Roman law and literature evidence high standards of civilization; on the other hand, the Romans institutionalized barbaric prac-tices. The major forms of entertainment both in the Republic and the Empire were chariot races, wild-animal shows, and gladiatorial combat. Chariot races were gala events in

Hadrian's Wall. Between A.D. 122 and 127, the Romans constructed an elaborate defensive system in Britain consisting of a wall of solid masonry and a series of forts. Built on high ground, Hadrian's Wall extended from the estuary of the Solway to that of the Tyne, a distance of 73 miles. (*Photograph by The British Tourist Authority*)

which the most skillful riders and the finest and best-trained stallions raced in an atmosphere of incredible excitement. The charioteers, many of them slaves hoping that victory would bring them freedom, became popular heroes. The rich staked fortunes on the races, and the poor bet their last coins.

The Romans craved brutal spectacles. One form of entertainment pitted wild beasts against each other or against men armed with spears. Another consisted of battles, sometimes to the death, between highly trained gladiators. The gladiators, mainly slaves and condemned criminals, learned their craft at schools run by professional trainers. Some gladiators entered the arena armed with a sword, others with a trident and a net. If the spectators were displeased with a losing gladiator's performance, they would call for his execution.

Over the centuries, these spectacles grew more bizarre and brutal. Hundreds of tigers were set against elephants and bulls; wild bulls tore apart men dressed in animal skins; women battled in the arena; dwarfs fought each other. During the reign of Emperor Titus, five thousand beasts were slaughtered in one day. In fact, much of the African trade was devoted to supplying the animals for these contests.

Signs of Trouble

The pax Romana was one of the finest periods in world history. But even during the Time of Happiness, signs of trouble appeared that would grow to crisis proportions in the third century.

Internal Unrest

The Empire's internal stability was always subject to question. Were the economic foundations of the Empire strong and elastic enough to endure hard blows? Could the Roman Empire retain the loyalty of so many diverse nationalities, each with its own religious and cultural traditions? And were the mass of people committed to the values of Greco-Roman civilization, or would they withdraw their allegiance and revert to their native traditions if imperial authority weakened?

During the pax Romana, dissident elements did come forth, particularly in Gaul, Judea, and Egypt. The Jews fought two terrible and futile wars to try to liberate their land from Roman rule. Separatist movements in Gaul were also crushed by Roman forces. To provide free bread for Rome's poor, Roman emperors exploited the Egyptian peasantry. Weighed down by forced labor, heavy taxes, requisitions, and confiscations, Egyptian peasants frequently sought to escape from farmwork.

The unrest in Egypt, Gaul, and Judea demonstrated that not all people at all times welcomed the grand majesty of the Roman peace, that localist and separatist tendencies persisted in a universal empire. In the centuries that followed, as Rome staggered under the weight of economic, political, and military difficulties, these native loyalties reasserted themselves. Increasingly the masses and even the Romanized elite of the cities withdrew their support from the Roman world-state.

Social and Economic Weaknesses

A healthy world-state required empirewide trade to serve as an economic base for political unity, expanding agricultural production to feed the cities, and growing internal mass markets to stimulate industrial production. But the economy of the Empire during the pax Romana had serious defects. The means of communication and transportation were slow, which hindered long-distance commerce. Roman roads, built for military rather than commercial purposes, were often too narrow for large carts and in places were too steep for any vehicles. Many nobles, considering it unworthy for a gentleman to engage in business, chose to squander their wealth rather than invest it in commercial or industrial enterprises. Thus deprived of the stimulus of capital investment, the economy could not expand.

Limited employment opportunities resulted from the Greco-Roman civilization's failure to improve its technology substantially. Scarce employment left the masses with little purchasing power; this, in turn, adversely affected business and industry. Many unemployed inhabitants of Italian towns lived on free or cheap grain provided by the state. To feed this unemployed proletariat, the government kept the price of grain artificially low, discouraging farmers from expanding grain production and forcing many of them to seek other livelihoods. As more farmers left the countryside, the towns became swollen with an impoverished proletariat, and rural areas eventually faced a serious shortage of laborers.

Ultimately, only a small portion of the population—the middle and upper classes of the cities: landlords, merchants, and administrators—reaped the benefits of the Roman peace. They basked in luxury, leisure, and culture. The urban poor, on the other hand, shared little in the political and cultural life of the city and derived none of the economic gains. The privileged class bought off the urban poor with bread and circuses, but occasionally mass discontent expressed itself in mob violence. Outside the cities, the peasantry, still the great bulk of the population, was exploited to provide cheap food for the city dwellers. Between town and countryside, an enormous cultural gap existed. In reality, the cities were small islands of high culture surrounded by a sea of peasant barbarism.

Such a parasitical, exploitative, and elitist social system might function in periods of peace and tranquility, but could it survive crises? Would the impoverished people of town and country—the overwhelming majority of the population—remain loyal to a state whose benefits barely extended to them and whose sophisticated culture, which they hardly comprehended, virtually excluded them?

Cultural Stagnation and Transformation

Perhaps the most dangerous sign for the future was the spiritual paralysis that crept over the ordered world of pax Romana. A weary and sterile Hellenism underlay the Roman peace. The ancient world was undergoing a transformation of values that foreshadowed the end of Greco-Roman civilization.

During the second century A.D., Greco-Roman civilization lost its creative energies, and the values of classical humanism were challenged by mythic-religious movements. No longer regarding reason as a satisfying guide to life, the educated elite subordinated their intellect to feelings and imagination. People no longer found the affairs of this world to have purpose; they placed their hope in life after death. The Roman world was undergoing a religious revolution and was seeking a new vision of the divine.

The application of reason to nature and society, as we have seen, was the great achievement of the Greek mind. But, despite its many triumphs, Greek rationalism never entirely subdued the mythic-religious mentality, which draws its strength from human emotion. The masses of peasants and slaves remained attracted to religious forms. Ritual, mystery, magic, and ecstasy never lost their hold on the ancient world—nor, indeed, have they in our own scientific and technological society. During the Hellenistic Age the tide of rationalism gradually receded, and the nonrational, an ever-present undercurrent, showed renewed vigor. This resurgence of the mythical mentality could be seen in the popularity of the occult, magic, alchemy, and astrology. Feeling themselves controlled by heavenly powers, burdened by danger and emotional stress, and fearing fate as fixed in the stars, people turned for deliverance to magicians, astrologers, and exorcists.

They also became devotees of the many Eastern religious cults that promised personal salvation. More and more people felt that the good life could not be achieved by individuals through their own efforts; they needed outside help. Philosophers eventually sought escape from this world through union with a divine presence greater than human power. Increasingly the masses, and then even the educated elite, came to believe that the good life could not be found on earth but only in a world beyond the grave. Believing themselves to be isolated souls wandering aimlessly in a social desert, people sought refuge in religion. Reason had been found wanting; the time for faith and salvation was at hand.

What brought about the resurgence of the mythical mentality? We have seen that the city-state provided individuals with a sense of belonging and purpose. They found self-fulfillment and self-realization as citizens. The decline of the city-state and its absorption first into Hellenistic kingdoms and later into the Roman Empire left something vital missing in people's lives. Gone were the exhilaration of city-state politics and the sense of community that the city-state had provided. The Roman Empire had imposed peace and stability, but it could not alleviate the feelings of loneliness, anxiety, impotence, alienation, and boredom that had been gaining ground in the Mediterranean world since the fourth century B.C.

As Roman emperors became increasingly autocratic, opportunities for political activity decreased precipitously, and interest in public affairs waned. More than ever before, individuals felt that they had no personal control over their own lives. Their political significance lost, the psychological security provided by the city gone, individuals felt abandoned and isolated. The Roman world-state, vast, remote, and autocratic, could never provide that sense of community, that air of excitement, that feeling of belonging to something larger than oneself, that had derived from an individual's attachment to a city. Nothing replaced the old ideal of civic liberty and civic participation that had generated cultural creativity.

A spiritual malaise had descended upon the Greco-Roman world. Among the upper classes, the philosophic and scientific spirit withered; rational and secular values were in retreat. Deprived of the excitement of politics and bored by idleness and pleasure, the best minds, says historian M. I. Rostovtzeff,

lost faith in the power of reason. . . . Creative genius dwindled; science repeated its previous results. The textbook took the place of research; no new artistic discoveries were made, but echoes of the past were heard . . . [writers] amuse[d] the mind but [were] incapable of elevating and inspiring it.[9]

The Spread of Mystery Religions

The proliferation of oriental mystery religions was a clear expression of this transformation of classical values. During the Hellenistic era, slaves, merchants, and soldiers brought many

Sacred Relief: Mithras Sacrifices a Bull. The spread and popularity of mystery religions during the Empire was one sign of spiritual malaise. Mithras, god of the soldiers, and his cult were widespread. Of all the mystery religions, Mithraism was Christianity's most serious rival. (*Cincinnati Art Museum, Gift of Mr. and Mrs. Fletcher E. Nyce, 1968*)

religious cults westward from Persia, Babylon, Syria, Egypt, and Asia Minor. The various mystery cults possessed many common features. Their rites were secret, revealed only to members. Converts underwent initiation rites and were bound by oath to secrecy. The initiates, in a state of rapture, attempted to unite with the deity after first purifying themselves through baptism (sometimes with the blood of a bull), fasting, having their heads shaved, or drinking from a sacred vessel. Communion was achieved by donning the god's robe, eating a sacred meal, or visiting the god's sanctuary. This sacramental drama propelled initiates through an intense mystical experience of exaltation and rebirth; cultists were certain that their particular savior-god would protect them from misfortune and ensure their soul's immortality.

Of special significance was the cult of Mithras, which had certain parallels with early Christianity and was its principal competi-tor. Originating in Persia, Mithraism spread westward into the Roman Empire. Because it stressed respect for the masculine virtues of bravery and camaraderie, it became particularly popular with the army. The god Mithras, whose birthdate was celebrated on December 25, had as his mission the rescuing of humanity from evil. He was said to demand high standards of morality, to judge souls after death, and to grant eternal life to his faithful followers.

The popularity of magic and mystery demonstrates that many people in Roman society either did not comprehend or had lost faith in the rational and secular values of classical humanism. Religion proved more comforting to the spirit. People felt that the gods could provide what reason, natural law, and world affairs could not: a sure way of overcoming life's misfortunes and discouragements, a guarantee of immortality, a sense of belonging to a community of brethren who cared, an exciting outlet for bottled-up emotions, and a sedative for anxiety at a time when dissatisfaction with the human condition showed itself in all phases of society and life.

Spiritualization of Philosophy

The religious orientation also found expression in philosophy, which demonstrated attitudes markedly at odds with classical humanism. These attitudes, commonly associated with religion, included indifference to the world, withdrawal, and pessimism about the earthly state. From trying to understand nature and individuals' relationships to one another, the philosophers more and more aspired for communion with a higher reality. Like the mystery religions, philosophy reached for something beyond this world in order to comfort the individual.

Stoicism was the principal philosophy of the pax Romana, and its leading exponents were Seneca, Epictetus (A.D. c. 60–c. 117), and Marcus Aurelius. Perpetuating the rational tradition of Greek philosophy, Rome's early Stoics saw the universe as governed by reason and esteemed the human intellect. Like Socrates, they sought the highest good in this world, not in an afterlife, and envisioned no power above human reason. Moral values were obtained from reason alone. The individual was self-sufficient, and depended entirely on rational faculties for knowing and doing good.

But with time, Roman Stoics increasingly viewed philosophy as a means of gaining spiritual consolation and inner strength to endure life's misfortunes. Their thought revealed a sense of weariness with the world and of the sadness of life. Many such tired souls would be attracted by Christianity. In urging compassion, mercy, and forgiveness, Seneca revealed a Christian-like concern for his fellows.

The Stoic conception of God underwent a gradual transformation that reflected the religious yearnings of the times. For the early Stoics, God was an intellectual necessity, an impersonal principle that gave order to the universe. For later Roman Stoics, God had become a moral necessity that comforted and reassured people. While maintaining the traditional Stoic belief that the individual can attain virtue through unaided reason, Epictetus and Marcus Aurelius came close to seeking God's help to live properly. The gap between Greek philosophy and Christianity was narrowing. Marcus Aurelius, the last of the great Stoics, maintained that reason, the noblest part of human nature, came from universal Reason or God; that by heeding the promptings of reason, by directing one's actions according to right reason, one obeyed God. This religious turn in Stoicism was clearly reflected in the thought of Epictetus, who wrote concerning the person who has recognized God in and through reason,

. . . why should not such a man call himself a citizen of the universe? Why should he not call himself a son of God? And why shall he fear anything that happens among men? . . . but to have God as our maker, and father, and guardian— shall this not suffice to deliver us from griefs and fears?[10]

Despite its spiritual leanings, Stoicism did not seek refuge in life after death, did not conceive of God as a personal savior with whom a person enters into communion, and did not turn to revelation as a guide to life. But in Neo-Platonism, which replaced Stoicism as the dominant school of philosophy in the Late Roman Empire, religious yearnings were transformed into a religious system that transcended reason.

Plotinus (A.D. c. 205–c. 270), the most influential spokesman of Neo-Platonism, went far beyond Marcus Aurelius' natural religion; in aspiring to the ecstatic union of the soul with God, he subordinated philosophy to mysticism. Plato's philosophy, we have seen, contained both a major and a minor key. The major key stressed a rational interpretation of the human community and called for reforming the polis on the basis of knowledge, whereas the minor key urged the soul to rise to a higher world of reality. Although Plotinus retained Platonic rationalism (he viewed the individual as a reasoning being and used rational argument to explain his religious orientation), he was intrigued by Plato's otherworldliness.

What Plotinus desired was union with the One or the Good, sometimes called God—the source of all existence. Plotinus felt that the intellect could neither describe nor understand the One, which transcended all knowing, and that joining with the One required a mystical leap, a purification of the soul so that it could return to its true eternal home. For Plotinus, philosophy became a religious experience, a contemplation of the eternal. In comparison to this union with the divine One, of what value was knowledge of the sensible world or a concern for human affairs? For Plotinus this world was a sea of tears and troubles from which the individual yearned to escape. Reality was not in this world, but beyond it, and the principal goal of life was not comprehension of the natural world nor the fulfillment of human potential nor the betterment of the human community, but knowledge of the One. Thus, his philosophy broke with the essential meaning of classical humanism.

Plotinus' philosophy, concludes historian of philosophy W. T. Stace, "is founded upon . . . the despair of reason." It seeks to reach the Absolute not through reason but through "spiritual intoxication." This marks the end of philosophy in the ancient world.

For philosophy is founded upon reason. It is the effort to comprehend, to understand, to grasp the reality of things intellectually. Therefore it cannot admit anything higher than reason. To exalt intuition, ecstasy, or rapture, above thought—this is the death of philosophy. . . . In Neo-Platonism, therefore, ancient philosophy commits suicide. This is the end. The place of philosophy is taken henceforth by religion.[11]

By the Late Roman Empire, mystery religions intoxicated the masses, and mystical philosophy beguiled the educated elite. Clas-

sical civilization was undergoing a transformation. Philosophy had become subordinate to religious belief; secular values seemed inferior to religious experience. The earthly city had raised its eyes toward heaven. The culture of the Roman world was moving in a direction in which the quest for the divine was to predominate over all human enterprises.

The Decline of Rome

Third-Century Crisis

At the death of Marcus Aurelius in A.D. 180 the Empire was politically stable, economically prosperous, and militarily secure. In the third century, the ordered civilization of the pax Romana ended. Several elements caused this disruption. The Roman Empire was plunged into military anarchy, was raided by Germanic tribes, and was burdened by economic dislocations. In addition, Eastern religions that undermined the rational foundations of Greco-Roman civilization pervaded the Roman world.

The degeneration of the army was a prime reason for the third-century crisis. During the great peace, the army had remained an excellent fighting force, renowned for its discipline, organization, and loyalty. In the third century A.D., however, there was a marked deterioration in the quality of Roman soldiers. Lacking loyalty to Rome and greedy for spoils, soldiers used their weapons to prey on civilians and to make and unmake emperors. From A.D. 235 to 285, military mutiny and civil war raged, and many emperors were assassinated. The once stalwart army neglected its duty of defending the borders and disrupted the internal life of the Empire.

Perhaps this change in attitude can be explained by liberal granting of citizenship. In A.D. 212, citizenship was extended to virtually all freeborn inhabitants of the Empire. Previously, army recruits had been drawn from provincials who were attracted by the promise of citizenship and its advantages. These recruits generally were men of a high caliber

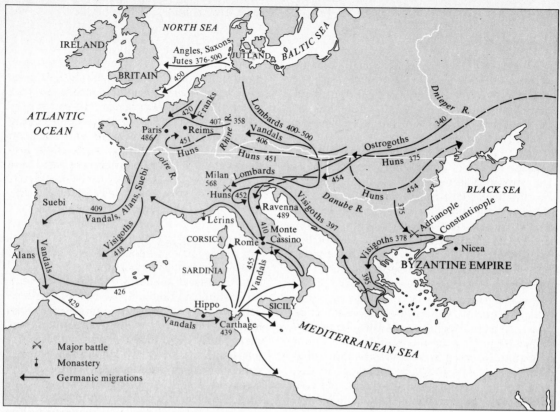

Map 7.2 Incursions and Migrations, c. A.D. 300–500

who were interested in bettering themselves and their families' lot. With citizenship no longer an inducement for enlistment, says Edward T. Salmon,

recruits were now only too likely to be drawn from the lowest and most primitive elements . . . men of the rough and reckless type, who were joining the army chiefly in order to get weapons in their hands with which they would be able to extort for themselves an even greater share of the Empire's collective wealth . . . men who knew little and cared less about Rome's mission and who, when not preying upon the civilians, had not the slightest compunction about preying upon one another.[12]

Taking advantage of the military anarchy, Germanic tribesmen crossed the Rhine-Danube frontier to loot and destroy. The Goths raided coastal cities of Asia Minor and Greece and even burned much of Athens.

In the west, other Germanic tribes penetrated Gaul, Spain, and Italy, and engaged the Romans in a full-scale battle near Milan. At the same time that the European defense lines were being breached, a reborn Persian Empire, led by the Sassanid Dynasty, attacked and for a while conquered Roman lands in the east. Some sections of the Empire, notably in Gaul, attempted to break away; these moves reflected an assertion of local patriotism over Roman universalism. The "city of mankind" was crumbling.

These eruptions had severe economic repercussions. Cities were pillaged and destroyed, farmlands ruined, and trade disrupted. To obtain funds and supplies for the military, emperors confiscated goods, exacted forced labor, and debased the coinage by minting more currency without an increase in the supply of precious metal. These measures led many citizens to withdraw their loyalty from Rome and brought ruin to the middle class. As inflation and devaluation cheapened the value of money, some parts of the Empire turned to barter as a medium of exchange.

Invasions, civil war, rising prices, a debased coinage, declining agricultural production, disrupted transportation, and the excessive demands of the state caused economic havoc and famine in the cities. The urban centers of the ancient world, creators and disseminators of high civilization, were caught in a rhythm of breakdown. As cities decayed, the center of life gravitated back to the countryside. Large, fortified estates owned by the emperor or wealthy aristocrats provided refuge for the uprooted and destitute of town and country.

The majority of citizens had no deep investment in urban life. The Roman army, consisting principally of peasants and barbarian volunteers, felt no deep commitment to the cities and their culture either. In the countryside, people were not much affected by classical civilization, which had made little headway against native languages, religions, and manners. Even the emperors, traditional guardians of the cities, began to seek their support in the food-producing countryside and in the peasant-dominated army.

During the third century A.D., the spiritual crisis intensified as the rational foundations of Greco-Roman civilization eroded further. People turned increasingly to the mystery cults, which offered relief from earthly misery, a sense of belonging, and a promise of immortality. In philosophy, creative energies were directed not toward a greater understanding of nature or society, but toward a knowledge of God, which philosophers were teaching to be the path to happiness. Hellenism was breaking down.

Diocletian and Constantine: The Regimented State

The emperors Diocletian (A.D. 285–305) and Constantine (A.D. 306–337) tried to contain the awesome forces of disintegration. At a time when agricultural production was steadily declining, they had to feed the city poor and an army of 400,000 strung out over the Empire. They also had to prevent renewed outbreaks of military anarchy and to defend the borders against barbarian attacks. Their solution was to tighten the reins of government and to squeeze more taxes and requisitions out of the citizens. In the process they transformed Rome into a bureaucratic, regimented, and militarized state.

Ruling like an oriental despot, Diocletian completed a trend that had been developing for generations. He imitated the pomp of the East and wore magnificent robes and jewels; he demanded that subjects prostrate themselves in his presence. Cities lost their traditional right of local self-government, which consolidated a trend started earlier. To ensure continuous production of food and goods, as well as the collection of taxes, the state forced unskilled workers and artisans to hold their jobs for life and to pass them on to their children. For the same reasons, peasants were turned into virtual serfs, bound to the land that they cultivated. An army of government agents was formed to hunt down peasants who fled the land to escape crushing taxes and poverty.

Also frozen into their positions were city officials (*curiales*). They often found it necessary to furnish from their own pockets the difference between the state's tax demands and the amount that they could collect from an already overtaxed population. This system of a hereditary class of tax collectors and of crippling taxes to pay for a vastly expanded bureaucracy and military establishment enfeebled urban trade and industry. These conditions killed the civic spirit of townsmen, who desperately sought escape. By overburdening urban dwellers with taxes and regulations, Diocletian and Constantine shattered the vitality of city life on which Roman prosperity and civilization depended.

Rome was governed by an oriental despotism, a highly centralized monarchy regimenting the lives of its subjects. Whereas Augustus had upheld the classical ideal that the commonwealth was a means of fostering the good life for the individual, Diocletian adopted the oriental attitude that the individual lives for the state. The absolutism inherent in the concept of the Principate had completely and irrevocably asserted its ascendancy over the republican elements that had endured in Augustus's settlement.

To guard against military insurrection, Diocletian appointed a loyal general to govern the western provinces of the Empire, while he ruled the East; although both emperors bore the title Augustus, Diocletian remained superior. By building a new imperial capital, Constantinople, at the Bosporus, a strait where Asia meets Europe, Constantine furthered this trend of dividing the Empire into eastern and western halves.

Barbarian Invasions

By imposing some order on what had been approaching chaos, Diocletian and Constantine prevented the Empire from collapsing. Rome had been given a reprieve. A long period of peace might have brought economic recovery, but misfortune continued to burden Rome and the process of breakdown and disintegration resumed. In the last part of the fourth century the problem of guarding the frontier grew more acute.

The Huns, a savage Mongol people from central Asia, swept across the plains of Russia and put pressure on the Visigoths, a Germanic tribe that had migrated into southeastern Europe. Terrified of the Huns, the Goths sought refuge within the Roman Empire. Hoping to increase his manpower and unable to stop the panic-stricken Germans, Emperor Valens permitted them to cross the Danube frontier. But two years later, in 378, the Goths and the Romans fought each other in a historic battle at Adrianople. The barbarian calvary defeated the Roman legions, an indication that Rome could no longer defend its borders. The Goths were in the Empire to stay.

Other Germanic tribes increased their pressure on the Empire's borders. Attracted by the warmer climate, riches, and advanced civilization of the Roman Empire, they also were looking for new lands to farm and were frightened by the advent of the Huns. The borders finally collapsed at the end of 406, as Vandals, Alans, Suebi, and other tribes joined the Goths in devastating and overrunning the Empire's western provinces. In 410, the Visigoths sacked Rome.

Economic conditions continued to deteriorate. Cities in Britain, Gaul, Germany, and Spain lay abandoned. Other metropolises saw their populations dwindle and production stagnate. The great network of Roman roads was not maintained, and trade in the West almost disappeared or passed into the hands of Greeks, Syrians, and Jews from the east.

In 451 Attila (c. 406–453), called "the Scourge of God," led his Huns into Gaul, where he was defeated by a coalition of Germans and the remnants of the Roman army. He died two years later, having come within a hairsbreadth of turning Europe into a province of a Mongolian empire. But Rome's misfortunes persisted. In 455, Rome was again sacked, this time by the Vandals. Additional regions fell under the control of Germanic chieftains. Germanic soldiers in the pay of Rome gained control of the government and dictated the choice of emperor. In 476, German officers overthrew the Roman Emperor Romulus and placed a German on the throne. This act is traditionally regarded as the end of the Roman Empire in the west.

The Underlying Reasons for Decline

What were the underlying causes for the decline and fall of the Roman Empire in the west? Surely no other question has intrigued the historical imagination more than this one. Implicit in the answers suggested by historians and philosophers is a concern for their own civilization. Will it suffer the same fate as Rome?

To analyze so monumental a development as the fall of Rome, some preliminary observations are necessary. First, the fall of Rome

Arch of Constantine. Constantine managed to bring the Empire under his control for almost a quarter of a century. He tightened the screws of regimentation and built a capital at Constantinople (Byzantium); he tolerated and later was converted to Christianity. (*ENIT/Italian Government Travel Office*)

was a process lasting hundreds of years; it was not a single event that occurred in A.D. 476. Second, only the western half of the Empire fell. The eastern half—wealthier, more populous, less afflicted with civil wars, and less exposed to barbarian invasions—survived as the Byzantine Empire until the middle of the fifteenth century. Third, no single explanation suffices to account for Rome's decline; multiple forces operated concurrently to bring about the fall.

The Role of the Barbarians Was Rome's fall suicide or murder? Did the barbarians walk over a corpse, or did they contribute sub-stantially to Rome's decline and fall? Undoubtedly an Empire enfeebled by internal rot succumbed to the barbarian invasions. Perhaps a stronger Rome might have secured its borders, as it had done during the pax Romana. But the barbarian attacks occurred mainly in the west, and the western Empire, poorer and less populated than the eastern portion, reeled under these increasingly more numerous and more severe barbarian on-slaughts. Also, the pressures exerted by the barbarians along an immense frontier aggra-vated Rome's internal problems. The bar-barian attacks left border regions impover-ished and depopulated. The Empire imposed high taxes and labor services on its citizens in order to strengthen the armed forces, causing the overburdened middle and lower classes to hate the imperial government that took so much from them.

Spiritual Considerations The classical mentality, once brimming with confidence about the potentialities of the individual and the power of the intellect, suffered a failure of nerve. The urban upper class, upon whom the responsibility for preserving cosmopolitan Greco-Roman culture traditionally rested, became dissolute and apathetic, no longer taking an interest in public life. The aristocrats secluded themselves behind the walls of their fortified country estates; many did not lift a finger to help the Empire. The townsmen demonstrated their disenchantment by avoiding public service and by rarely organizing resistance forces against the barbarian invaders. The great bulk of the Roman citizenry, apathetic and indifferent, simply gave up, despite the fact that they overwhelmingly outnumbered the barbarian hordes.

Political and Military Considerations The Roman government itself contributed to this spiritual malaise through its increasingly autocratic tendencies, which culminated in the regimented rule of Diocletian and Constantine. The insatiable demands and regulations of the state in the Late Roman Empire sapped the initiative and civic spirit of its citizens. The ruined middle and lower classes withdrew their loyalty. For many the state had become the enemy, and its administration was hated and feared more than the barbarians.

Related to the political decline was the inability of the government to control ambitious military commanders who used their troops to seize the throne and its immense power. The internal security and stability of the Empire was thus constantly imperiled by army leaders more concerned with grandiose personal dreams than with defending the Empire's borders. These civil wars imposed terrible financial burdens on the Empire and gravely weakened the frontier defenses—an invitation to the Germans to increase their pressure.

The deteriorated quality of Roman soldiers was another reason why Rome failed to defend its borders, even though the German invaders were fewer numerically. During the third century the army consisted predominantly of the provincial peasantry. These nonurban, non-Italian, semicivilized soldiers, often the dregs of society, were not committed to Greco-Roman civilization. They had little comprehension of Rome's mission, and at times used their power to attack the cities and towns. The emperors also recruited large numbers of barbarians into the army to fill depleted ranks. Ultimately, the army consisted predominantly of barbarians, as both legionnaires and officers. Although these Germans made brave soldiers, they too had little loyalty to Greco-Roman civilization and to the Roman state. This deterioration of the Roman army occurred because many young citizens evaded conscription. No longer imbued with patriotism, they considered military service a servitude to be shunned.

Economic Considerations Among the economic causes contributing to the decline of the Roman Empire in the west were population decline, the failure to achieve a breakthrough in technology, the heavy burden of taxation, and the economic decentralization that abetted political decentralization.

The population of the Empire may have shrunk from 70 million during the pax Romana to 50 million in the Late Roman Empire. The epidemic during the reign of Marcus Aurelius, which might have been the bubonic plague, lasted fifteen years. A second plague struck the Empire during the reign of Commodus, Marcus Aurelius' son. Other plagues in the middle of the third century and constant warfare further reduced the population. The birthrate did not rise to compensate for these losses. Worsening economic conditions and a lack of hope in the future apparently discouraged people from increasing the sizes of their families.

The decline in population adversely affected the Empire in at least three important ways. At the same time that the population was declining, the costs of running the Empire were spiraling, which created a terrible burden for taxpayers. Second, fewer workers were available for agriculture, the most important industry of the Empire. Third, population decline reduced the manpower available for the army, forcing emperors to permit the establishment of Germanic colonies within the Empire's borders to serve as feeders for the army. This situation led to the barbarization of the army.

The Roman peace brought stability but it failed to discover new and better ways of producing goods and agricultural products. To be sure, some advances in technology did take place during the Hellenistic Age and the pax Romana: rotary mills for grain, screw-presses, and improvements in glass-blowing and field-drainage methods. But the high intellectual culture of Greece and Rome rested on a meager economic and technological foundation. The widespread use of slave labor probably precluded a breakthrough in technology, for slaves had little incentive to invent more efficient ways of producing. The upper classes, identifying manual labor with slavery, would not condescend to engage in the mechanical arts. This failure to improve the level of technology limited employment opportunities for the masses. Because the masses could not increase their purchasing power, business and industry were without a mass internal market that might have acted as a continual stimulus for the accumulation of capital and for economic expansion.

Instead of expanding industry and trade, towns maintained their wealth by exploiting the countryside. The Roman cities were centers of civilized life and opulence, but they lacked industries. They spent, but they did not produce. The towns were dominated by landlords whose estates lay beyond the city and whose income derived from corn, oil, and wine. Manufacturing was rudimentary, confined essentially to textiles, pottery, furniture, and glassware. The methods of production were simple, the market limited, the cost of transportation high, and agricultural productivity low—the labor of perhaps nineteen peasants was required to support one townsman. Such a fundamentally unhealthy economy could not weather the dislocations caused by uninterrupted warfare and the demands of a mushrooming bureaucracy and military.

With the barbarians pressing on the borders, the increased military expenditures overstrained the Empire's resources. To pay for the food, uniforms, arms, and armor of the soldiers, taxes rose, growing too heavy for peasants and townsmen. The state also requisitioned wood and grain and demanded that citizens maintain roads and bridges. The government often resorted to force to collect taxes and exact services. Crushed by these demands, many peasants simply abandoned their farms and sought the protection of large landowners, or turned to banditry.

Making the situation worse was the administrative separation of the Empire into east and west undertaken by Diocletian and Constantine. As a result, western emperors could no longer rely on financial aid from the wealthier east to finance the defense of the borders. Slow communications and costly transport continued to hamper the economic unity—an empirewide trade that was required for Roman political unity. Meanwhile, industries gravitated outward to search for new markets in the frontier army camps and for new sources of slaves in border regions. This dispersion further weakened the bonds of economic unity. Gradually, trade became less international and more local, and provincial regions grew more self-sufficient. The strife of the third century intensified the drift toward economic self-sufficiency in the provinces, a condition that promoted localism and separatism.

Contributing to the economic decentralization was the growth of industries on lat-

Chronology 7.1 The Roman Empire

27 B.C.	Octavian assumes the title *Augustus* and becomes, in effect, the first Roman emperor; start of the pax Romana
14 B.C.	The death of Augustus; Tiberius gains the throne
A.D. 66–70	The Jewish revolt; Romans capture Jerusalem and destroy the Second Temple
79	Eruption of Mount Vesuvius and destruction of Pompeii and Herculaneum
132–135	Hadrian crushes another revolt by the Hebrews
180	Marcus Aurelius dies; the end of the pax Romana
212	Roman citizenship is granted to virtually all free inhabitants of Roman provinces
235–285	Military anarchy; attacks by barbarians
285–305	Diocletian tries to deal with the crisis by creating a regimented state
378	Battle of Adrianople; the Goths defeat the Roman legions
406	Borders collapse, and barbarians pour into the Empire
410	Rome is sacked by Visigoths
455	Rome is sacked by Vandals
476	The end of the Roman Empire in the West

ifundia, the large fortified estates owned by wealthy aristocrats. Producing exclusively for the local market, these estates contributed to the impoverishment of urban centers by reducing the number of customers available to buy goods made in the cities. As life grew more desperate, urban craftsmen and small farmers sought the protection of these large landlords, whose estates grew in size and importance. The growth of latifundia was accompanied by the decline of cities and the transformation of independent peasants into virtual serfs.

These great estates were also new centers of political power that the imperial government could not curb. A new society was taking shape in the Late Roman Empire. The center of gravity had shifted from the city to the landed estate, from the imperial bureaucrats to the local aristocrats. These developments epitomized the decay of ancient civilization and presaged the Middle Ages.

Notes

1. Tacitus, *The Annals of Imperial Rome*, trans. by Michael Grant (Baltimore: Penguin Books, 1959), I. 3, p. 31.

2. Cited in David Magie, *Roman Rule in Asia Minor* (Princeton, N.J.: Princeton University Press, 1950), p. 490.

3. Seneca, *Epistles*, trans. by Richard M. Grummere (Cambridge, Mass.: Harvard University Press, Loeb Classical Library, 1917), Epistle 47, p. 307.

4. Sallust, *The Conspiracy of Cataline*, trans. by S. A. Handford (Baltimore: Penguin Books, 1963), p. 193.

5. Excerpted in Naphtali Lewis and Meyer Reinhold, eds., *Roman Civilization Sourcebook*, vol. 2, *The Empire* (New York: Harper Torch Books, 1966), p. 136.

6. *The Aeneid of Virgil*, trans. by Allen Mandelbaum (Berkeley: University of California Press, 1971), pp. 160–161.

7. *The Art of Love and Other Love Books of Ovid* (New York: Grosset & Dunlap, The Universal Library, 1959), pp. 117–118, 130–132, 135.

8. *The Satires of Juvenal*, trans. by Hubert Creekmore (New York: Mentor Books, 1963), ll. 242–248, 269–272, 302–305, pp. 58–61.

9. M. I. Rostovtzeff, *Rome* (New York: Oxford University Press, 1960), p. 322.

10. Epictetus, *The Discourses*, trans. by W. A. Oldfather (Cambridge, Mass.: Harvard University Press, Loeb Classical Library, 1925), p. 65.

11. W. T. Stace, *A Critical History of Greek Philosophy* (London: Macmillan, 1924), p. 377.

12. Excerpted in Mortimer Chambers, ed., *The Fall of Rome* (New York: Holt, Rinehart & Winston, 1963), pp. 45–46.

Suggested Reading

Carcopino, Jerome, *Daily Life in Ancient Rome* (1940). All phases of Roman society during the second century.

Chambers, Mortimer, ed., *The Fall of Rome* (1963). A valuable collection of readings.

Clarke, M. L., *The Roman Mind* (1968). Studies in the history of thought from Cicero to Marcus Aurelius.

Jones, A. H. M., *Augustus* (1970). An authoritative discussion of the Augustan settlement.

Katz, Solomon, *The Decline of Rome* (1955). A helpful introduction.

Lewis, Naphtali, and Meyer Reinhold, *Roman Civilization*, vol. 2 (1966). Primary sources.

MacMullen, Ramsay, *Constantine* (1969). An account of the man and his times.

Mazzarino, Santo, *The End of the Ancient World* (1966). Describes how many thinkers have viewed the idea of the death of Rome and offers a modern interpretation.

Paoli, R. E., *Rome: Its People, Life and Customs* (1963). Surveys all phases of Roman society—women, slavery, clothing, industry, law, medicine, and so on.

Rostovtzeff, Michael, *Rome* (1960). The concluding chapters offer a stimulating and controversial interpretation for the fall of the Empire.

Rowell, H. T., *Rome in the Augustan Age* (1962). The city and its people in the era of Augustus.

Starr, C. G., *Civilization and the Caesars* (1965). A fine interpretive essay on the collapse of classical humanism and the spread of religion in the four centuries from Cicero to Augustine.

Wheeler, Mortimer, Sir, *Roman Art and Architecture* (1964). An interpretive study, filled with insight.

White, Lynn, ed., *The Transformation of the Roman World* (1973). A useful collection of essays on the transformation of the ancient world and the emergence of the Middle Ages.

Review Questions

1. In what ways was Augustus a creative statesman?

2. The Roman world state completed the trend toward cosmopolitanism and universalism that had emerged during the Hellenistic Age. Discuss this statement.

3. Why is the pax Romana regarded as one of the finest periods in world history?

4. Describe the achievements of some Roman writers and scientists during the pax Romana.

5. What signs of trouble existed during the pax Romana?

6. Why were people attracted to mystery religions?

7. How was classical humanism in retreat in the second and third centuries A.D.?

8. Describe the crisis that afflicted Rome in the third century.

9. How did Diocletian and Constantine try to deal with the Empire's crisis?

10. What was the significance of the westward movement of the Huns? What effect did the Battle of Adrianople have on the Empire?

11. What role did the barbarians play in the decline of Rome?

12. Analyze the spiritual, military, political, and economic reasons for the decline of the Roman Empire.

13. Could creative statesmanship have saved the Roman Empire? Explain why it might or might not have saved the Empire.

8

*Early Christianity:
A World Religion*

*A*s confidence in human reason and hope for happiness in this world waned in the last centuries of the Roman Empire, a new outlook began to take hold. Evident in philosophy and in the popularity of oriental religions, this viewpoint stressed escape from an oppressive world and communion with a higher reality. Christianity evolved and expanded within this setting of declining classicism and heightening otherworldliness. As one response to a declining Hellenism, Christianity offered a spiritually disillusioned Greco-Roman world a reason for living—the hope of personal immortality. The triumph of Christianity marked a break with classical antiquity and a new stage in the evolution of the West, for there was a fundamental difference between the Hellenic and the Christian concepts of God, the individual, and the purpose of life.

Origins of Christianity

Judaism in the First Century B.C.

A Palestinian Jew named Jesus was executed by the Roman authorities during the reign of Tiberius (A.D. 14–37), who was Augustus' successor. At the time, few people paid much attention to what proved to be one of the most pivotal events in world history. In the quest for the historical Jesus, scholars have stressed the importance of both his Jewishness and the religious ferment that prevailed in Palestine in the first century B.C. Jesus' ethical teachings are rooted in the moral outlook of Old Testament prophets and, says Andrew M. Greeley, a student of religion, must be viewed as

a logical extension of the Hebrew Scriptures . . . a product of the whole religious environment of which Jesus was a part. Jesus defined himself as a Jew, was highly conscious of the Jewishness of his message and would have found it impossible to conceive of himself as anything but Jewish. . . . The teachings of Jesus, then, must be placed

154

squarely in the Jewish religious context of the time.[1]

In the first century B.C., four principal social-religious parties or sects existed among the Palestinian Jews: Sadducees, Pharisees, Essenes, and Zealots. Composed of the upper stratum of Jewish society—influential landed gentry and hereditary priests who controlled the temple in Jerusalem—the Sadducees insisted on a strict interpretation of Mosaic Law and the perpetuation of temple ceremonies. Challenging the Sadducees, the Pharisees adopted a more flexible attitude toward Mosaic Law; the Pharisees allowed for discussion and varying interpretations of the Law and granted authority to oral tradition as well as to written Scripture. Unlike the Sadducees, the Pharisees believed in life after death; the concept of personal immortality, a later addition to Hebrew religious thought probably acquired from Persia, had gained wide acceptance by the time of Jesus. The Pharisees had the support of the bulk of the Jewish nation. The third religious party, the Essenes, established a semimonastic community near the Dead Sea. Like the Pharisees, they believed in the physical resurrection of the body, but gave this doctrine a more compelling meaning by tying it to the immediate coming of God's kingdom. Another sect, the Zealots, demanded that the Jews neither pay taxes to Rome nor acknowledge the authority of the Roman emperor. Devoted patriots, the Zealots engaged in acts of resistance to Rome.

In addition to the afterlife, another widely recognized idea in the first century B.C. was the belief in a Messiah, a redeemer chosen by God to liberate Israel from foreign rule. In the days of the Messiah, it was predicted, Israel would be free, the exiles would return, and the Jews would be blessed with peace, unity, and prosperity. Jesus (c. 4 B.C.–c. A.D. 29) performed his ministry within this context of Jewish religious-national expectations and longings. The hopes of Jesus' early followers encompassed a lower-class dissatisfaction with the aristocratic Sadducees, a Pharisee emphasis on prophetic ideals and the afterlife, an Essene preoccupation with the end-of-days, a belief in the nearness of God and the need for repentance, and a conquered people's yearning for a Messiah who would liberate their land from Roman rule and establish God's reign.

Jesus: The Inner Man

Historians are able to speak with greater certainty about social-religious developments in Judea at the time of Jesus than they can about Jesus himself. In reconstructing what Jesus did and believed, the historian labors under a handicap, for the sources are few. Jesus himself wrote nothing, and nothing was written about him during his lifetime. In the generations following Jesus' death, both Roman and Jewish historians paid him scant attention. Consequently, virtually everything we know about Jesus derives from the Bible's New Testament, which was written decades after Jesus' death by devotees seeking to convey a religious truth and to propagate a faith.

Modern historians in quest of the historical Jesus have rigorously and critically analyzed the New Testament; their analyses have provided some insights into Jesus and his beliefs. Nevertheless, much about Jesus remains obscure. Very little is known about his childhood. Like other Jewish youths he was taught Hebrew religious-ethical thought and the many rules that governed daily life. At about the age of thirty, no doubt influenced by John the Baptist, Jesus felt called upon by God to preach the imminent coming of the reign of God and the need for repentance—a moral transformation so that a person could gain entrance into God's kingdom. "Now after John was arrested, Jesus came into Galilee, preaching the gospel of God, and saying, 'The time is fulfilled, and the kingdom of God is at hand; repent, and believe in the gospel.' " (Mark 1:14–15)[2]*

*The biblical quotations in this chapter are taken from the Revised Standard Version of the Holy Bible.

For Jesus, the coming of the kingdom was imminent; the process leading to the establishment of God's kingdom on earth had already begun. A new order would soon be established in which God would govern his people righteously and mercifully. Hence the present became critical for him—a time for spiritual preparedness and penitence—because an individual's thoughts, goals, and actions would determine whether he or she would gain entrance into the kingdom. People must change their attitudes, he said. They must eliminate base, lustful, hostile, and selfish feelings; they must stop pursuing wealth and power; they must purify their hearts and show their love for God and their fellow human beings.

Like the Hebrew prophets, Jesus saw ethics as the core of Mosaic Law: "So whatever you wish that men would do to you, do so to them; for this is the law and the prophets." (Matthew 7:12) Jesus did not intend to lead his fellow Jews away from their ancestral religion: " 'Think not that I have come to abolish the law and the prophets; I have come not to abolish them but to fulfil them.' " (Matthew 5:17)

Although Jesus did not seek to break with his past, he was distressed with the Judaism of his day. The rabbis taught the Golden Rule, as well as God's love and mercy for his children, but it seemed to Jesus that these ethical considerations were being undermined by an exaggerated rabbinical concern with ritual, restrictions, and the fine points of the Law, and that the center of Judaism had shifted from prophetic values to obedience to rules and prohibitions regulating the smallest details of daily life. Such legalism and ritualism, Jesus held, distorted the meaning of prophetic teachings. The proliferation of rules, Jesus felt, dealt only with an individual's visible behavior; rules did not penetrate to the person's inner being and lead to a moral transformation. Observing the Lord's command to rest on the Sabbath— for example, by not eating an egg laid on Saturday or by not lifting a chair on that day—did not purify a person's soul.

The inner person concerned Jesus, and it was an inward change that he sought. " 'For from within, out of the heart of man, come evil thoughts, fornication, theft, murder, adultery, coveting, wickedness, deceit, licentiousness, envy, slander, pride, foolishness. All these evil things come from within, and they defile a man.' " (Mark 7:21–23) Individuals must feel again that God is at hand; they must choose God's way by conquering their sinful selfishness and pride and by demonstrating compassion for their neighbors. To Jesus, the spirit of Mosaic Law was more important than the letter of the Law, and right living and a pure loving heart were more important than legal quibbling. With the fervor of a prophet, he urged a moral transformation of human character through a direct encounter between the individual and God.

By preaching active love for one's fellows and by stressing a personal and intimate connection between the individual and God, Jesus associated himself more with the Hebrew prophetic tradition than with the Hebrew rituals, rules, and prohibitions that served to perpetuate a national and cultural tradition of a distinct people. We have seen that Hebrew history reveals both universal and parochial components; Jesus' teachings are more indicative of the universalism inherent in the concept of the one God and in the prophets' teachings.

It was inevitable that Jewish scribes and priests, guardians of the faith, would regard Jesus as a threat to ancient traditions. To Jewish leaders, Jesus was a troublemaker, a subversive who was undermining respect for the Sabbath and religious rites, an arrogant man who claimed that he above all other men was favored by God, another in a long line of messiahs who had been condemned and executed. To the Romans who ruled Palestine, Jesus was a political agitator who could ignite Jewish messianic expectations into a revolt against Rome. (It is likely that several of Jesus' early followers were Zealots, and the Romans may have viewed Jesus as a Zealot leader.) After Jewish leaders turned

Jesus over to the Roman authorities, the Roman procurator, Pontius Pilate, sentenced him to death by crucifixion.

Some Jews, believing that Jesus was an inspired prophet or even the long-awaited Messiah, had become his followers—the chief of these were the Twelve Disciples. At the time of Jesus' death, Christianity was not a separate religion, but a small Hebrew sect with dim prospects for survival. What established the Christian movement and gave it strength was the belief of Jesus' followers that he was raised from the dead on the third day after he was buried. The doctrine of the resurrection enabled people to regard Jesus as more than a superb ethical soul, more than a prophet, more than the Messiah; it made possible belief in Jesus as a divine savior-god, who had come to earth to show people the way to heaven.

In the years immediately following the crucifixion, the religion of Jesus was confined almost exclusively to Jews, who could more appropriately be called Jewish-Christians. The word *Christian* came from a name given Jesus: *Christ* (the Lord's Anointed, the Messiah). Missionaries of this dissenting Christian movement within Judaism were called Apostles—those sent out to preach the gospel, or good news, about Christ. They addressed themselves to Jews and to converts to Judaism who, because they did not adhere fully to Mosaic Law, were not wholly accepted by the Jewish community. Before Christianity could realize the universal implications of Jesus' teachings and become a world religion, as distinct from a Jewish sect, it had to extricate itself from Jewish ritual, politics, and culture. This achievement was the work of a Hellenized Jew named Saul, known to the world as Saint Paul.

Saint Paul: From a Jewish Sect to a World Religion

Saint Paul (A.D. c. 5–c. 67) came from the Greek city of Tarsus in southeastern Asia Minor. He belonged to the Diaspora, or the

Saint Paul. Early Christian art brought to an end the classical concern with the visible real world. Mosaics such as this of Saint Paul of translucent glass transformed the interiors of churches into heavenly abodes. Bodies assumed unnatural poses and became spiritualized. (*Scala/Art Resource*)

"Dispersion"—the millions of Jews living outside Palestine. Though the Jews of the Diaspora retained their ancient faith, they also were influenced by Greek culture. An example is the Alexandrian Jew, Philo (c. 30 B.C.–c. A.D. 40), who tried to demonstrate that Hebrew Scripture could be explained and justified in terms of Greek philosophy. The Jews of the Diaspora were more receptive to foreign ideas, and had a broader conception of humanity than did the Palestinian Jews, who were noted for their intense nationalism and religious exclusiveness. Non-Jews, or *Gentiles*, coming into contact with Jews of the Diaspora, were often favorably impressed with Hebrew monotheism, ethics, and family life. Some Gentiles embraced Hebrew monotheism, but refused to adhere to provisions of the Law requiring circumcision and dietary regulations. Among these Gentiles and non-Palestinian Jews who were greatly influenced by the Greco-Roman milieu, Jesus' Apostles would find receptive listeners.

Reared in Tarsus, a stronghold of Greek culture, Saul knew Greek well, but it is unlikely that he had great familiarity with Greek literature and philosophy. Trained in the outlook of the Pharisees, the young Saul went to Jerusalem to study with Rabban Gamaliel, an outstanding Pharisee teacher. In Jerusalem, Saul persecuted the followers of Jesus, but then he underwent a spiritual transformation and became a convert to Jesus. Serving as a zealous missionary of Jewish Christianity in the Diaspora, Saint Paul preached to his fellow Jews in synagogues. Recognizing that the Christian message applied to non-Jews as well, Paul urged spreading it to the Gentiles.

Although neither the first nor the only missionary to the Gentiles, Saint Paul was without doubt the most important. In the process of his missionary activity—and he traveled extensively through the Roman Empire—he formulated doctrines that represented a fundamental break with Judaism and became the heart of this new religion. Paul taught that all people, both Jew and Gentile, were sinners, as a consequence of Adam's original defiance of God; that Jesus had come to earth to save all people from sin; that by dying on the cross, he had atoned for the sins of all and made it possible for all to have eternal life in heaven; and that by believing in Jesus, people could gain this salvation. Alone, the individual was helpless, possessed by sin, unable to overcome his or her wicked nature. Jesus was the only hope, said Paul. "Wretched man that I am! Who will deliver me from this body of death? Thanks be to God through Jesus Christ our Lord!" (Romans 7:24–25) Through the ritual of baptism—purification by water—individuals could enter into a personal union with Christ.

Christ: A Savior-God   To the first members of the Christian movement, Jesus was both a prophet who proclaimed the power and purpose of God and the Messiah whose coming heralded a new age. To Saint Paul, Jesus was a resurrected redeemer who held out the promise of salvation to the entire world, a savior-god who took on human flesh to atone for the sins of humanity by suffering death on the cross.

The idea of a slain savior-god was well known in the mystery religions of the eastern Mediterranean and in Gnosticism, a pre-Christian religious movement that synthesized many mythological and philosophical traditions. Like these religions, Christianity initiated converts into the mysteries of the faith, featured a sacramental meal, and developed a priesthood. But the similarities between Christianity and the mystery cults should not be overstressed, since the differences are more profound.

Unlike the cultic gods, Jesus had actually lived in history. Hence people could identify with him in a more personal way, which enormously increased the appeal of this new religion. Also, the deities of the mystery religions were killed against their will by evil powers. In Jesus, it was said, God had become a man and suffered pain and death out of compassion and pity to show a floundering humanity the way that would lead from sin to eternal life. This suffering savior evoked from a distressed humanity deep feelings of love and loyalty. Finally, Christianity, with its Hebraic heritage, would tolerate no other divinity but God. Pagans, on the other hand, often belonged to more than one cult, or at least recognized the divinity of the gods of other cults.

The Break with Judaism In attempting to reach the Gentiles, Saint Paul had to disentangle Christianity from a Jewish sociocultural context. Thus, he held that neither Gentile nor Jewish followers of Jesus were bound by the hundreds of rituals and rules that constitute Mosaic Law. For Saint Paul, there was no distinctive difference between Jew and Gentile; in his view, the ministry of Jesus was intended for all. In the wake of Jesus' coming, Paul insisted, Mosaic regulations were obsolete and a hindrance to missionary activity among the Gentiles.

To Paul, the new Christian community was the true fulfillment of Judaism; it was granted the promise that God had earlier bestowed on Israel; it was the means for moral transformation and eternal life. The Jews regarded their faith as a national religion, bound organically with the history of their people. For Paul, the new Christian community was not a nation but an *oikoumene*, a world community. To this extent, Christianity shared in the universalism of the Hellenistic Age. Jesus not only fulfilled the messianic aspirations of the Jews, but he also fulfilled the spiritual needs and expectations of all peoples.

In preaching the doctrine of a risen Savior and insisting that Mosaic Law had been superseded Paul, whatever his intentions, was breaking with his Jewish roots and transforming a Jewish sect into a new religion. Separating Christianity from Judaism enormously increased its appeal for non-Jews who were attracted to Hebrew ethical monotheism but repelled by circumcision, dietary regulations, and other strict requirements of Mosaic Law. Paul built on the personalism and universalism implicit in the teachings of Jesus (and the Hebrew prophets) to create a religion intended not for a people with its own particular history, culture, and land, but for all humanity.

Spread and Triumph of Christianity

By de-Judaizing Christianity, Saint Paul made the new religion fit for export to the Greco-Roman world. But its growth was slow. Originating in the first century, Christianity took firm root in the second, grew extensively in the third, and became the official religion of the Roman Empire at the end of the fourth century.

The Appeal of Christianity

The triumph of Christianity was related to a corresponding decline in the vitality of Hellenism and a shift in cultural emphasis—a movement from reason to emotion and revelation. Offering comforting solutions to the existential problems of life and death, religion demonstrated a greater capacity to stir human hearts than reason did. Hellenism had invented the tools of rational thought, but the power of mythical thought was never entirely subdued. By the Late Roman Empire, science and philosophy were unable to compete with mysticism and myth.

This deterioration of the classical outlook was demonstrated by the growing popularity of Eastern religions and the transformation of philosophy. Although the Greco-Roman world had conquered the East militarily, the oriental world, through its religions, waged a counteroffensive that eventually overwhelmed a decaying Greco-Roman civilization. Mystery cults, which promised personal salvation, were spreading and gaining followers. Stoicism and Epicureanism were performing a religious function by trying to help individuals overcome emotional stress, while Neo-Platonists yearned for a mystical union with the One. Astrology and magic, which offered supernatural explanations for the op-

Map 8.1 The Journeys of Saint Paul

erations of nature, were also popular. This drift away from rational and worldly values helped prepare the way for Christianity. In a culturally stagnating and spiritually troubled Greco-Roman world, Christianity gave to life a new meaning and offered to disillusioned men and women a new hope.

During the Hellenistic Age, the individual had struggled with the problems of alienation and community. With the decline of the independent city-state, the individual searched for a new frame of reference, a new form of attachment. The Roman Empire represented one possible allegiance. But for many people, it was not a satisfying relationship—the individual found it difficult to be devoted to so vast, remote, and impersonal a political organization. The Christian message of a divine Savior, a concerned Father, and brotherly love inspired men and women who were dissatisfied with the world of here-and-now, who felt no attachment to city or empire, who derived no inspiration from philosophy, and who suffered from a profound sense of loneliness. Christianity offered the individual

what the city and the Roman world-state could not: a profoundly personal relationship with God, an intimate connection with a higher world, and membership in a community of the faithful who cared for each other.

Stressing the intellect and self-reliance, Greco-Roman thought did not provide for the emotional needs of the ordinary person. Christianity addressed itself to this defect in the Greco-Roman outlook. The poor, the oppressed, and the slaves were attracted to the personality, life, death, and resurrection of Jesus, his love for all, and his concern for suffering humanity. They found spiritual sustenance in a religion that stretched out a hand of love, that taught that a person of worth need not be well-born, rich, educated, or talented. To people burdened with misfortune and terrified by death, Christianity held the promise of eternal life, a kingdom of heaven where they would be comforted by God the Father. Thus, Christianity gave to the common person what the aristocratic values of Greco-Roman civilization generally did not—a sense of dignity. Hellenic philosophy offered little compassion for the sufferer, but the cardinal principle of Christianity held that Jesus had endured earthly torments because of his love for all human beings.

Christianity's success was due not only to the appeal of its message but to the power of an institution. To retain the devotion of the faithful, to win new converts, to protect itself from opponents, and to administer its services, Christianity needed an organized body of followers. This body became the Christian church, which grew into a strong organization uniting the faithful. To city-dwellers—lonely, alienated, disillusioned with public affairs, stranded mortals groping for a sense of community—the church that called its members brother and sister filled an elemental need of human beings to belong. Another attraction for converts was the lack of painful or expensive initiation rites, which were standard requirements for entrance into Mithraism, a leading rival (see page 141 Chapter 7). Also, unlike Mithraism, the church welcomed women converts, who were often the first to join and brought their menfolk after them. Among other reasons, the church attracted women because it commanded that husbands treat their wives kindly, remain faithful, and provide for the children. The church won new converts and retained the loyalty of the old ones by providing social services for the poor and infirm, welcoming slaves, criminals, sinners, and other outcasts, and extending a hand of brotherhood and comfort during difficult times.

The ability of an evolving Christianity to assimilate elements from Greek philosophy and even from the mystery religions also contributed in no small measure to its growth. By becoming infused with Greek philosophy, Christianity was able to present itself in terms intelligible to those versed in Greek learning, and was thus able to attract some educated people. Because some Christian doctrines (a risen Savior-God, a Virgin and her child, life after death), practices (baptism), and holy days (December 25) either paralleled or were adopted from the mystery religions, it became relatively easy to win converts from these rivals.

Christianity and Rome

Generally tolerant of religions, the Roman government at first did not significantly interfere with Christianity. Indeed, Christianity benefited in many ways from its association with the Roman Empire. Christian missionaries, among them some of the Twelve Apostles who were the original followers of Christ, traveled throughout the Empire, over roads and across seas made safe by Roman arms. The common Greek dialect, the *koine*, spoken in most parts of the Empire, facilitated the task of missionaries. Had the Mediterranean world been fractured into separate and competing states, the spread of Christianity might well have faced an insurmountable obstacle. The universalism of the Roman Empire, which made citizenship available to peoples of many nationalities, prepared the way for the universalism of Christianity, which welcomed membership from all nations.

As the number of Christians increased, Roman officials started to pay the Christians more mind; they began to fear the Christians as subversives, preaching allegiance to God and not to Rome. To many Romans, Christians were enemies of the social order—strange people who would not accept the state gods, would not engage in Roman festivals, scorned gladiator contests, stayed away from public baths, glorified pacifism, refused to honor deceased emperors as gods, and worshiped a crucified criminal as Lord. Romans ultimately found in Christians a universal scapegoat for the ills burdening the Empire, such as famines, plagues, and military reverses. In an effort to stamp out Christianity, emperors resorted to persecution. Christians were imprisoned, beaten, starved, burned alive, torn apart by wild beasts in the arena for the amusement of the Romans, and crucified.

The persecutions fell into two main categories. The early persecutions, beginning with those incited under Emperor Nero in A.D.

64, were local and did not cause much loss of life; they were too sporadic to impede the growth of Christianity. But two centuries later, in A.D. 250, Emperor Decius unleashed a brief but brutal terror against the Christians that extended throughout much of the Empire. Decius' successors, Gallus (251–253) and Valerian (253–260), also issued anti-Christian edicts and had Christians murdered.

Christians lived in relative peace from 260 to 303, but then Diocletian (284–305) instituted the most severe persecution they had yet faced, lasting for three years in the west and longer in the east. The persecutions under the mid-third-century emperors and Diocletian caused the brutal deaths of many Christians. Some, fearful of torture and death, abandoned their faith. However, the persecutions did not last long enough to extirpate the new religion. Actually, they strengthened the determination of most of the faithful and won new converts who were awed by the extraordinary courage of the martyrs, who willingly died for their faith.

Unable to crush Christianity by persecution, Roman emperors decided to gain the support of the growing number of Christians within the Empire. In A.D. 313, Constantine, genuinely attracted to Christianity, issued the Edict of Milan granting toleration to Christians. By allowing for the free flow of Christian teachings and by instituting legislation favorable to the Church, Constantine and his successors accelerated the growth of Christianity and the Christianization of the Empire. By A.D. 392, Theodosius I had made Christianity the state religion of the Empire and declared the worship of pagan gods illegal. Persecution did not end, but its target had shifted from Christians to heretics.

Christianity and Greek Philosophy

Christianity synthesized both the Hebrew and the Greco-Roman traditions. Having emerged from Judaism, Christianity assimilated Hebrew monotheism and prophetic morality and retained the Old Testament as the Word of God. Without this Hebraic foundation,

Christianity cannot be understood. As the new religion evolved, it also assimilated elements of Greek philosophy. But there was a struggle between conservatives who wanted no dealings with pagan philosophy and those believers who recognized the value of Greek thought to Christianity.

To conservative church fathers, classical philosophy was all in error because it did not derive from divine revelation. They believed that whereas philosophers merely battled over words, Christianity possessed *the Word*, true wisdom revealed by God. As the final statement of God's truth, Christianity superseded both pagan philosophy and pagan religions. These conservatives feared that studying classical authors would contaminate Christian morality (did not Plato propose a community of wives and did not the dramatists treat violent passions?) and promote heresy (was not classical literature replete with references to pagan gods?). For these church fathers there could be no compromise between Greek philosophy and Christian revelation. They regarded their life's mission to be preaching the gospel of Jesus, which required no reinforcement from pagan ideas. "What indeed has Athens to do with Jerusalem?" asked Tertullian (A.D. 150–225). "With our faith, we desire no further belief. For this is our [first] faith that there is nothing which we ought to believe besides."[3]

Some early church fathers, however, defended the value of studying classical literature. Properly taught, such literature could aid in the moral development of children because it contained many examples of virtuous deeds. Some church fathers maintained that Greek philosophy contained a dim glimmer of God's truth, a pre-Christian insight into divine wisdom. Christ had corrected and fulfilled an insight reached by the philosophic mind. Knowledge of Greek philosophy, they argued, helped a Christian to explain his beliefs logically and to argue intelligently with pagan critics of Christian teachings.

Utilizing the language and categories of Greek philosophy, Christian intellectuals transformed Christianity from a simple ethical creed into a theoretical system, a theology.

This effort to express Christian beliefs in terms of Greek rationalism is referred to as the Hellenization of Christianity. Greek philosophy enabled Christians to explain in rational terms God's existence and revelation. Using philosophical concepts, church fathers attempted to show that the Trinity, although a mystery, did not violate the law of contradiction; that God the Father, God the Son, and God the Holy Spirit did not conflict with monotheism. They attributed the order and regularity of nature and the natural law, standing above human law—two cardinal principles of Stoic thought—to God the designer of the universe.

Christ was depicted as the divine *logos* (reason) in human form. The Stoic teaching that all people are fundamentally equal because they share in universal reason could be formulated in Christian terms—that all are united in Christ. Stoic ethics that stressed moderation, self-control, and brotherhood could be assimilated by Christian revelation. Particularly in Platonism, which drew a distinction between a world perceived by the senses and a higher order open to the intellect, Christian thinkers found a congenial medium for expressing Christian beliefs. The perfect and universal Forms, or Ideas, which Plato maintained were the true goal of knowledge and the source of ethical standards, were held by Christians to exist in God's mind.

That Greek philosophy exercised a hold over church doctrine is of immense importance; it meant that rational thought, the priceless achievement of the Greek mind, was not lost. But this Hellenization of Christianity was not a triumph of classicism over Christianity. The reverse is the essential truth: Christianity triumphed over Hellenism; Greek philosophy had to sacrifice its essential autonomy to the requirements of Christian revelation. Although Christianity made use of Greek philosophy, Christian truth rested on faith, not reason. As Tertullian stated, "And the Son of God died; it is by all means to be believed, because it is absurd. And He was buried, and rose again; the fact is certain because it is impossible."[4]

The Antioch Chalice. From the fourth century A.D., this cup is the earliest surviving Christian chalice. The transformation of the wine of the mass into the very blood of Christ was central to Christian worship. In later medieval times, historical kings and knights in literature would search for the original chalice of the Last Supper, the Holy Grail. (*The Metropolitan Museum of Art, The Cloisters Collection, 1950*)

Growth of Christian Organization, Doctrine, and Attitudes

Early in its history the church developed along hierarchical lines. Those members of the Christian community who had the authority to preside over the celebration of the Mass—breaking bread and offering wine as Christ had done in the Last Supper—were called either priests or bishops. Gradually the designation *bishop* was reserved for the one clergyman in the community with the authority to resolve disputes over doctrines and practices. Regarded as the successors to Christ's Twelve Apostles, bishops supervised religious activities within their regions. The most influential bishops ministered to the leading cities of the Empire—Rome, Alexandria, Antioch, and Milan.

The Primacy of the Bishop of Rome

The bishop of Rome, later to be called the pope, claimed primacy over the other bishops, maintaining that the Apostle Peter founded the Roman see (official seat of authority), and that both Peter and Paul were martyred in Rome. Moreover, as the traditional capital of the Empire, Rome seemed the logical choice to serve as the center of the church.

In developing the case for their supremacy over the church organization, bishops of Rome increasingly referred to the famous New Testament passage in which Jesus says to his Disciple Simon (also called Peter): " 'And I tell you, you are Peter, and on this rock I will build my church.' " (Matthew 16:18) Because *Peter* in Greek means *rock (petra)*, it was argued that Christ had chosen Peter to succeed him as ruler of the universal church. It was commonly accepted that Saint Peter had established a church in Rome and was martyred there, so it was argued further that the Roman bishop inherited the power that Christ had passed on to Peter. Thus, the argument continued, the bishop of Rome held a unique office: of all the bishops, only he had inherited the powers originally granted by Christ to Peter. Because the Apostles had been subordinate to Peter, so too must the bishops defer to Peter's successor. In the fourth and fifth centuries, popes took a leading part in doctrinal disputes that threatened to divide the church. More and more Christians came to esteem Rome as the champion of true Christianity.

The Rise of Monasticism

Not all Christians welcomed the growing wealth and power of the church. Inspired by Jesus' example of self-denial and seeking to escape from the agonies and corruptions of this world, some ardent Christians withdrew to deserts and mountains in search of spiritual renewal. In their zeal for holiness they sometimes practiced extreme forms of asceticism—self-flogging, wearing spiked corsets, eating only herbs, or living for years on a column thirty feet above the ground.

Gradually, colonies of these hermits sprang up, particularly in Egypt; in time, the leaders of these monastic communities drew up written rules for prayer and work. In the first half of the fourth century, Saint Pachomius set up several regulated monasteries in Egypt, and the first convent was founded about 320 in the Egyptian desert by Mary, Pachomius' sister. Saint Basil (c. 329–c. 379), a Greek who was bishop of Caesarea in Palestine, established the rule that became the standard of monasteries in the East. Basil required monks to refrain from bodily abuses and to engage in manual labor. Through farming, weaving, and construction, monks could make a monastery self-supporting and have the means to assist the needy. Basil forbade his monks to own personal property other than clothing and insisted that they spend much of their time in silence.

The monastic ideal spread from east to west. Saint Martin of Tours established a monastery in Gaul, which actively converted the pagan peasants. But the principal figure in the shaping of monasticism in the West was Saint Benedict, who founded a monastery at Monte Cassino, Italy, in 529. The rule of Saint Benedict called for the monks to live in poverty and to study, labor, and obey the abbot, the head of the monastery. Monks were required to pray often, work hard, talk little, and surrender private property. In imposing discipline and regulations, Benedict eliminated the excessive and eccentric individualism of the early monks; he socialized and institutionalized the spiritual impulse that led monks

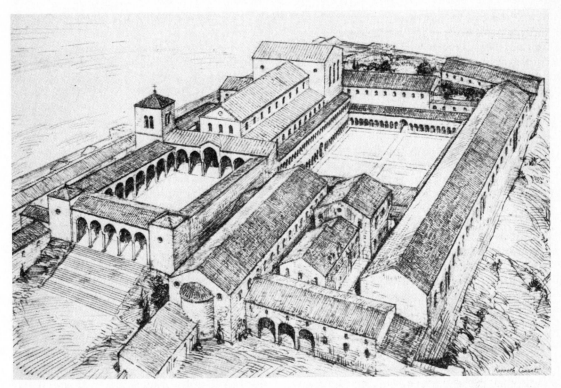

Plan of Monte Cassino Abbey. Founded by Saint Benedict in 529, Monte Cassino Abbey still serves as a religious community today, although the buildings have had to be rebuilt several times after the ravages of war. Benedict's rule instructed monks to live in poverty, to labor, to study, and to aid the sick and the poor. (*From Kenneth John Conant,* The Pelican History of Art: Carolingian and Romanesque Architecture, 800–1200 [*Penguin Books, 1959*], *Reprinted by permission of Penguin Books Ltd.*)

to withdraw from the world. Benedict demonstrated the same genius for administration that Romans had shown in organizing and governing their Empire. Benedict's rule became the standard for monasteries in Western Europe.

Doctrinal Disputes

Christ's sayings and actions were preserved by word of mouth. Sometime around A.D. 66–70, Saint Mark formulated the Christian message from this oral tradition and perhaps from some material that had been put in writing earlier. Later Saint Matthew and Saint Luke, relying heavily on Mark's account, wrote somewhat longer Gospels. The Gospels of Mark, Matthew, and Luke are called *synoptic* because their approach to Jesus is very similar. The remaining Gospel, written by Saint John, varies significantly from the Synoptic Gospels. The Synoptic Gospels, The Gospel According to Saint John, Acts of the Apostles, the twenty-one Epistles, including those written by Saint Paul, and Revelation constitute the twenty-seven Books of the Christian New Testament. Christians also accepted the Old Testament of the Hebrews as God's Word.

The early Christians had a Bible and a clergy to teach it. But Holy Writ could be interpreted differently by equally sincere believers, and controversies over doctrine threatened the unity of the early church. The most important controversy concerned how people viewed the relationship between God and Christ. Arius (A.D. 250–336), a Greek priest in Alexandria, led one faction; he denied the complete divinity of Christ—one of the basic tenets of the church. To Arius, Christ was more than man but less than God; the Father and the Son did not possess the same nature or essence. Arius said that there was no permanent union between God and Christ; the Father alone is eternal and truly God.

The Council of Nicaea (325 A.D.), the first assembly of bishops from all parts of the Roman world, was called to settle the controversy. The Council condemned Arius and ruled that God and Christ were of the same substance, coequal and coeternal. The position adopted at Nicaea became the basis of the Nicene Creed, which remains the official doctrine of the church. Although Arianism, the name given Arius' heresy, won converts for a time, it eventually lost supporters.

Another controversy arose over the relationship between Christ's divine and human natures. Some theologians, viewing Christ as a great ethical soul, tended to emphasize his human nature at the expense of his divine nature. Other theologians argued that Christ's human nature had been absorbed by his divine nature—in effect, that Christ possessed a single divine nature. The Council of Chalcedon in A.D. 451 formulated the orthodox position that Christ is truly God and truly man, and that two distinct natures, one divine and the other human, are joined and preserved in his person. The other views were declared heretical but continued to persist in the eastern part of the Empire.

The controversies over Christ's nature and his relationship to God were by no means theological hairsplitting. What was at stake was the central message of Christianity: Christ had descended to earth to show men and women the path to heaven, and they could achieve salvation by following the Son who was one with the Father.

Christianity and Society

While salvation was their ultimate aim, Christians still had to dwell within the world and deal with its imperfections. In the process, Christian thinkers challenged some of the mores of Greco-Roman society and formulated attitudes that would endure for centuries.

The first Christians condemned warfare, regarding acts of revenge and the shedding of blood as a violation of Christ's precepts. But after Roman emperors professed Christianity, Christians began to serve the government with greater frequency. With the barbarians menacing the borders, these officials could not advocate pacifism. Christian theorists began to argue that under certain circumstances—to punish injustice or to restore peace—war was just. But even such wars must not entail unnecessary violence.

Christians denounced the gladiator combats and contests between men and beasts as bloodlust and murder. Nevertheless, these spectacles persisted even after the majority of the population had converted to Christianity. When the games finally ended, it was probably due more to the growing poverty of the Western Empire than to the Christian conscience.

Sharing in the patriarchal tradition of Jewish society, Saint Paul subjected the wife to her husband's authority. "Wives, be subject to your husbands, as to the Lord. For the husband is the head of the wife as Christ is the head of the church." (Ephesians 5:22–23) Paul wanted women to remain quiet at church meetings. "If there is anything they desire to know, let them ask their husbands at home. For it is shameful for a woman to speak in church." (I Corinthians 14:35) But Paul also held that all are baptized in Christ: "There is neither Jew nor Greek, there is neither slave nor free, there is neither male nor female; for you are all one in Christ Jesus." (Galatians 3:28) Consequently, both men and women possessed moral autonomy. The early church held to strict standards on sexual matters. It condemned adultery and held virginity for spiritual reasons in high esteem.

Christians waged no war against slavery, which was widely practiced and universally accepted in the ancient world. Saint Paul commanded slaves to obey their masters, and many Christians were themselves slave owners. However, Christians taught that slaves too were children of God, sought their conversion, and urged owners not to treat them harshly.

Saint Augustine: The Christian World-View

During the early history of Christianity, many learned men, "fathers of the church," explained and defended church teachings. Most of the leading early fathers wrote in Greek, but in the middle of the fourth century, three great Latin writers—Saint Jerome, Saint Ambrose, and Saint Augustine—profoundly influenced the course of Christianity in the West.

As a youth, Saint Jerome (A.D. c. 340–420) studied Latin literature in Rome. Throughout his life, he remained an admirer of Cicero, Virgil, Lucretius, and other great Latin writers, and he defended the study of classical literature by Christians. Baptized in his mid-twenties, Jerome became attracted to the ascetic life and lived for a while as a hermit in the desert of Chalcis near Antioch. After becoming a priest, he visited holy places in Palestine and intensely studied the Scriptures in Constantinople. Returning to Rome, Jerome became secretary to Pope Damasus and spiritual adviser to a group of wealthy women attracted to the ascetic life. Facing criticism for his attacks on the luxurious living and laxness of the clergy, Jerome left Rome. He established a monastery near Bethlehem, where he devoted himself to prayer and study.

Saint Jerome wrote about the lives of the saints and promoted the spread of monasticism. But his greatest achievement was the translation of the Old and New Testaments from Greek and Hebrew into Latin. Jerome's

text, the common or Vulgate version of the Bible, became the official edition of the Bible for the western church.

Saint Ambrose (A.D. 340–397), bishop of Milan, Italy, composed religious hymns and wrote books on Scripture, dogma, and morality. In his work on the duties of the clergy, Ambrose provided humane rules for dealing with the poor, the old, the sick, and the orphaned. He urged clerics not to pursue wealth, but to exercise humility and to avoid favoring the rich over the poor. Ambrose sought to defend the autonomy of the church against the power of the state. Emperors are not the judges of bishops, he wrote. His dictum that "The Emperor is within the church, not above it" became a cardinal principle of the medieval church.

The most important Christian theoretician in the Late Roman Empire was Saint Augustine (A.D. 354–430), bishop of Hippo in North Africa. Born in the North African province of Numidia, Augustine attended school at Carthage where he studied the Latin classics. During his student days, Augustine took a concubine, by whom he had a son. Struggling to find meaning in a world that abounded with evil, Augustine turned to Manichaeism, an oriental sect whose central doctrine was the struggle of the universal forces of light and good against those of darkness and evil. But still Augustine, now a professor of rhetoric, felt spiritually restless. In Milan, Augustine, inspired by the sermons of Ambrose, abandoned Manichaeism, and devoted his life to following Christ's teachings. After serving as a priest, he was appointed bishop of Hippo in 395.

In his autobiography, the *Confessions*, Augustine described his spiritual quest and appealed to devotees of Manichaeism and to adherents of pagan philosophy to embrace Christianity. Augustine wrote *The City of God* at the turn of the fifth century when the Greco-Roman world-view was disintegrating and the Roman world-state was collapsing. Augustine became the principal architect of the Christian outlook that succeeded a dying classicism.

In 410, when Augustine was in his fifties, Visigoths sacked Rome—a disaster for which the classical consciousness was unprepared. Throughout the Empire people panicked. Pagans blamed the tragedy on Christianity. The Christians had predicted the end of the world, they said, and by refusing to offer sacrifices to ancient gods, Christians had turned these deities against Rome. Pagans also accused Christians of undermining the empire by refusing to serve in the army. Even Christians expressed anxiety. Why were the righteous also suffering? Where was the kingdom of God on earth that had been prophesied?

Augustine's *The City of God* was a response to the crisis of the Roman Empire in the same manner that Plato's *Republic* was a reaction to the crisis of the Athenian polis. But whereas Plato expressed hope that a state founded on rational principles could remedy the abuses of Athenian society, Augustine maintained that the worldly city could never be the central concern of a Christian. He said that the ideal state could not be realized on earth, that it belonged only to heaven. The misfortunes of Rome, therefore, should not distress a Christian unduly, for Christianity belonged to the realm of the spirit and could not be identified with any state. The collapse of Rome did not diminish the greatness of Christianity, for the true Christian was a citizen of a heavenly city that could not possibly be pillaged by ungodly barbarians, but would endure forever. Compared to God's heavenly city, the decline of Rome was unimportant. The welfare of Christianity was not to be identified with Rome's material progress or even its existence.

Augustine provided comfort to Christians anguished by Rome's misfortunes. They were assured that the decay or prosperity of Rome was ultimately meaningless compared to the bliss that awaited them in the heavenly city. They were told that Christianity was measured neither by Rome's successes nor by its failures. What really mattered in history, said Augustine, was not the coming to be or the passing away of cities and empires, but the individual's entrance into heaven or hell.

Yet Augustine was still a man of this world. He stipulated that although the earthly city was the very opposite of the heavenly city, it was a reality that people must face. Christians could not reject their city entirely, but must bend it to fit a Christian pattern. The city that someday would rise from the ruins of Rome must be based upon Christian principles. Warfare, economic activity, education, and the rearing of children should all be conducted in a Christian spirit. Although the City of Man was ever evil, imperfect, and of no consequence in comparison to the City of God, it was not about to disappear and be replaced by the Kingdom of God on earth. The church could not neglect the state, but must guide it to protect human beings from their own sinful natures. The state must employ repression and punishment to restrain people, who were inherently sinful, from destroying each other and the few good men and women that God had elected to save from hell. But the earthly city would always be inhabited predominantly by sinners, said Augustine. People should be under no illusion that it could be transformed into the City of God, for everywhere in human society we see

love for all those things that prove so vain and . . . breed so many heartaches, troubles, griefs, and fears; such insane joys in discord, strife, and war; such wrath and plots of enemies . . . such fraud and theft and robbery; such perfidy . . . homicide and murder, cruelty and savagery, lawlessness and lust; all the shameless passions of the impure—fornication and adultery . . . and countless other uncleanness too nasty to be mentioned; the sins against religion—sacrilege and heresy . . . the iniquities against our neighbors—calumnies and cheating, lies and false witness, violence to persons and property . . . and the innumerable other miseries and maladies that fill the world, yet escape attention.[5]

Yet, God, infinitely compassionate, still cared for his creation, said Augustine. By coming to earth as man in the person of Jesus Christ and by enduring punishment and suffering,

God had emancipated human beings from the bondage of original sin.

But Augustine did not hold that by his death Christ had opened the door to heaven for all. The majority of humanity remained condemned to eternal punishment, said Augustine; only a handful had the gift of faith and the promise of heaven. People could not by their own efforts overcome a sinful nature; a moral and spiritual regeneration stemmed not from human will power but from God's grace. And God determined who would be saved and who would be damned.

Whereas the vast majority of people, said Augustine, were citizens of a doomed earthly city, the small number endowed with God's grace constituted the City of God. These people lived on earth as visitors only, for they awaited deliverance to the Kingdom of Christ, where together with the good angels and God they would know perfect happiness. But the permanent inhabitants of the earthly city were destined for eternal punishment in hell. A perpetual conflict existed between the two cities and between their inhabitants; one city stood for sin and corruption, the other for God's truth and perfection.

For Augustine, the highest good was not of this world but consisted of eternal life with God. Augustine's distinction between this higher world of perfection and a lower world of corruption remained influential throughout the Middle Ages. However, the church, rejecting Augustine's doctrine that only a limited number of people are predestined for heaven or hell, emphasized that Christ had made possible the salvation of all who would embrace the opportunity.

Augustine repudiated the distinguishing feature of classical humanism—the autonomy of reason. For him, ultimate wisdom could not be achieved through rational thought alone; reason had to be guided by faith. Without faith there could be no true knowledge, no understanding. Philosophy had no validity if it did not first accept as absolutely true the existence of God and the authority of his revelation. Valid ethical standards could not be formulated by reason alone, but were

revealed to people by the living God. Christian truth did not rest on theoretical excellence or logical consistency; it was true because its source was God.

Augustine's belief contrasts with that of Socrates, who insisted that through rational reflection each individual could arrive at standards of good and evil. For the humanist Socrates, ultimate values were something that the individual could grasp through thought alone and could defend rationally. Augustine insisted that individuals, without divine guidance, lacked the capacity to comprehend ultimate truth or to regenerate themselves morally, and that without God they could not attain wisdom nor liberate themselves from sin.

Thus, against the classical view that asserted the primacy of reason, Augustine opposed the primacy of faith. But he did not necessarily regard reason as an enemy of faith, and he did not call for an end to rational speculation. Augustine possessed rare intelligence; a student of the classics and an admirer of Platonism, he respected the power of thought. What he denied of the classical view was that reason *alone* could attain wisdom. The wisdom that Augustine sought was Christian wisdom, knowledge of God and God's expectations for humanity. The starting point for this knowledge, he said, was belief in God and the Scriptures. For Augustine, secular knowledge for its own sake was of little value; the true significance of knowledge lay in its role as a tool for comprehending God's will. Augustine adapted the classical intellectual tradition to the requirements of Christian revelation.

With Augustine, the human-centered outlook of classical humanism—which for centuries had been undergoing transformation—gave way to a God-centered world-view. The fulfillment of God's will, not the full development of human talent, became the central concern of life.

Augustinian Christianity is a living philosophy because it still has something vital to say about the human condition. To those who believe that people have the intelligence and good will to transform their earthly city into a rational and just community that promotes human betterment, Augustine warns of human sinfulness, weakness, and failure. He reminds the optimist that progress is not certain, that people, weak and ever prone to wickedness, are their own worst enemies, that success is illusory, and that misery is the essential human reality.

Christianity and Classical Humanism: Alternate World-Views

Christianity and classical humanism are the two principal components of the Western tradition. The value that modern Western civilization places on the individual derives ultimately from classical humanism and the Judeo-Christian tradition. Classical humanists believed that individual worth came from the individual's capacity to reason, to shape his character and his life according to rational standards. Christianity also places great stress on the individual. In the Christian view, God cares for each person; he wants people to behave righteously and to enter heaven; Christ died for all because he loves humanity. Christianity espouses active love and genuine concern for fellow human beings. Without God, people are as Augustine described them—"foul, crooked, sordid, bespotted, vicious"; with God, the human personality can undergo a moral transformation and become loving, good, and ethically free.

But Christianity and classical humanism also represent two essentially different world-views. The triumph of the Christian outlook signified a break with the essential meaning of classical humanism; it pointed to the end of the world of antiquity and the beginning of an age of faith, the Middle Ages. With the victory of Christianity, the ultimate goal of life shifted. Life's purpose was no longer to achieve excellence in this world through the full and creative development of human talent, but to attain salvation in a heavenly city. A person's worldly accomplishments amounted to very little if he or she did not accept God and his revelation.

In the classical view, history had no ultimate end, no ultimate meaning; periods of happiness and misery repeated themselves endlessly. In the Christian view, history is filled with spiritual meaning. It is the profound drama of individuals struggling to overcome their original sin in order to gain eternal happiness in heaven. History began with Adam and Eve's defiance of God and would end when Christ returns to earth, when evil is eradicated, when God's will prevails.

Classicism held that there was no authority higher than reason; Christianity teaches that without God as the starting point, knowledge is formless, purposeless, and prone to error. Classicism held that ethical standards were laws of nature that reason could discover. Through reason, individuals could arrive at those values by which they should regulate their lives. Reason would enable them to govern desires and will; it would show them where their behavior was wrong and teach them how to correct it. Because individuals sought what was best for themselves, they would obey the voice of reason. Early Christianity, on the other hand, maintained that ethical standards emanated from the personal will of God. Without obedience to God's commands, people would remain wicked forever; the human will, essentially sinful, could not be transformed by the promptings of reason. Only when individuals turned to God for forgiveness and guidance—only then would they find the inner strength to overcome their sinful nature. People cannot perfect themselves through scientific knowledge; it is spiritual insight and belief in God that they require and that must serve as the first principle of their lives. For classicism, the ultimate good was sought through thought and action; for Christianity, ultimate good comes through knowing and loving God.

But Christian thinkers respected Greek philosophy and did not seek to eradicate the intellectual heritage of Greece. Rather, they sought to fit it into a Christian framework. By preserving the Greek philosophical tra-

Chronology 8.1 Early Christianity

A.D. 29	The crucifixion of Jesus
c. 34–64	Missionary activity of Saint Paul
c. 66–70	The Gospel According to Mark is written
250–260	A decade of brutal persecution of Christians by the Romans
313	Constantine grants toleration of Christianity
320	The first convent is founded
325	The Council of Nicaea rules that God and Christ are of the same substance, coequal and coeternal
392	Theodosius I makes Christianity the state religion
430	Death of Saint Augustine
451	The Council of Chalcedon rules that Christ is truly God and truly man
529	Monte Cassino is founded by Saint Benedict

dition, Christian thinkers performed a task of immense historical significance.

Christianity inherited the Hebrew view of the overriding importance of God for humanity: God makes life intelligible and purposeful. For the Christian, God is a living being, loving and compassionate, in whose company one seeks to spend eternity; one knows God essentially through faith and feeling. Although the Greek philosophers had a conception of God, it was not comparable to the God of Hebrews and Christians. For the Greek, God was a logical abstraction, a principle of order, the supreme good, the highest truth; God was a concept, impersonal, unfeeling, and uninvolved with human concerns. The Greeks approached God through the intellect, not the heart; they neither loved nor worshiped God. In addition, because religion was at the periphery, not the center, of classical humanism, the idea of God did not carry the same significance that it did for Christianity.

In the classical world, the political community was the avenue to justice, happiness, and self-realization. In early Christianity, the good life was not identified with worldly achievement but with life eternal, and the ideal commonwealth could only be one that was founded and ruled by Christ. It was entrance into God's kingdom that each person must make the central aim of life. For the next thousand years, this distinction between heaven and earth, this otherworldly, theocentric outlook would define the Western mentality.

In the Late Roman Empire, when classical values were in decay, Christianity was a dynamic and creative movement. Possessing both institutional and spiritual strength, Christianity survived the fall of Rome. Because it retained elements of Greco-Roman civilization and taught a high morality, Christianity served as a civilizing agent in the centuries that followed Rome's collapse. Indeed, Christianity was the essential shaper of the European civilization that emerged in the Middle Ages.

Notes

1. Andrew M. Greeley, "Hippie Hero? Superpatriot? Superstar? A Christmas Biography,"

New York Times Magazine (December 23, 1973), p. 28.

2. The biblical quotations are used with permission from The Holy Bible, Revised Standard Version (New York: Thomas Nelson & Sons, 1952). The Revised Standard Version is the text used for biblical quotations throughout, except when noted otherwise.

3. Tertullian, "On Prescription Against Heretics," Ch. 7, in Alexander Roberts and James Donaldson, *The Anti-Nicene Fathers* (New York: Charles Scribners Sons, 1918), III, p. 246.

4. Tertullian, "On the Flesh of Christ," in ibid., p. 525.

5. Saint Augustine, *The City of God*. An abridged version from the translation by Gerald G. Walsh, et al. (Garden City, N.Y.: Doubleday Image Books, 1958), p. 519.

Suggested Reading

Armstrong, A. H., and R. A. Markus, *Christian Faith and Greek Philosophy* (1960). A presentation of the dialogue between Christianity and Greek philosophy.

Chadwick, Henry, *The Early Church* (1967). A survey of early Christianity in its social and ideological context.

Cochrane, C. N., *Christianity and Classical Culture* (1957). A study of thought from Augustus to Augustine; difficult, but worth the effort.

Davies, J. G., *The Early Christian Church* (1967). A splendid introduction to the first five centuries of Christianity.

Dodds, E. R., *Pagan and Christian in an Age of Anxiety* (1965). Examines the philosophical and spiritual climate from the accession of Marcus Aurelius to the conversion of Constantine.

Enslin, M. S., *Christian Beginnings* (1956). Strong on the Jewish background to Jesus.

Grant, Michael, *Jesus* (1977). A recent examination of the Gospels.

Jaeger, Werner, *Early Christianity and Greek Paideia* (1961). How the church fathers perpetuated and transformed Greek ideas.

Latourette, K. S., *A History of Christianity* (1953). Clearly written and eminently readable.

Mattingly, Harold, *Christianity in the Roman Empire* (1967). A brief, well-informed survey.

Nock, A. D., *Early Christianity and Its Hellenistic Background* (1964). A superb scholarly treatment of the relationship of Christianity to the wider cultural setting.

Nock, A. D., *St. Paul* (1963). A highly respected account of the principal Christian Apostle to the Greco-Roman world.

Pelikan, Jaroslav, *The Christian Tradition* (1971), vol. 1, *The Emergence of the Catholic Tradition*. The first of a five-volume series on the history of Christian doctrine.

Review Questions

1. Why does the life of Jesus present a problem to the historian?

2. What were Jesus' basic teachings?

3. What is the relationship of early Christianity to Judaism?

4. What was the historical significance of the belief in Jesus' resurrection?

5. How did Saint Paul transform a Jewish sect into a world religion?

6. What factors contributed to the triumph of Christianity in the Roman Empire?

7. Why did some early Christian thinkers object to the study of classical literature? What arguments were advanced by the defenders of classical learning? What was the outcome of this debate? Why was it significant?

8. What arguments were advanced by the bishop of Rome to support his supremacy over the church organization?

9. What is the historical significance of Saint Basil, Saint Martin of Tours, and Saint Benedict?

10. What is the signficance of the controversy over Christ's nature and his relationship to God?

11. What were Saint Augustine's attitudes toward the fall of Rome, the worldly city, humanity, and Greek philosophy?

12. Compare and contrast the world-views of early Christianity and classical humanism.

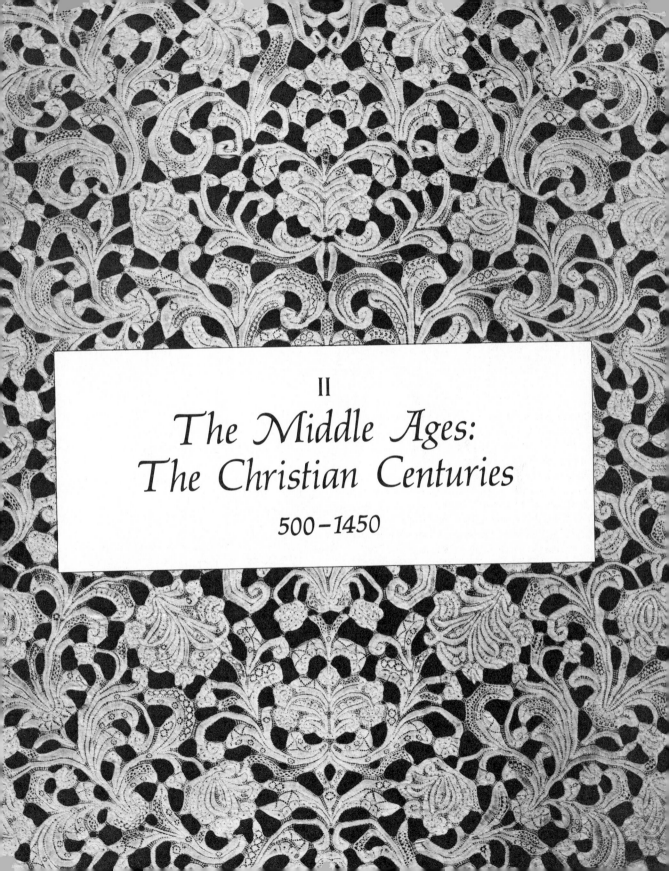

II
The Middle Ages:
The Christian Centuries

500–1450

9

The Rise of Europe: Fusion
of Classical, Christian,
and German Traditions

*T*he triumph of Christianity and the establishment of Germanic Kingdoms on once-Roman lands constituted a new phase in Western history: the end of the ancient world and the beginning of the Middle Ages, a period that spanned a thousand years. In the ancient world the locus of Greco-Roman civilization was the Mediterranean Sea; the heartland of medieval civilization shifted to the north, to regions of Europe that Greco-Roman civilization had barely penetrated. During the Middle Ages, a common European civilization evolved that integrated Christian, Greco-Roman, and Germanic elements. Christianity was at the center of medieval civilization; Rome was the spiritual capital, and Latin the language of intellectual life; Germanic customs pervaded social and legal relationships.

An Age of Transition

The Medieval East: Byzantium and Islam, an Overview

Three new civilizations based on religion emerged on the ruins of the Roman Empire: Byzantium, Islam, and Latin Christendom (western and central Europe). Although the Roman Empire in the west fell to the German tribes, the eastern provinces survived. They did so because they were richer and more populous and because the main thrust of the Germanic and Hunnish invaders had been directed at the west. In the eastern regions, Byzantine civilization took shape. Its religion was Christianity, its culture Greek, and its machinery of administration Roman. The capital, Constantinople, was built on the site of the ancient Greek city of Byzantium, on a peninsula in the Straits of the Bosporus, the dividing line between Asia and Europe. Constantinople was a fortress city perfectly situated to resist attacks from land and sea.

175

Hagia Sophia. The extensive interior mosaics that once transformed the vaults of Hagia Sophia into the golden sky of heaven linked this Byzantine structure with Early Christian architecture. But the heights and vast domed interior were new and the hallmark of the First Golden Age of Byzantine art. The emperors strongly identified themselves with Christ, and elaborate church ceremonies necessitated the presence of the emperor. Hagia Sophia provided the dramatic setting. © *Bruno Barbey/Magnum)*

Byzantium During the Early Middle Ages (500–1050), Byzantine civilization was economically and culturally far more advanced than the Latin West. At a time when few Westerners (Latin Christians) could read or write, Byzantine scholars studied the literature, philosophy, science, and law of ancient Greece and Rome. Whereas trade and urban life had greatly declined in the West, Constantinople was a magnificent Byzantine city of schools, libraries, open squares, and bustling markets.

Over the centuries, many differences developed between the Byzantine church and the Roman church. The pope resisted domination by the Byzantine emperor, and the Byzantines would not accept the pope as head of all Christians. The two churches quarreled over ceremonies, holy days, the display of images, and the rights of the clergy. The final break came in 1054; the Christian church split into the Roman Catholic in the West and the Eastern (Greek) Orthodox in the East, a division that still persists.

Political and cultural differences widened the rift between Latin Christendom and Byzantium. Latin Christians refused to recognize that the Byzantine emperors were, as they claimed, successors to the Roman emperors. In the Byzantine empire, Greek was the language of religion and intellectual life; in the West it was Latin.

Byzantine emperors were absolute rulers who held that God had chosen them to rule and to institute the Lord's will on earth. As successors to the Roman emperors, they claimed to rule all the lands once part of the Roman Empire. Emperor Justinian, who reigned from 527 to 565, sought to regain the lands in the western Mediterranean that had been conquered by Germanic invaders. During his reign, Byzantine forces retook North Africa from the Vandals, part of southern Spain from the Visigoths, and Italy from the Ostrogoths, establishing a western capital at Ravenna.

The long and costly wars drained the treasury, however, and led to the neglect of defenses in the Near East and the Balkan Peninsula. The Balkans were invaded by Slavic tribes from the Black Sea region and by Avars and Bulgars originally from Central Asia; Syria was ravaged by the Persians. Nor were the conquered territories in the west secure. The Germanic Lombards, who had moved into northern Italy in the late sixth century, conquered much Byzantine territory that had been recently recovered from the Ostrogoths, and by 629 the Visigoths had driven the Byzantines from Spain.

In the early seventh century, the Byzantines faced a renewed threat from the Persians, who seized the Byzantine provinces of Syria, Palestine, and Egypt. In an all-out effort, however, Emperor Heraclius (ruled 610–641) regained the provinces and in 627 crushed the Persians near the ruins of the ancient

Ivory of Romanos II. Sculpture survived during the Byzantine period in the form of religious ivory panels. The figures of the emperor and empress exhibit the favored style: the bodies are elongated, stiff, and weightless. (*Cabinet des Médailles, Paris/Hirmer Fotoarchiv*)

city of Nineveh. But an exhausted Byzantine Empire had become vulnerable to the Muslim Arabs, who had burst out of the Arabian Desert seeking to propagate their new faith (see page 181). By 642 the Arabs had stripped the Byzantine Empire of Syria, Palestine, and Egypt, and by the beginning of the eighth century, they had taken North Africa. Near the end of the seventh century and again in

Islamic Astrolabe. The astrolabe, which measured latitude, served both an astronomical and an astrological purpose; it was used to tell the time of day, to locate the position of the planets, and to prepare horoscopes. (*Mas, Barcelona*)

717, the Muslims besieged Constantinople. But the Byzantine fleet was armed with a new weapon, "Greek fire"—a fiery explosive liquid shot from tubes, which set enemy ships afire and made blazing pools of flame on the water's surface. Thus, the light Byzantine ships were able to repulse the better-built Arab ships.

The Arabs' failure to take Constantinople was crucial not only for the Byzantine Empire, but also for the history of Christianity. Had this Christian fortress fallen in the eighth century, the Arabs would have been able to overrun the Balkan Peninsula and sail up the Danube River into the European heartland. After this defeat, however, Islamic armies largely concentrated their conquests outside Europe.

From the late ninth to the early eleventh centuries, the Byzantine forces grew stronger and even took the offensive against the Muslims. But soon new enemies threatened. By 1071 the Normans from France had driven the Byzantines from Italy; in the same year, the Seljuk Turks defeated the Byzantines in Asia Minor and subjugated most of the peninsula, the heart of the Byzantine Empire. Internal dissensions, however, led to the breakup of the Seljuk Empire.

Seeking to exploit Seljuk weakness and to regain lost territories, the Byzantines appealed to Latin Christians for help. Although European Christians had little love for the Byzantines, they did want to free Christian holy places from the Muslims. For this purpose, they undertook a series of Crusades beginning in the late eleventh century (see Chapter 10). In 1204, during the Fourth Crusade, Latin Christian knights (greedy for wealth) and Venetian merchants (eager to gain control of the rich Byzantine trade) decided to take Constantinople rather than to fight the Muslims.

The Latin Christians looted the city, destroying sacred books, vandalizing churches, and carrying huge amounts of gold, jewels, and works of art back to western Europe. They also seized islands along Constantinople's major trade routes, set up kingdoms on Byzantine lands, and tried to force Latin forms of Christianity upon the Byzantine Greeks. The Orthodox Greeks resisted, and for nearly sixty years Latin and Greek Christians fought one another. Not until 1261 were the Westerners driven from Constantinople. The Byzantine Empire regained its independence, but its power was disastrously weakened. Crushing taxes, decreasing agricultural production, declining trade, and civil war continued to weaken the tottering empire.

The deathblow to the empire was dealt by another group of Turks. The Ottoman Turks had accepted Islam and had begun to build an empire. They drove the Byzantines from Asia Minor and conquered much of the Balkans. By the beginning of the fifteenth century, the Byzantine Empire consisted of only two small territories in Greece and the city

Mosque of Cordoba. The richness of Islamic culture and architecture is evident in Spain where Muslim rule lingered until the conquest of Granada in 1492. The arch of alternating stone would find its way into Christian churches, most memorably at Vezelay in southern France. (*Mas, Barcelona*)

of Constantinople. In 1453 the Ottoman Turks broke through Constantinople's great walls, looted the city, and slaughtered thousands of its inhabitants. After more than a thousand years, the Byzantine Empire had come to an end.

During its thousand-year history, Byzantium made a significant impact on world history. First, it prevented the Muslim Arabs from advancing into eastern Europe. Had the Arabs broken through Byzantine defenses, much of Europe might have been converted to the new faith of Islam. Another far-reaching effect arose under Justinian when the laws of ancient Rome were codified. This monumental achievement preserved Roman law's principles of reason and justice. Today's legal codes in much of Europe and Latin America

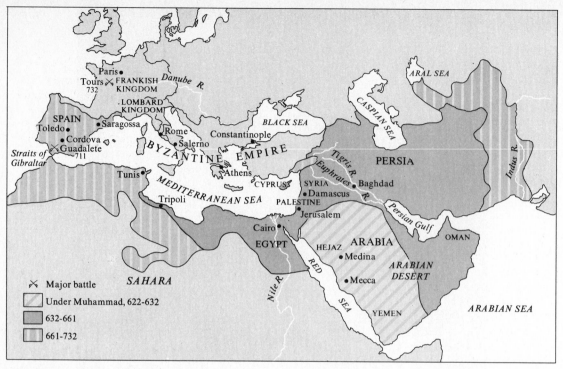

Map 9.1 The Expansion of Islam, 622–732

trace their roots to the Roman law recorded by Justinian's lawyers. The Byzantines also preserved the philosophy, science, mathematics, and literature of ancient Greece. Contacts with Byzantine civilization stimulated learning in both the Islamic world to the east and Latin Christendom to the west. Speros Vryonis, a student of Byzantine civilization, states: "The Byzantines carried the torch of civilization unextinguished at a time when the barbarous Germanic and Slav tribes had reduced much of Europe to near chaos: and they maintained this high degree of civilization until Western Europe gradually emerged and began to take form."[1] Byzantium also carried a higher civilization and Orthodox Christianity to the Slavic peoples, including the Russians, of eastern Europe. Byzantium gave the Slavs legal principles, art forms, and an alphabet—the Cyrillic, based on the Greek—that enabled them to write in their own languages.

Islam A second civilization to arise after Rome's fall was based on the vital new religion of Islam, which emerged in the seventh century among the Arabs of Arabia. Its founder was Muhammad (c. 570–632), a prosperous merchant in the trading city of Mecca. When Muhammad was about forty, he believed that he was visited by the Angel Gabriel, who ordered him to "recite in the name of the Lord!" Transformed by this vision, Muhammad was convinced that he had been chosen to serve as a prophet.

Although most desert Arabs worshipped tribal gods, in the towns and trading centers many Arabs were familiar with Judaism and Christianity, and some had accepted the idea of one God. Rejecting the many deities of the tribal religions, Muhammad offered the Arabs a new monotheistic faith, *Islam*, which means "surrender to Allah" (God).

Islam standards of morality and rules governing daily life are set by the Koran, which Muslims believe contains the words of Allah as revealed to Muhammad. Muslims believe that their religion is the completion and perfection of Judaism and Christianity. They regard the ancient Hebrew prophets as messengers of God and value their message of compassion and the oneness of humanity. Muslims also regard Jesus as a great prophet, but do not believe that he was divine.

The merchants of Mecca would not accept this new faith, and to escape persecution, Muhammad and his small band of followers left Mecca in 622 for Medina, a town about 200 miles away. Their flight, known as the *Hegira*, or "breaking of former ties," is one of the most important events in Muslim history and is commemorated by yearly pilgrimages. The date of the Hegira became year one of the Muslim calendar.

In Medina, Muhammad gained converts and won respect as a judge, rendering decisions on such matters as family relations, property inheritance, and criminal behavior. Preaching a holy war against unbelievers, Muhammad urged followers to raid the trading caravans from Mecca and to subdue unfriendly Bedouin tribes. He tried to convert the Jews of Medina, but they would not accept him as a prophet, and mocked his unfamiliarity with the Old Testament and the learned writings of the rabbis. For a time, Muhammad actively persecuted Arabian Jews, expelling several thousand from Medina, seizing Jewish property, beheading some 600 Jewish men, and enslaving women and children. Later, Muhammad permitted the Arabian Jews the free exercise of their religion and guaranteed the security of their property. In 630, Mecca surrendered to a Muslim army without a fight. Soon Bedouin tribes all over Arabia had embraced Islam and recognized the authority of the Prophet Muhammad.

In a little more than two decades, Muhammad had united the often feuding Arabian tribes into a powerful force dedicated to Allah and the spreading of the Islamic faith. After Muhammad's death in 632, his friend Abu Bakr became his successor, or caliph; regarded as the defender of the faith, whose power derived from Allah, the caliph governed in accordance with Muslim law as defined in the Koran. Islam gave the many Arab tribes the unity, discipline, and organization to succeed in their wars of conquest. Under the first four caliphs, who ruled from 632 to 661, the Arabs with breathtaking speed overran the Persian Empire, stripped Byzantium of some of its provinces, and invaded Europe. Muslim warriors believed that they were engaged in a holy war (*jihad*) to spread Islam to nonbelievers and that those who died in the jihad were assured a place in paradise. A desire to escape from the barren Arabian desert and to exploit the rich Byzantine and Persian lands was another compelling reason for expansion. In the east, Islam's territory eventually extended into India and to the borders of China; in the west, it encompassed North Africa and most of Spain but the Muslims' northward push lost momentum and was halted in 732 at the battle of Tours in southern France.

In the eighth and ninth centuries under the Abbasid caliphs, Muslim civilization entered its golden age. Islamic civilization creatively synthesized Arabic, Byzantine, Persian, and Indian cultural traditions. During the Early Middle Ages, when learning was at a low point in western Europe, the Muslims had forged a high civilization.

Muslim science, philosophy, and mathematics rested largely on the achievements of the ancient Greeks. The Muslims acquired Greek learning from the older Persian and Byzantine civilizations, which had kept alive the Greek inheritance. By translating Greek works into Arabic and commenting on them, Muslim scholars performed the great historical task of preserving the philosophic and scientific heritage of ancient Greece. Greek learning, supplemented by original contributions of Muslim scholars and scientists, was then passed on to Christian Europe.

There are numerous examples of Muslim brilliance in mathematics, science, and philosophy. Muslim mathematicians did original work in algebra and trigonometry; Muslim astronomers corrected the observations made by ancient astronomers, particularly Ptolemy. Building on the medical knowledge of the Greeks, Muslim physicians became the best-trained and most skillful doctors of the time. Surgeons performed amputations, removed cancerous tissue, devised new medicines, and used anesthetics in performing operations. The best Muslim hospitals had separate wards for fevers, surgical cases, eye diseases, and dysentery. Well ahead of their time were those Muslim doctors who recommended humane treatment for the mentally ill.

Muslim thinkers employed the categories of Greek philosophy to explain Islamic doctrine. Al-Farabi (c. 870–950), who wrote commentaries on Aristotle, offered proofs for God's existence based on Aristotelian logic that were later studied by medieval Christian philosophers. The most eminent Muslim thinker, Ibn-Sina, known to the West as Avicenna (980–1037), was a poet, doctor, scientist, and philosopher who wrote on every field of knowledge. His philosophic works, which relied heavily on Aristotle, had an important influence on medieval Christian thinkers. Another giant of Muslim learning was Ibn-Rushd, whom westerners call Averroës (1126–1198). Averroës insisted that the Koran did not oppose the study of philosophy and held that the ancient Greeks— even though they were not Muslims—had discovered truth. His commentaries on Aristotle were studied in western universities, where they sparked an important controversy (see Chapter 11).

The Arab Empire, stretching from Spain to India, was unified by a common language (Arabic), a common faith, and a common culture. By the eleventh century, however, the Arabs began losing their dominance in the Islamic world. The Seljuk Turks, who had taken Asia Minor from the Byzantines, also conquered the Arabic lands of Syria, Palestine, and much of Persia. Although the Abbasid caliphs remained the religious and cultural leaders of Islam, political power was exercised by Seljuk sultans. In the eleventh and twelfth centuries, the Muslims lost Sicily and most of Spain to Christian knights, and European Crusaders carved out kingdoms in the Near East.

In the thirteenth century came a new wave of invaders, the Mongols from Central Asia. Led by Genghis Khan, Mongolian archers, mounted on fast-moving ponies, poured across Asia into Muslim lands. By 1227, when Genghis Khan died, the eastern part of the Muslim world had fallen to the Mongols. After the death of Genghis Khan, some Mongol forces swept across Russia and threatened Central Europe; others continued to advance on Muslim lands in the Near East. Storming Baghdad in 1258, the Mongols burned, plundered, and killed with savage fury; among the 50,000 people slaughtered was the last Abbasid caliph. The Mongols devastated the palaces, libraries, and schools that had made Baghdad the cultural capital of the Islamic world. A year later they marched into Syria, again killing and looting. Their brutal advance westward was finally stopped in 1260 in Palestine by Egyptian forces.

By the beginning of the fourteenth century, the Muslim world seemed less threatened. In the Near East, the Muslims had recaptured the last Christian state founded by the Crusaders, while the Mongols, who had by this time converted to Islam, remained in Persia and were unable to advance westward. In the late fourteenth century, however, the Mongols under Tamerlane again menaced the Near East. Another bloody conqueror, Tamerlane cowed opposition with huge pyramids built from the skulls of thousands of slaughtered victims. After Tamerlane's death in 1404, his empire disintegrated and its collapse left the way open for the Ottoman Turks.

The Ottoman Empire reached its height in the sixteenth century with the conquest of Egypt, North Africa, Syria, and the Arabian coast. The Ottomans developed an effective system of administration, but their empire lacked the vitality that had kept the Muslim world more advanced than western Europe for most of the Middle Ages. Thus, the Ottomans did not restore the cultural brilliance, the thriving trade, or the prosperity that the Muslim world had known under the Abbasid Caliphs of Baghdad.

Although they experienced centuries of cultural greatness, neither Byzantium nor Islam made the breakthroughs in science, technology, philosophy, economics, and political thought that gave rise to the modern world. This process would be the singular achievement of Europe. During the Early Middle Ages, Latin Christendom was culturally far behind the two Eastern civilizations, but by the twelfth century it had caught up. In succeeding centuries it produced the movements that ushered in the modern age: Renaissance, Reformation, Scientific Revolution, Age of Enlightenment, French Revolution, and Industrial Revolution.

Western Europe: Political and Economic Transformation

From the sixth to the eighth centuries, Europe was struggling to overcome the disorders created by the breakup of the Roman Empire and the deterioration of Greco-Roman civilization. A new civilization with its own distinctive style was taking root. It consisted of elements from the Greco-Roman past, the traditions of the Germans, and the Christian outlook. But it would take centuries for this new civilization to bear fruit.

In the fifth century, German invaders founded kingdoms in North Africa, Italy, Spain, Gaul, and Britain—lands formerly belonging to Rome. Even before the invasions, the Germans had acquired some knowledge of, and attraction for Roman culture. Therefore, the new Germanic rulers did not seek to destroy Roman civilization, but to share in its advantages. For example, Theodoric the Great, the Ostrogoth ruler of Italy, retained the Roman senate, government officials, civil service, and schools; the Burgundians in Gaul and the Visigoths in Spain maintained Roman law for their conquered subjects; and Clovis, a Frankish ruler, wore Roman imperial colors and took Roman titles.

But the Germanic kingdoms, often torn by warfare, internal rebellion, and assassination, provided a poor political base on which to revive a decadent and dying classical civilization. Most of the kingdoms survived for only a short time and had no enduring impact.

In 533–534, Byzantium destroyed the Vandal kingdom in North Africa and the Vandals disappeared as a people; a similar fate befell the Ostrogoth kingdom in Italy two decades later. In the early eighth century, Muslim Arabs destroyed the Visigoth kingdom in Spain. An exception to this trend occurred in Gaul, where the most successful of the Germanic kingdoms was established by the Franks—the founders of the new Europe.

The Roman world was probably too far gone to be rescued, but even if this were not so, the Germans were culturally unprepared to play the role of rescuer. By the end of the seventh century the old Roman lands in the West showed a marked decline in central government, town life, commerce, and learning. The German invaders, while vigorous and brave, were essentially a rural and warrior people who were tribal in organization and outlook. Their native culture, without cities or written literature, was primitive in comparison to the literary, philosophic, scientific, and artistic achievements of the Greco-Roman world. The Germans were not equipped to reform the decaying Roman system of administration and taxation, to cope with the economic problems that had burdened the Empire, or to breathe new life into the dying humanist culture.

Roman ideas of citizenship and the legal state were totally alien to Germanic tradition. The Germans gave loyalty to their kindred and to a tribal chief, not to an impersonal state that governed citizens of many nationalities. The king viewed the land he controlled as a private possession that could be divided among his sons after his death—a custom that produced numerous and devastating civil wars and partitions. Unlike the Romans, the Germanic invaders had no trained civil servants to administer the state and no system of taxation to provide a secure financial base for government. Barbarian kings subdivided their kingdoms into districts and chose members of the great noble families to administer each district. These noble counts dispensed justice, maintained order, and collected taxes in their districts. The danger always existed that the counts would usurp the monarch's authority.

The Germans also found Roman law strange. Roman law incorporated elements of Greek philosophy and was written, whereas German law at the time of the invasions consisted of unwritten tribal customs. Roman law applied to all people throughout the Empire regardless of nationality; a German could be judged only by the law of his own tribe. Roman judges investigated evidence and demanded proof; German courts relied on trial by ordeal. In a typical ordeal, a bound defendant was thrown into a river. If he sank, he was innocent; floating was interpreted as divine proof of guilt, as the pure water had "rejected" the evildoer. Although primitive by Roman standards, Germanic law did help to lessen blood feuds between families. Before long the Germanic kingdoms began to put customary tribal law, which had absorbed and continued to absorb elements from Roman law, into writing. Replacing Roman law and spreading throughout Europe, Germanic law became an essential element of medieval society.

The distinguishing feature of classical civilization, the vitality of its urban institutions, had deteriorated in the Late Roman Empire. This shift from an urban to a rural economy accelerated under the kingdoms created by Germanic chieftains. While the German kings retained Roman cities as capitals, they did not halt the process of decay that had overtaken urban centers. These rulers settled their people in the countryside, not in towns; they did not significantly utilize cities as instruments of local government; and they failed to maintain Roman roads. Although towns did not vanish altogether, they continued to lose control over their surrounding countryside and to decline in wealth and importance. They were the headquarters of bishops, rather than centers of commerce and intellectual life. Italy remained an exception to this general trend. There Roman urban institutions persisted, even during the crudest period of the Early Middle Ages. Italian cities kept some metal currency in circulation and traded with each other and with Byzantium.

Shrinking commerce during the Early Middle Ages was part of the process of decline begun in the Late Roman Empire. Although commerce never wholly disappeared—and indeed experienced temporary periods of renewed activity—it was predominantly localized and was controlled by colonies of Jews, Syrians, and Greeks, a sign of the economic inertia of Latin Christians. From the last decade of the fifth century to the middle of the seventh century, Byzantine merchants established themselves in the West and exchanged papyrus, spices, and textiles for European slaves. However, this trade dropped off greatly in the second half of the seventh century because as Muslim power expanded to control the Mediterranean, Byzantine merchants had to turn eastward for markets. Thus the bonds between East and West weakened, and Europe shifted its axis northward away from the Mediterranean. Few goods exchanged hands and few coins circulated; people produced for themselves what they needed.

The Waning of Classical Culture

Greco-Roman humanism, which had been in retreat since the Late Roman Empire, continued its decline in the centuries immediately following Rome's demise. The old Roman upper classes abandoned their heritage and absorbed the ways of their Germanic conquerors; the Roman schools closed and Roman law faded into disuse. The human figure, which had been the subject for Greco-Roman artists, was supplanted by primitive, geometric shapes. Few people other than clerics could read and write Latin, and even learned clerics were rare. Knowledge of the Greek language in Europe was almost totally lost, and the Latin rhetorical style deteriorated. Many literary works of classical antiquity were either lost or neglected. European culture seemed much poorer than the high civilizations of Byzantium, Islam, and ancient Rome.

During this period of cultural poverty, the few persons who were learned generally did not engage in original thought, but salvaged and transmitted remnants of classical civilization. Given the context of the times, this was a considerable achievement. These individuals retained respect for the inheritance of Greece and Rome at the same time that they remained devoted to Christianity. In a rudimentary way, they were struggling to create a Christian culture that combined the intellectual tradition of Greece and Rome with the religious teachings of the Christian church.

An important figure in the intellectual life of this transitional period was Boethius (480–c. 525), a descendant of a noble family. Boethius had received a classical education at the Platonic Academy at Athens before Emperor Justinian closed it in 529. Later Boethius served the Ostrogothic king Theodoric I (c. 489–526), who ruled Italy. Recognizing that Greco-Roman civilization was dying, Boethius tried to rescue the intellectual heritage of antiquity. Boethius translated into Latin some of Aristotle's treatises on logic. In addition, Boethius wrote commentaries on Aristotle, Cicero, and Porphyry, a Neo-Platonist philosopher, as well as treatises on theology and textbooks on arithmetic, astronomy, and music. But his life was cut short when Theodoric had him executed in 524 or 525 for allegedly participating in a plot against the throne.

While in prison awaiting execution, Boethius wrote *The Consolation of Philosophy*, which is regarded as one of the masterpieces of world literature. After a sudden turn of fortune had deprived him of power, prestige, and possessions and had confronted him with the imminence of death, Boethius pondered the meaning of life: "Think you that there is any certainty in the affairs of mankind when you know that often one swift hour can utterly destroy a man?"[2] Alone in his dungeon, he turned not to Christ, but to the philosophical training of his youth for guidance and consolation. He derived comfort from Lady Philosophy, who reassured him, in the tradition of Socrates and the Stoics, that "if then you are master of yourself, you will be in possession of that which you will never wish to lose, and which Fortune will never be able to take from you."[3] No tyrant

can "ever disturb the peculiar restfulness which is the property of a mind that hangs together upon the firm basis of its reason."[4] In the life and thought of Boethius the classical tradition lived on. He was a bridge between a classical civilization too far gone to be revived and a Christian civilization still in embryo.

Until the twelfth century virtually all that Latin Christendom knew of Aristotle came from Boethius's translations and commentaries. Similarly, his work in mathematics, which contains fragments from Euclid, was the principal source for the study of that discipline in the Early Middle Ages. He also bequeathed to future generations basic philosophic definitions and terms. In his theological writings he attempted to demonstrate that reason did not conflict with orthodoxy, an early attempt to attain a rational comprehension of belief—to join faith to reason, as he expressed it. Boethius's effort to examine Christian doctrines rationally, a principal feature of medieval philosophy, would grow to maturity in the twelfth and thirteenth centuries. Writing in the sixth century, Boethius was a forerunner of this movement.

Cassiodorus (c. 490–575), a contemporary of Boethius, was born in southern Italy of a good family; he served three Ostrogoth kings. Although Cassiodorus wrote the twelve-volume *History of the Goths* and some theological treatises, his principal importance was as a collector of Greek and Latin manuscripts and as an advocate of higher education to improve the clergy's quality. In his educational writings he justified the importance of studying secular literature as an aid to understanding sacred writings. Even though his works were not original, they did rescue some ideas of the ancients from oblivion; these ideas would bear fruit again in later centuries. Cassiodorus's plans for founding a university in Rome modeled after the one in Alexandria did not materialize; in fact, six hundred years would elapse before universities would arise in Latin Christendom. Leaving political office, Cassiodorus retired to a monastery where he initiated the monastic practice of copying classical texts. Without this tradition, many key Christian and pagan works would undoubtedly have perished.

In Spain, Isidore of Seville (c. 576–636) compiled an encyclopedia, *Etymologiae*, covering a diversity of topics from arithmetic to God to furniture. Isidore derived his information from many secular and religious sources. Quite understandably his work contained many errors, particularly in its references to nature. For centuries, though, the *Etymologiae* served as a standard reference work and was found in every monastic library of note.

The translations and compilations made by Boethius, Cassiodorus, and Isidore, the books collected and copied by monks, and schools established in monasteries (particularly those in Ireland, England, and Italy) kept intellectual life from dying out completely in the Early Middle Ages. Amid the deterioration of political authority, the stagnation of economic life, and the decline in learning, a new civilization was emerging. German and Roman peoples intermarried, and Roman, German, and Christian traditions intermingled. But it was the church more than anything else that gave form and direction to the emerging civilization.

The Church: The Shaper of Medieval Civilization

The Church as Unifier

Christianity was the integrating principle, and the church was the dominant institution of the Middle Ages. During the Late Roman Empire, as the Roman state and its institutions decayed, the church gained in power and importance; its organization grew stronger and its membership increased. Unlike the Roman state, the church was a healthy and vital organism. The elite of the Roman Empire had severed their commitment to the values of classical civilization, whereas the church leaders were intensely devoted to their faith.

During the invasions of the fifth and sixth centuries, the church assumed many political functions formerly performed by the Roman state, and continued to convert the Germanic tribes. By teaching a higher morality, the church tamed the warrior habits of the German peoples. By preserving some of the high culture of Greece and Rome, it opened German minds to new ideas. When the Empire collapsed, the church retained its administrative system and preserved elements of Greco-Roman civilization. The church served as a unifying and civilizing agent and provided people with an intelligible and purposeful conception of life and death. In a dying world, the church was the only institution capable of reconstructing civilized life.

Thus, the Christian outlook was the foundation of medieval civilization, not the traditions of the German barbarians. People saw themselves as participants in a great drama of salvation. There was only one truth—God's revelation to humanity. There was only one avenue to heaven, and it passed through the church. God had established the church to administer the rites through which his love and protection (grace) was bestowed on people. Without the church, people would remain doomed sinners. To the medieval mind, society without the church was as inconceivable as life without the Christian view of God and the purpose of life. Membership in a universal church replaced citizenship in a universal empire. Across Europe, from Italy to Ireland, a new society centered on Christianity was forming.

Monks and the Papacy

Monks were instrumental in constructing the foundations of medieval civilization. During the seventh century, intellectual life on the Continent continued its steady decline. In the monasteries of England and Ireland, however, a tradition of learning persisted. In the early fifth century, Saint Patrick had converted the Irish to Christianity. In Ireland, Latin became firmly entrenched as the lan-

Monastery of Mont St. Michel. The monastic institutions throughout western Europe stood firm amid the intellectual and cultural confusion of the early Middle Ages. By copying ancient manuscripts and studying Latin, monks preserved elements of classical civilization. (*French Government Tourist Office*)

guage of both the church and scholars at a time when it was in danger of disappearing in many parts of the Continent. Irish clergymen preserved and cultivated both Greek and Latin and revived Latin's use during their missionary activities on the Continent. Irish scholars engaged in Biblical analysis, and in addition to copying manuscripts, they decorated them with an exquisite eye for detail. In England, the Anglo-Saxons, who converted to Christianity mainly in the seventh century, also established monasteries that kept learning alive. The Venerable Bede (673–735) wrote commentaries on Scripture and translated the fourth Gospel (Saint John's) into Anglo-Saxon. Bede is best known for his *Ecclesiastical History of the English People*, one of the finest historical works in the Middle Ages.

In the sixth and seventh centuries, Irish monks practiced their Christian missionary activities from monasteries on the Continent. Once converted, many Anglo-Saxons embraced Benedictine monasticism and, continuing the efforts of Irish monks, became the chief agents for the conversion of the people in Northern Europe. By converting pagans to Christianity, monks made possible a unitary European civilization based on a Christian foundation. By copying and preserving ancient texts, monks and nuns also kept alive elements of ancient civilization.

During the Early Middle Ages, when cities were in decay, monasteries were the principal cultural centers; they would remain so until the rebirth of towns in the High Middle Ages. By instructing peasants in superior methods of farming, monks were partly responsible for the reclamation of lands that had been neglected or devastated during the great invasions. Monasteries also offered succor to the sick and the destitute and served as places of refuge for travelers. To the medieval mind, the monk's selfless devotion to God, his adoption of poverty, and his dedication to prayer and contemplation represented the highest expression of the Christian way of life; it was the finest and most certain path to salvation. Regarding the monks as soldiers in the war against paganism, unorthodoxy, and heresy, the papacy protected monasteries and encouraged their spread.

The Early Middle Ages was a formative period for the papacy, as it was for society in general. The status of the papacy was closely tied to events in Italy. In the sixth century, the Byzantine Emperor Justinian, who viewed the breakup of Rome as only temporary, sought to regain western lands lost to the Germanic invaders. In 533–534, a Byzantine force led by Belisarius destroyed the Vandal kingdom in North Africa. The Byzantines then invaded Italy, breaking the power of the Ostrogoths. The destruction of the Ostrogoth kingdom opened the way for the Lombards, the last Germanic people to settle in once Roman lands. In the last part of the sixth century the Lombards invaded Italy and seized much of the territory that the Byzantines had regained from the Ostrogoths.

The Lombard invasion provided the papacy with an opportunity to free itself from Byzantine domination. Increasingly, popes assumed control over the city of Rome and the surrounding territory, while at the same time seeking to protect these lands from the Lombards. At this critical stage, Gregory I, the Great (590–604), became pope. A descendant of a prominent and wealthy Roman senatorial family and a monk, Gregory turned out to be one of the ablest of the medieval popes. He used Roman methods of administration to organize and administer effectively papal property in Italy, Sicily, Sardinia, Gaul, and other regions. The papacy owned huge estates worked by serfs, timberlands, and mines, which provided the income for maintaining the clergy, churches, monasteries, hospitals, and orphanages in Rome and other places. Because of Gregory's efforts, the papacy became the leading financial institution of the day.

Gregory tried to strengthen the pope's authority within the church, insisting that all bishops and the Byzantine church in Constantinople were subject to papal authority. Establishing monasteries, he tightened the bonds between the monks and the papacy, and it was he who dispatched Benedictine monks to England to win over the Anglo-Saxons. The newly established Anglo-Saxon church looked to Rome for leadership. Gregory realized that if the papacy were to lead Christendom effectively, it must exercise authority over churches outside of Italy—a policy adopted by popes who succeeded him.

In addition to providing the papacy with a sound financial base and strengthening its ties with monasteries and non-Italian churches, Gregory engaged in other activities. Gregory wrote commentaries on the books of the Bible and authored many works dealing with Christian themes—the duties of bishops, the lives of saints and monks, miracles, and purgatory. Because of his many writings, Gregory is regarded as a father of the Latin church. Gregory was also an astute diplomat, and he knew that the papacy required the political and military support of a powerful kingdom to protect it from its enemies, especially the Lombards. Accordingly he set his sights on an alliance with the Franks; finally materializing 150 years later, this alliance between the papacy and Frankish kings was instrumental in the shaping of medieval history.

The Kingdom of the Franks

From their homeland in the Rhine River Valley, the Frankish tribes had expanded into Roman territory during the fourth and fifth centuries. The ruler Clovis united the various Frankish tribes and conquered most of Gaul.

In 496, he converted to Roman Christianity. Clovis's conversion to Catholicism was an event of great significance. A number of other German kings had adopted the Arian form of Christianity, which the church had declared heretical. By embracing Roman Christianity, the Franks became a potential ally of the papacy.

After Clovis's death in 511, the Frankish lands suffered hard times. His kingdom was divided, and the Merovingian rulers (so named after Merovech, a semilegendary ancestor of Clovis) engaged in fratricidal warfare and brutal murder. In the seventh century the various Merovingian rulers had become ineffective and lost much of their power to great landowners. The real ruler of each Frankish realm was the Mayor of the Palace, the king's chief officer. One of these, Pepin II of Heristal (687–714), triumphed over his rival mayors and became ruler of Frankland. Pepin was the founder of the Carolingian dynasty (so named after Charlemagne, the greatest of the Carolingians).

Succeeding Pepin was his son Charles Martel, who served as Mayor of the Palace from 717 to 741. Charles Martel subjected all Frankland to Carolingian rule and repulsed the Muslims in southern Gaul. But Muslim Arabs and Berbers from North Africa, who had conquered Visigoth Spain in the early eighth century, crossed the Pyrenees into Frankish Gaul and advanced northward along the old Roman road. At the Battle of Tours in 732, the Franks defeated the Muslims. Although the Muslims continued to occupy the Iberian Peninsula, they would advance no farther north into Europe. Charles Martel was succeeded by his son Pepin the Short, who in 751 deposed the last Merovingian king. With the approval of the papacy and his nobles, Pepin was crowned king by Boniface, a prominent bishop.

In approving Pepin's royal accession, the papacy was continuing Gregory's earlier efforts to gain an ally in its struggle against the Lombards, who still had designs on papal territory. In 753, Pope Stephen II journeyed across the Alps to confer with Pepin, who

Book of Kells. The beauty of the Book of Kells lies in the intricate richness of its interlacing and abstract design. The Virgin and Child on this manuscript page illustrate a more primitive representation of the human form than that found in classical art; the barbarian kingdoms had brought artistic activity to a virtual standstill. (*The Board of Trinity College, Dublin*)

welcomed the pontiff with respect. The pope anointed Pepin again as king of the Franks and appealed to him to protect the papacy from the Lombards. Pepin invaded Italy, defeated the Lombards, and turned over captured lands to the papacy. Pepin's donation made the pope ruler of the territory between

Rome and Ravenna, which became known as the Papal States.

The Era of Charlemagne

The alliance between the Franks and the papacy was continued by Pepin's successor, Charlemagne (Charles the Great), who ruled from 768 to 814. Charlemagne continued the Carolingian policy of expanding the Frankish kingdom. He destroyed the Lombard kingdom and declared himself king of the Lombards. He added Bavaria to his kingdom, and after long, terrible wars, he forced the Saxons to submit to his rule and to convert to Christianity. He conquered a region in northern Spain, the Spanish March, that served as a buffer between the Christian Franks and the Muslims in Spain.

Immense difficulties arose in governing the expanded territories. Size seemed an insuperable obstacle to effective government, particularly since Charlemagne's administrative structure, lacking in trained personnel, was primitive by Islamic, Byzantine, or Roman standards. The empire was divided into about 250 counties administered by counts—nobles personally loyal to the ruler. Men from powerful families, the counts served as generals, judges, and administrators, implementing the king's decisions. To supervise the counts, Charlemagne created *missi dominici* (royal messengers)—generally two laymen and a bishop or abbot—who made annual journeys to the different counties. The purpose of the missi dominici was to prevent counts and their subordinates from abusing their power and from undermining Charlemagne's authority.

On Christmas Day in Rome in the year 800, Pope Leo crowned Charlemagne Emperor of the Romans. The initiative for the coronation probably came from the papacy, not from Charlemagne. The meaning of this event has aroused conflicting opinions among historians, but certain conclusions seem justified. The title signified that the tradition of a world empire still survived, despite the demise of

the western Roman Empire three hundred years earlier. But because it was the pope who crowned Charlemagne, this meant that the emperor had a spiritual responsibility to spread and defend the faith. Thus Roman universalism was fused with Christian universalism.

The Frankish empire, of course, was only a dim shadow of the Roman Empire. The Franks had no Roman law nor Roman legions; there were no cities that were centers of economic and cultural activity; officials were not trained civil servants with a world outlook, but were uneducated war chieftains with a tribal viewpoint. Yet Charlemagne's empire did embody the idea of a universal Christian empire, an ideal that would endure throughout the Middle Ages.

The crowning of a German ruler as Emperor of the Romans by the head of the church represented the merging of German, Christian, and Roman elements, which is the essential characteristic of medieval civilization. This blending of traditions was also evident on a cultural plane, for Charlemagne, a German warrior-king, showed respect for classical learning and Christianity, both non-Germanic traditions.

Carolingian Renaissance

Charlemagne felt that it was his religious duty to raise the educational level of the clergy so that they understood and could properly teach the faith. To do so, it was necessary to overcome the illiteracy or semiliteracy of clergymen and to prepare sacred Scriptures that were uniform, complete, and free of errors. Charlemagne also fostered education to train administrators who would be capable of overseeing his kingdoms and royal estates; such men had to be literate.

To achieve his purpose, Charlemagne gathered some of the finest scholars in Europe. Alcuin of Northumbria, England (735–804), was given charge of the Palace School attended by Charlemagne and his family, high lords, and youths training to serve the em-

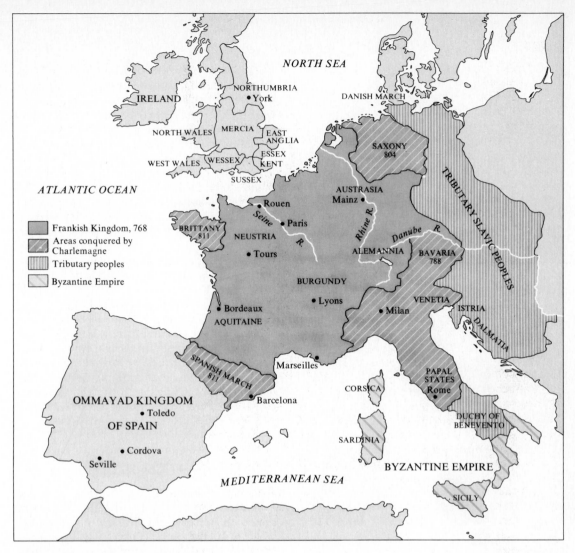

Map 9.2 The Carolingian World

peror. Alcuin was assigned the task of preparing a definitive text of the Bible from the various versions then in use. His text was an important achievement, for it was generally accepted, with modifications and corrections, as the standard version of the Bible throughout the Middle Ages.

The focus of the Carolingian Renaissance was predominantly Christian—an effort to train clergymen and improve their understanding of the Bible and the writings of the church fathers. This process raised the level of literacy and improved the Latin style. Most

important, monastic copyists continued to preserve ancient texts, which otherwise might never have survived—the oldest surviving manuscripts of many ancient works are Carolingian copies. Carolingian scholars thus helped to fertilize the cultural flowering known as the Twelfth-Century Awakening— the high point of medieval civilization.

Compared to the Greco-Roman past, to the cultural explosion of the twelfth and thirteenth centuries, or to the great Italian Renaissance of the fifteenth century, the Carolingian Renaissance seems slight indeed. Although the

Viking memorial stone. A migratory people, the Vikings did not produce monumental art. Viking art was simple but vital in its design and bold carving, as is illustrated in this memorial stone, which depicts a horseman and sailors. (*Antikvarisk-Topografiska Arkivet [ATA], Stockholm*)

Carolingian Renaissance did rediscover and revive ancient works, it did not recapture the spirit of Greece and Rome. Carolingian scholars did not engage in independent philosophical speculation or search for new knowledge, nor did they achieve that synthesis of faith and reason that would be constructed by the great theologians of the twelfth and thirteenth centuries. But we must bear in mind the cultural poverty that had pre-

vailed before the era of Charlemagne. The Carolingian Renaissance reversed the process of cultural decay that characterized much of the Early Middle Ages. Learning would never again fall to the low level it had reached in the centuries following the decline of Rome.

During the era of Charlemagne, a distinct European civilization had taken root. It blended the Roman heritage of a world empire, the intellectual achievement of the Greco-Roman mind, Christian otherworldliness, and the customs of the Germanic peoples. This nascent western European civilization differed from Byzantine and Islamic civilizations, and Europeans were growing conscious of the difference. But the new civilization was still centuries away from fruition.

Charlemagne's empire also engendered the ideal of a unified Latin Christendom—a single Christian community under one government. The ideal of a Christian world-state, Christendom, inspired many people, both clergy and laity, and would reach its peak from the eleventh to the thirteenth centuries.

The Breakup of Charlemagne's Empire

After Charlemagne's death in 814, his son Louis the Pious inherited the throne. Louis aimed to preserve the empire, but the task was virtually impossible. The empire's strength rested more on the personal qualities of Charlemagne than on any firm economic or political foundation. Moreover, the empire was simply too large and consisted of too many diverse peoples to be governed effectively. Along with facing Frankish nobles who sought to increase their own power at the emperor's expense, Louis had to deal with his own rebellious sons. After Louis died in 840, the empire was divided among the three sons who survived.

The Treaty of Verdun in 843 gave Louis the German the eastern part of the empire, which marked the beginning of Germany; to Charles the Bald went the western part, which was the start of France; and Lothair received the Middle Kingdom, which extended from

Rome to the North Sea. This Middle Kingdom would become a source of conflict between France and Germany into the twentieth century. As central authority waned, large landowners increasingly came to exercise authority in their own regions. Simultaneous invasions from all directions furthered this movement toward localism and decentralization.

In the ninth and tenth centuries, Latin Christendom was attacked on all sides. From bases in North Africa, Spain, and southern Gaul, Muslims ravaged coastal regions of southern Europe. The Magyars, Mongolian nomads, had crossed the steppes of Russia and established themselves on the plains of the Danube; their horsemen launched lightning raids into northern Italy, western Germany, and parts of France. Defeated in Germany in 933 and again in 955, the Magyars withdrew to what is now Hungary; they ceased their raids and adopted Christianity.

Still another group of invaders, the Northmen, or Vikings, sailed south from Scandinavia on their long wooden ships to plunder the coasts and river valleys of western Europe. These ferocious warriors spread terror wherever they landed. Superb seamen, the Vikings crossed the North Atlantic and settled in Iceland and Greenland; from there, they almost certainly travelled and landed on the coast of North America.

In pursuit of slaves, jewels, and precious metals hoarded in monasteries, these invaders plundered, destroyed, and murdered. Villages were devastated, ports were destroyed, and the population was decimated. Trade was at a standstill, coins no longer circulated, and farms were turned into wastelands. The European economy collapsed, the political authority of kings disappeared, and cultural life and learning withered.

These terrible attacks heightened political insecurity and accelerated anew the process of decentralization that had begun with the decline of Rome. During these chaotic times counts came to regard as their own the land that they administered and defended for their king. Similarly, the inhabitants of a district looked on the count or local lord as their ruler, for his men and fortresses protected

them. In their regions, nobles exercised public power formerly held by kings, an arrangement later designated as feudalism.

In instances where great lords failed to protect their territories from neighboring counts or from invaders, political power was further fragmented. In other areas local nobles chipped away at a count's authority in his county. In many regions the political unit shrank from the county to the *castellany*, the land close to a lord's castle. In such areas the local lord exercised virtually supreme authority; people turned to him for protection and for the administration of justice. Europe had entered an age of feudalism in which the essential unit of government was not a kingdom but a county or castellany, and political power was the private possession of local lords.

Feudal Society

Arising during a period of collapsing central authority, invasion, scanty public revenues, and declining commerce and town life, feudalism attempted to provide some order and security. Feudalism was not an organized system deduced logically from abstract principles, but an improvised response to the challenge posed by ineffectual central authority. Feudal practices were not uniform; they differed from locality to locality, and in some regions had barely taken root. Feudalism was a stopgap system of government that provided some order, justice, and law during an era of breakdown, localism, and transition. Feudalism would remain the predominant political arrangement until kings reasserted their authority.

Vassalage

Feudal relationships enabled lords to increase their military strength. The need for military support was the principal reason for the practice of vassalage, in which a man, in a solemn ceremony, pledged loyalty to a lord.

This feature of feudalism derived from an ancient German ceremony during which warriors swore personal allegiance to the head of the war-band. Among other things, the vassal gave military service to his lord, and received in return a *fief*, which was usually land. This fief was inhabited by peasants, and the crops that they raised provided the vassal with his means of support.

In return for the fief and the lords's protection, the vassal owed several obligations to his lord. These duties included rendering military assistance and supplying knights for his lord; sitting in the lord's court and judging cases, such as the breach of feudal agreements between the lord and his other vassals; providing lodgings when the lord traveled through the vassal's territory; giving a gift when the lord's son was knighted or when his eldest daughter married; and raising a ransom if the lord were captured by an enemy.

Generally, both lord and vassal felt honorbound to abide by the oath of loyalty. It became an accepted custom for a vassal to renounce his loyalty to his lord if the latter failed to protect him from enemies, mistreated him, or increased the vassal's obligations as fixed by the feudal contract. Similarly, if a vassal did not live up to his obligations, the lord would summon him to his court where he would be tried for treachery. If found guilty, the vassal could lose his fief and perhaps his life. Sometimes disputes between vassals and lords erupted into warfare. Because a vassal often held land from more than one lord and sometimes was himself a lord to vassals, situations frequently became awkward, complex, and confusing. On occasion, a vassal had to decide to which lord he owed *liege homage* (prime loyalty).

As feudalism evolved, the king came to be regarded as the chief lord, who had granted fiefs to the great lords, who in turn had divided them into smaller units and regranted them to vassals. Thus all members of the ruling class, from the lowliest knights to the king, occupied a place in the feudal hierarchy. In theory the king was the highest political authority and the source of land tenure, but in actual fact he was often less powerful than other nobles of the realm. Feudalism would decline when kings converted their theoretical powers into actual powers.

Feudal Law

Feudal law, which incorporated many features of traditional German law, differed markedly from Roman law. Roman law was universal, for it was enacted by a central government for a world empire; it was rational, for it sought to be in accord with natural law that applied to all; it was systematic, for it offered a framework of standards that applied to individual cases. Feudal law, on the other hand, was local, covering only a small region. And it was personal; in the Roman view the individual as a citizen owed obligations to the state, whereas under feudalism, a vassal owed loyalty and service to a lord according to the terms of a personal agreement made between them.

In the feudal view, lords and kings did not make law; rather, they discovered and confirmed it by examining ancient customs. Therefore, feudal patterns of landownership, military service, and wardship came to be regarded as an expression of ancient, unchanging, and inviolable custom. Consequently, if the vassal believed that his lord had violated the feudal agreement, that is, had broken faith with him and had transgressed upon traditions, the vassal would demand restoration of customary rights before an audience of his fellow vassals. Often lords battled each other, believing that they were defending their rights. Similarly, lords claimed the right to resist kings who did not honor their feudal agreements.

Feudal Warriors

Feudal lords viewed manual labor and commerce as degrading for men of their rank. They considered only one vocation worthy—

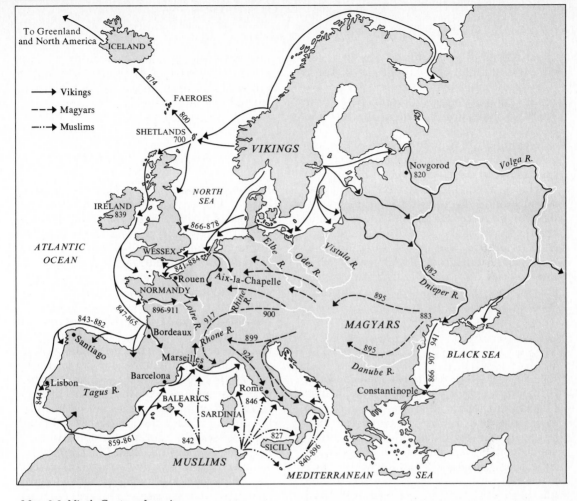

To Greenland
and North America

→ Vikings
--→ Magyars
-·-·→ Muslims

ICELAND

874

FAEROES

800

SHETLANDS
700

NORTH
SEA

IRELAND
839

ATLANTIC
OCEAN

866-878

WESSEX

841-884

Rouen

NORMANDY

896-911

847-865

843-882

Santiago

Bordeaux

Loire R.

917

Rhine R.

Aix-la-Chapelle

Elbe R.

Oder R.

Vistula R.

900

VIKINGS

Novgorod
820

Volga R.

882

Dnieper R.

895

MAGYARS

883

895

941

907

866

BLACK SEA

Lisbon

Tagus R.

Marseilles

Barcelona

BALEARICS

844

859-861

842

Rhone R.

899

924

Rome

846

SARDINIA

827

SICILY

840-896

Danube R.

Constantinople

MUSLIMS

MEDITERRANEAN   SEA

Map 9.3 Ninth-Century Invasions

that of warrior. Through combat, the lord demonstrated his valor, earned his reputation, measured his individual worth, derived excitement, added to his wealth, and defended his rights. Warfare was his whole purpose in life. During the twelfth century, to relieve the boredom of peacetime, nobles staged gala tournaments in which knights, fighting singly or in teams, engaged each other in battle to prove their skill and courage. The victors in these pageants not only gained honor from fellow nobles and admiring ladies, but also received prizes—falcons, crowns, and substantial amounts of money. The feudal glorification of combat became deeply ingrained in Western society, and has endured into the twentieth century. Over the centuries a code

of behavior, called *chivalry*, evolved for the feudal nobility. A true knight was expected to fight bravely, to demonstrate loyalty to his lord, and to treat other knights with respect and courtesy.

The church, in time, interjected a religious element into the warrior culture of the feudal knight. It sought to use the fighting spirit of the feudal class for Christian ends—knights could assist the clergy in enforcing God's will. To the Germanic tradition of loyalty and courage was added a Christian component; as a Christian gentleman, a knight was expected to honor the laws of the church and to wield his sword in the service of God. A knight was supposed to protect women, children, and the weak, and defend the church against heretics and infidels. The very ceremony of knighthood was placed within a Christian framework. A priest blessed the future knight's arms and prayed that the knight would always "defend the Just and Right."

Regarding the private warfare of lords as a lawless violence that menaced social life, the church in the eleventh century imposed strictures called "the Peace of God" and "the Truce of God." These restrictions limited feudal warfare to certain days of the week and certain times of the year. Thus the church tried to regulate warfare according to moral principles. Although only relatively effective, the Peace of God did offer Christian society some respite from plundering and incessant warfare.

Noblewomen

Feudal society was very much a man's world. In theory, women were held to be inferior to men; in practice, they were subjected to male authority. Fathers arranged the marriages of their daughters. Girls from aristocratic families were generally married at age sixteen or younger to men often twice their age; aristocratic girls who did not marry often had to enter a convent. The wife of the lord was at the mercy of her husband; if she annoyed him, she might expect a beating. But as the lady of the castle, she performed important duties. She assigned tasks to the servants, made medicines, preserved food, taught young girls how to sew, spin, and weave, and despite her subordinate position, took charge of the castle when her husband was away. Although the church taught that both men and women were precious to God and that marriage was a sacred rite, some clergymen viewed women as agents of the Devil—evil temptresses who, like the Biblical Eve, lured men into sin.

Feudalism had an enduring impact on Western civilization. It contributed to Western notions about honor, gentlemen, and romantic love (see Chapter 11). And most im-

portantly, the principle of limiting a king's power and the practice of parliamentary government also derived from feudal traditions (see Chapters 10 and 12).

Agrarian Society

Feudalism was built on an economic foundation known as *manorialism*. Although pockets of free peasantry remained, a village community (manor) consisting of serfs bound to the land became the essential agricultural arrangement in medieval society. The manorial village was the means of organizing an agricultural society with limited markets and money. Neither the lords who warred nor the clergymen who prayed performed economically productive work. Their ways of life were made possible by the toil of serfs.

The origins of manorialism can be traced in part to the Late Roman Empire, when peasants depended on the owners of large estates for protection and security. This practice developed further during the Early Middle Ages, especially during the invasions of Northmen, Magyars, and Muslims in the ninth and tenth centuries. Peasants continued to sacrifice their freedom in exchange for protection, or in some cases, they were too weak to resist the encroachments of local magnates. Like feudalism, manorialism was not a neat system, but consisted of improvised relationships and practices that varied from region to region.

A lord controlled at least one manorial village; great lords might possess hundreds. A small manor had a dozen families; a large one had as many as fifty or sixty. The manorial village was never completely self-sufficient, because salt, millstones, and metalware were generally obtained from outside sources; it did, though, constitute a balanced economic setting. Peasants grew grain and raised cattle, sheep, goats, and hogs; blacksmiths, carpenters, and stonemasons did the building and repairing; the village priest cared for the souls of the inhabitants; and the lord defended

Chronology 9.1 The Rise of Europe

496	Clovis adopts Roman Christianity
523	Boethius writes *Consolation of Philosophy*
540	Cassiodorus establishes a monastic library at Vivarium
596	Pope Gregory sends missionaries to convert the Anglo-Saxons
717	Charles Martel becomes Mayor of the Palace under a weak Merovingian king
732	Charles Martel defeats the Muslims at Tours
751	Pepin the Short, with the support of the papacy, deposes the Merovingian ruler and becomes king of the Franks
755	Pepin donates lands taken from Lombards to the papacy
768	Charlemagne becomes king of the Franks
774	Charlemagne defeats the Lombards
782	Alcuin of York heads Charlemagne's Palace School
c. 799	Charlemagne subdues the Saxons
800	Charlemagne is crowned Emperor of the Romans by Pope Leo III
814	Charlemagne dies and is succeeded by his son Louis the Pious
840	Death of Louis the Pious; the empire is divided among his sons
c. 840s	The height of Viking attacks
c. 890	Magyars invade central Europe

the manor and administered the customary law.

When a manor was attacked by another lord, the peasants found protection inside the walls of their lord's house. By the twelfth century, this building had in many places become a well-fortified stone castle. Poor roads, few bridges, and dense forests made travel difficult; thieves and warring knights made it unsafe. Peasants generally lived, worked, and died on the lord's estate and were buried in the village churchyard. Few persons had any contact with the world beyond the village of their birth.

In return for protection and the right to cultivate fields and to pass these holdings on to their children, the serf owed obligations to his lord, and his personal freedom was restricted in a variety of ways. Bound to the land, he could not leave the manor without the lord's consent. Before a serf could marry, he had to obtain the lord's permission and pay a fee. The lord could select a wife for his serf and force him to marry her. Sometimes a serf, objecting to the lord's choice, preferred to pay a fine: "Thomas of Oldbury came on summons and was commanded to take Agatha of Halesowen to wife; he said he would rather be fined."[5] These rules also applied to the serf's children, who inherited their parents' obligations. In addition to working his allotted land, the serf had to tend the fields reserved for the lord. Other services exacted by the lord included digging ditches, gathering firewood, building fences, repairing roads and bridges, and sewing clothes. Probably somewhat more than half the serf's workweek was devoted to fulfilling these labor obligations. Serfs also paid a variety of dues to the lord. These included the annual *capitation*, a tax considered a sign of servitude; the *taille*, a tax upon the serf's property; and the *heriot*, an inheritance tax imposed when a deceased serf's sons acquired the right to their father's lands. In addition, serfs paid *banalities* for using the lord's mill, bake-oven, and winepress—fees the serfs viewed as particularly odious.

Serfs derived some benefits from manorial relationships. They received protection during a chaotic era, and they possessed customary rights, which the lord often respected, to cottages and farmlands. If a lord demanded more services or dues than was customary, or if he interfered with their right to cottages or strips of farmland, the peasants might demonstrate their discontent by refusing to labor for the lord. Up to the fourteenth century, however, open rebellion was rare because lords possessed considerable military and legal power. The manorial system promoted attitudes of dependency and servility among the serfs; their hopes for a better life were directed toward heaven.

Medieval agriculture suffered from several deficiencies. Among them was the short supply of fertilizer; farmers depended solely on animal manure. Inadequate wood ploughs and primitive methods of harnessing draft animals resulted in low yields. Yet as the Middle Ages progressed, important improvements in agriculture (discussed in Chapter 10) did take place that had wide ramifications for medieval economic and social life.

Manorialism and feudalism presupposed an unchanging social order—clergy who prayed, lords who fought, and peasants who toiled. People believed that society functioned smoothly when each person accepted his or her status and performed his or her proper role. Consequently, a person's rights, duties, and relationship to law depended on one's ranking in the social order. To change position was to upset the organic unity of society. And no one, serfs included, should be de-

prived of the traditional rights associated with his or her rank. This arrangement was justified by the clergy:

God himself has willed that among men, some must be lords and some serfs, in such a fashion that the lords venerate and love God, and that the serfs love and venerate their lord following the word of the Apostle; serfs obey your temporal lords with fear and trembling; lords treat your serfs according to justice and equity.[6]

The revival of an urban economy and the re-emergence of central authority in the High Middle Ages would undermine feudal and manorial relationships.

Notes

1. Speros Vryonis, Jr., *Byzantium and Europe* (New York: Harcourt, Brace & World, 1967), p. 193.

2. Boethius, *The Consolation of Philosophy*, trans. by W. V. Cooper (New York: Modern Library, 1943), p. 26.

3. Ibid., p. 29.

4. Ibid., p. 34.

5. Quoted in G. G. Coulton, *Medieval Village, Manor, and Monastery* (New York: Harper Torchbooks, 1960), p. 82.

6. Quoted in V. H. H. Green, *Medieval Civilization in Western Europe* (New York: St. Martin's Press, 1971), p. 35.

Suggested Reading

Barber, Richard, *The Knight and Chivalry* (1982). The world of the feudal warrior.

Bark, W. C., *Origins of the Medieval World* (1960). The Early Middle Ages as a fresh beginning.

Dawson, Christopher, *The Making of Europe* (1957). Stresses the role of Christianity in shaping European civilization.

Duby, Georges, *The Early Growth of the European Economy* (1974). By a leading French medievalist.

Focillon, Henri, *The Year 1000* (1971). Conditions of life toward the end of the Early Middle Ages.

Ganshof, F. L., *Feudalism* (1964). A concise treatment of feudal institutions.

Keen, Maurice, *The Pelican History of Medieval Europe* (1969). A brief survey.

Laistner, M. L. W., *Thought and Letters in Western Europe A.D. 500 to 900* (1957). A comprehensive survey of European thought in the Early Middle Ages.

Latouche, Robert, *The Birth of Western Economy* (1966). Economic decline during the Early Middle Ages.

Lewis, A. R., *Emerging Medieval Europe* (1967). Good discussions of economic and social changes.

Lot, Ferdinand, *The End of the Ancient World* (1961). The transition from the ancient world to the Middle Ages.

Morrall, John B., *The Medieval Imprint* (1971). A brief survey.

Rowling, Marjorie, *Life in Medieval Times* (1973). All phases of medieval daily life.

Southern, R. W., *The Making of the Middle Ages* (1953). A brief survey.

Thompson, J. W., and Johnson, E. N., *An Introduction to Medieval Europe* (1937). Still a valuable text.

Tierney, Brian, *Western Europe in the Middle Ages* (1970). An outstanding text.

Zacour, Norman, *An Introduction to Medieval Institutions* (1969). Comprehensive essays on all phases of medieval society.

Review Questions

1. In what ways were Greco-Roman ideas and institutions alien to Germanic traditions?

2. How was the Roman world in the West transformed by the seventh century?

3. The civilization of Latin Christendom was a blending of Christian, Greco-Roman, and Germanic traditions. Explain this statement.

4. What was the significance of monks to medieval civilization?

5. Explain the significance of the following Frankish rulers: Clovis, Charles Martel, and Pepin the Short.

6. What crucial developments occurred during the reign of Charlemagne? Why were they significant?

7. What were the causes and effects of the breakup of Charlemagne's empire?

8. What conditions led to the rise of feudalism? How did feudal law differ from Roman law?

9. What conditions led to the rise of manorialism? What obligations did a serf have to the lord? What did the serf derive in return?

10

The High Middle Ages:
Vitality and Renewal

*B*y the end of the eleventh century, Europe showed many signs of recovery and vitality. The invasions of Magyars and Vikings had ended, and powerful lords and kings imposed greater order in their territories. Improvements in technology and the clearing of new lands increased agricultural production. More food, the fortunate absence of plagues, and the limited nature of feudal warfare contributed to a population increase. The revival of long-distance trade and the emergence of towns were other visible signs of economic expansion. Offensives against the Muslims—in Spain, in Sicily, and (at the end of the century) in the Holy Land—demonstrated Europe's growing might and self-confidence. So too did the German conquest and colonization of lands on the northeastern frontier of Latin Christendom.

Reform movements strengthened the bonds between the church and the people and increased the power of the papacy. During the High Middle Ages (1050–1270) the pope, as vice regent of Christ, sought to direct, if not to rule, all Christendom. European economic and religious vitality was paralleled by a cultural flowering in philosophy, literature, and the visual arts. The civilization of Latin Christendom had entered its golden age.

Economic Expansion

The High Middle Ages was a period of economic vitality. It witnessed an agricultural revolution, a commercial revolution, the rebirth of towns, and the rise of an enterprising and dynamic middle class.

An Agricultural Revolution

During the Middle Ages, important advances were made in agriculture. Many of these innovations occurred in the early Middle Ages, but were only gradually adopted and were

Eleventh-Century Calendar: Almanac Illustration of January. The innovation of the heavy plow helped spark an agricultural revolution. Increased productivity, in turn, contributed to the growth of towns and trade. (*The Bettmann Archive*)

not used everywhere; however, in time, they markedly increased production. By the end of the thirteenth century, medieval agriculture had reached a technical level far superior to that of the ancient world.

One innovation was a heavy plow that cut deeply into the soil. This new plow enabled farmers to work more quickly and effectively. As a result, they could cultivate more land, including the heavy moist soils of northern Europe that had offered too much resistance to the light plow. Another important advance in agricultural technology was the invention of the collar harness. The old yoke harness worked well with oxen, but it tended to choke horses which, because they move faster and have greater stamina than oxen, are more valuable for agricultural work. The introduction of the horseshoe to protect the soft hoofs of horses added to their ability to work on difficult terrain.

Two other developments were the widening use of the watermill by the tenth century and the introduction of windmills, which came into use in the twelfth century. Both inventions saved labor in grinding grain, and they replaced ancient hand-worked mills.

The gradual emergence of the three-field system of managing agricultural land, particularly in northern Europe, increased production. In the old, widely used two-field system, half the land was planted in autumn with winter wheat, while the other half was left fallow to restore its fertility. In the new three-field system, one third of the land was planted in autumn with winter wheat, a second third was planted the following spring with oats and vegetables, and the last third remained fallow. The advantage of the three-field system was, first, that two thirds of the land was farmed and only one third was not in use. Second, the diversification of crops made more vegetable protein available.

Increased agricultural production reduced the number of deaths by starvation and dietary disease and thus contributed to a population increase. Grain surpluses also meant that draft animals and livestock could survive the winter. The growing number of animals provided a steady source of fresh meat and milk and increased the quantity of manure for fertilizer.

Soon the farmlands of a manorial village could not support its growing population. Consequently, peasants had to look beyond their immediate surroundings and colonize trackless wastelands. Lords vigorously promoted this conversion of uncultivated soil into agricultural land because it increased their incomes. Monastic communities also actively engaged in this enterprise. Almost everywhere, peasants were draining swamps, clearing forests, and establishing new villages. Their endeavors during the eleventh and twelfth centuries brought vast areas of Europe under cultivation for the first time. New agricultural land was also acquired through expansion, the most notable example being the organized settlement of lands to the east by German colonists.

The colonizing and cultivation of virgin lands contributed to the decline of serfdom. Lords owned vast tracts of forests and swamps that would substantially increase their incomes if cleared, drained, and farmed. But serfs were often unwilling to move from their customary homes and fields to do the hard labor needed to cultivate these new lands. To lure serfs away from their villages, lords promised them freedom from most or all personal services. In many cases the settlers fulfilled their obligations to the lord by paying rent rather than by performing services or providing foodstuffs, thus making the transition from serfs to freemen. In time, they came to regard the land as their own. As a result of these changing economic conditions, the percentage of French peasants who were serfs had fallen from 90 percent in 1050 to about 10 percent in 1350.

The improvement in agricultural technology and the colonization of new lands altered the conditions of life in Europe. Surplus food and the increase in population freed people to work at nonfarming occupations, making possible the expansion of trade and the revival of town life.

The Revival of Trade

Expanding agricultural production, the termination of Viking attacks, greater political stability, and an increasing population produced a revival of commerce. During the Early Middle Ages, Italians and Jews kept alive a small amount of long-distance trade between Catholic Europe and the Byzantine and Islamic worlds. In the eleventh century, sea forces of Italian trading cities cleared the Mediterranean of Muslim fleets. As in Roman times, goods could circulate once again from one end of the sea to the other. The cities of Venice, Amalfi, Genoa, and Pisa grew prosperous from the lucrative Mediterranean

trade. The expanding population of northern Europe provided a market for Eastern silks, sugar, spices, and dyes, and Italian merchants were quick to exploit this demand.

By the beginning of the eleventh century the European economy showed unmistakable signs of recovery from the disorders of the previous century. During the next two centuries, local, regional, and long-distance trade gained such a momentum that some historians describe the period as a commercial revolution that surpassed the commercial activity of the Roman Empire during the pax Romana. A class of traders emerged that had business contacts in other lands, know-how, and ambition.

Crucial to the growth of trade were international fairs, where merchants and craftsmen set up stalls and booths to display their wares—swords, leather saddles, tools, rugs, shoes, silks, spices, furs, fine furniture, and other goods. Because of ever-present robbers, lords provided protection for merchants carrying their wares to and from fairs. Each fair lasted about three to six weeks; then the merchants would move on to another site. The Champagne region in northeastern France was the great center for fairs.

The principal arteries of trade flowed between the eastern Mediterranean and the Italian cities, between Scandinavia and the Atlantic coast, between northern France, Flanders, and England, and from the Baltic Sea in the north to the Black Sea and Constantinople via Russian rivers. The fine woolen cloth manufactured in Flanders provided the principal stimulus for commerce along the Atlantic coast, and Flemish merchants prospered. In exchange for Flemish cloth, Scandinavians traded hunting hawks and fur; the English traded raw wools; and the Germans traded iron and timber. A wine trade also flourished between French vineyards and English wine merchants.

Because of their strategic position, Italian towns acted as middlemen between the trade centers of the eastern Mediterranean and those of Latin Christendom. Luxury goods from as far away as India and China were transported to Italy by Italian ships, and then taken overland to parts of Germany and France. In addition, the Italians extended their trade and increased their profits by sailing westward into the Atlantic Ocean and then north to the markets of Spain, the Netherlands, and England. On return voyages they brought back wool and unfinished cloth, which in turn stimulated the Italian textile industry. Since individual businessmen often lacked sufficient capital for these large-scale enterprises, groups of merchants formed partnerships. By enabling merchants to pool their capital, reduce their risks, and expand their knowledge of profit-making opportunities, these arrangements furthered commerce.

Increased economic activity led to other advances in business techniques. Underwriters insured cargoes; the development of banking and credit instruments made it unnecessary for merchants to carry large amounts of cash. The international fairs not only were centers of international trade, but also served as capital markets for international credit transactions. The arrangements made by fair-going merchants to settle their debts held the origin of the bill of exchange. The development of systematic bookkeeping, without which no large-scale commercial activity can be conducted on a continuous basis, was another improvement in business techniques. So too was the formation of a body of commercial law that defined the rules of conduct for debts and contracts.

The Rise of Towns

In the eleventh century, towns emerged anew throughout Europe, and in the next century they became active centers of commercial and intellectual life. Towns were a new and revolutionary force—socially, economically, and culturally. Towns contributed to the decline of manorialism because they provided new opportunities, other than food producing, for commoners. A new class of merchants and

craftsmen came into being. This new class—the middle class—was made up of people who unlike the lords and serfs, were not affiliated with the land. The townsman was a new man with a different value system from that of the lord, the serf, or the clergyman.

One reason for town growth was the increased food supply arising from advances in agricultural technology. Surplus farm production meant that the countryside could support an urban population of artisans and professionals. Another reason for the rise of urban centers was the expansion of trade. Towns emerged in locations that were natural for trade—sea coasts, riverbanks, crossroads, and market sites; they also sprang up outside fortified castles and monasteries and on surviving Roman sites. The colonies of merchants who gathered at these places were joined by peasants skilled in crafts or willing to work as laborers. From a medieval record comes this description of the emergence of a town.

After this castle was built, certain traders began to flock to the place in front of the gate to the bridge of the castle, that is merchants, tavern-keepers, then other outsiders drifted in for the sake of food and shelter of those who might have business transactions with the count, who often came there. Houses and inns were erected for their accommodation, since there was not room for them within the chateau. These habitations increased so rapidly that soon a large ville came into being.[1]

Medieval towns were protected from outside attack by thick high walls, towers, and drawbridges. Most towns had a small population; the largest ones—Florence, Ghent, and Paris—had between 50,000 and 100,000 inhabitants. Covering only small areas, these walled towns were crowded with people. The narrow and crooked streets were lined with the booths and wares of merchants and artisans and were strewn with refuse. During the day the streets were jammed with mer-

Map 10.1 Medieval Trade Routes ▶

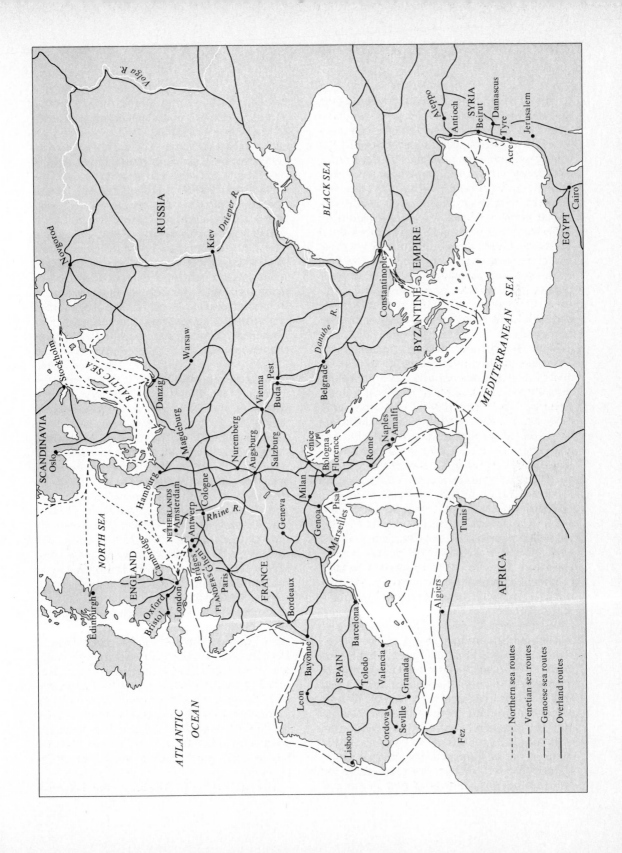

ATLANTIC OCEAN

SCANDINAVIA
Oslo
Stockholm
BALTIC SEA
NORTH SEA
Edinburgh
ENGLAND
Cambridge
Oxford
Bristol
London
NETHERLANDS
Amsterdam
Antwerp
Bruges
Ghent
FLANDERS
Hamburg
Cologne
Rhine R.
Paris
FRANCE
Geneva
Bordeaux
Bayonne
Leon
Lisbon
SPAIN
Toledo
Cordova
Seville
Barcelona
Valencia
Granada
Fez
AFRICA
Algiers
Tunis
Marseilles
Genoa
Pisa
Milan
Salzburg
Augsburg
Nuremberg
Magdeburg
Danzig
Novgorod
RUSSIA
Kiev
Dnieper R.
Volga R.
Warsaw
Vienna
Pest
Buda
Belgrade
Danube R.
BLACK SEA
Constantinople
BYZANTINE EMPIRE
Venice
Bologna
Florence
Rome
Naples
Amalfi
MEDITERRANEAN SEA
EGYPT
Cairo
SYRIA
Aleppo
Antioch
Beirut
Damascus
Tyre
Acre
Jerusalem

------- Northern sea routes
— — — Venetian sea routes
—·—·— Genoese sea routes
————— Overland routes

chants hawking their goods, women carrying baskets, men carting produce and merchandise, beggars pleading, and children playing. A festive occasion such as a procession honoring a patron saint sometimes brought traffic to a standstill; a hanging or a beheading was looked on as another festive occasion and always attracted a huge crowd. At night, the streets were deserted; few people ventured forth because the few elderly watchmen were no match for the numerous thieves.

Merchants and craftsmen organized guilds to protect their members from outside competition. The merchant guild in a town prevented outsiders from doing much business. A craftsman new to a town had to be admitted to the guild of his trade before he could open a shop. Competition between members of the same guild was discouraged. To prevent any guild member from making significantly more money than another member, a guild required that its members work the same number of hours, pay employees the same wages, produce goods of equal quality, and charge customers a just price. These rules were strictly enforced. Guilds also performed social and religious functions. Guildsmen attended meetings in the guildhall, celebrated holidays together, and marched in processions. The guilds cared for members who were ill or poor and extended help to widows and children of deceased members.

Because many towns were situated on land belonging to lords or on the sites of old Roman towns ruled by bishops, these communities at first came under feudal authority. In some instances, lords encouraged the founding of towns, for urban industry and commerce brought wealth to the region. However, tensions soon developed between merchants who sought freedom from feudal restrictions and lords and bishops who wanted to preserve their authority over the towns. Townsmen, or burghers, refused to be treated as serfs bound to a lord and liable for personal services and customary dues. The burghers wanted to travel, trade, marry, and dispose of their property as they pleased; they wanted

to make their own laws and levy their own taxes. Sometimes by fighting, but more often by payments of money, the townsmen obtained charters from the lords giving them the right to set up their own councils. These assemblies passed laws, collected taxes, and formed courts that enforced the laws. Towns became more or less self-governing city-states, the first since Greco-Roman days.

The leading citizens of the towns were the merchant-bankers, called patricians. Some patricians in the prosperous Italian towns enjoyed great wealth, owned considerable real estate, and engaged in business transactions involving large sums. These people generally dominated town politics; often the patricians obtained country estates and merged with the feudal aristocracy. Successful doctors and lawyers, in many instances the sons of patricians, also belonged to the urban elite. Below them on the social scale were master craftsmen in the more lucrative crafts (goldsmiths, for example) and large retailers. Then came small retailers, masters in the less profitable crafts, and journeymen training to be masters. At the bottom were the laboring poor—the bulk of the population—who were unprotected by guilds, had no special skills, and were subject to unemployment.

In a number of ways, towns loosened the hold of lords on serfs. Seeking freedom and fortune, serfs fled to the new towns where, according to custom, lords could no longer reclaim them after a year and a day. Enterprising serfs earned money by selling food to townsmen. When they acquired a sufficient sum, they bought their freedom from lords, who needed cash to pay for goods bought from merchants. Lords increasingly began to accept fixed cash payments from serfs in place of labor services or foodstuffs. As serfs met their obligations to lords with money, they gradually became rent-paying tenants and, in time, were no longer bound to the lord's land. The manorial system of personal relations and mutual obligations was disintegrating.

The activities of townsmen made them a

new breed; they engaged in business and had money and freedom. Their world was the market rather than the church, the castle, or the manor. Townsmen were freeing themselves from the prejudices both of feudal aristocrats who considered trade and manual work degrading and of the clergy who cursed the pursuit of riches as an obstacle to salvation. The townsmen were critical, dynamic, and progressive—a force for change. Medieval towns nurtured the origins of the bourgeoisie, the urban middle class, which would play a crucial role in modern European history.

The Rise of States

The revival of trade and the growth of towns were signs of a growing vitality in Latin Christendom. Another sign of strength was the greater order and security provided by the emergence of states. While feudalism fostered a Europe that was split into many local regions, each ruled by a lord, the church envisioned a vast Christian commonwealth, *Respublica Christiana,* governed by an emperor who was guided by the pope. During the High Middle Ages, the ideal of a universal Christian community seemed close to fruition. Never again would Europe possess such spiritual unity.

But there were forces at work propelling Europe in a different direction. Aided by educated and trained officials who enforced royal law, tried people in royal courts, and collected royal taxes, kings expanded their territory and slowly fashioned strong central governments. Gradually, subjects began to transfer their prime loyalty away from the church and lords to the person of the king. These developments laid the foundations of European states. Not all areas followed the same pattern. While England and France achieved a large measure of unity during the Middle Ages, Germany and Italy remained divided into numerous independent territories.

England

After the Roman legions abandoned England in the fifth century, the Germanic Angles and Saxons invaded the island and established several small kingdoms. In the ninth century, the Danes, one group of the Northmen who raided western Europe, conquered most of Anglo-Saxon England. But the Saxon kingdom of Wessex, ruled by Alfred the Great (871–899), survived. To resist the Danes, Alfred strengthened his army and built a fleet; to stem the decline in learning that accompanied the Danish invasions, Alfred, like Charlemagne, founded a palace school to which he brought scholars from other areas. Alfred himself studied Latin and translated a work of Pope Gregory I into Anglo-Saxon. He also had other works translated into Anglo-Saxon, including Boethius' *Consolation of Philosophy.* Alfred's descendants gradually regained land from the Danes and re-established Anglo-Saxon control over the island.

In 1066 the Normans—those Northmen who had first raided and then settled in France—conquered Anglo-Saxon England. Determined to establish effective control over his new kingdom, William the Conqueror, duke of Normandy, kept a sixth of conquered England for himself. In accordance with feudal practice, he distributed the rest among his Norman nobles, who swore an oath of loyalty to William and provided him with military assistance. But William made certain that no feudal baron had enough land or soldiers to threaten his power. The Norman conquest had led to the replacement of an Anglo-Saxon aristocracy with a Norman one.

To strengthen royal control, William retained Anglo-Saxon administrative practices. The land remained divided into *shires* (counties) administered by *sheriffs* (royal agents). This structure gave the king control over local government. To determine how much money he could demand, William ordered a vast census taken of people and property in every village. This data, compiled in the *Domesday Book,* listed the quantities of tenants, cattle,

Battle of Hastings from the Bayeux Tapestry. The Battle of Hastings (1066) resulted in the conquest of England by William, duke of Normandy. As a result of the Norman Conquest, England was unified at a stroke. William's victory also led to the introduction of the French language to England. This fused with Anglo-Saxon to produce Middle English. Otherwise, English would have remained a Germanic dialect. (*Anderson/Art Resource*)

sheep, pigs, and farm equipment throughout the realm. Thus, better than any other monarch of his day, William knew what the assets of his kingdom were. Because William had conquered England in one stroke, his successors did not have to travel the long, painful road to national unity followed by French monarchs.

A crucial development in shaping national unity was the emergence of *common law*. When Henry I became king in 1100, England had conflicting baronial claims and legal traditions that were a barrier to unity. There was the old Anglo-Saxon law, the feudal law introduced by the Normans from France, the church law, and the commercial law emerging among the town businessmen. During the reigns of Henry I (1100–1135) and Henry II (1154–1189), royal judges traveled to different parts of the kingdom. Throughout England, important cases began to be tried in the king's court rather than in local courts, thereby increasing royal power. The decisions of royal judges were recorded and used as guides for future cases. In this way, a law common to the whole land gradually came to prevail over the customary law of a specific locality. Because common law applied to all England, it served as a force for unity. It also provided a fairer system of justice. The common law remains the foundation of the English legal system.

Henry II made trial by jury a regular judicial procedure for many cases heard in the king's court, laying the foundations of the modern system. Henry II also ordered representatives of a given locality to report under oath to visiting royal judges any local persons who were suspected of murder or robbery. This indictment jury was the ancestor of the modern grand jury system.

Paralleling the development of a strong judicial system was the growth of an efficient financial administration. The Exchequer, the royal accounting office, was formed during the early years of Henry I's reign. Its officials saw to the collection of all revenues owed the king. These officials, like the judges, formed a class of professional administrators personally loyal to the king.

King John (1199–1216) inadvertently precipitated a situation that led to another step in the political development of England. Fighting a costly and losing war with the king of France, John had coerced his vassals into giving him more and more revenue; also he had punished some vassals without a proper trial. In 1215, the angry barons rebelled and compelled John to fix his seal to a document called the Great Charter, or *Magna Carta*. The Magna Carta is celebrated as the root of the unique English respect for basic rights and liberties. Although essentially a feudal document directed against a king who had violated feudal practices, the Magna Carta stated certain principles that could be interpreted more widely.

Over the centuries, these principles were expanded to protect the liberties of Englishmen against governmental oppression. The Magna Carta stated that no unusual taxes "shall be imposed in our kingdom except by the common consent of our kingdom." In time, this right came to mean that the king could not levy taxes without the consent of Parliament, the governmental body that represents the English people. The Magna Carta also provided that "no freeman shall be taken or imprisoned . . . save by the lawful judgment of his peers or by the law of the land." The barons who drew up the document had intended it to mean that they must be tried by fellow barons. As time passed, these words were regarded as a guarantee of trial by jury for all men, a prohibition against arbitrary arrest, and a command to dispense justice fully, freely, and equally. Implied in the Magna Carta is the idea that the king cannot rule as he pleases, but must govern according to the law, and that not even the king can violate the law of the nation. Centuries afterward, when Englishmen sought to limit the king's power, they would interpret the Magna Carta in this way.

In Anglo-Saxon England the tradition had emerged that the king should consider the advice of the leading men in the land. Later, William the Conqueror continued this practice by seeking the opinions of leading nobles and bishops. In the thirteenth century it became accepted custom that the king should not decide major issues without consulting these advisors as assembled in the Great Council. Lesser landowners and townsmen also began to be summoned to meet with the king. These two groups were eventually called the House of Lords (bishops and nobles) and the House of Commons (knights and burghers). Thus the English Parliament had evolved, and by the mid–fourteenth century it had become a permanent institution of government.

Frequently in need of money but unable to levy new taxes without the approval of Parliament, the king had to turn to that body for help. Parliament used this control over money matters to increase its power. The tradition grew that the power to govern rested not with the king alone, but with the king and Parliament together.

During the Middle Ages, England became a centralized and unified state. But the king did not have unlimited power; he was not above the law. The rights of the people were protected by certain principles implicit in the common law and the Magna Carta, and by the power of Parliament.

France

In the 150 years following Charlemagne's death, the western part of his empire, which was destined to become France, faced terrible ordeals. Charlemagne's heirs fought each other for the crown; the Vikings raided everywhere their ships would carry them; Muslims from Spain plundered the southern coast; and strong lords usurped power for themselves. With the Carolingian family unable to maintain the throne, the great lords elected the king. In 987, they chose Hugh Capet (987–996), the count of Paris. Because many great lords held territories far larger than those of Hugh, the French king did not seem a threat to noble power. But Hugh strengthened the French monarchy by having the lords also elect his son as his co-ruler. This practice endured until it became understood that the crown would remain with the Capetian family.

With the accession of Louis VI (1108–1137), a two-hundred-year period of steadily increasing royal power began. Louis started this trend by successfully subduing the barons in his own duchy. A decisive figure in the expansion of royal power was Philip Augustus (1180–1223). Philip struck successfully at King John of England (of Magna Carta fame), who held more territory in France than Philip did. When William, duke of Normandy in western France, had conquered England in 1066, he became ruler of England and Normandy; William's great-grandson Henry II had acquired much of southern France through marriage to Eleanor of Aquitaine in 1152. By stripping King John of most of his French territory (Normandy, Anjou, and much of Aquitaine), Philip trebled the size of his kingdom and became stronger than any French lord.

Louis IX (1226–1270)—pious, compassionate, conscientious, and a genuine lover of peace—was perhaps the best-loved French monarch of the Middle Ages. Departing from feudal precedent, Louis issued ordinances for the entire realm without seeking the consent of his vassals. One ordinance prohibited private warfare among the nobility. Another promoted the nationwide circulation of coins produced by royal mints. These ordinances furthered royal power and promoted order.

Under Louis IX and his successors, the power of the French monarch continued to grow. Kings added to their lands by warfare and marriage; they devised new ways of raising money, including taxing the clergy. A particularly effective way of increasing the monarch's power was by extending royal justice. In the thirteenth century, the king's court, *Parlement*, became the highest court in France. Quarrels between the king and his vassals were resolved in the Parlement, and many cases previously tried in lords' courts were transferred to the king's court. Moreover, since the decision of feudal courts could be appealed to the Parlement, lords no longer had the last say on legal questions.

In the beginning of the fourteenth century, Philip IV (the Fair) engaged in a struggle with the papacy (see pages 255–256). Seeking to demonstrate that he had the support of his subjects, Philip convened a national assembly called the *Estates General*, representing clergy, nobility, and townsmen. It would be called again to vote funds for the crown. But unlike the English Parliament, the Estates General never became an important body in French political life, and it never succeeded in controlling the monarch. While the basis for limited monarchy had been established in England, no comparable checks on the king's power developed in France. By the end of the Middle Ages, French kings had succeeded in creating a unified state. But regional and local loyalties remained strong and persisted for centuries.

Germany

After the destruction of Charlemagne's empire, its German territories were broken into large duchies. Following an ancient German practice, the ruling dukes elected one of their own as king. The German king, however, had little authority outside his own duchy. Some German kings tried not to antagonize the dukes, but Otto the Great (936–973) was determined to control them. He entered into an alliance with German bishops and archbishops who could provide him with fighting men and trained administrators—a policy continued by his successors.

In 951, Otto marched into northern Italy in an attempt to assert his influence. Ten years later, he returned to protect the pope from his Italian enemies. In 962, in emulation of the coronation of Charlemagne, the pope crowned Otto "Emperor of the Romans." (Later the title would be changed to Holy Roman emperor.)

The revival of the empire meant that the history of medieval Germany was closely tied to that of Italy and the papacy. Otto and his successors wanted to dominate Italy and the pope—an ambition that embroiled the Holy Roman emperor in a life-and-death struggle

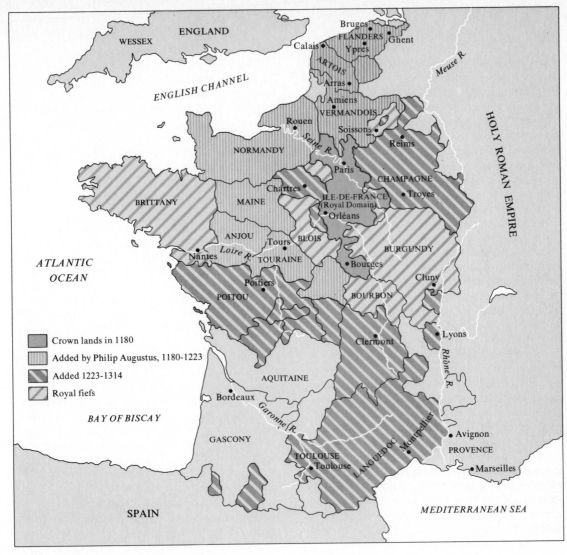

Map 10.2 The Kingdom of France, 1180–1314

Legend:
- Crown lands in 1180
- Added by Philip Augustus, 1180-1223
- Added 1223-1314
- Royal fiefs

with the papacy. The papacy allied itself with the German dukes and the Italian cities, enemies of the emperor. The intervention in papal and Italian politics was the principal reason why German territories did not achieve unity in the Middle Ages.

The Emergence of Representative Institutions

One great contribution of the Middle Ages to the modern world was the representative institution. Representative assemblies, or par-

liaments, had their beginnings at the end of the twelfth century in the Spanish kingdom of León. In the thirteenth century, they had developed in other Spanish kingdoms—Castile, Aragon, Catalonia, Valencia—and in Portugal, England, and the Holy Roman Empire. In the fourteenth century, parliaments arose in France and the Netherlands.

Kings generally came to accept the principles that parliamentary consent was required for levying taxes and that the king should consult parliament about important laws and obtain its approval. The parliaments had usually grown out of royal dependence on the nobility for military support. Because of this dependence, monarchs considered it wise to listen to the opinions of the lords. Consequently, it became customary for the king to summon councils to discuss matters of war and peace and other vital questions. As the high clergy also constituted an important group in the realm, they too were consulted. And as towns gained in wealth and significance, townsmen also were asked to royal councils. Leading nobles came to represent the nobility as an order of society; members of the upper clergy—archbishops, bishops, and abbots—represented the entire clergy; and deputies from the towns represented their fellow townsmen. An important tradition had been established: the duty of the monarch to seek advice and consent on issues of concern to his subjects. Perhaps the practice of representative government was influenced by those church lawyers who held that the pope should seek the guidance of the Christian community as expressed in church councils—meetings of representatives of the secular and regular clergy.

To be sure, in succeeding centuries parliaments would either be ignored or dominated by kings. Nevertheless, the principle of constitutional government—government by consent—was woven into the fabric of Western society. The representative parliament is unique to Western civilization; it has no parallel in the political systems of the non-European world. Originating in the Middle Ages, the representative assembly is a distinct achievement and contribution of Western civilization.

The Growth of Papal Power

Accompanying economic recovery and increased political stability in the High Middle Ages was a growing spiritual vitality marked by several developments. The common people were showing greater devotion to the church.

Within the church, reform movements were attacking clerical abuses, and the papacy was growing more powerful. A holy war against the Muslims was drawing the Christian community closer together. During this period, the church tried with great determination to make society follow divine standards; that is, it tried to shape all institutions and expressions of the intellect according to a comprehensive Christian outlook.

The Sacraments

As the sole interpreters of God's revelation and the sole ministers of his sacraments, the clergy imposed and supervised the moral outlook of Christendom. Divine grace was channeled through the sacraments, which could be administered only by the church, the indispensable intermediary between the individual and God. For those persons who resisted its authority, the church could impose the penalty of excommunication (expulsion from the church and denial of the sacraments, without which there could be no salvation).

Through the seven sacraments, the community of the church encompassed the individual from birth to death. The rite of baptism cleansed the individual—usually an infant—of the stain of original sin. Confirmation granted the young adult additional grace to that received at baptism. Matrimony made marriage a holy union. Extreme unction was administered to the dying in an effort to remove the remains of sin. The sacrament of the Eucharist, derived from the Gospel accounts of Christ's Last Supper, took place within a liturgical service, the Mass; in a solemn ceremony, the bread and wine were miraculously transformed into the substance of the body and blood of Christ, which the priest administered, allowing the faithful to partake of Christ's saving grace. The sacrament of penance required a sinner to show sorrow for his sin, to confess it to a priest,

Map 10.3 The Holy Roman Empire, c. 1200 ▶

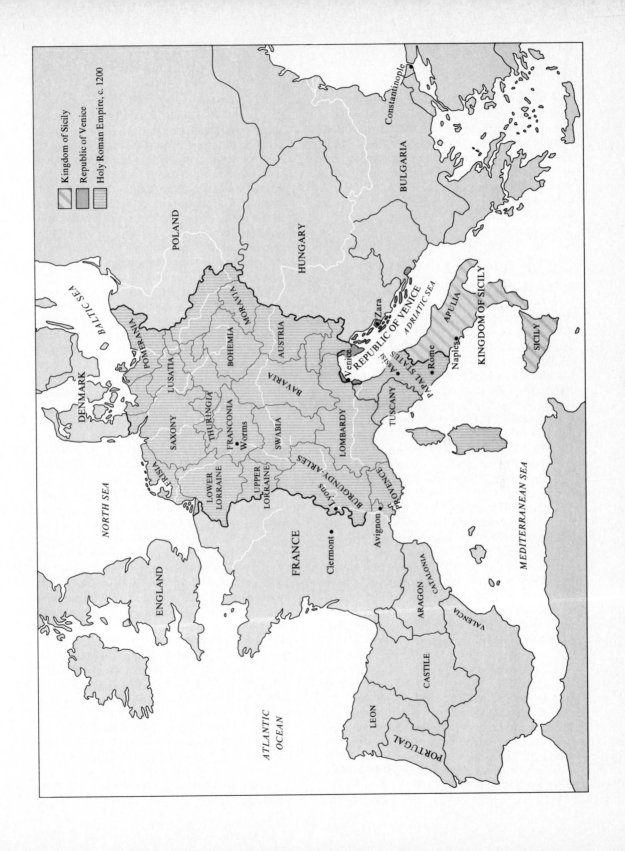

Kingdom of Sicily
Republic of Venice
Holy Roman Empire, c. 1200

BALTIC SEA

DENMARK

NORTH SEA

POMERANIA

POLAND

LUSATIA

SAXONY

THURINGIA

MORAVIA

BOHEMIA

FRANCONIA
Worms

FRISIA

LOWER
LORRAINE

UPPER
LORRAINE

SWABIA

BAVARIA

AUSTRIA

HUNGARY

ENGLAND

ATLANTIC
OCEAN

FRANCE

Clermont

LYONS

BURGUNDY-ARLES

PROVENCE

Avignon

LOMBARDY

TUSCANY

Venice

REPUBLIC OF VENICE

Zara

ADRIATIC SEA

ASSISI

PAPAL STATES

Rome

Naples

APULIA

KINGDOM OF SICILY

SICILY

Constantinople

BULGARIA

PORTUGAL

LEON

CASTILE

ARAGON

CATALONIA

VALENCIA

MEDITERRANEAN SEA

and to perform an act of penance—prayer, fasting, almsgiving, or a pilgrimage to a holy shrine; through the priest the sinner could receive absolution and be rescued from spending eternity in hell. This sacrament enabled the church to enforce its moral standards throughout Latin Christendom. The final sacrament, ordination, was used in consecrating men in holy orders.

The Gregorian Reform

By the tenth century, the church was Western Europe's leading landowner, owning much of Italy and vast properties in other lands. However, the papacy was in no position to exercise commanding leadership over Latin Christendom. The office of pope had fallen under the domination of aristocractic families; they conspired and on occasion murdered in order to place one of their own on the wealthy and powerful throne of Saint Peter. As the papacy became a prize for Rome's leading families, it was not at all unusual for popes themselves to be involved in conspiracies and assassinations. Also weakening the authority of the papacy were local lords, who dominated churches and monasteries by appointing bishops and abbots and by collecting the income from church taxes. These bishops and abbots, appointed by lords for political reasons, lacked the spiritual devotion to maintain high standards of discipline among the priests and monks.

What raised the power of the papacy to unprecedented heights was the emergence of a reform movement, particularly in French and German monasteries. High-minded monks called for a reawakening of spiritual fervor and the elimination of moral laxity among the clergy, especially a concern for worldly goods, the taking of mistresses, and a diminishing commitment to the Benedictine rule. Of the many monasteries that participated in this reform movement, the Benedictine monks of Cluny in Burgundy, France, were the most influential.

Founded in 910, Cluny soon established daughter houses in France, Germany, England, and Italy, which were supervised by the mother monastery. Cluniac monks attempted to impose Christian ideas on society. The monks demanded that clergymen should not take wives or mistresses, and that they should not purchase their offices in the church. The monks tried to liberate their monasteries from the control of lords and commanded them to use their arms not for personal advantage but for Christian ends—the protection of the church and the unfortunate.

In the middle of the eleventh century, popes came under the influence of the monastic reformers. In 1059, a special synod convened by the reform-minded Pope Nicholas II moved to end the interference of Roman nobles and German Holy Roman emperors in the selection of the pope. Henceforth, a select group of clergymen called *cardinals* would essentially be responsible for choosing the pontiff.

The reform movement found its most zealous exponent in the person of Hildebrand, who became Pope Gregory VII in 1073. For Gregory, human society was part of a divinely ordered universe governed by God's universal law. As the supreme spiritual leader of Christendom, the pope was charged with the mission of establishing a Christian society on earth. As successor to Saint Peter, the pope had the final word on matters of faith and doctrine. All bishops came under his authority; so did kings, whose powers should be used for Christian ends. The pope was responsible for instructing rulers in the proper use of their God-given powers, and kings had the solemn duty to obey these instructions. If the king failed in his Christian duty, the pope could deny him his right to rule. Responsible for implementing God's law, the pope could never take a subordinate position to kings.

Like no other pope before him, Gregory VII made a determined effort to assert the pre-eminence of the papacy over both the church hierarchy and secular rulers. This determination led to a bitter struggle between the papacy and German monarch and future

Holy Roman emperor Henry IV. The dispute was a dramatic confrontation between two competing versions of the relationship between secular and spiritual authority.

Through his reforms, Gregory VII intended to improve the moral quality of the clergy and to liberate the church from all control by secular authorities. He forbade priests who had wives or concubines to celebrate mass, deposed clergy who had bought their offices, excommunicated bishops and abbots who received their estates from a lay lord, and expelled from the church lay lords who invested bishops with their office. The appointment of bishops, Pope Gregory insisted, should be controlled entirely by the church.

This last point touched off the conflict, called the *Investiture Controversy*, between Henry and Pope Gregory. Bishops served a dual function. On the one hand, they belonged to the spiritual community of the church; on the other, as members of the nobility and holders of estates, they were also integrated into the feudal order. Traditionally, emperors had both granted bishops their feudal authority and invested them with their spiritual authority. In maintaining that no lay rulers could confer ecclesiastical offices on their appointees, Pope Gregory threatened Henry's authority.

Seeking allies in the conflict with feudal nobility in earlier times, German kings had made vassals of the upper clergy. In return for a fief, bishops had agreed to provide troops for a monarch in his struggle against the lords. But if kings had no control over the appointment of bishops—in accordance with Pope Gregory's view—they would lose the allegiance, military support, and financial assistance of their most important allies. To German monarchs, bishops were officers of the state who served the throne. Moreover, by agreeing to Gregory's demands, German kings would lose their freedom of action and be dominated by the Roman pontiff. Henry IV regarded Gregory VII as a fanatic who trampled on custom, meddled in German state affairs, and threatened to subordinate kingship to the papacy.

Emperor Henry IV and His Anti-Pope, Clement III, Expelling Pope Gregory VII, Twelfth Century. Papal intervention in political matters led to violent opposition from monarchs in England, France, and Germany. None was as bitter as the conflict between Henry IV and Gregory VII. The *Republica Christiana* foundered. (*The Granger Collection*)

With the approval of the German bishops, Henry called for Pope Gregory to descend from the throne of Saint Peter. Gregory in turn excommunicated Henry and deposed him as king. German lands were soon embroiled in a civil war, as German lords used the quarrel to strike at Henry's power. The princes declared that they would not recognize Henry as king if the ban of excommunication were not lifted, and they invited Gregory to meet with them in Germany. Henry, who did not want Gregory to come to Germany and stir up his rebellious subjects, shrewdly planned to journey to Italy and appeal to Gregory to remove the stigma of excommunication. As Christ's vicar, Gregory was obligated to forgive a humble penitent. In midwinter, the German monarch crossed the Alps into northern Italy and headed for the castle of Canossa, where Gregory was staying. After three days the pope forgave Henry. This act of humility was, in a way, a victory for Henry, because with the ban of excommunication removed, he was able to deal more effectively with his rebellious lords. The image of the German emperor pleading for forgiveness, however, had the effect of increasing the prestige of the papacy enormously.

But the civil war persisted. The lords declared Henry deposed and elected Rudolf as his successor. Gregory, again disillusioned with Henry, recognized Rudolf as the new king. Not to be outdone, Henry, with the support of his warrior-bishops, declared Pope Gregory deposed. Finally Henry's troops crossed the Alps, successfully attacked Rome, and installed a new pope who, in turn, crowned Henry Emperor of the Romans. Gregory died in exile.

The papacy had resiliency, however. Gregory's successors were energetic men who skillfully promoted papal interests. Finally in 1122, the church and Emperor Henry V reached a compromise. Bishops were to be elected exclusively by the church and to be invested with the staff and the ring—symbols of spiritual power—by the archbishop, not the king. This change signified that the bishop owed his role as spiritual leader to the church only. But the king would grant the bishop the scepter, an act that would indicate that the bishop was also the recipient of a fief and the king's vassal, owing feudal obligations to the crown. This compromise, called the *Concordat of Worms,* recognized the dual function of the bishop as a spiritual leader in the church and a feudal landowner. Similar settlements were reached with the kings of France and England.

The Investiture Controversy had important consequences both for German territories and for the papacy. As a result of the civil war, the great German lords strengthened their control over their lands, thereby thwarting the unifying and centralizing efforts of the monarchy. The conflict with the papacy kept Germany, unlike England and France, from emerging from the Middle Ages as a unified state. Despite the exile of Gregory VII and the appointment of a new pope by Henry IV, the Investiture Controversy was no defeat for the papacy. The Concordat of Worms recognized that the church was an independent body headed by the papacy, over which rulers had no authority. Moreover, Gregory's vision of a Christendom guided by the pope, and of the state subordinate to and in the service of the papacy, persisted. Future popes, sharing his vision, would raise the papacy to new heights of power.

The conflict between the papacy and the German rulers continued after the Concordat of Worms—a contest for supremacy between the heir of Saint Peter and the heir of Charlemagne. German monarchs aimed at controlling the papacy and the prosperous north Italian cities. When Frederick I (1152–1190), known as Frederick Barbarossa ("Red Beard"), tried to assert authority over these cities, they resisted. In 1176, the armies of an alliance of Italian cities supported by the pope decisively defeated Frederick's forces. The Italian infantry showed that it could defeat knights on horseback, and Frederick was compelled to recognize the independence of the Italian cities. His numerous expeditions to Italy weakened his authority; German princes strengthened themselves at the expense of the monarchy, thereby continuing to preclude German unity.

Frederick did, however, achieve a diplomatic triumph. He arranged for his son, Henry VI, to marry the heiress to the kingdom of Sicily. Consisting of the island of Sicily and most of the Italian mainland south of Rome, the kingdom was well run and economically advanced. The papacy waged a relentless struggle to separate Sicily from the Holy Roman Empire. In attempting to join Sicily to Germany, Henry and his successors severely strained German resources. Taking advantage of the emperor's difficulties in Sicily, German princes continued to consolidate their power at home.

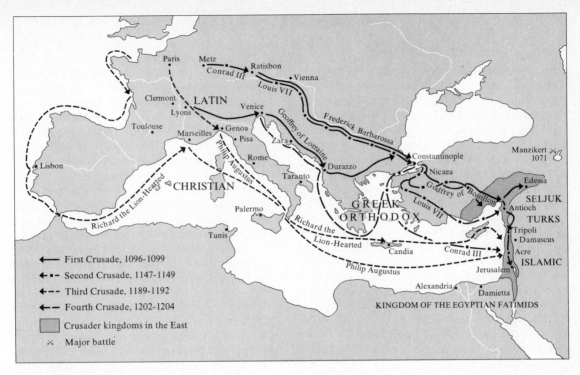

Map 10.4 The Routes of the Crusades

The Crusades

Like the movement for spiritual renewal associated with the Cluniac reformers, the Crusades—wars to regain the Holy Land from the Muslims—were an outpouring of Christian zeal and an attempt by the papacy to assert its pre-eminence. The Crusades were another sign—like the renewal of commerce and the growth of towns—of growing vitality and self-confidence. The victims of earlier Muslim attacks, Latin Christians now took the offensive.

The Crusades were also part of a general movement of expansion that took place in Europe during the High Middle Ages. Latin Christians were venturing forth as pioneers to open new lands to cultivation and as conquerors to expand the borders of Christendom.

By the middle of the eleventh century, Genoans and Pisans had driven the Muslims from Sardinia. In 1087, they successfully attacked the North African port of Tunis, a leading base for Muslim pirates, and forced the Emir of Tunis to free Christian captives and to favor Genoese and Pisan merchants. By 1091, Normans had taken Sicily from the Muslims and southern Italy from Byzantium. With the support of the papacy, Christian knights engaged in the long struggle to drive the Muslims from Spain; by 1248, after more than two centuries of conflict, only the small southern kingdom of Granada remained in Muslim hands. Germans conquered and colonized lands south of the Baltic coast inhabited by non-Christian Slavs, Balts, and Prussians. German settlers brought with them Christianity and German language and culture. They cleared vast tracts of virgin land for farming and established towns in a region where urban life had virtually been unknown.

In the eleventh century the Seljuk Turks, who had earlier embraced Islam, conquered vast regions of the Near East, including Anatolia, a province of the Byzantine Empire. With the death of the Turkish sultan in 1092, the Seljuk Empire broke up, which reduced the pressure on Byzantium. Seeking to strengthen his army in preparation for the reconquest of Anatolia, Byzantine Emperor Alexius appealed to the West for mercenaries.

Pope Urban II, at the Council of Clermont (in France) in 1095, exaggerated the danger confronting Eastern Christianity. He called for a holy crusade against the heathen Turks, whom he accused of defiling and destroying Christian churches. Several months later he expanded his objectives to include the conquest of Jerusalem. A Christian army, mobilized by the papacy to defend the faith and to regain the Holy Land from nonbelievers, accorded with the papal concept of a just war; it would channel the energies of Europe's warrior class in a Christian direction. A crusade against the Muslims also held the promise of bringing the Eastern church, which had formally broken with Rome in 1054, under papal leadership. In organizing a crusade for Christian ends, Urban II, like Pope Gregory in his struggle with Henry IV, sought to demonstrate the supremacy of the papacy.

What motivated the knights and others who responded to Urban's appeal? No doubt the Crusaders regarded themselves as armed pilgrims dedicated to rescuing holy places from the hated Muslims. Through the years Christian pilgrims had made the journey to Jerusalem to do penance for crimes against the church and to demonstrate their piety. These pilgrims and other devout Christians found it deplorable that Christian holy places were controlled by heathen Muslims. Moreover, Urban declared that participation in a crusade was itself an act of penance, an acceptable way of demonstrating sorrow for sin. In their enthusiasm to recruit warriors, popular preachers went even further; they promised cancellation of penalties for sin. To a knight, a crusade was no doubt a great adventure that promised glory and plunder, but it was also an opportunity to remit sins by engaging in a holy war. The enthusiasm with which knights became Christian warriors demonstrated the extent to which the warrior mentality of the nobles had become penetrated by Christian principles.

Stirred by popular preachers, the common people also became gripped by the crusading spirit. The most remarkable of the evangelists was Peter the Hermit. Small and thin, with a long gray beard caked with mud, Peter rode his donkey through the French countryside arousing the religious zeal of plain folk. Swayed by the old man's eloquence, thousands of poor people abandoned their villages and joined Peter's march to Jerusalem. As this army of the poor crossed Germany, the credulous peasants expected to find Jerusalem just beyond the horizon; some thought that Peter was leading them straight to heaven. While Peter's army made its way to Constantinople, another army of commoners recruited in Germany began their crusade by massacring the Jews of the Rhineland, despite the efforts of bishops to protect them. Unlike Peter's army, these commoners never reached Constantinople; after plundering Hungary, they were slaughtered by Hungarians (Magyars). Camped in the suburbs of Constantinople, Peter's restless recruits crossed into Turkish territory where they also were massacred. Faith alone could not win Jerusalem.

Departing later than the commoners, an army of knights assembled in Constantinople in the spring of 1097. After enduring the long march through Anatolia, the Christian army arrived at Antioch in Syria, which they captured after a long siege. In June 1099, three years after leaving Europe, the Crusaders stood outside the walls of Jerusalem. Using siege weapons, they broke into the city and slaughtered the Muslim and Jewish inhabitants.

Weakened by local rivalries and religious quarrels, the Muslim world failed to unite against the Christian invaders who, in addition to capturing Jerusalem, carved out four principalities in the Near East. But how long could these Christian states, islands in a Muslim sea, endure against a Muslim counteroffensive?

Never resigned to the establishment of Christian states in their midst, Muslim leaders called for a *jihad*, or holy war. In 1144, one

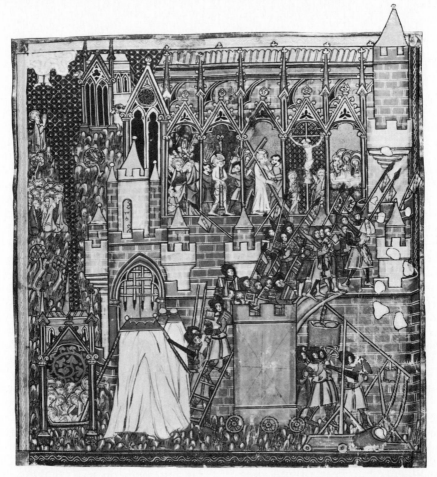

Capture of Jerusalem. "Mad with joy, we reached the city of Jerusalem on the Tuesday, eight days before the Ides of June, and laid seige to it," wrote one crusader. Two months later, the crusaders broke into the city and massacred its inhabitants. (*Bibliothèque Nationale, Paris*)

of the Crusader states, the County of Edessa, fell to the resurgent forces of Islam. Alarmed by the loss of Edessa, Pope Eugenius II called for a second crusade. In 1147, King Louis VII of France and Emperor Conrad III of Germany led their forces across the Balkans into Asia Minor. Both armies, traveling independently, were decimated by Seljuk Turks, and only a fraction of the Christian forces reached their destination. The Second Crusade was a complete failure.

After 1174, Saladin, a brilliant commander, became the most powerful leader in the Muslim Near East, and in 1187 he invaded Pal-

estine. Saladin annihilated a Christian army near Nazareth and captured Jerusalem in 1189. In contrast to Christian knights of the First Crusade, who filled Jerusalem with blood and corpses, Saladin permitted no slaughter. The capture of Jerusalem led to the Third Crusade, in which some of Europe's most prominent rulers participated—Richard I, the Lion Hearted, of England, Philip Augustus of France, and Frederick Barbarossa of Germany. The Crusaders captured Acre and Jaffa, but Jerusalem remained in Muslim hands.

Other crusades followed, but the position of the Christian states in the Near East continued to deteriorate. In 1291, almost two centuries after Pope Urban's appeal, the last Christian strongholds in the Near East had fallen.

The Crusades had some immediate effects on Latin Christendom. They increased the wealth of the Italian cities that had furnished transportation for the Crusaders and had benefited from the increased trade with the East. They may have contributed to the decline of feudalism and the strengthening of monarchy, because many lords were killed in battle or squandered their wealth financing expeditions to the Holy Land. Although the call for the Crusades demonstrated the growing power of the papacy, in the long run the crusading movement may have diminished the papacy in the eyes of Christendom. In time, popes corrupted the crusading ideal, employing it for political reasons as a weapon against European rulers.

The two centuries of conflict between Christendom and Islam did not produce many significant results. The Crusades did foster trade between Latin Christendom and the East, but the revival of trade had already begun and would have proceeded without the Crusades. The Crusades stimulated an interest in geography and travel and became a theme in literature, but they did not significantly influence European cultural progress. The Crusaders had no contact with Muslim centers of learning in the Near East; it was through Spain and Sicily that Muslim learning penetrated Latin Christendom and helped stimulate the cultural awakening of the twelfth and thirteenth centuries. Over the centuries, people have praised the Crusades for inspiring idealism and heroism; others have castigated the movement for corrupting the Christian spirit, for unleashing religious intolerance and fanaticism that would lead to strife in future centuries.

Dissenters and Reformers

Freedom of religion is a modern concept; it was totally alien to the medieval outlook.

Regarding itself as the possessor and guardian of divine truth, the church felt a profound obligation to purge Christendom of heresy—beliefs that challenged Christian orthodoxy. To the church, heretics had committed treason against God and were carriers of a deadly infection. Heresy was the work of Satan; lured by false ideas, people might abandon the true faith and deny themselves salvation. The church could never create a Christian world community if heretics rebelled against clerical authority and created divisions among the faithful. In the eyes of the church, heretics not only obstructed individual salvation, but also undermined the foundations of society.

To compel obedience, the church used its power of excommunication. An excommunicated person could not receive the sacraments or attend church services—fearful punishments in an age of faith. In dealing with a recalcitrant ruler, the church could declare an interdict on his territory, which in effect denied the ruler's subjects the sacraments (although exceptions could be made). The church hoped that the pressure exerted by an aroused populace would compel the offending ruler to mend his ways.

The church also conducted heresy trials. Before the thirteenth century, local bishops were responsible for locating heretics and putting them on trial. In 1233 the papacy established the Inquisition, a court specially designed to fight heresy. Accused heretics were presumed guilty until proven innocent, were not told the names of their accusers, and were not permitted lawyers. To wrest a confession from the accused, torture was permitted. Accused persons who persisted in their beliefs were turned over to the civil authorities to be burned at the stake.

The Waldensians   Dissent in the Middle Ages was often reformist in character. Inspired by the Gospels, reformers criticized the church for its wealth and involvement in worldly affairs; they called for a return to the simpler, purer life of Jesus and the Apostles. Reform movements drew support from the new class of town dwellers; the church often rebuked the way of life in towns and only slowly adjusted to the townsmen's spiritual needs.

In their zeal to emulate the moral purity and material poverty of the first followers of Jesus, these reform-minded dissenters attacked ecclesiastical authority. The Waldensians, followers of Peter Waldo, a rich merchant of Lyon, were a case in point. In the 1170s, Peter distributed his property to the poor and attracted both male and female supporters. Like their leader, they committed themselves to poverty and to preaching the Gospel in the *vernacular*, or native tongue, rather than in the church's Latin, which many Christians did not understand. The Waldensians considered themselves true Christians, faithful to the spirit of the apostolic church. Repelled by Waldensian attacks against the immorality of the clergy and by the fact that these laymen were preaching the Gospel, ecclesiastical authorities condemned the movement as heretical. Despite persecution, however, the Waldensians continued to survive as a group in northern Italy.

The Cathari   Catharism was the most radical heresy to confront the medieval church. This belief represented a curious mixture of Gnosticism and Manichaeism—Eastern religious movements that had competed with Christianity in the days of the Roman Empire—and of doctrines condemned as heretical by the early church. Carried to Italy and southern France by Bulgarian missionaries, Catharism gained followers in regions where opposition to the worldliness and wealth of the clergy was already strong.

Cathari tenets differed considerably from those of the church. The Cathari believed in an eternal conflict between the forces of the god of good and those of the god of evil. Because the evil god, whom they identified with the God of the Old Testament, created the world, this earthly home was evil. The soul, spiritual in nature, was good, but it was trapped in wicked flesh. Because sexual activity was responsible for imprisoning the spirit in the flesh, the Cathari urged abstinence to avoid the birth of still another wicked hu-

man. They also abstained from eggs, cheese, milk, and meat because these foods were the products of sexual activity. The Cathari taught that since the flesh is evil, Christ would not have taken a human form; hence he could not have suffered on the cross nor have been resurrected. Nor could God have issued forth from the evil flesh of the Virgin. According to Catharism, Jesus was not God but an angel. In order to enslave people, the evil god created the church, which demonstrated its wickedness by pursuing power and wealth. Repudiating the church, the Cathari organized their own ecclesiastical hierarchy.

The center for the Catharist heresy was southern France, where a strong tradition of protest existed against the moral laxity and materialism of the clergy. When the Cathari did not submit to peaceful persuasion, Innocent III called on kings and lords to exterminate Catharism with the sword. Lasting from 1208 to 1229, the war against the Cathari was marked by brutality and fanaticism.

The Franciscans and the Dominicans   Driven by a zeal for reform, devout laymen condemned the clergy for moral abuses. Sometimes their piety and resentment exploded into heresy; other times it was channeled into movements that served the church. Such was the case with the two great orders of friars, Franciscans and Dominicans.

Like Peter Waldo, Saint Francis of Assisi (c. 1181–1226) came from a wealthy merchant family. After undergoing an intense religious experience, Francis abandoned his possessions and devoted his life to imitating Christ. Dressed as a beggar, he wandered into villages and towns preaching, healing, and befriending. Unlike the monks who withdrew into walled fortresses, Francis proclaimed Christ's message to the poor of the towns. Like Peter Waldo, he preached a religion of personal feeling; like Jesus, he stretched out a hand of love to the poor, to the helpless, to the sick, and even to lepers whom everyone feared to approach. The saintly Francis soon attracted disciples called *Little Brothers*, who followed in the footsteps of their leader.

To suspicious churchmen the Little Brothers seemed another heretical movement protesting against a wealthy and worldly church. However, Francis respected the authority of the priesthood and the validity of the sacraments. Recognizing that such a popular movement could be useful to the church, Innocent III allowed Francis to continue his mission. Innocent hoped that the Franciscans would help keep within the church those laymen who had deep religious feelings but were dissatisfied with the leadership of the traditional hierarchy.

As the Franciscans grew in popularity, the papacy exercised greater control over their activities; in time the order was transformed from a spontaneous movement of inspired laymen into an organized agent of papal policy. The Franciscans served the church as teachers and missionaries in eastern Europe, North Africa, the Near East, and China. The papacy set aside Francis's prohibition against the Brothers owning churches, houses, and lands corporately. His desire to keep the movement a lay order was abandoned when the papacy granted the Brothers the right to hear confession. Francis's opposition to formal learning as irrelevant to preaching Gospel love was rejected when the movement began to urge university education for its members. Those who protested against these changes as a repudiation of Francis's spirit were persecuted, and a few were even burned at the stake as heretics.

The Dominican order was founded by Saint Dominic (c. 1170–1221), a Spanish nobleman who had preached against the Cathari in southern France. Believing that those well-versed in Christian teaching could best combat heresy, Dominic, unlike Francis, insisted that his followers engage in study. In time, the Dominicans became some of the leading theologians in the universities. Like the Franciscans they went out into the world to preach the Gospel and to proselytize. Dominican friars became the chief operators of the Inquisition. For their zeal in fighting heresy, they were known as the watchdogs of the Lord.

Innocent III: The Apex of Papal Power

During the pontificate of Innocent III (1198–1216), papal theocracy reached its zenith. More than any earlier pope, Innocent made the papacy the center of European political life; in the tradition of Gregory VII, he forcefully asserted the theory of papal monarchy. As head of the church, Vicar of Christ, and successor of Saint Peter, Innocent claimed the authority to intervene in the internal affairs of secular rulers when they threatened the good order of Christendom. According to Innocent, the pope, "lower than God but higher than man . . . judges all and is judged by no one."[2] And again: "Princes have power in earth, priests over the soul. As much as the soul is worthier than the body, so much worthier is the priesthood than the monarchy. . . . No king can reign rightly unless he devoutly serve Christ's vicar."[3]

Innocent applied these principles of papal supremacy in his dealings with the princes of Europe. When King Philip Augustus of France repudiated Ingeborg of Denmark the day after their wedding and later divorced her to marry someone else, Innocent placed an interdict on France to compel Philip to take Ingeborg back. For two decades, Innocent III championed Ingeborg's cause until she finally became the French queen. When King John of England rejected the papal candidate for archbishop of Canterbury, Stephen Langton, Innocent first laid an interdict on the country. Then he excommunicated John, who expressed his defiance by confiscating church property and by forcing many bishops into exile. However, when Innocent urged Philip Augustus of France to invade England, John backed down. He accepted Innocent's nominee for archbishop, returned the property to the church, welcomed the exiles back, and as a sign of complete capitulation, turned his kingdom over to Innocent to receive it back as a fief. Thus, as vassals of the papacy, John and his successors were obligated to do homage to the pope and to pay him a feudal

Chronology 10.1 The High Middle Ages

910	The founding of Abbey of Cluny
962	Otto I crowned Emperor of the West, beginning the Holy Roman Empire
987	Hugh Capet becomes king of France
1054	The split between the Byzantine and the Roman churches
1061–1091	The Norman conquest of Sicily
1066	The Norman conquest of England
1075	Start of the Investiture Controversy
1096	Start of the First Crusade
c. 1100	Revival of the study of Roman law at Bologna
1163	Start of the construction of the Cathedral of Notre Dame
1198–1216	Pontificate of Innocent III; the height of the church's power
1267–1273	Saint Thomas Aquinas writes *Summa Theologica*
c. 1321	Dante completes the *Divine Comedy*

tribute. Innocent also laid interdicts on the Spanish kingdoms of Castile and León and on Norway.

Pope Innocent also sought to separate Sicily from the Holy Roman Empire. When the candidacy for Holy Roman emperor was disputed, Innocent backed young Frederick II, king of Sicily and grandson of Frederick Barbarossa. In return for Innocent's backing, Frederick agreed to give up Sicily. When Frederick (1215–1250) emerged victorious over his rival, Otto of Brunswick, Innocent thought that the Holy Roman emperor would finally be subservient to the papacy. But Frederick, breaking his promise, refused to renounce Sicily. Subsequently, a furious struggle was waged between Frederick II (and his heirs) and the successors of Innocent III. The outcome was a disaster for the Holy Roman emperor who lost Sicily and saw his authority over the German princes evaporate. Once again, because of the Italian adventures of the emperors, Germany stayed fragmented; it would remain broken into separate and independent territories until the last part of the nineteenth century.

Innocent called the Fourth Crusade to demonstrate anew that the papacy was the shepherd of Christendom. In 1202, ten thousand Crusaders gathered in Venice prepared to depart for the East. But the Venetians who had agreed to provide transport and food would not set sail because the Crusaders produced less money than the agreement had called for. The wily Venetians then proposed a new deal. They would allow the Crusaders to postpone payment in exchange for their cooperation in capturing the trading port of Zara, a rival of Venice controlled by the king of Hungary. Infuriated by this attack against a Christian city, Innocent excommunicated the Crusaders and the Venetians. But anxious to save the Crusade, he quickly lifted the sentence on the soldiers.

Again the Crusade was diverted. Alexius IV, pretender to the throne of Byzantium, offered the Venetians and the Christian army a huge sum in exchange for their aid in restoring his throne. While some Crusaders rejected the bribe and sailed to Syria to fight the Muslims, the bulk of the crusading army attacked Constantinople in 1204. In a contradictory display of barbarism, they looted and defiled churches and massacred citizens. This shameful behavior, along with the belief that the papacy was exploiting the crusading ideal to extend its own power, weakened both the papacy and the crusading zeal of Christendom.

After the disastrous Fourth Crusade, Innocent's attention turned to the Cathari. Unable to eliminate the Catharist heresy in southern France through preaching, Innocent decided on force. An army of crusading knights headed by a papal legate assembled in northern France; it headed south, massacring heretics. Soon command of the crusading army passed to Simon de Montfort, a minor baron with great ambition. De Montfort slaughtered suspected heretics throughout the county of Toulouse and for a short time he held the title of count of Toulouse. The crusading knights had effectively broken the power of the nobles who had protected the heretics. Innocent III sent legates to the region to arrest and try the Cathari. Under his successor, Dominican and Franciscan inquisitors completed the task of exterminating them.

The culminating expression of Innocent's supremacy was the Fourth Lateran Council, called in 1215. Composed of about twelve hundred clergy and representatives of secular rulers, the council issued several far-reaching orders. It maintained that the Eastern Orthodox church was subordinate to the Roman Catholic church; it prohibited the state from taxing the clergy, and declared laws detrimental to the church null and void. The council made bishops responsible for ferreting out heretics in their dioceses and ordered secular authorities to punish convicted heretics. It insisted on high standards of behavior for the clergy and required that each Catholic confess his or her sins to a priest at least once a year.

Christians and Jews

Latin Christendom's growing self-consciousness, which found expression in hostility to Muslims and condemnation of heresy, also sparked a hatred of Jews—a visibly alien group in a society dominated by the Christian world-view. In 1096, bands of Crusaders massacred Jews in French and German towns. One contemporary wrote:

I know not whether by a judgment of the Lord, or by some error of mind, they rose in a spirit of cruelty against the Jewish people scattered throughout these cities and slaughtered them without mercy, . . . asserting it to be their duty against the enemies of the Christian faith. . . . The Jews of [Mainz], knowing of the slaughter of their brethren, . . . fled in hope of safety to Bishop Rothard. . . . He placed the Jews in the very spacious hall of his own house, . . . [but the crusaders] attacked the Jews in the hall with arrows and lances. Breaking the bolts and doors, they killed the Jews, about seven hundred in number, who in vain resisted the force and attack of so many thousands. They killed the women, also, and with their swords pierced tender children of whatever age and sex.[4]

In 1290, Jews were expelled from England, and in 1306 from France. Between 1290 and 1293, expulsions, massacres, and forced conversions led to the virtual disappearance of a centuries-old Jewish community life in southern Italy. In Germany, savage riots periodically led to the torture and murder of Jews.

Several factors contributed to anti-Jewish feelings during the Middle Ages. To medieval Christians, the refusal of the Jews to embrace Christianity was an act of wickedness, particularly since the church taught that the coming of Christ had been prophesied by the Old Testament. Related to this prejudice was the depiction of the crucifixion in the Gospels. In the minds of medieval Christians, the crime of deicide—the killing of God—eternally stained the Jews as a people. The flames of hatred were fanned by the false allegation that Jews, made bloodthirsty by the spilling of Christ's blood, tortured and murdered Christians, particularly children, to obtain blood for ritual purposes. This blood libel was widely believed by the credulous masses and incited numerous riots that led to the murder, torture, and expulsion of countless Jews, despite the fact that popes condemned the charge as groundless.

The role of Jews as money lenders also contributed to animosity toward them. As Jews were increasingly excluded from international trade and were barred from the guilds, and in some areas from landholding, virtually the only means of livelihood open to them was money lending. This activity, which was forbidden to Christians, aroused the hatred of individual peasants, clergy, lords, and kings who did the borrowing.

The policy of the church toward the Jews was that they should not be harmed, but that they should live in humiliation. Hence the Fourth Lateran Council barred Jews from public office, required them to wear a distinguishing badge on their clothing, and ordered them to remain off the streets during Christian festivals. Christian art, literature, and religious instruction depicted the Jews in a derogatory manner. Deeply etched into the minds and hearts of Christians, the distorted image of the Jew as a contemptuous creature persisted in the popular mentality into the twentieth century.

Despite their precarious position, medieval Jews maintained their faith, expanded their tradition of biblical and legal scholarship, and developed a flourishing Hebrew literature. The work of Jewish translators, doctors, and philosophers would contribute substantially to the flowering of medieval culture in the High Middle Ages.

Europe in the High Middle Ages showed considerable vitality. The population increased, long-distance trade revived, new towns emerged, states started to take shape, and papal power increased. The culminating expression of this recovery and resurgence was the cultural awakening of the twelfth and thirteenth centuries, the high point of medieval civilization and a great creative period in Western history.

Notes

1. Quoted in J. W. Thompson, *Social and Economic History of the Middle Ages* (New York: Frederick Ungar, 1959), 2:772.

2. Excerpted in Brian Tierney, ed., *The Crisis of Church and State, 1050–1300* (Englewood Cliffs, N.J.: Prentice-Hall, 1964), p. 132.

3. Quoted in James Westfall Thompson and Edgar Nathaniel Johnson, *An Introduction to Medieval Europe* (New York: W. W. Norton, 1937), p. 645.

4. A. C. Krey, ed., *The First Crusade: The Accounts of Eye-Witnesses and Participants* (Princeton, N.J.: Princeton University Press, 1921), pp. 54–55.

Suggested Reading

Gimpel, Jean, *The Medieval Machine* (1977). Technological advances in the Middle Ages.

Lopez, R. S., *The Commerical Revolution of the Middle Ages* (1976). Commercial and industrial expansion in the High Middle Ages.

Mayer, H. E., *The Crusades* (1972). A short scholarly treatment.

Mundy, J. H., *Europe in the High Middle Ages 1150–1309* (1973). All phases of society in the High Middle Ages.

Pernoud, Regine, ed., *The Crusades* (1964). A compilation of original sources.

Petit-Dutaillis, Charles, *The Feudal Monarchy in France and England* (1964). A comparative study of the development of French and English medieval institutions.

Pounds, N. J. G., *An Economic History of Medieval Europe* (1974). A lucid survey.

Rorig, Fritz, *The Medieval Town* (1971). A study of medieval urban life.

Schafer, William, ed., *The Gregorian Epoch* (1964). A useful collection of readings on the Cluniac Movement, Gregory VII, and the Investiture Controversy.

Strayer, J. R., *On the Medieval Origins of the Modern State* (1970). Characteristics of medieval state-building.

Synan, Edward A., *The Popes and the Jews in the Middle Ages* (1965). An exploration of Jewish-Christian relations in the Middle Ages.

Tierney, Brian, ed., *The Crisis of Church and State, 1050–1300* (1964). Contains many documents illustrating this crucial medieval development.

Trachtenberg, Joshua, *The Devil and the Jews* (1961). The medieval conception of the Jew and its relationship to modern anti-Semitism.

White, Lynn, Jr., *Medieval Technology and Social Change* (1964). A study of medieval advances in technology.

Review Questions

1. What advances in agriculture occurred during the Middle Ages? What was the effect of these advances?

2. What factors contributed to the rise of towns? What was the significance of the medieval town?

3. Identify and explain the importance of the following: William the Conqueror, common law, Magna Carta, and Parliament.

4. Identify and explain the significance of the following: Hugh Capet, Philip Augustus, Louis IX, and Estates General.

5. Why did Germany not achieve unity during the Middle Ages?

6. What is the significance of the medieval representative institution?

7. What were the goals of Cluniac reformers?

8. What was Gregory VII's view of the papacy? How was the Investiture Controversy resolved? What was the significance of this controversy?

9. What prompted Urban II to call a crusade against the Turks? What prompted lords and commoners to go on a crusade? What was the final importance and outcome of the Crusades?

10. Why did the church regard Waldensians and Cathari as heretics?

11. What were the achievements of Saint Francis and Saint Dominic?

12. Papal power reached its height under Innocent III. Discuss this statement.

13. What factors contributed to the rise of anti-Semitism during the Middle Ages? How does anti-Semitism demonstrate the power of mythical thinking?

14. The High Middle Ages showed many signs of recovery and vitality. Discuss this statement.

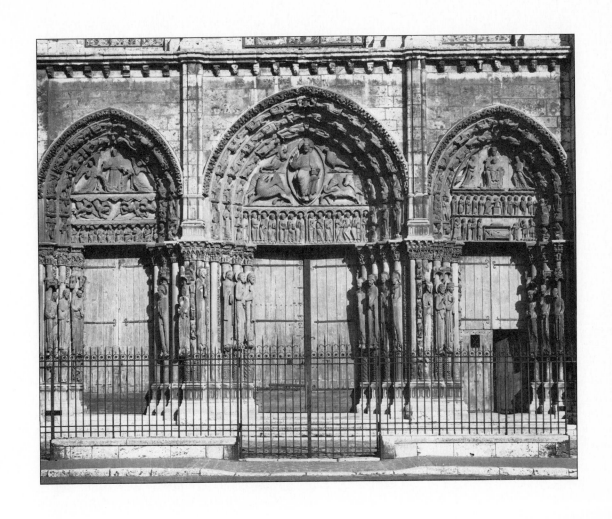

11

The Flowering of Medieval Culture:
The Christian Synthesis

*T*he high point of papal power in the Middle Ages coincided with a cultural flowering in philosophy, the visual arts, and literature. Creative intellects achieved on a cultural level what the papacy accomplished on an institutional level—the integration of society around a Christian viewpoint. The High Middle Ages saw the restoration of some of the learning of the ancient world, the rise of universities, the emergence of an original form of architecture (the Gothic), and the erection of an imposing system of thought called *scholasticism*. Medieval theologian-philosophers fashioned Christian teachings into an all-embracing philosophy that represented the spiritual essence, the distinctive style of medieval civilization. They achieved what Christian thinkers in the Roman Empire had initiated and what the learned men of the Early Middle Ages were groping for—a synthesis of Greek philosophy and Christian revelation.

Revival of Learning

In the late eleventh century, Latin Christendom began to experience a cultural revival; all areas of life showed vitality and creativeness. In the twelfth and thirteenth centuries, a rich civilization with a distinctive style united an educated elite in the lands from Britain to Sicily. Gothic cathedrals, an enduring testament to the creativeness of the religious impulse, were erected throughout Europe. Universities sprang up in scores of cities. Roman authors were again read and their style imitated; the quality of written Latin—the language of the church, learning, and education—improved, and secular and religious poetry, both in Latin and in the vernacular, abounded. Roman law emerged anew in Italy, spread to northern Europe, and regained its importance (lost since Roman times) as worthy of intellectual scholarship. Some key works of ancient Greece were translated into Latin and studied in universities. Pursuing the ra-

Map 11.1 Medieval Centers of Learning

tional tradition of Greece, men of genius harmonized Christian doctrines and Greek philosophy.

Several conditions contributed to this cultural explosion known as the Twelfth-Century Awakening. As attacks of Vikings, Muslims, and Magyars ended and kings and great lords imposed more order and stability, people found greater opportunities for travel and communication. The revival of trade and the growth of towns created a need for literacy and provided the wealth required to support learning. Growing contact with Islamic and Byzantine cultures led to the translation into Latin of ancient Greek works preserved by these Eastern civilizations. The Twelfth-Century Awakening was also kindled by the legacy of the Carolingian Renaissance, whose cultural lights had dimmed but never wholly vanished in the period of disorder following the dissolution of Charlemagne's empire.

In the Early Middle Ages the principal educational centers were the monastic schools. During the twelfth century, cathedral schools in towns grew in importance. Their teachers, paid a stipend by a local church, taught grammar, rhetoric, and logic. But the chief expression of expanding intellectual life was the university, a distinct creation of the Middle Ages.

The origins of the medieval university are obscure and varied. The first universities were not planned but grew up spontaneously. They arose as students eager for knowledge gathered around prominent teachers. The renewed importance of Roman law for business and politics, for example, drew students to Bologna to study with acknowledged masters.

The university was really a guild or corporation of masters or students who joined together to defend their interests against episcopal or town authorities or the townspeople. A university might emerge when students united because of common needs, such as protection against townspeople who overcharged them for rooms and necessities. Organized into a body, students could also make demands on their instructors. At Bologna, professors faced fines for being absent or for giving lectures that drew fewer than five students; they were required to leave behind a deposit as security to ensure their return if they took a journey. A corporation of students formed the University at Bologna. The University of Paris, which evolved from the Cathedral School of Notre Dame, was the creation of a corporation of masters.

University students attended lectures, studied for examinations, and earned degrees. They studied grammar, rhetoric, logic, arithmetic, geometry, astronomy, music, and, when prepared, church law and theology, which was considered the queen of the sciences. The curriculum relied heavily on Latin translations of ancient texts, principally the works of Aristotle. In mathematics and astronomy, students read Latin translations of Euclid and Ptolemy, while students of med-

icine studied the works of two great medical men of the ancient world, Hippocrates and Galen.

But sometimes students followed other pursuits. They turned to drinking, gambling, and fighting, instead of studying. At Oxford University, it was reported that students "went through the streets with swords and bows and arrows . . . and assaulted all who passed by."[1] Fathers complained that their sons preferred "play to work and strumming a guitar while the others are at their studies."[2] Students often faced financial problems, and they knew whom to ask for help: "Wellbeloved father, to ease my debts . . . at the tavern, at the baker's, with the doctor . . . and to pay . . . the laundress and the barber, I send you word of greetings and of money."[3]

Universities performed a vital function in the Middle Ages. Students learned the habit of reasoned argument. Universities trained professional secretaries and lawyers, who administered the affairs of church and state; these institutions of learning also produced theologians and philosophers, who shaped the climate of public opinion. The learning disseminated by universities tightened the cultural bonds that united Christian Europe, and established in the West a tradition of learning that has never died; there is direct continuity between the universities of our own day and medieval universities.

The Medieval World-View

A distinctive world-view based essentially on Christianity evolved during the Middle Ages. This outlook differed from both the Greco-Roman and the modern scientific and secular views of the world. In the Christian view, not the individual but the Creator determined what constituted the good life. Thus, reason that was not illuminated by revelation was either wrong or inadequate, for God had revealed to his children the proper rules for the regulation of individual and social life. Ultimately, the good life was not of this world but came from a union with God in a higher

College of Henricus Allemagna, School of Bologna, Second Half of Fourteenth Century. The core of the medieval curriculum included the *trivium* and the *quadrivium*. Students mastered grammar, rhetoric, and dialectic—the "three ways" (trivium)—and then pro- ceeded to mathematics, geometry, astronomy, and music (the quadrivium). The technique of teaching was the *disputatio*, or oral disputation between master and student. (*Bildarchiv Preussischer Kulturbesitz*)

world. This Christian belief as formulated by the church made life and death purposeful and intelligible. It was the outlook that dominated the thought of the Middle Ages.

The Universe: Higher and Lower Worlds

Medieval thinkers sharply differentiated between spirit and matter, between a realm of grace and an earthly realm, between a higher world of perfection and a lower world of imperfection. Moral values were derived from the higher world, which was also the final destination for the faithful. Two sets of laws operated in the physical universe, one for the heavens and one for the earth. The cosmos was a giant ladder with God at the summit; earth, composed of base matter, stood just above hell.

From Aristotle and Ptolemy, medieval thinkers inherited the theory of an earth-centered universe—the geocentric theory—which they impregnated with Christian symbolism. The geocentric theory held that revolving around the motionless earth at uniform speeds were seven transparent spheres in which were embedded each of the seven "planets"—the moon, Mercury, Venus, the sun, Mars, Jupiter, and Saturn. A sphere of fixed stars enclosed this planetary system. Above the firmament of the stars were the three heavenly spheres: the outermost, the Empyrean Heaven, was the abode of God and the Elect; through the Prime Mover—the sphere below—God transmitted motion to the planetary spheres; the first heavenly sphere was the invisible Crystalline Heaven. (See illustration on page 235.)

An earth-centered universe accorded with the Christian idea that God created the universe for men and women and that salvation was the essential aim of life. Because God had created people in his image, they deserved this central position in the universe. Although they might be living at the bottom rung of the cosmic ladder, only they, of all living things, had the capacity to ascend to heaven, the realm of perfection. Everything depended on how well they played their role in the drama of salvation.

Also acceptable to the Christian mentality was the sharp distinction drawn by Aristotle between the world above the moon and the one below it. Aristotle held that terrestrial bodies on earth were made of four elements—earth, water, air, fire. Celestial bodies that occupied the region beyond the moon were composed of a fifth element, the ether, too clear, too pure, too perfect to be found on earth. The planets and stars existed in a world apart; they were made of the divine ether and followed laws of nature that did not apply to earthly objects. Whereas earthly bodies underwent change—ice converting to water, a burning log converting to ashes—heavenly objects were incorruptible, immune to all change. Unlike earthly objects, they were indestructible.

Heavenly bodies also followed different laws of motion than earthly objects did. Aristotle said that it was natural for celestial bodies to move eternally in uniform circles, such motion being considered a sign of perfection. According to Aristotle, it was also natural for heavy bodies (stone) to fall downward and for light objects (fire, smoke) to move upward toward the celestial world; the falling stone and the rising smoke were finding their natural place in the universe.

This view of the universe would be shattered by the Scientific Revolution of the sixteenth and seventeenth centuries. The Scientific Revolution removed earth from its central position in the universe and made it just another planet that revolves about the sun. It dispensed with the medieval division of the universe into higher and lower worlds and postulated the *uniformity* of nature and of nature's laws: the cosmos knows no privilege of rank; heavenly bodies follow the same laws of nature as earthly objects do. Space is geometric and homogeneous, not hierarchic, heterogeneous, and qualitative. The universe was no longer conceived as finite and closed but as infinite, and the operations of nature were explained mathematically.

The Individual: Sinful but Redeemable

At the center of medieval belief was the image of a perfect God and a wretched and sinful human being. God had given Adam and Eve freedom to choose; rebellious and presumptuous, they had used their freedom to defy God. In doing so, they made evil an intrinsic part of the human personality. But God, who has not stopped loving human beings, has shown them the way out of sin. God became man and died so that human beings might be saved. Men and women are weak, egocentric, and sinful. With God's grace they can overcome their sinful nature and gain salvation; without grace, they are utterly helpless.

The medieval individual's understanding of self related to a comprehension of the universe as a hierarchy culminating in God. On earth, the basest objects were stones devoid of souls; higher than stones were plants, which possessed a primitive type of soul that allowed for reproduction and growth. Still higher were animals that had the capacity to move. The highest of the animals were human beings who, unlike other animals, could grasp some part of universal truth. Far superior to them were the angels who, without difficulty, apprehended God's truth. At the summit of this graduated universe was God, who was pure Being, without limitation, and the source of all existence. God's revelation reached down to humanity through the hierarchic order. From God, revelation passed to the angels, who were also arranged hierarchically. From the angels, the truth reached men and women, grasped first by prophets and apostles and then by the multitudes. Thus, all things in the universe, from angels to men and women to the lowest earthly objects, occupied a place peculiar to their nature and were linked by God in a great, unbroken chain.

Medieval individuals derived a sense of security from this hierarchical universe in which the human position was clearly defined. True, they were sinners who dwelt on a corruptible earth at the bottom of the cosmic hierarchy. But they *could* ascend to the higher world of perfection beyond the moon. As children of God, they enjoyed the unique privilege that each human soul was precious; all individuals commanded respect insofar as they were not formal heretics. (A heretic forfeited dignity and could be justly executed.)

Medieval thinkers also arranged knowledge in a hierarchic order: knowledge of spiritual things surpassed all worldly knowledge, all human sciences. Therefore, the true Christian understood that the study of the individual and society cannot proceed properly unless guided by the Creator's teachings. To know what God wanted of the individual was the summit of self-knowledge and led to entrance into heaven. Thus, God was both the source and the end of knowledge; by God alone it exists, and only through God can it be perfected. The human capacity to think and to act freely constituted the image of God within each individual; it ennobled man and woman and offered them the promise of associating with God in heaven. As the only creatures to possess these traits, human beings had been granted " 'dominion over the fish of the sea, and over the birds of the air, and over the cattle, and over all the earth, and over every creeping thing that creeps upon the earth.' " (Genesis 1: 26–27) But the ultimate end of knowledge was always to gain salvation.

True, human nobility derived from intelligence and free will. But if individuals used these attributes without recognizing their debt to God, if they forgot that they were never his equal—in short, if they committed the sin of pride—they brought misery on themselves. To challenge the divine will with human will constituted contempt for God and a violation of the divine order. Such sinful behavior invited self-destruction. To save themselves from damnation, people must demonstrate the purity of their intentions in obeying God's moral laws. They must appeal to God for forgiveness and for the strength to do right.

In the medieval view, neither nature nor man could be understood apart from God and his revelation. All of reality emanated from God and was purposefully arranged in a spiritual hierarchy. Three great expressions of this view of life were scholastic philosophy, the *Divine Comedy* of Dante, and the Gothic cathedral.

Philosophy-Theology

Medieval philosophy, or *scholasticism*, attempted to apply reason to revelation. It was an attempt to explain and clarify Christian teachings by means of concepts and principles of logic derived from Greek philosophy. Scholastics tried to show that the teachings of faith, although not derived from reason, were not contrary to reason. They tried to prove through reason what they already held to be true through faith. For example, the existence of God and the immortality of the soul, which every Christian accepted as articles of faith, could also, they thought, be demonstrated by reason. In struggling to harmonize faith with reason, medieval thinkers constructed an extraordinary synthesis of Christian and Greek thought.

The scholastic masters used reason not to challenge faith but to serve faith—to elucidate, clarify, and buttress it. They did not break with the central concern of Christianity, that of earning God's grace and achieving salvation. Although this goal could be realized solely by faith, scholastic thinkers insisted that a science of nature did not obstruct the pursuit of grace and that philosophy could assist the devout in the contemplation of God. They did not reject Christian beliefs that were beyond the grasp of human reason and therefore could not be deduced by rational argument. Instead, they held that such truths rested entirely on revelation and were to be accepted on faith. To medieval thinkers, reason did not have an independent existence, but ultimately had to acknowledge a suprarational, superhuman standard of truth. They wanted rational thought to be directed by faith for Christian ends and guided by scriptural and ecclesiastical authority. Ultimately, faith had the final word.

Not all Christian thinkers welcomed the use of reason. Regarding Greek philosophy as an enemy of faith, a fabricator of heresies, and an obstacle to achieving communion of the soul with God, conservative theologians opposed the application of reason to Christian revelation. In a sense the conservatives were right. By giving renewed vitality to Greek thought, medieval philosophy nurtured a powerful force that would eventually shatter the medieval concepts of nature and society and weaken Christianity. Modern Western thought was created by philosophers' refusal to subordinate reason to Christian orthodoxy. Reason proved a double-edged sword: it both ennobled and undermined the medieval world-view.

Saint Anselm and Abelard

An early scholastic, Saint Anselm (1033–1109) was abbot of the Benedictine monastery of Le Bec in Normandy. He used rational argument to serve the interests of faith. Like Augustine before him and other thinkers who followed him, Anselm said that faith was a precondition for understanding. Without belief there could be no proper knowledge. He developed philosophical proof for the existence of God. Anselm argued as follows: We can conceive of no being greater than God. But if God were to exist only in thought and not in actuality, his greatness would be limited; he would be less than perfect. Hence he exists. Anselm's motive and method reveal something about the essence of medieval philosophy. He does not begin as a modern might: "If it can be proven that God exists, I will adopt the creed of Christianity; if not, I will either deny God's existence (atheism) or reserve judgment (agnosticism)." Rather, Anselm accepts God's existence as an established fact because he believes what Holy Scripture says and what the church teaches. He then proceeds to employ logical argument to demonstrate that God can be known not only through faith but also through reason. He would never use reason to subvert what he knows to be true by faith. In general, this attitude would characterize later medieval thinkers, who also applied reason to faith.

As a young teacher of theology at the Cathedral School of Notre Dame, Peter Abelard (1079–1142) acquired a reputation for brilliance and combativeness. His tragic affair with Héloise, whom he tutored, has become one of the geat romances in Western literature. Héloise had a child and entered a nunnery; Abelard was castrated on orders of Canon Fulbert, Héloise's guardian, and sought temporary refuge in a monastery. After resuming his career as a teacher in Paris, Abelard again had to seek refuge, this time for writing an essay on the Trinity that church officials found offensive. After further difficulties and flights, he again returned to Paris to teach dialectics. Not long afterward, his most determined opponent, Bernard of Clairvaux, accused Abelard of using the method of dialectical argument to attack faith. To Bernard, a monk and mystic, subjecting revealed truth to critical analysis was fraught with danger:

. . . the deepest matters become the subject of undignified wrangling. . . . Virtues and vices are discussed with no trace of moral feelings, the sacraments of the Church with no evidence of faith, the mystery of the Holy Trinity with no spirit of

humility or sobriety: all is presented in a distorted form, introduced in a way different from the one we learned and are used to.[4]

Hearkening to Bernard's powerful voice, the church condemned Abelard and confined him to a monastery for the rest of his days.

Abelard believed that it was important to apply reason to faith and that careful and constant questioning led to wisdom. In *Sic et Non* (Yes and No), he took 150 theological issues and, by presenting passages from the Bible and the church fathers, showed that there were conflicting opinions. He suggested that the divergent opinions of authorities could be reconciled through proper use of dialectics. But like Anselm before him, Abelard did not intend to refute traditional church doctrines. Reason would buttress, not weaken, the authority of faith. He wrote after his condemnation in 1141:

I will never be a philosopher, if this is to speak against St. Paul; I would not be an Aristotle if this were to separate me from Christ. . . . I have set my building on the cornerstone on which Christ has built his Church. . . . I rest upon the rock that cannot be moved.[5]

Saint Thomas Aquinas: The Synthesis of Reason and Christianity

The introduction into Latin Christendom of the major works of Aristotle created a dilemma for religious authorities. Aristotle's comprehensive philosophy of nature and man, a product of human reason alone, conflicted in many instances with essential Christian doctrine. For Aristotle, God was an impersonal principle that accounted for order and motion in the universe. For Christianity, not only was God responsible for order in the physical universe, but he was also a personal being—a loving Father concerned about the deeds of his children. Whereas Christianity taught that God created the universe at a specific point in time, Aristotle held that the universe was eternal. Nor did Aristotle believe

God as Architect of the Universe, French Old Testament Miniature, Thirteenth Century. To the medieval mind, God was the origin of all. The universe was a known hierarchical system, and a "chain of being" extended downward to the lowest forms. Human beings, because of their immortal souls, could ascend toward God or, as a result of sinning, could descend into hell. (*Österreichische Nationalbibliothek, Vienna*)

in the personal immortality of the soul, another cardinal principle of Christianity. Church officials feared that the dissemination of Aristotle's ideas and the use of Aristotelian logic would endanger faith. At various times in the first half of the thirteenth century they forbade teaching the scientific works of Aristotle at the University of Paris. Because the ban did not apply throughout Christendom and was not consistently enforced in Paris, Aristotle's philosophy continued to be studied.

Rejecting the position of conservatives who insisted that philosophy would contaminate faith, Saint Thomas Aquinas (c. 1225–1274) upheld the value of human reason and natural knowledge. He set about to reconcile Aristotelianism with Christianity. Aquinas taught at Paris and organized the Dominican school of theology in Naples. His greatest work, *Summa Theologica,* is a systematic exposition of Christian thought. As a devout Catholic and member of the Dominican order, he of course accepted the truth of revelation. Belief in God and the fulfillment of his commands, Aquinas always maintained, are necessary for achieving salvation. He would not use reason to refute revelation.

Aquinas divided revealed truth into two categories: beliefs whose truth can be demonstrated by reason, and beliefs that reason cannot prove to be either true or false. For example, he believed that philosophical speculation could prove the existence of God and the immortality of the human soul, but that it could not prove or disprove the doctrines of the Trinity, the Incarnation, and the Redemption; these articles of faith wholly surpassed the capacity of human reason. But this fact did not detract from their certainty. Doctrines of faith did not require rational proof to be valid. They were true because they originated with God, whose authority is unshakable.

Can the teachings of faith conflict with the evidence of reason? For Aquinas, the answer was emphatically no. He said that revelation could not be the enemy of reason because revelation did not contradict reason, and reason did not corrupt the purity of faith. Revelation supplemented and perfected reason. If there appeared to be a conflict between philosophy and faith, it was certain that reason had erred somewhere, for the doctrines of faith were infallible. Since *both* faith and reason came from God, they were not in competition with each other but, properly understood, supported each other and formed an organic unity. Consequently, reason should not be feared, for it was another avenue to God. Because there was an inherent

agreement between true faith and correct reason—they both ultimately stemmed from God—contradictions between the two were only a misleading appearance. Although philosophy had not yet been able to resolve the dilemma, for God no such contradictions existed. In heaven, human beings would attain complete knowledge as well as complete happiness. While on earth, however, they must allow faith to guide reason; they must not permit reason to oppose or undermine faith.

Because reason was no enemy of faith, its application to revelation should not be feared. As human reasoning became more proficient, said Aquinas, it also became more Christian, and apparent incompatibilities between faith and reason disappeared. Recognizing that both faith and reason point to the same truth, the wise person accepts the guidance of religion in all questions that relate directly to knowledge needed for salvation. There also existed a wide range of knowledge that God had not revealed and that was not required for salvation. Into this category fell much knowledge about the natural world of things and creatures, which human beings had perfect liberty to explore.

Thus, in exalting God, Aquinas also paid homage to human intelligence, proclaimed the value of rational activity, and asserted the importance of physical reality revealed through human senses. Therefore, he valued the natural philosophy of Aristotle. Correctly used, Aristotelian thought would provide faith with valuable assistance. To synthesize Aristotelianism with the divine revelation of Christianity was Aquinas's great effort. That the two could be harmonized he had no doubt. He made use of Aristotelian categories in his five proofs of God's existence. In his first proof, for example, Aquinas argued that a thing cannot move itself. Whatever is moved must be moved by something else, and that by something else again. "Therefore, it is necessary to arrive at a first mover, moved by no other; and this everyone understands to be God."[6]

Aquinas also found a place for Aristotle's

conception of man. Aristotle, said Aquinas, was correct to regard man as a natural being and to devise for man a natural system of ethics and politics. Aristotle, however, did not go far enough. Aquinas said that, in addition, human beings are also special children of God. Consequently, they must define their lives according to the standards God has set. Aquinas insisted that much of what Aristotle had to say about man is accurate and valuable, for he was a gifted philosopher; but he possessed no knowledge of God. The higher insight provided by revelation did not disqualify what natural reason had to say about human beings, but improved upon it.

Aquinas upheld the value of reason. To love the intellect was to honor God and not to diminish the truth of faith. He had confidence in the power of the rational mind to comprehend most of the truths of revelation, and he insisted that in nontheological questions about specific things in nature—those questions not affecting salvation—people should trust only to reason and experience.

Aquinas gave new importance to the empirical world and to scientific speculation and human knowledge. The traditional medieval view based largely on Saint Augustine drew a sharp distinction between the higher world of grace and the lower world of nature, between the world of spirit and the world of sense experience. Knowledge derived from the natural world was often seen as an obstacle to true knowledge. Aquinas altered this tradition by affirming the importance of knowledge of the social order and the physical world. He gave to human reason and to worldly knowledge a new dignity. Thus, the City of Man was not merely a sinful place from which people tried to escape in order to enter God's city; it was worthy of investigation and understanding. But Aquinas remained a medieval and not a modern thinker, as historian Steven Ozment explains:

Aquinas brought reason and revelation together, but strictly as unequals. . . . In this union, reason, philosophy, nature, secular man and the state ultimately had value only in subservience to the *higher goals of revelation, theology, grace, religious man, and the church. . . . Thomist theology was the most sophisticated statement of the medieval belief in the secondary significance of the lay and secular world, a congenial ideology for a church besieged by independent and aggressive secular political powers.*[7]

Strict Aristotelianism: The Challenge to Orthodoxy

Some teachers in the Faculty of Arts at Paris found Aquinas's approach of Christianizing or explaining away Aristotle unacceptable. Unlike Aquinas, they did not seek to reconcile Aristotle's philosophy with Christian dogma. They held that certain Aristotelian propositions contradicting faith were philosophically true, or at least could not be proven false. These teachers maintained that it was impossible to refute these propositions by natural reason alone—that is, without recourse to faith. For example, by reason alone Aristotle had demonstrated that the world was eternal and that the processes of nature were unalterable. The first doctrine conflicted with the Christian belief that God created the universe at a point in time; the second conflicted with the belief that God could work miracles.

But these teachers did not take the next step and argue that Aristotle was correct and faith wrong. They only maintained that Aristotle's arguments could not be refuted by natural reason, and that the philosopher—as a philosopher, not as a Christian—based his judgments on rational arguments only, not on miracles and revelation. These strict Aristotelians did not deny the truths of faith, but they did assert that natural reason could construct conclusive proofs for propositions that the church had explicitly stated to be false.

In 1277, the Bishop of Paris condemned 219 propositions, many of them taught by these expositors of Aristotle at the University of Paris. Included in the condemnation were some propositions held by Aquinas. This move attempted to prevent Aristotle's philosophical naturalism from undermining Christian beliefs. Consequently, the condemnation was a triumph for conservative theologians who had grown increasingly worried about the inroads made by Aristotelianism. To them, even the Christian Aristotelianism of Aquinas was suspect.

Condemnations generally hinder the pursuit of knowledge, but ironically the condemnation of 1277 may have had the opposite effect. It led some thinkers to examine critically and reject elements of Aristotle's natural philosophy. This development may have served as a prelude to modern science, which, born in the sixteenth and seventeenth centuries, grew out of a rejection of Aristotelian physics.

Science

During the Early Middle Ages, few scientific works from the ancient world were available to western Europeans. Scientific thought was at its lowest ebb since it had originated more than a thousand years earlier in Greece. In contrast, both Islamic and Byzantine civilizations preserved and in some instances added to the legacy of Greek science. In the High Middle Ages, however, many ancient texts were translated from Greek and Arabic into Latin, and entered Latin Christendom for the first time. The principal centers of translation were Spain, where Christian and Muslim civilizations met, and Sicily, which had been controlled by Byzantium up to the last part of the ninth century and then by Islam until Christian Normans completed conquest of the island by 1091.

In the thirteenth and fourteenth centuries, a genuine scientific movement did occur. Impressed with the naturalistic and empirical approach of Aristotle, some medieval schoolmen spent time examining physical nature. Among them was the Dominican Albert the Great (Albertus Magnus). Albert (c. 1206–1280) was born in Germany, studied at Padua, and taught at the University of Paris, where Thomas Aquinas was his student. To Albert, philosophy meant more than employing

Greek reason to contemplate divine wisdom: it also meant making sense of nature. Albert devoted himself to editing and commenting on the vast body of Aristotle's works.

While retaining the Christian stress on God, revelation, the supernatural, and the afterlife, Albert (unlike many earlier Christian thinkers) considered nature a valid field for investigation. In his writings on geology, chemistry, botany, and zoology, Albert, like Aristotle, displayed a respect for the concrete details of nature by using them for empirical evidence:

I have examined the anatomy of different species of bees. In the rear, i.e. behind the waist, I discovered a transparent, shining bladder. If you test this with your tongue, you find that it has a slight taste of honey. In the body there is only an insignificant spiral-shaped intestine and nerve fibers which are connected with the sting. All this is surrounded with a sticky fluid.[8]

Showing a modern-day approach, Albert approved of inquiry into the material world, stressed the value of knowledge derived from experience with nature, sought rational explanations for natural occurrences, and held that theological debates should not stop scientific investigations. He pointed to a new direction in medieval thought.

Another scholar of the scientific movement was Robert Grosseteste (c. 1175–1253), chancellor of Oxford University. He declared that the roundness of the earth could be demonstrated by reason. In addition, he insisted that mathematics was necessary in order to understand the physical world, and he carried out experiments on the refraction of light.

Another Englishman, the monk and philosopher Roger Bacon (c. 1214–1294), foreshadowed the modern attitude of using science to gain mastery over nature. He recognized the practical advantages that might come from science and prophesied:

Machines for navigation can be made without rowers so that the largest ships on rivers or seas will be moved by a single man in charge with

greater velocity than if they were full of men. Also oars can be made so that without animals they will move with unbelievable rapidity. . . . Also flying machines can be constructed so that a man sits in the midst of the machine revolving some engine by which artificial wings are made to beat the air like a flying bird. Also a machine small in size can be made for walking in the sea and rivers, even to the bottom without danger.[9]

Bacon valued the study of mathematics and read Arabic works on the reflection and refraction of light. Among his achievements were experiments in optics and the observation that light travels much faster than sound. In searching for the cause of the rainbow, he demonstrated some understanding of the inductive method of reasoning. His description of the anatomy of the vertebrate eye and optic nerves was the finest of that era, and he recommended dissecting the eyes of pigs and cows to obtain greater knowledge of the subject.

The study of the ancient texts of Hippocrates and Galen and their Islamic commentators, particularly Avicenna's *The Canon of Medicine,* which synthesized Greek and Arabic medicine, elevated medicine to a formal discipline. Although these texts contained numerous errors and contradictions, they had to be mastered, if only to be challenged, before modern medicine could emerge. In addition, medieval doctors dissected animals and, in the late fourteenth century, human bodies. From practical experience, medieval doctors, monks, and laypersons added to the list of plants and herbs that would ease pain and hasten healing.

Medieval scholars did not make the breakthrough to modern science. They kept the belief that the earth was at the center of the universe and that different sets of laws operated on earth and in the heavens. They did not invent analytic geometry or calculus or arrive at the modern concept of inertia (see Chapter 17). Medieval science was never wholly removed from a theological setting. Modern science self-consciously seeks the advancement of specifically scientific knowl-

edge, but in the Middle Ages, many questions involving nature were raised merely to clarify a religious problem.

Medieval scholars and philosophers did, however, advance knowledge about optics, the tides, and mechanics. They saw the importance of mathematics for interpreting nature, and they performed experiments. By translating and commenting on ancient Greek and Arabic works, medieval scholars provided future ages with ideas to reflect on and to reject, a necessary precondition for the emergence of modern science.

Medieval thinkers also developed an anti-Aristotelian physics that some historians of science believe influenced Galileo, the creator of modern mechanics, more than two centuries later. To explain why heavy objects do not always fall downward—why an arrow released by a bow moves in a straight line before it falls—Aristotle said that when the arrow leaves the bow, it separates the air, which then moves behind the arrow and pushes it along. Aristotle, of course, had no comprehension of the law of *inertia* which, as formulated by Isaac Newton in the seventeenth century, states that a body in motion will continue in a straight line unless interfered with. Unable to imagine that a body in motion is as natural a condition as a body at rest, Aristotle maintained that an outside force must maintain continual contact with the moving object. Hence, the flying arrow requires the "air-engine" to keep it in motion.

In the fourteenth century, Jean Buridan, a professor at Paris, rejected Aristotle's theory. Buridan argued that the bowstring transmits to the arrow a force called *impetus,* which keeps the arrow in motion. Whereas Aristotle attributed the arrow's motion to the air, which was external to the arrow, Buridan found the motive force to be an agent imparted to the arrow by the bowstring. Although still far from the modern theory of inertia, Buridan's impetus theory was an advance over Aristotle's air-engine. In the impetus theory, a moving body requires a cause to keep it in motion. In the theory of inertia, once a body is in motion, no force is required to keep it moving in a straight line. The state of motion is as natural as the state of rest.

In other ways, late medieval physics went beyond Aristotle, particularly in the importance given to expressing motion mathematically. The extent to which late medieval thinkers influenced the thinkers of the Scientific Revolution is a matter of debate. Some historians regard modern science as the child of the Middle Ages. Other historians believe that the achievements of medieval science were slim and that modern science is very little indebted to the Middle Ages.

Recovery of Roman Law

During the Early Middle Ages, western European law essentially consisted of Germanic customs, some of which had been put into writing. Some elements of Roman law endured as custom and practice, but the formal study of Roman law had disappeared. The late eleventh and twelfth centuries saw the revival of Roman law, particularly in Bologna, Italy. Irnerius lectured on the *Corpus Juris Civilis*, codified by Byzantine jurists in the sixth century. He made Bologna the leading center for the study of Roman law. Irnerius and his students employed the methods of organization and logical analysis that scholastic theologians used in studying philosophical texts.

Unlike traditional Germanic law, Roman law assumed the existence of universal principles that could be grasped by the human intellect and expressed in the law of the state. Roman jurists had systematically and rationally structured the legal experience of the Roman people. The example of Roman law stimulated medieval jurists to organize their own legal tradition. Intellectuals increasingly came to insist upon both a rational analysis of evidence and judicial decisions based upon rational procedures. Law codes compiled in parts of France and Germany and in the kingdom of Castile were influenced by the recovery of Roman law.

Roman legal experience contained political principles that differed markedly from feudal practices. According to feudal tradition lords, by virtue of their large estates, were empowered to exercise political authority. Roman jurists, on the other hand, had attributed governmental powers to the state and had granted wide powers to the emperor. The *Corpus Juris Civilis* stated that the power to make laws had originally resided with the Roman people, but that they had surrendered this power to the emperor. Medieval lawyers in the service of kings used this concept to justify royal absolutism, holding that the monarch possessed the absolute powers that the Roman legal tradition had granted to the Roman emperor. This strong defense of the monarch's power helped kings to maintain their independence from the papacy.

Roman law also influenced the law of the church (canon law), which was derived from the Bible, the church fathers, church councils, and the decisions of popes. In the last part of the eleventh century, church scholars began to codify church law and were helped by the Roman legal tradition.

Literature

Medieval literature was written both in Latin and in the vernacular. Much of medieval Latin literature consisted of religious hymns and dramas depicting the life of Christ and saints. A typical hymn by Saint Thomas Aquinas follows.

Sing, my tongue, the Savior's glory
Of his Flesh the mystery sing;
Of the Blood, all price exceeding,
Shed by our immortal King,
Destined for the world's redemption,
From a noble womb to spring.[10]

Medieval university students, like their modern counterparts, lampooned their elders and social conventions, engaged in drinking bouts, and rebelled against the rigors of study.

French Tapestry of a Courtier and His Lady. The courtly love tradition, in which women were worshipped and untouchable, inspired poetry. By inviting poets to their courts and writing poetry themselves, noblewomen actively influenced the rituals and literature of courtly love. (*Musée de Cluny/Lauros-Giraudon/Art Resource*)

And they put their feelings into poetry written in Latin.

We in our wandering,
Blithesome and squandering;
*　　Tara, tantara, teino!*

Eat to satiety,
Drink with propriety;
*　　tara, tantara, teino!*

Laugh till our sides we split,
Rags on our hides we fit;
*　　Tara, tantara, teino!*

Jesting eternally,
Quaffing infernally;
*　　Tara, tantara, teino!*[11]

The High Middle Ages saw the emergence of a vernacular literature. The French *chansons de geste*—epic poems of heroic deeds that had first been told orally—were written in the vernacular of northern France. These poems dealt with Charlemagne's battles against the Muslims, with rebellious nobles, and with feudal warfare. The finest of these epic poems, *The Song of Roland*, expressed the vassal's loyalty to his lord and the Christian's devotion to his faith. Roland, Charlemagne's nephew, was killed in a battle with the Muslims.

The *Nibelungenlied*, the best expression of the heroic epic in Germany, is often called "the *Iliad* of the Germans." Like its French counterpart, it dealt with heroic feats.

In stories of our fathers, high marvels we are
*　　told*
Of champions well-approved in perils manifold.
Of feasts and merry meetings, of weeping and
*　　of wail,*
And deeds of gallant daring I'll tell you in my
*　　tale.*[12]

Pisa Cathedral and Tower. Italian Gothic architecture remained very conservative. The basilican style, which had emerged in the Early Christian era, prevailed. The flying buttresses and extensive use of stained glass never took firm root in Italy. (*Alinari/Art Resource*)

The *roman*—a blending of old legends, chivalric ideals, and Christian concepts—combined love with adventure, war, and the miraculous. Among the romans were the tales of King Arthur and his Round Table. Circulating by word of mouth for centuries, these tales spread from the British Isles to France and Germany. In the twelfth century, they were put into French verse.

Another form of medieval poetry, which flourished particularly in Provence in southern France, dealt with the romantic glorification of women. Sung by *troubadours*, many of them nobles, the courtly love poetry expressed a changing attitude toward women. Although medieval men generally regarded women as inferior and subordinate, courtly love poetry ascribed to noble ladies superior qualities of virtue. To the nobleman, the lady became a goddess worthy of all devotion, loyalty, and worship. He would honor her and serve her as he did his lord; for her love he would undergo any sacrifice. Troubadours sang love songs that praised ladies for their beauty and charm and expressed both the joys and pains of love:

I sing of her, yet her beauty
is greater than I can tell,
with her fresh color, lively eyes,
and white skin, untanned
and untainted by rouge.
She is so pure and noble
that no one can speak ill of her.

But above all, one must praise,
it seems to me, her truthfulness,
her manners and her gracious speech
for she never would betray a friend. . . .[13]

Noblewomen actively influenced the rituals and literature of courtly love. They often invited poets to their courts and wrote poetry

242

Reims façade. In Reims Cathedral, the High Gothic style makes a complete statement: the portals are deeply recessed with rich sculpture. The towers are symmetrical with an elaborate, heavily sculpted, connecting screen, and the rose window facing the front is so large that it serves as a translucent wall. (*Jean Roubier*)

themselves. They demanded that knights treat them with gentleness and consideration, and that knights dress neatly, bathe often, play instruments, and compose (or at least recite) poetry. To prove worthy of his lady's love, a knight had to demonstrate patience, charm, bravery, and loyalty. By devoting himself to a lady, it was believed, a knight would ennoble his character.

Courtly love did not involve a husband-wife relationship, but a noble's admiration and yearning for another woman of his class. Among nobles, marriages were arranged for political and economic reasons. The rituals of courtly love, it has been suggested, provided an expanded outlet for erotic feelings condemned by the church. They also expanded the skills and refined the tastes of the noble. The rough warrior acquired wit, manners, charm, and skill with words. He was becoming a courtier and a gentleman.

Written in the vernacular, *The Canterbury*

Tales of Geoffrey Chaucer (c. 1340–1400) is a masterpiece of English literature. Chaucer chose as his theme twenty-nine pilgrims en route from London to the religious shrine at Canterbury. In describing the pilgrims, Chaucer displayed humor, charm, an understanding of human nature, and a superb grasp of the attitudes of the English. Few writers have pictured their times better.

An Oxford Cleric, still a student though,
One who had taken logic long ago,
Was there; his horse was thinner than a rake,
And he was not too fat, I undertake,
But had a hollow look, a sober stare;
The thread upon his overcoat was bare.
He had found no preferment in the church
And he was too unworldly to make search
For secular employment. By his bed
He preferred having twenty books in red
And black, of Aristotle's philosophy,
To having fine clothes, fiddle or psaltery. . . .
The thought of moral virtue filled his speech
And he would gladly learn, and gladly teach.
. . . .
A worthy woman *from beside* Bath *city*
Was with us, somewhat deaf, which was a
    pity.
In making cloth she showed so great a bent
She bettered those of Ypres and of Ghent. . . .
A worthy woman all her life, what's more
She'd have five husbands, all at the church
    door,
Apart from other company in youth;
No need just now to speak of that, forsooth.[14]

The greatest literary figure of the Middle Ages was Dante Alighieri (1265–1321) of Florence. Dante appreciated the Roman classics and wrote not just in Latin, the traditional language of intellectual life, but also in Italian, his native tongue. In this respect he anticipated the Renaissance. In the tradition of the troubadours, Dante wrote poems to his beloved Beatrice:

My lady carries love within her eyes:
    All that she looks on is made pleasanter;
Upon her path men turn to gaze at her;
He whom she greeteth feels his heart to rise,
    And droops his troubled visage, full of
     sighs,
    And of his evil heart is then aware:
    Hate loves, and Pride becomes a wor-
     shipper.
O women, help to praise her in somewise.
Humbleness, and the hope that hopeth well,
    By speech of hers into the mind are
     brought,
    And who beholds is blessed often-
     whiles.
    The look she hath when she smiles
    Cannot be said, nor holden in the thought;
    'Tis such a new and gracious miracle.[15]

In the *Divine Comedy*, Dante synthesized the various elements of the medieval outlook and summed up, with immense feeling, the medieval understanding of the purpose of life. Written while Dante was in exile, the *Divine Comedy* describes the poet's journey through hell, purgatory, and paradise. Dante arranges hell into nine concentric circles; in each region, sinners are punished in proportion to their earthly sins. The poet experiences all of hell's torments—burning sand, violent storms, darkness, and fearful monsters who whip, claw, bite, and tear sinners apart. The ninth circle, the lowest, is reserved for Lucifer and traitors. Lucifer has three faces, each a different color, and two batlike wings. In each mouth he gnaws on the greatest traitors in history—Judas Iscariot, who betrayed Jesus, and Brutus and Cassius, who assassinated Caesar. Those condemned to hell are told: "All hope abandon, ye who enter in."

In purgatory, Dante meets sinners who, although they undergo punishment, will eventually enter paradise. In paradise, an abode of light, music, and gentleness, the poet, guided by Beatrice, meets the great saints and the Virgin Mary. For an instant, he glimpses the Vision of God. In this indescribable mystical experience, the aim of life is realized.

Architecture

Two styles of architecture evolved during the Middle Ages: Romanesque and Gothic. The Romanesque style predominated in the eleventh and greater part of the twelfth centuries. Romanesque buildings—many of them monasteries as well as churches—contained massive walls supporting stone barrel vaults, rounded arches, and small windows. A construction of thick walls with few gaps for windows was necessary to hold up the great weight of the roofs. The interiors of Romanesque churches were dark, with an air of mystery, and the columns and walls were decorated with sculptured religious scenes. The development of the pointed arch allowed for supports that lessened the bearing pressure of the roof on the walls. This new style, the Gothic, allowed buildings to have lofty, vaulted ceilings, and huge windows, which made the interior lighter than Romanesque churches. The Romanesque church produced an impression of massive solidity; the Gothic cathedral, one of soaring grace.

Although Gothic cathedrals displayed a new style, they retained many architectural features that had been traditional in Christian churches for nearly a millennium. For instance, their floor plans are cruciform—in the shape of a cross. The head of the cross, where the altar is located, almost always faces east, the direction of the rising sun, itself a symbol of resurrection and rebirth.

The Gothic cathedral gave a visual expression of the medieval view of a hierarchical universe. Historian Joan Gadol concludes: "Inside and out, the Gothic cathedral is one great movement upward through a mounting series of grades, one ascent through horizontal levels marked by arches, galleries, niches, and towers. . . . the material ascends to the spiritual, the natural is assumed into the supernatural—all in a gradated rise."[16]

Magnificently designed stained-glass windows depicted scenes from the Bible and the lives of saints for the edification of the people, many of whom were illiterate. The subtle

Rose Window, Amiens Cathedral. Inseparable from the quest for height was the new aesthetic of light. The stained glass window became a signature of the Gothic style; it transformed the quality of light admitted, infusing the interior with a spiritual atmosphere. (*Bildarchiv Foto Marburg*)

light of the stained glass windows evokes a religious experience. Light was a principal medieval metaphor for God. Although light itself is usually invisible, it enables human beings to see; similarly, God is invisible, but his existence makes possible the world of space and time.

Reims Smiling Angel. This angel of the Annunciation is more lifelike than the elongated jamb statues of the earliest Gothic sculpture. Its head turns in a natural way. Pathos, shared suffering, would soon appear in sculpture, but only the Renaissance would see statues divorced from their architectural setting. (*Jean Roubier*)

The space of a Gothic cathedral is symbolic, too. The complex interior space seems to thrust upward at the same time it seems to surge forward. The sense of weightless upward thrust implies the immanence and energy of God. Much of the impression of upward movement is created by the springing pointed arches, which are more dynamic than the earlier round-headed ones. The proportions throughout the interior are tall and narrow. Long, thin vertical colonnettes extend, almost unbroken, from the floor to the vaults of the ceiling.

Soaring height seems effortless in a Gothic cathedral because the individual parts of the interior look light. Walls that are actually ten feet thick or more appear thin because of the slim, crisp colonnettes that articulate them. Walls are opened up by delicate carved decoration, called *tracery*, and the upper reaches of the walls are filled with large stained-glass windows. There is so much tracery and such large windows that scarcely any wall space is left visible.

The reduction in wall space is made possible by the flying buttresses on the building's exterior. These great arcs of masonry distribute the weight and thrust of the stone vaults out to the exterior walls. Esthetically, the light cage of buttresses surrounding the cathedral keeps the exterior silhouette looking as airy and diffuse as the interior space.

Some Gothic cathedrals took more than fifty years to complete. Only in an age of intense religious faith could such energy have been spent to glorify God. These vast building projects, many of them in northern France, were made possible by unprecedented economic prosperity. Cathedrals, which acted as headquarters for all the surrounding churches serving the laity, raised funds from a variety of sources. Cathedrals owned income-producing properties, such as farmland, mills, and forests; they received donations from pilgrims visiting the relics of famous saints; clerics also collected tolls and taxes on goods shipped to fairs through their region.

The Gothic style was to remain vigorous until the fifteenth century, spreading from France to England, Germany, Spain, and beyond. Revived from time to time thereafter, it has proved to be one of the most enduring styles in Western art and architecture.

Not too long ago some intellectuals viewed the Middle Ages as a period of ignorance and superstition, an era of cultural sterility that stood between the high civilizations of ancient Greece and Rome and the modern West. This view of the Middle Ages as a dark age has been abandoned, and quite properly so, for the High Middle Ages saw the crystallization of a rich and creative civilization. To be sure, its religious orientation set it apart both from classical civilization and from our own modern secular and scientific civilization. But the *Summa Theologica* of Aquinas, the *Divine Comedy* of Dante, and the Gothic cathedral all attest to the creativeness of the medieval religious spirit.

Notes

1. Quoted in G. G. Coulton, *Life in the Middle Ages* (New York: Macmillan, 1928), 1:74.

2. Quoted in Charles Homer Haskins, *The Rise of Universities* (Ithaca, N.Y.: Cornell University Press, 1957), p. 79.

3. Quoted in Coulton, *Life in the Middle Ages*, 3:113.

4. Quoted in Anders Piltz, *The World of Medieval Learning* (Oxford, England: Blackwell, 1981), p. 83.

5. Quoted in David Knowles, *The Evolution of Medieval Thought* (New York: Vintage Books, 1964), p. 123.

6. *Summa Theologica*, Part I, Question 2, Art. 3.

7. Steven Ozment, *The Age of Reform* (New Haven, Conn.: Yale University Press, 1980), p. 20.

8. Quoted in Piltz, *The World of Medieval Learning*, p. 176.

9. Quoted in A. C. Crombie, *Medieval and Early Modern Science* (Garden City, N.Y.: Doubleday Anchor Books, 1959), 1:55–56.

10. Excerpted in Charles W. Jones, ed., *Medieval Literature in Translation* (New York: Longmans, Green, 1950), p. 903.

11. Quoted in Haskins, *The Rise of Universities*, pp. 86–87.

12. *The Fall of the Nibelungers*, trans. by William Nanson Lettsom (London: Williams & Norgate, 1890), p. 1.

13. Excerpted in Anthony Bonner, ed., *Songs of the Troubadours* (New York: Schocken Books, 1972), pp. 42–43.

14. Geoffrey Chaucer, *The Canterbury Tales*, trans. Neville Coghill (Baltimore: Penguin Books, 1958), pp. 27, 31.

15. Dante Alighieri, *The New Life*, trans. Dante Gabriel Rossetti (London: Elis & Elvey, 1899), pp. 82–83.

16. Joan Gadol, *Leon Battista Alberti, Universal Man of the Early Renaissance* (Chicago: The University of Chicago Press, 1969), pp. 149–150.

Suggested Reading

Baldwin, John W., *The Scholastic Culture of the Middle Ages* (1971). A useful survey for the introductory student.

Brooke, Christopher, *The Twelfth-Century Renaissance* (1969). Surveys schools, learning, theology, literature, and leading figures.

Copleston, F. C., *Aquinas* (1955). A study of Aquinas's thought.

——, *A History of Medieval Philosophy* (1974). A lucid, comprehensive survey of medieval philosophy.

Crombie, A. C., *Medieval and Early Modern Science*, 2 vols. (1959). All phases of medieval science.

Dales, R. C., ed. *The Scientific Achievement of the Middle Ages* (1973). A collection of readings from original sources.

Gilson, Etienne, *Reason and Revelation in the Middle Ages* (1966). A superb, brief exposition of the medieval philosophic tradition.

Haskins, C. H., *The Renaissance of the 12th Century* (1957). Reprint of a still-useful work.

Knowles, David, *The Evolution of Medieval Thought* (1964). One of the best of its kind.

Mâle, Emile, *The Gothic Image* (1958). A valuable study of medieval art.

Pieper, Josef, *Scholasticism* (1964). Written with intelligence and grace.

Piltz, Anders, *The World of Medieval Learning* (1981). A clearly written, informative survey of medieval education and learning.

Wieruszowski, Helene, *The Medieval University* (1966). A good survey, followed by documents.

Review Questions

1. What factors contributed to the revival of learning in the late eleventh and twelfth centuries?

2. What was the significance of medieval universities?

3. Compare and contrast medieval universities with universities today.

4. Describe the essential features of the medieval view of the universe. How does it differ from the modern view of the universe?

5. The medieval individual's understanding of himself or herself was related to a comprehension of the universe as a hierarchy culminating in God. Explain this statement.

6. What were scholastic philosophers trying to accomplish?

7. Does the scholastic goal have any relevance for us today?

8. Aquinas did not consider reason to be an enemy of faith. Explain this statement.

9. What was the significance of Aquinas's thought?

10. What would Socrates have thought of Aquinas?

11. What did the Middle Ages contribute to the growth of science?

12. What was the significance of the revival of Roman law?

13. Describe what each of the following tells about the attitudes and interests of medieval people: troubadour poetry, *The Canterbury Tales*, *Divine Comedy*, and Gothic cathedrals.

12

The Late Middle Ages:
Crisis and Dissolution

An Age of Adversity

The Decline of the Church
Conflict with France
Critique of Papal Power
The Great Schism
Fourteenth-Century Heresies

Breakup of the Thomistic Synthesis

The Middle Ages and the Modern World: Continuity and Discontinuity

By the opening of the fourteenth century, Latin Christendom had experienced more than 250 years of growth. On an economic level, agricultural production had expanded, commerce and town life had revived, and the population had increased. On a political level, kings had become more powerful, bringing greater order and security over large areas. On a religious level, the papacy had demonstrated its strength as the spiritual leader of Christendom, and the clergy had been reformed. On a cultural level, a unified world-view blending faith and reason had been forged.

During the Late Middle Ages, roughly the fourteenth and early fifteenth centuries, medieval civilization was in decline. The fourteenth century, an age of adversity, was marked by crop failures, famine, population decline, plagues, stagnating production, unemployment, inflation, devastating warfare, and abandoned villages. Violent rebellions by the disadvantaged of towns and countryside were ruthlessly suppressed by the upper classes. This century witnessed flights into mysticism, outbreaks of mass hysteria, and massacres of Jews; it was an age of pessimism and general insecurity. The papacy declined in power, heresy proliferated, and the synthesis of faith and reason, erected by Christian thinkers during the High Middle Ages, began to disintegrate. All these developments were signs the stable and coherent civilization of the thirteenth century was drawing to a close.

But all was not decline and gloom. On the positive side, representative institutions developed and thinkers showed a greater interest in the world of nature. And in Italy, the dynamic forces of urbanism and secularism were producing a period of cultural and humanistic flowering known as the *Renaissance*.

An Age of Adversity

In the Late Middle Ages, Latin Christendom was afflicted with severe economic problems.

The earlier increases in agricultural production did not continue. Limited use of fertilizers and limited knowledge of conservation exhausted the topsoil. As more grazing lands were converted to the cultivation of cereals, animal husbandry decreased, causing a serious shortage of manure needed for arable land. Intermittent bouts of prolonged heavy rains and frost also hampered agriculture. From 1301 to 1314, there was a general shortage of food, and from 1315 to 1317, famine struck Europe. Throughout the century, starvation and malnutrition were widespread.

Other economic problems abounded. A silver shortage, caused by technical problems in sinking deeper shafts in mines, led to the debasement of coins and a spiraling inflation, which hurt the feudal nobility in particular. Prices for manufactured luxury goods, which the nobility craved, rose rapidly. At the same time, the dues that the nobility collected from peasants diminished. To replace their revenues, lords and knights turned to plunder and warfare.

Compounding the economic crisis was the Black Death, or bubonic plague. This disease was carried by fleas on black rats and probably first struck Mongolia in 1331–1332. From there it crossed into Russia. Carried back from Black Sea ports, the plague reached Sicily in 1347. Spreading swiftly throughout much of Europe, the plague attacked an already declining and undernourished population. The first crisis lasted until 1351, and other serious outbreaks occurred in later decades. The crowded cities and towns had the highest mortalities. Perhaps twenty million people—about one-quarter to one-third of the European population—perished in the worst human disaster in recorded history.

Deprived of many of their intellectual and spiritual leaders, the panic-stricken masses drifted into immorality and frenzied forms of religious life. Hysteria and popular superstition abounded. Flagellants marched from region to region beating each other with sticks and whips in a desperate effort to appease God, who they believed had cursed them with the plague. Black magic, witchcraft, and sexual license found eager supporters.

Great Plague. The Black Death, or bubonic plague, devastated Europe, carrying off entire villages. A new piety swept through European art in the plague's aftermath. The elegant French courtly love style was replaced by tightly swaddled infants and suffering saints. (*Bibliothèque Royale Albert I, Brussels*)

Dress became increasingly ostentatious and bizarre; art forms concentrated on morbid scenes of decaying flesh, dances of death, and the torments of Hell. Sometimes this hysteria was directed against Jews, who were accused of causing the plague by poisoning wells. Terrible massacres of Jews occurred despite the pleas of the papacy.

The millions of deaths caused production of food and goods to plummet and some prices to soar. Nobles tried to make peasants bear the brunt of the crisis, as the value of land decreased and agricultural income lessened. A law decreed in England in 1349 required peasants to work for lords at fixed wages. Similar regulations of wages in German, Spanish, and Portuguese principalities aggravated tensions between peasants and nobles.

Economic and social tensions, some of them antedating the Black Death, escalated into rebellions. Each rebellion had its own specific causes, but a general pattern characterized the uprisings in the countryside. When kings and lords, breaking with customary social relationships, imposed new and onerous regulations, the peasants rose in defense of their traditional rights. In 1323, the lords' attempt to reimpose old manorial obligations infuriated the free peasants of Flanders, whose condition had improved in earlier decades. The peasants' revolt lasted five bloody years. In 1358, French peasants took up arms in protest against the plundering of the countryside by soldiers. Perhaps 20,000 peasants died in the uprising known as the *Jacquerie*. In 1381, English peasants revolted, angered over legislation that tied them to the land and imposed new taxes. John Ball, who claimed to be a priest, expressed egalitarian sentiments:

My good friends, things cannot go on well in England, nor ever will until everything shall be in common; when there shall neither be vassal nor lord, and all distinctions leveled; when the lords shall be no more masters than ourselves. But ill have they used us! and for what reason do they thus hold us in bondage? Are we not all descended from the same parents, Adam and Eve? and what can they show, or what reasons give, why they should be more the masters than ourselves? except, perhaps, in making us labor and work, for them to spend. . . . They have handsome manors, when we must brave the wind and rain in our labors in the field; but it is from our labor they have wherewith to support their pomp.[1]

Like the revolts in Flanders and France, the uprising in England failed. To the landed aristocracy, the peasants were sinners attacking a social system ordained by God. Possessing superior might, the nobility suppressed the peasants, sometimes with savage cruelty.

Social unrest afflicted the towns as well as the countryside. The wage earners of Florence (1378), the weavers of Ghent (1382), and the poor of Paris (1382) rose up against the ruling oligarchy. These revolts were generally initiated not by the poorest and most downtrodden, but by those who had made some gains and were eager for more. The rebellions of the urban poor were crushed just as the peasant uprisings were.

Fourteenth-century Europeans suffered because of the numerous long wars that devastated towns and farmlands and seriously hampered economic life. To deprive an invading army of food, fields were laid waste. The invaders also decimated farmlands in order to destroy the enemy's morale, and bands of discharged soldiers plundered the countryside.

In earlier centuries, wars had generally been short and small in scale, sparing noncombatants from the worst effects. In the fourteenth century this trend changed. The most destructive war was the series of conflicts between France and England known as the Hundred Years' War (1337–1453). Because English kings had ruled parts of France, conflicts between the two monarchies had been common. By 1214 the French monarchy had succeeded in acquiring most English territories in France. In 1328 the Capetian dynasty came to an end with the death of Charles IV, the son of Philip IV, the Fair. An assembly of French barons gave the crown to Philip VI of Valois, nephew of Philip the Fair. Edward III, king of England, insisted that he had a superior claim to the throne because his mother was Philip the Fair's daughter. Edward's attempt to gain the French throne was one reason for a new conflict. Another was the effort of the French monarch to squeeze taxes from Flemish towns, like Bruges, which had grown rich as trade and cloth-making centers. Dependent on English wool and resentful of the French monarchy's demands, the Flemish towns threw their support behind Edward III.

In the opening phase of the war, the English inflicted terrible defeats on French knights at the battles of Crécy (1346) and Poitiers (1356). Using longbows, which allowed them to shoot arrows rapidly, English archers cut down wave after wave of charging French cavalry. The war continued on and off

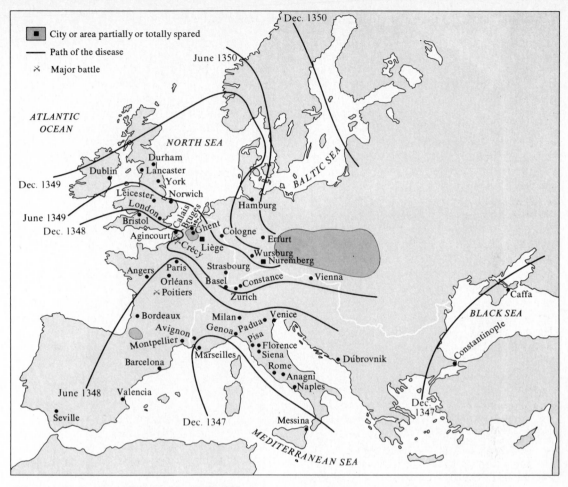

Map 12.1 Path of the Black Death, 1347–1350

throughout the fourteenth century. During periods of truce, gangs of unemployed soldiers roamed the French countryside killing and stealing, actions that precipitated the Jacquerie.

After the battle of Agincourt (1415), won by the English under Henry V, the English controlled most of northern France. It appeared that England would shortly conquer France and join the two lands under one crown. At this crucial moment in French history, a young and illiterate peasant girl, Joan of Arc (1412–1431), helped to rescue France. Believing that God commanded her to drive the English out of France, Joan rallied the demoralized French troops, leading them in battle. In 1429, she liberated the besieged city of Orléans. Imprisoned by the English, Joan was condemned as a heretic and a witch in 1431 by a hand-picked church court. She was burned at the stake. The English intended to undermine the French cause by demonstrating that Joan was not divinely chosen. But Joan's life and death inspired the French people with a sense of devotion to their country. The reorganized and aroused French army recaptured Paris. By 1453, the English were driven from all French territory except for the port of Calais.

During the Hundred Years' War, French kings introduced new taxes that added substantially to their incomes. These monies furnished them with the means to organize a professional army of well-paid and loyal

Charles d'Orléans in the Tower of London. The battle of Agincourt gave the English control over much of northern France: Although relatively short-lived, the English victory became a source of high patriotism; Shakespeare would immortalize it in *Henry V*. In contrast, the French nobleman Charles d'Orléans captured there and imprisoned in the Tower for the next twenty-five years wrote melancholy poems. (*The British Library, Royal Ms. 16, F. II, folio 73*)

troops. By evoking a sense of pride and oneness in the French people, the war also contributed to a growing, but still incomplete, national unity. The English too emerged from the war with a greater sense of solidarity.

However, the war had terrible consequences for the French peasants. Thousands of farmers were killed and valuable farmland was destroyed by English armies and marauding bands of mercenaries. In another portentous development, the later stages of the Hundred Years' War saw the use of gunpowder and heavy artillery.

The Decline of the Church

The principal sign of fragmentation in the Late Middle Ages was the waning authority and prestige of the papacy. In the High Middle Ages, the papacy had been the dominant institution in Christendom, but in the Late Middle Ages, its power disintegrated. The medieval ideal of a unified Christian commonwealth guided by the papacy shattered. Papal authority declined in the face of the growing power of kings who championed the parochial interests of states. Papal prestige and its capacity to command waned as it became more embroiled in European politics. Many pious Christians felt that the pope behaved more like a secular ruler than like an Apostle of Christ. Political theorists and church reformers further undermined papal authority.

Conflict with France

Pope Boniface VIII (1294–1303) vigorously upheld papal claims to supremacy over secular rulers. In the famous bull *Unam Sanctam,* he declared:

> . . . if the earthly power errs, it shall be judged by the the spiritual power, . . . but [the pope] can be judged only by God not by man. . . . Whoever therefore resists this power so ordained by God resists the ordinance of God. . . . Therefore, we declare, state, define, and pronounce that it is altogether necessary to salvation for every human creature to be subject to the Roman Pontiff.[2]

But in trying to enforce this idea of papal supremacy on proud and increasingly more powerful kings, Boniface suffered defeat and humiliation.

Philip IV of France (1285–1314) and Edward I of England (1272–1307) taxed the churches in their lands to raise revenue for the war they planned to wage. In doing so, they disregarded the church prohibition against the taxing of its property by the state without papal permission. In the bull *Clericis laicos,* Boniface decreed that kings and lords who impose taxes on the clergy, and clergy who pay them, would incur the sentence of excommunication. Boniface badly miscalculated. Far from bowing to the pope's threat, both Edward and Philip acted forcefully to assert their authority over the churches in their kingdoms. Boniface backed down from his position, declaring that the French king could tax the clergy in times of national emergency. Thus the matter was resolved to the advantage of the state.

A second dispute had more disastrous

Portrait of Joan of Arc. A witch to the English and a heroine to the French, this simple, illiterate peasant girl rallied French forces to reverse the tide of English supremacy in France. She was burned at the stake in 1431 by the English. Her life and death became the impetus France needed to reorganize and finally to drive the English by 1453 from all French territory except Calais. Joan was made a saint by the Roman Catholic church in the twentieth century. (*Archives Nationales, Paris*)

consequences for Boniface. Philip tried and imprisoned a French bishop despite Boniface's warning that this was an illegal act and a violation of church law and tradition, which held that the church, not the state, must judge the clergy. Philip summoned the first meeting of the Estates General to gain the backing of the nation. Shortly afterwards, Boniface issued the bull *Unam Sanctam,* previously quoted, and threatened to excommunicate Philip. The outraged monarch decided to seize Boniface and to replace him with a new pope. Aided by Italian mercenaries and enemies of Boniface, French conspirators attacked the papal summer palace at Anagni in September 1303 and captured the pope. Although Boniface was released, this terrible event proved too much for him, and a month later he died.

Boniface's successors, Benedict XI (1303–1304) and Clement V (1305–1314) tried to conciliate Philip. In particular, Clement agreed to suppress the Templars, a wealthy religious-military order to whom the French crown was in debt. Another victory for Philip was Clement's decision to remain at Avignon, a town on the southeastern French frontier, where he had set up a temporary residence.

From 1309 to 1377, a period known as the *Babylonian Captivity*, the popes were all French. During this time, the papacy, removed from Rome and deprived of revenues from the Papal States in Italy, was often forced to pursue policies favorable to France. Worsening the papal image was growing anti-papalism among laymen, who were repelled by the luxurious style of living at Avignon and by the appointment of high churchmen to lands where they did not know the language and where they demonstrated little concern for the local population. Under these circumstances, more and more people questioned the value and necessity of the papacy.

Critique of Papal Power

The conflict between Boniface and Philip provoked a battle of words between proponents of papal supremacy and defenders of royal rights. In his treatise, *On Ecclesiastical Power*, Giles of Rome (c. 1245–1316) vigorously supported the doctrine of papal power. Because the spiritual is inherently superior to the temporal, he argued, the pope has the authority to judge temporal rulers. All temporal lords ought to be governed by spiritual and ecclesiastical authority, and especially by the pope, who heads the church.

Defenders of royal prerogatives challenged the pope's claim to primacy over both secular rulers and the clergy. In taking this position, they weakened the medieval church. *On Kingly and Papal Power* (1302) by John of Paris (c. 1241–1306) attacked the theory of papal monarchy championed by Giles of Rome and

asserted the independence of the French monarchy. For John, the church was primarily a spiritual body charged with administering the sacraments; as such, its authority did not extend to temporal affairs. Indeed, clerical interference in secular affairs threatened the state's stability. While granting that "the priest is superior to the ruler in dignity," John maintained that "it is not necessary to be superior to him in all things." Since both rulers and priests derive their power from God, said John, they are each superior in their own spheres. "The priest is, therefore, superior in spiritual matters and conversely, the ruler is superior in temporal matters."[3]

The most important critique of clerical intrusion into worldly affairs was *The Defender of the Peace* (1324) by Marsiglio of Padua (c. 1290–c. 1343). Marsiglio held that the state ran according to its principles, which had nothing to do with religious commands originating in a higher realm. Religion dealt with a supranatural world and with principles of faith that could not be proved by reason, said Marsiglio. Politics, on the other hand, dealt with a natural world and with the affairs of the human community. And political thinkers should not try to make the earthly realm conform to articles of faith. For Marsiglio, the state was self-sufficient; it needed no instruction from a higher authority. Thus Marsiglio denied the essential premises of medieval papal political theory: that kings received their power from God; that the pope, as God's vicar, was empowered to guide kings; that the state, as part of a divinely ordered world, must conform to and fulfill supranatural ends; and that the clergy were above the laws of the state. Marsiglio felt that the church should be a spiritual institution with no temporal power.

The Great Schism

The Avignon popes were often competent men who, despite the hard times that had overtaken the papacy, tried to bolster papal power. They tightened their hold over church administration by reserving for themselves certain appointments and collections of fees formerly handled by local bishops. Through a deliberate effort at financial centralization, including the imposition of new taxes and the more efficient collection of old ones, the Avignon popes increased papal income substantially.

Pope Gregory XI returned the papacy to Rome in 1377, ending the Babylonian Captivity. But the papacy was to endure an even greater humiliation—the Great Schism. Elected pope in 1378, Urban VI immediately displayed tactlessness, if not mental imbalance, by abusing and even imprisoning cardinals. Fleeing from Rome, the cardinals declared that the election of Urban had been invalid and elected Clement VII as the new pope. Refusing to step down, Urban excommunicated Clement who responded in kind. To the utter confusion and anguish of Christians throughout Europe, there were now two popes—Urban ruling from Rome and Clement from Avignon.

Prominent churchmen urged the convening of a general council—the Council of Pisa—to end the disgraceful schism. Held in 1409 and attended by hundreds of churchmen, the Council of Pisa deposed both Urban and Clement and elected a new pope. Neither deposed pope recognized the council's decision, so that Christendom then had three popes! A new council was called at Constance in 1414. In the struggle that ensued, each of the three popes either abdicated or was deposed in favor of an appointment by the council. In 1417, the Great Schism ended.

During the first half of the fifteenth century, church councils met at Pisa (1409), Constance (1414–1418), and Basel (1431–1449) in order to end the schism, combat heresy, and reform the church. The Conciliar movement attempted to transform the papal monarchy into a constitutional system in which the pope's power would be regulated by a general council. Supporters of the movement held that the papacy could not reform the church as effectively as a general council representing the clergy. But the Conciliar movement ended

in failure. As the Holy Roman emperor and then the French monarch withdrew support from the councils, the papacy regained its authority over the higher clergy. In 1460, Pope Pius II condemned the Conciliar movement as heretical.

The papacy was deeply embroiled in European power politics and the worldly life of Renaissance Italy and often neglected its spiritual and moral responsibilities. Many devout Christians longed for a religious renewal, a return to simple piety; the papacy barely heard this cry for reform. The papacy's failure to provide creative leadership for reform made possible the Protestant Reformation of the sixteenth century. The Reformation, by splitting Christendom into Catholic and Protestant, destroyed forever the vision of a Christian world commonwealth guided by Christ's vicar, the pope.

Fourteenth-Century Heresies

Another threat to the medieval ideal of a universal Christian community came from radical reformers questioning the function and authority of the entire church hierarchy. These heretics in the Late Middle Ages were forerunners of the Protestant Reformation.

The two principal dissenters were the Englishman John Wycliffe (c. 1320–1384) and the Czech John Huss (c. 1369–1415). By stressing a personal relationship between the individual and God and by claiming the Bible itself, rather than church teachings, to be the ultimate Christian authority, they challenged the fundamental position of the medieval church: that the avenue to salvation passed through the church alone. They attacked the wealth of the higher clergy and sought a return to the spiritual purity and material poverty of the early church. To Wycliffe, the wealthy, elaborately organized hierarchy of the church was unnecessary and wrong. The splendidly dressed and propertied bishops had no resemblance to the simple people who first followed Christ. Indeed, these worldly bishops headed by a princely and tyrannical

pope were really anti-Christians, the "fiends of Hell." Wycliffe wanted the state to confiscate church property and the clergy to embrace poverty. By denying that priests changed the bread and wine of communion into the substance of the body and blood of Christ, Wycliffe and Huss rejected the sacerdotal power of the clergy. Although both movements were declared heretical and Huss was burned at the stake, the church could not crush the dissenters' followers or eradicate their teachings. The doctrines of the Reformation would parallel the teachings of Wycliffe and Huss to some extent.

Breakup of the Thomistic Synthesis

In the Late Middle Ages, the papacy lost power, as kings, political theorists, and religious dissenters effectively challenged papal claims to supreme leadership. Also breaking down was the great theological synthesis constructed by philosophers. The process of fragmentation seen in the history of the church also took place in philosophy.

Saint Thomas Aquinas's system culminated the scholastic attempt to show the basic agreement of philosophy and religion. In the fourteenth century, a number of thinkers cast doubt on the possibility of synthesizing Aristotelianism and Christianity, that is, reason and faith. Consequently, philosophy grew more analytical and critical. Denying that reason could demonstrate the truth of Christian doctrines with certainty, philosophers tried to separate reason from faith. Whereas

Left: **Hubert and/or Jan van Eyck: The Last Judgment,** c. **1420.** The major concern of medieval people was the salvation of their souls. At the Last Judgment, the good would be drawn to heaven for an eternity of bliss, while the damned would be sealed in hell. The Flemish artist depicts in graphic detail this final division. (*The Metropolitan Museum of Art, Fletcher Fund, 1933*)

Aquinas had said that reason proved or clarified much of revelation, fourteenth-century thinkers asserted that the basic propositions of Christianity were not open to rational proof. Whereas Aquinas had held that faith supplements and perfects reason, some philosophers were now proclaiming that reason often contradicts faith.

Duns Scotus (1265–1308), an English Franciscan, held that human reason cannot prove that God is omnipotent, that he forgives sins, that he rewards the righteous and punishes the wicked, or that the soul is immortal. These Christian doctrines, which scholastic philosophers believed could be proven by reason, were for Scotus the province of revelation and faith, not reason.

To be sure, this new outlook did not urge abandoning faith in favor of reason. Faith had to prevail in any conflict with reason because faith rested on God, the highest authority in the universe. But the relationship between reason and revelation was altered. Articles of faith, it was now held, had nothing to do with reason; they were to be believed, not proved. Reason was not an aid to theology, but a separate sphere of activity. This new attitude snapped the link between reason and faith that Aquinas had so skillfully forged. The scholastic synthesis was disintegrating.

A principal proponent of this new outlook was William of Ockham (c. 1280–1349). In contrast to Aquinas, Ockham insisted that natural reason could not prove God's existence, the soul's immortality, or any other essential Christian doctrine. Reason could only say that God probably exists and that he probably endowed man with an immortal soul. But it could not prove these propositions with *certainty*. The tenets of faith were beyond the reach of reason, said Ockham; there was no rational foundation to Christianity. For Ockham, reason and faith were different ways of proceeding; it was neither possible nor helpful to join reason to faith. He did not, however, seek to undermine faith—only to disengage it from reason.

In the process of proclaiming the authority of theology, Ockham also furthered using reason to comprehend nature. Ockham's approach, separating natural knowledge from religious dogma, made it easier to explore the natural world empirically without fitting it into a religious framework. With Ockham, then, we see a forerunner of the modern mentality: a separation of reason from religion, and a growing interest in the empirical investigation of nature.

Medieval civilization began to decline in the fourteenth century, but no new dark age descended on Europe; its economic and political institutions and technological skills had grown too strong. Instead, the waning of the Middle Ages opened up possibilities for another stage in Western civilization—the modern age.

The Middle Ages and the Modern World: Continuity and Discontinuity

In innumerable ways the modern world is linked to the Middle Ages. European cities, the middle class, the state system, English common law, universities—all had their origins in the Middle Ages. During that period, important advances were made in business practices. By translating and commenting on the writings of Greek and Arabic thinkers, medieval scholars preserved a priceless intellectual heritage, without which the modern mind could never have evolved. And between the thought of the scholastics and that of early modern philosophers there are numerous connecting strands.

During the Middle Ages, Europeans began to take the lead over the Muslims, the Byzantines, the Chinese, and all the other peoples in the use of technology. Medieval technology and inventiveness stemmed in part from Christianity, which taught that God had created the world specifically for human beings to subdue and utilize. Consequently, medieval people tried to employ animal power and laborsaving machinery to relieve human drudgery. Moreover, Christianity taught that God was above nature, not within it, so for the Christian there was no spiritual obstacle to exploiting nature as there was, for example, for the Hindu. Unlike classical humanism, the Christian outlook did not consider manual work degrading—even monks combined study with manual labor.

Believing that God's law was superior to state or national decrees, medieval philosophers provided a theoretical basis for opposing tyrannical kings who violated Christian principles. The idea that both the ruler and the ruled are bound by a higher law would, in a secularized form, become a principal element of modern liberal thought.

The Christian stress on the sacred worth of the individual and on the higher law of God has never ceased to influence Western civilization. Although in modern times the various Christian churches have not often taken the lead in political and social reform, the ideals identified with the Judeo-Christian tradition have become part of the common Western heritage. As such, they have inspired social reformers who may no longer identify with their ancestral religion.

Feudal traditions lasted long after the Middle Ages. Up to the French Revolution, for instance, French aristocrats enjoyed special privileges and exercised power over local government. In England, the aristocracy controlled local government until the Industrial Revolution transformed English society in the nineteenth century. Retaining the medieval ideal of the noble warrior, aristocrats continued to dominate the officer corps of European armies through the nineteenth century and even into the twentieth. Aristocratic notions of duty, honor, loyalty, and courtly love have also endured into the twentieth century.

Feudalism also contributed to the history of liberty. According to feudal theory the king, as a member of the feudal community, was duty-bound to honor agreements made by his vassals. Lords possessed personal rights that the king was obliged to respect. Resentful of a king who ran roughshod over customary

feudal rights, lords also negotiated contracts with the crown, such as the famous Magna Carta, to define and guard their customary liberties. To protect themselves from the arbitrary behavior of a king, feudal lords initiated what came to be called *government by consent* and the *rule of law*.

Thus, in the Middle Ages there gradually emerged the ideas that law was not imposed on inferiors by an absolute monarch, but required the collaboration of the king and his subjects; that the king, too, was bound by the law; and that lords had the right to resist a monarch who violated agreements. Related to these ideas, representative institutions also emerged with which the king was expected to consult on the realm's affairs. The most notable was the British Parliament which, although it was subordinate to the king, became a permanent part of the state. Later, in the seventeenth century, Parliament would successfully challenge royal authority. Continuity, therefore, exists between the feudal tradition of a king bound by law and the modern practice of limiting the authority of the head of state.

Although the elements of continuity are concrete, the characteristic outlook of the Middle Ages is as different from that of the modern age as it was from that of the ancient world. Religion was the integrating feature of the Middle Ages, whereas science and secularism determine the modern outlook. The period from the Italian Renaissance of the fifteenth century through the eighteenth-century Age of Enlightenment constituted a breaking away from the medieval worldview—a rejection of the medieval conception of nature, the individual, and the purpose of life.

Medieval thought began with the existence of God and the truth of his revelation as interpreted by the church, which set the standards and defined the purposes for human endeavor. The medieval mind rejected the fundamental principle of Greek philosophy—the autonomy of reason. Without the guidance of revealed truth, reason was seen as feeble.

The Polos Embarking from Venice. The journey of the Polos to the court of the great Khan sees the medieval world almost at an end. The exploration of the East would soon be followed by voyages to Africa and the discovery of the New World. Commerce and trade would transform the western economy. The role of the individual would change from that of a functioning member in an ordered political and spiritual realm to that of an explorer of new worlds: physical, intellectual, and artistic. (*Bodleian Library, Oxford, Ms. Bodley 264, fol. 218R*)

Scholastics reasoned closely and carefully, drew fine distinctions, and at times demonstrated a critical attitude. They engaged in genuine philosophical speculation, but they did not allow philosophy to challenge the basic premises of their faith. Unlike either ancient or modern thinkers, medieval schoolmen believed ultimately that reason alone could not provide a unified view of nature or society. A rational soul had to be guided by a divine light. For all medieval philosophers, the natural order depended on a supernatural order for its origin and purpose. To understand the natural world properly it was necessary to know its relationship to the higher world.

In the modern view, both nature and the human intellect are self-sufficient. Nature is a mathematical system that operates without miracles or any other form of divine intervention. To comprehend nature and society, the mind needs no divine assistance; it accepts no authority above reason. The modern mentality finds it unacceptable to reject the conclusions of science on the basis of clerical authority and revelation, or to base politics, law, or economics on religion; it refuses to accept dogma uncritically and insists on scientific proof.

The medieval philosopher arranged both nature and society into a hierarchic order. Heaven was the source of moral values, and the church was responsible for teaching and upholding these ethical norms. Kings acquired their right to rule from God. The entire social structure constituted a hierarchy: the clergy guided society according to Christian standards; lords defended Christian society from its enemies; serfs, at the bottom of the social order, toiled for the good of all. There was also a hierarchy of knowledge. A lower form of knowledge derived from the senses, and the highest type of knowledge, theology, dealt with God's revelation. To the medieval mind this hierarchic ordering of nature, society, and knowledge had a divine sanction.

Rejecting the medieval division of the universe into higher and lower realms and superior and inferior substances, the modern view came to regard the universe as one and nature as uniform; the modern thinker studies mathematical law and chemical composition, not grades of perfection. Spiritual meaning is not sought in an examination of the material world. Roger Bacon, for example, described seven coverings of the eye and then concluded that God had fashioned the eye in this manner in order to express the seven gifts of the Spirit. This way of thinking is alien to the modern outlook.

The modern West also broke with the rigid division of medieval society into three orders: clergy, nobles, and commoners. Opposing the feudal principle that an individual's obligations and rights are a function of his or her rank in society, the modern West stressed equality of opportunity and equal treatment under the law. It rejected the idea that society should be guided by clergymen who possess a special wisdom, by nobles who were entitled to special privileges, and by a king who received his power from God.

The modern West also rejected the personal and customary character of feudal law. As the modern state developed, law assumed an impersonal and objective character. For example, if the lord demanded more than the customary forty days of military service,

the vassal might refuse to comply, seeing the lord's request as an unpardonable violation of custom and agreement and an infringement on his liberties. In the modern state with a constitution and a representative government, if a new law increasing the length of military service is passed, it merely replaces the old law. People do not refuse to obey it because the government has broken faith or violated custom.

In the modern world, the individual's relationship to the universe has been radically transformed. To medieval thinkers, human beings ranked below angels, but were superior to inanimate objects, plants, and animals. People in the Middle Ages knew why they were on earth and what was expected of them; they never doubted that heaven would be their reward for living a Christian life. J. H. Randall, Jr., a historian of philosophy, eloquently sums up the medieval world-view:

> *The world was governed throughout by the omnipotent will and omniscient mind of God, whose sole interests were centered in man, his trial, his fall, his suffering and his glory. Worm of the dust as he was, man was yet the central object in the whole universe. . . . And when his destiny was completed, the heavens would be rolled up as a scroll and he would dwell with the Lord forever. Only those who rejected God's freely offered grace and with hardened hearts refused repentance would be cut off from this eternal life.* [4]

This comforting medieval vision is alien to the modern outlook. Today, in a universe fifteen billion years old in which the earth is a tiny speck floating in an endless cosmic ocean, where life evolved over tens of millions of years, many Westerners no longer are certain that human beings are special children of God; that heaven is their ultimate goal; that under their feet is Hell; that God is an active agent in human history. To many intellectuals the universe seems unresponsive to the religious supplications of people, and life's purpose is sought within the limits of earthly existence. Almost ruthlessly, science and secularism have driven Christianity and

Chronology 12.1   The Late Middle Ages

September 1303	The French attack the papal summer place at Anagni
1309–1377	The "Babylonian Captivity"; the popes are all French and influenced by the French monarchy
1323–1328	The peasants revolt in Flanders
1328	The end of France's Capetian dynasty; Edward III of England tries to gain the French throne
1337–1453	The Hundred Years' War between England and France
1346	The battle of Crécy—the French are defeated by the British
1347–1351	The Black Death reaches Italian ports and ravages Europe
1356	The battle of Poitiers—the French are defeated by the English
1358	The Jacquerie, the French peasants' revolt
1377	Pope Gregory XI returns the papacy to Rome
1378	The Florentine laborers revolt
1378–1417	The Great Schism; Christendom has two and then three popes
1381	The English peasants revolt
1382	The weavers revolt in Ghent
1415	The battle of Agincourt—the French are defeated by Henry V of England; John Huss, Bohemian religious reformer, is burned at the stake
1429	Joan of Arc liberates Orléans
1431	Joan of Arc is condemned as a witch
1453	The English are driven from France, except Calais; the end of the Hundred Years' War
1460	Pope Pius II condemns the Conciliar movement as heretical

faith from their central position to the periphery of human concerns.

The modern outlook emerged gradually in the period from the Renaissance to the eighteenth-century Age of Enlightenment. Mathematics rendered the universe comprehensible. Economic and political thought broke free of the religious frame of reference. Science became the great hope of the future. The thinkers of the Enlightenment wanted to liberate humanity from superstition, ignorance, and traditions that could not pass the test of reason. Rejecting the Christian idea of a person's inherent sinfulness, they held that the individual was basically good, and that evil resulted from faulty institutions, poor education, and bad leadership. Thus the concept of a rational and free society in which individuals could realize their potential slowly emerged.

In the following chapters, we will examine how the medieval conception of the cosmos, society, and the individual gradually crumbled before the onset of science and secularism. Western thinkers abandoned religious interpretations of nature and sought to transform institutions so that they followed rational norms. This effort kindled enormous enthusiasm and hope, for it held the promise of emancipating men and women from abuses of the past. But the path to a rational and free society became choked with obstacles— some created by the very success of reason and freedom. People began to lose confidence in reason and weakened their commitment to freedom; this change engulfed Western civilization in a spiritual crisis that still persists.

Notes

1. Jean Froissart, *Chronicles of England, France, Spain* (London: Henry G. Bohn, 1849), p. 653.

2. Excerpted in Brian Tierney, ed., *The Crisis of Church and State 1050–1300* (Englewood Cliffs, N.J.: Prentice Hall, 1964), p. 189.

3. Excerpted in Ralph Lerner and Muhsin

Mahdi, *Medieval Political Philosophy* (New York: The Free Press, 1963), pp. 413–414.

4. J. H. Randall, Jr., *The Making of the Modern Mind* (Boston: Houghton Mifflin, 1940), p. 34.

Suggested Reading

Bowsky, W. M., ed., *The Black Death* (1971). A collection of readings on the impact of the plague.

Ferguson, W. K., *Europe in Transition 1300–1520* (1962). The transition from Middle Ages to Renaissance.

Hay, Denys, *Europe in the Fourteenth and Fifteenth Centuries* (1966). A good survey of the Late Middle Ages.

Hilton, Rodney, *Bond Men Made Free* (1977). An analysis of medieval peasant movements.

Holmes, George, *Europe: Hierarchy and Revolt, 1320–1450* (1975). A good survey of the period.

Huizinga, Johan, *The Waning of the Middle Ages* (1924). An old but still valuable discussion of late medieval culture.

Lerner, Robert E., *The Age of Adversity* (1968). A short, readable survey of the fourteenth century.

McFarlane, K. B., *John Wycliffe and the Beginnings of English Nonconformity* (1952). The man and his influence.

Mollat, Guillaume, *The Popes at Avignon* (1963). The papacy in the fourteenth century.

Ozment, Steven, *The Age of Reform, 1250–1550* (1980). An intellectual and religious history of Late Medieval and Reformation Europe.

Perroy, Edouard, *The Hundred Years' War* (1965). The best treatment of the conflict.

Spinka, M., *John Hus and the Czech Reform* (1941). A reliable work on Huss and the Hussite wars.

Review Questions

1. What economic problems made the fourteenth century an age of adversity?

2. What were the principal reasons for peasant uprisings in the fourteenth century?

3. What was the fundamental issue at stake in the conflict between Boniface VIII and Philip IV?

4. How did John of Paris and Marsiglio of Padua challenge the pope's claim to primacy over secular authority?

5. Identify and explain the historical significance of the Babylonian Captivity, Great Schism, and Conciliar movement.

6. Why did the church regard Wycliffe and Huss as heretics?

7. What was the significance of Ockham's philosophy?

8. What is the legacy of the Middle Ages to the modern world?

9. How does the characteristic outlook of the Middle Ages differ from that of the modern age?

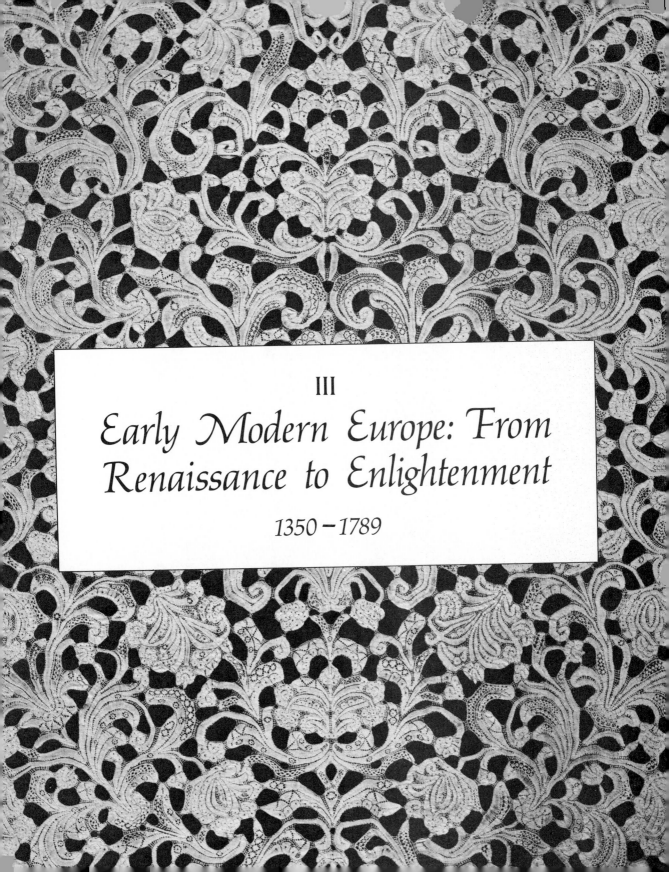

III

Early Modern Europe: From Renaissance to Enlightenment

1350 – 1789

13

The Renaissance: Transition to the Modern Age

*F*rom the Italian Renaissance of the fifteenth century through the Age of Enlightenment of the eighteenth century, the outlook and institutions of the Middle Ages disintegrated and distinctly modern forms emerged. The radical change in European civilization could be seen on every level of society. On the economic level, commerce and industry expanded greatly, and capitalism largely replaced medieval forms of economic organization. On the political level, central government grew stronger at the expense of feudalism. On the religious level, the rise of Protestantism fragmented the unity of Christendom. On the social level, the prosperous people in both city and country gained in numbers and strength and were preparing for political and cultural leadership. On the cultural level, the clergy lost its monopoly over learning, and the otherworldly orientation of the Middle Ages gave way to a secular outlook in literature and the arts. Theology, the queen of knowledge in the Middle Ages, surrendered its crown to science. Reason, which in the Middle Ages had been subordinate to revelation, asserted its independence.

Many of these tendencies manifested themselves dramatically during the Renaissance. The word *renaissance* means rebirth and it is used to refer to the attempt by artists and thinkers to recover and apply the ancient learning and standards of Greece and Rome. In historical terms, the Renaissance is both a cultural movement and a period. As a movement it was born in the city-states of northern Italy and spread to the rest of Europe. As a period it runs from about 1350 to 1600. Until the late fifteenth century the Renaissance was restricted to Italy. What happened there in the fourteenth and fifteenth centuries sharply contrasts with civilization in the rest of Europe, which until the end of the fifteenth century still belonged to the Late Middle Ages.

The nineteenth-century historian Jacob Burckhardt in his classic study, *The Civilization* of the Renaissance in Italy (1860), held that the Renaissance is the point of departure for the modern world. During the Renaissance, said Burckhardt, individuals showed an increasing concern for worldly life and self-consciously aspired to shape their destinies, an attitude that is the key to modernity.

Burckhardt's thesis has been challenged, particularly by medievalists who view the Renaissance as an extension of the Middle Ages, not as a sudden break with the past. These critics argue that Burckhardt neglected important links between medieval and Renaissance culture. A distinguishing feature of the Renaissance, the revival of classical learning, had already emerged in the High Middle Ages to such an extent that historians speak of "the renaissance of the twelfth century." The Renaissance owes much to the legal and scholastic studies that flourished in the Italian universities of Padua and Bologna before 1300. Town life and trade, hallmarks of Renaissance society, were also a heritage from the Middle Ages.

To be sure, the Renaissance was not a complete and sudden break with the Middle Ages. Many medieval ways and attitudes persisted. Nevertheless, Burckhardt's thesis that the Renaissance represents the birth of modernity has much to recommend it. Renaissance writers and artists themselves were aware of their age's novelty. They looked back on the medieval centuries as a "Dark Age" that followed the grandeur of ancient Greece and Rome, and they believed that they were experiencing a rebirth of cultural greatness. Renaissance artists and writers were fascinated with the cultural forms of Greece and Rome; they sought to imitate classical style and to capture the secular spirit of antiquity. In the process they broke with medieval artistic and literary forms. They valued the full development of human talent and expressed a new excitement about the possibilities of life in this world. This outlook represents a new trend in European civilization.

The Renaissance, then, was an age of transition that saw the rejection of certain elements of the medieval outlook, the revival of classical cultural forms, and the emergence of distinctly modern attitudes. This rebirth began in Italy during the fourteenth century and gradually spread north and west to Germany, France, England, and Spain during the late fifteenth and the sixteenth centuries.

Italy: Birthplace of the Renaissance

The city-states of northern Italy that spawned the Renaissance were developed urban centers where people had the wealth, freedom, and inclination to cultivate the arts and to enjoy the fruits of worldly life. In Italy, moreover, reminders of ancient Rome's grandeur were visible everywhere. Roman roads, monuments, and manuscripts intensified the Italians' links to their Roman past.

Political Evolution of the City-States

During the Middle Ages the feudal states of northern Italy had been absorbed into the Holy Roman Empire. They continued to owe nominal allegiance to the German emperor during the early Renaissance. But its protracted wars with the papacy had sapped the empire of vitality. Its subsequent weakness meant that the states of northern Italy were able to develop as autonomous political entities. Also promoting this development was the weakening of the papacy in the fourteenth century (see pages 254–258).

The city-states that developed in northern Italy were similar in their size and their varied types of governments to those of ancient Greece. Among the more important city-states were Rome, Milan, Florence, Venice, Mantua, Ferrara, Padua, Bologna, and Genoa. These city-states markedly differed from most of Europe in two fundamental respects. First, by the late eleventh and twelfth centuries

Map 13.1 Italian City-States, c. 1494 ▶

DUCHY OF
SAVOY

DUCHY OF
MILAN

DUCHY OF
MANTUA

REPUBLIC OF VENICE

OTTOMAN EMPIRE

Milan
Lodi
Pavia
Turin

M. OF
MANTUA
Mantua

Padua
Venice

SALUZZO

Po R.

Ferrara
D. OF FERRARA

DALMATIA

REP. OF GENOA

Genoa

D. OF MODENA

Bologna

Ravenna

REP. OF LUCCA

Arno R.

REP. OF
FLORENCE
Florence

FLORENCE

Pisa

Urbino

Siena

Assisi

ADRIATIC SEA

REP. OF
SIENA

Tiber R.

PAPAL STATES

CORSICA

Rome

Bari

KINGDOM OF
NAPLES

Naples
Salerno

SARDINIA

Palermo

KINGDOM OF
SICILY

M E D I T E R R A N E A N   S E A

the city-states had developed as flourishing commercial and banking centers and had monopolized the trade in Mediterranean areas, which included trade between the Orient and the West. So the merchant fleets, especially those of Venice and Genoa, carried goods from ports in the eastern Mediterranean westward into the Atlantic and from there north to the Baltic Sea. Unlike that of the rest of Europe, the wealth of these cities lay not in land, but in commerce and industry. When popes, monarchs, and feudal magnates of Europe needed money, they borrowed it from Italian, especially Florentine, merchant-bankers.

Second, the predominance of business and commerce within these city-states meant that the feudal nobility, who held the land beyond the city walls, played a much less important part in government than they did elsewhere in Europe. By the end of the twelfth century the city-states had ceased to be dominated by the feudal nobility, or landed aristocracy. The aristocracy and the rich merchants had to share power, and when their alliances broke down, as they often did, the two groups struggled for power based on their opposing interests and outlooks. The interests of the smaller merchants and the artisans in the towns also had to be catered to. When they were not, these groups rioted and rebelled, as they did, for instance, in 1378 during the revolt of the *Ciompi* (the wool-workers) in Florence.

Politically these city-states were inherently unstable. They managed to keep both papacy and Empire at bay, sometimes by playing one giant against the other in the manner of Third World nations today. But the price of this continued independence was that the city-states, without any externally imposed power structure, had to seek solutions to their own instability. This instability arose from two sources—the internal conflict between merchants and nobles and the external rivalry between the city-states themselves. Out of this situation came experiments in the form and technique of government. The origins of modern political thought and practice can be

discerned in this experimentation, thus forging an important connection between the Renaissance and the modern age.

The political experimentation that went on in the northern Italian city-states can usefully, if only roughly, be divided into two periods— the first (1300–1450) marked by the defense of republicanism and the second (1450–1550) by the triumph of despotism. By the end of the twelfth century the city-states had adopted a fairly uniform pattern of republican self-government built around the office of a chief magistrate. He was elected by the citizens on the basis of a broad franchise, and he ruled with the advice of two councils—a large public one and a small secret one. His powers were tightly circumscribed by the constitution; with his term of office restricted ordinarily to six months, he could be removed from government or punished at the end of his tenure.

The city-states not only developed republican institutions; they self-consciously devised important theories to defend and justify their liberty and self-government in the face of their external enemies, the papacy and the Empire. To the emperor they argued that their customary feudal subjection to his authority must be radically adjusted to fit the changed reality that they were in fact self-governing. To the papacy they argued that Christ had denied all political jurisdiction to the clergy, including the pope, and so undercut the papal claim to political control in Italy and elsewhere.

However, the republicanism of the city-states, with their internal instability and their rivalry, proved precarious. During the fourteenth and early fifteenth centuries the republican institutions in one city after another toppled in favor of rule by despots. Three conditions were responsible for this development. First, class war between rich merchants and nobles caused one group or the other, or both, to seek a resolution of the crisis by turning to one-man rule. Second, the economic disasters, famine, and disease of the period from 1350 to 1450 encouraged the drift toward despotism. Northern Italy

Presentation of the Infant Jesus in the Temple, attributed to Giotto (c. 1266/76–1337). The monumentality of Giotto's figures and their dramatic glances and gestures were received with awe in Florence. Renaissance artists were strongly influenced by Giotto's work. (*Isabella Stewart Gardner Museum, Boston*)

was particularly hard hit by the bubonic plague. The citizenry lost faith in the ability of short-term republican governments to cope with such emergencies and put their trust in long-term, one-man rule. Third, and perhaps most important, the city-states had come to rely on mercenary troops, whose leaders, the notorious *condottieri*—unschooled in and owing no loyalty to the republican tradition—simply seized power during emergencies.

Some city-states held out against the trend toward despotism for a long time; among those that did, Florence was by far the most successful. In the process, the Florentines developed new arguments and theories for the maintenance of republicanism and liberty

(see pages 279–281). But by the mid-fifteenth century, even Florentine republicanism was giving way before the intrigues of a rich banking family—the Medici. They had installed themselves in power in the 1430s with the return of Cosimo de' Medici from exile. Cosimo's grandson, Lorenzo the Magnificent, completed the destruction of the republican constitution in 1480, when he managed to set up a government staffed by his own supporters.

The one city-state where republicanism survived until the advent of Napoleon was Venice. Protected from the rest of Italy by lagoons, Venice during the Middle Ages controlled a far-flung and exceptionally lucrative seagoing trade and a maritime empire stretching along the Adriatic and the eastern Mediterranean seas. Venice's maritime commercial successes were matched by political ones at home. For centuries, Venice managed to govern itself without major upheaval; its republican constitution made this stability possible. Its chief executive offices, the Council of Ten, were elective, but after 1297, both these offices and the electorate were narrowly restricted by law to old patrician families. Venice was an aristocratic republic. The government proved remarkably effective because the ruling elite was able to engender a sense of public duty in its young that passed on from one generation—and one century— to the next. Venetian government, because it was at once stable and republican, served as a powerful model to republican theorists in seventeenth- and eighteenth-century Europe.

The city-states, excepting Venice, were not only internally unstable, but they were also constantly at war with one another. By the middle of the fifteenth century, however, five major powers had emerged from the fighting: the kingdom of Naples and Sicily in the south; the Papal States, where the popes had built up, bit by bit, a territory running across the center of the Italian peninsula; and in the north the city-states of Florence, Venice, and Milan. In 1454 these five powers, largely through the efforts of Cosimo de' Medici, concluded the Peace of Lodi. For the next forty years they were relatively peaceful, until the French king Charles VIII invaded northern Italy in 1494.

The Peace of Lodi endured so long because of diplomacy. The essential techniques of modern diplomacy were worked out and applied in the second half of the fifteenth century in Italy. The practices of establishing embassies with ambassadors, sending and analyzing intelligence reports, consulting and negotiating during emergencies, and forming alliances all developed during this period. Some historians also see this time in Italian history as the seedbed for the notion of balance of power—a pattern that eventually became fundamental to the diplomacy of all

Europe. Later, in the early modern period, European governments formed alliances so that no single state or group of allied states could dominate the Continent. Some elements of this balance of power were anticipated in the struggles among the Italian city-states.

Renaissance Society

Paralleling the new developments in relations among city-states was the new way of life emerging within the city-states. Prosperous merchants played a leading role in the political and cultural life of the city. With the expansion of commerce and industry, the feudal values of birth, military prowess, and a fixed hierarchy decayed in favor of ambition and individual achievement, whether at court, in the counting house, or inside the artist's studio. Not that the old feudal, chivalric code was destroyed—rather, it was transformed to serve different purposes.

The new urban, commercial oligarchies could not justify their power in the old way, through heredity. Moreover, they had to function within the inherently unstable political climate of the city-states. Faced with this dual problem, the oligarchs fell back on the feudal idea of honor and developed elaborate codes. These codes differed in significant ways from their medieval antecedents. First came a depreciation (although never a complete elimination) of birth as a basis of merit, with a corresponding emphasis on effort, talent, and (in the case of the artist) creative genius. Second, honor was no longer defined in narrow, largely military terms, but was expanded to include both the civic and courtly virtues of the worthy citizen and courtier and the artistic achievement of the painter, sculptor, architect, and poet.

The new code, however, remained elitist and even aristocratic. Indeed, because of their very newness and insecurity, the new oligarchs of the Renaissance were all the more anxious to adopt the aristocratic outlook of the old nobility. The *nouveaux riches* (new rich) aped the feudal aristocracy in dress and manners, even as they accommodated the code of knightly chivalry to the demands of a new urban and commercial culture. Renaissance society was a highly unstable compound of old and new.

Marriage and Family Life   City life profoundly altered family structure, marriage patterns, and relations between the sexes. Elsewhere in Europe most people still lived on the land and tended to marry early in order to produce large families to work the fields. But in cities, early marriage could be a liability for a man who was attempting to make his fortune. The results were that older men married young brides, which meant that wives usually outlived their husbands. Because a widow inherited her husband's property, she was not pressed to remarry and she brought up her children in a single-parent household.

The large number of single, relatively prosperous, and leisured adults probably explains why Renaissance cities were notorious for sodomy, prostitution, and triangles involving an older husband, a young wife, and a young lover. Such sexual behavior was encouraged by the relative anonymity of the large cities and by the constant influx of young men of talent from the country districts.

Single-parent households might also account for the high incidence of homosexuality during the Renaissance. Historian David Herlihy maintains that sons became attached to their mothers in the absence of their fathers and their heterosexual development was stifled. Whether one accepts this Freudian interpretation or not, Herlihy's other conclusion has much to recommend it: that so many women were responsible for nurturing their children may have encouraged the development of the Renaissance idea of a gentleman, which emphasized civility, courtliness, and an appreciation of art, literature, and the feminine graces.

Whatever the effect on their sons, upper-class women enjoyed greater freedom in greater numbers than they had since the Fall of Rome. If they were married, they had the income to pursue pleasure in the form of clothes, conversation, and romance. If a well-to-do husband died while his wife was still young, she had no financial reasons to remarry. She was then free, to a degree previously unknown, to go her own way.

Patronage of the Arts   Members of the urban upper class became patrons of the arts, providing funds to support promising artists and writers. Urban patricians whose wealth was based upon commerce and banking, not land, had become dominant in both republican Florence and despotic Milan. Unable to claim power by birth or to rely on traditional loyalties, they looked to culture to provide the trappings and justification of power.

For the newly rich, art could serve a political function. In its sheer magnificence, art could manifest power and cast that spell over subjects or citizens that all governments must depend on to some extent. Art could also serve as a focus of civic pride and patriotism, just as literature could (see page 277). Just as they contended on the battlefield, insecure rulers competed for art and artists to bolster their egos. Art became a desirable political investment, especially when in the fifteenth century, economic investments were not offering as much return as they had a century or two before. The popes, too, invested in art. Having lost the battle for temporal dominion in Europe, the papacy concentrated on increasing its direct dominion in Italy by consolidating and expanding the Papal States. As an adjunct to this policy, the popes heaped wealth on artists to enhance their own papal prestige and perhaps to recover some of their shattered self-esteem. So the popes became the most lavish patrons of all, as the works of Michelangelo and Raphael testify.

The result of this new patronage by popes and patricians was an explosion of artistic creativity. The amount and especially the nature of this patronage also helped to shape both art and the artist. Portraiture became a separate genre for the first time since antiquity and was developed much further than ever

Michelangelo Buonarroti (1475–1564): The Dying Slave. The human figure inspired the greatest works of Michelangelo. As a Neo-Platonist, he saw a constant struggle between the soul of the individual and the body that entrapped it. *The Dying Slave* was part of a monument for Pope Julius. (*Louvre/Cliché des Musées Nationaux*)

before. Patrician rivalry and insecurity of status, fed by the Renaissance ethic of achievement and reward, produced a scramble for honor and reputation. This pursuit fostered the desire to be memorialized in a painting, if not in a sculpture. A painter like Titian was in great demand.

The great artists emerged as famous men by virtue of their exercise of brush and chisel. In the Middle Ages, artists had been regarded as craftsmen who did lowly (manual) labor and who, as a result, were to be accorded little if any status. Indeed, they remained anonymous for the most part. But the unparalleled Renaissance demand for art brought artists public recognition for the first time. They enjoyed this status until the Industrial Revolution, when art once more depreciated in value. Artistic fame did not come without effort, and the drive for it, stimulated again by the Renaissance ethos of competition and by the humanist ethic, may have spurred artists to greater creative achievements than might otherwise have developed.

Secularism   Renaissance society was marked by a growing secular outlook. Intrigued by the active life of the city and eager to enjoy worldly pleasures that their money could obtain, wealthy merchants and bankers moved away from the medieval preoccupation with salvation. To be sure, they were neither nonbelievers nor atheists, but increasingly religion had to compete with worldly concerns. Consequently, members of the urban upper class paid religion less heed, or at least did not allow it to interfere with their quest for the full life. The challenge and pleasure of living well in this world seemed more exciting than the promise of heaven. This outlook found concrete expression in Renaissance art and literature.

Individualism   Individualism was another hallmark of Renaissance society. Urban life released people of wealth and talent from the old constraints of manor and church. The urban elite sought to assert their own personalities, to discover and to express their own peculiar feelings, to demonstrate their unique talents, to win fame and glory, and to fulfill their ambitions. This Renaissance ideal was explicitly elitist. It applied only to the few, entirely disregarding the masses; it valued what was distinctive and superior in an individual, not what was common to all men; it was concerned with the distinctions of the few, not the needs or rights of the many. Individualism became deeply embedded in the Western soul, and was expressed in artists who sought to capture individual character, in explorers who ventured into uncharted seas, in conquerors who carved out empires in the New World, and in merchant-capitalists who amassed fortunes.

The Renaissance Outlook: Humanism and Secular Politics

Humanism

The most characteristic intellectual movement of the Renaissance was *humanism,* an educational and cultural program based on the study of ancient Greek and Roman literature. The humanist attitude toward antiquity differed from that of medieval scholars. Medieval scholars sought to fit classical learning into a Christian world-view. Renaissance humanists, in contrast, did not subordinate the classics to the requirements of Christian doctrines; rather, they valued ancient literature for its own sake—for its clear and graceful style, for its insights into human nature. From the ancient classics, humanists expected to learn much that could not be provided by medieval writings—how to live well in this world and how to perform one's civic duties, for example. For the humanists the classics were a guide to the good life, the active life. To achieve self-cultivation, to write well, to speak well, and to live well, it was necessary to know the classics. In contrast to scholastic philosophers who used Greek philosophy to

prove the truth of Christian doctrines, Italian humanists used classical learning to nourish their new interest in a worldly life.

Whereas medieval scholars were familiar with only some ancient Latin writers, Renaissance humanists restored to circulation every Roman work that could be found. Similarly, whereas knowledge of Greek was very rare in Latin Christendom during the Middle Ages, Renaissance humanists increasingly cultivated the study of Greek in order to read Homer, Demosthenes, Plato, and other ancients in the original.

Although predominantly a secular movement, Italian humanism was not un-Christian. True, humanists often treated moral problems in a purely secular manner, but when they did deal with religious and theological questions, they did not challenge Christian belief or question the validity of the Bible. They did, however, attack scholasticism for its hairsplitting arguments and preoccupation with trivial questions. They stressed instead a purer form of Christianity based on the direct study of the Bible and writings by the church fathers.

A principal source of humanism was the study of law that flourished in the thirteenth and fourteenth centuries in Bologna, Padua, and Ravenna. Not only did students learn the law; they also learned rhetoric—how to argue and how to speak. In these adjuncts to legal study lie some origins of humanism. Using classical Roman models for their arguments, teachers and students went beyond their textbook exercises to make comments on contemporary political issues. Here was the earliest regular use of classical sources to make a judgment or to point to a moral for the present. The Roman classics in the hands of the legists and rhetoricians became source books for the defense of liberty and independence, first against emperors and popes and later against the threat of home-grown despots. So well developed did this tradition become that it eventually outgrew the bounds of the legal studies where it was first nurtured and took the form of a separate enterprise. Men of letters, prehumanists, wrote chronicles of their cities, glorifying the historical struggle against tyranny. Political advice books, based on classical Roman wisdom that instructed rulers and citizens in how to oppose tyranny, also appeared rather steadily starting in the fourteenth century.

An early humanist, sometimes called the father of humanism, was Petrarch (1304–1374). Petrarch and his followers carried the recovery of the classics further by making a systematic attempt to discover the classical roots of medieval Italian rhetoric. Petrarch's own efforts to learn Greek were largely unsuccessful, but by encouraging his students to master the ancient tongue, he advanced humanist learning. Petrarch was particularly drawn to Cicero, the ancient Roman orator. Following the example of Cicero, Petrarch insisted that education should consist not only of learning and knowing things, but also of learning how to communicate one's knowledge and how to use it for the public good. Therefore, the emphasis in education should be on rhetoric and moral philosophy, wisdom combined with eloquence. This was the key to virtue in the ruler, the citizen and the republic. Petrarch helped to make Ciceronian values dominant among the humanists. His followers set up schools to inculcate the new Ciceronian educational ideal.

Implicit in the humanist educational ideal was a radical transformation of the Christian idea of men and women. According to the medieval (Augustinian) view, men and women were not only incapable of attaining excellence through their own efforts and talents, but it was wrong and sinful for them even to try. Human beings were completely subject to divine will. In contrast, the humanists, recalling the classical Greek concept of *arete,* made the achievement of excellence through individual striving the end not only of education, but of life itself. Because individuals were capable of this goal, moreover, it was their duty to pursue it as the end of life. The pursuit was not effortless; indeed, it took extraordinary energy and skill.

People, then, were capable of excellence in every sphere and duty-bound to make the effort. This emphasis on human creative powers was one of the most characteristic and influential doctrines of the Renaissance. A classic expression of it is found in *Oration on the Dignity of Man* (1486) by Giovanni Pico della Mirandola (1463–1494). Man, said Pico, has the freedom to shape his own life. Pico has God say to man: "We have made you a creature" such that "you may, as the free and proud shaper of your own being, fashion yourself in the form you may prefer."[1]

Pico also spells out another implication of man's duty to realize his potential: through his own exertions, man can come to understand and control nature. One of the new and powerful Renaissance images of man was as the *magus,* the magician. The vision of the mastery of nature continued to inspire experimentalists, like Francis Bacon, and natural philosophers, like Robert Boyle and Isaac Newton, until at least the early eighteenth century. A major psychological driving force of the scientific revolution, this vision stemmed in large part from the philosophy of Italian humanists like Pico.

The attack on the medieval scholastics was implicit in the humanist educational ideal. From the humanist perspective, scholasticism failed not only because its terms and Latin usage were barbarous, but also because it did not provide useful knowledge. This humanist emphasis on the uses of knowledge also offered a stimulus to science and art.

So hostile were the humanists to all things scholastic and medieval that they reversed the prevailing view of history. The Christian view saw history as a simple unfolding of God's will and providence. The humanists stressed the importance of human actions and human wills in history—of people as active participants in the shaping of events. The humanists rejected the providentialist scheme in favor of a cyclical view deriving from the ancients, particularly Aristotle, Polybius, and Cicero. History alternated between times of darkness and times of light, of ignorance and illumination, of decline and rebirth.

This cyclical view allowed the humanists

to characterize the epoch preceding their own as a period of declension from classical heights. Equally, it allowed them to see themselves and their own time as representing a period of rebirth, the recovery of classical wisdom and ideals. On the basis of this cyclical view, the humanists invented the notion of the Middle Ages as that period separating the ancient world from their own by a gulf of darkness. To the humanists, then, we owe the current periodization of history into ancient, medieval, and modern. There was also an element in the humanist view of today's idea of progress: they dared to think that they, "the moderns," might even surpass the ancient glories of Greece and Rome.

The humanist emphasis on historical scholarship yielded a method of critical inquiry that in the right hands could help to undermine traditional loyalties and institutions. The work of Lorenzo Valla (c. 1407–1457) provides the clearest example of this trend. Educated as a classicist, Valla trained the guns of critical scholarship on the papacy in his most famous work, *Declamation Concerning the False Decretals of Constantine*. The papal claim to temporal authority rested on a document that purported to verify the so-called Donation of Constantine, whereby when the Emperor Constantine moved the capital to Constantinople in the fourth century, he had bestowed on the pope dominion over the entire western Empire. But Valla proved that the document was based on an eighth-century forgery because the language at certain points was unknown in Constantine's own time and did not come into use until much later.

Also embedded in the humanist re-evaluation of individual potential was a new appreciation of the moral significance of work. For the humanist the honor, fame, and even glory bestowed by one's city or patron for meritorious deeds was the ultimate reward for effort. The humanist pursuit of praise and reputation became something of a Renaissance cult.

In fourteenth- and fifteenth-century republican Florence, at least until the Medici took control, Petrarchan humanism was not

Lorenzo de' Medici. The Medici preferred to wield power behind the scenes through secret alliances and intrigue. Lorenzo, who became head of the family in his teens, fostered the fiction of the good citizen; this portrait of him is by Agnolo Bronzino. (*Scala/Art Resource*)

meant for a court elite. Humanism was meant rather as a civic idea—to educate and inform citizens so that they could contribute to the common good to the greatest possible extent. In this sense, humanism was put in the service of republican values and the republican cause, and the mixture of the two is what has come to be called *civic humanism* by recent historians. This civic ideal developed furthest in the Florentine republic.

By the second half of the fifteenth century, as the Medici gained increasing control, the civic ideal was being replaced by another that was more fitting to the times, the ideal of princely rule. This princely ideal borrowed much from civic humanism, even though it was directed toward princes and courtiers and not toward citizens. The emphasis on the pursuit of virtue and honor was still there. Like the ideal gentleman, the ideal prince evolved through a humanistic education that would prepare him for the struggle between virtue and fortune so that virtue would prove victorious.

But the similarities between the civic and princely ideals were not as important as the differences. The aim of princely rule was no longer liberty, but peace and security. The best means to this end was no longer a republic, but hereditary monarchy. This new princely ideal was reflected in a new spate of advice books; the most influential of these was *The Book of the Courtier,* written between 1513 and 1518 by Baldassare Castiglione (1478–1529). These books promoted the notion that the ideal ruler should be universally talented and skillful, equally commanding on the battlefield, at court, and in the state, and virtuous throughout. These advice books, especially Castiglione's, were to serve as indispensable handbooks for courtiers and would-be gentlemen not only in Renaissance Italy, but throughout Europe. This ideal held sway until well into the seventeenth century, when the type finally began to give way before a new idea of virtue and virtuosity.

A Revolution in Political Thought

One advice book transcended the class of these works: *The Prince,* written in 1513 by the Florentine Niccolò Machiavelli (1469–1527). Machiavelli's book offered a critique of the humanist ideal of princely rule and in so doing made some fundamental contributions to political theory. Indeed, Machiavelli may be called the first major modern political thinker. To Machiavelli the humanist ideal is naive in its insistence on the prince's virtues and eloquence to the exclusion of all other considerations. He attacks the medieval and humanist tradition of theoretical politics:

Since my intention is to say something that will prove of practical use to the inquirer, I have thought it proper to represent things as they are in real truth, rather than as they are imagined. Many have dreamed up republics and principalities which have never in truth been known to exist; the gulf between how one should live and how one does live is so wide that a man who neglects what is actually done for what should be done learns the way to self-destruction.[2]

Politics, Machiavelli argues, requires the rational deployment of force as well as, and even prior to, the exercise of virtue.

On this point, Machiavelli's advice is quite specific. He wrote *The Prince* in part as a plea. Since 1494, Italy had fallen prey to France and Spain. Their great royal armies overpowered the mercenary armies of the city-states and went on to lay waste to Italy in their struggle for domination of the peninsula. To prevent this, Machiavelli says, the Italians must relinquish humanistic Christian utopianism and unite behind a leader—the prince—whose first act would be to disband the mercenaries and forge a new citizen army, worthy of the glorious Roman past and capable of repelling the "barbarian" invasion. "Mercenaries," Machiavelli claims, "are useless and dangerous." They are "useless" because "there is no . . . inducement to keep them on the field apart from the little they are paid, and this is not enough to make them want to die for you." And they are "dangerous" because their leaders, the infamous *condottieri,* "are anxious to advance their own greatness" at the expense of the city-state. Reliance on mercenaries is the sole cause of "the present ruin of Italy,"[3] and the cure lies in the creation of a national militia, led by a prince.

This prince must be both wily and virtuous—not (as humanists had said) virtuous alone: "The fact is that a man who wants to act virtuously in every way necessarily comes to grief among so many who are not virtuous." So Machiavelli scandalized Christian Europe by asserting that "if a prince wants to maintain his rule he must learn how not to be virtuous, and to make use of this or not according to his need."[4] Even more shocking, the prince must know how to dissemble, that is, to make all his actions appear virtuous, whether they are so or not. In ironic parody of conventional advice-book wisdom, Machiavelli argues that a ruler must cultivate a *reputation* for virtue rather than virtue itself. In this connection Machiavelli arrived at a fundamental political truth—that politics (and especially the relationship between ruler and ruled) being what it is, the road to success for the prince lies in dissimulation. "Everyone sees what you appear to be, few experience what you really are. And those few dare not gainsay the many who are backed by the majesty of the state."[5] Here again the Renaissance arrived at modernity.

Machiavelli broke with both the scholastic and the humanist traditions of political thought. He was a secularist who tried to understand and explain the state without recourse to Christian teachings. Influenced by classical thought and especially the works of Livy, he rejected the prevailing view that the state is God's creation and that the ruler should base his policies on Christian moral principles. For Machiavelli, religion was not the foundation for politics but merely a useful tool in the prince's struggle for success. The prince might even dissemble, if he thought he had to, in matters of the faith, by appearing pious, whether or not he was, and by playing on and exploiting the piety of his subjects.

Renaissance Art

The most graphic image of the Renaissance is conveyed through its art, particularly architecture, sculpture, and painting. Renaissance examples of all three art forms reflect a style that stressed proportion, balance, and harmony. These artistic values were achieved through a new, revolutionary conceptualization of space and spatial relations. Renaissance art also reflects to a considerable extent the values of Renaissance humanism, a return to classical models in architecture, to the rendering of the nude human figure, and to a heroic vision of human beings.

Medieval art sought to represent spiritual aspiration; the world was a veil merely hinting at the other perfect and eternal world. Renaissance art did not stop expressing spiritual aspiration, but its setting and character differ altogether. This world is no longer a shroud, but becomes the *place* where people live, act, and worship. The reference is less to the other world and more to this world, and people are treated as creatures who find their spiritual destiny as they fulfill their human one.

The Middle Ages had produced a distinctive art known as the Gothic. By the fourteenth and fifteenth centuries, Gothic art had evolved into what is known as the International Style, characterized by careful drawing, flowing and delicate lines, harmonious composition, and delightful naturalistic detail.

Renaissance art at its most distinctive represents a conscious revolt against this late Gothic trend. This revolt produced revolutionary discoveries that served as the foundation of Western art up to this century. In art, as in philosophy, the Florentines played a leading role in this esthetic transformation. They, more than anyone else, were responsible for the way artists saw and drew for centuries and for the way most Western people still see or want to see.

Early Renaissance Art

The first major contributor to Renaissance painting was the Florentine painter Giotto (c. 1266/76–1337). Borrowing from Byzantine painting, he created figures modeled by alterations in light and shade. He also developed several techniques of perspective, representing three-dimensional figures and objects in two-dimensional surfaces, so that they appear to stand in space. Giotto's figures also look remarkably alive (see page 273). They are drawn and arranged in space to tell a story, and the expressions they wear and the illusion of movement they convey heighten the dramatic effect. Giotto's best works were *frescoes*, wall paintings painted

Botticelli (1444–1510): The Birth of Venus. Botticelli was a member of the Florentine group of Neo-Platonists. They tried to harmonize Greco-Roman ideals with those of Christianity. The nude goddess is Venus, but the modest tilt of the head is the traditional pose of the Virgin Mary. To Botticelli the beauty of Venus and the purity of Mary were identical. (*Alinari-Scala/Art Resource*)

while the plaster was still wet or *fresh*. Lionized in his own day, Giotto had no immediate successors, and his ideas were not taken up and developed further for almost a century.

By the early fifteenth century the revival of classical learning had begun in earnest. In Florence it had its artistic counterpart among a circle of architects, painters, and sculptors who sought to revive classical art. The leader of this group was an architect, Filippo Brunelleschi (1377–1446). He abandoned Gothic prescriptions altogether and designed churches (Florence Cathedral, for instance) reflecting classical models. To him, we also owe a scientific discovery of the first importance in the history of art: the rules of perspective. Giotto had revived the ancient technique of foreshortening; Brunelleschi completed the discovery by rendering perspective in mathematical terms. Brunelleschi's

devotion to ancient models and his new tool of mathematical perspective set the stage for the further development of Renaissance painting.

Brunelleschi's young Florentine friend Masaccio (1401–1428) took up the challenge. Faithful to the new rules of perspective, Masaccio was also concerned with painting statuesque figures and endowing his paintings with a grandeur and simplicity whose inspiration is classical. Perspective came with all the force of religious revelation.

Early Renaissance artists were dedicated to representing things as they are, or at least as they are seen to be. Part of the inspiration for this was also classical. The ancient ideal of beauty was the beautiful nude. Renaissance admiration for ancient art meant that artists for the first time since the Fall of Rome studied anatomy; they learned to draw the human form by having models pose for them, a practice fundamental to artistic training to this day. Another member of Brunelleschi's circle, the Florentine sculptor Donatello (1386–1466), also showed renewed interest in the human form and conscious rejection of Gothic taste.

Another approach to the observation of nature—besides the imitation of the ancients—developed in northern Europe, principally in the Netherlands. Its original exponent was Jan van Eyck (c. 1390–1441), who worked mostly in what is now Belgium. Van Eyck's art developed out of the International Style. Within that style there was an interest in the faithful depiction of objects and creatures in the natural world. Van Eyck carried this tendency so far that it became the principal aim of his art: his pictures are like photographs in their infinitely scrupulous attention to the way things look. Unlike his contemporaries in Florence, van Eyck subordinated anatomy and perspective to appearance and showed no interest in classical models. In his concern to paint what he saw, he also developed oil painting. At that time, most paints were egg-based, but oil-based paints allowed him to obtain more lifelike and virtuoso effects (see page 258). The technique spread quickly to Italy, with astonishing results.

Late Renaissance Art

The use of perspective posed a fundamental problem for Renaissance painters: how to reconcile perspective with composition and the search for harmony. A chief interest of later fifteenth-century Italian painting lay in the various ways in which artists tackled this problem.

Among the Florentine artists of the second half of the fifteenth century who strove for a solution of this question was the painter Sandro Botticelli (c. 1444–1510). One of his most famous pictures depicts not a Christian legend, but a classical myth—*The Birth of Venus*. Representing, as it does, the way that beauty came into the world, this painting is another expression of the Renaissance desire to recover the lost wisdom of the ancients. Botticelli has succeeded in rendering a perfectly harmonious pattern—but at the cost of sacrificing solidity and anatomical correctness. In *The Birth of Venus*, what the viewer notices are the graceful, flowing lines that unify and vivify the painting. Even the liberties that Botticelli took with nature—for example, the unnatural proportions of Venus's neck and shoulders—enhance the esthetic outcome.

New approaches to this problem of perspective and composition were developed by the three greatest artists of the Renaissance—Leonardo da Vinci (1452–1519), Michelangelo Buonarroti (1475–1564), and Raphael Santi (1483–1520). All of them were closely associated with Florence, and all of them were contemporaries.

Leonardo was a scientist and engineer, as well as a great artist. He was an expert at fortifications and gunnery, an inventor, an anatomist, and a naturalist. He brought this close observation of nature to his paintings and combined it with powerful psychological insight to produce works that although few in number, were of unsurpassed genius. Among the most important of these are *The Last Supper* and *La Gioconda* (the Mona Lisa). The Mona Lisa is an example of an artistic invention of Leonardo's—what the Italians call *sfumato*. Leonardo left the outlines of the face a little vague and shadowy; this freed it of any wooden quality, which more exact drawing would impart, and thus made it more lifelike and mysterious. Here was a major breakthrough in solving the problem of perspective. The artist must not be too exact and rigid in adhering to the rules; he must introduce a correcting softness and atmosphere to achieve a reconciliation between perspective and the demands of design.

Michelangelo's route to artistic harmony was through a mastery of anatomy and drawing. His model in painting came from sculpture; his paintings are sculpted drawings. He was of course a sculptor of the highest genius whose approach to his art was poetic

Leonardo da Vinci (1452–1519): Mona Lisa. Leonardo da Vinci's paintings are few in number and difficult to interpret. Psychological mystery characterizes the *Mona Lisa*. Poets, essayists, and art historians have not fully explained her smile. Like most of his paintings, it is in an unfinished state. (*Louvre/Cliché des Musées Nationaux*)

and visionary. Instead of trying to impose form on marble, he thought of sculpting as releasing the form from the rock. Among his greatest sculptures are *David, Moses,* and *The Dying Slave* (page 276). Michelangelo was also an architect and, patronized by the pope, he designed the dome of the new St. Peter's basilica in Rome. But perhaps his most stupendous work was the ceiling of the Sistine Chapel in the Vatican, commissioned by Pope Julius II. In four years, working with little assistance, Michelangelo covered the empty

space with the most monumental sculpted pictures ever painted, pictures that summarize the Old Testament story. The Creation of Adam is the most famous of these superlative *frescoes.*

Raphael, the last of these three artistic giants, was the complete master of design in painting. His balanced compositions sacrifice nothing to perspective. Rather, perspective becomes just another tool, along with *sfumato* and mathematical proportion, for achieving harmony. Raphael is especially famous for the sweetness of his Madonnas. But he was capable of painting other subjects and of conveying other moods as well, as his portrait of his patron, *Pope Leo X with Two Cardinals,* reveals.

Renaissance painting came late to Venice, but when it arrived in the late fifteenth and early sixteenth centuries, it produced a tradition of sustained inventiveness whose keynote was the handling of color. Giovanni Bellini (c. 1431–1516) may be said to have discovered color as a tool of composition. He borrowed perspective from Florentine painting, but he used color too as a principal means of achieving unity and harmony.

This use of color was extended in a revolutionary direction by another Venetian, Giorgione (c. 1478–1510), to whom only five paintings can be ascribed with absolute certainty. Until Giorgione, landscape had functioned primarily as decorative and sometimes imaginative background, as in the Mona Lisa. But Giorgione made landscape a part of the subject of his paintings and, through his handling of light and color, used it to unify and integrate his canvases. According to art historian E. H. Gombrich, "This was almost as big a step forward . . . as the invention of perspective had been."[6] Perhaps Giorgione's greatest experiment in this respect was *The Tempest.*

The bewitching effects of color were carried to their fullest development by Titian (c. 1477–1576), a leading Venetian painter. He was a complete professional for whom the brushstroke was all. His portraits were magical in their ability to capture both features and personality. Titian also defied artistic convention by deliberately using unbalanced groups of figures and by achieving harmony not through positioning, but by means of light and color.

The Spread of the Renaissance

The Renaissance spread to Germany, France, England, and Spain in the late fifteenth and the sixteenth centuries. In its migration northward, Renaissance culture adapted itself to conditions unknown in Italy, such as the growth of the monarchical state and the strength of lay piety. In England, France, and Spain, Renaissance culture tended to be court-centered and hence antirepublican, as it was, for instance, under Francis I in France and Elizabeth I in England. In Germany and the Rhineland, no monarchical state existed, but a vital tradition of lay piety was present in the Low Countries. For example, the Brethren of the Common Life was a lay movement emphasizing education and practical piety. Intensely Christian and at the same time anticlerical, the people in such lay movements found in Renaissance culture tools for sharpening their wits against the clergy— not to undermine the faith, but rather to restore it to its Apostolic purity.

Thus, northern humanists were profoundly devoted to ancient learning, just as the humanists in Italy had been. But nothing in northern humanism compares to the paganizing trend associated with the Italian Renaissance. The northerners were chiefly interested in the problem of the ancient church and, in particular, the question of what constituted original Christianity. They sought a model in light of which they might reform the corrupted church of their own time.

Everywhere, two factors operated to accelerate the spread of Renaissance culture after 1450: growing prosperity and the printing press. Prosperity, brought on by peace and

Raphael (1483–1520): Pope Leo X. Raphael is often called the great synthesizer because he emulated Michelangelo in *The School of Athens* and Leonardo da Vinci in many paintings of the Madonna and Christ child. His portraits of individual statesmen, like this one of Pope Leo X with Cardinals Giulio de' Medici and Luigi de' Rossi, are among his most perceptive works psychologically. (*Alinari-Scala/Art Resource*)

the decline of famine and plague, led to the founding of schools and colleges. The sons (women were excluded) of gentlemen and merchants were sent to school to receive a humanistic education imported from Italy. The purpose of such education was to prepare men for a career in the church or the civil service of the expanding state and for acceptance into higher social spheres.

Printing with movable type, which was invented in the middle of the fifteenth century, quickened the spread of Renaissance ideas. Back in the Late Middle Ages the West had learned, through the Muslims from the Chinese, of printing, paper, and ink. However, in this block printing process, a new block had to be carved from wood for each new impression, and the block was discarded as unusable as soon as a slightly different impression was needed. About 1445, Johann Gutenberg (c. 1398–1468) and other printers in Mainz in the Rhineland invented movable metal type to replace the cumbersome blocks. It was possible to use and reuse the separate pieces of type, as long as the metal in which they were cast did not wear down, simply by arranging them in the desired order. This invention made books, and hence ideas, more quickly available, cheaper, and more numerous than ever before; it also made literacy easier to achieve. Printing provided a surer basis for scholarship and prevented the further corruption of texts through handcopying. By giving all scholars the same text to work from, it made progress in critical scholarship and science faster and more reliable.

Humanism outside Italy was less concerned with the revival of classical values than with the reform of Christianity and society through a program of Christian humanism. The Christian humanists cultivated the new arts of rhetoric and history, as well as the classical languages—Latin, Greek, and Hebrew. But the ultimate purpose of these pursuits was more religious than it had been in Italy, where secular interests predominated.

Erasmian Humanism

To Erasmus (c. 1466–1536) belongs the credit for making Renaissance humanism an international movement. He was educated in the Netherlands by the Brethren of the Common Life, which was one of the most advanced religious movements of the age, combining mystical piety with rigorous humanist pedagogy. Erasmus traveled throughout Europe as a humanist educator and Biblical scholar. Like other Christian humanists, Erasmus trusted the power of words and used his pen to attack scholastic theology and clerical

abuses and to promote his philosophy of Christ. His weapon was satire, and his *Praise of Folly* and *Colloquies* won him a reputation for acid wit vented at the expense of conventional religion.

True religion, Erasmus argued, does not depend on dogma, ritual, or clerical power. Rather it is revealed clearly and simply in the Bible and therefore is directly accessible to all people, from the wise and great to the poor and humble. Nor is true religion opposed to nature. Rather, people are naturally capable of both apprehending and living according to the good as set out in the Scriptures. A perfect harmony between human nature and true religion allows humanity to attain, if not perfection, at least the next best thing, peace and happiness in this life.

This clear but quiet voice was drowned out by the storms of the Reformation, and the Erasmian emphasis on the individual's natural capacities fell down before a renewed emphasis on human sinfulness and dogmatic theology. Erasmus was caught in the middle and condemned on all sides; for him, the Reformation was both a personal and historical tragedy. He had worked for peace and unity and was treated to a spectacle of war and fragmentation. Erasmian humanism, however, survived these horrors as an ideal, and during the next two centuries, whenever thinkers sought toleration and rational religion (Rabelais and Montaigne, for instance), they looked back to Erasmus for inspiration.

Germany and France

German and French humanists pursued Christian humanist aims. They used humanist scholarship and language to satirize and vilify medieval scholastic Christianity and to build a purer, more Scriptural Christianity. These northern humanists had great faith in the power of words. The discovery of accurate Biblical texts, it was hoped, would lead to a great religious awakening. Protestant reformers, including Martin Luther, relied on humanist scholarship.

Medieval and Renaissance Art

Figure 1 Rose Window, Chartres Cathedral. (*Robert Harding Associates*)

Figure 2 *May* from *Les Très Riches Heures* of Jean, Duke of Berry, 1413–1416. *(Chantilly, Musée Condé/Giraudon/Art Resource)*

Figure 3 Master of the Prayer Books: *Dance of Mirth,* c. 1500. In Guillaume de Lorris and Jean de Meun, *Roman de la Rose.* (*The British Library, Harley MS. 4425, fol. 14v*)

Figure 4 Jan van Eyck: *St. Barbara*, 1437. (*Koninklijk Museum, Antwerp*)

Medieval sources tell us that the builders of Gothic cathedrals consciously intended their churches to symbolize heavenly realms. Much of the uplifting experience in viewing the churches' interiors comes from the luminous light of their stained-glass windows (Figure 1). Their colored atmosphere seems as tangible as the massive stone buildings themselves. Light was one of the main metaphors that medieval people used for God. The interior space of a Gothic cathedral (Figure 6) is symbolic too, with its soaring height implying the indwelling presence and energy of God. (See a discussion of Gothic architecture on pages 245–246.)

The Gothic style, which originated in the twelfth century, remained vigorous for the next three hundred years in some parts of Europe. In Italy, however, the style was replaced earlier with a new, humanist style in the early fifteenth century. In Florence, Filippo Brunelleschi (c. 1377–1446) designed San Lorenzo (Figure 5), the parish church of Cosimo de' Medici, in 1418. Although the interior retained many traditional features of Christian churches, such as a cross-shaped floor plan, its ornamentation was radically new. Brunelleschi introduced "correct" classical ornaments: coffered ceilings, rounded arches and Greek Corinthian capitals (the tops of columns decorated with carved acanthus leaves)—all found in such ancient buildings as the Pantheon (Figure 8 in the first art essay, "Greek Art and Roman Reflections"). In an attempt analogous to that of his contemporaries who were philosophers and writers, Brunelleschi sought to create a synthesis between antique forms and the Christian architectural heritage.

Painters also developed a new style during the fifteenth century. Representations of God, Jesus, angels, and saints gained a new immediacy as artists placed them in recognizable,

Figure 5 *Top:* Filippo Brunelleschi: San Lorenzo, Florence, 1421. (*Scala/Art Resource*)

Figure 6 *Bottom:* Nave and Choir, Notre Dame Cathedral, Paris, Built 1163–c. 1200. (*Jean Roubier*)

everyday settings and attempted to re-create in painting many of the effects of perceiving forms in light and space. Artists of the Northern Renaissance, such as Jan van Eyck (active 1422–1441), worked in an area now encompassed by Belgium, primarily in Bruges. Van Eyck's work is distinguished for his acute study of the effects of encompassing light, which influenced later Italian artists, especially those of the Venetian school. He also adapted traditional symbols to include concrete contemporary detail. For example, *St. Barbara* (Figure 4) is traditionally designated by the presence of a tower, the site of her martyrdom. Van Eyck's representation has a tower under construction and shows technology of his time, including scaffolding and the great wheels designed to hoist stone blocks.

Italian artists of the early fifteenth century, like Fra Angelico (1387–1455), tended to reduce detail and emphasize consistent, believable space. The loggia (roofed, open gallery) of his *Annunciation* (Figure 7), is constructed in accordance with the new perspective system so that the figures of Mary and the Angel Gabriel seem to inhabit a space similar to the one that our eyes and mind would perceive in viewing such a scene. Raphael (1483–1520), who worked a half-century later, shows further development of Renaissance illusionism in his *Annunciation* (Figure 8). The figures are also set in a consistent, measurable space, but the interior space is larger in relation to the figures and their poses are somewhat more complex and animated. Raphael's treatment of light, color, and landscape owes much to the innovations of van Eyck.

Many changes in monumental painting were reflected in book illumination. Illustrated manuscripts produced during the Late Middle Ages and the Renaissance, such as the *Très Riches Heures* (Figure 2) and the *Roman de la Rose* (Figure 3), are magnificent miniature works of art. These exquisite book illuminations show the new naturalistic mode of representation. Painted in part by the Limbourg brothers for the Duke of Berry during

Figure 7 *Left:* Fra Angelico: *The Annunciation,* c. 1440–1450. Fresco, San Marco, Florence. (*Scala/Art Resource*)

Figure 8 *Above:* Raphael: *The Annunciation.* The Vatican, Rome. (*Scala/Art Resource*)

the years 1413–1416, then completed seventy years later by another artist, the *Très Riches Heures* is an exceptional example of a Book of Hours, or personal prayers for each liturgical hour of the day; these books often contained other texts, such as Psalms and masses.

Figure 2 represents a month from the calendar at the beginning of the manuscript, and depicts the members of the Duke's court celebrating the first of May. The figures lie in the space beyond the "window" of the simple border. In the background, the artist has included in accurate and minute architectural detail a view of one of the Duke's residences.

Almost a century later, the Flemish Master of the Prayer Books (c. 1500) illustrated a copy of the *Roman de la Rose,* of which the *Dance of Mirth* is a page; the manuscript was commissioned by Count Engelbert II of Nassau, a governor of the Netherlands. Both manuscripts contain rich colors and fine detail, but the later *Dance of Mirth* shows the more natural and animated poses of contemporary Renaissance paintings. The border framing the scene with true renditions of iris, moth, and snail represents a Flemish revolution in manuscript style; it forms a space independent from the rest of the page. The flowers and the other subjects contrast with the more formalized trees in the *May* scene, just as the faces and figures in their dance evidence more expression than the sober, less individualistic faces in *May.*

In contrast to the fine detail of manuscripts are the massive sculptures by Michelangelo (1475–1564), who flourished during the Italian High Renaissance. His works were commissioned by Popes, including Julius II for whom he painted the Sistine Chapel ceiling. Michelangelo's *Moses* (Figure 9) was made for Pope Julius's tomb. This project, like many other grandiose High Renaissance schemes, was too costly and elaborate to complete; the original plans called for about forty figures arranged upon an immense pyramid. Michelangelo designed the *Moses* to occupy one corner, which explains the prominence of the right angle formed by the figure's knee. In the final form of the tomb, completed in 1547, forty-two years after its conception, there are only six figures, and *Moses* appears in the center.

—Katherine Crum

Figure 9 Michelangelo: *Moses*, 1513–1516. Marble, 100 1/2 in. high. San Pietro in Vincoli, Rome, in the mausoleum of Pope Julius II (*Alinari/Art Resource*)

French thinkers of the next generation exploited and carried the humanist legacy in more radical directions. Among them, two were outstanding: Michel de Montaigne (1533–1592) and François Rabelais (c. 1494–1553). Both thought and wrote in reaction to the religious wars resulting from the Reformation. In the face of competing religious dogmatisms—Catholic, Protestant, and sectarian—Montaigne advanced a skepticism in which he maintained that one can know little or nothing with certainty. He therefore advocated political quietism and acceptance of Christianity on faith. This skepticism also entailed tolerance. An individual was not fully responsible for his or her beliefs, since they were the product of frail reason and force of circumstance. Thus, people should not be punished for their beliefs. The only ones who deserved to be severely dealt with were the dogmatists in religion, because their certainty and self-righteousness flew in the face of a fundamental epistemological fact—that "reason does nothing but go astray in everything, and especially when it meddles with divine things."

Montaigne was not a systematic philosopher but devoted himself to what he could learn by Socratic self-examination, the results of which he set down in his *Essays*. In their urbane and caustic wit and their intense self-absorption, the *Essays* betray a crucial shift in humanist thought that became more pronounced in the next century. Gone is the optimism and emphasis on civic virtue of the High Renaissance. In their place come skepticism and introspection, the attempt to found morality on the self rather than on public values. This shift represented a retreat from the idealism of Renaissance humanism, no doubt produced by the increasing scale and violence of religious war.

Rabelais took a different route from Montaigne's. In response to religious dogmatism, Rabelais asserted the essential goodness of the individual and the right to be free to enjoy the world rather than being bound down, as Calvin later would have it, by fear of a vengeful God. Rabelais's folk-epic,

Erasmus by Hans Holbein the Younger (c. 1497–1543). The brilliance and honesty of Erasmus's philosophical treatises endeared him to both conservative Catholic and Protestant reformers. He travelled freely throughout Europe in his pursuit of truth. (*The Metropolitan Museum of Art, Robert Lehman Collection, 1975* [1975.1.138])

Gargantua and Pantagruel, in which he celebrates earthly and earthy life, is the greatest French work of its kind and perhaps the greatest in any literature. Rabelais said that once freed from religion, people could, by virtue of their native goodness, build a paradise on earth and disregard the one dreamed up by theologians. In *Gargantua and Pantagruel*, Rabelais imagined a monastery where men and women spend their lives "not in laws, statutes, or rules, but according to their own free will and pleasure." They slept and ate when they desired and learned to "read, write, sing, play upon several musical instruments, and speak five or six . . . languages and compose in them all very quaintly." Only one rule did they observe: "DO WHAT THOU WILT."[7]

Spanish Humanism

Spanish humanism represents a special case. The church hierarchy gained such a tight grip in Spain during the late fifteenth and early sixteenth centuries that it monopolized humanist learning and exploited it for its own repressive purposes. There was little or no room for a dissenting humanist voice such as there was in Germany, France, or England. The mastermind behind this authoritarian Spanish humanism was Cardinal Francisco Jiménez de Cisneros (1436–1517). Jiménez founded the University of Alcalá not far from Madrid for the instruction of the clergy. He also sponsored and published the Complutensian Polyglot Bible with Hebrew, Latin, and Greek texts in parallel columns. Jiménez, like Christian humanists elsewhere, sought the enlightenment of the clergy through a return to the pure sources of religion, and he saw his Polyglot Bible as furnishing a principal means of realizing that goal.

A century after Jiménez, Miguel de Cervantes Saavedra (1547–1616) produced his great novel, *Don Quixote,* in which he satirizes the ideals of knighthood and chivalry. Don Quixote, the victim of his own illusions, roams the countryside looking for romance and the chance to prove his knightly worth. To Quixote's servant, Sancho Panza, Cervantes assigns the role of pointing up the inanity of his master's quest by always acting prudently and judging according to common sense. Despite his earthy realism, however, Panza must share his master's misfortunes—so much for realism in a world run by men full of illusions. Cervantes's satire is very gentle. That knightly valor was still a valid subject for satire indicates how wedded Spain was even in the early seventeenth century to the conservative values of its crusading past.

English Humanism

Christian humanism in England sharply contrasted to that in Spain. It was developed by secular men in government as much as by clerics, and its objectives were often opposed to authority and tradition. Various Italian humanists came to England during the fifteenth century as bishops, merchants, court physicians, or artists. Englishmen also studied in Italy, especially in Florence, and introduced the serious humanistic study of the classics at Oxford University toward the end of the century.

The most influential humanist of the early English Renaissance was Sir Thomas More (1478–1535), who studied at Oxford. His impact arose from both his writing and his career. Trained as a lawyer, he became a successful civil servant and member of Parliament. His most famous book is *Utopia,* the major utopian treatise to be written in the West since Plato's *Republic* and one of the most original works of the entire Renaissance.

Many humanists had attacked private wealth as the principal source of pride, greed, and human cruelty. But More was the only one to carry this insight to its logical conclusion: in *Utopia,* he called for the elimination of private property. He had too keen a sense of human weakness to think that people could become perfect, but he used *Utopia* to call attention to contemporary abuses and to suggest radical reforms. He exploited the satirical and ironical potential of recent overseas discoveries by setting *Utopia* among a non-Christian people, which made his criticism more caustic and pointed. More succeeded Cardinal Wolsey as Lord Chancellor under Henry VIII. But when the king broke with the Roman Catholic church, More resigned, unable to reconcile his conscience with the king's rejection of papal supremacy. Three years later, in July 1535, More was executed for treason for refusing to swear an oath acknowledging the king's ecclesiastical supremacy.

William Shakespeare (1564–1616), widely

Chronology 13.1 The Renaissance

1200–1300	Bologna, Padua, and Ravenna become centers of legal studies
1300–1450	Republicanism reigns in northern Italian city-states
1304–1374	Petrarch, "Father of humanism"
1378	The Ciompi revolt in Florence
1407–1457	Lorenzo Valla issues the *Declamation Concerning the False Decretals of Constantine*
c. 1445	Johann Gutenberg invents movable metal type
1454	The Peace of Lodi is signed
1494	Charles VIII of France invades northern Italy; Pope Julius II commissions frescoes by Michelangelo in the Vatican's Sistine Chapel
1513	Machiavelli writes *The Prince*
1528	*The Courtier*, by Baldassare Castiglione, is published
1535	Sir Thomas More, English humanist and author of *Utopia*, is executed for treason

considered the greatest playwright the world has ever produced, gave expression to Renaissance values—honor, heroism, and the struggle against fate and fortune. But there is nothing conventional about Shakespeare's treatment of characters possessed of these virtues. His greatest plays, the tragedies (*King Lear, Julius Caesar,* and others), explore a common theme: men, even heroic men, despite virtue, are able only with the greatest difficulty, if at all, to overcome their human weaknesses. What fascinates Shakespeare is the contradiction between the Renaissance image of nobility, which is often the self-image of Shakespeare's heroes, and man's capacity for evil and self-destruction. Thus Ophelia says of Hamlet, her lover, in the play of the same name:

O, what a noble mind is here o'erthrown!
The courtier's, soldier's, scholar's, eye, tongue, sword;
The expectancy and rose of the fair state,
The glass of fashion and the mould of form,
The observ'd of all observers, quite, quite down!
[And] I, of ladies most deject and wretched,

That suck'd the honey of his music vows,
Now see that noble and most sovereign reason,
Like sweet bells jangled, out of tune and harsh;
That unmatch'd form and feature of blown youth
Blasted with ecstasy. O, woe is me,
T' have seen what I have seen, see what I see![8]

The plays are thus intensely human, but so much so that humanism fades into the background. Thus, art transcends doctrine to represent life itself.

The Renaissance and the Modern Age

The Renaissance, then, marks the birth of modernity—in art, in the idea of the individual's role in history and in nature, and in society, politics, war, and diplomacy. Central to this birth is a bold new view of human nature: individuals in all endeavors are free of a given destiny imposed by God from the outside—free to make their own destiny guided only by the example of the past, the force of present circumstances, and the drives of their own inner nature. Individuals, set free from theology, are seen to be the products, and in turn the shapers, of history. Their future is not wholly determined by providence, but is partly the work of their own free will.

Within the Italian city-states where the Renaissance was born, rich merchants were at least as important as the church hierarchy and the old nobility. The city-states were almost completely independent because of the weakness of church and empire. So the northern Italians were left free to invent new forms of government in which merchant oligarchs, humanists, and *condottieri* played a more important part than the priests and nobles who dominated politics in the rest of Europe. Of course this newness and lack of tradition produced, along with the inventiveness, disorder and violence. Condottieri grabbed power from hapless citizens, and republics gave way to despotism.

But the problems created by novelty and instability demanded solutions, and the wealth of the cities called forth the talent to find them. Commercial wealth and a new politics produced a new culture: Renaissance art and humanism. Talented individuals—scholars, poets, artists, and government officials—returned to classical antiquity, which in any case lay near to hand in Italy and Greece. Ancient models in art, architecture, literature, and philosophy provided the answers to their questions. This return to antiquity also entailed a rejection of the Middle Ages as dark, barbarous, and rude. The humanists clearly preferred the secular learning of ancient Greece and Rome to the clerical learning of the more recent past. The reason for this was obvious: the ancients addressed the same problems faced by the humanists; the scholastics did not.

The revival of antiquity by the humanists did not mean, however, that they identified completely with it. The revival itself was done too self-consciously for that. In the very act

of looking back, the humanists differentiated themselves from the past and recognized that they were different. They were in this sense the first modern historians, because they could study and appreciate the past for its own sake and to some degree on its own terms.

In the works of Renaissance artists and thinkers the world was, to a large extent, depicted and explained without reference to a higher supernatural realm of meaning and authority. This is clearly seen in Machiavelli's analysis of politics. Closely associated with this secular element in Renaissance culture was a new realism that beckoned toward the modern outlook. What else is Machiavelli's new politics but a politics of realism, dealing with the world as he finds it rather than as it ought to be? This realism also manifests itself in the realm of art, where mathematical perspective renders the world in its spatial dimension and gives it a solidity and drama that constitute a modern visual and esthetic realism. The sources for both the esthetic and the political realism were the cultural forms of ancient Greece and Rome.

Renaissance humanism exuded a deep confidence in the capacities of able people, instructed in the wisdom of the ancients, to understand and change the world. Renaissance realism, then, was mixed with idealism, and this potent combination departed sharply from the medieval outlook. In place of Christian resignation there grew a willingness to confront life directly and a belief that able humans can succeed even against great odds.

This new confidence is closely related to another distinctive feature of the Renaissance—the cult of the individual. Both prince and painter were motivated in part by the desire to display their talents and to satisfy their ambitions. This individual striving was rewarded and encouraged by the larger society of rich patrons and calculating princes who valued ability. Gone was the medieval Christian emphasis upon the virtue of self-denial and the sin of vainglory. Instead, the Renaissance placed the highest value upon self-expression and self-fulfillment, upon the realization of individual potential, especially of the gifted few. The Renaissance fostered an atmosphere in which talent, even genius, was allowed to flourish. The ideal, at least, was meritocracy.

To be sure, the Renaissance image of the individual and the world, bold and novel, was the exclusive prerogative of a small, well-educated urban elite and did not reach down to include the masses. Nevertheless, the Renaissance set an example of what people might achieve in art and architecture, taste and refinement, education and urban culture. In many fields the Renaissance set the cultural standards of the modern age.

Notes

1. Giovanni Pico della Mirandola, *Oration on the Dignity of Man,* trans. by A. Robert Caponigri (Chicago: Henry Regnery, 1956), p. 7.

2. Niccolò Machiavelli, *The Prince,* trans. by George Bull (Harmondsworth, England: Penguin Books, 1961), pp. 90–91.

3. Ibid., pp. 77–78.

4. Ibid., p. 91.

5. Ibid., p. 101.

6. E. H. Gombrich, *The Story of Art,* 12th ed. (London: Phaidon, 1972), p. 250.

7. François Rabelais, *Gargantua and Pantagruel,* trans. by Sir Thomas Urquhart (1883), Bk. I, Ch. 57.

8. From *Hamlet, Prince of Denmark,* in *The Complete Plays and Poems of William Shakespeare,* ed. by William Allan Neilson and Charles Jarvis Hill (Boston: Houghton Mifflin, 1942), p. 1067.

Suggested Reading

Baron, Hans, *The Crisis of the Early Italian Renaissance* (1966). Influential interpretation of the origins of civic humanism.

Bouwsma, William J., *Venice and the Defense of Republican Liberty* (1968). The Venetian origins of Western republicanism.

Brucker, Gene A., *Renaissance Florence* (rev. ed., 1983). An excellent reader.

Burckhardt, Jacob, *The Civilization of the Renaissance in Italy* (1860). 2 vols. (1958). The first major interpretative synthesis of the Renaissance; still an essential resource.

Burke, Peter, *Popular Culture in Early Modern Europe* (1978). A fascinating account of the social underside from the Renaissance to the French Revolution.

Caspari, Fritz, *Humanism and the Social Order in Tudor England* (1968). Relations between thought and society.

Eisenstein, Elizabeth, *The Printing Press as an Agent of Change,* 2 vols. (1978). The definitive treatment—informative, argumentative, and suggestive.

Gilbert, Felix, *Machiavelli and Guicciardini* (1965). Florentine political and historical writing in the fifteenth and early sixteenth centuries.

Ginzburg, Carlo, *The Cheese and the Worms* (1982). A lively, penetrating account of the cosmos as seen from the point of view of a sixteenth-century Italian miller.

Harbison, E. Harris, *The Christian Scholar in the Age of Reformation* (1956). Relations between humanism and Protestantism.

Huizinga, Johan, *Erasmus and the Age of Reformation* (1957). A readable study of the greatest northern European humanist.

Maclean, Ian, *The Renaissance Notion of Woman* (1980). The birth of modern ideas and attitudes regarding women.

Pocock, J. G. A., *The Machiavellian Moment* (1975). A heady adventure in the history of ideas, tracing republicanism from its Italian Renaissance origins through the English and American revolutions.

Pullen, B., *A History of Early Renaissance Italy* (1973). A solid, brief account.

Skinner, Quentin, *The Foundations of Modern Political Thought,* 2 vols. (1978). The first volume covers the Renaissance; highly informed.

Wittkower, R., *Architectural Principles in the Age of Humanism* (1952). Architecture as the expression of Renaissance values and ideas.

Review Questions

1. What does the word *renaissance* mean, and where and when did it first occur?

2. What is the connection between the Renaissance and the Middle Ages? What special conditions gave rise to the Italian Renaissance?

3. Which forms of government predominated among the Italian city-states? In the end, which was the most successful? Why?

4. In what ways did the social patterns of Renaissance Italy depart from those of the rest of Europe?

5. What are some connections between Renaissance society and Renaissance art and culture?

6. What is *humanism* and how did it begin? What did the humanists contribute to education and history?

7. What is the difference between civic humanism and the princely ideal of government, and from what does this difference come?

8. How can it be said that Machiavelli invented a new politics by standing the ideal of princely rule on its head?

9. What is *perspective*? To whom do we owe the discovery of its rules?

10. What is the basic difference between Early and Late Renaissance painting?

11. What factors encouraged the spread of the Renaissance into the western European monarchies and the Rhineland?

12. To what key invention do we owe the rise of the printing press? What were the effects of the printing press on European civilization?

13. Why is the Renaissance considered the departure from the Middle Ages and the beginning of modernity?

14

The Reformation: Shattering of Christendom

*B*y the early sixteenth century the one European institution that alone transcended geographic, ethnic, linguistic, and national boundaries was under severe attack from reformers. For centuries the Catholic church, with its center in Rome, had extended its influence into every aspect of European society and culture. As a result, however, the church's massive wealth and power appeared to take predominance over its commitment to the search for holiness in this world and salvation in the next. Encumbered by wealth, addicted to international power, and desiring to protect their own interests, the clergy, from the pope on down, became the center of a storm of criticism. Humanists, made self-confident by the new learning of the Renaissance, called for the reform and renewal of the church, setting the stage for the Protestant Reformation. Eventually, though, that movement came to deviate quite significantly from what the Renaissance humanists had in mind.

Schooled in the techniques of criticism developed during the Renaissance, humanists first used those techniques on the documents that supposedly justified papal authority. Thus did they refute the Donation of Constantine (see page 279). But the fraud that especially vexed the humanists lay not on parchments, but in the very practices by which the church governed the faithful.

However, the Protestant Reformation did not originate in elite circles of humanistic scholars. Rather, it began in the mind of Martin Luther (1483–1546), an obscure German monk and a brilliant theologian. Luther rejected the church's claim to be the only vehicle for human salvation and defied the pope's right to silence, reprimand, and excommunicate any Christian who rejected papal authority or denied the truth of certain of the church's teachings. In a public defiance, undertaken after much soul-searching, Luther instituted a rebellion against the church's authority that in less than one decade shattered irrevocably the religious unity of Christendom. The Reformation, begun in 1517, dominated European history throughout much of the sixteenth century.

The Renaissance breathed new energy into European intellectual life and in the process discarded the medieval preoccupation with theology. Similarly, the Reformation marked the beginning of a new religious outlook. Personal faith, rather than adherence to the practices of the church, became central to the religious life of European Protestants. Local congregations and national churches came to replace the international church, which survived the Reformation but had vast areas of its wealth and power dismantled. Like the Renaissance humanists, some Protestant leaders were trained in ancient learning, but they gave humanism a religious meaning. Renaissance humanists had sought to reinstitute the wisdom of ancient times; Protestant reformers wanted to restore the spirit of early Christianity, in which faith seemed purer, believers more sincere, and clergy uncorrupted by luxury and power. By the 1540s the church initiated its own internal reformation, but it came too late to stop the movement toward Protestantism in some parts of northern and western Europe.

During the Late Middle Ages various attempts were made to reform the church from within. These movements were generated by bishops, monks, and scholars who assumed that the church's difficulties stemmed from the inefficiency and corruption of the papacy. These reformers sought to wrest power from the popes and to place it in the hands of a general council of the church's hierarchy. This was indeed one of the aims, in addition to ending the Great Schism and combatting heresy, of the Conciliar movement in the first half of the fifteenth century. However, the councils of Constance and of Basel (see page 257) failed to leave a meaningful inheritance to the church, largely because the special interests of kings and nations undercut their authority. The defeat of the Conciliar movement prevented the church from reforming itself from within and made possible a more general reformation.

Background to the Reformation: The Medieval Church in Crisis

During the Early Middle Ages the church had served as the great unifying and civilizing force in Latin Christendom. Culturally, and even administratively, it performed functions formerly carried out by the Roman Empire. By the fourteenth century, however, the usefulness and authority of its popes and bishops, as well as the vitality of its teachings, were being doubted. As kings increased their power and as urban centers with their sophisticated laity grew in size and numbers, people began to question the authority and independence of the international church and its clergy.

Several areas of the church's power were being closely examined. In theory, both popes and kings derived their authority from God. But where did one authority begin and the other leave off? According to Christian teachings, popes could instruct monarchs in the proper use of their authority: lay kings must serve and not challenge the church. But increasingly, monarchs did challenge the church's supremacy in worldly matters. The church also taught that new ideas must bend to the primacy of theology. But new learning in the hands of laymen endangered the supremacy of the monasteries and clergy-dominated universities as centers of learning. Lay scholarship also threatened the church's teachings on matters of authority. As national economies and local elites grew stronger, trouble brewed over the issue of paying taxes to a distant spiritual ruler in Rome whose wealth seemed more than sufficient. The manner in which church officials were appointed, with greater emphasis on their social place than their piety, also led to widespread attacks on the church's leadership.

By the Late Middle Ages the church had entered a time of crisis. During this period, political theorists rejected the pope's claim to supremacy over kings. The central idea of medieval Christendom—a Christian commonwealth led by the papacy—increasingly

The Sacred Heart of Jesus, Hand-colored Woodcut Sold as an Indulgence, Nuremberg, 1480s. The practice of selling indulgences to erase purgatory time disgusted Martin Luther. The veneration of relics—objects associated with the life of Christ or his saints, even bones or hair—was also condemned. Rival churches would often claim to have the "only authentic" head of a certain saint. (*The Metropolitan Museum of Art, New York; bequest of James Clarck McGuire, 1931*)

fell into disrepute. Theorists were arguing that the church was only a spiritual body, and therefore its power did not extend to the political realm. They said that the pope had no authority over kings, that the state needed no guidance from the papacy, and that the clergy were not above secular law.

Political theories were aimed at the educated elite, but the common people of town and countryside also expressed dissatisfaction with the church. By the Late Middle Ages, new material forces were affecting large segments of European society. Towns and cities contributed to the growth of an indigenous culture that focused on vernacular languages and regional dialects, rather than on the Latin of the monks and their schools. The townspeople had achieved a new wealth and a new self-confidence that made them resent any interference by bishops in their economic affairs. Urban centers also challenged the role of monasteries as economic innovators and centers of commercial life. By the early fourteenth century the church no longer held the initiative in worldly matters. When economic and social crises enveloped Europe in the second half of the fourteenth century, new reformers, despairing of the church's traditional privileges and even of its teachings, cast doubt on its authority.

For all these social and economic reasons, Latin Christendom during the late fourteenth century witnessed the first systematic attacks ever launched against the church. Church corruption—such as the selling of indulgences, nepotism (the practice of appointing one's relatives to offices), the holding of many bishoprics, and the sexual indulgence of the clergy—was nothing new. What was new and startling was the willingness of educated and uneducated Christians to attack these practices publicly. In *The Canterbury Tales*, Chaucer singles out two of his characters, who held clerical offices, for special scorn: the pardoner, who sold indulgences, that is, the remission of time spent in purgatory for one's sins; and the summoner, who served writs to appear in church courts. Chaucer paints a black picture of their arrogance and corruption. Less corrupt figures, such as his prioress, are let off with only mild caricatures. But in this first major English poem, Chaucer made the point that the church was corrupt.

Millenarianism

The peasant revolts of the Late Middle Ages frequently assumed a heretical cast. These movements foreshadowed the popular unrest so characteristic of the German Reformation.

In many instances, they combined heretical beliefs with hatred for church officials and protest against social and economic inequities and injustices. These popular heretical protest movements often took a doctrine accepted by the offical church and reinterpreted it to express their vision of a society where religion ensures justice for the poor and oppressed. For instance, the church preached that at some time in the future the world would end and Christ would come again to finally judge all men. Those whom Christ chose to be with him would be called saints, and they would reign with him in heaven. But medieval reformers, many drawn from, and followed by the poorer segments of European society, interpreted that doctrine to mean that Christ would condemn the rich and propertied and would establish a new society where the poor would inherit the earth. For a thousand years, a millennium, the poor would rule in Christ's kingdom.

Millenarianism, as this radical interpretation of the Last Judgment is called, gave its believers religious justification for attacking established institutions and institutional corruption. That Christ would rule with the poor in a future paradise meant that the society of their own day must be ruled by Antichrist. For many later medieval reformers, the concept of Antichrist, or the image of the "whore of Babylon" taken from the Bible, became a shorthand for the corruption of the church. When in the early sixteenth century Luther and other reformers called the pope himself the Antichrist, or the whore of Babylon, they were appealing to a tradition of reform and protest that had existed in the West for centuries.

Wycliffe and Huss

The two most serious attempts to reform the church, prior to Luther, occurred in the late fourteenth century in England and Bohemia. In both cases the leaders of these movements, John Wycliffe in England and John Huss in Bohemia, were learned theologians who attacked some church doctrines and practices (see Chapter 12). By expressing their ideas in learned and precise language, Wycliffe and Huss made heresy intellectually respectable. By incorporating popularly held beliefs, they appealed to the common people and sought and found mass support.

John Wycliffe (c. 1320–1384), a master at Oxford University, attacked the church's authority at its root by arguing simply that the church did not control the individual's eternal destiny. He said that salvation came only to those who possess faith, a gift freely given by God and not contingent on participating in the church's rituals or on receiving its sacraments. From this position, which in effect made the clergy far less important, Wycliffe attacked the church's wealth and argued that all true believers in Christ were equal and were, in effect, Christ's priests. To make faith accessible to them, Wycliffe translated portions of the Bible into English.

Wycliffe received powerful support from members of the English nobility, who hated the church's economic and secular power. However, when his ideas were taken up by articulate peasants and spoken during the abortive Peasants' Revolt of 1381, Wycliffe lost many powerful backers. In the end his attempt to reform the church by bringing it under secular control failed. But partly because he retained strong supporters and because he was more interested in scholarship than leadership, Wycliffe survived the failure of his movement and died a natural death. His ideas remained alive in popular religious beliefs, and his movement, the Lollards, helped foster Protestantism in England during the sixteenth century.

A harsher fate awaited the Bohemian (Czech) reformer, John Huss, who was burned at the stake in 1415. Partly under the influence of Wycliffe's writings Huss, in his native Prague, attacked the church for its wealth and power. After his execution, his followers broke with Rome and for a brief time nationalized the Bohemian church. This movement, like the Lollards in England, prepared the ground for the success of the Protestant Reformation. Until well into the seventeenth century, Bohemia remained a battleground of popular Protestantism against the official church.

Mysticism and Humanism

Wycliffe's and Huss's intensely practical attempts to initiate reform coincided with a powerful new religiosity that also made its appearance in the fourteenth century. All religions can inspire mystical experience, although in Western Christianity it often appears at times of acute institutional crisis. Late medieval mystics sought an immediate and personal communication with God; such experiences inspired them to advocate concrete reforms for the purpose of renewing the church's spirituality. Interesting from the viewpoint of the Protestant Reformation's later appeal to women, many late medieval mystics were women who, by virtue of their sex, had been deprived of an active role in governing the church. First mysticism and then Protestantism offered women a way of expressing their independence in religious matters.

The church hierarchy inevitably regarded this form of intense religiosity with some suspicion. For if individuals can experience God directly, they would seemingly have little need for the church and its rituals. In the fourteenth century, these mystical movements seldom became heretical. But in the sixteenth and seventeenth centuries, radical reformers often found in Christian mysticism a powerful alternative to institutional control and even to the necessity of a priesthood.

The Brethren of the Common Life, in the Low Countries, propounded a religious movement known as the *devotio moderna*, which was inspired by mysticism. A semi-monastic order of laity and clergy, the Brethren expressed their practical piety by dedicating their lives to the service of the entire community. With their teaching, they trained a new generation of scholars and humanists who became, during the late fifteenth century, some of the church's severest critics. Signif-

icantly, the Brethren's new schools flourished in the most heavily urbanized part of western Europe. For the linen merchants of Antwerp or the drapers of Amsterdam, a new religiosity was all too welcome by the late fifteenth century. They had grown increasingly disillusioned not only with the church taxes but also with the inefficiency of the church when compared to their own strenuous economic life.

Both mysticism and humanistic Christianity seemed for a time to offer sufficient alternatives to the scholasticism of the clergy. Certainly Erasmus thought that the critical gaze of the humanist would be sufficient to show the clergy the folly of their ways, which he ridiculed in *The Praise of Folly* (1510). Yet mysticism, with its emphasis on inner spirituality, and humanism, with its emphasis on classical learning, could not in themselves capture the attention of thousands of ordinary Europeans. A successful reform movement required leaders of an active and aggressive temperament who could do battle with political realities and win lay support against the local and international power of the church.

The Lutheran Revolt

Only an attack on papal and clerical authority could alter the power and practices of the church. Such an attack would have to involve winning over the multitudes, appealing to princes, and making heresy respectable. This feat required someone who had experienced the personal agony of doubting the church's power to give salvation and who could translate that agony into language understandable to all Christians. Martin Luther had experienced just such a personal crisis, and he possessed the will and the talent to offer it as an example for other Christians. Luther wrote voluminously and talked freely to his friends and students. Using this mass of recorded material, historians have been able to reconstruct the life and personality of this Augustinian monk who began the Reformation.

Luther's father, born a peasant, apparently was unusually ambitious. Hans Luther left the land, became a miner, and finally a manager and lessee of several mines, in an industry that was booming in late-fifteenth-century Germany. Like many newly successful individuals, Hans Luther had ambitious plans for his son; he wanted Martin to study law at the university in order to attain the status of an educated man. Luther's mother came from a burgher family and displayed an intense piety, thus putting him in closer touch with German popular religion and piety than was common among his contemporary scholars.

At the prestigious University of Erfurt, Luther embarked on an intellectual career that was to make him one of the foremost theologians and Biblical scholars of his day. As a young student, Luther fulfilled his father's wish and studied law. His earlier education gave him a fine grounding in classical learning, which served him throughout his life. At the university, Luther developed an interest in theology and philosophy, particularly the teachings of the fourteenth-century philosopher William of Ockham (see Chapter 12). Ockham had stressed the difference between faith and reason; he had insisted that truth learned through revelation was a matter of faith that might not be capable of demonstration by human reason; thus church teachings, and consequently salvation, rested entirely on faith. Since the church supported the synthesis of faith and reason achieved by the scholastics, notably Thomas Aquinas, it regarded Ockham's notions with suspicion.

At the age of twenty-one, Luther suddenly abandoned his legal studies to enter the Augustinian monastery at Erfurt. All the steps that led to this rebellion against parental authority are not known, but the actual decision was made swiftly. In later life, Luther recounted that the decision had been made in fear, as a vow to Saint Anne in the midst of a fierce lightning storm, by a young man convinced that his death at that moment would bring him eternal damnation. Why Luther presumed his damnation is not

Portrait of Martin Luther, 1546: School of Lucas Cranach (1472–1553). Martin Luther's personal struggle to attain spiritual peace through faith led to the fragmentation of Christendom. For him, the time was right for reform. The church was worldly and corrupt, and a nationalistic temper made many European monarchs and aristocrats hostile toward Roman authority. (*Busch Reisinger Museum, Harvard University, Gift, Paul J. Sachs and Meta Sachs*)

known, but his guilt conspired with his vivid imagination to kindle what must have been a growing resentment against his father's domination. Luther began his search for spiritual and personal identity, and therefore for salvation, within the strict confinement and discipline of the monastery. He pursued his theological studies there and prepared for ordination into the priesthood.

The Break with Catholicism

As he studied and prayed, Luther grew increasingly terrified about the possibility o his damnation. As a monk he sought union with God, and he understood the church's teaching that salvation depended upon faith, works, and grace. He participated in the sacraments of the church, which according to its teaching were intended to give grace. Indeed, after his ordination, Luther administered the sacraments. Yet he felt the weight of his sins, and nothing the church could offer seemed to relieve that burden.

Seeking solace and salvation, Luther increasingly turned to reading the Bible. Two passages seemed to speak directly to him: "For in it the righteousness of God is revealed through faith for faith: as it is written, 'He who through faith is righteous shall live.'" (Romans 1:17); and "They are justified by his grace as a gift, through the redemption which is in Christ Jesus." (Romans 3:24). In these two passages, Luther found, for the first time in his adult life, some hope for his own salvation. Faith, freely given by God through Christ, entitles the recipient to salvation.

The emphasis on faith alone in the Scriptural passages conformed to Luther's earlier interest in Ockham's teachings. But more important, the concept of salvation by faith alone seemed to provide an answer to his spritual quest. Practicing good works, along with prayer, fasting, pilgrimages, the Mass, and the other sacraments—had never brought Luther peace of mind. He concluded that no amount of good works, however necessary for maintaining the Christian community, would bring salvation. Through reading the Bible and through faith alone, the Christian could find the meaning of earthly existence. For Luther, the true Christian was a courageous figure who faced the terrifying quest for salvation armed only with the hope that God had granted the gift of faith. The new Christian served others not to trade good works for salvation, but solely to respond to the demands of Christian love.

During his personal struggle over the possibility of salvation, Luther had not lived as a cloistered monk. Pursuing his theological studies, he became a professor at the nearby university at Wittenberg and a preacher in that city's church. From approximately 1513 onward, Luther shared his personal and intellectual struggle with his students and his congregations. At the University of Wittenberg and in the province of Saxony in general, Luther found an audience receptive to his views, and his popularity and reputation grew as a result. Before 1517, he was considered a dynamic and controversial preacher whose passionate interest lay in turning Christians away from their worldly interests and from reliance on good works, while focusing their attention on Christ and the truth contained within Scripture. After 1517, he became a figure of international reputation and eventually a publicly condemned heretic in the eyes of the church.

The starting point for the Reformation was Luther's attack in 1517 on the church's practice of selling indulgences. The church taught that some individuals go directly to heaven or hell, while others go to heaven only after spending time in purgatory; this waiting period is necessary for those who have sinned excessively in this life but who have had the good fortune to repent before death. To die in a state of mortal sin meant to suffer in hell eternally. Naturally people worried about how long they might have to spend in purgatory. Indulgences were intended to remit portions of that time and were granted to individuals by the church for their prayers, attendance at Mass, and almost any good works—including monetary offerings to the church. This last good work was the most controversial, since it could easily appear that people were buying their way into heaven.

In the autumn of 1517 a monk named Tetzel was selling indulgences in the area near Wittenberg. Some of the money he obtained was for rebuilding St. Peter's Basilica in Rome, but the rest was for paying off debts incurred by a local archbishop in purchasing his office from the pope. Although Luther did not know about this second purpose, he was incensed both by Tetzel's crude manner and by his flagrant exploitation of the people's ignorance and money. Luther launched his attack on

Tetzel and the selling of indulgences by tacking on the door of the Wittenberg castle church his ninety-five theses.* Luther's theses (propositions) challenged the entire notion of selling indulgences, not only as a corrupt practice but also as a theologically unsound assumption—namely, that salvation can be earned by good works. In the ninety-five theses the outline of Luther's later theology is already evident, and his reliance on faith as the only means to salvation is implicitly stated.

At the heart of Luther's argument in the ninety-five theses and in his later writings was the belief that the individual achieves salvation through personal religiosity, a sense of contrition for sins, and trust in God's mercy. He also believed that church attendance, fasting, pilgrimages, charity, and other good works did not earn salvation. The church, on the other hand, held that *both* faith and good works were necessary for salvation. Luther further insisted that every individual could discover the meaning of the Bible unaided by the clergy, although the church maintained that only the clergy could read and interpret the Bible properly. Luther argued that in matters of faith there was no difference between the clergy and the laity. Each person could receive faith directly and freely from God. But the church held that the clergy were intermediaries between individuals and God and that in effect Christians reached eternal salvation through the clergy. For Luther, no priest, no ceremony, no sacrament could bridge the gulf between the Creator and his creatures, and the possibility of personal damnation remained a distinct reality. Hope lay only in a personal relationship between the individual and God, as expressed through faith in God's righteousness. No church could mediate that faith for the individual, and to that extent Luther's theology destroyed the foundations of the church's spiritual power.

* Some scholars debate whether this public display ever occurred. If it did not, the document was nevertheless widely circulated almost immediately.

But if faith alone, freely given by God, brings salvation to the believer, how can a person know if he or she has faith? Luther seemed content to assert that the search itself was a sign that God had favored a pious and penitent supplicant. Yet in Luther's doctrine of faith the notion of predestination is barely beneath the surface. The predestination argument continues today. God, of course, is all-knowing and eternal and his will is absolute. Not only does he give faith to whomever he chooses, but he does so for his own inscrutable reasons. Since God's existence, and therefore his will, is timeless, he knows the fate of each individual even as he or she is searching for salvation. In that sense every person is predestined either for heaven or for hell. But the problem remains, how can one know if one has been chosen? Luther said simply that no one could ever really know. Subsequent reformers would make much of the doctrine of predestination in their struggle to systematize Protestant doctrine and to create an identifying experience for all true Christians.

Although Luther did not realize it in 1517, the Reformation had begun. Quickly translating the theses from Latin into German, his students printed and distributed them, first in Saxony and eventually throughout Germany. Local church authorities recognized in Luther a serious threat and prepared to silence him. But Luther was tenacious; he began to write and preach his theology with increasing vigor.

At this point, politics intervened. Recognizing that his life might be in danger if he continued to preach without a protector, Luther appealed for support to the prince of his district, Frederick, the elector of Saxony. The elector was a powerful man in international politics—one of seven lay and ecclesiastical princes who chose the Holy Roman emperor. Frederick's support convinced church officials, including the pope, that this monk would have to be dealt with cautiously.

The years 1518–1519 were momentous ones for the Holy Roman Empire. Before his death in 1519, the Holy Roman Emperor Maximilian

Print Shop, Sixteenth-Century Print. Neither the Renaissance nor the Reformation would have been so widespread without printing, which was invented in Nuremberg in the 1450s. The printed word was the medium for the rapid transmission of Luther's and Calvin's revolutionary treatises, first in Germany and Switzerland and then elsewhere in Europe. (*BBC Hulton Picture Library/Bettmann Archive*)

I wanted to see his grandson, Charles, king of Spain, elected to succeed him. The papacy at first opposed Charles's candidacy, even looking to Frederick of Saxony as a possible alternative. Frederick wisely declined to be a candidate; as one of the seven electors, his vote was courted by the contenders—Charles, Francis I of France, and Henry VIII of England. Charles bribed his way onto the throne. But during this crucial election period and for some years afterward, he had to proceed cautiously on issues that might offend powerful German princes.

These political considerations explain the delay in Luther's official condemnation and excommunication by the pope. When in 1520 the pope finally acted against him, it was too late; Luther had been given the needed time

to promote his views. He proclaimed that the pope was Antichrist and that the church was the "most lawless den of robbers, the most shameless of all brothels, the very kingdom of sin, death and Hell."[2] When the papal bull excommunicating him was delivered, Luther burned it.

No longer members of the church, Luther and his followers established congregations for the purpose of Christian worship. Christians without the church needed protection, and in 1520 Luther published the *Address to the Christian Nobility of the German Nation*. In it, he appealed to the emperor and the German princes to reform the church and to cast off their allegiance to the pope, who he argued had used taxes and political power to exploit them for centuries. His appeal produced some success; the Reformation flourished on the resentment against foreign papal intervention that had long festered in Germany. Luther also wrote to the German people and conveyed the meaning of his personal experience as a Christian. In *The Freedom of the Christian Man* (1520), Luther called on his followers to strive for true spiritual freedom through faith in Christ, to discipline themselves to live as law-abiding members of society, to obey legitimate political authority, and to perform good works according to the dictates of Christian love. In these treatises Luther made it clear that he wanted to present no threat to legitimate political authority, that is, to the power of the German princes.

In 1521, Charles V, the Holy Roman emperor, who was a devout Catholic, summoned Luther to Worms, giving him a pass of safe conduct. There Luther was to answer to the charge of heresy, both an ecclesiastical and a civil offense. On his journey, Luther received a warm public response from great crowds of people. But the emperor and his officials coldly demanded that he recant. Luther's reply, delivered after some deliberation, is undoubtedly his most famous statement: "Unless I am convinced of error by the testimony of Scripture or by clear reason . . . I cannot and will not recant anything, for it is neither safe nor honest to act against one's conscience. God help me. Amen." Shortly after this confrontation with the emperor, Luther went into hiding to escape arrest. During that one-year period he translated the New Testament into German. With this work he offered his compatriots the opportunity to take the same arduous spiritual odyssey that he had and to join him as a new type of Christian. These people were eventually called *Protestants*, those who protested against the established church, or in the case of the nobility, actually took up arms against it.

The Appeal and Spread of Lutheranism

Once Luther recognized the need for followers, he appealed to every level of German society for support. And he was successful. His brilliance as a theologian was matched by his ability to bridge the gap between his sophisticated version of Christianity and the beliefs and aspirations of all Christians. Spread rapidly by the new printing press, the tenets of Protestantism offered the hope of revitalization and renewal not only for true religion but for society and government.

Lutheranism appealed to the devout, who resented the worldliness and lack of piety of many clergy. But the movement found its greatest following among German townspeople who objected to money flowing from their country to Rome in the form of church taxes and payment for church offices. In addition, the Reformation provided the nobility with the unprecedented opportunity to confiscate church lands, to eliminate church taxes, and to gain the support of their subjects by serving as leaders of a popular and dynamic religious movement. The Reformation also gave the nobles a way of resisting the Catholic Holy Roman emperor, Charles V, who wanted to extend his authority over the German princes. Resenting the Italian domination of the church, many other Germans who supported Martin Luther believed that they were freeing German Christians from foreign control.

Lutheranism also drew support from the peasantry, who saw Luther as their champion against their oppressors—feudal lay and ecclesiastical lords and the townspeople. Indeed, in his writings and sermons Luther often attacked the greed of the princes and bemoaned the plight of the poor. Nevertheless, Luther was a political conservative who hesitated to challenge secular authority. To him, the good Christian was an obedient citizen.

Although Luther had spoken forcefully about the discontent of Christians with their church, he never understood that in the minds of the poor and socially oppressed, the church's abuses were visible signs of the exploitation encountered in their daily lives. Wealthy and powerful feudal lords who governed them and prosperous townspeople who bought their labor for the lowest possible wages were no different from the venal clergy; indeed, in some cases the lord was a local bishop.

In the early sixteenth century, a rapid population explosion throughout Europe had produced severe inflation coupled with high unemployment and low wages. These conditions seriously affected the poor. The peasantry in Germany was probably worse off than in England and the Low Countries; and in the German states, the feudal power of lords over every feature of peasant life remained unbroken. In 1524, the long-suffering peasants openly rebelled against their lords. The Peasants' Revolt spread to over one-third of Germany; some 300,000 people took up arms against their masters.

Undoubtedly, Luther's successful confrontation with the authorities had served to inspire the peasants, and he had at one time chastised the nobles for failing to care for the poor as commanded in the Gospel. But he had no intention of associating his movement with a peasant uprising at the risk of alienating the nobility who supported him. Luther virulently attacked the rebellious peasants, urging the nobility to become "both judge and executioner" and to "knock down, strangle, and stab . . . and think nothing so venomous, pernicious, Satanic as an insurgent . . . Such wonderful times are these that a prince can merit heaven better with bloodshed than another with prayer."[3] By 1525 the peasants had been put down by the sword. Thousands died or were left homeless, and many were permanently alienated from the Lutheran Reformation.

The Peasants' Revolt was not the last violent confrontation for the German Reformation. Catholic power also threatened. Initially, the Holy Roman emperor hesitated to intervene militarily, a delay that proved crucial. His involvement in international power politics at first precluded him from acting in Germany: he was at war with France over control of portions of Italy, and Turkey threatened his territories in the east, particularly Austria. Soon, however, Catholic and Protestant princes in various territories of the empire were waging intermittent warfare over its religious fate.

Religious strife was only settled, and then in a piecemeal fashion, by the Peace of Augsburg (1555). It decreed by the famous dictum *cuius regio, eius religio* ("whoever rules, his religion") that each territorial prince should determine the religion of his subjects. Broadly speaking, northern Germany became largely Protestant, while Bavaria, Baden-Württemberg, and other southern territories remained in the church. The victors were the local princes. Toward the end of his life, Charles V expressed his bitter regret for not having intervened more forcefully in those early years. The decentralization of the empire and its division into Catholic and Protestant areas would block German unity until the last part of the nineteenth century.

The Spread of the Reformation

Nothing better illustrates people's dissatisfaction with the church in the early sixteenth century than the rapid spread of Protestantism. There was a pattern to this phenomenon. Protestantism grew strong in northern Europe—northern Germany, Scandinavia, the Netherlands, and England; it failed in the Romance countries, although not without a struggle in France. In general, Protestantism was an urban phenomenon, and it prospered where local magistrates supported it and where the distance from Rome was greatest.

Protestantism also appeared simultaneously in different places—a sure indication of its popular roots. For example, in the Swiss city of Zurich, the priest and reformer Ulrich Zwingli (1484–1531) preached a form of Christianity very close to that of Luther and claimed that he developed his ideas independently of Luther. Zwingli and Luther both

Map 14.1 The Protestant and the Catholic Reformations ▶

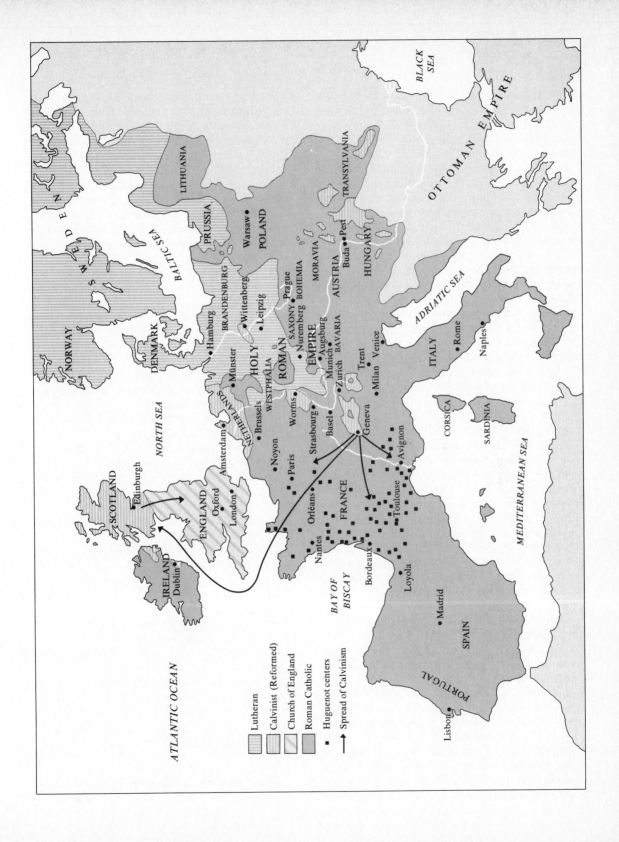

BLACK SEA

OTTOMAN EMPIRE

LITHUANIA

PRUSSIA

Warsaw • POLAND

TRANSYLVANIA

NORWAY

SWEDEN

BALTIC SEA

BRANDENBURG

Wittenberg • Prague BOHEMIA MORAVIA Buda • • Pest

DENMARK

Hamburg • Leipzig SAXONY • Nuremberg AUSTRIA HUNGARY

Münster HOLY ROMAN EMPIRE Augsburg • Munich

WESTPHALIA • Worms Zurich BAVARIA Trent

NETHERLANDS Brussels • • Basel • Venice Milan •

Amsterdam • Strasbourg • • Geneva

NORTH SEA Noyon • • Paris Avignon •

SCOTLAND Orléans • FRANCE Toulouse •

Edinburgh • Oxford • ENGLAND

London •

IRELAND

Dublin • Nantes •

Bordeaux •

BAY OF BISCAY Loyola •

ATLANTIC OCEAN

Madrid •

SPAIN

PORTUGAL

Lisbon •

ADRIATIC SEA

ITALY • Rome

Naples •

CORSICA SARDINIA

MEDITERRANEAN SEA

Lutheran

Calvinist (Reformed)

Church of England

Roman Catholic

■ Huguenot centers

→ Spread of Calvinism

sought a ceremonial alternative to the doctrine of transubstantiation—the priest's transformation of communion bread and wine into the substance of Christ's body and blood—and the enormous power it gave to the priesthood. But the two reformers came to differ bitterly over the exact form of the ceremonial. Zwingli turned the communion service into a feast of commemoration. In their quarrel we see the fate that awaited many reformers. Once free to read and interpret the Bible for themselves, they could not agree on its meaning, or on the ritual expressions they would give to their new versions of Christianity.

Zwingli died on the battlefield defending the Reformation. His teachings laid the foundation for a strong reformation in Switzerland, and the major reform movement of the next generation, Calvinism, benefitted from Zwingli's reforms.

Calvinism

The Reformation's success outside Germany derived largely from the work of John Calvin (1509–1564), a French scholar and theologian. For decades, French humanists had attacked the corruption of the church. Their views found sympathy at the court of the French king, Francis I. His sister, Margaret of Navarre, had helped foster this critical humanism, and her intellectual circle looked favorably on Luther's writings. By the 1530s, Lutheran treatises circulated widely in Paris. Some university students, including the young John Calvin, were impressed by the reformer's ideas.

Calvin was born into a French family of substantial bourgeois status, although his father, somewhat like Luther's, was self-made and ambitious. A lawyer and administrator, the elder Calvin had served the civil and ecclesiastical authorities of the city of Noyon until a dispute over finances led to his excommunication. He desired prosperous careers for his sons. John first studied to be a priest and then, at his father's insistence, took up the study of law at the University

of Orléans. Unlike the rebellious Luther, Calvin waited until his father's death to return to Paris and resume his theological studies.

Sometime in 1533 or 1534, Calvin met French followers of Luther and became convinced of the new theology's truth. He began to spread its beliefs immediately after his conversion, and within a year he and his friends were in trouble with the civil and ecclesiastical authorities. Calvin was arrested, but was released because of insufficient evidence.

King Francis I, a bitter rival of the Holy Roman emperor, could countenance Protestantism in Germany, but he had no intention of permitting disruptive religious divisions in his own France. Riots had already broken out in Paris between Catholics and supporters of the Reformation. In 1534 the French church, supported by royal decree, declared the Protestants heretics and subjected them to arrest and execution.

Within a year, young Calvin had abandoned his humanistic and literary studies to become a preacher of Reformation. Calvin explained his sudden conversion as an act of God—"He subdued and reduced my heart to docility, which, for my age, was over-much hardened in such matters."[4] From early in his religious experience, Calvin emphasized the power of God over sinful and corrupt humanity. Calvin's God thundered and demanded obedience, and the terrible distance between God and the individual was mediated only by Christ.

Calvin's understanding of God's relationship to the individual stressed its legal rather than its personal nature. Calvin said that God's laws must be rigorously obeyed; that social and moral righteousness must be earnestly pursued; that political life must be carefully regulated; and that human emotions must be strictly controlled. What psychological forces induced Calvin to embrace such a stern theology are not known, but they were not unique to him. The compelling force of Calvinist belief is an extraordinary aspect of the Protestant Reformation, and its historical consequences were great.

Like Luther, Calvin explained salvation in terms of uncertain predestination. He argued that although people are predestined to salvation or damnation, they can never know their fate in advance. This terrible decree could and did lead some to despair. For others—in a paradox difficult for the modern mind to comprehend—Calvinism gave a sense of self-assurance and righteousness that made *the saint*, that is, the truly predestined man or woman, into a new kind of European. Most of Calvin's followers seemed to believe that in having comprehended the fact of predestination, they had received a bold insight into their unique relationship with God.

The social and political implications of that insight were immediate: Calvinists became militant Protestants capable of ruling their town or city with the same iron will used to control their unruly passions. Again like Luther, Calvin always stressed that Christians should obey legitimate political authority. But Calvinists were individuals who assumed that only unfailing dedication to God's law could be seen as a sign of salvation; their obedience to human laws would always be contingent on their inner sense of righteousness. Thus, Calvinism made for stern men and women, active in their congregations and willing to suppress vice in themselves and others. Calvinism could also produce revolutionaries willing to defy any temporal authorities that were perceived to be in violation of God's laws. For Calvin, obedience to Christian law became the dominating principle of his life. Rigorous enforcement of the law ensured obedience to God's law; it also served as an alternative to the decrees and obligations formerly imposed by the Catholic church.

The political situation in France forced Calvin to leave. After his flight from Paris, he finally sought safety in Geneva, a small, prosperous Swiss city near the French border. There Calvin eventually established a Protestant church that did not hesitate to dominate the lives of many others less committed to the Reformation. Switzerland was a logical choice; its cities had long been in the vanguard of the Reformation. Before Calvin's arrival, Geneva's citizens were in revolt against their Catholic bishops. The French-born reformer Guillaume Farel led a small Protestant congregation there and implored Calvin to stay with him to continue the work of the Reformation. Together they became the leaders of the Protestant movement in Geneva. After many setbacks, Calvin emerged as the most dynamic agent of reform in the city. Until his death in 1564, his beliefs and actions dominated Geneva's religious and social life.

Calvin established a kind of theocracy—a society where the church regulates the political and social lives of its citizens. The older and more pious male members of the community governed the city. These elders of the Calvinist church imposed strict discipline in dress, sexual mores, church attendance, and business affairs; they severely punished irreligious or sinful behavior. This rigid discipline contributed to Geneva's prosperity; indeed, Calvin had instituted the kind of social discipline that the ruling merchants had always wanted. At every turn prosperous merchants, as well as small shopkeepers, saw in Calvinism a series of doctrines that justified the self-discipline they already exercised in their own lives and wished to impose on the unruly masses. They particularly approved of his economic views, for Calvin saw nothing sinful about commercial activities and even gave his assent to the practice of charging interest.

Geneva became the center of international Protestantism. Calvin trained a new generation of Protestant reformers of many nationalities, who carried his message back to their homelands. Calvin's *Institutes of the Christian Religion* (1536), in its many editions, became (after the Bible) the leading textbook of the new theology. In the second half of the sixteenth century, Calvin's theology of uncertain predestination spread into France, England, the Netherlands, and parts of the Holy Roman Empire.

Calvin always opposed any recourse to violence. Yet when monarchy became their persecutor, his followers felt compelled to respond. Calvinist theologians became the first political theoreticians of modern times to publish cogent arguments for opposition to monarchy, and eventually for political revolution. In France and later in the Netherlands, Calvinism became a revolutionary ideology, complete with an underground organization composed of dedicated followers who challenged monarchical authority. (In the seventeenth century, the English version of Calvinism—Puritanism—performed the same function.) In certain circumstances, Calvinism possessed the moral force to undermine the claims of the monarchical state over the individual.

France

Although Protestantism was illegal in France after 1534, its persecution was half-hearted and never systematic. The Protestant minority in France, the Huguenots, grew and became a well-organized underground movement that attracted nobles, urban dwellers, some peasants, and women especially. Huguenot churches, often under the protection of powerful nobles, assumed an increasingly political character in response to monarchy-sponsored persecution. By 1559, French Protestants were sufficiently organized and militant to challenge their persecutors, King Henry II and the Guise—one of the foremost Catholic families in Europe, tied by marriage and conviction to the Spanish monarchy and its rigorous form of Catholicism. Guise power in the French court meant that all Protestant appeals for more lenient treatment went unheeded, and in 1562 civil war erupted between Catholics and Protestants. What followed was one of the most brutal religious wars in the history of Europe. In 1572, an effort at conciliation through the marriage of a Protestant leader into the royal family failed when the Catholics, urged on by the queen mother, Catherine de' Medici, murdered the assembled Protestant wedding guests. Over the next week, a popular uprising against Protestants left thousands of them dead; the streets, according to eyewitness accounts, were stained red with blood. This slaughter,

known as the Saint Bartholomew's Day Massacre, inspired the pope to have a mass said in thanksgiving for a Catholic "victory." Such was the extent of religious hatred in Europe by the late sixteenth century.

After nearly thirty years of brutal fighting throughout France, victory went to the Catholic side—but only barely. Henry of Navarre, the Protestant bridegroom who in 1572 had managed to escape the fate of his supporters, became king, but only after he had reconverted to Catholicism. He established a tentative peace by granting Protestants limited toleration. In 1598 he issued the Edict of Nantes, the first document in any nation-state that attempted to institutionalize a degree of religious toleration. In the seventeenth century the successors of Henry IV (assassinated in 1610) gradually revoked the edict. The theoretical foundations of toleration, as well as its practice, remained weak in early modern Europe.

England

The Reformation was initiated in England not by religious reformers, but by the king himself. Henry VIII (1509–1547) removed the English church from the jurisdiction of the papacy because the pope had refused to grant him an annulment of his marriage to his first wife. The English Reformation began as a political act on the part of a self-confident Renaissance king. But its origins stretched back into the Middle Ages, and its character, once it got underway, became intensely religious and increasingly Protestant.

Unlike the French and Spanish kings, the English Tudors had never frightened the papacy. The Tudors had enjoyed a good measure of control over the English church, but they had never played a major role in European and papal politics. When Henry VIII decided that he wanted a divorce from the Spanish princess Catherine of Aragon, in 1527–1528, the pope in effect ignored his request. Henry had a shaky case from a theological point of view and not enough international political power to force his will on the papacy. As the pope stalled, Henry grew more desperate—he needed a male heir and presumed that the failure to produce one lay with his wife. At the same time, he desired the shrewd and tempting Anne Boleyn. But Spain's power over the papacy, symbolized by the Spanish army that had sacked Rome in 1525, ensured that Henry's pleas for an annulment would go unheeded.

Although anticlericalism and resentment toward the papacy was rife throughout Europe at this time, the English also possessed a tradition of popular opposition to the church that stretched back to Wycliffe in the fourteenth century. Aware of that tradition, Henry VIII arranged to grant himself a divorce by severing England from the church. To do so, he had to call Parliament, which in turn passed a series of statutes drawn up at his initiative and guided through Parliament by his minister, Thomas Cromwell. Beginning in 1529, Henry convinced both houses of Parliament to accept his Reformation, and so began an administrative and religious revolution. In 1534 he had himself declared supreme head of the Church of England. In 1536 he dissolved the monasteries and seized their property, which was distributed or sold to his loyal supporters. In most cases, it went to the lesser nobility and landed gentry.

In the eleven years following Henry's death in 1547, there were four monarchs. Henry VIII was succeeded by his son, Edward VI, who reigned from 1547 to 1553 and was a Protestant. On his death, he was succeeded by Mary (1553–1558), the daughter of Henry VIII and Catherine of Aragon. A devout Catholic, Mary persecuted Protestants in England. By the 1558 succession of Elizabeth I, Henry's second daughter (by Anne Boleyn), England was a Protestant country again.

The English, or Anglican, church as it developed in the sixteenth century differed little in its customs and ceremonies from the Roman Catholicism it replaced. And large sections of the English population, including aristocratic families, remained Catholic and even used their homes as centers for Catholic

Henry VIII. Henry VIII initiated the break with Rome. Ironically, earlier as a youthful monarch, he received from a grateful papacy the title "Defender of the Faith" for a published treatise against Martin Luther. *(National Portrait Gallery, London)*

rituals performed by clandestine priests. These divisions boded ill for the future.

In addition, the exact nature of England's Protestantism was a subject of growing dispute. Was the Anglican church to be truly Protestant? Was its hierarchy to be responsive to, and possibly even appointed by, the laity? Were its services and churches to be simple, lacking in "popish" rites and rituals and centered only around Scripture and sermon? Was Anglicanism to conform to Protestantism as practiced in Switzerland, either in Calvinist Geneva or Zwinglian Zurich? Clearly the clergy, especially the English bishops, would accept no form of Protestantism that might

Elizabeth I. The genius of Elizabeth I confounded her countrymen and the Catholic Church alike. Parliament wanted her to marry and give over power to her husband. The Catholic Church long held hopes for the English monarchy to reconcile with Rome. Elizabeth capitulated to no one and carefully charted a course that consolidated her personal power and allowed England to gain strength as a Protestant nation. Her portrait is by Nicholas Hilliard. (*Walker Art Gallery, Liverpool*)

limit their ancient privileges, ceremonial functions, and power.

Despite these religious issues, raised in large measure by the growing number of English Calvinists, or *Puritans* as they were called, Elizabeth's reign was characterized by a heightened sense of national identity. The English Reformation enhanced that sense, as did the increasing fear of invasion by Spain, a Catholic power with twice England's population and a vast colonial empire that was intent on returning England to the papacy.

Spain and Italy

In Spain, Protestantism met with no success. In the Middle Ages, church and state had successfully allied in a religious and nationalist crusade to drive out the Muslims, forging strong links between the Spanish monarchy and the church. The church augmented and justified the power and authority of the monarchy and at the same time retained its economic and political power. About one-quarter of the Spanish population held clerical office of one kind or another, and the church owned one-half of Spain's land. Furthermore, the church possessed judicial authority sanctioned by the state; its judicial arm, the Inquisition, enforced public and private morality.

Luther's works circulated in Spain for a brief time, but the Spanish authorities quickly and thoroughly stamped out Protestantism. After 1560, even the Inquisition was hard-pressed to find Protestants. The Spanish church was efficient, self-confident, and undoubtedly the most repressive in Europe. The absence of civil liberty and freedom of thought until very recently in modern Spain has historical roots in the Inquisition of the sixteenth century. Late in that century, Spain became the main defender of Catholicism on the Continent, and that imperial mission gradually sapped its vast military power. Yet Protestant antagonism toward Spain remained vital until well into the eighteenth century.

A similar pattern developed in Italy, where Luther's ideas were discussed in Italian humanist circles but gained no popular audience. The Italian humanists distrusted Luther's emphasis on human sinfulness, and church authorities persecuted the few converts. Attempts to reform the Italian church were largely unsuccessful, and even reform-minded popes in the 1520s and 1530s had little support among the Vatican's Italian bureaucracy.

The Radical Reformation

The mainstream of the Protestant Reformation can be described as *magisterial;* that is, the leading reformers generally supported established political authorities, whether they were territorial princes or urban magistrates. For the reformers, human freedom was a spiritual, not a social, concept. Yet the Reformation did help trigger revolts among the artisan and peasant classes of central and then western Europe. Indications are that church doctrine had not made great inroads into the folk beliefs of large segments of the European masses. Late medieval records of church interrogations, usually in towns and villages where heresy or witchcraft was suspected, show the people to have deviated to an extraordinary degree from official doctrines and beliefs. For example, some peasants held the very unchristian beliefs that Nature was God or that witches had as much spiritual power as priests did. By the 1520s, several radical reformers arose, often from the lower classes of European society, and attempted to channel popular religion and folk beliefs into a new version of reformed Christianity that spoke directly to the temporal and spiritual needs of the oppressed.

The proliferation of many radical groups throughout the Continent makes them difficult to classify. Nevertheless, some beliefs were common to the Radical Reformation. Like Lutherans and Calvinists, the radicals struggled with the problem of salvation. Luther argued that faith alone, freely given by God, provides salvation for the believer. Radical reformers proclaimed that God's will was known by his saints—those predestined for salvation. In a world where survival itself was often precarious for the poor and oppressed, the radicals argued that even ordinary men and women have certain knowledge of their salvation through the *inner light*—a direct and immediate communication from God to his chosen saints. That knowledge makes the saint free. For the radicals, such spiritual freedom justified their demands for social and economic freedom and equality. Protestantism, radically interpreted, proclaimed the righteousness and the priesthood of all believers. It said that all people can have faith if God wills it, and that God would

not abandon the wretched and humble of the earth.

The radicals said that the poor shall inherit an earth that at present is ruled by Antichrist, and that the end of the world has been proclaimed by Scripture. The saints' task is to purge this earth of evil to make it ready for Christ's Second Coming. For the radicals the faith-alone doctrine came to mean certain salvation for the poor and lowly, and the Scriptures became an inspiration for social revolution. Luther, Calvin, and the other reformers vigorously condemned the social doctrines that were preached by the radical reformers.

The largest group in the Radical Reformation prior to 1550 has the general name of *Anabaptists.* Having received the inner light—the message of salvation—the Anabaptist felt born anew and yearned to be rebaptized. This notion had a revolutionary implication: the first baptism—one's first Christian allegiance to an established church (Protestant or Catholic)—does not count. The Anabaptist is a new Christian, a new person led by the light of conscience to seek reform and renewal of all institutions in preparation for the Second Coming of Christ. Millenarian doctrines about the end of the world provided a sense of time, of urgency.

In 1534 the Anabaptists captured the city of Münster in Westphalia near the western border of Germany. They seized the property of nonbelievers, burned all books except the Bible, and in a mood of jubilation and sexual excess, openly practiced a repressive (as far as women were concerned) polygamy. All the while the Anabaptists proclaimed that the Day of Judgment was close at hand. The leaders at Münster were men totally unprepared for power, and their actions led to a universal condemnation of the radicals. Their defeat was achieved by an army led by the Lutheran prince, Philip of Hesse.

In early modern Europe, *Münster* became a byword for dangerous revolution. Determined to prevent these wild enthusiasts from gaining strength in their own territories, princes attacked them with ferocity. In Münster today, the cages still hang from the church steeple where the Anabaptist leaders were tortured and left to die as a warning to all would-be imitators.

By the late sixteenth century, many radical movements had either gone underground or grown quiet. But a century later, during the English Revolution (1640–1660), the beliefs and political goals of the Radical Reformation again surfaced, threatening to push the revolution in a direction that its gentry leaders desperately feared. Although the radicals failed in England too, they left a tradition of democratic and antihierarchical thought. The radical assertion that saints, who have received the inner light, are the equal of anyone, regardless of social status, helped shape modern democratic thought.

The Catholic Response

The church could never have predicted the force of the Protestant Reformation, especially the number of powerful noblemen attracted to it. When it developed, the papacy seemed incapable of responding with needed reforms of its own, perhaps because it feared the forces that would be unleashed within the church and might challenge its own power. In the first instance, the energy for reform came from ordinary clergy as well as lay people such as Ignatius Loyola (1491–1556). Trained as a soldier, this pious Spanish reformer sought to create a new religious order fusing the intellectual excellence of humanism with a reformed Catholicism that would appeal to powerful economic and political groups. Founded in 1534, the Society of Jesus, more commonly known as the Jesuits, became the backbone of the Catholic Reformation in southern and western Europe. The Jesuits combined traditional monastic discipline with a dedication to teaching and an emphasis on the power of preaching, and they sought to use both to win converts back to the Church.

The Jesuits sought to bypass local corruption and appealed to the papacy to lead a truly international movement to revive Christian universalism. The Jesuits saw most clearly the power of the bitter fragmentation produced by the Reformation, and they also saw one of the central flaws in Protestant theology. Predestination offered salvation especially to the literate and prosperous laity and also, at least in theory, to the poor.

But equally, it included the possibility of despair for the individual or of a life tormented by a fear of damnation. In response, the Jesuits offered hope—a religious revival based upon ceremony, tradition, and the power of the priest to offer forgiveness. In addition, they opened some of the finest schools in Europe. Just as the Lutherans in Germany sought to bring literacy to the masses so that they might read the Bible, the Jesuits sought to bring intellectual sophistication to the laity, especially to the rich and powerful. The Jesuits pursued positions as confessors to princes and urged them to press their efforts to strengthen the church in their territories. They even sought to develop a theology that permitted "small sins" in the service of an ultimately just cause. In this way the Jesuits, by the seventeenth century, became the greatest teachers in Europe, and also the most controversial religious group within the church—were they the true voice of a reformed church, or did they use religion simply as a disguise to seek political power of their own, to make themselves the Machiavellian servants of princes? It was a controversy that neither their contemporaries nor historians have been able to solve.

The Jesuits built schools and universities throughout Europe, designed churches, and even fostered a distinct style of art and architecture: cherubic angels grace the ornate decor of Jesuit churches; heaven-bound virgins beckon the penitent. This baroque style, so lavish and emotive, was intended to move the heart, just as the skilled preacher sought to move the intellect. The Protestant message had been heard: religion is ultimately a private, psychological matter that is not always satisfied by scholastic argumentation.

By the 1540s the Counter Reformation was well underway. This attempt to reform the church from within combined several elements that had always stood for renewal within traditional Catholicism. For example, the Jesuits were imitating such preaching orders of the Middle Ages as the Dominicans and the Franciscans, and Catholic reformers looked to Renaissance humanism like that of Erasmus as the key to the church's total reformation. The leaders of this Catholic movement attacked many of the same abuses that had impelled Luther to speak out, but they avoided a break with the doctrinal and spiritual authority of the clergy.

The Counter Reformation also took aggressive and hostile measures against Protestantism. The church tried to counter the popular appeal of Protestantism by offering dramatic, emotional, even sentimental piety to the faithful. For individuals who were unmoved by this appeal to sentiment or by the church's more traditional spirituality and who allied with Protestant heresy, the church resorted to sterner measures. The Inquisition expanded its activities, and wherever Catholic jurisdiction prevailed, unrepentant heretics were subject to death or imprisonment. Catholics did not hold a monopoly on persecution: wherever Protestantism obtained official status—in England, Scotland, and Geneva, for instance—Catholics or religious radicals also sometimes faced persecution. But the church possessed greater national power in certain countries, and hence its power to persecute was greater. This was an age when only skeptics or freethinkers valued religious toleration.

The censorship of printed literature was an inherent part of European intellectual life, lasting until well into the nineteenth century. By the 1520s the impulse to censor and burn dangerous books had surfaced dramatically. In the rush to eliminate heretical literature, the church condemned the works of reforming Catholic humanists as well as those by Protestants. Indeed not only books were burnt; Calvin executed by fire the naturalist and skeptic Michael Servetus, who opposed the doctrine of the Trinity; in 1600 the church burned Giordano Bruno for similar reasons.

El Greco (1541–1614): Portrait of a Cardinal (probably Don Fernando Niño de Guevara). The Spanish church fiercely opposed the Reformation. The Inquisition persecuted Protestants relentlessly. The tenseness of the sitter captures the wary militancy of Spanish Catholicism. The Cardinal's cool glance is belied by his claw-like hand. *(The Metropolitan Museum of Art, New York; bequest of Mrs. H. O. Havemeyer, 1929. The H. O. Havemeyer Collection)*

These victims were merely two famous men who fell in an age of persecution; thousands were imprisoned or executed. The Index of Prohibited Books became an institutional part of the church's life; it was finally abolished in 1966.

Much of the Catholic response to the Reformation entailed hostility and rejection. Yet within the church itself, reformers succeeded in putting through concrete changes. In 1545 the Council of Trent met to reform the church and to strengthen it to face the Protestant challenge. Over the many years that it was convened (until 1563), the Council modified and unified church doctrine; abolished many corrupt practices, such as the selling of indulgences; and vested final authority in the papacy, thereby ending the long and bitter struggle within the church over papal authority. The Council of Trent purged the church and gave it doctrinal clarity on such matters as the roles of faith and good works in attaining salvation. It passed a decree that the church shall be the final arbiter of the Bible and demanded that texts be taken literally wherever possible. Galileo was to experience great difficulties in the next century because that decree made the motion of the earth into a contradiction of Scripture (see pages 386–387). But the intention of the decree was to offer the church as a clear voice amid the babble of Protestant tongues. All compromise with Protestantism was rejected (not that Protestants were anxious for it). The Reformation had split western Christendom irrevocably.

The Reformation and the Modern Age

At first glance, the Reformation seems to have renewed the medieval stress on otherworldliness and reversed the direction toward a secularized humanism taken by the Renaissance. Yet a careful analysis shows decisively modern elements in Reformation thought, as well as antifeudal tendencies in its political history. The Reformation shattered the religious unity of Europe, the chief characteristic of the Middle Ages, and further weakened the church, the principal institution of medieval society, whose moral authority, rejected by millions, and political power waned considerably. Yet by the early seventeenth century, the policies of enlightened education, vigorous preaching, church building, cen-

sorship and persecution, had brought thousands of Germans and Bohemians, in particular, back to the church. To this day Europe remains a continent of Catholic and Protestant. Although doctrinal rigidity (and in some places church attendance) has largely disappeared, the split between the southern Catholic countries and the Protestant north is still alive in various customs and traditions.

By strengthening the power of monarchs and magistrates at the expense of religious bodies, the Reformation furthered the growth of the modern state. Protestant rulers totally repudiated the pope's claim to temporal power and extended their authority over Protestant churches in their lands. In Catholic lands, the church reacted to the onslaught of Protestantism by supporting the monarchies, but at the same time it preserved a significant degree of political independence. Protestantism did not create the modern secular state; it did, however, help to free the state from subordination to religious authority; such autonomy is an essential feature of modern political life.

Very indirectly, Protestantism contributed to the growth of political liberty—another ideal, although not always a reality, in the modern West. To be sure, neither Luther nor Calvin championed political freedom. Luther said that subjects should obey the commands of their rulers, and Calvinists created a theocracy in Geneva that closely regulated its citizens. Nevertheless, the Reformation provided a basis for challenging monarchical authority. During the religious wars, some Protestant theorists supported resistance to monarchs whose edicts, they believed, defied God's law. Moreover, the Protestant view that all believers—laity, clergy, lords, kings—were masters of their own spiritual destiny eroded hierarchical authority and accorded with emerging constitutional government.

The Reformation also contributed to the creation of an individualistic ethic. Protestants sought a direct and personal relationship with God and interpreted the Bible for themselves. Facing the prospect of salvation or damnation entirely on their own, without the church to

Chronology 14.1 The Reformation

1381	English peasants revolt; support John Wycliffe, early reformer
1414–1418	The Council of Constance
1431–1449	The Council of Basel
1517	Martin Luther writes his ninety-five theses and the Reformation begins
1520	Pope Leo X excommunicates Luther
1524–1526	The German peasants revolt
1529	The English Parliament accepts Henry VIII's Reformation
1534	Henry VIII is declared head of Church of England; King Francis I of France declares Protestants heretics; Ignatius Loyola founds the Society of Jesus; Anabaptists, radical reformers, capture Münster in Westphalia
1536	Henry VIII dissolves monasteries and seizes their properties; Calvin publishes *Institutes of the Christian Religion*
1536–1564	John Calvin leads the Reformation in Geneva with Guillaume (William) Farel
1545–1563	The Council of Trent
1553–1558	Mary, Catholic Queen of England, persecutes Protestants
1555	The Peace of Augsburg
1562–1598	French wars of religion between Catholics and Protestants are settled by the Edict of Nantes in 1598
1640–1660	The English Revolution

provide aid and security, and believing that God had chosen them to be saved, Protestants developed an inner confidence and assertiveness. This religious individualism was the counterpart of the intellectual individualism of the Renaissance humanists.

The Protestant ethic of the Reformation developed concurrently with a new economic system. Theorists have argued ever since about whether the new individualism of the Protestants brought on the growth of capitalism or whether the capitalistic values of the middle class gave rise to the Protestant ethic. In the middle of the nineteenth century, Karl Marx theorized that Protestantism gave expression to the new capitalistic values of the bourgeois: thrift, hard work, self-reliance, and rationality. Hence, Marx argued, the success of Protestantism can be explained by reference to the emergence of Western cap-

italism. In 1904, German sociologist Max Weber argued that Marx had got it backwards, that Protestantism encouraged the growth of capitalism, not vice versa.[5] Weber began with the assumption that religious beliefs do in fact have relevance to the way individuals act in the world. Religion is not primarily a series of doctrines, said Weber, but an ethic that possesses a spirit. Weber saw in the Protestant ethic of the reformation, as it evolved through the life experiences of its followers, the spirit of a nascent capitalism.

Weber acknowledged that capitalism existed in Europe before the Reformation—for example, the merchant-bankers in Italian and German towns. But, argued Weber, not all capitalism is the same, and in the West it has been a particular type of capitalism that has proved most dynamic. Weber saw the spirit of capitalism embodied in the entrepreneur, the *parvenu*, the self-made man. He strives for business success and brings to his enterprise self-discipline and self-restraint. He makes profit not for pleasure, but for more profit. He brings to his enterprise moral virtues of frugality and honesty. And he strives to render work and business efficient and planned, with profits carefully accumulated over time.

For Weber, Protestants made the best capitalists because predestination made them *worldly ascetics*—Christans forced to find salvation without assistance and through activity in this world. The reformers had condemned the monastery as an unnatural life, and their concomitant emphasis on human sinfulness established a psychology of striving that could only be channeled into worldly activity. So Protestants fulfilled their vocation, or calling, by service to the community or state and by dedication to this daily work. Commerce could become, if Weber is right, sanctified. But this ethic did little to alleviate the condition of the poor, which had worsened by the end of the sixteenth century.

By the late seventeenth century in Europe, the center of economic growth was shifting away from Mediterranean and Catholic countries toward northern Atlantic areas: England, the Netherlands, and parts of northern France. Protestant cities, with their freer printing presses, were also becoming centers of intellectual creativity. The characteristics of the modern world—individual expression, economic exploitation, and scientific learning—were to become most visibly present in western European Protestant cities like London, Amsterdam, and Geneva. Both the Protestant entrepreneur and the Protestant intellectual began to symbolize the most advanced forms of economic and creative life.

The tradition of individual striving for material gain, so much a part of Western culture today, developed out of what had once been a religious quest for salvation, made urgent in this world by the theology of the Protestant Reformation. Sixteenth-century Protestantism created a new, highly individual, spirituality. Survival in this world and salvation in the next came to depend on inner faith and self-discipline; for the prosperous, both eventually became useful in a highly competitive world where individuals rule their own lives and the labor of others and represent themselves and others in government.

Notes

1. John Dillenberger, Ed., *Martin Luther: Selections from His Writings* (New York: Doubleday, 1961), p. 46, taken from *The Freedom of a Christian* (1520).

2. Martin Luther, *Luther's Works*, Robert Schultz, ed. (Philadelphia: Fortress Press, 1967), 46:50–52.

3. François Wendel, *Calvin* (Paris: Presses Universitaires de France, 1950), p. 20.

4. See Max Weber, *Protestant Ethic and the Spirit of Capitalism*, trans. by Talcott Parsons (New York: Scribners, 1958).

Suggested Reading

Elton, G. R., *Reformation Europe, 1517–1559* (1966). A good, though very conservative, account.

Erikson, Erik H., *Young Man Luther* (1958). A psychological interpretation of Luther.

Grimm, Harold J., *The Reformation Era, 1500–1650*, 2nd ed. (1973). The best and most complete narrative available.

Huizinga, Johan, *Erasmus and the Age of Reformation* (1957). The best available survey.

Koenigsberger, H. G., and Mosse, George L., *Europe in the Sixteenth Century* (1968). Some very good chapters on the Reformation.

Neale, J. E., *The Age of Catherine de Medici* (1960). This book manages to make sense out of a complex period.

Scarisbrick, J. J., *Henry VIII* (1968). A very fair and balanced account of a most complex and willful monarch.

Spitz, Lewis William, *The Religious Renaissance of the German Humanists* (1963). Good coverage of the German humanists.

Tawney, R. H., *Religion and the Rise of Capitalism* (1962; reprint of 1926 ed.). Should be read by all students of Protestantism.

Weber, Max, *The Protestant Ethic and the Spirit of Capitalism,* trans. by Talcott Parsons (rev. ed. 1977). This classic essay argues the case for Protestantism as a force encouraging the development of capitalism. Written before World War I, it has never been surpassed.

Wendel, François, *Calvin* (1950). This is the standard biography.

Review Questions

1. Why did the Reformation begin in the early sixteenth century rather than in the fourteenth century at the time of Huss and Wycliffe? Describe the conditions and personalities responsible for starting the Reformation.

2. What personality traits did Martin Luther possess? Which traits seemed responsible for his role and actions in the Reformation? How did Luther's theology mark a break with the church? Why did many Germans become followers of Luther?

3. What role did the printing press play in the Reformation?

4. What were Calvin's major achievements?

5. In what ways did the radical reformers differ from the other Protestants?

6. What did *Münster* symbolize in early modern Europe?

7. Which features in Protestantism were likely to have made its followers more successful capitalists than their Catholic contemporaries?

8. How did the Reformation in England differ from that in Germany?

9. Why did France not become a Protestant country? Give the reasons and describe the circumstances.

10. What role did the Jesuits and the Inquisition play in the Counter Reformation? What did the Counter Reformation accomplish?

11. How did the Reformation weaken medieval institutions and traditions?

15

European Expansion:
Colonization, Commerce,
and Capitalism

*D*uring the period from 1450 to 1750, western Europe entered an era of overseas exploration and economic expansion that transformed society. By 1450, Europe had recovered from the severe contraction of the fourteenth century, produced by plague and marginal agriculture, and was resuming the economic growth that had been the pattern in the twelfth and early thirteenth centuries. This new period of growth, however, was no mere extension of the earlier one, but a radical departure from medieval economic forms.

Overseas exploration changed the patterns of economic growth and society. European adventurers discovered a new way to reach the rich trading centers of India by sailing around Africa. They also conquered, colonized, and exploited a new world across the Atlantic. These discoveries and conquests brought about an extraordinary increase in business activity and the supply of money, which stimulated the growth of capitalism. People's values were transformed into shapes that were alien and hostile to the medieval outlook. By 1750 the model Christian in northwestern Europe was no longer the selfless saint, but the enterprising businessman. The era of secluded manors and walled towns was drawing to a close. A world economy was emerging in which European economic life depended on the market in Eastern spices, African slaves, and American silver. During this age of exploration and commercial expansion, Europe generated a peculiar dynamism unmatched by any other civilization. A process was initiated that, by 1900, would give Europe mastery over most of the globe and wide-ranging influence over other civilizations.

The economic expansion from 1450 to 1650 or 1700 did not, however, raise the living standards of the masses. The vast majority of the people, 80 to 90 percent, lived on the land, and their main business was the production of primary goods—food, especially cereals, and wool. For most of these people, life hovered around the subsistence level, sometimes falling below subsistence during times of famine and disease. Whenever the standard of living improved, any surplus resources would soon be taken up by the survival of more children and hence more mouths to feed. The beneficiaries of the commercial expansion, those whose income rose, were the rich, especially the *nouveaux riches*.

In these respects, then, early modern Europe was comparable to an underdeveloped country today whose society consists of two main economic groups—a small, wealthy elite and a large and growing population that exists on the margin of subsistence and is wracked by recurrent hunger and disease. Developments during overseas exploration and economic expansion should be viewed in the context of these social conditions.

European Expansion

During the Middle Ages the frontiers of Europe had expanded, even if only temporarily in some instances. The Crusaders carved out feudal kingdoms in the Near East. Christian knights pushed back the Muslims on the Iberian Peninsula and drove them from Mediterranean islands. Germans expanded in the Baltic region at the expense of non-Christian Balts, Prussians, and Slavs. Genoa and Venice established commercial ports in the Adriatic Sea, the Black Sea, and the eastern Mediterranean. In the fifteenth and sixteenth centuries, western Europeans embarked on a second and more lasting movement of expansion that led them into the uncharted waters of the Atlantic, Indian, and Pacific oceans. Combined forces propelled Europeans outward and enabled them to dominate Asians, Africans, and American Indians.

Forces Behind Expansion

The population of western Europe increased rapidly between 1450 and 1600. This increase occurred at all levels of society, and among the gentry it was translated into land hunger. As the numbers of the landed classes exceeded the supply of available land, the sons of the aristocracy looked beyond Europe for the lands and fortunes denied them at home. Nor was it unnatural for them to do so by plunder and conquest—their ancestors had done the same thing for centuries. Exploits undertaken and accomplished in the name of family, church, and king were legitimate, perhaps the most legitimate, ways of earning merit and fame, as well as fortune. So the gentry provided the leadership—Cortés is an example—for the expeditions to the New World.

Merchants and shippers, as well as the sons of the aristocracy, also had reason to look abroad. Trade between Europe, Africa, and the Orient had gone on for centuries, but always through intermediaries who increased the costs and decreased the profits on the European end. Gold had been transported by Arab nomads across the Sahara from the riverbeds of West Africa. Spices had been shipped from India and the East Indies by way of Muslim and Venetian merchants. Western European merchants now sought to break those monopolies by going directly to the source—to West Africa for gold, slaves, and pepper, and to India for pepper, spices, and silks. Moreover, incentive grew for such commercial enterprise because between 1450 and 1600 the wealth of prosperous Europeans increased dramatically. This wealth was translated into new purchasing power and the capacity to invest in foreign ventures that would meet the rising demand among the prosperous for luxury goods.

The centralizing monarchical state also played its part in expansion. Monarchs, like Ferdinand and Isabella of Spain, who had successfully established royal hegemony at home looked for opportunities to extend their control overseas. The Spanish rulers looked over their shoulders at their neighbors, the Portuguese, and this competition spurred the efforts of both countries in their drive to the East. Later the Dutch, English, and French engaged in a century-long rivalry. From overseas empires came gold, silver, and commerce that paid for ever-more expensive royal government at home and for war against rival dynasties abroad.

Finally, religion helped in expansion. The crusading tradition was well established, especially on the Iberian Peninsula, where a five-hundred-year struggle known as the Reconquest had taken place to drive out the Muslims. Cortés, for example, saw himself as following in the footsteps of Paladin Roland, the great medieval military hero who had fought to drive back Muslim and pagan. The Portuguese too were imbued with the crusading mission. Prince Henry the Navigator hoped that the Portuguese expansion into Africa would serve two purposes: the discovery of gold and the extension of Christianity at the expense of Islam. In this second aim, his imagination was fired by the legend of Prester John, which told of an ancient Christian kingdom of fabled wealth in the heart of Africa. If the Portuguese could reach that land, Prince Henry reckoned, the two kingdoms would join in a crusade against Islam.

Thus, expansion involved a mixture of economic, political, and religious forces and motives. The West possessed a crusading faith; divided into a handful of competing, warlike states, it expanded by virtue of forces built into its structure and culture. Not only did the West have the will to expand, it also possessed the technology needed for successful expansion. This factor also distinguished the West from China and Islam and helps to explain why the West, not the Oriental civilizations, launched an age of conquest resulting in global mastery.

Not since the Early Middle Ages had there been such a rapid technological revolution as that which began in the fifteenth century. Europeans learned about gunpowder from the Chinese as early as the late thirteenth century, and by the fifteenth century its military application had become widespread. The earliest guns were big cannons meant to knock holes in the walled defenses characteristic of

The New World, Engraving by G. Mercator. The development of the sailing ship and the gunship allowed Spain and Portugal to roam the seas with impunity. Spain had hoped that the New World would provide an abundance of costly spices. However, the land and precious metals there more than made up for the lack of spices. (*The Hispanic Society of America, New York*)

the Middle Ages. In the sixteenth and seventeenth centuries, handheld firearms (particularly the musket) and smaller, more mobile field artillery were perfected. Dynastic and religious wars and overseas expansion kept demand for armaments high, and the armament industry was, as a result, important to the growth of trade and manufacturing.

Another technological development during the period from 1400 to 1650 was the sailing ship. The vessels of the ancient world had been driven principally by oars and human energy. Such vessels, called galleys, were suitable for the shorter distances, calmer waters, and less variable conditions of the Mediterranean, the Black, and the Red seas. But galleys were unsuitable for the Atlantic and other great oceans that Europeans began to ply in the early sixteenth century. In western Europe by the fifteenth century, moreover, labor was in short supply, making it difficult to recruit or condemn men to the galleys. For these reasons the Portuguese, the Dutch, and the English abandoned the galley in favor of the sailing ship.

The sail and the gun were crucially important in allowing Europeans to overcome non-Europeans and penetrate and exploit their worlds. Western Europeans combined these devices in the form of the gunned ship. Not only was the sailing vessel more maneuverable and faster in the open seas than the galley, but the addition of guns gave it another tactical advantage over its rivals. The galleys of the Arabs in the Indian Ocean and the junks of the Chinese were not armed with guns below deck for firing at a distance to cripple or sink the enemy. In battle they relied instead on the ancient tactic of coming up alongside the enemy vessel, shearing off its oars, and boarding to fight on deck.

The gunned ship gave the West naval superiority from the beginning. The Portuguese, for example, made short work of the Muslim fleet sent to drive them out of the Indian Ocean in 1509. That victory at Diu, off the western coast of India, indicated that the West not only had found an all-water route to the Orient but was there to stay. Material and religious motives led Europeans to explore and conquer; superior technology ensured the success of their enterprises.

The Portuguese Empire

Several reasons account for Portugal's overseas success. Portugal's long Atlantic coastline ensured that its people would look to the sea—initially for fishing and trade and then for exploration. A sunny climate also spurred seafaring and commercial expansion. Portugal was Northern Europe's closest supplier of subtropical products—olive oil, cork, wine, and fruit. The feudal nobility, typically antagonistic to trade and industry, was not as powerful in Portugal as elsewhere in Europe. Although feudal warriors had carved Portugal out of Moorish Iberia in the twelfth century, their descendants were blocked from further interior expansion by the presence of the strong Christian Kingdom of Castile in the east. The only other outlet for expansion was the sea.

Royal policy also favored expansion. The central government promoted trading interests, especially after 1385 when the merchants of Lisbon and the lesser ports helped establish a new dynasty in opposition to the feudal aristocracy. In the first half of the fifteenth century a younger son of the king, named Prince Henry the Navigator (1394–1460) by English writers, sponsored voyages of exploration and the nautical studies needed to undertake them. In these endeavors he spent his own fortune and the wealth of the church's crusading order that he headed. Prince Henry sought to revive the anti-Muslim crusade to which Portugal owed its existence as a Christian state. This connection between the medieval crusades and the early modern expansion of Europe ran through Portuguese and Spanish history.

As early as the fifteenth century the Portuguese expanded into islands in the Atlantic Ocean. In 1420 they began to settle Madeira and raise corn there, and in the 1430s they pushed into the Canaries and the Azores in search of new farmlands and slaves for their colonies. In the middle decades of the century they moved down the West African coast to the mouth of the Congo River and beyond, establishing trading posts as they went.

By the last quarter of the century they had developed a viable imperial economy among the ports of West Africa, their Atlantic islands, and Western Europe—an economy based on sugar, black slaves, and gold. Africans panned the gold in the riverbeds of central and west-

Map 15.1 Overseas Exploration and Conquest, c. 1400–1600 ▶

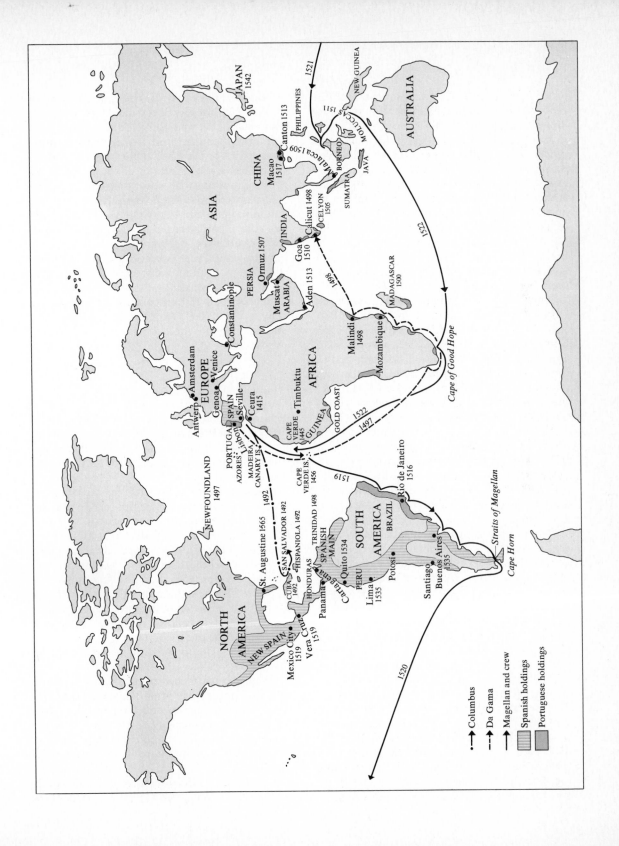

NEWFOUNDLAND
1497

NORTH
AMERICA

NEW SPAIN

Mexico City 1519
Vera Cruz 1519

St. Augustine 1565

SAN SALVADOR 1492
CUBA 1492
HISPANIOLA 1492
HONDURAS
TRINIDAD 1498
Panama Cartagena
Quito 1534
PERU
Lima 1535
Potosí
SPANISH
MAIN
Santiago
Buenos Aires 1535

SOUTH
AMERICA

BRAZIL

Rio de Janeiro 1516

Straits of Magellan
Cape Horn

1520

1519

1492

EUROPE
Amsterdam
Antwerp
Genoa Venice
SPAIN
Seville
PORTUGAL Lisbon
AZORES
MADEIRA
CANARY IS.

ASIA

Constantinople
PERSIA
Ormuz 1507
Muscat
ARABIA
Aden 1513

AFRICA

Timbuktu
CAPE VERDE
GUINEA
GOLD COAST
CAPE VERDE IS. 1456

CAPE VERDE
1445
Ceuta 1415

1497

1522

1498

Malindi 1498
Mozambique

MADAGASCAR
1500

Cape of Good Hope

1552

JAPAN
1542

CHINA
Macao 1517
Canton 1513

INDIA
Goa 1510
Calicut 1498
CEYLON 1505

SUMATRA

MALACCA 1509

BORNEO
PHILIPPINES
JAVA
MOLUCCAS 1511

NEW GUINEA

AUSTRALIA

1521

Columbus
Da Gama
Magellan and crew
Spanish holdings
Portuguese holdings

ern Africa, and the Portuguese purchased it at its source. They paid in cloth and slaves at a profit of at least 500 percent. Then the Portuguese transported the gold to Europe where they sold it for even more profit. Slaves figured not only in the purchase of gold but also in the production of sugar. In their Atlantic islands the Portuguese grew sugar cane, and little else by the end of the century, as a cash crop for European consumption, and slaves were imported from West Africa to do the work. There was also a lively trade in slaves to Portugal itself and elsewhere in southern Europe.

The Portuguese did not stop in western Africa. By 1488, Bartholomeu Dias had reached the southern tip of the African continent; a decade later Vasco da Gama sailed around the Cape of Good Hope and across the Indian Ocean to India. By discovering an all-water route to the Orient, Portugal broke the commercial monopoly of Eastern goods that Genoa and Venice had enjoyed.

In search of spices, the Portuguese went directly to the source, to India and the East Indies. As along the African coast, they established fortified trading posts—most notably at Goa on the western coast of India (Malabar) and at Malacca (now Singapore) in the Malay Peninsula.

Demand for spices was insatiable. Pepper and other spices are relatively unimportant items in the modern diet, but in the era before refrigeration, fresh meat was available only at slaughtering time, customarily twice a year. The rest of the year the only meat available, for those who could afford it at all, was dried, stringy, and tough; spices made meat and other foods palatable.

The infusion of Italian, particularly Genoese, investment and talent contributed to Portuguese expansion. As Genoese trade with the Near East, especially the Black Sea, shrank due to the Ottoman Turkish expansion, Genoese merchants shifted more and more of their capital and mercantile activities from the eastern to the western Mediterranean and the Atlantic, that is, to Spain and Portugal and their possessions overseas. This shift is

evident in the life of Christopher Columbus (1451–1506), a Genoese sailor, who worked in Portugal before finally winning acceptance for his scheme to find a westward route to the spices of the East at the court of Castile in Spain. Initially, much of the Genoese investment was in the sugar plantations in Portuguese colonies in the Atlantic. The Portuguese gained not only Genoese capital, but also the expertise to put it to use. The Genoese had established their own sugar colonies in Cyprus and Crete two centuries before, and they knew from long experience what would work. The plantation system based on slave labor was an Italian import; only now the slaves were black Africans instead of Slavs, as they had often been in the eastern Mediterranean.

The Spanish Empire

Spain stumbled onto its overseas empire, which nonetheless proved to be the biggest and richest of any until the eighteenth century. Columbus won the support of Isabella, queen of Castile. But on his first voyage (1492) he landed on the large Caribbean island that he named *Española* (Little Spain). To the end of his life, even after subsequent voyages, Columbus believed that the West Indies were part of the East. Two forthcoming events would reveal that Columbus had discovered not a new route to the East, but new continents: Vasco Nuñez de Balboa's discovery of the Pacific Ocean at the Isthmus of Panama in 1513 and Ferdinand Magellan's circumnavigation of the globe (1520–1521) through the strait at the tip of South America bearing his name.

The Spanish found no spices in the New World, but they were more than compensated by the abundant land and the large quantities of precious metals. Stories of the existence of larger quantities of gold and silver to the west lured the Spaniards from their initial settlements in the Caribbean to Mexico. In 1519, Hernando Cortés landed on the Mexican coast with a small army; during two years

Isabella and Ferdinand. With the marriage of Ferdinand of Aragon to Isabella of Castile, Spain came into being as a nation. At the Battle of Granada, they defeated the last of the Islamic forces on the Spanish mainland. Columbus courted and won the patronage of Isabella. Monies that had previously been used to fight Islam were diverted to exploration. The wealth of the New World would repay her patronage beyond all expectation. *(Copyright reserved to H.M. The Queen)*

of campaigning he managed to defeat the native rulers, the Aztecs, and to conquer Mexico for the Spanish crown. A decade later, Francisco Pizarro achieved a similar victory over the mountain empire of the Incas in Peru. Both Cortés and Pizarro exploited the hostility that the subject tribes of Mexico and Peru felt toward their Aztec and Incan overlords, a strategy that accounts in large part for the Spaniards' success.

For good reasons, the Mexican and Peruvian conquests became the centers of the Spanish overseas empire. First, there were the gold hoards accumulated over the centuries by the rulers for religious and ceremonial purposes. And when these supplies were exhausted, the Spanish discovered silver at Potosí in Upper Peru in 1545 and at Za-

catecas in Mexico a few years later. From the middle of the century, the annual treasure fleets sailing to Spain became the financial bedrock of Philip II's war against the Muslim Turks and the Protestant Dutch and English.

Not only gold and silver lured Spaniards to the New World. The crusading tradition also acted as a spur. Cortés, Pizarro, and many of their followers were *hidalgos*—lesser gentry whose status depended on the possession of landed estates and whose training and experience taught that holy war was a legitimate avenue to wealth and power. Their fathers had conquered Granada, the last Muslim kingdom in Spain, in 1492; they had expelled the Jews the same year and had carried the Christian crusade across to North Africa. The conquest and conversion of the

Silver mines at Potosí, Sixteenth Century. The Spanish conquest of the Incas and the Aztecs filled the coffers of Spain with gold and silver. The native population was decimated, and most native art and artifacts were destroyed, regarded as heathen work beneath the Europeans' consideration. *(In the Library of the Hispanic Society of America, New York)*

pagan peoples of the New World was an extension of the crusading spirit that marked the five previous centuries of Spanish history. The rewards were what they had always been: the propagation of the true faith, service to the crown, handsome land grants, and control over the inhabitants, who would work the fields. The land was especially attractive in the sixteenth century because the number of hidalgos was increasing with the general rise in population, and the amount of land available to them at home was as a result shrinking.

The conquerors initially obtained two kinds of grants from the crown, *encomiendas* and *estancias*. The latter were land grants, either of land formerly belonging to the native priestly and noble castes, or of land in remoter and less fertile regions. Encomiendas were royal grants of authority over the natives. Those who received such authority, the *encomenderos*, promised to give protection and instruction in the Christian religion to their charges. In return they gained the power to extract labor and tribute from the peasant masses, who were worked beyond their capacity.

The royal grants of encomiendas during the first generation of Spanish settlement were partially responsible for the decimation within a century of European occupation of the native population in the New World. Between 1500 and 1600 the number of natives shrank from about twenty million to little more than two million. The major cause of this catastrophe, however, was not forced labor but the diseases introduced from Europe—dysentery, malaria, hookworm, smallpox—against which the natives had little or no natural resistance. Beginning in the 1540s the position of the natives gradually improved as the crown withdrew grants that gave authority over the natives and took increasing responsibility for controlling the Indians.

Power and wealth gradually concentrated in fewer and fewer hands. As the Spanish landholders lost authority over the native population to royal officials and their associates, the latter gained substantially in power and privilege. As recurrent depressions ruined smaller landowners, they were forced to sell out to their bigger neighbors. On their conversion to Christianity, the Indians were persuaded to give more and more land to the church. Thus, Spanish America became permanently divided between the privileged elite and the impoverished masses.

One group suffered even more than the Indians: the blacks. The natives at least escaped the degradation of slavery. But blacks were imported from Africa in increasing numbers, especially as the Indian population declined, to work as slaves in the fields and the mines. The Portuguese and, in the eighteenth century, the British were the most important slave traders. Africans were captured by rival black tribes in western Africa, then enslaved and sold to Europeans in ports along the West African coast. The Africans were then herded onto ships for passage to the New World under such brutal conditions that only about half of them survived. Those who did were sold at auction in the ports of the Caribbean and North America; sellers and buyers considered the age and physical condition of the slaves, with little or no regard for any other aspects of their well-being—family ties for instance.

The Price Revolution

Linked to overseas expansion was another phenomenon—an unprecedented inflation during the sixteenth century, known as the *price revolution.* Evidence is insufficient on the general rise in prices. However, cereal prices multiplied by as much as eight times or more in certain regions in the course of the sixteenth century, and they continued to rise, although more slowly, during the first half of the next century. After 1650 prices leveled off or fell in most places; this pattern continued throughout the eighteenth century in England and off and on in France up to the Revolution. Economic historians have generally assumed that the prices of goods other than cereals increased by half as much as grain prices. Since people at that time did not understand why prices rose so rapidly, inflation was not subject to control. On the contrary, the remedies governments applied, like currency debasement, often worsened the problem.

Like colonization, the price revolution played an enormous role in the commercial revolution and did, in fact, partially result from the silver mining conducted in New Spain. The main cause of the price revolution, however, was the population growth during the late fifteenth and sixteenth centuries.

The population of Europe almost doubled between 1460 and 1620, and then it leveled off and decreased in some places. The patterns of population growth and of cereal prices thus match in the sixteenth and seventeenth centuries. Until the middle of the seventeenth century the number of mouths to feed outran the capacity of agriculture to supply basic foodstuffs, causing the vast majority of people to live close to subsistence. Until food production could catch up with the increasing population, prices, especially those of the staple food, bread, would continue to rise.

Why population grew so rapidly in the fifteenth and sixteenth centuries is not known, but the reasons why the population declined in the seventeenth century are. By then, the population had so outgrown the food supply that scarcity began to take its toll. Malnourishment, starvation, and disease pushed the death rate higher than the birth rate. With time, of course, prices lowered as population and hence demand declined in the 1600s.

The other principal cause of the price revolution was *probably* the silver that, beginning in 1552, flowed into Europe from the New World via Spain. But as a cause, the influx of silver lies on shakier ground than the inflationary effects of an expanding population. The increases in production and consumption following the growth in population would, to some degree, have necessitated an increase in the money supply to accommodate the greater number of commercial transactions. At some point it is assumed that the influx of silver exceeded the necessary expansion of the money supply and itself began contributing to the inflation. The most that can now be said is that the price revolution was caused by *too many people with too much money chasing too few goods*. The effects of the price revolution were momentous.

The Expansion of Agriculture

The greatest effects of the price revolution were on the land. Food prices, rising roughly twice as much as the prices of other goods, spurred ambitious farmers to take advantage of the situation and to produce for the expanding market. The opportunity for profit drove some farmers to work harder and manage their land better. The impact of the price revolution follows from that incentive.

The Old Pattern of Farming

The effects of the price revolution on farming were governed by the general social and po-

litical conditions operating in any given region or country. The effects in England were one sort; among the Dutch, another; in France, Spain, and the Mediterranean, still another; and in the Holy Roman Empire east of the Elbe River, in Poland, and in Russia, yet a fourth type. These differences must be compared against a background of European agriculture as it was practiced before the price revolution.

All over Europe, landlords held their properties in the form of manors. A particular type of rural society and economy had evolved on these manors in the Late Middle Ages. By the fifteenth century, much manor land was held by peasant-tenants according to the terms of a tenure known in England as *copyhold*. The tenants had certain hereditary rights in the land in return for the performance of certain services and the payment of certain fees to the landlord. Principal among these rights was the use of the commons—the pasture, woods, and pond. For the copyholder, access to the commons often made the difference between subsistence and real want, because the land tilled on the manor might not produce enough to keep a family.

Arable land was worked according to ancient custom. The land was divided into strips, and each peasant of the manor was assigned a certain number of strips. This whole pattern of peasant tillage and rights in the commons was known as the *open-field system*. After changing little for centuries, it was met head-on by the incentives generated by the price revolution.

Enclosure

In England, landlords aggressively pursued the possibilities for profit resulting from the inflation of farm prices. This pursuit required far-reaching changes in ancient manorial agriculture, changes that are called *enclosure*. The open-field system was geared to providing subsistence for the local village and, as such, prevented large-scale farming for a distant market. In the open-field system, the commons could not be diverted to the production of crops for sale. Moreover, the division of the arable land into strips made it difficult to engage in profitable commercial agriculture.

English landlords in the sixteenth century fought a two-pronged attack against the open-field system in their attempts to transform their holdings into market-oriented, commercial ventures. First they deprived their tenant peasantry of the use of the commons; then they changed the conditions of tenure from copyhold to leasehold. Whereas copyhold was heritable and fixed, leasehold was not. When a lease came up for renewal, the landlord could raise the rent beyond the tenant's capacity to pay. Restriction of rights to the commons deprived the poor tenant of critically needed produce. Both acts of the landlord forced peasants off the manor or into the landlord's employ as farm laborers.

With tenants gone, fields could be incorporated into larger, more productive units. Subsistence farming gave way to commercial agriculture—the growing of a surplus for the marketplace. Landlords would either hire laborers to work recently enclosed fields or rent these fields to prosperous farmers in the neighborhood. Either way, landlords stood to gain. They could hire labor at bargain prices because of the swelling population and the large supply of peasants forced off the land by enclosure. If the landlords chose to rent out their fields, they also profited. Prosperous farmers who themselves grew for the market could afford to pay higher rents than the previous tenants, the subsistence farmers; and they were willing to pay more because farm prices tended to rise even faster than rents.

The Yeomanry in England

The existence of prosperous farmers, sometimes called *yeomen,* in English rural society was crucial to the commercialization of farming. Yeomen were men who may not have owned much land themselves, but who rented enough to produce a marketable surplus,

sometimes a substantial one. They emerged as a discernible rural group in the High Middle Ages and were a product of the unique English inheritance custom, observed by peasantry and gentry alike, of *primogeniture.* The eldest son inherited the land, and the younger sons had to fend for themselves. Thus the land remained undivided, and the heirs among the peasantry often had enough land to produce a surplus for market. Many a gentleman landowner enclosed his fields not to work them himself, but to rent them to neighboring yeomen at rates allowing him to keep abreast of spiraling prices. Yeomen were better suited to work the land than the landlord, depending on it as they did for their livelihood.

One other process growing out of the price revolution promoted the commercialization of farming. Rising prices forced less businesslike landlords, who did not take advantage of the profit to be made from farming, to sell property in order to meet current expenses. The conditions of the price revolution thus tended to put an increasing amount of land into more productive hands. But rural poverty and violence increased because of the mass evictions of tenant farmers.

Convertible Husbandry

The effects of the price revolution on agriculture in the Netherlands were as dramatic and important as those in England. The Dutch population had soared and the majority of people had moved to the cities by the seventeenth century. As a result, a situation unique in all Europe—the problem of land use—became vitally important, especially as there was so little land to start with. The Dutch continued their efforts to reclaim land from the sea, which began in the Middle Ages. More significant, however, was their development in the fifteenth and sixteenth centuries, of a new kind of farming, known as *convertible husbandry.* This farming system employed a series of innovations that replaced the old three-field system of crop rotation,

Peter Brueghel the Younger (1564–1638): Harvesting Scene. England and the Netherlands underwent major agricultural changes in the sixteenth and seventeenth centuries. The enclosure system in England intensified land use and led to commercialization of agriculture. Convertible husbandry in the Netherlands ensured that the land was engaged for diversified agriculture, with no plots of land remaining unused. *(Nelson Gallery-Atkins Museum, Kansas City, Mo.; Nelson Fund)*

which had left one-third of the land unused at any given time. The new techniques used all the land every year and provided a more diversified agriculture.

The techniques combined soil-depleting cereals with soil-restoring legumes and grazing. For a couple of years, a field would be planted in cereals; in the third year, peas or beans would be sown to return essential nitrogen to the soil; for the next four or five years, the field became pasture for grazing animals, whose manure would further restore the soil for replanting cereals to restart the cycle. Land thus returned to grain would produce much more than land used in the three-field system. These devices for increasing productivity, when exported from the Netherlands and applied in England and France between 1650 and 1750, were essential in the complicated process by which these countries eventually became industrialized. For industrialization requires an agriculture productive enough to feed large, nonfarming urban populations.

Agricultural Change in Eastern Europe

In the Europe that stretches from the Elbe River across the Baltic plain to Russia, the effects of the price revolution were as dramatic as they were in England. The Baltic plain played an essential role in the European economy in the fifteenth, sixteenth, and early seventeenth centuries. Because western Europeans continued to outrun their food supply (in some places until the middle of the seventeenth century), they turned to the Baltic for regular shipments of grain.

Thus the landlords in the Baltic plain became commercial farmers producing for an international market. This trade led to a reorganization in the region south and east of the Baltic. There, as in England, enclosure to produce an agricultural surplus took place on a vast scale. But in contrast to the English experience, the peasant-tenants who had engaged in subsistence farming on these lands for generations were not evicted; nor did they become farm laborers working for low wages. Instead they remained on the land, and the terms of their tenure gradually shifted toward serfdom. As in Spain, a two-caste society emerged, a world of noble landlords and serfs. But unlike Spain's, this society produced for the marketplace.

The Expansion of Trade and Industry

The conditions of the price revolution also caused trade and industry to expand. Population growth exceeding the capacity of local food supplies stimulated commerce in basic foodstuffs, for example the Baltic trade with western Europe. Equally important as a stimulus to trade and industry was the growing income of landlords, merchants, and in some instances, peasants. This income created a rising demand for consumer goods, which helps explain several activities already mentioned. For example, the Portuguese spice trade with the East and the sugar industry in the Portuguese islands developed because prosperous people wanted such products. Rising income also created a demand for farm products other than cereals—meat, cheese, fruit, wine, and vegetables. The resulting land use reduced the area available for grain production and contributed to the rise in bread prices, which meant even larger profits.

Another factor in the commercial and industrial expansion was the growth of the state. With increasing amounts of tax revenue to spend, the expanding monarchies of the sixteenth and seventeenth centuries bought more and more supplies—ships, weapons, uniforms, paper—and so spurred economic expansion.

The Putting-Out System

Along with commercial and industrial expansion came a change in the nature of the productive enterprise. Just as the price revolution produced, in the enclosure movement, a reorganization of agriculture and agrarian society, it similarly affected trade and manufacturing. The reorganization there took place especially in the faster-growing industries—woolen and linen textiles—where an increasingly large mass market outpaced supply and thus made prices rise. This basic condition of the price revolution operated, just as it did in food production, to produce expansion. In the textile industries, increasing demand promoted specialization. For example, eastern and southwestern England made woolens, and northwestern France and the Netherlands produced linen.

Markets tended to shift from local to regional or even to international, a condition that gave rise to the merchant-capitalist. Unlike local producers, the merchant-capitalists' operations extended across local and national boundaries. This mobility allowed these capitalists to buy or produce goods where costs were lowest and to sell where prices and volume were highest. Because of the size and range of a business, an individual capitalist could control the traditional local producers, who increasingly depended on him for the widespread marketing of their expanded production.

This procedure, which was well developed by the seventeenth century, gave rise to what is known as the *putting-out system* of production. The manufacture of woolen textiles is a good example of how the system worked. The merchant-capitalist would buy the raw wool from English landlords who had enclosed their manors to take advantage of the rising price of wool. The merchant's agents collected the wool and took it (put it out) to nearby villages for spinning, dyeing, and weaving. The work was done in the cottages of peasants, many of whom had been evicted from the surrounding manors as a result of enclosure and therefore had to take what work they could get at the lowest possible wages. When the wool was processed into cloth, it was picked up and shipped to market.

The putting-out system represents an important step in the evolution of capitalism. It was not industrial capitalism, because there were no factories and the work was done by hand rather than by power machinery; nevertheless, the putting-out system significantly breaks with the medieval guild system. The new merchant-capitalists saw that the work was performed in the countryside, rather than in the cities and towns, to avoid guild restrictions (on output, quality, pay, and working conditions). The distinction between a master and an apprentice who will someday replace the master, which is assumed in the guild framework, had given place to the distinction between the merchant-owner (the person who provided the capital) and the worker (the one who provided the labor in return for wages and would probably never be an owner).

Enclosure also served to capitalize industry. Mass evictions lowered the wages of cottage workers because labor was plentiful. This condition provided additonal incentive on the part of the merchant-capitalist to invest in cottage industry. But the changes in farming were much more important in the economic development of Europe than the changes in industry, because agriculture represented a much larger share of total wealth than industry did.

Innovations in Business

Accompanying the emergence of the merchant-capitalist and the putting-out system was a cluster of other innovations in business life. Banking operations grew more sophisticated, making it possible for depositors to pay their debts by issuing written orders to their banks to make transfers to their creditors' accounts—the origins of the modern check. Accounting methods also improved. The widespread use of double-entry bookkeeping made errors immediately evident and gave a clear picture of the financial position of a commercial enterprise. Although known in the ancient world, double-entry bookkeeping was not widely practiced in the West until the fourteenth century. In this and other business practices the lands of southern Europe, especially Italy, were the forerunners; their accounting techniques spread to the rest of Europe in the sixteenth century.

The fourteenth century also saw the development of business practices related to shipping. A system of maritime insurance, without which investors would have been highly reluctant to risk their money on expensive vessels, evolved in Florence. By 1400, maritime insurance had become a regular item of the shipping business, and it was destined to play a major role in the opening of Atlantic trade. At least equally important to overseas expansion was the form of business enterprise known as the joint-stock company, which allowed small investors to buy shares in a venture. These companies made possible the accumulation of the large amounts of capital needed for large-scale operations, like the building and deployment of merchant fleets, which were quite beyond the resources of one person.

Map 15.2 Industrial Centers in the Sixteenth Century ▶

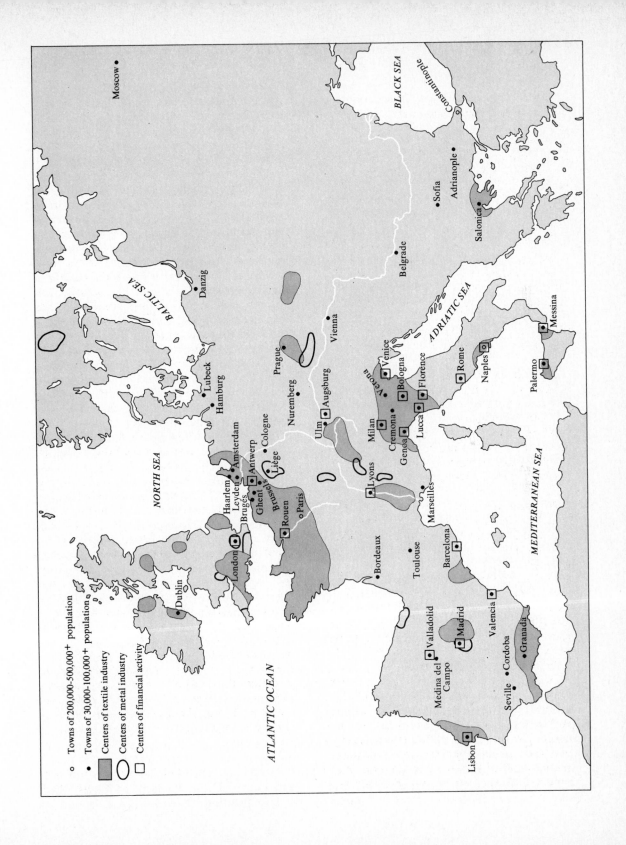

Towns of 200,000-500,000+ population ○

Towns of 30,000-100,000+ population ●

Centers of textile industry ▨

Centers of metal industry ◯

Centers of financial activity ☐

MOSCOW ●

BLACK SEA

Constantinople ○

Sofia ●

Adrianople ●

Salonica ▨

Danzig ●

Belgrade ●

Vienna ●

ADRIATIC SEA

Messina ☐

Prague

Venice ☐

Rome ☐

Palermo ●

Lübeck ●

Hamburg ●

Nuremberg ●

Augsburg ●

Ulm ●

Verona

Milan ●

Cremona ●

Bologna ☐

Florence ☐

Lucca ☐

Genoa ●

Naples ☐

BALTIC SEA

NORTH SEA

Amsterdam ●

Haarlem Leyden

Bruges Ghent Brussels

Antwerp

Cologne

Liège

Rouen ☐

Paris ○

Lyons ☐

Marseilles ●

MEDITERRANEAN SEA

London ◉

Dublin ●

Bordeaux ●

Toulouse ●

Barcelona ☐

Valencia ●

Madrid ◉

Valladolid ●

Medina del Campo ●

Seville ●

Cordoba ●

Granada ☐

Lisbon ☐

ATLANTIC OCEAN

Different Patterns of Commercial Development

The response to the price revolution in trade and industry differed in various parts of Europe—and the different responses hinged again on social and political conditions. In both the United Provinces (the Netherlands) and England there were far fewer strictures on trade and industry than in France and Spain. Thus, in the sixteenth and seventeenth centuries England and the United Provinces were better placed than France and Spain to take advantage of the favorable conditions for business expansion. In the United Provinces, this favorable position resulted from the weakness of feudal culture and values in comparison to commercial ones; other factors were its small land area and a far larger percentage of urban population than elsewhere in western Europe.

England's advantage derived from a different source: not the weakness of the landed gentry, but its habits. Primogeniture operated among those who owned large estates just as it did among the yeomanry, with much the same effect. Younger sons were forced to make their fortunes elsewhere. Those who did so by going into business would often benefit from an infusion of venture capital that came from their elder brothers' landed estates. And of course capital was forthcoming from such quarters because of the profitable nature of English farming. In a reverse process, those who made fortunes in trade would typically invest money in land and rise gradually into landed society. Those skills that had brought wealth in commerce would then be applied to new estates, usually with equal success.

England and the Netherlands In both England and the United Provinces the favorable conditions led to large-scale commercial expansion. In the 1590s the Dutch devised a new ship, the *fluit* or flyboat, to handle bulky grain shipments at the lowest possible cost. This innovation allowed them to capture the Baltic trade, which became a principal source

of their phenomenal commercial expansion between 1560 and 1660. Equally dramatic was their commercial penetration of the Orient. Profits from the European carrying trade built ships that allowed them first to challenge and then to displace the Portuguese in the spice trade with the East Indies during the early seventeenth century. The Dutch chartered the United East India Company in 1602 and established trading posts in the islands, which were the beginnings of a Dutch empire that lasted until World War II.

The English traded throughout Europe in the sixteenth and seventeenth centuries, especially with Spain and the Netherlands. The staples of this trade were raw wool and woolens, but increasingly they included such items as ships and guns. The seventeenth century saw the foundation of a British colonial empire along the Atlantic seaboard in North America from Maine to the Carolinas and in the West Indies, where the English managed to dislodge the Spanish in some places.

In both England and the United Provinces, government promoted the interests of business. In the late sixteenth and early seventeenth centuries the northern provinces of the Spanish Netherlands, centered around Holland, won their independence from Spain in a protracted struggle. Political power in these so-called United Provinces passed increasingly into the hands of an urban patriciate of merchants and manufacturers based in cities like Delft, Haarlem, and especially Amsterdam. These urban interests pursued public policies that served their pocketbooks. The southern provinces of the Netherlands (Flanders) and Antwerp, their commercial capital, remained under Spanish domination. From the 1590s the Dutch, as the inhabitants of the United Provinces were called, sent ships to close the Scheldt (the river linking Antwerp to the North Sea) to commercial traffic. This act dealt a fatal blow to the economic fortunes of the city that had dominated trade between northern and southern Europe and between England and the Continent in the late fifteenth and much of the sixteenth centuries. Antwerp's position of leadership as a trading

Frans Hals (c. 1580–1666): **Banquet of the Officers of the St. George Civic Guard Company.** Hals's painting captures the new merchant "princes" of the Netherlands. They lived the good life surrounded by worldly products of the best quality. They did not concern themselves with theories of "divine right." Instead, as merchants, they were most interested in profits. *(Frans Halsmuseum, Haarlem, The Netherlands)*

center passed to Amsterdam, and later to London and Hamburg. The founding of the Dutch East India Company and the Bank of Amsterdam in the first decade of the seventeenth century also stemmed from an alliance between business and government for their mutual interests. The Bank of Amsterdam expanded credit, lowered interest rates, and increased confidence. The Dutch East India Company regulated trade, reduced wasteful competition between formerly independent traders, and hence consolidated investment.

In seventeenth-century England the central government increasingly took the side of the capitalist producer. At the beginning of the century the king had imposed feudal fees on landed property, acted against enclosures, and granted monopolies in trade and manufacture to court favorites, which restricted opportunities for investment. Also the king spent revenues on maintaining an unproductive aristocracy. But by the end of the century, due to the revolutionary transfer of power from the king to Parliament, economic policy more closely reflected the interests of big business, whether agricultural or commercial. Landowners no longer paid feudal dues to the king. Enclosure went on unimpeded, in fact abetted, by parliamentary enactment. The Bank of England, founded in 1694, brought the same benefits to English investors that the Bank of Amsterdam had been offering the Dutch for almost a century.

The Navigation Act, first passed in 1651, allowed all English shippers to carry goods anywhere, replacing the old system that had restricted trade with certain areas to specific traders. The Act also required that all goods be carried in English ships, allowing merchants, as Christopher Hill writes, "to buy English and colonial exports cheap and sell them dear abroad, to buy foreign goods cheap and sell them dear in England."[1] English shippers also gained the profits of the carrying trade, one factor leading to the displacement of the Dutch by the English as the leading power in international commerce after 1660.

France and Spain France benefited from commercial and industrial expansion, but not to the same degree as England. A principal reason for this was the aristocratic structure of French society. Family ties and social intercourse between gentry and merchants, such as existed in England, were largely absent in France. Consequently, the French aristocracy remained contemptuous of commerce. Also inhibiting economic expansion were the guilds—remnants of the Middle Ages that restricted competition and production. In France there was relatively less room than in England for the merchant capitalist operating outside the guild structures.

Spain presents an even clearer example of failure to grasp the opportunities afforded by the price revolution. By the third quarter of the sixteenth century, Spain possessed the makings of economic expansion: unrivaled amounts of capital in the form of silver, a large and growing population, rising consumer demand, and a vast overseas empire. These factors did not bear fruit because the Spanish value system regarded business as a form of social heresy. The Spanish held in high esteem those gentlemen who possessed land gained through military service and crusading ardor, which enabled them to live on rents and privileges. So commerce and industry remained contemptible pursuits.

Numerous wars in the sixteenth century (with France, the Lutheran princes, the Ottoman Turks, the Dutch, and the English)

put an increasing strain on the Spanish treasury, even with the annual shipments of silver from the New World. Spain spent its resources on maintaining and extending its imperial power and Catholicism, rather than on investing in economic expansion. In the end, the wars cost even more than Spain could handle. The Dutch, for a time, and the English and the French, more permanently, displaced Spain as the great power. The English and the Dutch had taken advantage of the opportunities presented by the price revolution; the Spanish had not.

The Growth of Capitalism

What Is Capitalism?

The changes described—especially in England and the Netherlands—represent a crucial stage in the development of the modern economic system known as *capitalism*. This is a system of *private enterprise:* the main economic decisions (what, how much, where, and at what price to produce, buy, and sell) are made by private individuals in their capacity as either owners, workers, or consumers. Capitalism is also said to be a system of *free enterprise:* the basic decisions are not left to individuals only; these decisions are also made in response to market forces. People are free, in other words, to obey the law of supply and demand. When goods and labor are scarce, prices and wages rise; when they are plentiful, prices and wages fall.

In the Middle Ages, capitalistic enterprise had not been widespread because the market, and therefore the operation of market forces, were severely restricted. The vast majority of people lived as self-sufficient subsistence farmers (peasants or serfs) on the land. There was some trade and a few small cities, especially in Italy, where capitalistic enterprise was conducted, but this commerce accounted for only a tiny fraction of total economic activity. Even in the cities, capitalistic forms of enterprise were hampered by guild restrictions, which set limits on production, wages, and prices without regard for market forces. In addition, the economic decay of the fourteenth and early fifteenth centuries did not predispose those who had surplus money to gamble on the future.

But conditions changed in certain quarters beginning in the fifteenth and sixteenth centuries, generating the incentive to invest— to take risks for future profit rather than to consume. This process was due, more than anything else, to the economic situation prevailing in Europe between 1450 and 1600.

The Fostering of Mercantile Capitalism

Several conditions fostered a sustained incentive to invest and reinvest—a basic factor in the emergence of modern capitalism. One was the price revolution stemming from a supply of basic commodities that could not keep pace with rising demand. Prices continued to climb, creating the most powerful incentive of all to invest rather than to consume. Why spend now, those with surplus wealth must have asked, when investment in commercial farming, mining, shipping, and publishing (to name a few important outlets) is almost certain to yield greater wealth in the future? The price revolution reduced the risk involved in investment, thus helping to overcome the wealthy's resistance to engaging in capitalistic enterprise.

Another condition that encouraged investment was that wealth was distributed in a way that promoted investment. Three distinct patterns of distribution worked to this effect. First, inflation widened the gap between rich and poor during the sixteenth century; the rich who chose to invest garnered increasing amounts of wealth, which probably added to their incentive to go on investing. Because of the growing population and the resulting shortage of jobs, employers could pay lower and lower wages; thus, again, their profits increased, encouraging reinvestment. Merchant capitalists were an important group of investors who gained from these factors.

As they grew, they were able to exercise a controlling influence in the marketplace because they operated on a large scale, from regional to international; thus they were able to dictate terms of production and employment, displacing the local guilds. This displacement represents another factor in the pattern of wealth distribution (and redistribution) favorable to investment and growth. Mercantile capitalism did not benefit all alike; in fact it produced increasing inequities between rich and poor, owners and workers, independent merchant-capitalists and local guildsmen.

The second pattern of wealth distribution that encouraged investment grew out of the practice of primogeniture wherever (as in England) it was the unwritten custom. The concentration of inherited property in the hands of the eldest child (usually the oldest son) meant that he had sufficient wealth to be persuaded to invest at least part of it. Any younger sons were left to make their own way in the world and often turned their drive and ambition into profits.

Finally, a pattern of international distribution of wealth promoted investment in some lands. The classic example is that of Spain in relation, say, to England. Spain in the sixteenth century devoted its wealth and energies to religious war and empire and relied on producers elsewhere for many of its supplies. So Spanish treasure was exported to England to pay for imports, stimulating investment there rather than in Spain. Capitalism did not develop everywhere at the same pace, and as the Spanish case shows, the very conditions that discouraged it in one place encouraged it somewhere else.

Another stimulus for investment came from government—and this occurred in two ways. First, governments acted as giant consumers whose appetites throughout the early modern period were expanding. Merchants who supplied governments with everything from guns to frescoes not only prospered, but were led to reinvest because of the constancy and growth of government demand. Governments also sponsored new forms of investment, whether to supply the debauched taste for new luxuries at the king's court or to meet the requirements of the military. Private investors also reaped incalculable advantages from overseas empires. Colonies supplied cheap raw materials and cheap (slave) labor and served as markets for exports. They greatly stimulated the construction of both ships and harbor facilities and the sale of insurance.

The second government stimulus was state policies meant to increase investment, which they no doubt sometimes, although not always, did. Collectively, these policies constitute what is known as *mercantilism:* the conscious pursuit by governments of those courses supposed to augment national wealth and power. One characteristic expression of mercantilism was the pursuit of a favorable balance of international payments. According to conventional wisdom, wealth from trade was measured in gold and silver, of which there was believed to be a more or less fixed quantity. The state's goal in international trade became to sell more abroad than it bought, that is, to establish a favorable balance of payments. When the amount received for sales abroad was greater than that spent for purchases, the difference would be an influx of precious metal into the state. By this logic, mercantilists were led to argue for the goal of national sufficiency: a country should try to supply most of its own needs to keep imports to a minimum. This argument, of course, ignored the fact that in international trade, the more a country buys, the more it can sell. The English were the first to see this fact and relinquish mercantilistic thinking, if only for a time, during the second half of the seventeenth century.

Mercantilism did have a positive side. Governments increased economic activity by employing the poor, subsidizing new industries, and chartering companies to engage in overseas trade. Particularly valuable were the steps taken by states to break down local trade barriers, such as guild regulations and internal tariffs, in an attempt to create national markets and internal economic unity.

The English also saw that mercantilistic calculations of national wealth should be made over the long run. For example, Thomas Mun (1571–1641) argued that a country might import more than it exported in the short run and still come out ahead in the end, because raw materials that are imported and then reprocessed for export will eventually yield a handsome profit.

In addition, Thomas Mun was one of the first to see the virtues of *consumerism,* a phenomenon that is still extremely important for achieving sustained economic growth. Speaking of foreign trade, he maintained that the more English merchants did to advertise English goods to potential customers, the greater the overseas market for those goods would be. In other words, demand can be *created.* Just as there is an urge to invest and make profits, so there is an appetite to consume and enjoy the products of industry, and both inclinations have played their part in the growth of capitalism. Nor was the message restricted to the foreign market. Between 1660 and 1750 England became the world's first consumer society: more and more people had more and more money to spend, and they acquired a taste for conspicuous consumption (which had always before been confined to the aristocracy). Discretionary goods were available—lace, tobacco, housewares, flowers—and consumers wanted them. Concomitantly, just as today, the more stimulus there was to buy, the harder the consumer worked, which induced further growth.

The price revolution, the concentration of wealth in private hands, and government activity combined to provide the foundation for sustained investment and for the emergence of mercantile capitalism. This new force in the world should not be confused with industrial capitalism. The latter evolved with the first industrial revolution in eighteenth-century England, but mercantile capitalism paved the way for it.

Chronology 15.1 The Commercial Revolution

1394–1460	Henry the Navigator, prince of Portugal, encourages expansion into Africa for gold and his anti-Muslim crusade
1430	The Portuguese expand into the Canaries and the Azores
1488	Bartholomeu Dias reaches the tip of Africa
1492	Christopher Columbus reaches the Caribbean island of Española on his first voyage; the Jews are expelled from Spain; Granada, the last Muslim kingdom in Spain, is conquered, ending the reconquest
1497	Vasco da Gama sails around Cape of Good Hope (Africa) to India
1509	The Portuguese defeat the Muslim fleet at Diu in the Indian Ocean
1513	Balboa discovers the Pacific Ocean at the Isthmus of Panama
1519–1521	Hernando Cortés conquers the Aztecs in Mexico
1520–1521	Magellan's soldiers circumnavigate the globe
1531–1533	Francisco Pizarro conquers the Incas in Peru
1545	Silver is discovered by the Spaniards at Potosí, Peru
1552	Silver from the New World flows into Europe via Spain, contributing to a price revolution
1590s	The Dutch develop shipping carriers for grain
1602–1609	The Dutch East India Company is founded; the Bank of Amsterdam is founded, expanding credit
1651	The Navigation Act is passed in England to accomplish the goals of mercantilism
1694	The Bank of England is founded

Seventeenth-Century Decline and Renewal

Population began to decline in Spain as early as the 1590s, and by the second quarter of the seventeenth century, it was declining throughout Europe. The decline resulted because during the price revolution demand continued to outrun supply, prices rose, and real wages fell. The diet of the masses deteriorated because they could not earn enough to buy sufficient bread. Bad harvests produced massive famines, and cities were overgrown and increasingly unsanitary. When plague struck, as it continued to do periodically, it did so among a weakened populace and took more lives. Finally, there was the Thirty Years' War (1618–1648) which ravaged the Holy Roman Empire and reduced its population by at least one-third.

The economic consequences of these factors were quick to follow. Prices fell and there was general economic dislocation. The new Atlantic powers, however, responded in a way that would lead to their recovery—England by the last quarter of the century and France by the 1730s. English and French farmers turned increasingly to enclosure and the application of the Dutch technique of convertible husbandry. Initially, these efforts attempted to make up for falling prices by increasing productivity. But over the long run they had the effect of increasing production and of sustaining a growing population.

By the second quarter of the eighteenth century, the population of western Europe was once more growing—but with significant differences from the earlier increase. The food supply tended to keep pace with rising demand, so the prices of basic foodstuffs stabilized and even declined. This achievement had enormous impact on the subsequent history of France and England. At last, enough was produced to feed a growing population without a rise in prices. Less income would have to be spent on food at a time when national income was rising because of expanded production for the needs of a growing population.

Given these developments, who benefited, why, and to what effect? First of all, many peasants could for the first time produce a surplus for market. This increased production meant a rise in income. The largest farmers, curiously enough, probably did not benefit, unless they were also landlords; they had long been producing for the market, sometimes for generations, and their increased production did not make up for the falling off of farm prices.

Second, the landlords' income increased. They had land to rent to the growing number of farmers who engaged in commercial farming and whose growing profits enabled them to pay even higher rents. This tendency was especially prevalent in France. There, enclosure was not widespread, and inherited land was divided among all the children in a family, a practice called *partible inheritance*. As a result, more and more peasants, because of population growth, sought a livelihood from the soil.

Third, there was a growth in the incomes of everyone whose earnings were in excess

of the price of bread. This group would have included at least a majority of the urban population because, of course, bread prices were falling.

Thus the new agronomy produced a situation in which *more and more people had more and more money to spend on, or to invest in, things other than food*—namely, industry and its products. This increasing income manifested itself in rising demand for goods and services. This demand was one of the basic preconditions for the Industrial Revolution in the eighteenth and early nineteenth centuries, particularly in England. Before large-scale industry could come into being, a market for its products was necessary.

In the process of industrialization, England gained the advantage over France largely because of the different patterns that agriculture took in the two countries. Beginning in the 1780s, French agriculture could not sustain the pattern that it had shared with England from the 1730s. By the 1780s, too many people were living on the land in France to allow adequate surpluses in years of poor harvest. At such times, peasants produced only enough to feed themselves, if that, and shortages caused bread prices to soar. Peasant incomes shrank from the lack of a marketable surplus. And higher bread prices reduced consumer spending power. The momentum for industrialization weakened or dissolved, a situation prevailing until the next century. Partible inheritance in France slowed industrial development. Primogeniture and enclosure in England speeded it up.

Toward a Global Economy

The transformations considered in this chapter were among the most momentous in the world's history. In an unprecedented development that may never be repeated, one small part of the world, western Europe, had become lord of the sea-lanes, master of many lands throughout the globe, and the banker and profit-taker in an emerging world economy. Western Europe's global hegemony was to last well into this century. In conquering and settling new lands, Europeans exported Western culture around the globe, a process that accelerated in the twentieth century.

The effects of overseas expansion were profound. The native populations of the New World were decimated. As a result of the labor shortage, millions of blacks were imported from Africa to work as slaves on plantations and in mines. Black slavery would produce large-scale effects on culture, politics, and society to the present day.

The widespread circulation of plant and animal life had great consequences. Horses and cattle were introduced to the New World. (So amazed were the Aztecs to see man on horseback that at first they thought horse and rider were one demonic creature.) In return the Old World was introduced to corn, the tomato, and most important, the potato, which was to become a staple of the northern European diet. Manioc, from which tapioca is made, was transplanted from the New World to Africa where it helped sustain the population.

Western Europe was wrenched out of the subsistence economy of the Middle Ages and launched on a course of sustained economic growth. This transformation resulted from the grafting of traditional forms, like primogeniture and holy war, onto new forces, like global exploration, price revolution, and convertible husbandry. Out of this change emerged the beginnings of a new economic system, mercantile capitalism, which in large measure provided the economic thrust for European world predominance and paved the way for the Industrial Revolution of the eighteenth and nineteenth centuries.

Notes

1. Christopher Hill, *Reformation to Industrial Revolution* (Baltimore: Penguin, 1969), pp. 159–160.

Suggested Reading

Appleby, Joyce, *Economic Thought and Ideology in Seventeenth-Century England* (1978). The invention of a science of economics in the context of an emerging capitalist society.

Boxer, C. R., *The Portuguese Seaborne Empire 1415–1825* (1969). A comprehensive treatment.

Cipolla, Carlo M., *Guns, Sails and Empires* (1965). Connections between technological innovation and overseas expansion, 1400 to 1700.

Davis, David Brion, *The Problem of Slavery in Western Culture* (1966). Authoritative and highly suggestive.

Davis, Ralph, *The Rise of the Atlantic Economies* (1973). A reliable recent survey of early modern economic history.

Elliott, J. H., *The Old World and the New 1492–1650* (1972). The impact of America on early modern Europe.

Haley, K. H. D., *The Dutch in the Seventeenth Century* (1972). A very readable, informative survey.

Hanke, Lewis, *The Spanish Struggle for Justice in the Conquest of America* (1949). A treatment of the priestly view of Indian rights under Spanish rule.

Hill, Christopher, *Reformation to Industrial Revolution* (1969). A concise Marxist interpretation of English economic development.

Kamen, H., *The Iron Century* (1971). Insight into the social and class basis of economic change.

Parry, J. H., *The Age of Reconnaissance* (1963). A short survey of exploration.

Wilson, C., *England's Apprenticeship, 1600–1763* (1965). Authoritative account.

Review Questions

1. What are the links between the Middle Ages and early modern overseas expansion? What were the new forces for expansion operating in early modern Europe?

2. Compare Spanish and Portuguese overseas expansion in terms of their motives, their areas of expansion, and the character of the two empires.

3. What is the connection between the price revolution and overseas expansion? What was the principal cause of the price revolution? Why?

4. What was *enclosure*? How did the price revolution encourage it?

5. Compare open-field farming and enclosure in terms of who worked the land, how the land was worked, and what the results of each method were.

6. What was *convertible husbandry*, where did it originate, and why was it such an important innovation?

7. What factors favored Spanish agricultural and commercial development, and why, nevertheless, did it stall later?

8. Compare farming in England with that in France and Spain. Why did the English method yield the most?

9. What was the *putting-out system*? What were its advantages over the guilds and its long-term effects?

10. What is *mercantile capitalism*? What three patterns of the distribution of wealth fostered its development?

11. How did economic decline in the seventeenth century provide conditions for the subsequent economic recovery and progress? Where was this progress greatest, and why?

12. How did the commercial revolution produce a global economy? What were its effects?

16

The Rise of Sovereignty: Transition to the Modern State

From the thirteenth to the seventeenth century a new and unique form of political organization emerged in the West: the dynastic or national state, which harnessed the power of its nobility and the material resources of its territory. Neither capitalism nor technology could have enabled the West to dominate other lands and peoples had it not been for the power of the European states. They channeled and organized violence into the service of national power by directing the energies of the ruling elite into national service and international competition. A degree of domestic stability ensued, and the states encouraged commerce and industry, which could in turn be taxed. Although they nurtured the aristocracy, many states also required that both lord and peasant serve in national armies for the purpose of foreign conquest as well as for defense.

At every turn the pivotal figures in the development of states were the kings. Europeans, whether landed or urban, grudgingly gave allegiance to these ambitious, and at times ruthless, authority figures. In general, a single monarch seemed the only alternative to the even more brutal pattern of war and disorder so basic to the governing habits of the feudal aristocracy. In the process of increasing their own power, the kings of Europe not only subordinated the aristocracy to their needs and interests but also gained firm control over the Christian churches in their territories. Gradually, religious zeal was made compatible with and largely supportive of the state's goals, rather than papal dictates or even universal Christian aspirations.

Various components characterized the dynastic states of the early modern period. All states required a language that was dominant enough to be used for government. Moreover, states maintained standing armies as soon as the system of tax collection gave them a sufficient economic foundation to do so. If kings were to subdue local aristocrats and terrify other kings, armies were essential, and they were established by the seventeenth century in Spain, France, and finally late in the century in England. These domestic armies, often used in conjunction with foreign mercenaries, were crucial to the maintenance and extension of state power. In many early modern states a vast bureaucracy coordinated and administered the activities of the central government and its army. Another characteristic was that the creation of a strong central government required a struggle between the monarch and localized systems of power, feudal aristocrats, bishops, and even occasionally representative assemblies.

Where early modern European monarchs succeeded in subduing, destroying, or reconstituting local aristocratic and ecclesiastical power systems, dynastic states were formed. Where the monarchs failed, as they did in the Holy Roman Empire and Italy, no viable states evolved until well into the nineteenth century. Those failures derived from the independent authority of local princes or city-states, and in the case of Italy, from the decentralizing influence of papal authority. In the Holy Roman Empire, feudal princes found allies in the newly formed Protestant communities, and in such a situation, religion worked as a decentralizing force. Successful early modern kings had to bring the churches under their authority and subordinate religion to the needs of the state. They did so not by separating church and state (as was later done in the United States), but rather by linking their subjects' religious identity with the national identity. For example, in England by the late seventeenth century, to be a true Protestant was to be a true English subject, while in Spain the same equation operated for the Catholic (as opposed to the Muslim or the Jew, who came to be regarded as non-Spanish).

The elements that made up the early modern state evolved slowly and at first haltingly. In the thirteenth century, most Europeans still identified themselves with their localities: their villages, manors, or towns. They gave political allegiance to their local lord or bishop. They knew little, and probably cared less, about the activities of the king and his court, except when the monarch called on them for taxes or military service. By the late seven-

teenth century, in extreme contrast, aristocrats in many European countries defined the extent of their political power in terms of their relationship to king and court. By then the lives of very ordinary people were being affected by national systems of tax collection, by the doctrines and practices of national churches, and by conscription.

Increasingly prosperous town dwellers, the bourgeoisie, realized also that their prosperity hinged, in part, on court-supported foreign and domestic policies. If the king assisted their commercial ventures, the bourgeoisie gave their support to the growth of a strong central state. Only in two states, England and the Netherlands, did the strikingly successful bourgeoisie manage to redistribute political power so that by the late seventeenth century, it could be shared by a monarchy (or a social oligarchy) and a powerful representative assembly.

The Rise of Hapsburg Spain

The Spanish political experience of the sixteenth century stands as one of the most extraordinary in the history of modern Europe. Spanish kings built a dynastic state that burst through its frontiers and encompassed Portugal, part of Italy, the Netherlands, and enormous areas in the New World. Spain became an intercontinental empire—the first in the West since Roman times.

In the eighth and ninth centuries, the Muslims controlled all Spain except for some tiny Christian kingdoms in the far north. Beginning in the ninth century, the Christian states began a 500-year struggle—the Reconquest—to drive the Muslims from the Iberian Peninsula. By the middle of the thirteenth century, Granada in the south was all that remained of Muslim lands in Spain.

Hispania as a concept and geographical area existed in Roman times, and citizens of Portugal, Castile, Aragon, Catalonia, and Andalusia, to name only the larger and more important areas of the peninsula, recognized a certain common identity—no more, no less.

Until 1469, Spain had not existed as a political entity. In that year, Ferdinand, heir to the throne of Aragon, married his more powerful and prosperous cousin, Isabella, heiress of Castile. Yet even after the unification of Castile and the Crown of Aragon, relations among the various and fiercely independent provinces of Spain were often tense.

Rich from the wool trade and more populous than other provinces, Castile became the heart of Spain. But the Crown of Aragon (Catalonia, Aragon, and Valencia) supplied commercial expertise to the union, as well as control over the western Mediterranean. Ferdinand's Aragon also contributed a vibrant tradition of constitutional government characterized by a concern for individual and class rights, as distinct from the rights of kings. Perhaps no territory in Europe possessed a more vital set of representative and judicial institutions. Aragonese independence is best summed up in the famous oath said to be taken by its nobility to the king: "We who are as good as you swear to you who are no better than we to accept you as our king and sovereign lord, provided you observe all our liberties and laws; but, if not, not."[1] Obviously any monarch set upon increasing royal authority in Aragon would have to proceed cautiously.

Ferdinand and Isabella

Ferdinand and Isabella displayed extraordinary statecraft in managing the various areas within their newly formed land. The success of their rule (1479–1516) laid the foundations for Spanish empire and Spanish domination of European affairs throughout the sixteenth century. They used Castile as their power base and set about ridding it of its military caste—those aristocrats who, in effect, operated from their fortified castles like private kings waging at will their private wars. In contrast, Ferdinand and Isabella rationalized and modernized the Spanish state's government.

Beginning in the late fifteenth century, Castilian dominance over government and administration was recognized and continually preserved, yet Aragonese rights were left more or less intact. Ferdinand and Isabella never established a unified state: there was no common currency and no single legal or tax system. Commonality of interests, rather than of administration and law, united Spain; and certain policies of Ferdinand and Isabella contributed decisively to this unity. They sought the reconquest of Spanish territory still held by the Muslims, and concomitantly they sought to assert the uniquely Christian character of the peninsula, to bring the Spanish church into alliance with the state.

Given the territorial and legal divisions within Spain, it is understandable why the church became the only universal institution in Spain, and why its legal arm, the Inquisition, played such an important role in the intellectual and religious life of this most disparate of kingdoms. It was most important for the development of strong monarchy that the Spanish rulers bring the church's interests in line with their own. Ferdinand and Isabella's alliance with the church and their war against the Muslims in the southern portion of the peninsula were interrelated. A crusade against the Muslim infidel presupposed an energetic church and a deep and militant Catholicism with the rulers committed to the aims of the church, and the church to the aims of the rulers. While other Europeans, partly under the impact of the Renaissance, questioned the church's leadership and attacked its corruption, the Catholic Kings (as Ferdinand and Isabella were called) reformed the church, making it responsive to their needs and also invulnerable to criticism. Popular piety and royal policy led in 1492 to a victory over Granada, the last Muslim-ruled territory in Spain.

The five-hundred-year struggle for Christian hegemony in the Iberian Peninsula left the Spanish fiercely religious and strongly suspicious of foreigners. Despite centuries of intermarriage with non-Christians, by the early sixteenth century, purity of blood and

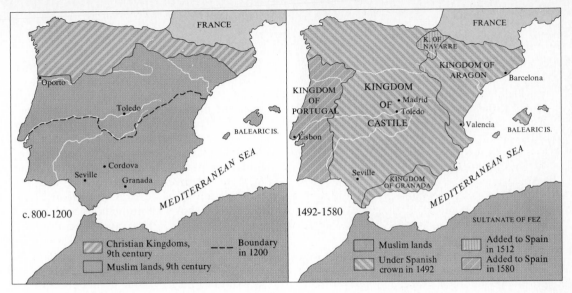

Map 16.1 Spain during the Ninth to Sixteenth Centuries

orthodoxy of faith became necessary for, and synonymous with Spanish identity. In 1492 the Jews and the Muslims were physically expelled from Spain or forced to convert. This process of detection and conversion was supervised by the church, or more precisely, by the Inquisition. Run by clerics but responsive to state policies, the Inquisition existed to enforce religious uniformity and to ferret out the increasing numbers of Muslims and Jews who ostensibly converted to Catholicism but who remained secretly loyal to their own religions. The Inquisition developed extremely sophisticated systems of interrogation, used its legal right to torture as well as burn heretics, and eventually extended its authority to Christians as well. It represented the dark side of Spanish genius at conquest and administration, and its shadow stretched down through the centuries well into the twentieth.

The wars against the Muslims gave the Spanish invaluable military experience and rendered their army one of the finest in Europe. The wars also created a pattern in the growth of the Spanish empire: it victories always lay in the south—in Italy, in Latin America, and against the Turks—while its defeats and setbacks occurred in the north—

in the Netherlands, in opposition to the Lutheran Reformation in the Holy Roman Empire, and against England.

With a superior army, with the great magnates pacified, and with the church and the Inquisition under monarchical control, the Catholic Kings expanded their interests and embarked on an imperialist foreign policy in Europe and abroad that had extraordinary consequences. Ultimately it made Spain dominant in the New World.

Ferdinand and Isabella gambled on Columbus's voyage and they won. Then, beginning in 1519, the conquistador Cortés defeated the Aztec nation with 600 foot soldiers and 16 horses, a feat that cannot be explained simply by citing the superior technology of the Spanish. This conquest rested primarily on the character and achievements of Spain's lesser gentry—the hidalgos. The willingness of the hidalgos to serve crown and church was equaled or surpassed only by their desire to get rich. Lured by gold and land, they made excellent soldiers and explorers in foreign lands; while at home they entered the governmental and ecclesiastical bureaucracies. They formed the core of a loyal civil service that was responsive to the needs of the monarchy and distrustful of and resentful toward

Titian (1477–1576): Portrait of the Emperor Charles V, 1548. With the wealth of the New World and the Hapsburg domination of the Holy Roman Empire, Charles V was the greatest ruler of his age. Titian's portraits revealed the characters of his subjects. (*Bayerischen Staatsgemäldesammlungen, Munich*)

the great nobles, or *grandees*. Spanish bureaucracy in the sixteenth century became a primary vehicle for social mobility, and the foreign and domestic policies initiated by Ferdinand and Isabella and continued by their successors received their greatest support from the gentry.

The Reign of Charles V: King of Spain and Holy Roman Emperor

Dynastic marriage constituted another crucial part of Ferdinand and Isabella's foreign policy. They strengthened their ties with the Austrian and Flemish (or Burgundian) kings by marrying one of their children, Juana (called *the Mad* for her insanity) to Philip the Fair, son of Maximilian of Austria, the head of the ruling Hapsburg family. Philip and Juana's son Charles (1516–1556) inherited the kingdom of Ferdinand and Isabella; through his other grandparents, he also inherited the Netherlands, Austria, Sardinia, Sicily, the kingdom of Naples, and Franche Comté. In 1519 he was also elected Charles V, Holy Roman Emperor. Charles became the most powerful ruler in Europe, but his reign also saw the emergence of political, economic, and social problems that eventually led to Spain's decline.

Charles's inheritance was simply too vast to be governed effectively, but that was only dimly perceived at the time. The Lutheran Reformation proved to be the first successful challenge to Hapsburg power. It was the first phase of a religious and political struggle between Catholic Spain and Protestant Europe that would dominate the last half of the sixteenth century.

Charles established a court filled with foreigners and spent much of his time in the northern provinces, while still collecting taxes in Castile. These policies produced a full-scale revolt in the Castilian towns in 1520 and 1521. Led by artisans and merchants, the revolt took on elements of a class war against the landed nobility. The nobles, in turn, rallied around Charles's royal army, and eventually the revolt was crushed. But the event and its outcome reveals much about the nature of Spanish absolutism. It relied on its aristocracy (unlike the French kings who tried to suppress their aristocrats), and it never encouraged the growth of a bourgeoisie.

The achievements of Charles V's reign rested on the twin instruments of army and bureaucracy. The Hapsburg empire in the New World was vastly extended and, on the whole, effectively administered and policed. Out of this sprawling empire with its newly enslaved native populations came the greatest flow of gold and silver ever witnessed by Europeans. Constant warfare in Europe, coupled with the immensity of the Spanish administrative network, required a steady intake of capital. However, this easy access to capital appears to have been detrimental in the long run to the Spanish economy (see Chapter 15). There was no incentive for the development of domestic industry, bourgeois entrepreneurship, or international commerce. Moreover, constant war engendered and perpetuated a social order geared to the aggrandizement of a military class, rather than to the development of a commercial class. And while war expanded Spain's power, it also increased the national debt. The weak economic foundation of Spanish power in the sixteenth century, combined with numerous expensive wars, sowed the seeds for the financial crises of the 1590s and beyond, and for the eventual decline of Spain as a world power. But also setting the stage for Spain's troubles were events in the two emerging powers to the north.

The Growth of French Power

Two states in the early modern period succeeded most effectively in consolidating the power of their central governments: France and England. Each became a model of a very different form of statehood. The French model emphasized, at every turn, the glory of the king and, by implication, the sovereignty of the state and its right to stand above the interests of its subjects. France's monarchy became *absolute*. Yet this evolution of the French state was a very gradual process, one not completed until the late seventeenth century.

When Hugh Capet became king of France in 987 he was, in relation to France's other great feudal lords, merely first among equals. He could demand military service from his vassals (only forty days a year) and was regarded as the protector of the church. But he only ruled over a small area around Paris, and the succession of his heirs to the kingship was by no means secure. Yet even at this early date, his title and his person were regarded as sacred. He was God's anointed, and his power, such as it was, rested on divine authority.

From this small power base, more symbolic than real, Hugh Capet's successors extended their territory and dominion at the expense of feudal lords' power. By 1328, when the Capetian family became extinct and the crown passed to the Valois family, the Capetians had made the French monarch the ruler of areas as distant from Paris as Languedoc in the south and Flanders in the north. To administer their territories, the Capetians established an efficient bureaucracy composed of townsmen and trustworthy lesser nobles who unlike the great feudal lords, owed their wealth and status directly to the king. These royal officials, an essential element of monarchical power, collected the king's feudal dues and administered justice. At the same time, French kings emphasized that they had been selected by God to rule, a theory known as the divine right of kings. This theory gave monarchy a sanctity that various French kings used to enforce their commands over rebellious feudal lords and to defend themselves against papal claims of dominance over the French church.

Yet medieval French kings never sought absolute power. Not until the seventeenth century was the power base of the French monarchy consolidated to the extent that kings and their courts could attempt to rule without formal consultations with their subjects. In the Middle Ages the French monarchs recognized the rights of, and consulted with, representative assemblies called *Estates*. These assemblies (whether regional or national) were composed of deputies drawn from the various elites: the clergy, the nobility, and significantly, the leadership of cities and towns in a given region. The Estates met as circumstance—wars, taxes, local disputes—warranted, and the nationally representative assembly, the *Estates General*, was always summoned by the king. In general, medieval French kings consulted these assemblies to give legitimacy to their demands and credibility to their administration. They also recognized that the courts—especially the highest court, the Parlement of Paris—had the right to administer the king's justice with a minimum of royal interference. Medieval kings did not see themselves as originators of law; they were its guarantors and administrators.

War came to serve the interests of a monarchy bent on consolidating its power and authority. As a result of the Hundred Years' War (1338–1453), the English were eventually driven from France and their claims to the French throne dashed. In the process of war and taxation to meet its burden, the French monarchy grew richer. The necessities of war enabled the French kings to levy new taxes, often enacted without the consent of the Estates General, and to maintain a large standing army under royal command. The Hundred Years' War also provoked allegiance to the king as the visible symbol of France. The war heightened the French sense of national identity; the English were a common enemy, discernibly different in manners, language, dress, and appearance.

With revenue and an army at their disposal, the French kings subsequently embarked on territorial aggrandizement. Charles VIII (1483–1498) invaded Italy in 1494. Machiavelli, a shrewd assessor of the implications of power, observed that while Italy's weakness derived from its lack of unity, the power of this new cohesive state of France derived in large measure from the strength of its prince and his huge and mostly native-born army. Although the French gained little territory from the Italian campaign, they did effectively challenge Spanish power in Italy and intimidate an already weakened papacy.

Religion and the French State

In every emergent state, tension existed between the monarch and the papacy. At issue was control over the church within that territory—over its personnel, wealth, and, of course, its pulpits, from which an illiterate majority learned what their leaders believed they should know, not only in matters of religious belief but also about questions of obedience to civil authority. The monarch's power to make church appointments could ensure a complacent church. A church that was willing to preach about the king's divine right and was tractable on matters of taxes was especially important in France because legally the church had to pay no taxes and only had to give donations to the crown. Centuries of tough bargaining with the papacy paid off when in 1516 Francis I concluded the Concordat of Bologna; Pope Leo X permitted the French king to nominate, and therefore effectively to appoint, men of his choice to all the highest offices in the French church.

The Concordat of Bologna laid the foundation for what became known as the *Gallican church*—a term signifying the immense power and authority of the Catholic church in France—which was sanctioned and overseen by the French kings. By the early sixteenth century, religious homogeneity had strengthened the central government at the expense of papal authority and of traditional privileges enjoyed by local aristocracy. This ecclesiastical and religious settlement lay at the heart of monarchical authority. Consequently, the Protestant Reformation threatened the very survival of France as a unified state. Throughout the early modern period the French kings had assumed that their states must be governed by one king, one faith, and one set of laws. Any alternative to that unity offered local power elites, whether aristocratic or cleric, the opportunity to channel religious dissent into their service. Once linked, religious and political opposition to any central government could be extremely dangerous.

Francis I (1515–1547) perceived that Protestantism in France would undermine the sacredness of his office, challenge his authority, and diminish his control over church officials. In 1534 the king, in conjunction with the court of Paris (the Parlement), declared Protestant beliefs and practices illegal and punishable by fine, imprisonment, and even execution. The Protestant reformer Calvin and his friends fled from Paris and eventually to Geneva (see Chapter 14), but they never abandoned the hope of converting Francis and France to the Protestant cause.

During the decades that followed, partly through the efforts of the Huguenot underground and partly because the French king and his ministers vacillated in their efforts at persecution, the Protestant minority grew in strength and dedication. By challenging the authority of the Catholic church, Protestants were also inadvertently challenging royal authority, for the French church and the French monarchy supported each other. Protestantism became the basis for a political movement of an increasingly revolutionary nature.

From 1562 to 1598, France experienced waves of religious wars that cost the king control over vast areas of the kingdom. Protestantism became for some adherents a vehicle for expressing their rage against the French church and the increasing power of the Valois kings. The great aristocratic families, the Guise for the Catholics and the Bourbons for the Protestants, drew up armies that scourged the land, killing and maiming their religious opponents. When entwined with religion, local grievances for a time proved capable of dismantling the authority of the central government. In Protestant urban centers, townsmen asserted their right to control local government, as well as to worship publicly in the Protestant manner. They allied with those aristocrats who would convert to the Reformation, for whatever reasons. The French Catholics, on the other hand, turned to the House of Guise for protection—a vivid reminder of the strength of feudal elites centuries after feudalism as an institution had

Francis I of France, by Joos Van Cleve (1485–1540). Francis I was a true Renaissance prince, power-hungry yet a patron of the arts. The aged Leonardo da Vinci ended his days at Francis's court at Amboise as guest of the French king. Francis was also a brilliant politician who helped found the Gallican Church through his Concordat of Bologna with Pope Leo X. Henceforth, the French monarchs alone were to appoint men of their choice to church offices in France. (*Cincinnati Art Museum; Bequest of Mary M. Emery*)

ceased to be the main expression of political authority.

In 1579, extreme Huguenot theorists published the *Vindiciae contra Tyrannos*. This theoretical statement combined with a call to action was the first of its kind in early modern times. It justified rebellion against, and even the execution of, an unjust king. European monarchs might claim power and divinely sanctioned authority, but by the late sixteenth century, their subjects had available the moral justification to oppose by force, if necessary, their monarch's will, and this justification rested on Scripture and religious conviction. Significantly, this same treatise was translated into English in 1648, a year before Parliament publicly executed Charles I, king of England.

The Valois kings floundered in the face of this kind of politico-religious opposition. The era of royal supremacy instituted by Francis I came to an abrupt end during the reign of his successor Henry II (1547–1559). Wed to Catherine de Medici, a member of the powerful Italian banking family, Henry occupied himself not with the concerns of government, but with the pleasures of the hunt. The sons who succeeded Henry—Francis II (1559–1560), Charles IX (1560–1574), and Henry III (1574–1589)—were uniformly weak. In this power vacuum, their mother Catherine emerged as virtual ruler—a queen despised for her foreign and nonaristocratic lineage, for the fact that she was a woman, and for her propensity for dangerous intrigue. One of the most hated figures of her day, Catherine de Medici defies dispassionate assessment. She ordered the execution of thousands of Protestants by royal troops in Paris—the infamous St. Bartholomew's Day Massacre (1572) which, with the blood bath that followed, became both a symbol and a legend in subsequent European history: a symbol of the excesses of religious zeal and a legend of Protestant martyrdom that gave renewed zeal to the cause of international Protestantism.

The civil wars begun in 1562 were renewed in the massacre's aftermath. They dragged on until the death of the last Valois king in 1589. The Valois failure to produce a male heir to the throne placed Henry, duke of Bourbon and a Protestant, in line to succeed to the French throne. Realizing that the overwhelmingly Catholic population would not accept a Protestant king, Henry (apparently without much regret) renounced his adopted religion and embraced the church. His private religious beliefs may never be known, but outward conformity to the religion of the Catholic majority was the only means to effect peace and re-establish political stability. Under the reign of Henry IV (1589–1610) the French

throne acquired its central position in national politics. Henry granted to his Protestant subjects and former followers a degree of religious toleration through the Edict of Nantes (1598), but they were never welcomed in significant numbers into the royal bureaucracy. Throughout the seventeenth century, every French king attempted to undermine the Protestants' regional power bases and ultimately to destroy their religious liberties.

The Consolidation of French Monarchical Power

The defeat of Protestantism as a national force set the stage for the final consolidation of the French state in the seventeenth century under the great Bourbon kings, Louis XIII and Louis XIV. Louis XIII (1610–1643) realized that his rule depended on an efficient and trustworthy bureaucracy, an ever-replenishable treasury, and constant vigilance against the localized claims to power by the great aristocracy and by the Protestant cities and towns. Many of the latter were capable of taking military action against the central government or even of forming alliances with foreign princes. Cardinal Richelieu, who served as Louis XIII's chief minister from 1624 to 1642, became the great architect of French absolutism.

Richelieu was the king's loyal servant; in this way he served the state. His morality rested on one sacred principle embodied in the phrase he invented: *raison d'état*, "reason of state." For Richelieu the state's necessities and the king's absolute authority were synonymous; one was inconceivable without the other. In accordance with his political philosophy, Richelieu brought under control the disruptive and antimonarchical elements within French society. He increased the power of the central bureaucracy, attacked the power of independent, and often Protestant, towns and cities, and persecuted the Huguenots. Above all, he humbled the great nobles by limiting their effectiveness as councilors to

Map 16.2 Europe, 1648 ▶

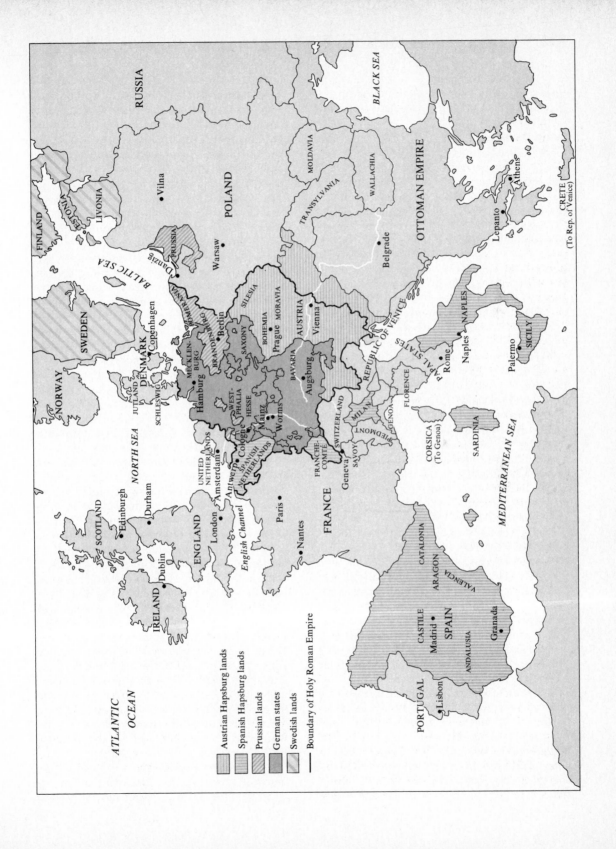

ATLANTIC OCEAN

NORWAY

SWEDEN

FINLAND

ESTONIA

LIVONIA

RUSSIA

Vilna

POLAND

Warsaw

Danzig

PRUSSIA

POMERANIA

BRANDENBURG

Berlin

MECKLEN-BURG

BALTIC SEA

Copenhagen

DENMARK

JUTLAND

SCHLESWIG

Hamburg

NORTH SEA

Edinburgh

SCOTLAND

Durham

Dublin

IRELAND

London

ENGLAND

English Channel

UNITED NETHERLANDS

Amsterdam

Antwerp

SPANISH NETHERLANDS

Cologne

WEST-PHALIA

HESSE

Mainz

Worms

Paris

Nantes

FRANCE

FRANCHE-COMTÉ

SAXONY

SILESIA

BOHEMIA

MORAVIA

Prague

BAVARIA

Augsburg

AUSTRIA

Vienna

SWITZERLAND

Geneva

SAVOY

PIEDMONT

MILAN

GENOA

GENOA

REPUBLIC OF VENICE

PAPAL STATES

FLORENCE

Rome

Naples

NAPLES

Palermo

SICILY

CORSICA (To Genoa)

SARDINIA

MEDITERRANEAN SEA

MOLDAVIA

TRANSYLVANIA

WALLACHIA

Belgrade

OTTOMAN EMPIRE

BLACK SEA

Athens

Lepanto

CRETE (To Rep. of Venice)

PORTUGAL

Lisbon

CASTILE

Madrid

SPAIN

ARAGON

CATALONIA

VALENCIA

ANDALUSIA

Granada

Austrian Hapsburg lands

Spanish Hapsburg lands

Prussian lands

German states

Swedish lands

Boundary of Holy Roman Empire

the king and by prohibiting their traditional privileges, like using a duel rather than court action to settle grievances.

Reason of state also guided Richelieu's foreign policy. Since the treaty of Cateau-Cambrésis (1559) that ended nearly a century of French-Spanish rivalry, both countries had ceased their armed hostilities to concentrate on the threat posed to internal order by the Protestant Reformation. This relative peace had enhanced Spanish power at the expense of the French, yet both countries were Catholic powers, interrelated by aristocratic marriages. When Richelieu came to power at the French court in 1624, the king and his mother were pursuing a policy of appeasement toward the Spanish. But reason of state, as Richelieu saw it, necessitated that France turn against Spain and enter on the Protestant and hence anti-Spanish side the war that was raging at the time in the Holy Roman Empire. The outcome of France's entry into the Thirty Years' War (1618–1648) produced a decided victory for French power on the Continent.

By the time of his death in 1642, Richelieu had established certain practices and policies that were continued by his successors to great effect. First, the avaricious and unprincipled Cardinal Mazarin, who took charge during the minority of Louis XIV (who was five years old when Louis XIII died) continued Richelieu's policies. Then Louis XIV (1643–1715) himself continued the work of his father's minister. The growth of royal absolutism produced a severe reaction among its victims: peasants who paid the burden of the state's taxes; aristocrats who bitterly resented their loss of power; and judges in the royal courts, the parlements, who resented attempts by the king and his ministers to bypass their authority.

Richelieu's policies, as administered by his corrupt successor Mazarin, produced a rebellious reaction, the *Fronde*—a series of street riots that eventually cost the government control over Paris and lasted from 1648 to 1653. Centered in Paris and supported by the great aristocracy, the courts, and Paris's poorer classes, the Fronde threatened to de-

velop into a full-scale uprising. And it might have but for one crucial factor: its leadership was fundamentally divided. Court judges (lesser nobility who had often just risen from the ranks of the bourgeoisie) deeply distrusted the great nobility and refused in the end to make common cause with them. And both groups feared disorder among the urban masses. The discontented elites could not unite, and as a result they could offer no viable alternative except disorder to the rule of absolute kings and their ministers.

When Louis XIV finally assumed responsibility for governing in 1661, he vowed that the events he witnessed as a child during the Fronde would never be repeated. In the course of his reign, he achieved the greatest degree of monarchical power ever witnessed during the early modern period. Indeed, no absolute monarch in Western Europe, before or possibly since, held so much personal authority or commanded such a vast and effective military and administrative machine. Louis XIV's reign represents the culmination of a process of increasing monarchical authority that had been underway for centuries. Yet Louis himself possessed such qualities of intelligence and cunning, coupled with a unique understanding of the capacities of his office, that some attention must be paid to this man who became the envy of his age.

Louis XIV's education had been practical, rather than theoretical. He knew that a hardworking monarch could dispense with chief ministers while still maintaining the effectiveness of his administration. Louis XIV worked long hours at being king, and he never undertook a venture without an eye to his personal grandeur. The sumptuous royal palace at Versailles was built for that reason; similarly, etiquette and style were cultivated there on a scale never before seen in any European court. A lengthy visit to Versailles, a necessity for any aristocrat who wanted his views and needs attended to, could bankrupt the less well-to-do.

Perhaps the most brilliant of Louis XIV's many policies was his treatment of the aristocracy. He simply dispensed with their services as influential advisers; indeed, Louis XIV would not have any minister assume the power that his father had accorded to Richelieu. He treated the aristocrats to elaborate rituals, feasts, processions, displays, and banquets; but amid all the clamor, their political power dwindled. The wiser members of the aristocracy stayed home and managed their estates; others made their way at court as minor functionaries and basked in the glory of the "Sun King."

Louis XIV's domestic policies centered around his incessant search for new revenues. Not only the building of Versailles, but also wars cost money, and Louis XIV waged them to excess. To raise capital, he used the services of Jean Baptiste Colbert, a brilliant administrator who improved methods of tax collecting, promoted new industries, and encouraged international trade. Such ambitious national policies were possible because Louis XIV had inherited an efficient system of administration introduced by Richelieu. Instead of relying on the local aristocracy to collect royal taxes and to administer royal policies, Richelieu had appointed the king's own men as *intendants*, functionaries dispatched with wide powers into the provinces. At first, their missions had been temporary and their success minimal, but gradually they became a permanent feature of royal administration. During the reign of Louis XIV, the country was divided into thirty-two districts controlled by intendants. Operating with a total bureaucracy of about a thousand officials and no longer bothering even to consult the parlements or Estates, Louis XIV ruled absolutely.

Why did such a system of absolute authority work? Did the peasants not revolt? Why did the old aristocracy not rise in rebellion? For the aristocrats, the loss of political authority was not accompanied by a comparable loss in wealth and social position; indeed, quite the contrary was true. During the seventeenth century, the French nobility—2 percent of the population—controlled approximately 20 to 30 percent of the total national income. The church, too, fared well under Louis, re-

Louis XIV by Lorenzo Bernini (1598–1680). The French king called in Italian Baroque architect and sculptor Bernini to redesign the Louvre. Louis rejected his designs for the palace and turned to the more solidly neoclassical work of Perrault. Bernini's bust would also not receive sanction as the official style, but it captures the Sun King and his grandiose ambitions. (*Château de Versailles/Alinari-Scala/Art Resource*)

ceiving good tax arrangements provided it preached about the king's divinely given rights. While there were peasant upheavals throughout the century, the sheer size of the royal army and police—over 300,000 by the end of Louis's reign—made successful revolt nearly impossible. When in the early 1700s a popular religious rebellion led by Protestant visionaries broke out in the south, royal troops crushed it. Thus, absolutism rested on the complicity of the old aristocracy, the self-aggrandizement of government officials, the church's doctrines, the revenues squeezed out of the peasantry, and the power of a huge military machine.

Yet Louis XIV's system was fatally flawed. Without any effective check on his power and dreams of international conquest, there was no limit imposed on the state's capacity to make war or on the ensuing national debt. Louis XIV coveted vast sections of the Holy Roman Empire; he also sought to check Dutch commercial prosperity and had designs on the Spanish Netherlands. By the 1680s, his domestic and foreign policies took on a violently aggressive posture. In 1685, he revoked the Edict of Nantes, forcing many of the country's remaining Protestants to flee. In 1689, he embarked upon a military campaign to secure territory from the Holy Roman Empire. And in 1701, he tried to bring Spain under the control of the Bourbon dynasty. Yet Louis XIV had underestimated the power of his northern rivals, England and the Netherlands. He viewed the apparent chaos of English politics during much of the seventeenth century as an inherent weakness of the English state. The combined power of England and the Netherlands in alliance with the Holy Roman Empire and the Austrians brought defeat to Louis XIV's ambitions.

Louis XIV's long wars emptied the royal treasury. By the late seventeenth century taxes had risen intolerably, and they were essentially levied on those least able to pay—the peasants. In the 1690s, the combination of taxes, bad harvests, and plague led to widespread poverty, misery, and starvation in large areas of France. Thus, for the great majority of French people, absolutism meant a decline in living standards and a significant increase in mortality rates. Absolutism also meant increased surveillance over the population: royal authorities censored books; spied on heretics, Protestants, and freethinkers; and even tortured and executed opponents of state policy.

By 1715, France was a tightly governed society whose treasury was bankrupt. Protestants had been driven into exile or forced to convert. Strict censorship laws closely governed publishing, causing a brisk trade in clandestine books and manuscripts. Direct taxes burdened the poor and were legally evaded by the aristocracy. Critics of state policy within the church had been effectively silenced. And over the long run, foreign wars had brought no significant gains.

In the France of Louis XIV, the dynastic state had reached maturity and had begun to display some of its classic characteristics: centralized bureaucracy; royal patronage to enforce allegiance; a system of taxation universally, but inequitably applied; and suppression of political opposition either through the use of patronage or, if necessary, through force. Another important feature was the state's cultivation of the arts and sciences as a means of increasing national power and prestige. Together, these policies enabled France and its monarchs to achieve political stability, to enforce a uniform system of law, and to channel the country's wealth and resources into the service of the state as a whole.

Yet at his death in 1715, Louis XIV left his successors a system of bureaucracy and taxation that was vastly in need of overhaul but was still locked into the traditional social privileges of the church and nobility to an extent that made reform virtually impossible. The pattern of war, excessive taxation of the lower classes, and expenditure in excess of revenues had severely damaged French finances. Failure to reform the system led to the French Revolution of 1789.

The Growth of Limited Monarchy and Constitutionalism in England

England achieved national unity earlier than any other major European state. Its fortunate geography freed it from the border disputes that plagued emerging states on the Continent. By an accident of fate, its administrative structure also developed in such a way as to encourage centralization. In 1066, William, duke of Normandy and vassal to the French king, had invaded and conquered England, acquiring at a stroke the entire kingdom. In contrast, the French kings took centuries to bring the territory of France under their domain.

The conquering Norman kings and their followers represented a distinct minority in England. Eventually they intermarried and merged with the larger population. In the first century of their rule, the Norman kings frequently lived in France for long periods and depended therefore on an efficient bureaucracy and on their own knowledge of the English kingdom to maintain their power.

Out of necessity, therefore, these medieval Norman kings consulted with their powerful subjects—archbishops, bishops, earls, and barons. By the middle of the thirteenth century, these consultations, or *parlays*, came to be called *parliaments*. Gradually the practice grew of inviting to these parliaments representatives from the shires—knights and burgesses. These lesser-than-noble but often wealthy and prominent representatives of the counties grew to see Parliament as a means of self-expression for redressing their grievances. In turn, the later medieval kings saw Parliament as an effective means of exercising control and of raising taxes. By 1297 the Lords and Commons (as the lower house was called) had obtained the king's agreement that no direct taxes could be levied without their consent. By the fourteenth century, Parliament had become a permanent institution of government. Its power was entirely subservient to the crown, but its right to question royal decisions had been established.

The medieval Parliament possessed two characteristics that distinguished it from its many Continental counterparts, such as the various French Estates. The English Parliament was national and not provincial, and more important, its representatives were elected across caste lines, with voting rights dependent on property and not on noble birth or status. These representatives voted as individuals, not collectively as clergy, nobles, or commoners, that is, as Estates. In the Middle Ages, Parliament and monarchy were in-

terdependent; they were seen not as rivals but as complementary forms of centralized government. Yet that very interdependence would ultimately lead to conflict.

Also emerging during the Middle Ages in England was the constitution—a set of precedents, laws, and royal acts that came to embody the basic principles of government. And in contrast to the French model, England grew to be a *constitutional* monarchy. This theoretical foundation—up to this time not written as a single constitution—grew out of legal practices and customs described under the generic title *common law*. As opposed to feudal law, which applied only to a local region, the common law extended throughout the realm and served as a force for unity.

The strength of the monarchy during the later Middle Ages received dramatic expression in English victories against France during the Hundred Years' War. The power of the English kings enabled them to rally the nobility, who in turn benefited enormously from pillaging France. Only after the revitalization of the French monarchy and its subsequent victories were the English aristocrats forced to take their skills and taste for war back home. The consequences of their return were devastating. Civil war ensued—the Wars of the Roses (1453–1485)—and the medieval war machine turned inward. Gangs of noblemen with retainers roamed the English countryside, and lawlessness prevailed for a generation. Only in 1485 did the Tudor family emerge triumphant.

The Tudor Achievement

Victory in the civil wars allowed Henry VII (1485–1509) to begin the Tudor dynasty. Henry and his successors strove to secure their power by remaking and revitalizing the institutions of government. Henry VII's goal was to bring an unruly nobility into check. Toward this end, he brought commoners into the government; these commoners, unlike the great magnates, could be channeled into royal service because they craved what the

King offered—financial rewards and elevated social status. Although they did not fully displace the aristocracy, commoners were brought into Henry VII's inner circle, into the Privy Council, into the courts, and eventually into all the highest offices of the government. The strength and efficiency of Tudor government was shown during the Reformation when Henry VIII (1509–1547) made himself head of the English church. He was only able to take this giant step toward increasing royal power because his father had restored order and stability. But Henry VIII's step still entailed a struggle (see Chapter 14).

The Protestant Reformation in England was a revolution in royal, as well as ecclesiastical government. It attacked and defeated a main obstacle to monarchical authority—the power of the papacy. At the same time, the Reformation greatly enhanced the power of Parliament. Henry used Parliament to make the Reformation because he knew that he needed the support of the lords, the country gentry, and the merchants. No change in religious practice could be instituted by the monarchy alone. Parliament's participation in the Reformation gave it a greater role and sense of importance than it had ever possessed in the past. Yet the final outcome of this administrative revolution enhanced monarchical power. By the end of his reign, Henry VIII easily possessed as much power as his French rival, Francis I. Indeed, up to the early seventeenth century the history of monarchical power in England, with its absolutist tendencies, was remarkably similar to the Continental pattern.

At Henry's death, the Tudor bureaucracy and centralized government was strained to its utmost, and it survived. The government weathered the reign of Henry's sickly son, Edward VI (1547–1553), with the extreme Protestantism of some of his advisers, and it survived the brief and deeply troubled reign of Henry's first daughter, Mary (1553–1558), who attempted to return England to Catholicism. At Mary's death, England had come dangerously close to the religious instability that undermined the French kings during the final decades of the sixteenth century.

Henry's second daughter, Elizabeth I (whose mother was Anne Boleyn), became queen in 1558. The Elizabethan period was characterized by a heightened sense of national identity. The English Reformation enhanced that sense, as did the increasing fear of foreign invasion by a Catholic power intent on returning England to the papacy. Such was the threat posed by Spain, possessor of twice England's population and of a vast colonial empire. The fear was real enough and was only abated by the defeat—more psychologically than militarily crippling—of the Spanish Armada in 1588. In the seventeenth century, the English would look back on Elizabeth's reign as a golden age. It was the calm before the storm, a time when a new commercial class was formed that, in the seventeenth century, would demand a greater say in government operations.

The Elizabethan age's capitalistic social and economic changes can be seen, in microcosm, by looking at the Durham region in northern England. From 1580 to 1640, a new coal-mining industry developed there through the efforts of entrepreneurs—gentlemen with minor lands whose industry and skill enabled them to exploit their mineral resources. The wool trade also prospered in Durham. By 1600 social and political tensions had developed. The wool merchants and the entrepreneurial gentry were demanding a greater say in governing the region. They were opposed by the traditional leaders of Durham society—the bishops and the dozen or so aristocratic families with major lands and access to the court in London.

This split is described as one between court and country. *Court* refers to the traditional aristocratic magnates, the hierarchy of the church, and royal officialdom. *Country* denotes a loose coalition of merchants and rising agricultural and industrial entrepreneurs from the prosperous gentry class, whose economic worth far exceeded their political power. The pattern found in Durham was repeated in other parts of the country, generally where industry and commerce grew and prospered. The agricultural and industrial gentry grew in social status and wealth. In the seventeenth century, these social and economic tensions would help foster revolution.

By the early seventeenth century in England the descendants of the old feudal aristocracy differed markedly from their Continental counterparts. Their insular isolation from the great wars of the Reformation had produced an aristocracy less military and more commercial in orientation. Furthermore, the lesser ranks of the land-owning aristocracy, gentlemen without titles (the gentry), had prospered significantly in Tudor times. In commercial matters they were often no shrewder than the great landed magnates, but they had in Parliament, as well as in their counties, an effective and institutionalized means of expressing their political interests. The great nobles, on the other hand, had largely abandoned the sword as the primary expression of their political authority without putting anything comparable in its place. Gradually, political initiative was slipping away from the great lords into the hands of a gentry that was commercially and agriculturally innovative, as well as fiercely protective of its local base of political power.

Religion played a vital role in this realignment of political interests and forces. Many of the old aristocracy clung to the Anglicanism of the Henrican Reformation, and in some cases to Catholicism. The newly risen gentry found in the Protestant Reformation of Switzerland and Germany a form of religious worship more suited to their independent and entrepreneurial spirit. They felt that it was their right to appoint their own preachers and that the church should reflect local tastes and beliefs, rather than a series of doctrines and ceremonies inherited from a discredited Catholicism. In late Tudor times gentry and merchant interests fused with Puritanism to produce a political-religious vision with ominous potential.

The English Revolution, 1640–1689

The forces threatening established authority were dealt with ineffectively by the first two Stuart kings—James I (1603—1625), and Charles I (1625–1649). Both believed, as did their Continental counterparts, in royal absolutism. Essentially, these Stuart kings tried to do in England what Louis XIII and later Louis XIV were to do in France: to establish court and crown as the sole governing bodies within the state. What the Stuarts lacked, however, was an adequate social and institutional base for absolutism. They did not possess the vast independent wealth of their French counterparts.

These kings had preached, through the established church, the doctrine of the divine right of kings. James I conducted foreign policy without consulting Parliament. Both tried to revitalize the old aristocracy and to create new peers to re-establish the feudal base of monarchical authority. After 1629, Charles brought his hand-picked advisers into government in the hope that they would purge the church of Puritans and the nation of his opponents. Charles disbanded Parliament and attempted to collect taxes without its consent. These policies ended in disaster.

The English Revolution broke out in 1640 because Charles I needed new taxes to defend the realm against a Scottish invasion. Parliament, finally called after an eleven-year absence, refused his request unless he granted certain basic rights: Parliament to be consulted in matters of taxation, trial by jury, *habeas corpus*, and a truly Protestant church responsive to the beliefs and interests of its laity. Charles refused, for he saw these demands as an assault on royal authority. The ensuing civil war was directed by Parliament, financed by taxes and the merchants, and fought by the New Model Army led by Oliver Cromwell (1599–1658), a Puritan squire who gradually realized his potential for leadership.

The New Model Army was unmatched by any ever seen before in Europe. Parliament's rich supporters financed it, gentleman farmers led it, and religious zealots filled its ranks along with the usual cross section of poor artisans and day laborers. This army brought defeat to the king, his aristocratic followers, and the Anglican church's hierarchy.

In January 1649, Charles I was publicly executed by order of Parliament. During the

Sir Christopher Wren (1632–1723): The Royal Hospital at Greenwich. The classical design of the Royal Hospital derives ultimately from Palladio and Michelangelo, but its blend of grave monumentality and simplicity reflect the taste of late-seventeenth-century England. The buildings are now part of the Royal Naval College: left, the Chapel; right, the Painted Hall. In the middle distance is the Queen's House, designed by Inigo Jones. (*A. F. Kersting*)

Interregnum of the next eleven years, one Parliament after another joined with the army to govern the country as a republic. In the distribution of power between the army and the Parliament, Cromwell proved to be a key element. He had the support of the army's officers and some of its rank and file, and he had been a member of Parliament for many years. His control over the army had only been secured, however, after its rank and file had been purged not of royalists, but of radical groups. Some of these radicals wanted to level society, that is, to redistribute property by ending monopolies and to give the vote to all male citizens. In the context of the 1650s, Cromwell was a moderate republican who also believed in religious toleration; yet history has painted him, somewhat unjustly, as a military dictator.

The English Revolution was begun by an agricultural and commercial bourgeoisie, urban merchants as well as landed gentry, who were imbued with the strict Protestantism of the Continental Reformation. But in the 1650s the success of their revolution was jeopardized by growing discontent from the poor or less prosperous who had made up the rank and file of the army and who demanded that their economic and social grievances be rectified. The radicals of the English Revolution—men like Gerrard Winstanley, the first theoretician of social democracy in modern times, and John Lilburne, the Leveller—demanded a redistribution of property, voting rights for the vast majority of the male population, and the abolition of religious and intellectual elites whose power and ideology supported the interests of the ruling classes. The radicals rejected Anglicanism, moderate Puritanism, and even, in a few cases, the lifestyle of the middle class; they opted instead for libertine and communistic beliefs and practices. The radicals terrified even devoted Puritans like Cromwell. By 1660 the country was adrift without effective leadership.

Parliament, having secured the economic interests of its constituency (gentry, merchants, and some small landowners), chose to return to court and crown and invited the exiled son of the executed king to return to the kingship. Having learned the lesson his father had spurned, Charles II (1660–1685) never instituted royal absolutism, although he did try to minimize Parliament's role in the government. His court was a far more open institution than his father's had been, for Charles II feared a similar death.

But Charles's brother James II (1685–1688) was a foolishly fearless Catholic and admirer of French absolutism. James gathered at his court a coterie of Catholic advisers and supporters of royal prerogative and attempted to bend Parliament and local government to the royal will. James's Catholicism was the crucial element in his failure. The Anglican church would not back him, and political forces similar to those that had gathered against his father, Charles I, in 1640 descended on him. The ruling elites, however, had learned their lesson back in the 1650s: civil war would produce social discontent among the masses. The upper classes wanted to avoid open warfare and preserve the monarchy as a constitutional authority, but not as an absolute one. Puritanism, with its sectarian fervor and its dangerous association with republicanism, was allowed to play no part in this second and last phase of the English Revolution.

In early 1688, Anglicans, some aristocrats, and opponents of royal prerogative (Whigs) formed a conspiracy against James II. Their purpose was to invite his son-in-law, William of Orange, *stadholder* of the Netherlands and husband of James's Protestant daughter Mary, to invade England and rescue its government from James's control. It was hoped that the final outcome of this invasion would be determined by William and his conspirators, in conjunction with a freely elected Parliament. This dangerous plan succeeded for three main reasons: William and the Dutch desperately needed English support against the threat of a French invasion; James had lost the loyalty of key men in the army, powerful gentlemen in the counties, and the Anglican church; and the political elite was committed and united in its intentions. James II fled the country, and William and Mary were declared king and queen by act of Parliament.

This bloodless revolution—sometimes called the Glorious Revolution—created a new political and constitutional reality. Parliament secured its rights to assemble regularly and to vote on all matters of taxation; the rights of *habeas corpus* and trial by jury (for men of property and social status) were also secured. These rights were in turn legitimated in a constitutionally binding document, the Bill of Rights (1689). All Protestants, regardless of their sectarian bias, were granted toleration. The Revolution Settlement of 1688–1689 resolved the profound constitutional and social tensions of the seventeenth century and laid the foundations of English government until well into the nineteenth century. The revolution, says historian J. H. Plumb, established "the authority of certain men of property, particularly those of high social standing either aristrocrats or linked with aristocracy, whose tap root was in land but whose side roots reached out to commerce, industry and finance."[2] Throughout the eighteenth century, England was ruled by kings and Parliaments

William and Mary in Triumph. This detail of the ceiling painting by Sir James Thornhill in the Painted Hall of the Royal Hospital (see page 360) shows William III and Mary II being received triumphantly after the ouster of James II in the Glorious Revolution of 1688–89. (*Royal Naval College, Greenwich*)

that represented the interests of an oligarchy whose cohesiveness and prosperity ensured social and political stability.

The English Revolution, in both its 1640 and its 1688 phases, secured English parliamentary government and the rule of law, and it also provided a degree of freedom for the propertied. In retrospect, we can see that absolutism according to the French model probably never had a chance in England. There were simply too many gentlemen there who possessed enough land to be independent of the crown, and yet not so much that they could control whole sections of the

kingdom. But to contemporaries, the issues seemed different: the English opponents of absolutism spoke of their rights, as granted by their ancient constitution and the feudal law, of the need to make the English church truly Protestant, and among the radicals, of the right of lesser men to secure their property. These opponents possessed an institution—Parliament—where they could express their grievances; eventually, they also acquired an army that waged war to secure the demands of the propertied classes. The result was limited monarchy as established in 1689 and a constitutional system based upon the laws made by Parliament and sanctioned by the king. Very gradually the monarchical element in that system would yield to the power and authority of parliamentary ministers and state officials.

The Revolution of 1688–1689 was England's last revolution. In the nineteenth and twentieth centuries, parliamentary institutions would be gradually and peacefully reformed to express a more democratic social reality. The events of 1688–1689 have rightly been described as "the year one," in that they fashioned a system of government that was not only resilient in Britain, but also capable of being adopted with modification elsewhere. The British system became a model for other forms of bourgeois representative government that were adopted in France and former British colonies, beginning with the United States.

The Netherlands: A Bourgeois Republic

One other area in Europe developed a system of representative government that also survived for centuries. The Netherlands, or Low Countries (Holland and Belgium), had been part of Hapsburg territory since the fifteenth century. When Charles V ascended to the Spanish throne in 1516, the Netherlands grew into an economic linchpin of the Spanish empire. Spain exported wool and bullion to the Low Countries in return for manufactured textiles, hardware, grain, and naval stores. Flanders, with Antwerp as its capital, was the manufacturing and banking center of the Spanish empire.

The Spanish monarchy exploited its colonies in both the old and new worlds to finance wars against the Turks and the Italian city-states, and by the 1540s, its crusade against Protestant Germany. In the northern Low Countries especially, this tax burden joined with administrative inefficiency, unemployment, and religious repression to create the conditions that sparked the first successful bourgeois revolution in history.

During the reign of Charles V's successor, Philip II, a tightly organized Calvinist minority, with its popular base in the cities and its military strategy founded on sea raids, at first harassed and then aggressively challenged Spanish power. In the 1560s the Spanish responded by trying to export the Inquisition into the Netherlands and by sending an enormous standing army there under the Duke of Alva. It was a classic example of overkill; thousands of once-loyal Flemish and Dutch subjects turned against the Spanish Crown. The people either converted secretly to Calvinism or aided the revolutionaries. Led by William the Silent (1533–1584), head of the Orange Dynasty, the seven northern provinces (Holland, Zeeland, Utrecht, Gelderland, Overijssel, Friesland, and Groningen) joined in the Union of Utrecht (1579) to protect themselves against Spanish aggression. Their determined resistance, coupled with the serious economic weaknesses of the overextended Spanish empire, eventually produced unexpected success for the northern colonies.

By 1609 the seven northern provinces were effectively free of Spanish control and loosely tied together under a republican form of government. Seventeenth-century Netherlands became a prosperous bourgeois state. Rich from the fruits of manufacture and trade in everything from flower bulbs to ships, the Dutch merchants ruled their cities and provinces with a fierce pride. By the early seventeenth century, this new nation of only one and a half million practiced the most innovative commercial and financial techniques in Europe.

In this fascinating instance, capitalism and Protestantism fused to do the work of princes; the Dutch state emerged without absolute monarchy, and indeed in opposition to it. From that experience, the ruling Dutch oligarchy retained a deep distrust of hereditary monarchy. The exact position of the House of Orange remained a vexing constitutional question until well into the eighteenth century. The oligarchs and their party, the Patriots, favored a republic without a single head, ruled by them through the Estates

Jan Vermeer (1632–1675): Young Woman with a Water Jug. Vermeer used many of the same objects in his light-filled, balanced interiors. The wall map is a reminder of Dutch trade. The rich oriental carpet, the stained glass, and the solid pitcher reflect a society that valued possessions having both beauty and utility (*The Metropolitan Museum of Art, Gift of Henry G. Marquand, 1889 (89.15.21)*)

General. The Calvinist clergy, old aristocrats, and a vast section of the populace—all for very different reasons—wanted the head of the House of Orange to govern as stadholder (head) of the provinces, in effect as a limited monarch in a republican state. These unresolved political tensions prevented the Netherlands from developing a form of republican government that might have rivaled the stability of the British system of limited monarchy. The Dutch achievement came in other areas.

Calvinism had provided the ideology of revolution and national identity. Capital, in turn, created a unique cultural milieu in the Dutch urban centers of Amsterdam, Rotter-

dam, Utrecht, and The Hague. Wide toleration without a centralized system of censorship made the Dutch book trade, which often disseminated works by refugees from the Spanish Inquisition and later by French Protestants, the most vital in Europe right up to the French Revolution. And the sights and sounds of an active and prosperous population, coupled with a politically engaged and rich bourgeoisie, fed the imagination as well as the purses of various artistic schools. Rembrandt van Rijn, Jan Steen, Frans Hals, Jan Vermeer, and Jan van del Velde are at the top of a long list of great Dutch artists—many of them also refugees. They left timeless images portraying the people of the only republican national state to endure throughout the seventeenth century.

The Failure of Spanish Power

The revolt in the Netherlands dealt a devastating blow to the Spanish economy, as well as to its northern defenses against France. Spain's most psychologically upsetting defeat of the century, however, was the destruction of the Armada in 1588 in an unsuccessful attempt to invade England. During the reign of Philip II, Spanish self-confidence was shaken and a long decline in political power began.

Philip II

In 1556, Charles V abdicated the Spanish throne in favor of his son, Philip, to whom he bequeathed an empire that was governed effectively, yet burdened by the specters of bankruptcy and heresy. Philip II (1556–1598) dedicated himself to the imposition of orthodoxy in Spain. He bided his time with foreign infidels and heretics, awaiting the day when the crown would possess the revenue necessary to launch an offensive against the Turks and against international Protestantism.

To Philip II, being truly Spanish meant

being Christian in faith and blood; the racist tendencies, already evident in the later fifteenth century, gained full expression during his reign. Increasingly, the country came to be ruled by an exclusive class of old Christians who claimed to be untainted because for centuries they had refused to marry Muslims or Jews. Traditional in their thinking and in their control over the church, the religious orders, and the Inquisition, the Old Christians tried to preserve an imperial system badly in need of reform.

Melancholic and standoffish by temperament, Philip II worked arduously and declined most of life's enjoyments. He pored over his ministers' reports, editing and commenting, yet in the end he was strangely indecisive. Some problems remained unsolved for years, as frustrated advisers begged in vain for the king to take action. A zeal for Catholicism ruled his private conduct and infused his foreign policy.

By the 1580s, Philip's foreign policy was overextended in every direction: the campaign against England was matched by unsuccessful attempts to intervene on the side of the Guise in the French wars of religion. Meanwhile, the military campaign in the Netherlands wrought a catastrophe. In 1576 the Spanish themselves were forced to flood and sack Antwerp, their leading commercial and banking city in northern Europe. Antwerp's trade gradually moved to Amsterdam, a Protestant stronghold, which replaced its southern rival as an international capital and as the center of the new Dutch national state.

At every turn in northern Europe, Philip II's policies proved futile. One dramatic event came to symbolize this malaise in the Spanish mind: the defeat of the powerful Armada by England, widely believed to be an inferior power. Spain had regarded an assault on England as a holy crusade against the "heretic and bastard" Queen Elizabeth. Some Spanish officials had reasoned that a successful invasion would ignite a Catholic uprising by (vastly overestimated) numbers of English Catholics. Philip II had longed for the opportunity to conquer England; it was the main

Protestant power in Europe, and Philip particularly resented its assistance to Dutch rebels.

Outfitted in Lisbon harbor and constantly delayed by shortages of equipment, the Armada was composed of 130 ships, only a fourth of the originally planned fleet. These main ships and numerous smaller vessels carried 22,000 seamen and soldiers. The English fleet numbered less than 75. Sailing from Lisbon in May 1588, the Armada was poorly equipped. Its ships were too large and cumbersome to negotiate the treacherous English Channel, where the English sailing ships easily outmaneuvered them. The English sent fire ships against the Armada, which broke its formation; a Spanish army to be launched from Flanders failed to make its rendezvous; and perhaps most decisively, strong winds drove the Armada out of striking position. The victory went to the English, and both sides believed it to be a sign from God.

This defeat had an enormous psychological effect on the Spanish. They openly pondered what they had done to incur divine displeasure. Protestant Europe, on the other hand, hailed this victory as a sign of its election, and the "Protestant wind" stirred by divine intervention entered the mythology of many a proud Englishman. In the rise and fall of nations, self-confidence has played a crucial, if inexplicable, role.

The End of the Spanish Hapsburgs

After the defeat of the Armada, Spain gradually and reluctantly abandoned its imperial ambitions in northern Europe. The administrative structure built by Charles V and Philip II did remain strong throughout the seventeenth century; nevertheless, by the first quarter of the century enormous weaknesses had surfaced in Spanish economic and social life. In 1596, Philip II was bankrupt, his vast wealth overextended by the cost of foreign wars. Bankruptcy reappeared at various times in the seventeenth century, while the agricultural economy, at the heart of any early modern nation, stagnated. The Spanish in their golden age had never devoted enough attention to increasing domestic production.

Although Spain retained vast portions of its empire during the seventeenth century, important pieces broke away. First, the northern Netherlands secured its virtual independence. Then, in 1640, Portugal successfully revolted, as did Catalonia, although Catalonia was eventually brought back into the empire. And from 1606 to 1650, Spanish trade with the Americas dropped by 60 percent.

Despite these setbacks, Spain was still capable of taking a very aggressive posture during the Thirty Years' War (1618–1648). The Austrian branch of the Hapsburg family joined forces with their Spanish cousins, and neither the Swedes and Germans nor the Dutch could stop them. Only French participation in the Thirty Years' War on the Protestant side tipped the balance decisively against the Hapsburgs. Spanish aggression brought no victories, and with the Peace of Westphalia (1648), Spain officially recognized the independence of the Netherlands and severed its diplomatic ties with the Austrian branch of the family. The latter signed a separate treaty with the French. Austria itself would develop under this central European branch of the Hapsburg dynasty as a dynamic state, but not until the eighteenth century.

Spain had only one great statesman in the seventeenth century—Gaspar de Guzmán, count of Olivares (d. 1645), whose skill and efficiency matched his craving to restore Spain's imperial glory. He served Philip IV for over twenty years until his aggressive foreign and domestic policies brought ruin. One strength of the Spanish monarchy had been its ability to favor Castile while respecting the liberties and privileges of the provinces, Aragon and Catalonia in particular. Olivares attempted to bring the provincial laws into conformity with those of Castile and to force greater provincial participation in Spanish affairs. Clearly neither the provincial assemblies, the *Cortes*, nor the provincial aristocrats wished to undo the status

quo, and Olivares's policies led to revolt in Catalonia.

By 1660 the imperial age of the Spanish Hapsburgs had come to an end. The rule of the Protestant princes had been secured in the Holy Roman Empire; the Protestant and Dutch Republic flourished; Portugal and its colony of Brazil were independent of Spain; and dominance over European affairs had passed to France. The quality of material life in Spain deteriorated rapidly, and the ever-present gap between rich and poor widened even more drastically. The traditional aristocracy and the church retained their land and power, but failed conspicuously to produce effective leadership.

In the second half of the seventeenth century, Spanish leadership grew markedly worse. Palace intrigue replaced diplomacy and statesmanship. The reign of Charles II (1665–1700), whose Hapsburg parents were related as uncle and niece, witnessed the total administrative and economic collapse of Castile. What vitality remained in Spain could be found in its periphery, in Catalonia and Andalusia. At his death in 1700, Charles II (whose marriages had been childless) declared in favor of a French successor, Philip of Anjou, Louis XIV's grandson.

Charles's act, coupled with Louis XIV's designs on the kingdom of Spain, provoked another European war. The War of the Spanish Succession (1701–1713) pitted the Holy Roman Empire, England, and the Netherlands against France. Its outcome defeated Louis's desire to unite Spain and France under the Bourbons. Philip V, although king of Spain, was forced to renounce his claim to the French throne. Spain retained its political independence, but the Hapsburg dynasty in Spain had come to an end. From 1700 until very recently the Spanish state has been ruled by either dictators or Bourbons.

Of all the sovereign states of Europe to emerge in the early modern period, Spain presents the greatest set of paradoxes. It was the least centralized of all the states of the sixteenth and seventeenth centuries. In that lay its strength and its weakness. In the six-

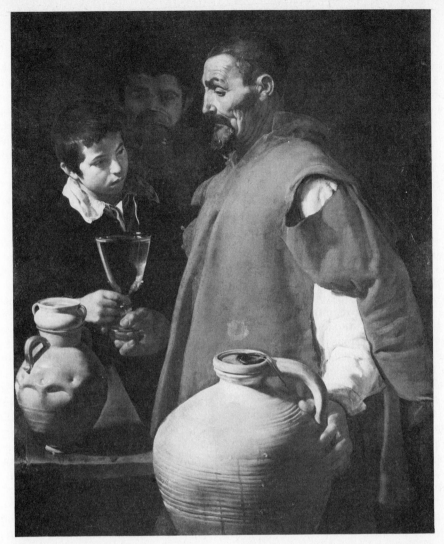

Diego Velázquez (1599–1660): The Water-Seller of Seville. The dramatic use of light makes Velázquez a Baroque artist, but his subject matter drawn from the lower classes shows the influence of Dutch genre scenes of everyday life. (*Victoria and Albert Museum*)

teenth century, Castile led the nation without crippling it. Spanish achievements in that century are nothing short of extraordinary in art, literature, navigation, exploration, administration, and even religious zeal. Then came the gradual and almost inexplicably precipitous decline in the seventeenth century, from which Spain has yet to recover.

The Spanish experience illustrates two observations in the history of the European state. First, the state as empire could only survive and prosper if the domestic economic base remained sound. The Spanish reliance on bullion from its colonies and its failure to cultivate industry and to reform the taxation system spelled disaster. Second, states with a vital and aggressive bourgeoisie flourished at the expense of societies where aristocracy and church dominated and controlled society and its mores—Spain's situation. The latter social groups tended to despise manual labor, profit taking, and technological progress. Although kings and dynastic families originally created them, after 1700 the major dynastic states were increasingly nurtured by the economic activities of the bourgeoisie. Bureaucracies drawn from the lesser aristocracy, however, still governed the states.

The Holy Roman Empire: The Failure to Unify Germany

In contrast to the French, English, Spanish, and Dutch experiences in the early modern period, the Germans failed to achieve national unity, which produced a legacy of frustration and antagonism toward the other powerful European states. The German failure to unify is tied to the history of the Holy Roman Empire. That union of various distinct central European territories was created in the tenth century when Otto I, in a deliberate attempt to revive Charlemagne's empire, was crowned Emperor of the Romans. Later the title was changed to Holy Roman emperor, with the kingdom consisting of mostly German-speaking principalities.

Most medieval emperors busied themselves not with administering their territories, but with attempting to secure control over the rich Italian peninsula and with challenging the rival authority of various popes. In the meantime, the German nobility extended and consolidated their rule over their peasants and over various towns and cities. Their aristocratic power remained a constant obstacle to German unity. Only by incorporating the nobility into the fabric of the state's power, into the court and the army, and by sanctioning their oppressive control over the peasants, would German rulers manage to create a unified German state. But that process of assimilation only commenced (first in Prussia) during the eighteenth century.

In the medieval and early modern periods the Holy Roman emperors were dependent on their most powerful noble lords—including an archbishop or two—because the office of emperor was an elected one, not the result of hereditary succession. German noble

princes—some of whom were electors—such as the archbishops of Cologne and Mainz, the Hohenzollern elector of Brandenburg, the landgrave of Hesse, and the duke of Saxony—were fiercely independent. All belonged to the empire, yet all regarded themselves as autonomous powers. These decentralizing tendencies were highly developed by the fifteenth century, when the emperors gradually realized that the outer frontiers of their empire were slipping away. The French had conducted a successful military incursion into northern Italy and on the western frontier of the empire. Hungary had fallen to the Turks, while the Swiss were hard to govern and, given their terrain, impossible to beat into submission. At the same time, the Hapsburgs maneuvered themselves into a position from which they could monopolize the imperial elections. The empire became increasingly German and Hapsburg, with Worms as the seat of imperial power.

The Holy Roman Empire in the reigns of the Hapsburg emperors Maximilian I (1493–1519) and Charles V (1519–1556) might have achieved a degree of cohesion comparable to that in France and Spain. Certainly the impetus of war—against France and against the Turks—required the creation of a large standing army and the taxation to maintain it. Both additions could have worked to the benefit of a centralized, imperial power. But the Protestant Reformation, begun in 1517, meshed in with the already well-developed tendencies toward local independence. As a result, it destroyed the last hope of Hapsburg domination and German unity. The German nobility were all too ready to use the Reformation as a vindication of their local power, and indeed Luther made just such an appeal to their interests.

At precisely the moment, in the 1520s, when Charles V had to act with great determination to stop the spread of Lutheranism, he was at war with France over its claims to Italian territory. Charles had no sooner won his Italian territories, in particular the rich city-state of Milan, when he had to make war against the Turks, who in 1529 besieged Vienna. Not until the 1540s was Charles V in the position to attack the Lutheran princes. By then they had had considerable time to solidify their position and had united for mutual protection in the Schmalkaldic League.

War raged in Germany between the Protestant princes and the imperial army led by Charles V. In 1551, Catholic France entered the war on the Protestant side, and Charles V had to flee for his life. Defeated and exhausted, Charles abdicated and retired to a Spanish monastery. The Treaty of Augsburg (1555) conferred on every German prince the right to determine the religion of his subjects. The princes had won their territories, and a unified German state was never constructed by the Hapsburgs.

When Emperor Charles V abdicated in 1556, he gave his kingdom to his son Philip and his brother. Philip inherited Spain and its colonies and Ferdinand acquired the Austrian territories. Two branches of the Hapsburg family were thus created, and well into the late seventeenth century they defined their interests in common and often waged war accordingly. The enormous international power of the Hapsburgs was checked only by their uncertain authority over the Holy Roman Empire. Throughout the sixteenth century the Austrian Hapsburgs barely managed to control these sprawling and deeply divided German territories. Protestantism, as protected by the Treaty of Augsburg, and the particularism and provinciality of the German nobility continued to prevent the creation of a German state.

The Austrian Hapsburg emperors, however, never missed an opportunity to further the cause of the Counter Reformation and to court the favor of local interests opposed to the nobility. No Hapsburg was ever more fervid in that regard than the Jesuit-trained Archduke Ferdinand II, who ascended to the throne in Vienna in 1619. He immediately embarked on a policy of religious intolerance and used Spanish officials as his administrators. His policies provoked a war within the empire that engulfed the whole of Europe.

The Thirty Years' War (1618–1648) began when the Bohemians, whose anti-Catholic tendencies can be traced back to the Hussite reformation, attempted to put a Protestant king on their throne. The Austrian and Spanish Hapsburgs reacted by sending an army into the kingdom of Bohemia, and suddenly the whole empire was forced to take sides along religious lines. The Bohemian nobility, after centuries of enforcing serfdom, failed to rally the rural masses behind them, and victory went to the emperor. Indeed, Bohemia suffered an almost unimaginable devastation; the ravaging Catholic army sacked and burned three-fourths of the kingdom's towns and practically exterminated its aristocracy.

Until the 1630s, it looked as if the Hapsburgs would be able to use the war to enhance their power and to promote centralization. But the intervention of Protestant Sweden, led by Gustavus Adolphus and encouraged by France, wrecked Hapsburg ambitions. The ensuing military conflict devastated vast areas of northern and central Europe. The civilian population suffered untold hardships: soldiers raped women and pillaged the land, and thousands of refugees took to the roads and forests. Partly because the French finally intervened directly, the Spanish Hapsburgs emerged from the Thirty Years' War with no benefits. At the Treaty of Westphalia (1648), their Austrian cousins reaffirmed their right to govern the eastern states of the kingdom with Vienna as their capital. Austria took shape as a dynastic state, while the German territories in the empire remained fragmented by the independent interests of their largely unreformed feudal nobility.

The Emergence of Austria and Prussia

Austria

As a result of the settlement at Westphalia, the Austrian Hapsburgs gained firm control over Hungary and Bohemia, where they installed a virtually new and foreign nobility. At the same time, they strengthened their rule in Vienna. In one of the few spectacular

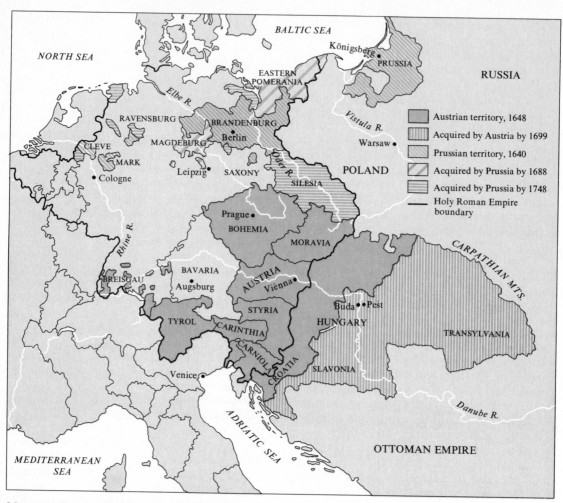

Map 16.3 The Growth of Austria and Brandenburg-Prussia, c. 1650–1750

successes achieved by the Counter Reformation, the ruling elites in all three territories were forcibly, or in many cases willingly, converted back to Catholicism. At long last, religious predominance could be used as a force—long delayed in eastern Europe because of the Protestant Reformation—for the creation of the Austrian dynastic state.

One severe obstacle to territorial hegemony remained: the military threat posed by the Turks, who sought to control much of Hungary. During the reign of Austrian Emperor

Leopold I (1658–1705), warfare against the Ottoman Empire—a recurrent theme in Hapsburg history beginning with Charles V—once again erupted, and in 1683 the Turks besieged the gates of Vienna. However, the Ottoman Empire no longer possessed its former strength and cohesiveness. A Catholic and unified Austrian army, composed of a variety of peoples from that kingdom and assisted by the Poles, managed to defeat the Turks and recapture the whole of Hungary and Transylvania and part of Croatia. Austria's right to govern was firmly accepted by the Turks at the Treaty of Karlowitz (1699).

The Austrian Hapsburgs and their victorious army had now entered the larger arena of European power politics. In 1700, at the death of the last Spanish Hapsburg, Leopold I sought to place his second son, Archduke Charles, on the Spanish throne. But this brought Leopold into a violent clash with Louis XIV. Once again Bourbon and Hapsburg rivalry, a dominant theme in early modern history, provoked a major European war.

In the War of the Spanish Succession the Austrians, with their army led by the brilliant Prince Eugene of Savoy, joined forces with the English and the Dutch. This war brought rewards in western Europe to the Austrian Hapsburgs, who acquired the Spanish Netherlands (Belgium today), as well as Milan and small holdings in Italy. But the Hapsburgs did not succeed in capturing the Spanish throne.

In the reign of Emperor Charles VI (1711–1740) Austria emerged as a major European power. Vienna became a cultural center in its own right. Austria's vast but loosely governed territories in the east, however, were not matched by territories in western and southern Europe.

Up to the early eighteenth century the Austrian Hapsburgs had struggled to achieve territorial hegemony and to subdue the dissident religious groups (Protestant and Turkish Muslim) that in very different ways threatened to undermine their authority. Warfare and the maintenance of a standing army had taken precedence over adminstrative reform and commercial growth. Yet military victory created the conditions within which centralization could occur.

The Austrian achievement of the eighteenth century, which made Austria a major force in European affairs, derived in large measure from the administrative reforms and cultural revival initiated by Charles VI (assisted militarily by Eugene of Savoy) and continued by his successors, Maria Theresa and Joseph II. These eighteenth-century monarchs embraced a style of government sometimes described as *enlightened* (see pages 421–423). They sought through education and liberal policies to catch up with the more established and older dynastic states of Europe.

Prussia

By the seventeenth century in northern Europe, the cohesive state governed by an absolute monarch (or by bourgeois oligarchs as in the Netherlands) had replaced feudalism as a system of government. Serfdom had disappeared in western Europe by the late sixteenth century, although it remained in parts of central and eastern Europe. The feudal aristocracy recouped their losses, however. No longer free to play at war or to control the lives of their peasants, progressive aristocrats improved their agricultural systems or sought offices and military commands in the service of the absolutist state. On the whole, western European aristocrats did not fare too badly under absolutism, but in the course of the early modern period, the state decisively checked their independent power.

Prussia was different. Prussia was a state, within the Holy Roman Empire, that had emerged very late in northern Europe (in the late seventeenth century). Like Austria, Prussia displayed certain unique characteristics. Although it did develop an absolute monarchy like France, its powerful aristocracy only acquiesced to monarchical power in exchange for guarantees of their feudal power over the peasantry. In 1653 the Prussian nobility granted the elector power to collect taxes for the maintenance of a powerful army, but only after he issued decrees rendering serfdom permanent.

The ruling dynasty of Prussia, the Hohenzollerns, had a most inauspicious beginning in the later Middle Ages. These rulers were little more than dukes in the Holy Roman Empire until 1415, when the Emperor Sigismund made one of them an imperial elector with the right to choose imperial successors. For centuries, the Hohenzollerns had made weak claims to territory in northern

Germany. They finally achieved control over Prussia and certain other smaller principalities by claiming the inheritance of one wife (1608) and by single-minded, ruthless aggression.

The most aggressive of these Hohenzollerns was the Elector Frederick William (1640–1688), who played a key role in forging the new Prussian state. Frederick William had inherited the territories of the beleaguered Hohenzollern dynasty, whose main holding, Brandenburg in Prussia, was very poor in natural resources. Indeed, Prussia had barely survived the devastation wrought by the Thirty Years' War, especially the Swedish army's occupation of the electorate.

A distaste for foreign intervention in Prussia, and for the accompanying humiliation and excessive taxes, prompted the *Junker* class (the landed Prussian nobility) to support national unity and strong central government. But they would brook no threat to their economic power over their lands and peasants. By 1672 the Prussian army, led by Junker officers, was strong enough to enter the Franco-Dutch war on the Dutch side. The war brought no territorial gains, but it allowed the elector to raise taxes. Once again the pattern of foreign war, taxes, and military conscription led to an increase in the power of the central government. But in Prussia, in contrast to western lands, the bureaucracy was entirely military. No clerics or rich bourgeois shared power with this Junker class. The pattern initiated by the Great Elector (Frederick William) would be continued in the reigns of his successors: Frederick I (d. 1713), Frederick William I, and Frederick the Great.

The alliance between aristocracy and monarchy was especially strengthened in the reign of Frederick William I (1713–1740). In the older dynastic states, absolute monarchs in every case tried to dispense with representative institutions once the monarchy's power could stand on its own. So, too, did Frederick William undercut the Prussian provincial assemblies, the *Landtage,* which still had power over taxation and army recruitment. Gradually, he rendered the Landtage superfluous.

But he was only able to do so by incorporating the landowning Junker class into the machinery of government—especially into the army—and by keeping the tax-paying peasants in the status of serfs.

In a nation where representative institutions in the twentieth century have struggled, often unsuccessfully, for survival, it is interesting that such institutions did exercise considerable influence in Prussia up to the early eighteenth century. Like the Austrians during the eighteenth century, the Prussians also embarked on a program of modernization, which has occasionally been described as enlightened.

Russia

Although remote from developments in western Europe, Russia in the early modern period took on some characteristics remarkably similar to those of western European states. Russia, also, relied on absolute monarchy reinforced by a feudal aristocracy. As in Europe, the latter's power to wreak havoc had to be checked and its energies channeled into the state's service. But the Russian pattern of absolutism breaks with the Western model and resembles that adopted in Prussia, where serfdom increased as the power of centralized monarchy grew. The award of peasants was the bribe by which the monarchy secured the aristocrats' cooperation in the state's growth.

Russian absolutism experienced a false start under Ivan IV, "The Terrible" (1547–1584). Late in the sixteenth century Ivan sought to impose a tsarist autocracy. He waged a futile war against Sweden and created an internal police force that was entrusted with the administration of central Russia. His failure in war and an irrational policy of repression (fueled in part by Ivan's mental instability) doomed his premature attempt to impose absolutism. Much of Ivan's state-building was

Map 16.4 The Expansion of Russia, 1300–1725 ▶

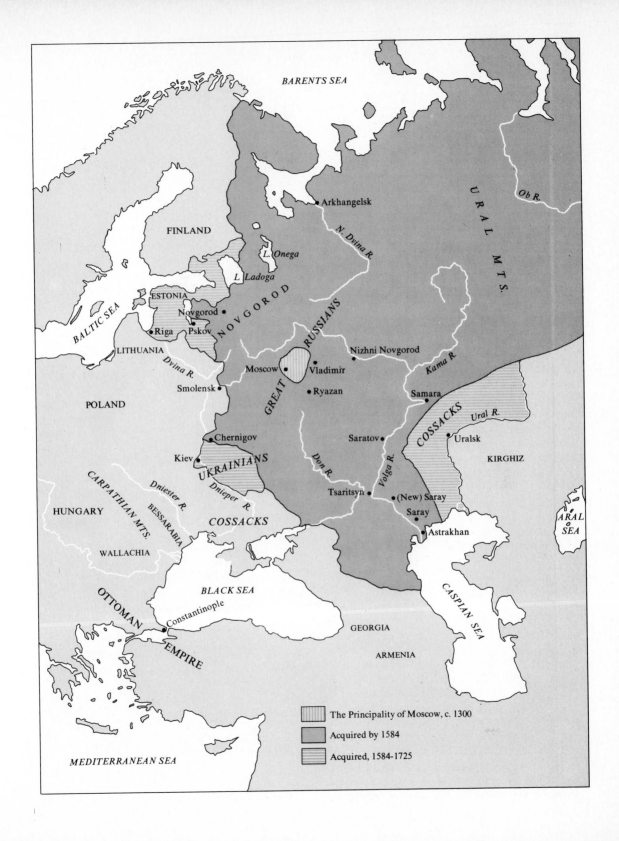

BARENTS SEA

FINLAND

L. Onega

L. Ladoga

ESTONIA

Novgorod

Riga

Pskov

BALTIC SEA

LITHUANIA

Dvina R.

POLAND

Smolensk

Arkhangelsk

N. Dvina R.

URAL MTS.

Ob R.

NOVGOROD

GREAT RUSSIANS

Moscow

Vladimir

Nizhni Novgorod

Kama R.

Samara

Ryazan

Chernigov

Saratov

COSSACKS

Uralsk

Ural R.

KIRGHIZ

Kiev

UKRAINIANS

Dniester R.

Dnieper R.

COSSACKS

CARPATHIAN MTS.

HUNGARY

BESSARABIA

WALLACHIA

Don R.

Volga R.

Tsaritsyn

(New) Saray

Saray

Astrakhan

ARAL SEA

OTTOMAN

EMPIRE

BLACK SEA

Constantinople

GEORGIA

ARMENIA

CASPIAN SEA

MEDITERRANEAN SEA

The Principality of Moscow, c. 1300

Acquired by 1584

Acquired, 1584–1725

St. Basil's Cathedral, Moscow. The cathedral of St. Basil is a fusion of native folk art and late Byzantine architecture. Russia in the seventeenth century had strong roots in its medieval past. Peter the Great forcefully rejected many traditions and made Russia turn to the West for inspiration. (*William Brumfield*)

undone with his death, which launched a "Time of Troubles"—a period of foreign invasion and civil warfare—that endured for years.

Order was restored in the country only in 1613 when the Romanov dynasty gained the support of the aristocracy. The accession of Michael Romanov as tsar marks the emergence of a unified Russian state. Of that dynasty, by far the most important ruler was Peter the Great (1689–1725). He ruthlessly suppressed the independent aristocrats, while inventing new titles and ranks for those loyal to the court. Both nobility and gentry were brought into the army by universal service obligations. The peasants were made the personal property of their lords, to be sold at will; thus, the distinction between serf and slave was obliterated. Finally, Peter brought the church under the control of the state by establishing a new office called the Holy Synod; its head was a government official.

From 1700 to 1707, taxes on the peasants multiplied five times over. Predictably, the money went toward the creation of a professional army along European lines and to making war. The preparation led this time to victory over the Swedes.

Peter succeeded in wedding the aristocracy to the absolutist state, and the union was so successful that strong Russian monarchs in the eighteenth century, like Catherine the Great, could embrace enlightened reforms without jeopardizing the stability of their regimes. Once again, repression and violence in the form of taxation, serfdom, and war led to the creation of a dynastic state—one that proved the least susceptible to reform, eventually to be dismantled in 1917 by the Russian Revolution.

The State and Modern Political Development

By the early seventeenth century, Europeans had developed the concept of a *state*—a dis-

tinctive political entity to which its subjects owed duties and obligations. That concept would become the foundation of the modern science of politics. The one essential ingredient of the Western concept of the state, as it emerged in the early modern period, was the notion of *sovereignty*; that is, within its borders the state was supreme, and all corporations and organizations—by implication even the church—were allowed to exist only by the state's permission.

The modern concept of the state first developed not in Renaissance Italy, as might be expected, but in France and England in the mid-1500s. In every instance where early modern theorists—with the exception of Calvinist revolutionaries—discussed a state, it was to instruct the prince in its governance. These theorists were responding to a new political reality: princes had become significantly more powerful than any other single group within a country. But simultaneously an entity larger than its component parts and even more important than its rulers had emerged; the state seemed increasingly to possess its own reason for existence. The art of government entailed molding the ambitions and strength of the powerful into their state's service. The state, its power growing through war and taxation, had become the basic unit of political authority in the West.

Significantly, the concept of human liberty, now so basic to Western thought, was not articulated first in the sovereign states of Europe. Rather, it was largely an Italian creation, discussed with great vehemence by the Italian theorists of the later Middle Ages and the Renaissance. These humanists lived and wrote in the independent city-states, and they often aimed their treatises against the encroachments of the Holy Roman emperor—in short, against princes and their search for absolute power. In the sixteenth and seventeenth centuries, the idea of liberty was generally found only in the writings of Calvinist opponents of absolutism. Not until the mid-seventeenth century in England was there a body of political thought arguing that human liberty could be ensured within the confines of a

Chronology 16.1 The Rise of Sovereignty

1453	The Hundred Years' War ends
1453–1485	The War of Roses in England between rival nobles
1469	Ferdinand and Isabella begin rule of Castile and Aragon
1485	Henry VII begins the reign of the Tudor dynasty in England
1517	The Protestant Reformation begins in Germany
1519	Charles V of Spain becomes Hapsburg emperor of the Holy Roman Empire
1553–1558	Queen Mary attempts to return England to Catholicism
1556–1598	Philip II of Spain persecutes Jews and Muslims
1559	The Treaty of Cateau-Cambrésis between France and Spain
1560s–1609	The Netherlands revolts from Spanish rule
1562–1598	Religious wars in France
1572	The St. Bartholomew's Day Massacre—Queen Catherine of France orders thousands of Protestants executed
1579	*Vindiciae contra Tyrannos*, published by Huguenots, justifies regicide
1588	The Spanish Armada is defeated by the English fleet
1590s	Boris Gudonov leads a reaction in Russia against Ivan IV, "The Terrible"
1593	Henry IV of France renounces his Protestantism to restore peace in France

powerful national state—one governed by mere mortals and not by divinely sanctioned and absolute kings. In general, despite the English and Dutch developments, absolutism in its varied forms (Spanish, French, Prussian) dominated the political development of early modern Europe.

Although first articulated in the Italian republics and then enacted briefly in England and more durably in the Netherlands, the republican ideal did not gain acceptance as a viable critique of absolutism until the European Enlightenment of the eighteenth century. In the democratic and republican revolutions of the late eighteenth century, western Europeans and Americans repudiated monarchical systems of government in response to the republican ideal. By then, princes and the aristocratic and military elites had outlived their usefulness in many parts of Europe. The states they had created, in large measure to further their own interests, had indeed become larger than their creators. Eventually the national states of western Europe, as well as of the Americas, proved able to survive and prosper without kings or aristocrats, while they retained the administrative and military mechanisms so skilfully and relentlessly developed by early modern kings and their court officials.

Chronology 16.1 continued

1598	The French Protestants are granted religious toleration by the Edict of Nantes
1624–1642	Cardinal Richelieu, Louis XIII's chief minister, determines royal policies
1640	The Portuguese revolt successfully against Spain
1640–1660	The English Revolution
1648	The Peace of Westphalia ends the Thirty Years' War
1648–1653	The Fronde, a rebellious reaction centered in Paris
1649	Charles I, Stuart king of England, is executed by an act of Parliament
1649–1660	England is co-ruled by Parliament and the army under Oliver Cromwell
1660	Charles II returns from exile and becomes king of England
1681	The Turks attack Vienna and are defeated; the Austrians recapture Hungary, Transylvania, and parts of Croatia
1685	Louis XIV of France revokes the Edict of Nantes
1688–1689	Revolution in England; end of absolutism
1701	Louis XIV tries to bring Spain under French control
1702–1713	The War of the Spanish Succession
1740	Frederick the Great of Prussia invades Silesia, starting war with Austria
1789	The French Revolution begins

Notes

1. J. H. Elliott, *Imperial Spain, 1469–1716* (New York: St. Martin's Press, 1963), p. 18.

2. J. H. Plumb, *The Growth of Political Stability in England: 1675–1725* (London: Macmillan, 1967), p. 69.

Suggested Reading

Anderson, Perry, *Lineages of the Abolutist State* (1974). An excellent survey, written from a Marxist perspective.

Elliott, J. H., *Imperial Spain, 1469–1716* (1963). An excellent survey of the major European power of the early modern period.

Goubert, Pierre, *Louis XIV and Twenty Million Frenchmen* (1966). An important reappraisal of the "Sun King," emphasizing the effects of his policies on ordinary French people.

Hill, Christopher, *God's Englishman* (1970). A biography of Oliver Cromwell.

Koenigsberger, H. G., and Mosse, G. L., *Europe in the Sixteenth Century* (1968). Some excellent chapters on the monarchies, the Dutch revolt, and the Hapsburgs.

Parker, Geoffrey, *Spain and The Netherlands, 1559–1659* (1979). A good survey of a complex relationship.

Plumb, J. H., *The Growth of Political Stability in England, 1675–1725* (1967). A basic book, clear and readable.

Shennan, J. H., *The Origins of the Modern European State* (1974). An excellent brief introduction.

Smith, Lacey Baldwin, *This Realm of England, 1399 to 1688* (revised ed., 1983). Still the best survey of England during this period.

Wedgwood, C. V., *William the Silent* (1944). A good biography of one of the founders of the Dutch republic.

Zagorin, Perez, *Rebels and Rulers, 1500–1660*, 2 vols. (1982). A good general survey of recent scholarship.

Review Questions

1. What role did the aristocracy play in the formation of the European states?

2. In what ways did early modern kings increase their power, and what relationship did they have to the commercial bourgeoisie in their countries?

3. What is meant by *raison d'état* and by the divine right of kings?

4. What role did religion and national churches play in creating the state?

5. Why did England move in the direction of parliamentary government, while most countries on the Continent embraced absolutism? Describe the main factors.

6. What made the Dutch state so different from its neighbors? Describe the differences.

7. What were the strengths and weaknesses of the Spanish state?

8. What makes the Prussian, Russian, and Austrian experiences of statehood roughly comparable?

9. Discuss the differences between the treatment of the peasants in eastern Europe and the treatment of those in western Europe.

10. Government has sometimes been described as being, in the final analysis, organized violence. Is that an adequate description of early modern European governments?

17

*The Scientific Revolution:
The Mechanical Universe*

*S*tarting in the late fourteenth century, the cohesive medieval world began to disintegrate, a process lasting to the late seventeenth century. Not only did the basic medieval institutions like feudalism weaken, but also the medieval view of the universe became transformed into the modern and scientific understanding of nature.

Three historical movements during the early modern period made this intellectual transformation, called the *Scientific Revolution*, possible. The Italian Renaissance created new literary and artistic styles that sought to portray people and nature as they are, and this effort aroused a curiosity that fostered investigation into physical phenomena. Then the Reformation shattered the unity of Christendom, and a different religious person, one intent on finding personal salvation without the assistance of priests or sacraments, came into existence. Protestant cities and countries inevitably found themselves in opposition to the Roman church and its teaching authority; very gradually the practitioners of the new science found a more congenial atmosphere for work in those Protestant centers. Both the Renaissance and the Reformation encouraged a sense of confidence in human ability to arrive at new truths about the physical environment. Finally, feudalism and manorialism were replaced by sovereign states and commercial capitalism. And by the late seventeenth century the leaders of those states actively encouraged science as a key to increasing human control over the environment. They saw that such control, particularly through agricultural experiments, might increase prosperity.

The unique contribution of the Scientific Revolution to the making of the modern world lay in its new mechanical conception of nature, which enabled Westerners to discover and to explain the laws of nature mathematically. They came to see nature as composed solely of matter whose motion, occurring in space and measurable by time, was governed by laws of force. This philosophically elegant construction renders the physical world knowable, and even possibly manageable.

The Scientific Revolution also entailed the discovery of a new, scientific methodology. Because of the successful experiments performed by scientists and natural philosophers such as Galileo Galilei (1564–1642), William Harvey (1578–1657), Robert Boyle (1627–1691), and Isaac Newton (1642–1727), Western science acquired its still-characteristic methodology of observation and experimentation. By the late seventeenth century, no one could entertain a serious interest in any aspect of the physical order without actually doing experiments or without observing, in a rigorous and systematic way, the behavior of physical phenomena. The mechanical concept of nature coupled with a rigorous methodology gave modern scientists the means to unlock and explain the secrets of nature.

Mathematics increasingly became the language of the new science. For centuries, Europeans had used algebra and geometry to explain certain physical phenomena. With the Scientific Revolution came a new mathematics, the calculus; but even more important, philosophers became increasingly convinced that all nature—physical objects as well as invisible forces—could be expressed mathematically. By the late seventeenth century, even geometry had become so complex that a gifted philosopher like John Locke (1632–1704), a friend and contemporary of Isaac Newton, could not understand the sophisticated mathematics used by Newton in the *Principia*. A new scientific culture had been born that during the eighteenth-century Enlightenment (see Chapter 18), achieved great importance as a model for progress in both the natural and human sciences.

Medieval Cosmology

The unique character of the modern scientific outlook is most understandable in contrast with what went before it—the medieval understanding of the natural world and its physical properties. That understanding rested on a blend of Christian thought with theories derived from ancient Greek writers like Aristotle and Ptolemy. The explanations given by Aristotle (384–322 B.C.) for the motion of heavy bodies permeated medieval scientific literature. In trying to understand motion, Aristotle had argued simply that it was in the nature of things to move in certain ways. A stone falls because it is absolutely heavy; fire rises because it is absolutely light. Weight is an absolute property of a physical thing; therefore, motion results from the properties of bodies, and not from the forces or laws of motion at work in nature. It follows (logically but incorrectly) that if the medium through which a body falls is taken as a constant, then the speed of its fall could be doubled if its weight were doubled. Only rigorous experimentation could refute this erroneous concept of motion; it was many centuries before such experimentation was undertaken.

Aristotle's physics fitted neatly into his cosmology, or world picture. The earth, being the heaviest object, lay stationary and suspended at the center of the universe. The sun, the planets, and the moon revolved in circles, or in combinations of circles, around the earth. Aristotle presumed that since the planets were round themselves, always in motion and seemingly never altered, the most "natural" motion for them should be circular.

Aristotle's physics and cosmology were unified. He could put the earth stationary at the center of the universe because he presumed its absolute heaviness; all other heavy bodies that he had observed do fall toward it. He presumed that the planets were made of a kind of luminous ether and were held in their circular orbits by luminous spheres, or "tracks." These spheres possessed a certain reality, although invisible to human beings, and hence they came to be known as the crystalline spheres.

Aristotle believed that everything in motion had been moved by another object that was itself in motion—a continuing chain of movers and moved. By inference, this belief led back

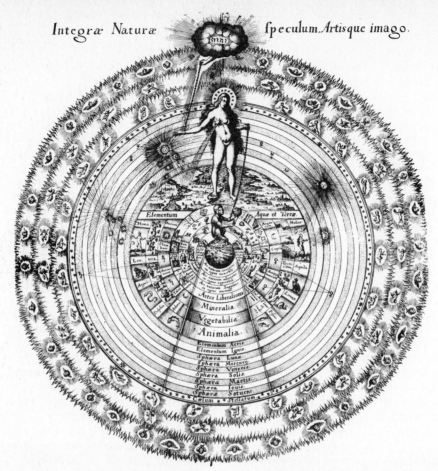

Integræ Naturæ   speculum.Artisque imago.

Utriusque Cosmi Historia, by Robert Fludd: The Universe. This engraving from the early seventeenth century illustrates the persistence of the medieval view of the universe. Christian theology had reinterpreted classical models from Aristotle and Ptolemy.

Here the hand of God is connected by a chain to the goddess Nature, who stands upon the earth, the center of the universe. (*By permission of the Houghton Library, Harvard University*)

to some object or being that began the motion. Christian philosophers of the Middle Ages argued that Aristotle's Unmoved Mover must be the God of Christianity. For Aristotle, who had no conception of a personal God or an afterlife, and who believed that the universe was eternal rather than created at a specific point in time, such an identification would have been meaningless.

Although Aristotle's cosmology never obtained the stature of orthodoxy among the ancient Greeks, by the second century A.D. in Alexandria, Greek astronomy became codified and then rigid. Ptolemy of Alexandria produced the *Almagest* (A.D. 150), a handbook of Greek astronomy based on the theories of

Aristotle. Central to that work was the assumption that a motionless earth stood at the center of the universe (although some Greeks had disputed the notion) and that the planets move about it in a series of circular orbits interrupted by epicycles. By the Late Middle Ages, Ptolemy's handbook, because of the support it lent to Aristotelian cosmology, had come to embody standard astronomical wisdom. As late as the middle of the seventeenth century, over one hundred years after Polish astronomer Nicolaus Copernicus had argued mathematically that the sun was the center of the universe, educated Europeans in most universities still believed the earth had that central position.

In the thirteenth century, mainly through the philosophical efforts of Thomas Aquinas (1225–1274), Aristotle's thought was adapted to Christian beliefs, often in tortured ways. Aquinas emphasized that order pervaded nature and that every physical effect had a physical cause. The tendency in Aquinas's thought and that of his followers, the scholastics, was to search for these causes—again to ask why things move, rather than how they move. But Aquinas denied that these causes stretched back to infinity. Instead, he insisted that nature proves God's existence; God is the First Cause of all physical phenomena. Despite the scholastic adaptations of Aristotle, the church still regarded Christian Aristotelianism with some suspicion, and in 1277 many of Aristotle's theories were condemned. That condemnation indirectly served to keep medieval science from falling totally under the influence of scholastic teachings.

Medieval thinkers integrated the cosmology of Aristotle and Ptolemy into a Christian framework that drew a sharp distinction between the world beyond the moon and an earthly realm. Celestial bodies were composed of the divine ether, a substance too pure, too spiritual to be found on earth; heavenly bodies, unlike those on earth, were immune to all change and obeyed different laws of motion than earthly bodies did. The universe was not homogeneous but was divided into a higher world of the heavens and a lower world of earth. Earth could not compare with the heavens in spiritual dignity, but God had nevertheless situated it in the center of the universe. Earth deserved this position of importance, for only here was the drama of salvation performed. This vision of the universe was to be shattered by the Scientific Revolution.

A New View of Nature

Renaissance Background

With the advent of the Renaissance, which began in Italy in the late fourteenth century, a new breed of intellectuals began to challenge medieval assumptions about human beings and nature. These thinkers were armed with a collection of newly discovered ancient Greek and Roman texts (see Chapter 13). The philosophy of Plato was seized on as an alternative to medieval scholasticism.

The great strength of Plato's philosophy lay in his belief that one must look beyond the appearance of things to an invisible reality that is simple, rational, and given to coherent, mathematical explanation. Plato's search for this fundamental reality would influence thinkers of the Scientific Revolution.

Renaissance Platonists interpreted Plato from a Christian perspective, and they believed that the Platonic search for truth about nature, about God's work, was but another aspect of the search for knowledge about God. The universities of Italy, as well as the independent academies founded in Italian cities, became centers where the Platonists taught, translated, and wrote commentaries about Plato's philosophy. These humanists tried to study the invisible world of Ideas and Forms that Plato claimed to be the essence of reality. Music and mathematics, they believed, provided contact with this universal, eternal, and unchanging higher reality. The leading thinkers of the Scientific Revolution found inspiration in the Platonic tradition that nature's truths apply universally and possess the elegance and simplicity of mathematics.

The thinkers of the Scientific Revolution also drew on a tradition of magic that reached back to the ancient world. In the first and second centuries A.D., various practitioners and writers elaborated on the mystical and magical approach to nature. Many of these anonymous students of magic were in contact with the Hermetic tradition. They believed that there had once been an ancient Egyptian priest, Hermes Trismegistus, who had possessed secret knowledge about nature's processes and the ultimate forces at work in the universe. In the second century A.D., this magical tradition was written down in a series of mystical dialogues about the universe. When Renaissance Europeans rediscovered these second-century writings, they erroneously assumed the author to be Hermes and his followers. Hence the writings seemed to be even older than the Bible.

This Hermetic literature glorified both the mystical and the magical. It prescribed that true knowledge comes from a contemplation of the One, or the Whole—a spiritual reality higher than, yet significantly for the development of science, embedded in nature. Some of these ancient writings argued that the sun was the natural symbol of this Oneness, and such an argument seemed to give weight to a heliocentric picture of the universe. The Renaissance followers of Hermes indulged in both what would now be called magic and what would be called science without seeing any fundamental distinction between them. The route that the searcher for nature's wisdom took did not matter as much as the quest did. As a result, in early modern Europe the practitioners of alchemy and astrology could also be mathematicians and astronomers, and the distinction we draw today between magic and science—between the irrational and the rational—would not have been understood by leading natural philosophers of the sixteenth and seventeenth centuries.

The Hermetic approach to nature also resembled Platonism in certain important ways. Both strove for perfection and a higher, spiritual reality, but the *magus,* or Hermetic magician, took certain shortcuts. The magus presumed that study and mental discipline were important, but that ultimate wisdom could come to its seeker through *gnosis,* an immediate, overpowering insight into the One, or God, or Nature. Important contributors to the Scientific Revolution, notably Johannes Kepler and Isaac Newton, grasped at the promise of such wisdom. Kepler believed in astrology, and Newton was profoundly interested in alchemy.

The Renaissance revival of ancient learning contributed a new approach to nature, one that was simultaneously mathematical, experimental, and magical. While the achievements of modern science depend on experimentation and mathematical logic, the compelling impulse to search for nature's secrets presumes a degree of self-confidence best exemplified and symbolized by the magician. Eventually, in one of the important by-products of the Scientific Revolution, the main practitioners of the new science would repudiate magic, largely because of its secretive quality and because of its associations with popular culture and religion. But the demise of magic should not obscure its initial role, among many other factors, as a stimulus for scientific inquiry and enthusiasm.

The Copernican Revolution

Nicolaus Copernicus was born in Poland in 1473. As a young man, he enrolled in the University of Cracow, where he may have come under the influence of Renaissance Platonism, which was spreading outward from the Italian city-states. Copernicus also journeyed to Italy, and in Bologna and Padua he may have been exposed to ancient Greek texts containing arguments for the sun being the center of the universe.

Copernicus' interest in mathematics and astronomy was stimulated by contemporary discussions of the need for calendar reform, and this topic required a thorough understanding of Ptolemaic astronomy. But the latter's mathematical complexity troubled Copernicus, trained, as he had been, in the new humanism. Copernicus believed that truth was the product of elegance and simplicity, and those qualities were lacking in Ptolemaic astronomy. In addition, Copernicus knew that Ptolemy had predecessors among the ancients who philosophized about a heliocentric universe or who held Aristotle in little regard. His Renaissance education gave Copernicus not a body of new scientific truth, but rather the courage to break with traditional truth taught in the universities.

Toward the end of his stay in Italy, Copernicus became convinced that the sun lay at the center of the universe. So he set out on a lifelong task to work out mathematical explanations of how the heliocentric universe operated. Because he did not want to engage in controversy with the followers of Aristotle, Copernicus published his findings only in 1543 in a work entitled *On the Revolutions of the Heavenly Spheres*. Legend says his book, which in effect began the Scientific Revolution, was brought to him on his deathbed.

The treatise retained some elements of the Aristotelian-Ptolemaic system. Copernicus never doubted Aristotle's basic notion of the perfect circular motion of the planets, or the existence of crystalline spheres within which the stars revolved, and he retained many of Ptolemy's epicycles. But Copernicus was trying to propose a heliocentric model of the universe that was mathematically simpler than Ptolemy's earth-centered universe. In this effort, Copernicus partially succeeded, for his system eliminated a significant number of Ptolemy's epicycles and cleared up some problems that had troubled astronomers.

Copernicus' genius was expressed in his ability to pursue an idea—a sun-centered universe—and to bring to that pursuit lifelong dedication and brilliance in mathematics. By removing the earth from its central position and by giving it motion—that is, by making the earth just another planet—Copernicus undermined the system of medieval cosmology and made the birth of modern astronomy possible.

But because they were committed to the Aristotelian-Ptolemaic system and to Biblical statements that supported it, most thinkers rejected Copernicus' conclusions. They also raised specific objections. The earth, they said, is too heavy to move. How, they asked, can an object falling from a high tower land directly below the point from which it was dropped if the earth is moving so rapidly?

Tycho and Kepler: The Laws of Planetary Motion

The most gifted astronomer in the generation after Copernicus, Tycho Brahe (1546–1601),

Tycho Brahe and His Observatory's Interior. Although Tycho Brahe remained a staunch Aristotelian, his observation of a new star in 1572 and a comet in 1577 challenged these traditional views. His precise scientific approach to astronomy and careful mathematical calculations were to be his greatest legacy. (*The British Library*)

never accepted the Copernican system. He did, however, realize more fully than any contemporaries the necessity for new observations. Aided by the king of Denmark, Tycho built the finest observatory in Europe to use in his work.

In 1572 he observed a new star in the heavens—a discovery that offered a direct and serious challenge to the Aristotelian assumption that the heavens are unalterable, fixed, and perfect. To this discovery of what eventually proved to be an exploding star, Tycho added his observations on the comet of 1577. He demonstrated that it moved unimpeded through the areas between the planets, that it passed right through the crystalline spheres. This discovery raised the question of whether such spheres existed, but Tycho himself remained an Aristotelian. Although his devotion to a literal reading of the Bible led Tycho to reject the Copernican sun-centered universe, he did propose an alternative system in which the planets revolved around the sun, but the sun moved about a motionless earth.

Tycho's fame ultimately rests on his skill as a practicing astronomer. He bequeathed to future generations precise calculations about the movements of heavenly bodies, which proved invaluable. These calculations were put to greatest use by Johannes Kepler (1571–1630), a German who collaborated with Tycho during the latter's final years. Tycho bequeathed his astronomical papers to Kepler, who brought to this data a scientific vision that was both experimental and mystical.

Kepler searched persistently for harmonious laws of planetary motion. He did so because he believed profoundly in the Platonic ideal: a spiritual force infuses the physical order; beneath appearances are harmony and unity; and the human mind can begin to comprehend that unity only through gnosis—a direct and mystical realization of unity—and through mathematics. Kepler believed that both approaches were compatible, and he managed to combine them. He believed in and practiced astrology (as did Tycho), and throughout his lifetime, Kepler tried to contact an ancient but lost and secret wisdom.

In the course of his studies and observations of the heavens, Kepler discovered the three basic laws of planetary motion. First, the orbits of the planets are elliptical, not circular as Aristotle and Ptolemy had assumed, and the sun is one focus of the ellipse. Unlike Tycho,

Kepler accepted Copernicus' theory and provided proof for it. Kepler's second law demonstrated that the velocity of a planet is not uniform, as had been believed, but increases as its distance from the sun decreases. Kepler's third law—that the squares of the times taken by any two planets in their revolutions around the sun are in the same ratio as the cubes of their average distances from the sun—brought the planets together into a unified mathematical system.

The significance of Kepler's work was immense. He gave sound mathematical proof to Copernicus' theory, eliminated forever the use of epicycles that had saved the appearance of circular motion, and demonstrated that mathematical relationships can describe the planetary system. But Kepler left a significant question unresolved: what kept the planets in their orbits? Why did they not fly out into space or crash into the sun? The answer would be supplied by Isaac Newton, who synthesized the astronomy of Copernicus and Kepler with the new physics developed by Galileo.

Galileo: Experimental Physics

At the same time that Kepler was developing a new astronomy, his contemporary Galileo Galilei (1564–1642) was breaking with the older physics of Aristotle. A Pisan by birth, Galileo lived for many years in Padua, where he conducted some of his first experiments on the motion of bodies. Guided by the dominant philosophy of the Italian Renaissance—the revived doctrines of Plato—Galileo believed that beyond the visible world lay universal truths, subject to mathematical verification. Galileo insisted that the study of motion entails not only the use of logic (as Aristotle had believed) but also the application of mathematics. For this Late Renaissance natural philosopher, mathematics became the language of nature. Galileo also believed that only after experimenting with the operations of nature can the philosopher formulate the harmonious laws of the universe and give them mathematical expression.

In his mechanical experiments, Galileo discovered that uniform force applied to bodies of unequal weights would produce, all other things being equal, a uniform acceleration. He demonstrated that bodies fall with arithmetic regularity. Motion could, therefore, be treated mathematically.

Galileo came very close to perceiving that inertia governs the motion of bodies, but his concept of inertia was flawed. He believed that inertial force was circular. He did not grasp what Newton would later proclaim, that bodies move in a straight line at a uniform velocity unless impeded. But Galileo's effect was enormous; he had suggested that terrestrial objects could in theory stay in motion forever.

Galileo established a fundamental principle of modern science—the order and uniformity of nature. There are no distinctions in rank or quality between the heavens and earth; heavenly bodies are not perfect and changeless as Aristotle had believed. In 1609, Galileo built a telescope through which he viewed the surface of the moon. The next year, in a treatise called *The Starry Messenger,* he proclaimed to the world that the moon "is not smooth, uniform, and precisely spherical as a great number of philosophers believe it and the other heavenly bodies to be, but is uneven, rough, and full of cavities . . . being not unlike the face of the earth, relieved by chains of mountains and deep valleys."[1] In addition, Galileo observed spots on the sun, providing further evidence that heavenly objects, like earthly objects, undergo change. There are no higher and lower worlds; nature is the same throughout.

Through his telescope Galileo also saw moons around Jupiter—a discovery that served to support the Copernican hypothesis. If Jupiter had moons, then all heavenly bodies did not orbit the earth. The moons of Jupiter removed a fundamental criticism leveled against Copernicus and opened up the possibility that indeed the earth, with its own

moon, might be just like the planet Jupiter, and both might in turn revolve around a central point—the sun.

With Galileo, the science of Copernicus and the assault on Aristotle entered a new phase. Priests began to attack Galileo from their pulpits in Florence, and they were backed by teachers within the academic community who routinely taught the old astronomy. These teachers saw a threat to their own power in Galileo's public notoriety and following among the laity. A secret group of priests and academics, named the "Liga," formed with the express purpose of silencing Galileo, and they used Aristotle and the Bible to attack him. Galileo had boldly defied this old elite and championed a new scientific learning for the laity; he proclaimed the new science as a new body of learning that required a new elite freed from the chains of tradition, knowledgeable in mathematics, and committed to experimentation. But in the early sixteenth century the Catholic church saw danger on every front: Protestants in Germany, recalcitrant people in nearly every state, laity demanding new schools offering practical education for their children. Now Galileo was supporting a view of the universe that conflicted with certain scriptural texts.

In 1632, Galileo's teachings were condemned and he was placed under house arrest. In this confrontation between the old clerical elite and the new secular elite, the old won out. But the price paid was high indeed. Science as preached by Galileo was not, as he knew perfectly well, inherently dangerous to Catholicism. But the clergy and their academic allies saw it as a challenge to their power, and they could enlist the papacy and the Inquisition in their support. As a result, students of the new science in Catholic countries looked to Protestant countries as places to live or publish their books. Censorship worked to stifle intellectual inquiry, and by the middle of the seventeenth century science had become, because of historical circumstance, an increasingly Protestant and northern European phenomenon.

The Newtonian Achievement

By the middle of the seventeenth century, largely because of the work of Copernicus, Kepler, and Galileo, Aristotle and Ptolemy had been dethroned. A new philosophy of nature and a new science had come into being whose essence lay in the mathematical expression of physical laws that describe matter in motion. Yet what was missing was an overriding law that could explain the motion observed in the heavens and on earth. This law was supplied by Isaac Newton.

Newton was born in 1642 in Lincolnshire, England, the son of a modest yeoman. He acquired a place at Trinity College, Cambridge, because of his intellectual promise, and there he devoted himself to natural philosophy and mathematics. His native talents were cultivated by tutors who gave him the latest works in philosophy to read; some of these works, in a form of Christian Platonism, emphasized the workings in the universe of spiritual forces derived from God. Newton's student notebooks survive and show him mastering these texts while also trying to understand the fundamental truths of Protestant Christianity as taught at Cambridge. Combining a Christian Platonism with a genius for mathematics, Newton produced an elegant synthesis of the science of Kepler and Galileo that eventually captured the imagination of European intellectuals.

In 1666, Newton formulated the mathematics for the universal law of gravitation, and in the same year, after rigorous experimentation, he determined the nature of light. The sciences of physics and optics were transformed. However, for many years, Newton did not publish his discoveries, partly because even he did not see the immense significance of his work. Finally, another mathematician and friend, Edmund Halley, persuaded him to publish under the sponsorship of the Royal Society. The result was the *Principia Mathematica* of 1687. In 1704, Newton published his *Opticks* and revealed his theory that light was corpuscular in nature and that it emanated from luminous bodies in a way that scientists later described as waves.

Of the two books, both monumental achievements in the history of science, the *Principia* made the greater impact on contemporaries. Newton not only formulated universal mathematical laws, but offered a philosophy of nature that sought to explain the essential structure of the universe: matter is always the same; it is atomic in structure, and in its essential nature it is dead or lifeless; and it is acted upon by immaterial forces that are placed in the universe by God. Newton said that the motion of matter could be explained by three laws: inertia, that a body remains in a state of rest or continues its motion in a straight line unless impelled to change by forces impressed upon it; acceleration, that the change in the motion of a body is proportional to the force acting upon it; and that for every action there is an equal and opposite reaction.

Newton argued that these laws apply not only to observable matter on earth but also to the motion of planets in their orbits. He showed that planets did not remain in their orbits because circular motion was "natural" or because crystalline spheres kept them in place. Rather, said Newton, planets keep to their orbits because every body in the universe exercises a force on every other body, a force that he called *universal gravitation*. Gravity is proportional to the product of the masses of two bodies and inversely proportional to the square of the distance between them. It is operative throughout the universe, whether on earth or in the heavens, and it is capable of mathematical expression. Newton was building his theory on the work of other scientific giants, notably Kepler and Galileo; yet no one before him possessed the breadth of vision, mathematical skill, and dedication to rigorous observation to combine this knowledge into one grand synthesis.

With Newton's discovery of universal gravitation, the Scientific Revolution reached its culmination. The universe could now be described as matter in motion; it was governed by invisible forces that operated everywhere, both on earth and in the heavens, and these forces could be expressed mathematically. The medieval picture of the world as closed, earth-bound, and earth-centered had been replaced by a universe seen to be infinite, governed by universal laws, and containing the earth as simply another planet.

But what was God's role in this new universe? Newton and his circle labored to create a mechanical world-picture dependent on the will of God, and in those efforts they were largely successful. Newton retained a central place for a providential deity who operates constantly in the universe; at one time he believed that gravity was simply the will of God operating on the universe. As Newton said in the *Opticks*, the physical order "can be the effect of nothing else than the wisdom and skill of a powerful ever-living agent."[2] Because of his deeply held religious convictions, Newton allowed his science to be used in the service of the established Anglican church. Newton, a scientific genius, was also a deeply religious thinker, who was committed to Protestant government.

Biology, Medicine, and Chemistry

The spectacular advances made in physics and astronomy in the sixteenth and seventeenth centuries were not matched in the biological sciences. Indeed, the day-to-day practice of medicine throughout western Europe changed little in the period from 1600 to 1700, for much of medical practice relied frequently on astrology.

Doctors clung to the teachings of the ancient practitioners Galen and Hippocrates. In general, Galenic medicine paid little attention to the discovery of specific cures for particular diseases. As a follower of Aristotle, Galen emphasized the elements that make up the body—he called their manifestations *humors*. A person with an excess of blood was sanguine; a person with too much bile was cho-

Sir Isaac Newton by Sir Godfrey Kneller (1646–1723). Newton's discovery of universal gravitation, a process that could be expressed mathematically, capped the Scientific Revolution. Pope's epitaph for him proclaimed, "Nature, and Nature's Laws lay hid in Night./ God said, 'Let Newton be!' and All was Light." (*National Portrait Gallery, London*)

leric. Health consisted of a restoration of balances among these various elements, so Galenic doctors often prescribed purges of one sort or another. The most famous of these was bloodletting, but sweating was also a favorite remedy. These methods were often as dangerous as the diseases they sought to cure, but they were taught religiously in the medical schools of Europe.

Despite the tenacity of Galenic medicine, innovators and reformers attempted during the sixteenth and seventeenth centuries to challenge and overturn medical orthodoxy. With an almost missionary zeal, Paracelsus (1493–1541), a Swiss-German physician and

Hermeticist, introduced the concept of diagnostic medicine. He argued that particular diseases can be differentiated and are related to chemical imbalances. His treatments relied on chemicals and not on bloodletting or the positions of the stars (although he did not discount such influences), and he proclaimed an almost ecstatic vision of human vitality and longevity. In most universities the faculties of medicine bitterly opposed his views, but by the mid-seventeenth century in England, and later in that century in France, Paracelsian ideas had many advocates. Support for Paracelsian medicine invariably accompanied an attack on the traditional medical establishment and its professional monopoly, and it often indicated support for the new science in general. The struggle between Galenists and Paracelsians quickly took on a social dimension; the innovators saw themselves pitted against a medical elite that, in their opinion, had lost its commitment to medical research and existed solely to perpetuate itself.

Victory came very slowly to the Paracelsians. In late-seventeenth-century France, the king himself intervened to allow medical students at the Sorbonne to read the writings of the medical reformers. But Paracelsian medicine was not really accepted until the eighteenth century. Universities like Leiden in The Netherlands adopted a new chemical approach to medicine and spawned a new generation of doctors who were capable of advancing daily medical practice beyond a slavish following of the ancient texts. Simultaneously, there was an upgrading in the social position of surgeons, who had been seen until then as lowly handworkers quite separate from and beneath medical practitioners. Gradually during the eighteenth century, enlightened doctors developed skill in both chemistry and surgery.

The medical reforms of the eighteenth century did not rest solely on the Paracelsian approach; they also relied heavily on the experimental breakthroughs made in the science of anatomy. A pioneer in this field was the Belgian surgeon Andreas Vesalius (1514–1564), who published *The Structure of the Human Body* in 1543. Opposing Galenic practice, Vesalius argued for observation and anatomical dissection as the keys to knowing how the human body works. By the late seventeenth century, doctors had learned a great deal about the human body, its structure, and its chemistry.

The study of anatomy yielded dramatic results. In 1628, William Harvey (1578–1657) announced that he had discovered the circulation of the blood. Harvey compared the functioning of the heart to that of a mechanical pump, and once again this tendency to mechanize nature, so basic to the Scientific Revolution in physics, led to a significant discovery. Yet the acceptance of Harvey's work was very slow, and the practical uses of his discovery were not readily apparent.

The mechanization of the world-picture entailed more than the destruction of the cosmology advanced by Aristotle and Ptolemy. What was also at stake were the explanations offered for everyday physical events. In the Aristotelian and medieval outlook, bodies moved because it was in their nature to do so. Aristotle had postulated "forms" at work in nature; Latin translations and scholastic commentaries identified these forms as spirits, invisible forces inherent in nature that produced changes as diverse as the growth in plants, the fall of heavy objects to the earth, or even (according to Catholic theologians) the transformation of bread and wine into the body and blood of Christ. The dethroning of Aristotelian explanations for physical phenomena assaulted whole systems of knowledge, often of a theological nature, that went to the heart of medieval belief about the nature of creation and God's relation to it.

Predictably, the final assault on the Aristotelian world view came from Protestant England. By the seventeenth century, English scientific reformers had begun to equate Aristotle with Catholic teachings. Robert Boyle (1627–1691), the father of modern chemistry, believed that Aristotle's physics amounted to little more than magic. Boyle wanted to abolish the spirits on which Catholic theology rested; he advocated that scientists adopt the zeal of the magicians without their secretive practices and their conjuring with spirits. As an alternative to spirits, Boyle adopted the atomic explanation that matter is made up of small, hard, indestructible particles that behave with regularity and explain changes in gases, fluids, and solids.

Boyle pioneered in the experimental method with such exciting and accurate results that by the time of his death, no serious scientist could attempt chemical experiments without following his guidelines. Thus the science of chemistry acquired its characteristic experimentalism; it was also based on an atomic theory of matter. But not until late in the eighteenth century was this new discipline applied to medical research.

Prophets and Proponents of the New Science

The spectacular scientific discoveries of the early modern period necessitated a complete rethinking of the social and intellectual role of scientific inquiry. Science needed prophets and social theorists to give it direction and to assess its implications. During the early modern period, three major reformers attempted, in disparate ways, to channel science into the service of specific social programs: Giordano Bruno (1548–1600), Francis Bacon (1561–1626), and René Descartes (1596–1650).

Bruno

Giordano Bruno's life is one of the most fascinating and tragic to be found in the turbulent world of the Reformation and Counter Reformation. Born in Italy, Bruno began his mature years as a monk and was burned at the stake by the church. What led him to this cruel fate was his espousal of new religious ideas, which were in fact as old as the second

century A.D., but which threatened the beliefs of the church. Bruno found in Hermetic philosophy, which he believed to be confirmed by Copernicus' heliocentric theory, the foundation of a new universal religion. He proposed that religion should be based on the laws found in nature and not on supernaturally inspired doctrines taught by the clergy.

Bruno was one of those Late Renaissance reformers who believed that the Hermetic philosophy, with its mystical approach to God and nature, held the key to true wisdom. The Hermetic philosophy accords the sun a special symbolic role because it infuses life into nature. On the basis of his belief, Bruno accepted Copernicus' sun-centered concept of the universe and began to write and preach about it all over Europe. Indeed, Bruno's fertile imagination, fired by Hermetic mysticism and the new science, led him to be one of the first Europeans to proclaim that the universe is infinite, filled with innumerable worlds. He also speculated that there might be life on other planets.

All of these notions were regarded by the church as dangerous. Bruno was in effect posing the Hermetic philosophy coupled with the new science as an alternative religious vision to either Protestantism or Catholicism. His sense of awe and enchantment with the natural order is similar to that found later among eighteenth-century freethinkers, who saw the scientific study and contemplation of nature, along with a vague sense of the Creator's majesty, as an alternative to organized religious worship. Bruno was a prophet of the new science to the extent that he saw its discoveries as confirming his belief in the wonders of creation. Creation was indeed so wondrous that it could be worshiped—the natural world could replace the supernatural as a fitting object for human curiosity and glorification.

Bacon

In contrast to Bruno's mysticism, the decidedly practical and empirical Francis Bacon stands as the most important English proponent of the new science, although not its most important practitioner. Unlike Bruno, Bacon became profoundly suspicious of magic and the magical arts, not because they might not work, but because he saw secrecy and arrogance as characteristic of their practitioners. Bacon was Lord Chancellor of England under James I, and he wrote about the usefulness of science partly in an effort to convince the crown of its advantages.

No philosopher of modern science has surpassed Bacon in elevating the study of nature into a humanistic discipline. In the *Advancement of Learning* (1605), Bacon argued that science must be open and free and all ideas must be allowed a hearing. Science must have human goals: the improvement of humanity's material condition and the advancement of trade and industry, but not the making of war or the taking of lives. Bacon also preached the necessity that science possess an inductive methodology grounded on experience; the scientist should first of all be a collector of facts.

Although Bacon was rather vague about how the scientist as a theorist actually works, he knew that preconceived ideas imposed on nature seldom yield positive results. An opponent of Aristotle, Bacon argued that university education should move away from the ancient texts and toward the new learning. As a powerful civil servant, Bacon was not afraid to attack the guardians of tradition. The Baconian vision of progress in science leading to an improvement of the human condition inspired much scientific activity in the seventeenth century, particularly in England.

Descartes

René Descartes, a French philosopher of the first half of the seventeenth century, went to the best French schools and was trained by the Jesuits in mathematics and scholastic philosophy. Yet in his early twenties, he experienced a crisis in confidence. He felt that everything he had been taught was irrelevant and meaningless.

Descartes began to search within himself for what he could be sure was clear and distinct knowledge. All he could know with certainty was the fact of his existence, and even that he knew only because he experienced not his body, but his mind: "I think, therefore I am." From this point of certitude, Descartes deduced God's existence. God exists because Descartes had in his mind an idea of a supreme, perfect being which, he reasoned, could only have been put there by such a being, not by any ordinary mortal. Therefore, God's existence means that the physical world must be real, for no Creator would play such a cruel trick and invent a vast hoax.

Descartes thus found confidence in the fact of his own existence and in the reality of the physical world, which he thought could best be understood through reason and mathematics. Scientific thought for Descartes meant an alternative to the chaos of conflicting opinions and the tyranny of truths learned, but not experienced, for oneself. Descartes, possibly as a result of knowing Bacon's ideas, also believed that "it is possible to attain knowledge which is very useful in life, and that, instead of that speculative philosophy which is taught in the schools, we may find a practical philosophy by means of which . . . we can . . . thus render ourselves the masters and possessors of nature"[3] (*Discourse on Method*).

Descartes has rightly been called the father of modern philosophy and one of the first prophets of modern science. He recognized the power that can come to individuals who ground knowledge not on the fact of God's existence, but on a willful assertion of their own ability as thinkers and investigators. Solely by applying their human minds to the world around them, human beings can achieve scientific knowledge that will make them the masters and possessors of nature. Descartes believed so fully in the power of unaided human reason that his practical science was largely deductive and not sufficiently based on rigorous experimentation. He thought that the scientist, aided by mathematics, could arrive at correct theories without necessarily testing them against experience.

The prophetic visions of Bruno, Bacon, and Descartes brought for the first time in the West the realization of the potential importance of scientific knowledge. Science could become the foundation of a new religiosity grounded on the practical study of nature— one that was eventually used by Enlightenment reformers to displace the authority of traditional religion. At the same time, science could also serve the needs of humanity. It could give to its practitioners a sense of power and self-confidence unimagined even by Renaissance proponents of individualism.

The Social Context of the Scientific Revolution

The Scientific Revolution reached its culmination during the second half of the seventeenth century in England at a time when that society was torn by revolution and civil war. That revolutionary context profoundly affected the direction of modern science. In the society that produced Boyle and Newton, the dreams of Bacon and Descartes were never actualized in ways they would have recognized, because social and political events intervened to shape science in ways they could not have expected.

By the 1640s, the influence of the writings of Kepler, Galileo, Bacon, and Descartes, had created in England a new science, with mechanical principles, mathematical theorems, and universal forces replacing the old world view. Just as the new science was developing as a recognized body of learning, political revolution erupted. In opposition to absolute monarchy and the established church, the Puritans sought social and political reform, the rule of Parliament, and a church governed by true Calvinists rather than by bishops. This Puritan Revolution played a crucial role in the formation of modern science.

René Descartes by Franz Hals (c. 1580–1666). Descartes is both the father of modern philosophy and the prophet of modern science. He placed his faith above all in the human intellect and its ability to achieve scientific knowledge, and made significant practical contributions in algebra. (*Royal Museum of Fine Arts, Copenhagen*)

The Puritan reformers championed the new science and encouraged young experimentalists to follow Bacon's call to put science in the service of humanity. The Puritan encouragement of science made it socially respectable, as well as religiously wholesome; the fear that mechanical notions might separate Creator from Creation seemed irrelevant. The Puritan promoters of science encouraged young gentlemen like Robert Boyle and his circle at Oxford to experiment and to use science to reform the university and improve the human condition, both material and spiritual.

As victory came to the Puritan side with the execution of Charles I in 1649, the revolution began to take a turn never intended by the Puritan reformers. The victorious army was dangerously close to becoming an independent force, and its ranks were made up of religious and political radicals. As representatives of the lower classes, they demanded a share in the reforms initiated by the Puritan landowners. They also questioned the social uses of the new science and advocated in its place the introduction of scientific learning closer to the folk practices and needs of the poor. Boyle and his scientific associates grew increasingly alarmed by these demands, and they in turn advocated their science as an alternative to the science and magic proposed by the radicals. Suddenly, the new science assumed a social and political meaning never imagined by its earliest proponents, yet similar to its role in modern industrial society.

Science, Boyle argued, must be conducted by cautious experimentation, and its benefits should be determined by scientists who are supported by the state. Despite Bacon's dreams, Boyle and his circle argued that science should focus on unraveling the mysteries of the universe and that the practical application of these theoretical insights, although desirable, should not be given highest priority. When science was applied practically, they said, it should not be primarily a means of redressing human ills, but should serve the interests of commerce and industry. Finally, natural philosophy, the understanding of nature underlying scientific research, should be compatible with the truths of Christianity. Boyle and his associates reacted violently against versions of the mechanical philosophy, as found in Descartes, that threatened to divorce science from religion.

The English Revolution anticipated a development that would become common: the channeling of science in the interest of the state and existing social arrangements. The Puritan reformers gave England a lead over much of Europe in scientific innovation. By the second half of the seventeenth century, many major scientific discoveries of the Scientific Revolution, particularly Newton's work, occurred within the intellectual milieu created by the English Revolution.

Newton adopted the experimental techniques first advocated by Boyle and his associates. He also embraced a highly spiritualized version of God's relationship to material creation—one taught in reaction to the reforming and democratizing tendencies within the English Revolution. As a result of his experimental rigor, his mathematical genius, and the philosophy of nature he learned as a young man at Cambridge, Newton articulated universal laws that became the foundation for the next century or more of European scientific inquiry.

The Newtonian synthesis came to mean more than simply a program for further scientific research. With his encouragement, Newton's followers preached the meaning of his science from their Anglican pulpits and also in countless books translated into every European language. They argued that Newtonian science should be used as a model for all human learning and, further, that the order and harmony of the Newtonian universe stood for the order and harmony that legally bound kings may impose on their subjects. The Newtonian universe would be constitutional at the same time that it was monarchical, and therein lay its appeal to Continental Europeans disillusioned with the excesses of absolute monarchy. What impressed them was the way in which the advocates of English science also accepted the principle of religious toleration and supported the rule of law binding both king and parliament. It was a model that thinkers we now describe as enlightened eagerly embraced.

According to this Newtonian model, just as God controls matter, people should control natural resources, trade, and industry—all for the purpose of serving their own interests. Order will result from the pursuit of self-interest, because order is inherent in the universe, which also means that society and government must be firmly controlled by legitimate authority. To challenge the existing social and political order, provided it operates according to constitutional law, would be, in effect, to challenge the harmony intended by God for both the human and the natural worlds.

The version of human progress suggested by the Newtonian synthesis laid great emphasis on the application of mechanical science to practical problems such as mining, hydrostatics, and the invention of mechanical devices. The Newtonians of the eighteenth century encouraged in their scientific lectures an approach to nature that made early industrialization possible, first in England and then gradually on the Continent.

Newtonian ideas, however, also encouraged European reformers to use the new science as an alternative to the doctrinal rigidity of established churches. The earliest supporters of Newtonian science in Europe before 1730 were committed to establishing learned journals or editing new encyclopedias intended to make learning accessible to as wide an audience as possible. In their eagerness to embrace the order, constitutional harmony, and progress promised by the Newtonian vision, however, European reformers of the eighteenth century were in one sense blind. Generally they failed to notice the dangers inherent in ruthlessly exploiting nature through the application of mechanical devices. The results of that exploitation only became apparent during the first decades of the nineteenth century in the industrialized areas of England and Scotland. By then, however, the Newtonian faith in the benefits offered by science, and the assumption that these benefits could be reaped without destroying the human and natural resources upon which they rested, had become nearly universal.

The Meaning of the Scientific Revolution

The Scientific Revolution was decisive in shaping the modern mentality; it shattered the medieval view of the universe and replaced it with a wholly different world-view. Gone was the belief that a motionless earth was at the center of a universe that was finite and enclosed by a ring of stars. Gone too was the belief that the universe was divided into higher and lower worlds and that different laws of motion operated in the heavens than operated on earth. The universe was now viewed as a giant machine operating according to universal laws that could be expressed mathematically; nature could be mastered.

The methodology that produced this new view of nature—the new science—played a crucial historical role in reorienting Western thought away from medieval theology and metaphysics and toward the study of physical and human problems. In the later Middle Ages, most men of learning were Aristotelians and theologians. But by the mid-eighteenth century, knowledge of Newtonian science and the dissemination of useful learning had become the goal of the educated classes. All knowledge, it was believed, could emulate scientific knowledge; it could be based on observation, experimentation, and rational deduction; it could be systematic, verifiable, progressive, and useful. At every turn the advocates of this new approach to learning hailed the scientists of the sixteenth and seventeenth centuries as proof that no institution or dogma had a monopoly on truth—the scientific approach would yield knowledge that might, if properly applied for the good of all people, produce a new and better age. Such an outlook gave thinkers new confidence in the power of the human mind to master nature and led them to examine European institutions and traditions with an inquiring, critical, and skeptical spirit. Thus inspired, the reformers of the eighteenth century would seek to create an Age of Enlightenment.

The Scientific Revolution ultimately weakened traditional Christianity. God's role in a mechanical universe was not clear. Newton had argued that God not only set the universe in motion but still intervened in its operations, thus leaving room for miracles. Others retained a place for God as Creator but regarded miracles as limitations on nature's mechanical perfection. Soon other Christian teachings came under attack as contrary to the standards of verification postulated by the new science. Applied to religious doctrines, Descartes's reliance on methodical doubt and clarity of thought and Bacon's insistence on careful observation led thinkers to question the validity of Christian teachings. Theology came to be regarded as a separate and somewhat irrelevant area of intellectual inquiry that was not fit for the interests of practical, well-informed people. Not only Christian doctrines but also various widespread and popular beliefs came under attack. Magic, witchcraft, and astrology, still widespread among the European masses, were regarded with disdain by elite culture. The Scientific Revolution widened the gap between the elite culture of the rich and landed and popular culture. The masses of people remained devoted to some form of traditional Christianity, while the uncertainty of a universe governed by devils, witches, or the stars continued to make sense to peasants and laborers who remained powerless in the face of nature or the domination of the rich and landed.

In Catholic countries, where the Scientific Revolution began, there was, by the early seventeenth century, a growing hostility toward scientific ideas. The mentality of the Counter Reformation enabled lesser minds to exercise their fears and arrogance against any idea they regarded as suspicious. Galileo was caught in this hostile environment, and the Copernican system was condemned by the church in 1616.

As a result, by the second half of the seventeenth century science had become an increasingly Protestant phenomenon. The major Protestant countries like England and the Netherlands accorded greater intellectual freedom and their presses were relatively free. Eventually, science also proved to be more compatible with the Protestant mind's emphasis on individual striving and the mercantile exploitation of nature for material gain.

Gradually the science of Newton became the science of western Europe: nature mechanized, analyzed, regulated, and mathematicized. As a result of the Scientific Revolution, learned Westerners came to believe more strongly than ever that nature could be mastered. Mechanical science—applied to canals, engines, pumps, and levers—had become the science of industry. Thus the Scientific Revolution, operating on both the intellectual and commercial levels, laid the groundwork for two major developments of the modern West—the Industrial Revolution and the Age of Enlightenment.

Notes

1. Excerpted in Stillman Drake, ed., *Discoveries and Opinions of Galileo* (New York: Doubleday, 1957), p. 28.

2. Excerpted in *Newton's Philosophy of Nature*, H. S. Thayer, ed. (New York: Hafner, 1953), p. 177.

3. Excerpted in Norman Kemp Smith, ed., *Descartes' Philosophical Writings* (New York: Modern Library, 1958), pp. 130–131.

Suggested Reading

Bernal, J. D., *Science in History* (1969). A learned classic on the meaning of science in history.

Briggs, Robin, *The Scientific Revolution of the Seventeenth Century* (1969). A clearly written survey with documents.

Butterfield, Herbert, *The Origins of Modern Science* (1957). A highly regarded analysis of the emergence of modern science.

Clark, G. N., *Science and Social Welfare in the Age of Newton* (1949). A standard work on the social uses of the new science.

Cohen, I. B., *The Birth of a New Physics* (1960). Authoritative, but difficult for the novice.

Drake, Stillman, ed., *Discoveries and Opinions of Galileo* (1957). A good place to start to learn Galileo's most important ideas.

Jacob, James R., *Robert Boyle and the English Revolution* (1977). Deals with the relationship between Boyle's science and the English Revolution.

Jacob, Margaret C., *The Newtonians and the English Revolution* (1976). Deals with the social meaning of Newton's science.

Kearney, Hugh, *Science and Social Change, 1500–1700* (1971). Includes a discussion of the social setting of the Scientific Revolution.

Koestler, Arthur, *The Watershed: A Biography of Johannes Kepler* (1960). A fascinating biography of a founder of modern science and a practitioner of magic.

Kuhn, Thomas, *The Structure of Scientific Revolutions* (1962). One of the first non-Marxist attempts to show that science has social implications.

Whitehead, Alfred North, *Science and the Modern World* (1960). An early and important meditation on the meaning of modern science.

Review Questions

1. What was the difference between the scientific understanding of the universe and the medieval understanding of it?

2. Describe the major achievements of Copernicus, Kepler, Galileo, and Newton.

3. How did the practice of medicine change during the Scientific Revolution? Describe the changes.

4. What were Bruno's differences with the church? Describe what happened.

5. Does modern science conform to Francis Bacon's ideals? List these ideals and discuss why each does/does not conform.

6. In what ways did the English Revolution shape modern science?

7. How did early modern Europeans perceive the new science as it was developing?

18

*The Age of Enlightenment:
Reason and Reform*

The eighteenth century is called the Age of Enlightenment or Age of Reason, for during this period an educated elite, expressing supreme confidence in the power of reason, attempted a rational analysis of European institutions and beliefs. The Enlightenment was heavily indebted to the discoveries of the seventeenth-century Scientific Revolution— to the experimental method pioneered by Galileo, Boyle, and Newton and to the mechanical picture of the universe formed by Newton. The Scientific Revolution seemed to show that order and mathematically demonstrable laws were at work in the physical universe. The thinkers of the Enlightenment, called *philosophes*, argued that it should be possible to examine *human* institutions with the intention of imposing a comparable order and rationality.

Late in the eighteenth century Immanuel Kant (1724–1804), a moderate German leader of the Enlightenment, was asked to define it. Kant argued that it was the bringing of "light into the dark corners of the mind," the dispelling of ignorance and superstition. Kant went to the heart of one aspect of the Enlightenment, that is, its insistence that each individual should reason independently without recourse to the authority of the schools, churches, and universities.[1]

Kant believed that this call for self-education meant no revolutionary disruption of the political order. In general, modern liberal and enlightened culture aimed at a gradual evolutionary transformation of the human condition; only a few radical thinkers during the eighteenth century were prepared to envision an immediate political disruption of the traditional authority of monarchy, aristocracy, and church. The mainstream of the Enlightenment was politically moderate, worshipful of the new science, critical of the clergy and all rigid dogma, tolerant in religious matters, and even loyal to enlightened monarchs who were prepared to keep the clerical censors away from the new books.

Philosophes were found most commonly in the major European cities, with Paris during the 1770s becoming the center of the Enlightenment. These embattled reformers developed a new style of writing philosophy, one that tried to make it understandable and even simple, sometimes entertaining. In the process the philosophes became journalists, propagandists, and in some cases brilliant literary stylists who made their various languages more readable for literate laymen and also the growing number of literate women.

Enlightenment culture relied heavily on the printing press as an agent of propaganda. Through it, reformers could address the increasingly large audiences found in the major European cities—London, Amsterdam, and Paris, in particular. Thanks to the power of the printed word, the Enlightenment was able to agitate for reform by addressing an educated and urban lay audience directly. In essays, monthly journals, works of fiction, and even mildly pornographic and anonymous tales, the philosophes attacked many of the abuses of eighteenth-century society—religious fanaticism and intolerance, the idleness and corruption of the aristocracy, the use of torture, terrible prison conditions, slavery, and violations of natural rights.

Although not profoundly original, the philosophes were bold in their criticism of existing institutions, especially the churches and the clergy. In essence, the philosophes were condemning all vestiges of medieval culture. Inevitably, modern liberal thought, as initiated by the Enlightenment, emerged as hostile to scholastic learning, priests, and eventually in some quarters, to Christianity itself. The philosophes expressed confidence in science and reason, espoused humanitarianism, and struggled for religious liberty and freedom of thought and person. Combining these values with a secular orientation and a belief in future progress, the philosophes helped to shape, if not to define, the modern outlook.

The Science of Religion

Christianity Under Attack

No single thread had united Western culture more powerfully than Christianity. Until the eighteenth century, educated people, especially rulers and servants of the state—however un-Christian their actions—had to give allegiance to one or another of the Christian churches. The Enlightenment's importance lies in the fact that it produced the first widely read and systematic assault on Christianity launched from within the ranks of the educated. The leaders of the Enlightenment sought to repudiate traditional Christianity and to put in its place a rational system of ethics and philosophy based on scientific truths.

The philosophes offered several approaches to the problem posed by religion. Moderates like Kant wanted simply to put a basic belief in God's existence and his providence in place of the formal dogmas of the Christian churches. *Deists* wanted God to be so removed from his creation as to be irrelevant to everyday human concerns. *Pantheists* or *materialists* wanted people to acknowledge Nature as if it were God; they wished to eliminate at a single stroke any form of religious belief and worship that remotely resembled Christianity. Members of this last group were labeled atheists by their enemies.

Most philosophes were deists who tried to make religion compatible with a scientific understanding of nature. Deists believed only those Christian doctrines that could meet the test of reason. For example, they considered it reasonable to believe in God, for only with a creator, they said, could such a superbly organized universe have come into being. But after God set the universe in motion, said the deists, he took no further part in its operations. Thus, while deists retained belief in God the Creator, they rejected clerical authority, revelation, original sin, and miracles. They held that Biblical accounts of the resurrection and of Jesus walking on water or waking the dead could not be reconciled with natural law. Deists viewed Jesus as a great moral teacher, not the son of God, and they regarded ethics, not faith, as the essence of religion; rational people, they said, served God best by treating their fellow human beings justly.

Whatever the remedy proposed to address the problem of religion, the effect was the same: the clergy of every denomination conducted a counteroffensive against the philosophes that went on throughout the eighteenth century. Nevertheless, in the last decade of the seventeenth century, the Enlightenment was well underway in England and in the Netherlands. Two factors were crucial in creating this new intellectual milieu: the Revolution of 1688–89 (see Chapter 16) and the relative freedom of the press in both countries. The Revolution of 1688–89 weakened the power of the established church in England. The church lost the right to prosecute heretics and to control the licensing of books. The Revolution also united England and the Netherlands in a war against French aggression and the absolutist regime of the French king, Louis XIV (d. 1715). Suddenly it seemed to educated people on both sides of the English Channel that the unchecked power of kings, supported as they were in European countries by established churches firmly in their control, was the most serious abuse of all time. It appeared as though only in those countries where the power of the clergy had been weakened, would true intellectual inquiry occur.

Skeptics and Freethinkers

The earliest examples of enlightened thinking show the importance of both the Revolution of 1688–89 and the war being waged against France. During the 1690s, the intellectual response to the unbridled power of Louis XIV joined with an assault on the power of the clergy; skeptics like Pierre Bayle (1647–1706) came to distrust all dogmas and to see superstition as a social evil far more dangerous than atheism. Bayle was a French Protestant forced to flee to the Netherlands as a result of Louis XIV's campaign against his coreligionists. Although a Calvinist himself, Bayle also ran into opposition from the strict Calvinist clergy, who regarded him as lax on doctrinal matters. He attacked his critics and persecutors in a new and brilliant form of journalism: his *Historical and Critical Dictionary* (1697), which was more an encyclopedia than a dictionary. Under alphabetically arranged subjects and in copious footnotes, Bayle gave the most recent learning of the day on various matters and never missed an opportunity to ridicule the dogmatic, the superstitious, or the just plain arrogant. In Bayle's hands, skepticism became a tool; rigorous questioning of accepted ideas became a method for arriving at new truths. As Bayle noted in his *Dictionary:* "it is therefore only religion that has anything to fear from Pyrrhonism [i.e., skepticism]."[2] In this same critical spirit, Bayle, in his dictionary article entitled "David," compared Louis XIV to Goliath. The message was clear enough: great tyrants and the clergy who prop them up should beware of self-confident, independently minded citizens who are skeptical of the claims of authority made by kings and churches and are eager to use their own minds to search for truth.

Bayle's *Dictionary*, which was in effect the first encyclopedia, had an enormous impact throughout Europe. Its very format captured the imagination of the philosophes. Here was a way of simply, even scientifically, classifying and ordering knowledge. In Paris during the 1740s, a group of publishers decided to produce a bigger and better encyclopedia than any of the others that had yet been published. They hired a young and impoverished hack writer named Denis Diderot to compile it, and thus began the rise to fame of one of the most important philosophes of the Enlightenment. Encyclopedias not only created an easy way of acquiring the most recent learning; they sometimes also established the literary careers of their editors.

Partly through Bayle's writings, *skepticism* became an integral part of the Enlightenment's approach to religion. In the middle of the eighteenth century, Scottish philosopher and historian David Hume (1711–1776) used skepticism to reject revealed religion and to arrive at a universal religion based on reason and common sense. In *An Enquiry Concerning Human Understanding* (1748), Hume argued that what is called *cause and effect* is not that at all. He said that the human mind associates events or ideas; they have no inherent association, and they were not designed by some outside force to be causes and effects.

The implications of skepticism as articulated by Bayle and Hume were clear: randomness, not the providential design argued by the clergy, governs human events, and it is the individual's job to impose order where none exists. All should be skeptical of assertions that "God ordains" certain human actions. Skepticism dealt a serious blow to revealed religion and seemed to point in the direction of "natural" religion, that is, toward a system of beliefs and ethics designed by rational people on the basis of their own needs.

The idea of natural religion had already been championed during the 1690s by the English freethinkers. These early representatives of the Enlightenment used the term *freethinking* to signal their hostility to established church dogmas and their ability to think for themselves.

They looked back to the English Revolution of mid-century for their ideas about government; many of the English freethinkers were republicans in the tradition established by important figures of the Interregnum. Indeed, the English freethinkers of the 1690s and beyond helped to popularize English republican ideas at home and in the American colonies, where in 1776 they would figure prominently in the thinking of American revolutionaries.

The freethinkers had little use for organized religion, or even for Christianity itself. For example, in 1696 the freethinker John Toland (1670–1722) published a tract called *Christianity Not Mysterious*, in which he argued that any religious doctrine that seemed to contradict reason or common sense—for example, Jesus' resurrection or the miracles of the Bible—ought to be discarded. Toland also attacked the clergy's power; in his opinion the Revolution of 1688–89 had not gone far enough in undermining the power of the established church and the king. Toland and his freethinking associates Anthony Collins and Matthew Tindal wanted England to be a republic governed by "reasonable" people who worshiped, as Toland proposed, not a mysterious God but intelligible Nature.

In science combined with skepticism and anticlericalism, thoughtful critics could find ample reason for abandoning all traditional authority. By 1700 a general 'crisis of confidence in established authority had been provoked by the works of Bayle and the freethinkers and of some seventeenth-century philosophers, such as Descartes. Once started in England and the Netherlands and broadcast via Dutch printers, the Enlightenment almost immediately became international.

Freemasons

As the Enlightenment's search for a new foundation of religious belief went on, some seekers inevitably attempted to found new clubs or societies. These groups tried to fulfill social and intellectual needs no longer being met by the traditional churches. In 1717 a group of London gentlemen, many of them very interested in the new science and in the spread of learning in general, founded the Grand Lodge, a collection of various Masonic lodges that had met in pubs around the city. From that date can be traced the origins of European Freemasonry and its spread into almost every European country.

Freemasonry was not originally intended to rival the churches. Nevertheless, the lodges became, especially on the Continent, alternative meeting places for men interested in the Enlightenment. Some French philosophes joined lodges in Paris, as did some clergy. In Vienna at the time of Mozart, who was a Freemason, and in Berlin during the reign of Frederick the Great, Masonic membership came to denote support for enlightened and centralized government, often in opposition to the local power of the clergy and the old aristocracy. For a few extreme rationalists bent on destroying the Christian churches, the Masonic lodges also seemed to function as a commendable alternative form of religion, complete with ritual, charitable funds, and sense of community. By the middle of the eighteenth century, perhaps as many as 50,000 men belonged to Masonic lodges in just about every major European city and in many towns as well. These lodges became places where men could gather and openly discuss their beliefs and the writings of the philosophes if they cared to do so. The ideals of equality and liberty took on meaning in these private gatherings, where the participants could reflect on the inequality they perceived in the world around them. Eventually some lodges admitted women as members.

Voltaire the Philosophe

The French possessed a vital tradition of intellectual skepticism going back to the late sixteenth century, as well as a tradition of scientific rationalism easily identified with Descartes. In the early eighteenth century, however, the French found it difficult to gain access to the new literature of Enlightenment because the French printing presses were among the most tightly controlled and censored in Europe. As a result a brisk but risky traffic developed in clandestine books and manuscripts subversive of authority, and French-language journals poured from Dutch presses.

As a poet and writer struggling for recognition in Paris, the young François Marie Arouet, known to the world as Voltaire (1694–1778), encountered some of the new ideas that were being discussed in private gatherings (called *salons*) in Paris. Care had to be taken in the French capital by those educated people who wanted to read books and discuss ideas hostile to the church or to the Sorbonne,

Bust of Voltaire by Jean-Antoine Houdon, (1741–1828). Voltaire (born François Marie Arouet) was the internationally famous supporter of the Enlightenment. He was poet, journalist, essayist, and utopian thinker. Superstition, the Catholic church, and arbitrary government were the constant targets of his critical pen. (*The Fine Arts Museums of San Francisco, Mr. and Mrs. E. John Magnin Gift*)

the clerically controlled university. Individuals had been imprisoned for writing, publishing, or owning books hostile to Catholic doctrine. Although Voltaire learned something of the new enlightened culture in Paris, it was in 1726, when he journeyed to London, that Voltaire the poet became Voltaire the philosophe.

In England, Voltaire became acquainted with the ideas of John Locke (1632–1704) and

Isaac Newton. From Newton, Voltaire learned the mathematical laws that govern the universe; he witnessed the power of human reason to establish general rules that seem to explain the behavior of physical objects. From Locke, Voltaire learned that people should believe only those ideas received from the senses. Locke's theory of learning, his epistemology, impressed many of the proponents of the Enlightenment. Again the implications for religion were most serious: if people believe only those things that they experience, they will be unable to accept mysteries and doctrines simply because they are taught by churches and the clergy. Voltaire experienced considerable freedom of thought in England and saw a religious toleration that stood in stark contrast to the absolutism of the French kings and the power of the French clergy. He also witnessed a freer mixing of bourgeois and aristocratic social groups than was permitted in France at this time.

Throughout his life Voltaire was a fierce supporter of the Enlightenment and a bitter critic of churches and the Inquisition. Although his own books were banned in France, he probably did more there than any other philosophe to popularize the Enlightenment and to mock the authority of the clergy. In *Letters Concerning the English Nation* (1733), Voltaire wrote about his experiences in England. He offered constitutional monarchy, new science, and religious toleration as models to be followed by all of Europe. In the *Letters* he praised English society for its encouragement of these ideals.

Voltaire never ceased to mock the purveyors of superstition and blind obedience to religious authority. In such works as *Candide* (1759) and *Micromegas* (1752), Voltaire castigated the clergy, as well as other philosophical supporters of the status quo who would have people believe that this was the best of all possible worlds.

Voltaire was a practical reformer who campaigned for the rule of law, a freer press, religious toleration, humane treatment of criminals, and a more effective system of government administration. His writings constituted a radical attack on aspects of eighteenth-century French society. Yet like so many of the philosophes, Voltaire feared the power of the people, especially if goaded by the clergy. He was happiest in the company of the rich and powerful, provided they tolerated his ideas and supported reform. Not surprisingly, Voltaire was frequently disappointed by eighteenth-century monarchs, like Frederick the Great in Prussia, who promised enlightenment but sought mainly to increase their own power and that of their armies.

Political Thought

With the exception of Machiavelli in the Renaissance and Thomas Hobbes and the republicans during the English Revolution, the Enlightenment produced the greatest originality in political thought witnessed in the West up to that time. Three major European thinkers and a host of minor ones wrote treatises on politics that remain relevant to this day: John Locke, *Two Treatises of Government* (1690), Montesquieu, *The Spirit of the Laws* (1748), and Jean Jacques Rousseau, *The Social Contract* (1762). All repudiated the divine right of kings and were concerned with checking the power of monarchy; each offered different formulas for achieving that goal. These major political theorists of the Enlightenment were also aware of the writings of Machiavelli and Hobbes and, although often disagreeing with them, borrowed some of their ideas.

Machiavelli had analyzed politics in terms of power, fortune, and the ability of the individual ruler; he did not call in God to justify the power of princes or to explain their demise. Machiavelli had also preferred a republican form of government to monarchy, and his republican vision never lost its appeal during the Enlightenment. Very late in the century, most liberal theorists recognized that the republican form of government, or at the least the virtues practiced by citizens in a

Map 18.1 Europe, 1715 ▶

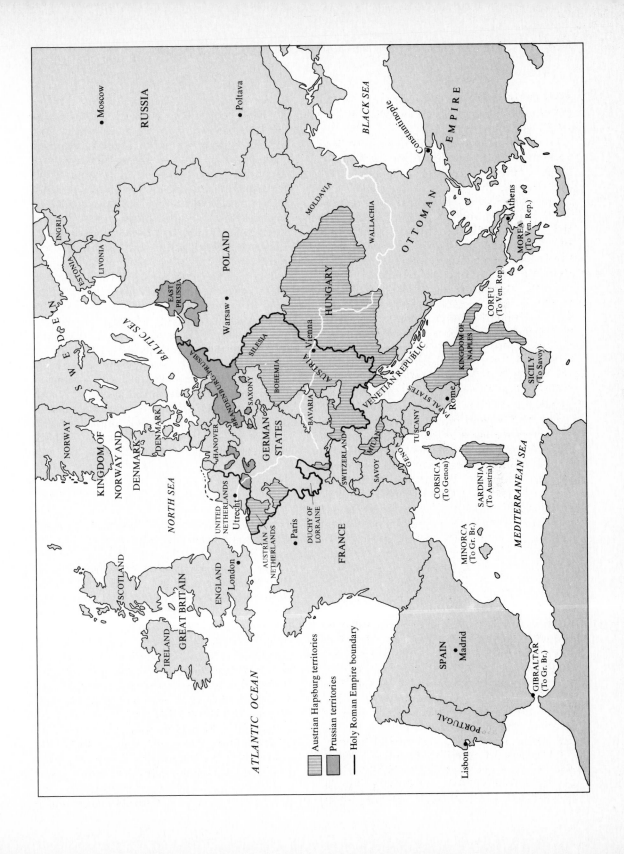

RUSSIA

• Moscow

• Poltava

BLACK SEA

Constantinople

OTTOMAN EMPIRE

INGRIA

LIVONIA

ESTONIA

MOLDAVIA

WALLACHIA

Athens

MOREA
(To Ven. Rep.)

POLAND

• Warsaw

EAST
PRUSSIA

S W E D E N

BALTIC SEA

HUNGARY

CORFU
(To Ven. Rep.)

SILESIA

SAXONY

BOHEMIA

Vienna

AUSTRIA

VENETIAN REPUBLIC

KINGDOM OF
NAPLES

SICILY
(To Savoy)

NORWAY

KINGDOM OF
NORWAY AND
DENMARK

DENMARK

HANOVER

GERMAN
STATES

BAVARIA

SWITZERLAND

MILAN

SAVOY

GENOA

PAPAL STATES

Rome

TUSCANY

NORTH SEA

UNITED
NETHERLANDS

Utrecht •

AUSTRIAN
NETHERLANDS

• Paris

DUCHY OF
LORRAINE

FRANCE

CORSICA
(To Genoa)

SARDINIA
(To Austria)

MINORCA
(To Gr. Br.)

MEDITERRANEAN SEA

SCOTLAND

IRELAND

GREAT BRITAIN

ENGLAND

London •

ATLANTIC OCEAN

SPAIN

Madrid •

GIBRALTAR
(To Gr. Br.)

PORTUGAL

Lisbon •

Austrian Hapsburg territories

Prussian territories

Holy Roman Empire boundary

republic, offered the only alternative to the corruption and repression associated with absolutist monarchy.

Enlightenment political thinkers were ambivalent toward much of the writing of Thomas Hobbes (1588–1679). All, however, liked the fact that Hobbes championed self-interest as a valid reason for engaging in political activity and that he produced a secular theory of politics, refusing to bring God into his system to justify the power of kings. Hobbes said that their power rested not on divine right but on a contract made with their subjects. Hobbes made that contract unbreakable—once established, the power of the government, whether king or parliament, was absolute. But Hobbes published his major work, *Leviathan,* in 1651, soon after England had been torn by civil war; as a result he was obsessed with the issue of political stability. He feared that left to their own devices, men would kill one another; the "war of all against all"[3] would prevail without the firm hand of a sovereign to stop it. Enlightenment theorists, beginning with John Locke, denied that governments possessed absolute power over their subjects, and to that extent they repudiated Hobbes. Many European thinkers of the eighteenth century, including Rousseau, also rejected his gloomy view that human nature is greedy and warlike.

Locke

Probably the most widely read political philosopher during the first half of the eighteenth century was John Locke. His *Two Treatises of Government* were seen as a justification for the Revolution of 1688–89 and the notion of government by consent of the people. Although they were published in 1690, Locke had written his treatises before the Revolution, but that was not known during the Enlightenment.

Locke's theory, in its broad outlines, stated that the right to govern derived from the consent of the governed and was a form of contract. When people gave their consent to a government, they expected it to govern justly, to protect their property, and to ensure certain liberties for the propertied. If a government attempted to rule absolutely and arbitrarily—if it violated the natural rights of the individual—it reneged on its contract and forfeited the loyalty of its subjects. Such a government could be legitimately overthrown. Locke believed that a constitutional government that limited the power of rulers was the best defense of property and individual rights.

Late in the eighteenth century, Locke's ideas were used to justify liberal revolutions both in Europe and in America. Indeed, the importance of Locke's political philosophy was not simply his recourse to contract theory as a justification of constitutional government; it was also his assertion that the community may take up arms against its sovereign in the name of the natural rights of liberty and property. Locke's ideas about the foundation of government had greater impact on the Continent and in America in the eighteenth century than they did in England.

Montesquieu

Baron de la Brède et de Montesquieu (1689–1755) was a French aristocrat who, like Voltaire, visited England late in the 1720s and who knew the writings of Locke. Montesquieu had little sympathy for revolutions, but he did approve of constitutional monarchy. His primary concern was to check the unbridled authority of the French kings. In opposition to the Old Regime, Montesquieu proposed a balanced system of government with an executive branch offset by a legislature whose members were drawn from the landed and educated elements in society. Montesquieu genuinely believed that the aristocracy possessed a natural and sacred obligation to rule and that their honor called them to serve the community. He also aimed to fashion a government that channeled the interests and energies of its people, a government that was not bogged down in corruption and inefficiency. His writings, particularly *The Spirit of the Laws,* established Montesquieu as a major philosophe whose philosophy possessed republican tendencies and as a critic of the Old Regime in France. Once again, innovative political thinking highlighted the failures of absolutist government and pointed to the need for some kind of representative assembly in every European country.

Rousseau

Not until the 1760s did democracy find its champion in Jean Jacques Rousseau (1712–1778). Rousseau based his politics on contract theory—the people choose their government and, in so doing, they effectively give birth to civil society. But Rousseau further demanded that the contract be constantly renewed, and that government be made immediately and directly responsible to the will of the people. *The Social Contract* opened with this stirring cry for reform: "Man is born free; and everywhere he is in chains," and it went on to ask how that can be changed. Freedom is in the very nature of man; "to renounce liberty is to renounce being a man, to surrender the rights of humanity and even its duties."[4]

Rousseau's political ideal was the small Greek city-state, for in these ancient communities people participated actively and directly in politics and were willing to sacrifice self-interest to the needs of the community. To the ancient Greek, said Rousseau, the state was a moral association that made him a better person, and good citizenship was the highest form of excellence. In contrast, modern society, said Rousseau, was prey to many conflicting interests; the rich and powerful used the state to preserve their interests and power, and the poor and powerless viewed it as an oppressor. Consequently, the obedience to law, the devotion to the state, and the freedom that had characterized the Greek city-state had been lost.

In the *Social Contract*, Rousseau tried to resolve the conflict between individual free-dom and the demands of the state. His solution was a small state, modeled after the Greek city-state. Such a state, said Rousseau, should be based on the *general will*—that which is best for the community, which expresses the community's common interests. Rousseau wanted laws of the state to coincide with the general will; people would have the wisdom to arrive at law that served the common good, but to do so they would have to set aside selfish interests for the good of the community. For Rousseau freedom consisted of obeying laws prescribed by citizens inspired by the general will. Citizens themselves must constitute the lawmaking body; lawmaking cannot be entrusted to a single person or a small group.

For Rousseau, those who disobey laws—who act according to their private wills rather than in accordance with the general will as expressed in law—degrade themselves and undermine the community. Therefore government has the right to force citizens to be obedient—to compel them to exercise their individual wills in the proper way. Rousseau believed that government has the right to enforce freedom, but he did leave the problem of minority rights unresolved.

No philosopher of the Enlightenment was more dangerous to the Old Regime than Rousseau. His ideas were perceived as truly revolutionary—as a direct challenge to the power of kings, churches, and aristocrats. Although Rousseau thought that many leaders of the Enlightenment had been corrupted by easy living and the life of the salons, with their attendant elegant ladies and dandies, he nevertheless earned an uneasy place in the ranks of the philosophes. In the French Revolution, his name would be invoked to justify democracy, and of all the philosophes, Rousseau would probably have been least horrified by the early phase of that revolutionary upheaval.

Rousseau also saw society as the corrupter of human beings who, left to their own devices, were inherently virtuous and freedom loving. A wide spectrum of opinion in the Enlightenment also saw society if not as corrupting, then at least as needing constant reform. Some enlightened critics were prepared to work with those in power in an effort to bring about concrete social reforms. Other philosophes believed that the key to reform lay not in social and political institutions, but in a change in mentality brought about by education and propaganda.

Social Thought

Psychology and Education

Just as Locke's *Two Treatises of Government* was instrumental in shaping the political thought of the Enlightenment, his *Essay Concerning Human Understanding* (1689) provided the theoretical foundations for an unprecedented interest in education. Locke's view that at birth the mind is blank, a clean slate or *tabula rasa*, held two important implications. First, if human beings were not born with innate ideas, then they were not, as Christianity taught, inherently sinful as a result of Adam and Eve's defiance of God. Second, a person's environment was the decisive force in shaping that person's character and intelligence. Nine of every ten men, wrote Locke, "are good or evil, useful or not, [because of] their education." Such a theory was eagerly received by the reform-minded philosophes, who preferred attributing wickedness to faulty institutions, improper rearing, and poor education—which could be remedied—rather than to a defective human nature.

"Locke has unfolded to man the nature of human reason," Voltaire wrote in his *Letters.* For the Enlightenment, the proper study of humanity addressed the process by which people can and do know. Locke had said that individuals take the data produced by their senses and reflect on it; in that way they arrive at complex ideas. Education obviously requires, in addition to an environment that promotes learning, the active participation of students. Merely receiving

knowledge not tested by their own sense experience is inadequate.

More treatises were written on education during the eighteenth century than in all previous centuries combined. On the Continent where the clergy controlled many schools and all universities, the educated laity began to demand state regulation and inspection of all educational facilities. This insistence was one practical expression of the growing discontent with the clergy and their independent authority. By the second half of the century, new schools and universities in Prussia, Belgium, Austria, and Russia attempted to teach practical subjects suited to the interests of the laity. Predictably, science was given a special place in these new institutions. Yet in 1762, one French author estimated that fewer than one-tenth of all school-age boys in France received a proper education. France was one of the more advanced European countries; by 1789 probably about half of the men and about 20 percent of the women were literate.

Prussia and Scotland excelled in the field of education, but for very different reasons. In Prussia, Frederick the Great decreed universal public education for boys as part of his effort to surpass the level of technical expertise found in other countries. His educational policy was another example of his using the Enlightenment to increase the power of the central government. In Scotland the improvements in education were largely sponsored by the established Calvinist church. The heirs of the Protestant Reformation, with its emphasis on the Bible and hence on the printed word, were fully capable of sponsoring progressive educational policies without the help of the Enlightenment.

In the teaching of medicine, the University of Leiden in the Netherlands became the most advanced institution in Europe in the eighteenth century. Indeed, its scientific faculty presented Newtonian physics and the latest chemistry to a generation of doctors and engineers assembled from all over Europe. A new medical school was also founded in Vienna. Many Scottish students, often trained in Leiden, brought their knowledge home to make Edinburgh University a major center for medical students.

Locke's doctrine that knowledge comes primarily through experience found its most extreme expression in the writings of Rousseau on education. In *Émile* (1762), Rousseau argued that individuals learn from nature, from people, or from things. Indeed Rousseau wanted the early years of a child's education to be centered on developing the senses, not spent chained to a schoolroom desk. Later, attention would be paid to intellectual pursuits, then finally to morality. Rousseau grasped a fundamental principle of modern psychology—the child is not a small adult, and childhood is not merely preparation for adulthood but a particular stage, with its own distinguishing characteristics, in human development. Children, said Rousseau astutely, should be permitted to behave like children.

Rousseau appealed especially to women to protect their children from social convention, that is, to teach their children about life. There were problems with Rousseau's educational system. He would render the family into the major educational force and he wanted its products to be cosmopolitan and enlightened, singularly free from superstition and prejudice. In the process, women (whom Rousseau would confine to the home) would bear the burden of instilling enlightenment, although they had little experience of the world beyond the family. Rousseau's contradictions sprang in large measure from his desperate search for an alternative to the formal educational systems that existed in his day. In the field of education, the reality of most European schools fell far below the ideal put forward by the philosophes.

Humanitarianism

Crime and Punishment   No society founded on the principles of the Enlightenment could condone the torture of prisoners and the inhumanity of a corrupt legal system. On that all the philosophes were clear, and they had plenty of evidence from their own societies on which to base their condemnation of torture and the inhumanity of the criminal justice system.

If education of children in the eighteenth century was poor, the treatment of criminals was appalling. Conditions differed little whether an individual was imprisoned because of unpaid debts or for being a bandit or murderer. Prisoners were often starved or exposed to disease, or both. On the Continent, where torture was still legal, prisoners could be subjected to brutal interrogation or to random punishment—treatment comparable to anything found today in many dictatorships. In 1777 an English reformer, John Howard, published a report on the state of the prisons in England and Wales: "the want of food is to be found in many country gaols. In about half these, debtors have no bread; although it is granted to the highwayman, the housebreaker, and the murderer; and medical assistance, which is provided for the latter, is withheld from the former." Torture was illegal in England, except in cases of treason, but the prison conditions were often as harmful to the physical and mental health of their inmates as torture was.

Although there is something particularly reprehensible about the torturer, his skills were consciously applauded in many countries during the eighteenth century. Fittingly, the most powerful critique of the European system of punishment came from Italy, where the Inquisition and its torture chambers had reigned with little opposition for centuries. In Milan during the early 1760s, the Enlightenment had made very gradual inroads, and in a small circle of reformers the practices of the Inquisition and the relationship between church and state in the matter of criminal justice were avidly discussed.

Out of that intellectual ferment came one of the most important books of the Enlightenment, *Of Crime and Punishment* (1764) by the Milanese reformer Cesare Beccaria (1738–1794). For centuries, sin and crime had been wedded in the eyes of the church; the function of the state was to punish the second because it was a manifestation of the first. Beccaria cut through that thicket of moralizing and argued that the church should concern itself with sin; it should abandon its prisons and courts. The state should concern itself with crimes against society, and the purpose of punishment should be to reintegrate the individual into society.

Beccaria also went further and inquired into the causes of crime. Abandoning the concept of sin Beccaria, rather like Rousseau, who saw injustice and corruption in the very fabric of society, regarded private property as the root of social injustice and hence the root of crime. Pointedly he asked: "What are these laws I must respect, that they leave such a huge gap between me and the rich? Who made these laws? Rich and powerful men. . . . Let us break these fatal connections. . . . let us attack injustice at its source."[5]

Beccaria's attackers labeled him a *socialist*—the first time (1765) that that term was used—by which they meant that Beccaria paid attention only to people as social creatures and that he wanted a society of free and equal citizens. In contrast, the defenders of the use of torture and capital punishment, and of the necessity of social inequality, argued that Beccaria's teachings would lead to chaos and to the loss of all property rights and legitimate authority. These critics sensed the utopian aspect of Beccaria's thought. His humanitarianism was not directed toward the reform of the criminal justice system alone; he sought to restructure society in such a way as to render crime far less prevalent and, whenever possible, to re-educate its perpetrators.

When Beccaria's book and then the author himself turned up in Paris, the philosophes greeted them with universal acclaim. By the 1760s, Paris had become the center of the Enlightenment, and that period is commonly called the High Enlightenment. All the leaders of the period—Voltaire, Rousseau, Diderot, and the atheist d'Holbach—embraced one or another of Beccaria's views. But if the criminal justice system as well as the schools were subject to scrutiny by enlightened critics, what did the philosophes have to say about

slavery, the most pernicious of all Western institutions?

Slavery   On both sides of the Atlantic during the eighteenth century there was growing criticism of slavery. At first it came from religious thinkers like the Quakers, whose own religious version of enlightenment predated the European-wide phenomenon by several decades. The Quakers were born out of the turmoil of the English Revolution, and their strong adherence to democratic ideas grew out of their conviction that the light of God's truth works in every man and woman. Many philosophes on both sides of the Atlantic knew Quaker thought, and Voltaire, who had mixed feelings about slavery, and Benjamin Franklin, who condemned it, admired the Quakers and their principles.

On the problem of slavery the Enlightenment was strangely ambivalent. In an ideal world—just about all philosophes agreed—slavery would not exist. But such was not the world, and given human wickedness, greed, and lust for power, Voltaire thought that slavery as well as exploitation might be inevitable: "the human race," Voltaire wrote in his *Philosophical Dictionary* (1764), "constituted as it is, cannot subsist unless there be an infinite number of useful individuals possessed of no property at all."[6] Denis Diderot thought that slavery was probably immoral, but given that the French empire subsisted in part on its slaves, their rights could not be discussed, he argued, in a monarchy. Indeed, not until 1794 after the first years of the French Revolution and only after agonized debate, did the French government, no longer a monarchy, finally abolish slavery.

It must be remembered that Enlightenment political thinkers, among them Locke (who condoned slavery) and Montesquieu (whose ideas were used to condone it), rejected God-given political authority and argued for the rights of property-holders and for social utility as the foundations of good government. Those criteria, property and utility, played right into the hands of the proslavery apologists. They particularly cited Montesquieu, who had said

figure . 1.

Slaves Processing Sugar in a Colonial Plantation. This diagram shows slaves running machinery to grind sugar cane into pulp. In the colonies of European countries in the New World and other lands, subjected peoples were used to perform hard labor in the plan- tations and mines. The immorality of slavery was raised initially by religious thinkers and then taken up by Diderot in his *Encyclopédie*. (*Courtesy of the University of Minnesota Libraries*)

that in tropical countries where sloth was "natural," slavery might be useful and even necessary to force people to work. Montesquieu was uncertain about the morality of slavery, but he had also argued that in despotisms the individual would lose little by willingly choosing enslavement. Proslavery propagandists argued, as well, that since most African tribes were despotic, the slaves in European colonies were in effect better off.

Yet the Enlightenment must also be credited with bringing the problem of slavery into the forefront of public discussion in Europe and in the American colonies. The utility argument cut both ways. If the principle held, as so many philosophes argued, that human hap- piness was the greatest good, how could slavery be justified? In his short novel *Candide*, Voltaire has his main character, Candide, confront the spectacle of a young Negro who has had his leg and arm cut off merely because it is the custom of a country. Candide's philosophical optimism is shattered as he reflects on the human price paid by this slave who harvested the sugar that Europeans enjoyed so abundantly. Throughout the eighteenth century the emphasis placed by the Enlightenment on moral sensibility produced a literature that used shock to emphasize over and over again, and with genuine revulsion, the inhumanity of slavery.

By the second half of the century, again

in that ferment of intellectual creativity described as the High Enlightenment, strongly worded attacks on slavery were issued by a new generation of philosophes. With Rousseau in the vanguard, they condemned slavery as a violation of the natural rights of man. In a volume issued in 1755, the great *Encyclopedia* of the Enlightenment, edited by Diderot, condemned slavery in no uncertain terms: "There is not a single one of these hapless souls . . . who does not have the right to be declared free . . . since neither his ruler nor his father nor anyone else had the right to dispose of his freedom."[7] That statement made its way into thousands of copies and various editions of an encyclopedia that was probably the most influential publication resulting from the French Enlightenment.

The *Encyclopedia*'s wide circulation (about 25,000 copies were sold before 1789), often despite the vigorous efforts of censors to stop it, probably tipped the scales to put the followers of the Enlightenment in the antislavery camp. But that victory for humanitarian principles must be seen as clouded by much ambiguous language, coming straight from the pens of some of Europe's supposedly most enlightened thinkers, and downright prejudice against the Negro as a non-European.

Women   The men of the Enlightenment also had some ambiguous things to say about women. Not entirely unlike slaves, women had few property rights within marriage, and their physical abuse by husbands was widely regarded as beyond the purview of the law. Women's education was slighted, and social theorists had for centuries regarded them as inferior. The origins of that sexual inequality intrigued the earliest political theorists, Hobbes and Locke. Both saw that neither nature nor Scripture gave the father dominion in the household. As Hobbes said in *Leviathan,* "in the state of nature, if a man and woman contract so, as neither is subject to the command of the other, the children are the mother's."[8] Yet this perception was never taken up by any of the major philosophes, and indeed neither Hobbes nor Locke concerned

himself with correcting the legal inferiority of women.

Yet by the middle of the eighteenth century, many French philosophes had begun to think about the condition of women and, in the cases of Voltaire and Diderot, had taken up with women, outside of marriage, who were in several areas their intellectual equals. Diderot fretted, as a result, about the poor education accorded to women; yet he also distrusted their apparent commitment to the old religiosity. By the 1750s in Paris, rich women had become the organizers of fashionable salons where writers and enlightened reformers gathered for free and open conversation; Diderot attended such a salon. But Baron d'Holbach, who led the most famous gathering of the 1770s, specifically excluded women because he believed that they lowered the tone and seriousness of the discussion. Rousseau, who had little use for Paris and its fashionable salons, also disdained the elegant women of the drawing rooms.

Rousseau's own conception of women specifically excluded them from the social contract, in that he saw nature as having given men dominion over women and children. Outside the family, in civil society, that dominion is never absolute; it rests on the will of the majority (presumably of men, because in *The Social Contract* Rousseau never mentions women as a part of civil society). In *A Discourse on Political Economy* (1755), Rousseau insists that the patriarchal structure of the family is natural; the primary function of the family is to "preserve and increase the patrimony of the father."[9] Yet Rousseau does allot to women the education of children, and at the end of the eighteenth century, many women saw Rousseau as an ally because his views would lead to an improvement in their domestic status and conceivably in their educational benefits.

With his characteristic skepticism, Hume saw all this ambiguity about women as resulting from men's desire to preserve their power and patrimony. Since men had no guarantees that the children their wives bore were in fact fathered by them, the only re-

Mme. Geoffrin's Salon. The High Enlightenment in the 1740s had Paris as its capital. The new thinking concentrated on social inequalities, especially those that stiffled talented human beings. The salons of exclusive Parisian society, such as that of Mme. Geoffrin, became the forum for the next generation of philosophers after Voltaire and Diderot. (*Lauros-Giraudon/Art Resource*)

course was to try to repress women sexually. According to Hume the necessity "to impose a due restraint on the female sex"[10] led to sexual inequality. But Hume was never troubled sufficiently by that inequality to discuss the point in any detail. And Kant, who defined the Enlightenment so eloquently, argued that the differences between men and women were simply natural. In *Observations on the Feeling of the Beautiful and Sublime* (1764), Kant argued with characteristic idealism that "women have a strong inborn feeling for all that is beautiful, elegant, and decorated . . . they love pleasantry and can be entertained by trivialities." Predictably, Kant concluded that "laborious learning or painful pondering, even if a woman should greatly succeed to it, destroys the merits that are proper to her sex." In that treatise, Kant came dangerously close to denying women any need to know the new science or to speculate: "her philosophy is not to reason, but to sense."[11] This major philosophe almost denied women a right to enlightenment.

Only late in the century, after the French Revolution had begun, did any thinker representative of the Enlightenment challenge Rousseau's views on women. Educated in enlightened circles and familiar with radical philosophes like the American revolutionary Thomas Paine, the English feminist Mary Wollstonecraft (1759–1797) extended the principles of the Enlightenment to the position and status of women. With devastating logic, her *Vindication of the Rights of Woman* (1792) called for "a revolution in female manners— time to restore to them their lost dignity— and make them, as part of the human species, labor by reforming themselves, to reform the world." She mocked the notion of sexual virtues, such as the beauty and modesty of which Kant had written. She believed, somewhat in the manner of Rousseau, only without his one-sex conclusions, that society had corrupted women: "from the tyranny of man the greater part of female follies proceed." Wollstonecraft viewed this corruption as analogous to the evils stemming from property rights and the vast inequalities in privilege and opportunity between the rich and the poor. True to Enlightenment ideals, Wollstonecraft did not attack property rights as such, but she did urge a significant reduction in the gap between the wealthy and the poor. Again in keeping with enlightened prescriptions, she urged that equal public education be made available to both men and women. For Wollstonecraft, feminism brought with it a commitment to universal human values, to excellence in learning—which she had never had the opportunity to pursue—and to "the power of generalizing ideas, of drawing comprehensive conclusions from individual observations."[12] Although she explicitly wrote for middle- and upper-class women and her work had little impact during her lifetime, Wollstonecraft's *Vindication* became a text on which nineteenth-century reformers and socialists could and did build.

Economic Thought

The Enlightenment's emphasis on property as the foundation for individual rights and its search for uniform laws inspired by Newton's scientific achievement led to the development of the science of economics. Appropriately, that intellectual achievement occurred in the most advanced capitalistic nation in Europe, Great Britain. Not only were the British in the vanguard of capitalist expansion; by the third quarter of the eighteenth century that expansion had brought on the start of the Industrial Revolution. Its new factories and markets for the manufacture and distribution of goods provided a natural laboratory where theorists, schooled in the Enlightenment's insistence on observation and experimentation, could observe the ebb and flow of capitalist production and distribution. In contrast to its harsh criticisms leveled against existing institutions and old elites, the Enlightenment on the whole approved of the independent businessman—the entrepreneur. And there was no one more approving than Adam Smith (1732–1790), whose *Wealth of Nations* (1776) became a kind of bible for those who would have capitalist activity stand as uniformly worthwhile, never to be inhibited by outside regulation.

Throughout the seventeenth century in England there had been a long tradition of economic thought. The resulting ideology stressed independent initiative and the freedom of market forces to determine the value of money and the goods it can buy. By 1700 English economic thought was already well ahead of what could be found on the Continent, with the exception of some Dutch writings. That sophistication undoubtedly reflected the complexity of market life in cities like London and Amsterdam.

One important element in seventeenth-century economic thought, as well as in the most advanced thinking on ethics, was the role of self-interest. Far from being viewed as crude or socially dangerous, it was seen as a good thing, to be accepted and even encouraged. In the mid-seventeenth century, Hobbes took the view that self-interest lay

Map 18.2 European Expansion, 1715 ▶

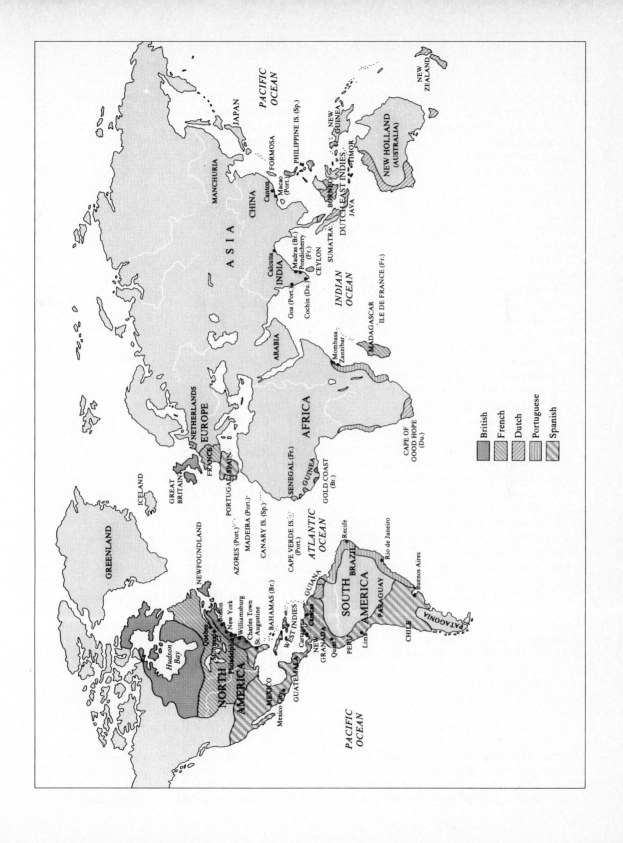

at the root of political action, and by the end of the century, Locke argued that government, rather than primarily restraining the extremes of human greed and the search for power, should first reflect the interests of its citizens. By the middle of the eighteenth century, enlightened theorists all over Europe—especially in England, Scotland, and France—had decided that self-interest was the foundation of all human actions and that at every turn government should assist people in expressing their interests and thus in finding true happiness.

Of course in the area of economic life, government had for centuries regulated most aspects of the market. The classic economic theory behind such regulation was mercantilism. Mercantilists believed that a constant shortage of riches—bullion, goods, whatever—existed, and that governments must so direct economic activity in their states as to compete successfully with other nations for a share of the world's scarce resources. There was also another assumption implicit in mercantilist theory: that money has a "real" value, which governments must protect. Its value is not to be determined solely by market forces.

It required enormous faith in the inherent usefulness of self-interest to assert that government should cease regulating economic activity, that the market should be allowed to be free. That doctrine of *laissez faire*—to leave the market to its own devices—was made the centerpiece of Adam Smith's massive economic study on the origins of the wealth of nations.

As a professor in Glasgow, Scotland, Smith actually went out and observed factories at work; he was one of the first theorists to see the importance of the division of labor in making possible the manufacture of more and cheaper consumer goods. Smith viewed labor as the critical factor in a capitalist economy: the value of money, or of an individual for that matter, rested on the ability to buy labor or the by-products of labor, namely goods and services. According to *The Wealth of Nations*, "Labor is the real measure of the ex-

changeable value of all commodities."[13] The value of labor is in turn determined by market forces, by supply and demand. Before the invention of money or capital, labor belonged to the laborer, but in the money and market society that had evolved since the Middle Ages, labor belonged to the highest bidder.

Smith was not distressed by the apparent randomness of market forces. Beneath this superficial chaos he saw order—the same order he saw in physical nature through his understanding of the new science. He used the metaphor of "the invisible hand" to explain the source of this order; by that he probably meant Newton's regulatory God, made very distant by Smith, who was a deist. That hand would invisibly reconcile self-interest to the common or public interest. With the image of the invisible hand, Smith expressed his faith in the rationality of commercial society and laid the first principle for the modern science of capitalist economics. He did not mean to license the oppression of the poor and the laborer. Statements in *The Wealth of Nations* such as: "Landlords, like all other men, love to reap where they never sowed," or "Whenever there is great property, there is great inequality,"[14] reveal Smith to be a moralist. Yet he knew of no means to stop the exploitation of labor. He believed that its purchase at market value ensured the working of commercial society, and he assumed that the supply of cheap labor was inexhaustible.

The thought of Adam Smith includes extreme versions of two tendencies within Enlightenment thought. The first was the search for laws of society that would imitate the laws postulated by the new science. The second, which was not shared by all philosophes, was an unshakable belief in progress: "In the progress of society . . . each individual becomes more expert in his own peculiar branch, more work is done upon the whole, and the quantity of science is considerably increased by it."[15] Knowledge is progressive, and by implication, the human condition also yields to constant improvement. Smith ignored the appallingly low life-expectancy rates in the new factory towns, and in the process bequeathed a vision of progress wedded to capitalism that remains powerful in some quarters to this day.

The High Enlightenment

More than any other political system in western Europe, the Old Regime in France was directly threatened by the doctrines and reforming impulse of the Enlightenment. The Catholic church was deeply entrenched in every aspect of life—landownership, control over universities and presses, and access to both the court and, through the pulpit, the people. For decades the church had brought its influence to bear against the philosophes, yet by 1750 the Enlightenment had penetrated learned circles and academies in Paris and the provinces. After 1750, censorship of the press was relaxed by a new censor deeply influenced by Enlightenment ideals. In fact, censorship had produced the opposite of the desired effect: the more irreligious and atheistic the book or manuscript was, the more attractive and sought-after it became.

By the 1740s, the fashion among proponents of the Enlightenment was to seek an encyclopedic format for presenting their ideas. This form of writing was the natural byproduct of the Enlightenment's desire to encompass all learning. After Bayle's *Dictionary*, the first successful encyclopedia was published in England by Ephraim Chambers in 1728, and before too long a plan was underway for its translation into French. A leading Freemason in France, the Chevalier Ramsay, even advocated that all the Masonic lodges in Europe should make a financial contribution to this effort, but few, if any, responded to the call.

Four aggressive Parisian publishers took up the task of producing the encyclopedia. One of them had had some shady dealings in clandestine literature that had acquainted him with the more irreligious and daring philosophes in Paris, which is how he knew

the young Denis Diderot (1713–1784). Out of that consortium of publishers and philosophes came the most important book of the Enlightenment, Diderot's *Encyclopedia*. Published in 1751 and in succeeding years and editions, the *Encyclopedia* initiated a new stage in the history of Enlightenment publishing. In the process it brought to the forefront pantheistic and materialistic ideas that until that time, only the most radical freethinkers in England and the Netherlands had openly written about. The new era thus ushered in is called the *High Enlightenment*. It permeated exclusive Parisian society, and it was characterized by a violent attack on the church's privileges and the very foundations of Christian belief. From the 1750s to the 1780s, Paris became the capital of the Enlightenment. The philosophes were no longer a persecuted minority (Diderot had spent six months in jail for his philosophical and libertine writings). Instead, they became cultural heroes. The *Encyclopedia* had to be read by anyone claiming to be educated.

In his preface to the *Encyclopedia*, Diderot's collaborator, Jean d'Alembert (c. 1717–1783), summed up the principles on which it had been compiled. In effect, he wrote a powerful summation of the Enlightenment's highest ideals. He also extolled Newton's science and gave a short description of its universal laws. The progress of geometry and mechanics in combination, d'Alembert wrote in his preface, "may be considered the most incontestable monument of the success to which the human mind can rise by its efforts."[16] In turn, he urged that revealed religion should be reduced to a few precepts to be practiced; religion should, he implied, be made scientific and rational. The *Encyclopedia* itself was self-consciously modeled on Bacon's admonition that the scientist should first of all be a collector of facts; in addition, it gave dozens of examples of useful new mechanical devices.

D'Alembert's preface also praised the psychology of Locke: all that is known, is known through the senses. He added that all learning should be catalogued and made easily and readily available, that the printing press should serve the needs of enlightenment, and that literary societies should be set up that would encourage men of talent. D'Alembert added that "they should banish all inequalities that might exclude or discourage men who are endowed with talents that will enlighten others."[17]

During the High Enlightenment, reformers dwelt increasingly on the Old Regime's inequalities that seemed to stifle men of talent. The aristocracy and the clergy were not always talented and seldom were they agitators for enlightenment and reform. Their privileges seemed increasingly less rational. By the 1780s, Paris had spawned a new generation of philosophes for whom Voltaire, Diderot, and Rousseau were aged or dead heroes. But these young authors found the life of the propagandist to be poor and solitary, and they looked at society's ills as victims rather than reformers. They gained firsthand knowledge of the injustices catalogued so brilliantly by Rousseau in *The Social Contract.*

The High Enlightenment's systematic, sustained, and occasionally violent attacks on the clergy and the irrationality of privilege link that movement with the French Revolution. The link did not lie in the comfortable heresies of the great philosophes, ensconced as they were in the fashionable Parisian salons. Rather, it lay in the way those heresies were interpreted by a new generation of reformers, Marat and Robespierre among them, who in the early days of the Revolution used the Enlightenment as a mirror against which they reflected the evils of the old order.

European Political and Diplomatic Developments

Warfare

The dreams of the philosophes, articulated in almost every area of human experience, seemed unable to forestall troublesome developments in power politics, war, and di-

plomacy. The century was dominated by two areas of extreme conflict: Anglo-French rivalry over control of territory in the New World and hegemony in northern Europe; and intense rivalry between Austria and Prussia over control of central Europe. These major powers, with their imperialistic ambitions, were led by cadres of aristocratic ministers or generals; the Enlightenment did little to displace the war-making role that had belonged to the aristocracy since the Middle Ages.

Yet even in international affairs there was a growing realization, not unrelated to the propaganda of the philosophes, that extreme power held by one state would threaten the order and stability of the whole of Europe. By the early eighteenth century, every European state identified France, by virtue of its sheer wealth and size, as the major threat to European stability.

By this time, France and England were the great rivals in the New World, although colonization had been well underway since the early sixteenth century. Spain had been the first sovereign state to establish an empire in America; located principally in South America and Central America, this empire was based on mining, trade, and slaves. The English and Dutch had followed, first as settlers and then also as slave traders, but their colonies lay to the north—in Virginia, New Amsterdam (later to become New York), and New England. Further north, the French explored and exploited Canada and the region now known as the Midwestern United States. By the early eighteenth century, the Dutch and the Spanish had largely dropped out of the race for colonies in North America, leaving the field to the French and the English.

By the middle of the eighteenth century, the rivalry of these two powers for territory in the New World infected European rivalry in the Old World. Earlier the British had sought to contain the French colossus and to ensure their historic trading interests in

Map 18.3 Europe, 1789 ▶

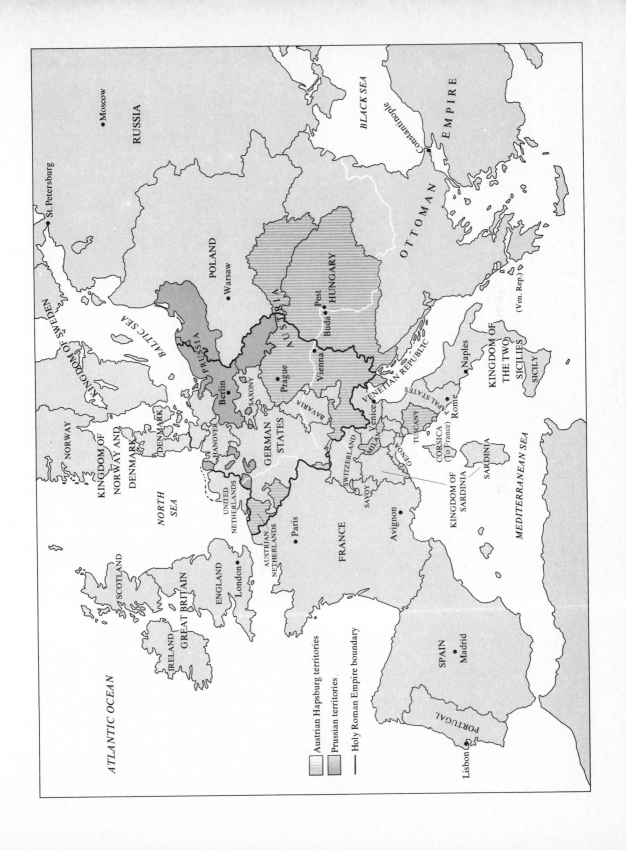

ATLANTIC OCEAN

RUSSIA

Moscow

St. Petersburg

BLACK SEA

Constantinople

OTTOMAN EMPIRE

KINGDOM OF SWEDEN

POLAND

Warsaw

BALTIC SEA

PRUSSIA

Berlin

SAXONY

Prague

AUSTRIA

Vienna

Buda

Pest

HUNGARY

(Ven. Rep.)

KINGDOM OF THE TWO SICILIES

SICILY

Naples

NORWAY

KINGDOM OF NORWAY AND DENMARK

DENMARK

HANOVER

GERMAN STATES

BAVARIA

VENETIAN REPUBLIC

Venice

MILAN

GENOA

PAPAL STATES

Rome

TUSCANY

CORSICA (To France)

SARDINIA

NORTH SEA

UNITED NETHERLANDS

AUSTRIAN NETHERLANDS

SWITZERLAND

SAVOY

Paris

FRANCE

Avignon

KINGDOM OF SARDINIA

MEDITERRANEAN SEA

SCOTLAND

IRELAND

GREAT BRITAIN

ENGLAND

London

SPAIN

Madrid

PORTUGAL

Lisbon

Austrian Hapsburg territories

Prussian territories.

Holy Roman Empire boundary

the Low Countries and the Rhineland by allying with the Dutch Republic and the Austrians, who controlled what is today called Belgium. This alliance of the Maritime Powers (Britain and the Netherlands) with Austria provided the balance of power against France for the entire first half of the eighteenth century.

The English obsession with the security of the Low Countries and with the protection of the market there for English grain and wool led Britain to intervene in Dutch internal affairs. The French were given to invading the Netherlands; they actually did so during the War of the Spanish Succession (1701–1713) and during the War of the Austrian Succession (1740–1748). As a result of the constant French threats, England sought to secure a government in The Hague that would be favorable to British interests, and in 1747 assisted in the restoration of the Dutch stadtholderate to William IV for that purpose. From that time on, the central government in the Netherlands remained cordial to British interests, although Dutch merchants were frequently hostile to that relationship.

The other major European rivalries broke out into hostilities in the 1740s. Wars between Prussia and Austria and between Austria and France were fought because these major powers wanted to secure their areas of domination both in Europe and in the New World. The wars signaled the rise of Prussia to the status of a major power but left the control of northern Europe open to negotiation. If any power could be described as the loser in that decade, it was the French. The wars exposed weaknesses in the French military system, without resolving the larger question of hegemony in Europe and the New World.

The wars also had an unexpected result. In the 1740s it became clear to the English and their Austrian allies that the Dutch did not possess the will or the resources to guard their southern borders adequately. No longer viewed as the centerpiece in the anti-French alliance, the Dutch Republic appeared to be best suited to a weak and ineffectual neutrality.

With the weakening of this tie with the Netherlands, Austria grew discontented with its old allies, while realizing that it was mortally threatened by the growing power of Prussia. In 1740, Frederick the Great of Prussia launched an aggressive foreign policy against neighboring states—the Austrian state of Silesia, in particular. The forces of the new Austrian queen, Maria Theresa, were powerless to resist this kind of military onslaught. In two years, Prussia had acquired what was probably the largest territory captured by any Continental European state in that era. Silesia augmented the Prussian population by 50 percent, and Frederick also acquired a relatively advanced textile manufacturing area. The Austrians never forgave his transgression.

In 1756, Maria Theresa formed an alliance with France against Prussia; the ensuing Seven Years' War (1756–1763) involved every major European power. Austria's alliance with France in 1756, which ended the historic rivalry between France and the house of Hapsburg, is known as the "diplomatic revolution." The Austrians had grown to fear Prussia in the north more than they feared the French. From the Austrian point of view, Prussia had stolen Silesia in 1740, and its restoration was more important than preserving historic rivalries with France. On the French side, King Louis XV longed for an alliance with a Roman Catholic power and for peace in Europe so that France would be better able to wage war against Britain in the New World.

For their part, the British had long since grown disaffected with the Austrians, and they sought and won a new ally in Frederick the Great. He stood at the head of a new state that was highly belligerent yet insecure, for all the European powers had reasons to want to keep Prussia weak and small. The Seven Years' War—which seesawed back and forth, with French, Austrian, and Russian forces ranged against Frederick's Prussians—changed things little in Europe, but it did reveal the extraordinary power of the Prussian war machine. Prussia joined the ranks of the Great Powers.

Hostilities in North America tipped the

balance of power there in favor of the English. From 1754 to 1763 the French and the English fought over their claims in the New World. England's victory in this conflict—known in American history as the French and Indian War—led ultimately to the American Revolution. England secured its claim to control the colonies of the eastern seaboard, a market that would enrich the English industrialists of the next generation enormously—although, from the colonists' viewpoint, unjustly.

The Dutch Revolution of 1747–1748—the only one to occur in western Europe outside of a city-state or colony in the period from 1689 to 1787—was the only indication to be seen there that the Great Powers or the merchant capitalists had anything to fear from their home populations (or from their slave populations), or that the ideas advanced by the philosophes might be put into practice. Unrest began in Amsterdam in 1747 when minor philosophes, freemasons, journalists, and devotees of English ideas shared in leading an artisan-based democratic uprising that failed utterly to achieve its goals. That minor ripple went unnoticed by the many kings, aristocrats, and oligarchs who ruled so comfortably elsewhere. A generation later, their complacency would wither as democratic revolutions swept first through the American colonies and then through every western European state on the Continent. The wars in the mid-1700s, though destructive in many ways, seemed to confirm the internal security and stability of the ruling elites that controlled their respective states.

Enlightened Despotism

Although some of the enlightened prescriptions for the operation of modern society, such as laissez faire, remain current, one ideal commonly discussed and occasionally advocated by the philosophes has long since fallen by the wayside. It was extinguished in large measure by the democratic revolutions of the late eighteenth century.

Enlightened despotism, although apparently a contradiction in terms, was used as a phrase by the French philosophe Diderot as early as the 1760s. Wherever this phrase is used by the philosophes, it refers to an ideal shared by many of them: the strong monarch who would implement rational reforms, who would remove obstacles to freedom and allow the laws of nature to work, particularly in trade, commerce, and book censorship. When historians use the term *enlightened despotism,* they generally are describing the reigns of specific European monarchs and their ministers—Frederick the Great in Prussia; Catherine the Great in Russia; Charles III of Spain; Maria Theresa and, to a greater extent, her son Joseph II in Austria; and Louis XV of France.

These eighteenth-century monarchs listed above instituted specific reforms in education, trade, and commerce and against the clergy. This type of enlightened government must be understood in context: these countries developed late relative to the older states of Europe. Prussia, Austria, and Russia had to move very quickly if they were to catch up to the degree of centralization achieved in England and France. And when monarchies in France and Spain also occasionally adopted techniques associated with enlightened despotism, they generally did so to compete against a more advanced rival—for example, France against England and Spain against France.

Austria   In the course of the eighteenth century, Austria became a major centralized state as a result of the reforms of Charles VI and his successors (see Chapter 16). Although Catholic and devout at home, Charles allied abroad with Protestant Europe against France. In the newly acquired Austrian Netherlands, he supported the progressive and reforming elements in the nobility that opposed the old aristocracy and clergy.

His daughter Maria Theresa (1740–1780) continued this pattern, and the Austrian administration became one of the most innovative and progressive on the Continent.

Maria Theresa, Empress of Austria, by Martin Van Meytens (detail). *Enlightened despot* is used to describe European rulers like Maria Theresa. The philosophes hoped that such monarchs would initiate reforms to guarantee basic freedoms and allow the laws of nature to work. Maria Theresa continued reforms and cultural revivals begun by Charles VI, but always with the purpose of increasing her own power. (*Collection of the John and Mabel Ringling Museum of Art, Sarasota, Florida*)

Many of its leading ministers, like the Comte du Cobenzl in the Netherlands or Gerard van Swieten, Joseph II's great reforming minister, were Freemasons. This movement often attracted progressive Catholics (as well as Protestants and freethinkers) who despised what they regarded as the medieval outlook of the traditional clergy.

Dynastic consolidation and warfare did contribute decisively to the creation of the Austrian state. But in the eighteenth century, the intellectual and cultural forces known as the Enlightenment enabled the state to establish an efficient system of government and a European breadth of vision. With these attributes, Austria came to rival (and in Spain's case to surpass) the older, more established states in Europe. Frustrated in their German territories, the Austrian Hapsburgs concentrated their attention increasingly on their eastern states. Vienna gave them a natural power base, while Catholic religiosity gradually united the ruling elites in Bohemia and Hungary with their Hapsburg kings. Hapsburg power created a dynastic state in Austria, yet all efforts to consolidate the western Empire and to establish effective imperial rule met with failure. The unification of Germany would proceed very slowly and come from somewhat unexpected quarters.

Prussia Under the most famous and enlightened Hohenzollern of the eighteenth century, Prussian absolutism (see Chapter 16) acquired some unique and resilient features. Frederick II, the Great, (1740–1786) pursued a policy of religious toleration and, in so doing, attracted French Protestant refugees, who had manufacturing and commercial skills. Intellectual dissidents, such as Voltaire, were also attracted to Prussia. Voltaire eventually went home disillusioned with this new Prussian "enlightened despotism," but not before Frederick had used him and in the process acquired a reputation for learning. By inviting various refugees from French clerical oppression, Frederick gave Berlin a minor reputation as a center for Enlightenment culture. But along with Frederick's courtship of the French philosophes with their enlightened ideals, there was the reality of Prussian militarism and the servitude of its peasants.

Yet the Hohenzollern dynasty succeeded in creating a viable state built by the labor of its serfs and the power of its Junker-controlled army; and this state would manage to survive as a monarchy until the First World War. By the middle of the eighteenth century, this small nation of no more than 2.5 million inhabitants exercised inordinate influence in European affairs because of its military prowess.

Prussian absolutism rested on the army and the Junker class, and its economy was state directed and financed. Its court expenses were held to a minimum—most state expenditures went into maintaining an army of 200,000 troops—the largest in relation to population for all Europe.

Russia   Russia during the eighteenth century made significant strides, under various monarchs, toward joining the European state system. During the reign of Peter the Great (1682–1725), the Russians established strong diplomatic ties in almost every European capital. In addition, the Russian metal industry became vital to European development. The English, who lacked the forest lands and wood necessary to fire smelting furnaces, grew dependent on Russian-produced iron.

Catherine the Great (1762–1796) consciously pursued policies intended to reflect her understanding of the Enlightenment. These presented contradictions. She entered into respectful correspondence with philosophes, but at the same time she extended serfdom to the entire Ukraine. She promulgated a new, more secular, educational system and sought at every turn to improve Russian industry, but her policies rested on the aggrandizement of the agriculturally based aristocracy. The Charter of Nobility in 1785 forever guaranteed the aristocracy's right to hold the peasants in servitude. The Enlightenment, as interpreted by this shrewd monarch, completed the tendency to monarchical absolutism that had been well underway since the sixteenth century.

The Effects of Enlightened Despotism

Enlightened despotism was, in reality, the use of Enlightenment principles by enlightened monarchs to enhance the central government's power and thereby their own.

These eighteenth-century monarchs knew, in ways their predecessors had not, that knowledge is power; they saw that application of learned theories to policy can produce useful results.

But did these enlightened despots try to create more humanitarian societies in which individual freedom flourished on all levels? In this area, enlightened despotism must be pronounced a shallow deployment of Enlightenment ideals. For example, Frederick the Great decreed the abolition of serfdom in Prussia, but had no means to force the aristocracy to conform because he desperately needed their support. And in the 1780s, Joseph II instituted liberalized publishing laws in Austria, until he heard of artisans reading pamphlets about the French Revolution. He quickly retreated and reimposed censorship. In the 1750s, Frederick the Great had also loosened the censorship laws, and writers were free to attack traditional religion, but they never were allowed to criticize the army, the key to Frederick's aggressive foreign policy. Catherine the Great gave Diderot a pension, but she would hear of nothing that compromised her political power, and her ministers were expected to give her unquestioning service.

Finally, if the Enlightenment means the endorsement of reason over force, peace and cosmopolitan unity over ruthless competition, then the foreign policies of these enlightened despots were uniformly despotic. The evidence lies in a long series of aggressions, including Frederick's invasion of Silesia in 1740, Austria's secret betrayal of its alliance with the English and Dutch and the ensuing Seven Years' War, and Austria's attempt in the 1770s to claim Bavaria. In short, the Enlightenment provided a theory around which central and eastern European states that were only recently unified could organize their policies. The theory also justified centralization over the power of local elites grown comfortable through centuries of unopposed authority. There were no major philosophes who did not grow disillusioned with enlightened monarchs on the rare occasions when their actions could be observed at close range. The Enlightenment did provide new principles for the organization of centralized monarchical power, but centralization with economic rationalization and management did not make their practitioners or beneficiaries any more enlightened. Enlightened despotism was extinguished largely by the democratic revolutions of the late eighteenth century.

The American Revolution

England's victory over France in the French and Indian War (1754–1763) set in motion a train of events that culminated in the American Revolution. The war had drained the British treasury, and now Britain had the additional expense of paying for troops to guard the new North American territories that it had gained in the war. As strapped British taxpayers could not shoulder the whole burden, Parliament members thought it quite reasonable that American colonists help pay the bill; they reasoned that Britain had protected the colonists from the French and was still protecting them in their conflicts with Indians. New colonial taxes and import duties were imposed by Parliament. Particularly galling to the colonists were the Stamp Act (which placed a tax on newspapers, playing cards, liquor licenses, and legal documents) and the Quartering Act (which required colonists to provide living quarters and supplies to English troops stationed in America).

Vigorous colonial protest compelled the British Parliament to repeal the Stamp Act, yet new taxes were imposed that raised the price of many everyday articles, including tea. The stationing of British troops in Boston, the center of rebelliousness, worsened tensions. In March 1770, a crisis ensued after a squad of British soldiers fired into a crowd of Bostonians who had been taunting them and pelting them with rocks and snowballs. Five Bostonians died, and six were wounded. A greater crisis occurred in 1773 when Par-

liament granted the East India Company exclusive rights to sell tea in America. The colonists regarded this as yet another example of British tyranny. When a crowd of Bostonians dressed as Indians climbed aboard East Indian ships and dumped about 90,000 pounds of tea overboard, the British responded with a series of repressive measures, including suppressing self-government in Massachusetts and closing the port of Boston.

The quarrel turned to bloodshed in April and June 1775. On July 4, 1776, delegates from the various colonies adopted the Declaration of Independence, written mainly by Thomas Jefferson. Applying Locke's theory of natural rights, this document declared that government derives its power from the consent of the governed, that it is the duty of a government to protect the rights of its citizens, and that people have the right to "alter or abolish" a government that deprives them of their "unalienable rights."

Why were the American colonists so ready to revolt? For one thing, they had brought with them a highly idealized understanding of English liberties; long before 1776 they had extended representative institutions to include small property owners who probably could not have voted in England. The colonists had come to expect representative government, trial by jury, and protection from unlawful imprisonment. Each of the thirteen colonies had an elected assembly that acted like a miniature parliament; in these assemblies, Americans gained political experience and quickly learned to be self-governing.

Familiarity with the thought of the Enlightenment and the republican writers of the English Revolution also contributed to the Americans' awareness of liberty. The ideas of the philosophes traversed the Atlantic and influenced educated Americans, particularly Thomas Jefferson and Benjamin Franklin. Like the philosophes, American thinkers expressed a growing confidence in reason, valued freedom of religion and of thought, and championed the principle of natural rights.

Another source of hostility toward estab-

The Signing of the Declaration of Independence, July 4, 1776 (detail) by John Trumbull. The success of the American Revolutionary War was hailed as a victory of liberty over tyranny. Jefferson and Franklin were intimately familiar with the thinking of the Enlightenment and stressed a confidence in reason, freedom of religion and thought, and the existence of natural rights. (*Copyright Yale University Art Gallery*)

lished authority among the American colonists was their religious traditions, particularly that of the Puritans, who believed that the Bible was infallible and its teachings a higher law than the law of the state. Like their counterparts in England, American Puritans challenged political and religious authorities who, in their view, contravened God's law. Thus Puritans acquired two habits that were crucial to the development of political liberty—dissent and resistance. When transferred to the realm of politics, these Puritan tendencies would lead Americans to resist authority that they considered unjust.

American victory came in 1783 as a result of several factors. George Washington proved a superior leader, able to organize and retain the loyalty of his troops. France, seeking to avenge its defeat in the Seven Years' War, helped the Americans with money and provisions and then in 1778 entered the conflict. Britain had difficulty shipping supplies across three thousand miles of ocean, was fighting the French in the West Indies and elsewhere

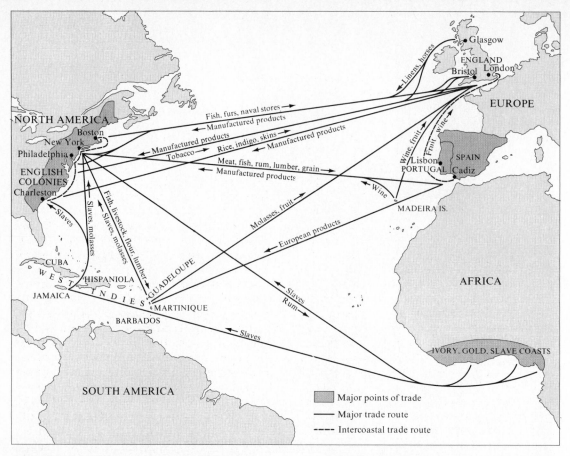

Map 18.4 Trade Routes Between the Old and New Worlds

at the same time, and ultimately lacked commitment to the struggle.

Reformers in other lands quickly interpreted the American victory as a successful struggle of liberty against tyranny. During the Revolution the various states drew up constitutions based on the principle of popular sovereignty and included bills of rights that protected individual liberty. Rejecting both monarchy and hereditary aristocracy, the Constitution of the United States created a republic in which power derived from the people. A system of separation of powers and checks and balances set safeguards against the abuse of power, and the Bill of Rights provided for protection of individual rights. To be sure, the ideals of liberty and equality were not extended to all people—slaves knew nothing of the freedom that white

Americans cherished, and women were denied the vote and equal opportunity. But to reform-minded Europeans, it seemed that Americans were fulfilling the promise of the Enlightenment; they were creating a freer and better society.

The Enlightenment and the Modern World

Enlightenment thought was the culmination of a trend instituted by Renaissance artists and humanists who attacked medieval otherworldliness and gave value to individual achievement and the worldly life. It was a direct outgrowth of the Scientific Revolution, which provided a new method of inquiry and verification and demonstrated the power and self-sufficiency of the human intellect. If nature were autonomous—that is, if it operated according to natural laws that did not require divine intervention—then the human intellect could also be autonomous. Through its own powers, it could uncover those general principles that operate in the social world as well as in nature.

The philosophes sought to analyze nature, government, religion, law, economics, and education through reason alone, without any reference to Christian teachings, and they rejected completely the claims of clerics to a special wisdom. The philosophes broke decisively with the medieval view that the individual is naturally depraved, that heaven is the true end of life, and that human values and norms derive from a higher reality and are made known through revelation. Instead, they upheld the potential goodness of the individual, regarded the good life on earth as the true end of life, and insisted that solely by the light of reason, individuals could improve themselves and their society. The outlook of the philosophes, as expressed by the French materialist, the Baron d'Holbach, demonstrates that the passage from medieval to modern, if not complete, was irreversible:

[In the past, the] human mind, confused with its theological opinions, forgot itself, doubted its own powers, mistrusted experience, feared truth, disdained its reason, and abandoned her direction, blindly to follow authority. Man was a mere machine in the hands of his tyrants and priests, who alone had the right of directing his actions; always led like a slave, he ever had his vices and character. These are the true causes of the corruption of morals, to which religion ever opposes only ideal barriers, and that without effect. Ignorance and servitude are calculated to make men wicked and unhappy. Knowledge, reason, and liberty can alone reform them, and make them happier; but every thing conspires to blind them, and confirm their errors. Priests cheat them, tyrants corrupt, the better to enslave them. . . . To learn the true principles of morality, men have no need of theology,
of revelation, or gods: They have need only of reason.[18]

The political philosophies of Locke, Montesquieu, and Rousseau held an entirely new and modern concept of the relationship between the state and the individual: states should exist not simply to accumulate power unto themselves, but also to enhance human happiness. From that perspective, monarchy and even oligarchy not based upon merit began to seem increasingly less useful. And if happiness be a goal, then it must be assumed that some sort of progress is possible in history.

The philosophes were generally optimistic about the future, believing that advances in science, a growing concern for natural rights, and an enlightened attitude toward torture, intolerance, and other injustices would usher in an age of human betterment. The philosophes insisted that people plan for the future victory of enlightenment by fostering education, judicial reform, political maturity, and even the creation of new religions that would be more civil than godly and more interested in humanity and nature than in heaven and sectarian dogma.

The philosophes wanted a freer, more humane, and more rational society, but they feared the people and their potential for revolutionary action. As an alternative to revolution, most philosophes offered science as the universal improver of the human condition. Faith in reform without the necessity of revolution proved to be a doctrine for the elite of the salons. In that sense the French Revolution can be said to have repudiated the essential moderation of philosophes like Voltaire, d'Alembert, and Kant. Yet the Enlightenment established a vision of humanity so independent of Christianity and so focused on the needs and abuses of present society that no established institution, once grown corrupt and ineffectual, could long withstand its penetrating critique. To that extent the writings of the philosophes point toward the democratic revolutions of the late eighteenth century.

Chronology 18.1 The Enlightenment

1685	Revocation of the Edict of Nantes; persecution of Protestants in France
1687	Publication of Newton's *Principia*
1688–89	Revolution in England; weakening of the clergy's power and loosening of censorship
1690	Publication of Locke's *Second Treatise of Civil Government*
1717	Founding of the Grand Lodge, London; the beginning of organized Freemasonry
1733	Voltaire publishes *Letters Concerning the English Nation*
1740	Frederick the Great invades Silesia; the War of Austrian Succession ensues
1748	Hume publishes *An Enquiry Concerning Human Understanding;* Montesquieu publishes *The Spirit of the Laws*
1749–50	French advocates of the Enlightenment become increasingly critical of their government
1751	Publication of Diderot's *Encyclopedia* in Paris
1762	Rousseau publishes *Émile*
1768–1774	The Russo-Turkish War
1775	The American Revolution begins
1776	Adam Smith publishes *Wealth of Nations*
1785	The Russian Charter of Nobility; the servitude of the peasants is guaranteed
1789	The French Revolution begins

Notes

1. "An Answer to the Question: 'What Is Enlightenment?' " in Hans Reiss, ed., *Kant's Political Writings* (Cambridge, England: Cambridge University Press, 1970), pp. 54–60.

2. Pierre Bayle, *Historical and Critical Dictionary*, Richard H. Popkin, ed. (New York: Bobbs-Merrill, 1965), p. 195.

3. Thomas Hobbes, *Leviathan*, C. B. Macpherson, ed. (Harmondsworth, England: Penguin Books, 1977), p. 189.

4. Jean Jacques Rousseau, *The Social Contract and Discourses* (New York: Dutton, 1950), pp. 3, 9.

5. Quoted in Franco Venturi, *Utopia and Reform in the Enlightenment* (Cambridge, England: Cambridge University Press, 1971), p. 101.

6. Voltaire, *Philosophical Dictionary*, Theodore Besterman, ed. (Harmondsworth, England: Penguin, 1974), p. 183.

7. Quoted in David B. Davis, *The Problem of Slavery in Western Culture* (Harmondsworth, England: Penguin, 1970), p. 449.

8. Quoted in Rosemary Agonito, ed., *History of Ideas on Women: A Source Book* (New York: G. P. Putnam's Sons, 1977), p. 101.

9. Ibid., p. 118.

10. Ibid., p. 124.

11. Ibid., p. 130.

12. Ibid., pp. 154–155.

13. Excerpted from Adam Smith, *The Wealth of Nations*, George Stigler, ed. (New York: Appleton, 1957), p. 3.

14. Ibid., p. 98.

15. Ibid., p. 7.

16. Jean Le Rond d'Alembert, *Preliminary Discourse to the Encyclopedia of Diderot*, trans. by Richard N. Schwab (New York: Bobbs-Merrill, 1963), p. 22.

17. Ibid., pp. 101–102.

18. Excerpted in Frank E. Manuel, ed., *The Enlightenment* (Englewood Cliffs, N.J.: Prentice-Hall, 1965), 60–61.

Suggested Reading

Anderson, M. S., *Europe in the Eighteenth Century, 1713–1783* (1961). A good general survey of the century with excellent chapters on cultural and intellectual life.

Becker, Carl, *The Heavenly City of the Eighteenth-Century Philosophers* (1932). Still a provocative assessment of the Enlightenment's relation to Christianity.

Cassirer, Ernst, *The Philosophy of the Enlightenment* (1951). A classic and basic account of Enlightenment philosophy; difficult reading.

Goldmann, Lucien, *The Philosophy of the Enlightenment: The Christian Burgess and the Enlightenment* (1968). Intended as a corrective to Cassirer, by a prominent European Marxist historian.

Hazard, Paul, *The European Mind, 1680–1715* (1963). Indispensable for the early period of the Enlightenment.

The Institute for Research in History, ed., *Women and the Enlightenment* (1984). A collection of essays asking the question: "Did women have an Enlightenment?"

Jacob, Margaret, *The Radical Enlightenment: Pantheists, Freemasons and Republicans* (1981). A study of the radical materialists and their contribution to the Enlightenment, especially in the first half of the century.

Venturi, Franco, *Utopia and Reform in the Enlightenment* (1971). A difficult but rewarding book, focussed on the more extreme reformers of the age.

Wangermann, Ernst, *The Austrian Achievement, 1700–1800* (1973). An excellent case study of the strengths and weaknesses of the most enlightened of European monarchies.

Review Questions

1. What is meant by the Age of Enlightenment? Where did the Enlightenment begin, and what contributed to its spread?

2. How did Christianity come under attack by deists, skeptics, freethinkers, and materialists?

3. In what ways does Voltaire exemplify the philosophes?

4. Why was Freemasonry important in the eighteenth century? Did its secrecy violate the ideals of the Enlightenment?

5. Describe the essential characteristics of the political thought of each of the following: Hobbes, Locke, Montesquieu, and Rousseau. Make relevant comparisons and contrasts.

6. Describe Locke's theory of learning. What was its significance for the Enlightenment?

7. How did the philosophes come to terms with the status of slaves and criminals?

8. Compare the views of Rousseau and Wollstonecraft on the position of women in society.

9. The philosophes approved of capitalism. Defend or refute this statement.

10. What made the High Enlightenment different from what went before it? Describe how it differed. How did the *Encyclopedia* exemplify the High Enlightenment?

11. List the major military conflicts of the eighteenth century. Discuss the significance of each.

12. Enlightened despotism was in reality the use of Enlightenment principles by monarchs to enhance the central government's power and thereby their own. Discuss this statement.

13. In what ways was the American Revolution based on Enlightenment principles?

14. The Enlightenment was a pivotal period in the shaping of the modern mentality. Discuss this statement.

Index